JAZZWOMEN

JAZZ

Profiles in Popular Music

Jeffrey Magee and Glenn Gass, co-editors

WOMEN

CONVERSATIONS WITH TWENTY-ONE MUSICIANS

Wayne Enstice and Janis Stockhouse

Preface by Cobi Narita and Paul Ash

Indiana University Press | Bloomington and Indianapolis

This book is a publication of

Indiana University Press
601 North Morton Street
Bloomington, IN 47404-3797 USA

http://iupress.indiana.edu

Telephone orders   800-842-6796
Fax orders   812-855-7931
Orders by e-mail   iuporder@indiana.edu

The paper used in this publication meets the
minimum requirements of American National
Standard for Information Sciences—
Permanence of Paper for Printed Library
Materials, ANSI Z39.48-1984.

Manufactured in the United States of America

**Library of Congress Cataloging-in-
Publication Data**

Enstice, Wayne, date
   Jazzwomen : conversations with twenty-one
musicians / Wayne Enstice and Janis Stockhouse ;
preface by Cobi Narita and Paul Ash.
p. cm. — (Profiles in popular music)
Includes bibliographical references (p.), selected
discographies, and index.
   ISBN 0–253-34436–0 (cloth : alk. paper)
   1. Women jazz musicians—Interviews. I.
Stockhouse, Janis, date II. Title. III. Series.
   ML395.E572 2004
   781.65′092′273—dc22
2003022615

1 2 3 4 5 09 08 07 06 05 04

Dedicated to
Eleanor Enstice
for her unconditional love.

CONTENTS

I believe I was invited to write this preface because of my own work on behalf of women in "the music," as producer, advisor, fan, and friend. But since Paul and I are like "one," and he has worked on every project with me, Paul and I wrote this preface together.

We know almost all of the subjects as people, and appreciate how Wayne and Janis managed to reach even the most private of them. Their conversations range far beyond the biographical—to their feelings, motivations, musical approaches, and attitudes. These women were obviously comfortable with their questioners. Wayne and Janis came prepared, having delved deeply into the music and history of each, bringing them closer to the essence of each musician.

The twenty-one portraits, arranged alphabetically—a great diplomatic concept—go beyond the usual suspects of the popular singers and pianists. There are enough instrumentalists to make a swinging band. Their ages and musical styles are wide-ranging, but Paul and I would pay anything to see them together on a stage.

The aspiring musician reader will learn about study, influences, and career moves. The social historian will gather more information of the glass ceiling, color barriers, and the musician's life. The casual reader will enjoy visits with twenty-one nice people, sitting comfortably in their homes, talking about their lives and their music.

Allow us to mention one interview in particular, that of Abbey Lincoln, my heart (Paul's, too). Abbey is so totally open in this interview, it's mind-boggling. Abbey is very frank about her attitudes and some very private thoughts on race, women's role in jazz, and other singers. (She is one of the strongest women I know.) This interview will be cited in every review of this book, and to me is worth the price of the entire volume. But then, so is every interview . . .

With love,
Cobi Narita and Paul Ash
Nobuko Cobi Narita, Founder and President,
Jazz Center of New York, Inc., and Universal Jazz
Coalition, Inc.; Founder and Past President,
International Women in Jazz, Inc.
Paul Ash, President, Sam Ash Music Stores

Acknowledgments

To succeed, jazz bands depend on a cooperative spirit dedicated to a common vision. A similar sense of community underscored the realization of this book, as a constellation of colleagues, associates, friends, and family members have shored and shepherded us over the eight-year stretch this project took to complete. Foremost among them are the musicians who generously consented to be interviewed. Our indebtedness only deepened each time the need surfaced for yet another lengthy session to iron out knotty historical or narrative problems. In addition to their gifts of time and gracious receptivity, gratitude of the highest order is extended to them for the inspired music they make, which sustained and centered this endeavor.

It makes eminent good sense that Nobuko Cobi Narita, among the most indefatigable of advocates for jazz and its players, made contributions to this volume that are second only to the musicians' in their importance. Cobi was an invaluable resource as we conducted field research. She continues to be a trusted advisor, and on occasion she has assumed on our behalf the improvised role of jazz diplomat. We are privileged to have the preface she composed with Paul Ash inaugurate our book. We are beholden to Marie Enstice, who had our welfare quite literally at her fingertips as she painstakingly transcribed countless hours of recorded interviews. On the home front, especially when the pitch of frustration was elevated, her influence was never less than salutary. Our special thanks as well for research and development grants from the University of Cincinnati, University Research Council, and the Lilly Foundation in Indianapolis.

We would be remiss not to single out several additional principals who played a key role. David Baker, Distinguished Professor of Music at Indiana University, was indispensable for his musical expertise and the constancy of encouragement he furnished. His colleague in the School of Music at Indiana University, Professor Patrick Harbison, was more than generous in his support of this project, and his discernment as an informal editor of selected portions of this book was greatly appreciated. We were very well served by Cephas Bowles, General Manager of WGBO-FM in Newark, New Jersey, as he repeatedly dipped into the deep pockets of his rolodex. We benefited enormously from Artists' Representative Suzi Reynolds, who was a model of unselfish effort in her devotion to the career and legacy of Teri Thornton. Kirsten Inquilla is recognized for repeatedly opening her Bronx flat for two weary travelers. Timothy Enstice is advanced equal attention for trenchant editorial observations delivered with unvarnished clarity.

Many others were instrumental in their willingness to share pithy insights, timely information, pertinent counsel, or welcome amenities. They include Kendra Gjerdingen, Bloomington, Indiana attorney; William Hays, English teacher at Bloomington High School North; Jane

Henson, Co-Director, ERIC Clearinghouse for Social Studies/Social Science Education; and Oscar Treadwell, Cincinnati-based jazz historian.

Finally, we could not envision undertaking the final phases of this project without the editorial team assembled at Indiana University Press, led by Music Editor Gayle Sherwood. The relish with which they have conducted the publication process, from their ambitious vision for the uses and dissemination of this work to the professional attention they have lavished on the manuscript at each stage of production, has been of inestimable value in confirming for us the worthiness of our original conception.

"Am I in it?" jazz pianist Dorothy Donegan asked beseechingly.

Enthralled by Ms. Donegan's performance at the Jazz Showcase in Chicago, I decided between sets to ask her to sign my special copy of the book I had co-authored, *Jazz Spoken Here.*[1] This was my jazz memorabilia copy. I had dozens of signatures and courtesy notes, not only from musicians who were in the book, but also from many who were not—the result of repeated occasions of this sort when a jazz concert inspired me to seek a memento.

I walked across the darkened room to the table where Dorothy Donegan was seated and made my request. It was then that she put that question to me—a question, I must admit, that disconcerted me because of the endearing, almost plaintive way this diminutive seventy-something musician asked it. I made an effort to gracefully extricate myself, but with the excitement from her first set still palpable in the room, my attempt at an explanation rang hollow. Seemingly unfazed, Dorothy Donegan listened politely and then graced the flyleaf with her signature.

That uncomfortable incident lingered with me beyond that evening in Chicago, because it reawakened an issue I thought had been put to rest. *Jazz Spoken Here* is a book I am proud of, and yet there was one characteristic of it that, in retrospect, I wish I could have modified: the exclusive focus on men. That shortcoming was a matter of chance. The book collected interviews with well-known musicians who performed in Arizona from 1975 to 1982; to my knowledge, there were no female counterparts who participated in that statewide circuit. Nevertheless, the book's monolithic take on gender could be interpreted as unwittingly complicit with what might be called a "politics of exclusion" that extends from the male dominance of the jazz world. The potential for irony in this situation was not lost on me, because not only was I familiar with the accomplishments of jazzwomen in the idiom, I was equally aware that they generally were not accorded joint privileges of visibility (recordings, gigs, scholarship). Stirred by the poignancy of these realizations, it seemed necessary to ask whether I could by any stretch of the definition play a reparative role.

My top priority as a jazz fan is to listen. When, though, I am prompted to think philosophically about the music, my staunchness moves me first to inveigh against the marginalization of jazz and the people who play it. Such a fit of pique passes, however, when I remember that no matter how late I get to the rummage sale, no one will pick up the jazz records before I arrive.

In this case, however, my partisan sentiments were redirected to inequities within the music. I observed that jazz has had mass appeal in this country only on those occasions when its entertainment values have locked into popular taste. As a consequence, even most *male* jazz musicians (excepting a handful of icons) have generally languished beyond the periphery of public awareness. Still, for those of us who look beneath the pervasive topcoat of pop culture, the male jazz player is available for discovery. Reigning as countercultural heroes since at least the inception of bop, the men of the music have seen their work spawn a satellite industry, complete with independent labels and a specialized press. But what of the heroines? How about the talented women who have had the courage to enter the predatory waters of the jazz life? Where is the comparative historical conscience, the equivalent critical corpus, in relation to their work? (On the basis of regular bookstore browsing, I speculate that for each book published annually on a woman jazz player, you could fill a phone booth with the tomes on men.) As my preoccupations intensified, the outcome seemed inevitable. An arc could be traced from my indelible encounter with Dorothy Donegan to the insistent urgings I now felt to embark on a new book.[2]

To undertake a theme of such breadth, my hunch was that I needed a partner—someone who was ardent about the music, preferably a musician, and it seemed patently obvious that this unknown person should be a woman. The question was, how to find her? The answer came in mid-1995, when I attended a concert featuring bop trumpeter Red Rodney, hosted by the Bloomington (Indiana) High School North Jazz Band. When the band director, Janis Stockhouse, walked onstage, it was as if a co-author had been plunked on my doorstep. A phone call from out of the blue and one meeting over coffee later, Janis agreed to join me. The next step was to see if the musicians would follow suit.

We began with a litmus test in the form of an introductory letter and response card mailed to a core list of women jazz musicians on the East and West coasts. The first indication that our project might have promise came when most everyone in this initial group agreed to be interviewed. As our contacts proliferated and our pool of subjects grew, Janis and I sealed our compact and developed our research methods. The majority of the forty-one interviews were conducted by Janis and me as a team.[3] Interview sites were most commonly the musicians' living quarters, where we would meet with the least interruption, and where our subjects were most inclined to relax.

The conversations averaged three hours in length. The longest single interview was with Marian McPartland. (This eight-hour session befitted Ms. McPartland's rich professional life, which serves as a microcosmic lens on much of the last century's jazz history.) Several of the musicians' stories required more than one meeting to record. The longest total interview was with Teri Thornton. Taped on three separate occasions, this interview spanned the full five years of our fieldwork, as we sadly watched the strapping, vibrant performer we had met in 1995 gradually succumb to terminal cancer. More recently we lost the superb organist Shirley Scott, and Clora Bryant has stopped playing because of health constraints. The remainder of the musicians are active, and many are in the prime of their careers. At this writing, two are emerging artists (Ingrid Jensen and Virginia Mayhew), and we were fortunate to record conversations with two of today's most important and acclaimed jazz musicians (Regina Carter and Maria Schneider) when they were on the cusp of visibility.

The opportunity in conversation to learn about these musicians was a thrill that never wore off. We asked questions mindful of what our readers would do if they were in our place. A small percentage of the questions were formalized by preliminary research. Most of what we asked, however, arose spontaneously during the improvised discussions, as we drew on knowledge acquired from a lifetime's consumption of jazz books, periodicals, and liner notes. Areas of questioning included each musician's formative years, career development, influences, and musical philosophy. These topics were complemented by a list of gender-based inquiries about the social conditions of the music, especially with reference to sexism on and off the bandstand.

Selections of music were played and discussed as part of the interview protocol, except where circumstances or a musician's preference precluded it. In all cases when music was used, the musicians were given prior information about the recordings so that the emphasis would be on anecdotes or analysis rather than identification.

In contrast to the excitement of meeting the musicians and entering into a conversation worth repeating, the transcribing and editing phases were painstaking. A close reading ensured that each portrait would find the fullness of the musicians' expression intact, in context, and accurate. To verify our content, we furnished each musician a copy of her chapter to review and amend. Securing the musicians' imprimatur during this final round ratified the project's collaborative spirit.[4]

The twenty-one women featured in this book were chosen to represent a cross-section of styles, career stations, and instruments. Some of the musicians have had sufficient media exposure to strike a familiar chord with the layperson, but most will not be known beyond the inner circle of the jazz world, and a few may have escaped the notice of even the seasoned listener. Instrumentalists were favored over vocalists in our selection of interviews, because women playing jazz on a horn or drums have had a much higher glass ceiling to shatter. (This is not to deny the musical caliber of the vocalists we have featured, several of whom are fine instrumentalists and composers in their own right.) Organizationally and thematically, we envisioned the book as a collective, one that might figuratively recall the formation of a jazz band. To the extent that this notion of convening an all-star women's band in print echoes the solidarity we witnessed among women in the jazz community, it is an apt metaphor. Nonetheless, we are mindful of the irony that our format, with its exclusive focus on women, mimics the gender-imposed ghettoization that many of these fine performers have chronically suffered in their careers.

Given the high level of musicianship and ambition that these women embody, the depth of their plight is startling, especially in the face of apparent social strides over the last century. Indeed, throughout our years of research, incredulity would regularly creep in that the need for such a book persists at all at this juncture in history. That it does, we are persuaded, is undeniable. Until critical mass tips the scales more equitably, we expect that accounts of this kind will contribute more to advancing the visibility of these dedicated professionals, many of whom are neglected treasures in American music, than to reinforcing stereotypes about them as a class.

Although, as mentioned earlier, books on women in jazz are scarce, there nonetheless have been several important works that preceded *Jazzwomen,* and we are indebted to them (please see "Suggestions for Further Reading"). By conducting trailblazing research on historical and social dimensions affecting the lives of women in jazz, our predecessors freed Janis and me to concentrate on our book's defining emphasis: the music these jazzwomen play, and how that music emerged from a splice of choice and circumstance.

This book may be considered a companion volume to the aforementioned *Jazz Spoken Here.* It departs from the previous work, however, in the urgency with which I felt that these stories needed to be chronicled. In the final analysis, the print record of each musician's voice as embodied in *Jazzwomen* (and complemented by the aural riches of the accompanying compact disc) is meant as a modest but telling corrective for an unjust lacuna in the history of a music we love.

Wayne Enstice, 2003

Notes

1. With Paul Rubin (Baton Rouge: Louisiana State University Press, 1990).

2. It saddens me to report that Ms. Donegan, who was unwittingly a catalyst for this book, died before arrangements could be made to interview her.

3. Scheduling conflicts resulted in my working alone on eight of the interviews included in this collection.

4. The views and ideas of the authors are not necessarily those of the interviewees within this book. The authors believe their data to be reliable, but they have not investigated the accuracy of every story or incident expressed therein. Therefore, the accuracy is not warranted or guaranteed.

Notes on the Selected Discographies

The discography of recommended listening that follows each chapter reflects the authors' judgments as to which recordings by each featured musician best meet three criteria: they are musically excellent (excluded recordings should not necessarily be construed as weaker efforts); they are representative of the mature mainstream of the musician's work; and at this writing they remain in print. Within these criteria we have attempted to furnish a degree of variety (instrumental settings, personnel, etc.), and, where appropriate, consideration has been given to representing more than one period in a musician's output. We have purposely kept the listings brief to make manageable the reader's initial encounter with a musician. In each case, the listing that bears an asterisk (*) is recommended as the best place to start in your review of a particular musician's work, and also the best choice for your library if you purchase only one recording by the artist in question.

JAZZWOMEN

Jane Ira Bloom

Jane Ira Bloom

Soprano saxophonist and composer Jane Ira Bloom has received international recognition for her novel explorations of sound as affected by motion and space. Whether she is swinging her own instrument in wide arcs or writing compositions that have the performers spinning as they play, the musical outcome of sound moving through space creates a breathtaking three-dimensional sonic experience. Also a pioneer in the use of live electronics, Bloom has carved a niche for herself as an innovative contemporary composer and a blue-chip saxophonist.

Born in 1955, this Massachusetts native began saxophone at an early age, and took private lessons during high school at the Berklee School of Music. She earned college degrees from Yale; while there, she frequented Boston jazz clubs and recorded her first two albums[1] for Outline Records, a label she founded.

Moving to New York City in 1977, Bloom honed her skills studying with saxophone master George Coleman. Her growth during this period as both a saxophonist and a composer is documented on three convincing records in the early '80s. One of them, *Mighty Lights,*[2] received five stars from *Down Beat* and established her as a new voice to be reckoned with on the soprano saxophone.

In tandem with her conception that music suggests shapes in space, in the late 1980s Bloom began to blend electronic tools such as digital delays, multiverb, and pitch shifters into her already swirling method of performing. As the first musician commissioned by the NASA Art Program, she composed *Rediscovery,* a four-part suite saluting the space shuttle *Discovery,* which was premiered at Cape Canaveral in the fall of 1989. As a result of her NASA collaboration, Asteroid *6083 Janeirabloom* was named in her honor.

Producing all of her own albums in the '90s, Bloom issued several highly regarded recordings on the Arabesque label. Her 1992 CD, *Art & Aviation,* was cited as one of the year's best jazz albums by *Jazz Times,* and her 1999 release, *The Red Quartets,* elicited widespread critical acclaim. In 2003, her pursuit of intersections between music and art was memorably celebrated in *Chasing Paint: Jane Ira Bloom Meets Jackson Pollock.*[3]

Bloom is a formidable improviser whose virtuosity has transcended the physical limits of the temperamental soprano saxophone. Using foot pedals to effortlessly switch in and out of the acoustic mode, she intersperses electronic whirs and ripplets to create a fascinating synthesis of musical sounds. Her sumptuous tone is more vocal than instrumental, and her hypnotic treatment of ballads breathes fresh life into chestnuts from the Great American Songbook.

Recent critical attention confirms Bloom's growing stature as a singular musician. In 2001, she won the *Down Beat* Critics Poll for best soprano saxophonist of the year, the Charlie Parker Fellowship for Jazz Innovation, the IWJ Jazz Masters Award,[4] and the Doris Duke/Chamber Music America Jazz Composition Award. She has written for the American Composers' Orchestra,[5] for the Pilobolus Dance Company, and for television and film features. More recently she premiered "Unexpected Light" for soprano saxophone and string quintet, and she has formed a new world music ensemble including Chinese pipa master Min Xiao-Fen. In 2003, Bloom was the winner of the highly regarded Jazz Journalists Soprano Saxophonist of the Year Award.

Recorded October 27, 1995, and March 24, 2000

JS: Jane, let's go back in time and imagine that as a youngster you never saw a soprano saxophone and music was not a part of your life. If that were the case, what would you be like today?

JIB: Good question! (*Laughs.*) I've got to think about that one. I might be a bit crazier than I am today. I might be a pretty wild person. (*Laughs.*) Music, for me, even from the time when I was very young was a very expressive outlet for whatever is inside gettin' out. It was how I identified myself. I felt even from the earliest time that I had music inside me. And if that wasn't there, who would I have been? Boy, no one's ever asked me that question. I kind of wonder very seriously whether I might've had some mental problems. (*Laughs.*)

JS: As a youngster, were you drawn more toward one kind of music than another?

JIB: Let me think about that. I knew I had the ability to improvise from a very young age. Something I loved to do. From the get-go, I was inventing things, even when I studied piano very early on. It was just a part of playing music. Even at a younger age I was observing the personality types and what it takes to be a classical musician or an improviser. I hadn't made any decisions about it, but I have to say, probably in all honesty, I think my intuition was heading me toward a place that was freer, that was in the jazz world.

WE: Did you improvise in other ways? Were you involved in the visual arts or play-acting? If I were your friend, what would we do of an afternoon when you were nine?

JIB: That's a good question. You're right, visual things: drawing. Toward high school I had a very strong affinity for photography. Very abstract. People tell me that if you saw my photographs they look like what I play. (*Laughs.*)

JS: As a musician, were you classically trained?

JIB: Yes. But I wasn't trained to be this or that. In my early education I didn't feel that my teachers were trying to teach me to be a classical player or a jazz player or an "anything" player. They were trying to train me to play the instrument so that I could do whatever I needed to do on it. I realize now, in retrospect, that was tremendously important.

JS: Which of your teachers were particularly praiseworthy?

JIB: Wind ensembles with Frank Battisti at the New England Conservatory were a big influence. But I'm talking specifically about Joe Viola. I mean, he really was my main point of contact.

JS: When did you begin your studies with Joe Viola?

JIB: When I was in ninth grade. I had studied alto saxophone in public school, and I was ready for a serious teacher. He was head of the Woodwind Department at Berklee, and I went into Boston to study with him privately. We spent a long time talking about improvisation, but the main point of study with him was woodwind technique: how to blow a saxophone, how to sight-read. I continued to study with him through college. So after eight to ten years I was still checking him out. (*Laughs.*) I count him as a teacher, a friend, and a mentor to this day.

JS: Do you associate your choice of the soprano with Viola?

JIB: It's absolutely associated with him. He's it. I wouldn't be playing it if it weren't for him. No question about it. When I heard him play the soprano, it was the most beautiful sound I'd ever heard. I said, "I want to do *that,* I want to sound like that." That was Joe Viola. He's the major, major source.[6]

JS: Did you learn about the Paris Conservatory solos and etudes?

JIB: Did I learn about French literature for the saxophone and sax quartet because of where the saxophone came from? My answer is yes. I spent a lot of time working on traditional etude material, again, to help hone my facility on the instrument, and also because I liked it. It was fun! We did jazz studies, too, simultaneously, but to me it was all one thing.

JS: How did you learn about the blues or what kind of a scale to play on a C minor 7 chord?

JIB: I didn't learn it from instructional books on how to play jazz, which is, right now, very common. It came from listening and an overwhelming passion for this sound I heard on records early on. As soon as I could get to hear it live, I would hear it live. My inroads to this music were through my ears. After studying with various teachers, I learned how to label things. My ears came first—the intuitive response to the music, and how to play it. It came secondarily from the page.

JS: What records did you listen to?

JIB: They were my mother's record collection. Ella Fitzgerald—you know, the American Songbook—Nelson Riddle, those kinds of things. That knowledge of the song tradition informs everything that I do. The American Songbook was something that was very primal for me at the beginning of my very first musical sounds. It's had a way of impacting on my music whether it's in the most traditional expression of those songs, like the versions that are on *The Red Quartets,*[7] or whether that sense of melody creeps into my more contemporary writing, even in pieces like "Emergency" or "Five Full Fathoms."[8]

WE: As a person interested in ideas, your approach to music at times draws on the world of science and technology, as applied to, for example, space exploration. Do you feel an affinity for science?

JIB: I'm a curious person. I was never a science jock when I was in school, but I have to say that those things interest me truly as a layperson. I was always interested in the core questions that are behind things like physics and space exploration. I don't approach it as, say, an engineer approaches it—you know, all the nuts and bolts of how you get people into space. It was definitely from an artist's point of view that I was interested in space exploration. What interested me was the wonder of it.

WE: Tell us about your involvement with NASA.

JIB: A group of seven of us, an "art team" it was called,[9] would go down to NASA—this was just after the *Challenger* accident. This group of artists was brought in to observe firsthand the launch and the mission of the shuttle *Discovery*'s return to flight. Then we went to Edwards Air Force Base to watch the landing as well. From our experiences we were to contribute a work of art to their traveling space art collection. It was a formative experience for me, talking about art and science collaborating.

WE: What influenced you particularly—the sounds of the launch, the high-tech systems, or just the space-age environment?

JIB: Hard to nail it down, but if you could imagine the artists being there with sketchbooks, and I was there with my tape recorder. Just recording anything I heard, trying to be perceptually aware. You know, you can't miss things like the sound of that launch or the sonic boom. The roar of a shuttle engine coming at you six seconds after you see it. That's fascinating. (*Laughs.*) I actually recorded the sound of the launch, and the guys at the Kennedy Space Center were saying, "Ah, this is nothing compared to what the *Apollo* engines used to sound like. You shoulda heard them." That's being very literal, but the other part of it is simply being a part of the experience of documenting the important historic role of men and women going into space. Being there when history is being made.

WE: Undoubtedly, it was a creative milestone for you.

JIB: It was. One of the most exciting experiences of my life was being part of that program, and it still resonates with me today. The orchestral piece that I wound up writing for NASA involved motion, it involved spatial electronics, it involved as much as I could think of that was as technically challenging in my own art form as the event that I was observing. I still write pieces thinking about it. One of the nice perks about being associated with the program was that I'd get press releases with photos about all the latest things that were coming out of the planetary program and the space program. I remember one press release I got was the announcement that the *Hubble* had discovered one of the most distant galaxies. I still have the sheet somewhere. But it so impressed me, you know, just reading about this thing, that I wrote a piece which is on *Art and Aviation*, called "Most Distant Galaxy."

WE: Another piece on *Art and Aviation* is "Hawkins' Parallel Universe," which sounds like it's based on "Body and Soul." What's the connection between Coleman Hawkins and a parallel universe?

JIB: Everybody thinks it's Stephen Hawking, the physicist. And you're right, "Body and Soul." Parallel universe? Well, to my ears, Coleman Hawkins was such an innovator in his time. He used to pick notes that were so out of the galaxy of his own time that I felt that I should write a piece and take it one step further—look for notes and rhythms that pushed my hearing outside the tonal centers and eighth-note jazz feel.

WE: What was the musical impetus for your participation in the NASA program?

JIB: Working with electronics. It was a passion of mine in the context of my own work as a jazz artist. Interestingly enough, the jazz community found it *very* strange. There's a certain segment of the jazz community that looks askew at involving electronic devices in jazz expression, for various reasons. It's not considered pure. To me it felt perfectly natural to use what I knew to take me to places I didn't know through music.

WE: Do you consider yourself to be a non-conformist in the jazz world?

JIB: I seem to have singular interests in things that are not always shared by other people. (*Laughs.*) I find it completely comfortable to play jazz concerts in planetariums. It makes perfect sense to me to write a piece of music about a painting. I don't think twice about it if I feel that live electronics are part of the palette of sound that I hear coming out of the saxophone. It doesn't faze me a bit to know that that's part of who I am or what my sound is.

WE: Returning to your chronology, didn't you start a record company early in your career?

JIB: Yes. Outline Records came about in the mid-'70s, when I was just getting ready to leave college and realizing, as a member of the music community in New Haven, that if I wanted to have a career I was going to have to promote myself. I was not alone among musicians who felt at the time that they didn't see any major record companies signing new, unknown artists, and if we wanted to document music that we felt was important, we'd have to do it ourselves. So at that time there was a group of us that went about the process of learning how to make records, or "LPs" in those days. How you record it, how you send it to a manufacturer, how you write the liner notes, get the album printed, and get it distributed. It's kinda like cottage-industry jazz. So I decided to start my own record company. I had been rehearsing and performing with a bassist in New Haven by the name of Kent McLagen. We were very serious about the original music we were playing and felt it was worth documenting. We recorded in 1976 in New Haven, and that was my "calling card" to the critics and to the distributors in New York. It was a way of introducing myself, in a sense, before I got here in 1977. That's how Leonard Feather and Nat Hentoff heard of my work.

WE: Could an independent jazz musician today fare as well?

JIB: Good question. It's a different world today; it was a smaller jazz world. That's the important thing. They weren't as inundated with product as they are today, and it also was an underground-jazz movement. This was *counter* to anything that was going on commercially at the time, and there really wasn't *that much* going on, you know, in terms of commercial jazz recording in the '70s. The music was underground, and this was a way of bringing it forth.

WE: During your last years at Yale, you drove into New York to study with George Coleman. Why did you choose him as a teacher?

JIB: I wanted to learn how to play fast. I was nineteen or twenty years old, and he had a harmonic sensibility that was, as John Pareles said about Sonny Rollins, "just a higher degree of calculus" than I understood. I wanted to get near it, I wanted to know what it was, and I wanted to know how he could do it with such *horrendous* speed. I don't know if that's what ultimately I learned with George, but I sure learned a lot from being around him and being next to that sound. You know, you think you're gonna learn something and you learn something else.

JS: Do you still practice regularly?

JIB: Absolutely. That's what I *love* to do.

JS: What would a typical practice session involve?

JIB: Sound and technique. Some people like to practice playing songs. I like to practice in almost a kinesthetic way. I do things at home that you'd never want to hear anybody do in public. I feel badly for whoever is in the room upstairs. It's like batting with a doughnut on. It's like reaching for intervals that you can't quite hear, playing at tempos that you can't quite cut. So that when you are with your instrument in a musical environment, you feel like the weight is off, you feel free as a bird, you feel lighter. It's an interesting but technical kind of approach. You're just constantly making sure that all your kinesthetic ability as a woodwind player is together so that you can express what you need to express spontaneously. To get your ideas through to your fingers as easily as you can. You know, try to make the instrument disappear.

WE: With the instrument transparent, what kinds of things are you thinking on the bandstand?

JIB: If things are going great, you're not thinking about anything. It's probably something close to what Zen practitioners describe as that alpha state where you're just completely in the doing of something. There's no impediment between what's inside and what's in your hands. It just becomes a sound, somehow. You wait for those moments. Those moments usually start happening when you've played with people for a long amount of time or when you've been on the road and playing several nights in a row. They don't happen when you just play casually. I think that's what keeps us all going—looking for those moments. It's like a quest. (*Laughs.*)

JS: You've coined the term "parameters of music." Please define that for us.

JIB: It occurred to me that in the writing of music we think about rhythm, we think about pitch, we think about harmony, we think about timbre. These are all very important parameters of musical thought. One thing we tend not to think about as much is space. I mean spatial relationships. How sound changes when it moves. There's a correlative, I guess, to thinking about time and its flow and relativity. Anyway, that's what led me to a lot of thinking and pursuing of a vocabulary of Doppler-like sounds, where you move and play at the same time. Henry Brant was probably the father in terms of new-music classical compositional thinking about spatial arrangements of sound. Or thinking about why sound works well in one environment and not in another—because of the space that surrounds it. And then it led me to think about what music would be like in zero gravity, where the relationship between sound and listener, the perceptual relationships, may not be linear because of the omnidirectional nature of the space. There's no gravity, there's no up and down.

JS: How has your solo voice, informed by the musical parameters you defined, been extended into other forms?

JIB: Well, I suppose from my own musical experience I have tried to open up the process of what you think about, what you write about, what you can do when you play. Letting jazz players know that movement can be part of improvising, too. Making sound change when you move. It hadn't actually been thought about—I mean, Sonny Rollins has been doing it for years, but nobody ever thought about it, really. I've spent some time teaching this kind of unique vocabulary that I've developed to other musicians in larger instrumental contexts. Taking movement and almost choreographing it for whole sections of orchestral and big band instruments. I began writing for orchestras in 1989. And I had a few experiences integrating improvisers with classically trained musicians in orchestras, trying to find some common vocabulary for them to meet on in music. You know, oftentimes when music is written for improvisers and orchestras, the improvisers are on one side, the orchestra's on the other—never the twain shall meet. I wrote a few pieces where I tried to dig into that, bringing improvisers into the orchestral sections and orchestral sections into the improvising.

That's been a new area that culminated in this rather large work that I wrote for the American Composers Orchestra in 1993.

JS: Did you perform with this ensemble at the premiere?

JIB: Yes. I was there with five or six key improvisers who I work with. They were involved in some loose improvisational sections in the orchestra and some very carefully defined choreographic sections where whole sections of brass—trumpets, trombones, French horns—stand and turn to create these Doppler-like sound effects.

JS: You convinced classical players to do that?

JIB: I got the finest orchestra in New York to do it. (*Laughter.*) They were such good sports. The American Composers Orchestra, which is just one of the primo new-music orchestras here in New York City. We also had about twelve to twenty brass in the balcony in Carnegie Hall so that the sound was spinning as well through the hall. It was like sound-surround. You know, Gabrieli taken to the nth degree. You wondered what I have been contributing? Maybe that's something.

WE: When you choreographed sections of this orchestra, was it more reminiscent of the lateral movements of the old Jimmie Lunceford band, or a "wave" occurring at a baseball stadium?

JIB: A little of both. There was no wave, up and down movement, because you could have a lot of serious train wrecks. But what was involved in the choreography of the sound was unison turning, if you can imagine, 180 and 360 degrees together. There were occasional times when I did choreograph it so that it was paced, so that sound would move around from instrument to instrument. And there was a spatial element to it, too—swirling the sound spatially between instruments that were on the stage and brass that was in the balconies. But usually it was on the same plane in arcs of 180 degrees or 360 degrees left, right, and with varying degrees of motion or speeds.

WE: I remember reading about a concert you gave at the Einstein Planetarium.[10] Evidently when the lights went down, the audience could not see the musicians. Is a performance of your music hurt if the band isn't visible?

JIB: The sound is sculptural in a sense. There's a strong visual element in my thinking that translates sonically. I've always felt it's very painterly—I think in strokes, in physical-sound strokes. So even when you turn the lights off you can feel it.

WE: Anthony Braxton composed a piece for four orchestras, thereby moving into the area of so-called serious twentieth-century music. Are you also wishing to produce fully annotated works and leave the jazz label behind?

JIB: No, no, no. You see, already you're putting lines in there and there are none. Perhaps where I have musical differences with someone like Anthony Braxton is because I'm really less interested in what's on the page. I'm less interested in the amount of writing, notating, that you'll see come out of Anthony or many twentieth-century composers. I'm still approaching it as a jazz player. I'm interested in how this information that's on the page can get off the page. How composition feeds an improvisational process, how it informs it, how it bounces off it, even when I'm writing for large orchestra. It probably has more to do with Duke Ellington than it does with the classical tradition. It's using composition as a springboard for your imagination and the improvisatory spirit of the ensemble you are playing with, and specific to those people that you're playing with. That's a very important difference when you're playing music as a composer-improviser, or improvising composer, or whatever you are.

WE: You said I'm putting lines in where there are none. Well, educate me. My understanding is that although classical musicians in past centuries were known to improvise, their counterparts today interpret exactly what's written. So isn't classical music practice today in stark contrast to the world of improvising jazz?

JIB: It's interesting, because I think I've been trying to merge them! Not to the extent, again, that I think some of my contemporaries are, because within the realm of writing and improvising, I'm much more interested in the improvising emphasis. But I think because of my generation's exposure to all kinds of music, they have *allowed* more formal writing aspects to become a part of their music as improvisers. And that was not so in the past. For example, going out on a contemporary new-music jazz gig in the year 2000 might call on you to be able to play things in written form that formerly only a contemporary classical musician would be able to cut. The year 2000 improviser not only has to be able to read that but also get ideas about how to improvise from it, without chord changes. (*Laughs.*) The level of proficiency, whether it's intervallic playing or the complexity of the rhythmic writing, looks a lot more like what you'd see in contemporary classical music. It's entering into the jazz world's palette.

JS: Is the converse true? Are jazz elements increasingly a feature in classical concerts?

JIB: Improvisation is out there, for sure. I see many contemporary new-music concerts now where there's an *electric guitarist* improvising in the context of a classical music ensemble! I think of the work that the "Bang on a Can" organization is doing in New York. Just sensational new-music musicians who are equally gifted as improvisers. Not in the tradition of jazz, per se, but they are comfortable in a world of improvisation.

WE: Isn't the term "improvisation" relative in jazz? For example, since you are so aware of your sound patterns and those of your group, don't you improvise within a familiar "corral of consciousness," if you will, rather than building everything fresh each time out?

JIB: "Corral of consciousness" is a good phrase, because that made me think of something else. You think that when you play with other musicians it can overly limit your choices and directions. But one of the things that improvisers learn over the years is that you play with certain people because they inspire you to go in directions you've never been in before. That's when good collaborations are really happening. Musically I've been the kind of person who likes to surprise my own ears. It's like having a love for the unexpected—even in your own work. In your own melodic line writing or in your own improvisations, you keep working toward surprising yourself.

WE: Jazz musicians put a premium on having a sound. What's the relationship between a musical identity and the surprises you're talking about?

JIB: The surprises aren't in the sound. You are who you are. There's no way, no matter how hard you try (*laughs*) to change that. But the surprising comes, I guess, in the mind/body relationship with playing, how you combine thought and feeling to improvise. That little bit of prompt from the head that nudges your intuition over here. I don't know; I feel like I'm talking philosophy. It's almost like I'm feeling and talking about an area where I'm not used to using words. For musicians, that kind of abstract thought is usually left in a musical place because sometimes in the talking of it there's a certain demystification of something that we like to leave unspoken. I've had a good education—I can put sentences together—but there's a reason why less is more, verbally speaking, for most improvisers. There's a reason Monk left those notes out. That's the way we think, and that's where we feel comfortable. You're really stretching me here. (*Laughs.*) I'm trying real hard not to give you stock answers. (*Laughs.*) I've done a lot of these interviews, but you're asking me some pretty thought-provoking questions, and I'm trying to think of another angle on things.

WE: A lot of what we've discussed has been about bold new ideas in jazz and improvised music. How about all the attention in the press about jazz being in a cul-de-sac? And, collaterally, all the coverage given the neo-traditionalists, spearheaded by Wynton Marsalis?

JIB: In my observations, I do think that there's been a period of music that's gone by that's actually mirrored, politically, what's going on in our country. There's a certain conservatism that is a reflection of the society, a period of almost like revisionism, instead of progression. And a different point of view from musicians about how they learned their music, how they came to it, and what their expectations were in playing this music. Their economic expectations, particularly. The educational place where people come from to play has changed, and I think the society itself has had an impact on the people, who they are and what they've been doing. Then again there's the point of view that jazz musicians have always been in an alternative place in the world despite what happens in the mainstream environment. Somehow it always manages to hold true to itself and do what it has to do if it's generated by musicians and for musicians. The problem comes in things being imposed on the musical community that are external to the music and the musicians. I belong to a music community that has felt that we had to lay low for quite a long time, and continue to do our work underground.

JS: How would you describe that community?

JIB: A lot of music experimenters. People pushing the boundaries of what they can do on their instruments as improvisers as well as extending the kinds of music that impact on their music.

JS: Who are some of those people?

JIB: I came out of New Haven with a bunch of musicians who happened to be there at the same time. Fascinating people. Gerry Hemingway comes to mind, David Mott comes to mind, Leo Smith, George Lewis, Anthony Davis. I was talking to Gerry at a party the other day. He made an observation which I have to agree with. He said that in New Haven the community was buzzing in the mid-'70s with musicians who were all very unique individuals. Nobody sounded like other people. Everyone had their own train of thought about the direction to follow in their music. And Gerry was saying the interesting thing is that twenty years have gone by, and if you look at this group of people you'll notice that they really were single-minded. They pursued their vision despite some pretty insurmountable odds and a lot of pressure to do other things. Abbey Lincoln says, "There are rewards for people who follow their vision." Something to that effect. The rewards aren't always apparent in the living of it. (*Laughs heartily.*)

WE: While we're on a social theme, let me ask you about sexual politics. Has gender been an issue for you in your life as a professional musician?

JIB: Of course it's an issue. Anybody who told you it isn't has a few more years to live. (*Laughs.*) It's a matter of covert discrimination. It's not *spoken*. That's what's so insidious about it. It's the phone calls that you *don't* get. It's the things that are never spoken in front of you, but you wonder why you never got the opportunities, or why you're never thought of among the list of musicians in a promoter's mind when a festival is being prepared. It's the sin of omission, and that's what's so deadly about it. That's why you have to talk about it and why you have to keep reminding people, "Why not?"

WE: Did you go through a period when you changed your conduct to conform to the male-dominated jazz world?

JIB: No. I've been myself. I've felt pretty comfortable with my femininity. Whoever it is I am, I've always felt pretty comfortable with that. And I've had a good relationship in my home life, so that's been a stabilizing factor for me. But the one thing—and again this is sociological, it's not musical—after a while, you simply miss being around women. And I don't just mean other women in the band. You miss interacting with women in the music business as well; there are very few that I know. Frankly, you just get lonely for the company of women. It's as simple as that.

JS: In school bands, girls quite often don't want to take a solo. They also gravitate toward flutes and clarinets because they don't have many role models for brass instruments or the saxophone.

JIB: It's a competition issue. It's not even about music. It's tough. Like you said, the role models for women brass players are few and far between. Women traditionally in jazz have been in certain prescribed areas—as vocalists, as pianists, and playing "feminine" instruments: violins, harps. So it's hard for young women to see that it's okay to lead. There is a history of women who did play brass instruments, who played the reeds and played the trombone and trumpets, drums and bass. Some of them were in the original Sweethearts of Rhythm. It's not like they didn't exist in this music. But there was no support system for these women. Talk about an uphill battle—they just couldn't survive. Jazz history has omitted them, but, believe me, they've been around. The women who made the strongest impact in the tradition of the music were vocalists. They are the ones that we think of right off the bat in the tradition of the music, and they've had an *enormous* impact on the music. *Enormous.* Miles Davis *loved* the way Shirley Horn sang. You can hear it in his phrasing. How that's happened in the instrumental world isn't quite as apparent yet. But it will be, at least to my ears right now. With a little more perspective, it will be.

JS: Do you still appear at women's jazz festivals?

JIB: I'm playing at the Mary Lou Williams Jazz Festival at the Kennedy Center this May. I played there about five years ago or so when it first started, and I'm gonna go back and play again. Isn't it something that there still *are* women's jazz festivals? I thought they would be gone by now. You know, if you'd asked me this question in 1976 when I embarked on my career—if we would hit the year 2000 and I would still be getting interviews about the state of women in jazz—I would have said, "No way." We would be as fully integrated into the jazz world by then as women have been in other fields. It's a sad comment on the state of sexism in our society right now that we're still having this conversation.

WE: To balance all the talk about "young lions," do we need to start identifying "young lionesses"?

JIB: Oh, I could have shot whoever it was that came up with that phrase. There's a lot of joking around in the jazz community about that phrase. Even the guys don't like that word; it was getting so silly.

WE: Allow me to read part of a response by Chick Corea to a recording by Alice Coltrane:[11] "By the way, what dawned on me before I knew it was Alice was the fact that it was a woman playing. I couldn't tell so much by the way she struck a single note or a phrase, but how she embroidered the piano; her lacework reminded me of a woman crocheting some very hip clothing." In view of this comment, should we lend credence to the idea that if someone plays behind a curtain we could tell if it was a man or woman on the basis of the way she or he handled form?

JIB: It doesn't matter. Even if they *could* tell it was a man or woman, it doesn't matter. What matters, and that you're missing from the quote, is that the sexism is in the covert language of what femininity is. That's the disgraceful thing about that quote. There are now a few more women critics, but if you read much jazz criticism written by men, you'll find *in* the language denigrating covert references to women that they don't even know about. "Swirling sounds of sexual whatever"—that's a little more obvious; but if you look through the language, certain writers aren't even aware that it's affecting even the vocabulary that they come up with to talk about music that is generated by a woman. It's very disturbing.

JS: I'm assuming that you don't have children.

JIB: No. It's interesting you mention it because probably the closest I'm doing to nurturing right now is teaching. I'm around young people a lot now. I'm passing it along that way. It's a musical way, but that's how I'm sharing what I've learned with a whole other generation of musicians. Boy, is the take different now, too. (*Laughs.*)

JS: In what way is "the take" different?

JIB: It's a different world than the one when I came up. I think I'm very much a product of the '60s in terms of my thought about what it means to be an artist, what it means to "do your own thing" despite all the odds. How you piece together this mysterious process called "learning how to be an improviser." Improvising a career, essentially. In the year 2000, a whole educational system, all kinds of literature, and how successful you can be financially at it, has grown up around trying to teach young people how to play. At the same time, some of the mystery's been taken out of it. The mystery that's involved in the process of what it means to be an improviser that changes how you think about what you're doing.

WE: In terms of professional visibility, do you get the exposure you feel you deserve?

JIB: I've had my fair share, yeah. At first curiosity, and then, hopefully, as the years have gone by it's been focused more on the strength of the body of the work that I've been doing. I've made ten albums under my own name over the course of my twenty or so years. For a jazz musician that isn't a lot, but I like to say that I don't record that much, but what I choose to record I try to make choice, you know, try to make it last. So it's how you're able to sustain a body of work. You know, you may have a great moment, but can you sustain a whole lifetime of good work?

JS: Do you have projects in mind that you'd like to record, but you're not sure people would buy?

JIB: I have all kinds of ideas for album projects. I still call them albums, isn't that interesting? I wonder if I can get them made, because they're just abstract concepts. I've written a series of pieces about Jackson Pollock. And a painter series, including artists like Miró and Van Gogh. You'd think that would be a neat thing to think about, and play about, and write about, but it may not always translate into singable melodies. It has other things going on in it—sounds that physically move and melodic lines that ebb and flow with an elastic time feel. And the way to record it, because of my interest in spatial things, might demand a more technical kind of recording than jazz budgets are able to offer.

WE: Your work is organized classically, while Pollock's denied conventions of Western order. Did his approach push your music into new areas?

JIB: I think so. It sort of gets into changing the interdependence of the parts. I started thinking about the unconscious ways that musicians communicate with one another and how you could "throw sound" around the bandstand like paint. Yeah, I think it does take inspiration from him.

JS: Is New York still the place of choice for a jazz player to conduct business?

JIB: Well, I think it's just a marketplace issue. If you're in New York you're extremely visible, that's all. And if you need to go through various steps to get a certain amount of visibility, whether it's to record or to get press or whatever, this is the place where you'll get it. But that has nothing to do with the musical content of what you do, and how easy it is now to make CDs. It's difficult to have an established working unit functioning and rehearsing and performing in New York. So if you live somewhere else, you actually have an advantage.

JS: New York used to be the prime testing ground. Is that still true?

JIB: That's why I came here, and indeed I have met a lot of people who have been great to work with and inspirational. But you know what's interesting is a generation of musicians, perhaps my age and older, they hit a certain point and they start to move out, start to move back to the states where they came from. When they've reached a certain measure of success, they're looking to get out of New York, as long as they're getting the phone calls. Most successful jazz musicians now live near airports and faxes and e-mails. Jazz musicians want to have a nice place to live just like anybody else.

WE: Let's take a deeper look at the music you make. In terms of your influences on the soprano sax, would I be correct to list Bechet, Lacy, and Coltrane?

JIB: None of the above. That was just not a big part of my listening. Or why I played the soprano at all. I have to say in all truthfulness, that's not the lineage that I followed to get to the soprano. The fact that the soprano's lineage was not as full as other instruments in jazz intrigued me because I was interested in developing something new. So if you're interested in a new sound or creating something new, it's a good place to be.

I took my inspiration much more from other instruments, whether it was other saxophone players or singers. I like the trumpet. I listened a lot to Miles and Booker Little. I found that more informative to the kind of sound that I was trying to develop on the instrument than listening to other soprano players.

WE: Can you be more specific about how Davis and Little influenced you as you were developing your sound?

JIB: It was their phrasing. I love the sense of struggle that I hear in trumpet playing, which I like communicating to the saxophone in the voice of it. Pacing, phrasing, breath length, intensity, attention to the detail of the attack and the decay of a sound.

WE: Decay?

JIB: Yeah. That's something that's very important on a brass instrument like the trumpet. You know, attack is tremendously important to what makes a trumpet a trumpet, but also, when you listen to Miles, not only how he starts a note but how he leaves it. That's a lot to think about. There's a whole world of sound just in that. But I always loved the trumpet, and it's probably why I so enjoyed my collaboration with Kenny Wheeler (on *Art and Aviation* and *The Nearness*). I say to people, "Boy, I wish I could do on the saxophone what he does on trumpet."

WE: The soprano has the reputation of scaring musicians away. But Joe Viola has apparently said that the soprano is no more difficult to play than other saxes.[12]

JIB: He's right about that. But the other thing he always said about the soprano is that it has a smaller window of accuracy. It's more exacting. That's why it's talked about among saxophone players with such a sense of struggle.

WE: The soprano has the least amount of metal of all the saxes. Does its relative lack of materiality appeal to you, especially since you want the instrument to be transparent?

JIB: Never thought of it that way. Something for me to think about. There is the quality of the upper register of the instrument that's very difficult to keep in tune, and also there are technical difficulties with locating the pitch and the sound. It's almost like you have to pick it right out of the air—that upper register. Soprano is the only instrument that could be described that way. That has some of the quality that you're describing—it doesn't feel solid, you know. But the solidity of the sound has to be inside *you,* the voice, the singer, the player.

WE: Continuing our discussion about the nature of your work, what is the content of your music?

JIB: Melody is. Maybe it comes via the line of George Gershwin, I don't know. But over the years, that's what I've seen as my through-line: melodic content. How to write melodic line comes, I think, from there. This is something that moves people, moved me, you know, and it's something I try to carry with me in all the writing that I do.

WE: Is beauty an issue for you? For example, the tone quality of your sound or the carefully wrought grace of the lines you play?

JIB: It's a word that doesn't seem to be comfortable in the jazz idiom. I can relate to the fact that I'm comfortable with my sound, just having a sound, and letting that be what it is, you know. I wouldn't have latched on to the word "beauty" because it connotes just the very words you used to describe the careful shaping of something. I think the way I approach having a sound on the instrument, or having the sound of an ensemble, has a little more spontaneity in it than careful artifice.

WE: Your output seems so diverse. Is eclecticism at the heart of your aesthetic?

JIB: Well, there are a lot of directions. I seem to find a couple of interesting threads, and a lot has to do with being a saxophone player, a single line player, a linear thinker. A lot of melodic writing I've done has found its way from basic tenets of writing popular American song, and I transpose that to ideas of stringing notes together in ways that create motion and flow without always having to use eighth notes. The regularity of a jazz eighth-note feel is the identifiable characteristic of a lot of jazz solos. I've been interested in writing and playing music that uses a lot of curves, a lot of ebb and flow, accelerando and deaccelerando, making fives and sevens try to feel as natural as an eighth note, and a sixteenth note. That kind of thing. But trying to make it feel right instead of writing seven notes for the sake of doing something other than four or eight.

JS: To compose, do you notate a melody or arrive at it when you improvise?

JIB: Usually I'm right at the piano.

JS: Once you've got the melody, do you struggle to put a harmonic structure to it?

JIB: Sometimes. Sometimes it goes the other way round. Sometimes the chords come first and then the linear writing. Harmony is a very interesting thing for me. It's internal. I almost don't even think in terms of major 7 and G7 chords, even though I know exactly what they are. I hear voicings, which is interesting. I'm very much informed by having listened to jazz harmony for a long time, but I hear these voicings. I start to write out voicings instead of writing out chords, which is a different approach. Then I go back and name them according to the chord names. Again, I think, this is because I'm a line player. My very first album was saxophone and bass duets. Very simple lines, almost like the equivalent of charcoal line drawing. I began recording in '76, and if I look at what I do today, I've filled in a lot of colors since then, but the essence of what I'm writing still stems from that place in 1976.

JS: Do you enjoy doing a slow B-flat blues to end a set?

JIB: Absolutely. One of my all-time favorite things to do is to play really slow ballads. It's something that I've come to as I've gotten a bit older. I've done it throughout my career on record and in performance, but as I've gotten older I feel more comfortable about trying to say more with less. I think that's just something that comes with a little bit of seasoning—you know, being around for a while, not feeling like you have to play this many notes to get across an idea. Pick the right ones.

JS: In performance, do you gravitate toward your own compositions?

JIB: I think it's a pretty full mix these days because I'm making a special effort to think more about recording some standard repertoire. But I try to record standards arranged with my point of view. If you hear the ballads that I record, you'll see I usually either write something or I arrange them in a way that takes it at a slightly different angle. Or it shows a little something about why I want to play it and why it's different from the way Coleman Hawkins played it.

WE: In *The Nearness,* I could swear that your rendition of "In the Wee Small Hours of the Morning" duplicates the phrase lengths in Sinatra's version.

JIB: Well, I certainly listened a lot to it. (*Laughs.*) I listen to him all the time.

WE: When playing standards, are you singing the lyrics in your mind?

JIB: In a way, yeah. Likewise some of those recordings of songs that I learned from Abbey Lincoln—I hear her voice so strong in my head. Or when I'm playing "How Deep Is the Ocean," you can bet I'm hearing Billie Holiday. Those voices are vivid to me.

WE: Before we conclude, I want to ask you about the absence of electronics on your most recent recording, *The Red Quartets.*

JIB: I'll tell you an interesting thing I observed about the music—actually Fred [Hersch] and I commented on this after we listened to *The Red Quartets.* I've been through a whole period of time where I use electronics in performance quite regularly. The music on *The Red Quartets* didn't call for it, but the thing that I found out was that my ideas using electronics have come full circle. For example, in the recording of "Emergency," where Fred and I are improvising together, what we did acoustically was to imitate sounds that I do often with the electronics. So coming from electronic sounds to discovering acoustic sounds that imitate the electronic sounds you are making, to me, that's full circle.

It made perfect circular sense to me because if you listen to *Mighty Lights,* before I had ever gotten involved in using live electronics, you can hear the Doppler effects, you know, me swinging the horn around the microphones. Before I even knew what the heck I was doing. It just felt right. It was after that that I started to get more conscious about how I could integrate electronics into these intuitive ideas that I had about movement. And then to spend a lot of time in that electronic world with that idea; and then to come back and reexamine where it came from; and then to reinvent the electronic sounds acoustically just makes beautiful sense to me. (*Laughs.*)

Mighty Lights. Enja 4044 807519 (1982).

*Art and Aviation. Arabesque AJ0107 (1992). (Excellent recording with live electronics.)

The Red Quartets. Arabesque AJ01444 (1999). (Exquisite recording in a quartet format, but no live electronics.)

Chasing Paint: Jane Ira Bloom Meets Jackson Pollock. Arabesque AJ0158 (2003).

Notes

1. *We Are,* 1978; *Second Wind,* 1980.

2. 1982; Enja Records (with Ed Blackwell, Charlie Haden, Fred Hersch).

3. 2003; Arabesque Recordings.

4. International Women in Jazz.

5. "Einstein's Red/Blue Universe," commissioned in 1994.

6. Joe Viola died on April 11, 2001. Ms. Bloom's recent recording *Chasing Paint* (Arabesque) is dedicated to Mr. Viola's memory.

7. "Time after Time" and "How Deep Is the Ocean."

8. "Emergency" and "Five Full Fathoms" are on *The Red Quartets.*

9. The art team was six visual artists and Jane.

10. Bill Shoemaker, "Jane Ira Bloom," *Down Beat,* July 1992, pp. 62, 63.

11. Leonard Feather, "Blindfold Test," *Down Beat,* November 26, 1970, p. 30.

12. Emilio Lyons and Fred Bouchard, "The Sax Doctor Meets the Bald Soprano," *Down Beat,* August 1994, p. 53.

JoAnne Brackeen

Photo by David Spitzer. Used by permission.

JoAnne Brackeen

The only woman to hold a chair in Art Blakey's Jazz Messengers, pianist/composer JoAnne Brackeen played with that most imitated of all combos from 1969 to 1971. Music critic Leonard Feather predicted that Brackeen's postbop playing would be as important to the 1980s as Bill Evans's and Herbie Hancock's contributions were to the 1960s.[1] This trailblazer for women in jazz has twenty-five albums as a leader and more than three hundred compositions to her credit.

Born in Ventura, California, in 1938, the former JoAnne Grogan learned her instrument by playing along with records. After moving to Los Angeles at sixteen, she began performing in earnest at local jazz clubs. Blessed with a towering six-foot frame, she was able to pass for older, allowing her the opportunity to play with established saxophonists Harold Land and Teddy Edwards.

She married tenor player Charles Brackeen in 1960, and five years later the burgeoning family moved to New York City. Her early years in New York were devoted to raising four children and paying her dues to break into the insular world of jazz. Following the period with Blakey, she had stints with Joe Henderson and, in the mid-'70s, the Stan Getz Quartet. Brackeen's exposure with Getz, especially her performance on the Grammy-winning *Stan Getz Gold*,[2] brought her critical acclaim and the attention of a much wider audience.

Brackeen has been an established leader since the late 1970s, primarily in the trio format. Her keyboard presence is marked by a percussive attack, even at slower tempos. On bright pieces, Brackeen's biting, jackhammer-like articulation in complex right-hand lines is countered by rumbling chordal progressions in the left. The close, rhythmic two-handed interplay generates a dense, at times tumultuous, barrage of sound that can consume a listener with its unrelenting tension. Brackeen's command of the piano is superbly displayed on her tour de force solo recordings, such as *Live at Maybeck*[3] or the more recent *Popsicle Illusions*.[4]

Brackeen's unique compositions range from the ethereal to the jubilant. A master of polyrhythms, in her 1990 composition "Picasso,"[5] for example, this unconventional pianist treats the listener to a metric excursion as she artfully and playfully shifts between six different time signatures. More a consolidator than an innovator, Brackeen frequently borrows from avant-garde vocabulary to create stunning musical mosaics that are marked by dissonant harmonies and disjointed but buoyant melodies.

Brackeen has been cited repeatedly in the polls as one of the world's leading jazz pianists, and since 1994 she has been a professor at the Berklee College of Music. Showered with honors over the years, she was recently featured in Ken Burns's TV documentary "Jazz," as well as in Robert Doerschuk's "88 Giants of Jazz Piano." JoAnne Brackeen's 1999 recording, *Pink Elephant Magic*,[6] received a Grammy nomination, and in 2001 she was the recipient of the ABI award[7] for "Woman of the Year."

Recorded June 21, 1996, and April 18, 1999

WE: JoAnne, what is the primary source of your music?

JB: My breath. All knowledge is in the breath, and it also feeds the body. Now I find out that it heals the body. It's your connection with the Earth. Music is energy and the air is energy, and so it all comes from one thing. And much of the study I do of music is that way. I never went to music school. I am *in* music school, and I got born here; Earth is the music school for me.

WE: When did you first decide upon a career in music?

JB: I never decided that. I heard music when I was two or three and I really liked it. I mean, it didn't seem like anything separate. So if something's not separate, it's hard to say when you decided. It's like saying when you decided to breathe. But it's always been magical for me. The most sparkly color feeling, a feeling of home, a feeling of what I belong to.

JS: Does your whole life revolve around music?

JB: Everything is music. I couldn't really separate music from life. You know, one time I was doing this record date for the MPS label.[8] It was in the Black Forest of Germany. We went into the studio, and I did the whole thing in about four hours. When I went back to my hotel, I don't know what happened, but for about a half an hour everything was sound. And I wasn't asleep. It was *amazing.* As a matter of fact, I didn't even know I was hearing it until it started to leave. It was like a full circle; it had all rhythm and all sound. I don't know if it's like some special thing in that area, but if someone was walking down the hallway of the hotel, or a horn honked outside or something, I could hear it later. It was just coming from that space into those sounds. It was all sound, but it was inaudible. Then as I came out of this state it started to fade into various sounds. It divided into separate sounds in the Earth, like into the separate things you normally hear. So then I realized that that's what people talk about—like a cosmic sound? There is no sound that isn't music; they just take different forms and rhythm and pitches.

WE: Did you feel that you were the origin of the sound?

JB: No. The sound is the origin of us, in the full-circle state. Yet it's the realization that you *aren't* the sound. That's what happens when you come back into the Earth. This thing is what everybody is, I assume. I don't think I'm that different from anybody.

WE: Everybody is this sound?

JB: Yeah.

WE: Are you saying that one is, or one is not, the sound?

JB: One is *only* the sound. An Earth experience was like one little tiny experience, for a hundred or something years. You come to Earth and separate the sounds. You're supposedly separate, but you're not really separated.

WE: Is sound all around us?

JB: There isn't any place where it isn't. But at the same time, it's the silence, too. It's inaudible.

WE: Silence is a part of sound, correct?

JB: The sound comes after. I know that from writing my tunes, because when I write, I write in the space where there's no sound. Total silence. The sound is the reflection of that quality of silence—there's all different kinds of qualities of it. So that's where I get my tunes, my songs.

WE: Now that you know that everything is sound, why continue to make music?

JB: Because I live as a separate. I'm not feeling that now. But I know it now.

JS: Have you had another experience similar to the Black Forest incident?

JB: I don't remember that one happening again. And it didn't happen before. I don't know if it will happen—it doesn't matter. It's like you grew a hand and your hand is there. I mean, you don't lose it. It's there, it's yours, and you use it. So you're not in the process of growing a hand, you're not in the process of being in that state, but then you come out the other end and you have something you didn't have before.

JS: Although you're separate, I take it that you're also aware of how you are unified with a larger entity?

JB: Yeah. In a very intricate, intimate way. I just use it. Anything that I do on a deep level, that would be a part of it.

JS: Do you want your music to move people toward a similar awareness?

JB: I want to take them in these spaces so they can know them, because if they go in these spaces it gives them continuous inspiration for what they do. It doesn't matter what field. The creative music that we're doing now that I guess you can call jazz—there's a whole lot of music called jazz, but I mean the kind that is creative, spontaneous—I think is the highest art form we have. I want my music to feed people what they need. If one lives to 120, that sounds like old, but that's a very short period of time to try, you know.

JS: You have quite a mission.

JB: Yeah! It's like I really love being here, and I love everything that's here.

WE: Let's talk about your development as a musician. When did you start playing piano?

JB: I started *really* when I was eleven, but in my head I heard all this music. I didn't know what chords were, but I knew what sounds were and I said, "Ooh, I want this to happen next," and it usually didn't happen. So the thing I can do in composing is I can put it how I want it.

WE: How did you respond to music classes in high school?

JB: They were boring. You know how impatient you are when you're young. That's horrible because already school is taking up six hours of your time—to waste six hours and get home and that's all you have left, and you can't have a say whether you have to go to school every day. Maybe in some country somewhere they will develop a form of learning that's not like that, because I think learning's very fascinating. But the way that we've evolved to this point, or had when I went to school, was pretty boring. When the music class came, well, there was a big grand piano in the room next door so I could go play the whole hour.

WE: Despite your lack of interest in the type of formal schooling you received, you did graduate from high school.

JB: The only reason I did was I figured I *owed* that to my parents. Because of that I decided, okay, I will just get all these A's and everything because they wanted me to take the courses that you take to go to college. So I did that and I had an A average. It was no big problem, I'll tell you that. I never did anything extra. I did all my homework in the class.

WE: If the choice would have been yours to make, would you have quit school?

JB: I would have left; I was like eleven when I really saw what was going on. From an eleven-year-old's point of view, if it's bad, I think it's pretty bad. And I think I'm pretty normal. I would have stopped going to any kind of high school. For the masses of people, they had certain things prescribed and it didn't matter what the person needed to learn or what they wanted to learn, they had to learn what was put there. And the people taught in such a boring way that you almost could have learned the whole course in three or four hours without having bothered to go through fifteen weeks, or however long a semester was. I had three good teachers out of my whole experience.

WE: After high school, you were accepted into the Los Angeles Conservatory. But you attended for only a brief time?

JB: Yeah. About three days. I thought they were wasting my time. I could go to the piano and practice and work on what I needed to. I was already working and had been working for some time. I learned to play when I was eleven, and I started working when I was eleven. I really could play. I could play once I just did it.

JS: Since you didn't go to music school, how did you learn music theory?

JB: When I was eleven, I had transcribed Frankie Carle solos. I already could hear the sound before I had a piano, so I guess that would be what you would call a proof. I copied about eight or ten solos note for note. Then I knew how to play so I didn't have to do that anymore.

WE: Frankie Carle is not going to be on many people's list of jazz players.

JB: Oh, I didn't know what jazz was. My parents had two piano players' recordings in the house, Carmen Cavallaro and Frankie Carle. I preferred Frankie Carle. At that time, he sounded more in the Fats Waller vein. He might still be alive; he was last year at ninety-six or ninety-seven. I called him about three years ago and told him how I learned to play the piano, and I sent him my CD. He was writing letters back.

WE: So in terms of basics, like fingering, you just did it whole cloth, by yourself?

JB: Yeah. You can't play unless you get a good position.

WE: Is your fingering unorthodox?

JB: Probably. I mean, I do it different every time.

WE: Have other musicians commented on it?

JB: Sometimes classical pianists are in the audience, and they are always in awe of my technique. I think that's real funny. I can play scales with the right fingering, in quotes, "the right fingering." But that's about as far as it goes. Because I don't play at the keyboard.

There's this energy right *above* the keyboard. It's maybe one inch above? You know, like an aura. If you've ever looked at someone and saw aura, it keeps moving. It looks like a kaleidoscope. So it's off the keyboard. There's an energy in there. I play the form of the energy, and it lands on the keys and it makes the sound I hear. I don't play from the keys, I play from that form.

WE: Do you sense a form of energy for each note?

JB: Well, I'm sure it's for each note, but that isn't the way it appears. It appears like a phrase. Like a sentence. Not like a letter.

WE: Are these sensations common to musicians you work with?

JB: Well, when I have a band I try to use people who are in that same type of thing. What would you call groups of people? It's like different tribes (*chuckles*), so to speak. And if you're of that tribe, it isn't just that you go to your instrument, you're born that way. And when you go to sleep, you can go to that place. You can go and be working with somebody when you're asleep.

WE: How about your working relationship with, for instance, Eddie Gomez?

JB: Okay, talk about psychic—there you go; there's one right there. I know that, in the state when you're not awake, we go to some of the same places.

WE: Have you and Eddie Gomez talked about this?

JB: I know it.

JS: Along the same lines, my research has given me the impression that the first time you heard Ornette Coleman's music, it sounded "right" to you.[9]

JB: The greatest sound for me ever, and I never had that experience again. This is the only person who had *that,* because he had all the feeling there of the tones and the pitch and the rhythm. Especially the orchestral things or the string quartet things that he did. He has a wider scope of sound for me. You have to go up so high to fly a jet plane and then you have to go higher to fly on a rocket and so on. He goes at the highest level of anything that I heard. That doesn't mean that I particularly like the way he's doing it or who he does it with. It just means the pure musicality that comes out of it. It goes to a place that I know. I came in that way. I didn't do anything to get that way.

JS: Ornette is often referred to as an avant-garde musician, a label that can scare listeners away. Interestingly, you've been quoted as saying you've always been avant-garde.

JB: Me? I never called myself that. I just play. It's simple, it's natural, and I think of avant-garde as being something that's not simple and natural. Also, a lot of times people call something avant-garde because they think that the person who plays that way doesn't know what the basics are. I'm not one of those. And neither is Ornette.

JS: Do you think Ornette is "natural"?

JB: Of course. I don't think, I know. Music is like animals: they know. We know, too. People need a school where they can learn to perceive first, and then when you read, it all can make sense. Then people can't fool you so much. Politicians would be totally different. People need to know how to perceive first, and you can start that when a child is born, before they're born.

JS: Could you clarify your thought that "music is like animals?"

JB: If I look at a bird I see music, and I don't think that the bird is avant-garde.

JS: Do you think that the use of the label "avant-garde" has marginalized Coleman's influence?

JB: Well, they had some of the most advanced music there was, and a lot of people that developed after that used a lot of the principles that they were using. Like Miles Davis. I never heard him play phrases—maybe they developed just simultaneously—but it was kind of odd that after Don Cherry was playing these different kinds of phrasings, then suddenly Miles is starting to do that. I didn't know Miles that well, but I know Ornette was always paying attention to Miles, and I think it was mutual. So there's a lot of influence that came from Ornette directly that nobody acknowledges, even now. But what about Monk? You know, I mention Monk to my students now, and many of them don't even like him. But somebody's gonna come along and take what Monk did and go on. We don't have that extension either. We've got a lot of extensions of Trane right now. But we don't have any extensions of Ornette.

JS: Did you see Ornette's predecessor, Charlie Parker, perform?

JB: I *saw* him, but I didn't see him in a physical form.

WE: How did you manage that?

JB: With my eyes closed. (*Laughs.*)

WE: You saw him playing?

JB: Yeah, I see a lot of things that way. It's not something I like to do, it's just something that happens.

JS: Aside from three good instructors in high school, has there been an important teacher in your life?

JB: No. And that's why I teach.[10] I really know what to teach because I know what I would've wanted when I was three or four. I look at each person and teach them according to how I see they can learn the quickest way. I have almost been fired from some places because the student learns too much and starts working and then doesn't go back the next year to the school. But if you only have 120, at the maximum, years to live, then why should somebody be wasting your time, you know? If I could teach somebody in three months what would take them five years to learn, I feel I'm doing the universe a favor, and that's who *I* work for. I work for the universe. The universe made me, so I give back to the universe.

WE: While we're talking about teaching, did Harold Land, Dexter Gordon, or others coach you when you started doing gigs in Los Angeles in the late '50s and early '60s?[11]

JB: Of course. But people didn't teach like they do now. They wouldn't tell you anything. If anything, they would keep the knowledge away. You had to search for it. It was the opposite. And also, you didn't get up on the bandstand simply because you were the right race and the right age and had the right face and the right figure. You had to be able to *play*. The jazz critics were not able to make or break a musician yet. It was in the hands of the musicians.

WE: Has that changed?

JB: Ooh! Has that ever changed! (*Laughs.*) Not just critics, people who produce the concerts now. There was much more respect for the art form. It wasn't something that slammed your face on the front of *Newsweek* and everybody knows your name and now you're rich and famous. And that means you can play. In those days they didn't have that.

WE: Elaborate if you will on the point about being the "right race," etc.

JB: Now it's best, more in vogue, if you are a certain race and a certain age, and if you look a certain way and your personality is a certain way. That isn't what music is based on, and in the past, in the '40s and '50s when people were playing, even into the '60s, you had to really be able to play to get on the bandstand and to work in what would be a major group. And major groups were really the only groups that were creative and had that ability and played. But nowadays it's like you don't have to know so much, and it can go by what you look like. How you look on the magazine cover. It doesn't have to do so much with ability and what they do with their ability. When I was coming up, the whole thing was not like that. I mean, you couldn't exist on the bandstand if you couldn't play because the people on the bandstand would play you right off. They would play, and all of a sudden you wouldn't know what you were doing or where you were.

WE: Has this affected your career in a negative way?

JB: If I said the word "superstar," an image would come to your mind, I'm sure.

JS&WE: (*In unison*) Miles Davis.

JB: Okay, and you can probably name fifty others. As far as I know, America has never had a superstar woman playing any instrument. The other day, I was trying even to think of any woman instrumentalist *by herself* on the cover of any American jazz magazine. Not a singer, and while she's alive. By herself. You can look it up. You can do your research. I don't know, I've just never seen it. I mean, I've been on the cover, but I had to share it. Geri Allen's been on the cover with somebody else. In Europe we can get on the cover by ourself, but not here. Men can be on the cover if they play or if they sing; the women only can be on the cover if they sing. It's not just that, it's the whole career—the way that they hire and the amounts of money they pay. I'm lookin' for women to start makin' it, too. Not because they're women; it's a mix. Just don't take away the naturalness that we got born with, and that's what they've done. But it's part of just growing; this country is new.

WE: But how about your career, specifically?

JB: When you ask how is *my* career going, I feel like I'm a pioneer, number one, because there's nobody in my age group that played the kind of music that I play and had their own group and does what I do. As far as I know, there *wasn't* anybody doing that before me. Maybe musically, but not where they went through the regular bands—Art Blakey, Freddie Hubbard, Stan Getz, Joe Henderson, all of that, and then they came out. As far as I know, I'm the only woman that ever did that in my era.

WE: What about Mary Lou Williams?

JB: No. I'm talking about doing *all* of it just as if I wasn't a woman, you know. And I never deviated. So as far as I know, I'm the first one. The only person I could think of, and she never went on and continued in a working musical career, was Alice Coltrane. Now you have them coming up—twenty years down the line they have started to trickle through. You have Geri Allen, Renee Rosnes, Terri Lyne Carrington, Cindy Blackman, Jane Bunnett, people like that. So I call myself a pioneer, and being a pioneer, you can imagine what that's like. That's not so easy.

WE: Don't you think women musicians of an earlier era helped pave the way?

JB: I think people like Mary Lou Williams, Dorothy Donegan, Marian McPartland, who were major talents, didn't have nearly the opportunities that awaited me in the '60s and '70s, etc. It was much harder for them than for me. They had to create their own opportunities to a large extent.

WE: Have you had problems with other musicians because you're a woman?

JB: No. Not very much of that. If I had that, it would be from people who are younger, and not for long. Actually, I found that changed. That completely changed. All the young people got *really* perceptive. I had a member or two in my band where that happened, and well, what happens now is if anybody has any indication of that, they're out.

WE: You mean resisting you because you're a woman?

JB: No, not even that. Say if we're playin' together and I play some idea that's kind of, for them at the moment, complicated, and they interpret that I made a mistake because they can't hear what I played. So then in turn what they do is change their position of where they were playing to where they thought I was now, and then, you know, I'm out there. But all the while they could be thinking that. That doesn't happen now. The younger musicians are *very* perceptive. My ideas are not hard or that complex.

WE: You're talking about your ideas. I was talking about your gender.

JB: No, I was just talking about *that.* I felt some of it had to do with gender. If that had been a guy playing he would have thought twice; he would have said I wonder what that idea was. What was that? Oh, okay, that was an idea of 5/4 superimposed over the 4/4, and she did that for three or four measures—he would have wondered what that was. But I've had some people where they just thought it was wrong—that would have to happen over and over for me to feel that way 'cause that could happen to anybody anytime, but if it happened every time we played some tune, then they're out. But I don't have to worry about that now because the people don't do that. That's been a change in the last five years. Younger people are much better prepared and are ready for anything. They're not looking at all if you're a woman or man. Actually I had some people where the opposite happened—it's partly why I use younger people in my group—I had some of the people say: "Well, look, I've played too long, I don't have to bother with learning this hard music that you play. I'm not going to do that anymore. That's too hard for me and I'm not gonna do it. I'm too old for that." I've had some people that are big names say that. So, of course, I don't use them. I respect what they have to say, but I'm wondering at the same time. I would be very bored if I felt that way. Maybe I'm not old enough; maybe I have to be older to get that way. Not chronologically, but another way.

WE: How do you select your band members?

JB: Sometimes their name pops out when it's written somewhere. It lights up. That's how I got Ravi Coltrane. I saw his name written somewhere, and it went just like that.

WE: In your opinion, are women musicians today still getting less than their due?

JB: How could anybody get their due as long as there's such a thing that you have to be this in order to be that, and one of the things you can't be is a woman?

JS: To continue with your chronology, do you think that coming up in the 1950s was an advantage musically?

JB: If I had to think of an advantage that I had over what's going on today, then that would've been it. 'Cause, you know, we had Horace Silver—did he sound like Thelonious Monk? Did Monk sound like Bud Powell? Did Bud Powell sound like Oscar Peterson? Did any of them sound like Herbie Hancock? It's like people were going inside and finding their music, and so I am fortunate. I just mentioned some piano players, but we could have gone through drummers or horn players and whatever. So we really had the distinct advantage that that was our whole world. So when we come into *this* world, it has its humorous points.

JS: Why did you leave Los Angeles?

JB: Because more of the music was here in New York, and the musicians were here. And also more seriousness here. More creativity here.

JS: You were married to Charles Brackeen at the time. Did you both come to New York with jobs lined up?

JB: Oh, no. Just like in a covered wagon. Actually we took a train.

WE: How did you make the contact with Art Blakey?

JB: That's a fun story. I lived in the East Village around the corner from this club called Slugs. It had these wood shavings all over the floor; it was like a dollar to get a beer. Almost all the major bands worked there. One time Art Blakey was working there. I walked in and it just sounded *great*. I just loved the way he played. But the piano player wasn't playing. He was just sitting up there. I think he was new; I don't know whether he didn't know the tune or he got lost or whatever. I just felt like, you know, sometimes it sounds great, but at this time it sounded like a piano should have been playing. So without even thinking, I just walked up to the stand and I said to the piano player, "Do you mind if I play some?" I didn't even think; everybody else was playing. I was just thinking of the sound of the music, you know. He said no, it was okay. So I played. I think I went through the whole set. At the end of the set Art looked up, and they said he saw a new face. So, then I was in the band. I had no idea.

WE: Were the two of you close?

JB: He used to call me his adopted daughter. Like he was the first person that I ever met that would talk about the thoughts that were in my head. I would never say them because nobody talked about them. Not only did he say them, he had such a sense of humor. So when he said I was his adopted daughter, I really felt that.

WE: Did you write tunes for the band?

JB: I wrote tunes, but the band couldn't play them. (*Laughter.*) I played them right after I left Art's band. You know, I was in Stan Getz's band, and actually Stan might have played a couple of tunes, but mostly he would give the trio a chance to play them. That was, like, Billy Hart and Clint Houston. Later that was my band.

JS: Did Getz's style constrain your playing at all?

JB: Stan Getz had certain constraints. You had to fit in a certain form. Inside of that form, you could develop. With Art, you could just open. But with Joe Henderson, after Stan, that was the most open band.

JS: More open than Art?

JB: Well, yeah. Because Art always had a group, your solos couldn't go on forever. Joe would leave the bandstand for twenty minutes and that's your solo.

JS: Getz often appeared melancholy or angry. What was he like to work with?

JB: You know, it just reminds me of this picture that Jimmy Rowles drew of Stan. He had this picture of twenty people, and it was called "A Nice Bunch of Guys." That was Stan Getz. (*Laughs.*) He always had a different personality.

JS: So you weren't as close with Getz as you were with Art Blakey?

JB: With Stan it was kinda strange. We were both really psychic. You could be in the front of the plane, and if you'd say anything about him, all of a sudden he'd come wandering up. But I was the same way. So if he would say something, there'd be these symbols; in some case it could be the name of a person or it would be a symbol. If he would give a symbol that I didn't care for, then I would either say or wear a symbol that he didn't care for, and nobody ever said anything. It was like this underground communication, but we never spoke about it. I can give you an example. I'm not going to tell you what *he* said, because it involves other people's names that I knew that he suddenly didn't like, and they're really good musicians. But if he was upset—who knows what reason he wanted to be upset at me—he would make sure I was in earshot and he would say this name. Now, how he knew I knew what that name meant to him and what it was supposed to mean to me, I don't know; but I knew. I knew he hated women to wear hats, so if he would just one time say that word within earshot of me, then that night I would wear a hat. Then he'd stop. Then it would reoccur. This went on *all* the time.

JS: Did you speak to each other musically on the bandstand?

JB: Oh, yeah! One time he got up on the bandstand and said one of these things, or did one of these things, and it was really the wrong time to do it. We were down in New Orleans; I can't remember what it was, but it was one of those little signals. We had many of them. They weren't all verbal. He could leave something out or he could make a certain movement. Whatever it was he did, it was really off center for the band to have experienced at that moment, and he *knew* it. We were playing, and in my own mind I was about to go up to the microphone and say something to the audience to clarify whatever had happened. 'Cause it was something that was being withheld from the audience. He knew he did it— every time he knew and every time I knew—I don't think anyone else in the band knew it. Then he called "Lush Life." I remember I had to play behind him on "Lush Life." I would play these delicate, beautiful chords that sound great with him. But this time I played some Cecil Taylor–type chords and runs. They also sounded great with him, but it was totally out, and it was not what he wanted to go on behind him, so he stopped whatever it was. He fixed it up. He repaired it very quickly. I remember just playing this *outrageous* thing behind him, so he stopped. He didn't think I would do that on the stand. I mean, he thought it was limited to wearing the hats. So he was going to go one step further and see how far this can go. He saved himself from me getting up and announcing something to the audience, but at the same time he didn't save himself from having that musical experience.

JS: Is it fair to say that there were tense moments like that from time to time in the band?

JB: Oh, every night. Stan never let up. He was total intrigue.

JS: Fascinating portrait of him.

JB: Yeah. But the main thing was the music. He was incredible. You know, the pitch and the sound he played in was just amazing. And also, he always had great bands. That's a part of, I guess, being a bandleader that people seemed to be able to do in those days.

JS: What were bandleaders able to do in those days?

JB: Instead of hiring the people that the press put on the top of *Jazz Times* or *Down Beat,* they actually hired people who really could play the best with their band or that they wanted to give that opportunity to and they knew had the talent. These days you can see anything behind anyone. You can go see a *great* horn player or singer, and the band or part of the band is like really weak. But in those days, that didn't happen.

JS: You didn't have any big band experience like so many of your elders when you were coming up. Is that something you'd like to rectify?

JB: Sometime, if I get accomplished what I want to do, I would like to do it. I just think that some of my tunes would sound great arranged for an orchestra, rather like symphonies. I wrote a string quintet and a string quartet, and I need to write one more so it makes a whole program. After that a big band would be great.

JS: Are you writing these string pieces in a classical form?

JB: I just wrote 'em; I made my own form. I use the same kind of phrases that I improvise with. I'm sure if Ornette listened to it, it wouldn't sound like classical music to him, but unless you listen to a lot of music you might think it sounds more like classical. All I did was just write the same way that I hear and play. One part of this has a two-minute section where I said, okay, I'll play for two minutes. And I don't have any clock or anything, right? I said, okay, I'm gonna play the violin part. So I played it and put it into the tape recorder. Then I said, okay, I'll play the viola part, same thing. No form, no key, no nothing. I did all four voices like that, and it sounds great. I think that some kind of writing can be like that—spontaneous writing. You just hear it and go play the separate parts, and then you put them together. I hope I live long enough, 'cause all these ideas that I've had since I was little, you know, slowly and surely they're . . .

JS: What ideas?

JB: Well, there are some songs that I wrote and recorded—"Haiti B"[12] and "Egyptian Dune Dance"[13]—that started out in different meters. That was, like, back in the '70s and '80s, when that was not so widespread. I mean, Max Roach was doing some of that, and John McLaughlin, but I didn't listen that much to them for that thing, and they didn't do it in the way that I'd started to do it. But now everybody's doing it. Now I have to go back and relearn what I started doing, like, twenty years ago, but I had four children to raise and I had to play what people would pay for. I have to go back and learn my own vocabulary.

JS: Was it just unusual meters that you were working with?

JB: And harmonies.

JS: Are you saying that your harmonies were more advanced early on and people are only now beginning to pick up on them?

JB: Yeah. I had to be careful what I played when I worked with Stan and other people. I couldn't use what I might want to use. I had to always monitor and edit it. So that stuff I started *way, way* back, and nobody would accept it. Now it's acceptable; in fact, it's preferable. In fact, they think it's the new thing now. Another one who thought like that was Art Blakey. When I was in his band we were on the road in Japan, and after the gig, you know, we'd go back to our rooms and do stuff. I had some of Miles's albums with Tony Williams on it. You know, everybody's listening to Tony. And Art plays the way he plays, right? But he came and heard what we were listening to, and for about three nights in a row he played everything that Tony plays. And another thing that people don't know is that Stan Getz could play what John Coltrane played. On July 4th, 1976, we were playing in Hamburg, Germany. We were playing "La Fiesta."[14] At the end of the tune he started playing like Trane, and you would not believe it. Something like Trane and Albert Ayler; on, and on, and on. Totally, totally out and perfect. I had a tape of it, but he confiscated it.

WE: Why is that important?

JB: Well, it's interesting. It's like Art Blakey was prepared to play in his era anything that was gonna happen in the future. Stan Getz never let anybody even know he could do that, and you'd call his thing very conservative, very lyrical. I would, too. I found out later on that he used to go listen to Trane all the time. But he didn't want anyone to know that. So I was just trying to say that the stuff that I was doing twenty years ago is now coming to pass, and these people think it's totally their new thing, their new vocabulary. So I have to go back into what I was doing. At last we can do this and people will listen and call it valid. But I don't have to worry cause my kids are self-supporting now. (*Laughter.*)

WE: Out of curiosity, when did you finally get free of monitoring and editing your playing?

JB: In the '90s.

WE: Now that you no longer have to be careful about what you play, how would you describe your piano conception?

JB: Well, when I play I don't hear the piano; I hear the sound of an orchestra and some things that are not in an orchestra. Sometimes I also get angry that there's not more notes, tones in between each tone. What I try to play is not there. One time I was writing a tune and trying to play the piano and I said, "Well, I can't play this." So I just sang it into the tape recorder. Then when I played it back I discovered it's all half tones, so that's why I couldn't play it. I said okay, go back to the piano and forget it.

JS: I want to ask you about some of the tunes you wrote on the album *Where Legends Dwell.*[15] What's behind the title "Edgar Irving Poe"?

JB: That's my name for Eddie Gomez. 'Cause you know when he talks, he's so prolific. It's like it's a book already written and edited. Listen, Eddie is one of these super geniuses. He'll tell you he wants to rehearse: "Oh, I gotta rehearse, I gotta rehearse." So, what would take somebody else three or four hours in a couple of days, he does in twenty minutes. He's got it. I don't know how he does that.

JS: Tell us about "Picasso."

JB: Oh, that was interesting, too. When I finished writing the tune, I said I know where this tune is from. If I look on a map, I can find where this tune is. So I looked at the American Express Book where they've got all these different countries. I saw Malaga. I said I know this is where this tune is from, so I put the title at the top of the tune. But to me the tune didn't sound like a city, it sounded like a person, so I couldn't get it, you know. And then an artist friend came over here, and he said, "Oh, I just went to see the Picasso show." And when he said "Picasso," I said that's the name of my tune. Later on, I was walking down Fifth Avenue and I went in a bookstore; and here's a book of Picasso, and he was born in Malaga.

WE: Let's talk about your *Maybeck*[16] recording on Concord. The way you interspersed your originals and standards was striking. Did you plan that out?

JB: No. When I got there I was so tired. I was just gonna go play a concert, so I hadn't decided anything yet. And then I walked into that room—it's all wood and these two great pianos. I said to Dick Whittington,[17] "Oh, wow! This has got to be a live record date, all these wood walls." And he was looking at me, like, kinda crazy. I said, "Let's call Carl[18] and see if he'll do it." It's like four o'clock Sunday afternoon, and Dick just looked at me and his jaw dropped open, you know, like all right, this girl is crazy. He called up and Carl Jefferson wanted to do it. So I went to sleep; I was really tired. I had done a lot of touring right before then. When I woke up it was about 6:30. They said, "Oh, the sound truck's here, it's going to be a date." So then I just wrote out something that would work. Because for a concert, I don't plan it. If it's a recorded concert, usually I would work on it and try to get things a certain way, but I had no idea I would want to record until four o'clock that afternoon.

[We turned to our first piece of music, "Syl-o-gism," performed by Mary Lou Williams, from *Zoning,* 1995; Smithsonian Folkways Recordings. Original recording released 1974.]

JB: That was *nice.* I like that. At first you didn't show me who it was and I thought, okay, it sounds something like Ahmad Jamal—you know, he'd emphasize the rhythm section and then he'd come in. She was playing a real lyrical tune, but she had, like, a note you don't expect and a time that you don't expect. That was in the '70s, but now in the '90s the piano player really plays the rhythms exactly like a drummer. So that would differentiate this 'cause hers was more loose; now they really nail that down. You might think of Jackie Terrason, somebody like that. So the piano player has more responsibility now in the rhythmical department, not the rhythms, but the way that they play them.

WE: Did you get to hear Mary Lou Williams in performance?

JB: She used to work at The Cookery; we used to always go over there in the '60s. I think that if the opportunities had been more open for women, that she would have been, like, really even a lot more than she was. If you go and hear somebody play, and they play the whole night one way and then when the people leave they start playing some other stuff that's *really* great, then you know. That's what I used to hear. I never did hear that on any recording that she did, but she had it, you know. She was studying to the end. If you didn't hear her, you didn't know that.

[Next we played "Eventually," by the Ornette Coleman Quartet, from *The Shape of Jazz to Come,* 1959; Atlantic Records.]

JB: It's the music that makes the most sense to me. Where that music comes from is where I came from right before I entered the Earth, and it's where I will go to when I finish this time around. Nothing's missing. It's all there for me. And it's the only music I've ever heard like that.

WE: How do you respond to people who say Ornette doesn't swing?

JB: That just means that he's at level one thousand and they're at level one or two, and they might have to come up to maybe level seventy-five to one hundred to even perceive what might be there.

WE: What happened the first time you heard Ornette?

JB: It was the first time I heard music that sounded like, "Wow! This is my family, this is my home."

WE: Was it a revelation, as if lightning struck?

JB: Well, that makes it sound separate. It makes it sound like you don't love something else. It just seemed like so a part of me. That's the best way to put it. Not like lightning; that sounds like some spectacular, "Oh, I love that." It wasn't like that. It was, "Wow! There really is something here like me." Not personality so much as just your nature.

WE: Obviously, then, you feel you are part of that tribe?

JB: I am. I was born that way. It's not a matter of learning or anything, it's just, like, that's the way you hear.

WE: How can you tell if someone is part of the tribe?

JB: Only the group knows.

[Next we listened to Bud Powell playing "Parisian Thoroughfare," from *The Amazing Bud Powell, Volume One,* recorded 1951; Blue Note Records.]

JB: You remember I was telling you that when I was little I used to listen to music and want something to go a certain way, and then it wouldn't go that way so I started composing? But with Bud Powell, everything he ever played, whatever I wanted to hear that would come next, he would always play exactly that. But it was more like an era; the music that we just heard from Ornette doesn't sound so much like an era. Bud, of course, was playing directly Bird-type of lines.

JS: So in comparison to the Bebop era, Ornette and his group stand as an isolated phenomenon?

JB: Well, it's too much of an era. It's like a whole—maybe it's two hundred years or something. Whereas Bud Powell was twenty years, or whatever that was. That's how I learned to play jazz. I transcribed Powell's solos. But it was nothing for me, because those are the notes I would hear in my head first. He was just playing them.

JS: You mean it was easy for you?

JB: Yeah. Every note; I never had any question. So many piano players I'd say, "Oh, wow, it was such a nice phrase, why don't they use this note or that note, or why didn't they start this phrase here and there?" But with him it was like everything was just there, just perfect. Monk had that for me too.

Selected Discography

Six Ate (originally released as *Snooze*). Candid CHCD 71009 (1975).
Fi-Fi Goes to Heaven. Concord CCD4316 (1987). (With Branford Marsalis.)
Live at Maybeck Recital Hall, Vol. 1. Concord CCD 4409 (1989). (Solo piano.)
*Pink Elephant Magic. Arkadia 70371 (1999).

Notes

1. Leonard Feather, *The Passion for Jazz* (New York: Horizon Press, 1980), p. 144.
2. Inner City.
3. Concord.
4. Arkadia.
5. From *Where Legends Dwell,* 1992; Concord.
6. Concord.
7. American Biographical Institute.
8. *Mythical Magic,* 1978.
9. Bob Blumenthal, "First Comes the Sound/JoAnne Brackeen," *Down Beat,* August 1982, pp. 26–27, 55.
10. JoAnne Brackeen is a professor at Berklee School of Music in Boston.
11. Linda Dahl, *Stormy Weather: The Music and Lives of a Century of Jazzwomen* (New York: Limelight Editions, 1984, 1982), p. 171.
12. Recorded on *Tring-A-Ling,* 1977; Choice Records.
13. Recorded on *Special Identity,* 1981; Antilles Records.
14. Written by Chick Corea.
15. Ken Music.
16. *Live at Maybeck Recital Hall, Vol. 1,* 1989; Concord Records.
17. Owner of Maybeck Hall.
18. Carl Jefferson, owner of Concord Records.

Clora Bryant

Clora Bryant

Criminally unsung, the name of pioneering trumpet player Clora Bryant does not appear in many of the popular guides to jazz. Nevertheless, this ardent student of Dizzy Gillespie, and an accomplished musician in her own right, has been among a handful of pathfinders for future generations of female instrumentalists. Bryant's pluckiness and passion to perform have enabled her to suffer indignities because of her race, gender, and choice of instrument, and to piece together a long and colorful, if unheralded, career in jazz.

Born May 30, 1927, in Denison, Texas, Bryant first picked up the trumpet at age fifteen. She progressed so rapidly that upon graduation from high school she had her choice of music scholarships. Opting to specialize in jazz, she enrolled at Prairie View A&M University, a historically black college near Houston. Bryant joined the school's swing band, the Prairie View Co-Eds, which toured the Chitlin' Circuit.[1] One of many all-girl groups during World War II, the Co-Eds distinguished themselves not only by the quality of their music-making, but also because the members were all African-American college women.

After one year at Prairie View, Bryant moved to California, where her older brother introduced her to the Central Avenue jazz scene. Inspired by hearing trumpeter Howard McGhee for the first time, she began collecting 78 RPM bop records. Bryant memorized the solos of her trumpet idols en route to her own status as a featured soloist with the West Coast all-girl bands the Sweethearts of Rhythm and the Queens of Swing.

She married bass player Joe Stone in 1949, and began sitting in at jam sessions, where she entered into a musical fraternity with many legendary bebop players. The 1950s found Bryant raising two sons and playing at Central Avenue's best jazz venues, including gigs with Eric Dolphy and Art Pepper at the Lighthouse Cafe in Hermosa Beach. In 1957, a small Hollywood label recorded her lone album as a leader, *Clora*

Bryant . . . Gal with a Horn.[2] First and foremost a trumpet player, she reluctantly agreed to sing on all eight tracks in order to get her album produced.

Because she was a woman who played the trumpet, club owners and even audiences of the '50s and '60s regarded Bryant as more of a novelty act than a serious musician. Clearly this was undeserved, as she has a driving bebop trumpet style reminiscent of Gillespie's. Possessing a powerful sound and sassy rhythmic sense, she ventures daringly into the atmosphere at the apex of solos, while her treatment of ballads is disarmingly tender.

In 1989 Bryant became the first female jazz instrumentalist to tour Russia. She has since co-authored a book on Central Avenue jazz and has played a key role in the revitalization and preservation of Central's old jazz quarter. In 1991 she initiated the drive for Dizzy Gillespie's star in Hollywood's Walk of Fame. The crowning glory of Bryant's musical career occurred more recently. On May 6, 2002, at the Kennedy Center in Washington, D.C., Dr. Billy Taylor presented Clora with the prestigious Mary Lou Williams Women in Jazz Award.

Recorded July 31, 1997

JS: Clora, to what do you attribute your lack of recognition as a jazz musician?

CB: Well, I never had a good manager. The reason why I didn't get a full-time manager is because of what you would have to do—the couch scene. (*Chuckles.*) I figured if I had a union card I shouldn't have to go that route. I think that is what really held me back.

JS: At what point were you in a position to really launch your career?

CB: That would have been the year that I did my album, 1957—the only record that I have in my name. Before the record came out, I went to Canada. I was ready. The record got three stars in *Down Beat,* but when I came back from Canada the record company was out of business.

JS: Am I correct in understanding that you had been in Canada a few years prior to that?

CB: Yes. When I first went there in 1954, I had my husband and my two oldest kids, and you know, it was the strangest thing when we got to Canada. The people there in Montreal acted like they'd never seen a black family before. We'd go down the street and we'd look like the Pied Piper. (*Laughter.*) People would be coming out of the buildings, they would be hanging out of the upstairs windows, they would be putting on brakes and making U-turns, and coming out of stores—you wouldn't believe it! My oldest son, Charles, has light hair and blue eyes, and they would rub his hair. They would say *frisé,* that's French for kinky. He was a blond, but his hair wasn't straight. They wanted to feel what it was like, I guess. It got to the place where my husband would not walk down the street with us. He said, "I'm not going out."

JS: Was it heckling or friendly curiosity?

CB: It was curiosity, but it became like a heckle because it was every time we went out. We could not go *anywhere* together as a family. After a while my husband couldn't get any work. They started calling him my "pimp," so my mother-in-law came and got the kids and brought them back to LA. About a month later he asked me to send him home, which I did.

I stayed there a year and a half and worked. That was very profitable, because I learned a lot about the business.

WE: When you went to Canada in 1954, did you have a stage act already formed?

CB: I had started doing my act in 1952 in Los Angeles, before I went to New York City in 1953 or Canada in 1954. I played the trumpet and sang. I would pick my music and have arrangements made for me. At that time Prez Prado's song "Cherry Pink and Apple Blossom White" was famous, and that would always get the house, as they say. That was a big number for me, especially in Canada, 'cause I would sing it in French.

WE: Didn't your act eventually include impersonations, including one of Louis Armstrong?[3]

CB: Yeah. I would do Jimmy Cagney, Mario Lanza—"Be My Love"—and Maurice Chevalier. But Louis was more effective because I played the trumpet. So I just zeroed in on that. One time Louis brought his own band onstage with me. That was a thrill. His band was in the big room at the Riviera, and we were in the lounge. So he and Lucille would come in between shows and sit back there and listen. Finally one night—he didn't say anything to me about it; none of the guys knew, either—we hear this music coming through the casino. "Basin Street Blues"—I guess he knew which song I was on. He came through the casino and up on the stage with me. I almost wet my pants. I almost dropped the horn. I wanted to faint. Oh, I didn't know what to do. (*Laughs.*) The guys said, "I didn't know if I should shit or go blind." That was a thrill! Here he comes with Barney Bigard, Trummy Young. Oh, man! Then he starts telling the people about me, what I was doing and how much he admired me. I started looking around to see who he was talking about. That was fun. Louis was a fun person.

WE: But Louis wasn't just a smiling face, was he?

CB: No. You see, I don't look at people like that when they're like that onstage. I don't see them as being clowns, because I know where they're coming from. Louis came from down south, where you had to do those kinds of things to get over. My dad had taken me to see minstrel shows. Back then we had what's called sideshows with the carnivals. We had midnight rambles in the theaters, and I knew what the guys had to do just to get onstage. Just before I came along they were blackening their faces, imitating the whites imitating them. That's what the minstrelsy era was about.

WE: Why would the black performers stoop to that?

CB: They weren't stooping when they blackened their faces. The black entertainers were reacting to the actions of the whites in blackface just so they could get onstage. Because when the white guys started blackening their faces and doing an impression of us, we couldn't get on the stage. The women didn't do it; just the men—the comedians. Bert Williams was blackface—he would blacken his face because he was a light man. He'd blacken his face and whiten his lips. That was in the early '20s. He was one of the first black acts on Broadway. People like Pigmeat Markham and Step 'n Fetchit did what they call "Uncle Tom stuff." That was the only way they could get through. But while those guys were doing that stuff, they were making good money. Step 'n Fetchit would come over on Central Avenue driving a purple Rolls-Royce one night and another color the next night, but he had to scratch his head and say "Yassah, boss" and all that kind of stuff to get it. They did what they had to do. I understand that. Although in my own town, to my knowledge, I only experienced one thing that woke me up to what was really happening as far as prejudices and things are concerned. I had to go in the *back* door of a *white* church to play for them.

WE: When you were in high school?

CB: Yes. I couldn't understand. "Why do I have to go to the back door?" I understood that in the department store downtown you couldn't try on any clothes. I understood that they wouldn't serve you, you'd have to go to the back door of a restaurant, but go to the back door of a church? That was beyond my comprehension. And, you know, everybody is supposed to feel like we were all created equal. It broke my heart. I was crushed. I could hardly play. "Ave Maria" was *really* shaking that day. (*Laughter.*)

WE: Clora, I have the impression you grew up in a closely knit family. Is the notion of family important to you?[4]

CB: Without my family, I couldn't have done the music. And without music, I couldn't have done my family.

WE: Why couldn't you have made music without your family?

CB: My mother died when I was three, so my father raised me and my two brothers. That was my whole point of wanting to get married and have kids—to have another family unit. As I grew up I always said, "Why isn't my mother here to love me?" My dad would say, "She's gone to heaven," but it never satisfied me. I wanted something of my own that I could love and nurture. I always knew that I'd have a family, and I always knew that when I did I'd take them on the road with me. I nursed them backstage, you know. It jelled. Without my family I would have been nothing.

WE: Do you think the presence of a family made the content of what you played richer?

CB: I do believe. I think I drew from inside of me what my kids had given to me. Not my husband, because he was a musician, too, and he was, you know, out there on the road all the time. Like I tell everybody, I worked behind Billie Holiday on Central Avenue, and we'd sit in the dressing room and she'd always want to talk about family. She'd want to talk about marriage, 'cause she always wanted to get married and have a family. My marriage was down the tubes, so to speak, but I could talk about my kids. In fact, Billie babysat my daughter when we rehearsed, you know. She was a beautiful lady. She was just misunderstood. She's kinda like me. But, you see, I didn't use the things that happened to me when I was a little girl—I didn't let that become a chain around my neck. By being without a mother, losing my father at one time, and being abused by my uncle, that could have given me all kinds of excuses to say, "Well, I didn't do that because I was this and that."

WE: What were the circumstances when your father left home?

CB: It was 1942; I was fifteen. He worked in a hardware store and was accused of stealing paint. He didn't do it, but a black man couldn't deny the charges. This was the South, so that would be like saying a white is lying. The police beat him up. They put him on a freight train and sent him out of town. He ended up in Yuma, Arizona. He came back before my senior year because he always said he'd be back to see me graduate, and he was.

WE: What influence did your father have on your life?

CB: My dad instilled in me that I was special. That I could be whoever I wanted to be, that I could do whatever I wanted to do—I just had to have the motivation. My dad only had a fifth-grade education, but he was *smart* as far as knowing from his heart and how to handle things. He grew up down south. His mother had been a slave. He had a lot of "mother's wit"—that's what we call it down south. My dad was in the Navy in the First World War. He served on the USS *Utah,* which is at the bottom of the ocean at Pearl Harbor. When I was coming up, we had to make the bed where the dime would bounce on the bed. He would go around with his white glove. That's why I made sure I had my table cleaned before you guys came today. (*Laughter.*) We had to have our clothes folded a certain way or he'd do like Joan Crawford: he'd dump them on the floor. We had to have the hangers hanging in the same direction. We had to swab the deck every day. I can draw on so many things that my dad taught me that you don't find in books and you don't learn in universities. I tell everybody I went to the University of Charles Bryant.

JS: You started on the trumpet at age fifteen. Had you received any formal musical training prior to that?

CB: Very little. I just knew the scales, and my aunt had bought one of those cards that you put in the back of the piano keys and I picked the notes out on the piano. I would learn something and teach my brother. We had a white lady who came over from a little town called Sherman, which is ten miles from my home. She'd come in the black neighborhood and teach kids. When I was about nine, that lady heard me and my brother on my aunt's piano, so she came over across the street and wanted to know who was playing the piano. I said it was me and my brother. She said, "I'd like to teach you guys." I said, "Well, my dad doesn't have any money. We can't afford it." There were two young girls across the street. She said, "As long as their mother and father pay for their lessons, I'll come over and teach you guys for free." She'd catch the train to Dennison and teach these girls, and then she'd take an extra hour to teach us.

WE: The first big band you played with was the Prairie View Co-Eds.[5] Tell us about some of your experiences with that group.

CB: With the Co-Eds, every weekend we'd leave campus and play somewhere: Houston, Dallas, Fort Worth, San Antonio, Austin, Corpus Christi, Galveston, Port Arthur. Then the summer of 1944 came the East Coast tour, when we went to New York. That was the first time that I'd been away from home. We stayed at one house where they kept a goat in the house, and you know how goats smell. We traveled in three station wagons, and we slept in the station wagons that night. We went through some changes traveling like that. We'd pull up to a service station and the guy would come out with a rifle: "You better get your ass outta here or I'll fill it full of lead." We'd want to use the bathroom. "We don't have no bathroom for niggers; go on out there in the field and squat."

JS: What did you think of New York City when you first saw it?

CB: Coming into New York is what I remember. (*Laughs.*) We came in those three station wagons, and we had a chaperon who must have weighed three hundred pounds. We had three flats in my station wagon—I rode with the chaperon 'cause I was the youngest one in the band. And, boy (*laughs*), it was at the height of traffic, you know, and people were blowing their horns. They saw the Texas license plates, and they talked about us like dogs! Then we pulled up to the hotel where bebop started, in a club called Minton's. We stayed at the Cecil Hotel. I didn't get to go in the club because I was too young, but the other girls went in. They were able to hear some of the transition from swing to bop. I didn't get to be a part of that 'cause my chaperon was over me like a mother hen.

WE: Between your father and this chaperon, you led a fairly sheltered life!

CB: I really did. We had played Houston before we left; we played opposite Nat Towles's Band. Joe Louis's wife, Marva, was doing an act. She was singing, and Nat Towles's Band was playing behind her. In the band was a guy that married Sarah Vaughan, a good-looking trumpet player. I was sitting backstage and talking, and he came over to me—he knew we were going to New York that summer on a tour—so he said, "When you get to New York I'll come backstage and I'll take you to dinner." I said, "Great." I mean, what do I know?

(*Laughs.*) When we get to New York, he comes backstage and he asked Mrs. Von Charleton—that was our chaperon's name—if he could take me to dinner. He wanted me to go meet his aunt. Oh, well, if you say somethin' like that down south, you want your lady friend to meet your family, you could do no wrong. So Mrs. Von Charleton said, "Sure." We went to dinner, then he took me to this place and this lady comes to the door. He said to me, "Go on in, I'll be in in a minute." He's standing at the door talking to the lady—I guess he was paying her. (*Laughs.*) So she gives him a key to this room and we go in. I said, "Was that your aunt?" I thought it was so strange 'cause he didn't introduce me to the lady who I thought was his aunt, you know. He said, "No, but she'll be here in a minute." Then he starts taking his jacket off. I said, "What are you doing?" He said, "I'm just gonna get comfortable; pull your sweater off." I said, "No, where's your aunt?" He said, "Oh, she'll be here in a minute." And then he came over and he tried to kiss me, and I *screamed*. This lady must have been standing outside the door, 'cause she busted in and said, "I *thought* that girl was too young. Get her outta here." (*Laughs.*) He had taken me to a room to have sex—I didn't know what was going on! He tried to hold my arm, but I jerked it loose from him, and I read him up and down about he and his aunt. He said, "I didn't know you didn't know that's what taking you to see my aunt meant." I said, "How would I know? I just turned seventeen, and I'm straight out of Texas."

WE: While we're in this subject area, is it true that you had another startling experience when you played a short stint with the Sweethearts of Rhythm?[6]

CB: They [the Sweethearts of Rhythm] played the Million Dollar Theater, and they were traveling in a bus. Miss Jones was going to ask my dad if I could travel with them. But the first day that I played with them, I went home that night and told my dad about the girls feeling each other's boobs and butts. It was a shock. I had never seen it before; I didn't know what was going on. They were trying to decide whose sleeping mate I was going to be in the bunk on this bus, you know. My dad said, "You come home." So at each intermission I had to come home from downtown LA out to the West Side.

JS: Did all the women in the band act like that?

CB: I didn't say everybody, no.

WE: Let's revisit the fact that your career never really took off. You had developed connections with some great musicians, such as Dizzy Gillespie, Duke Ellington, and Count Basie. Why didn't they hire you for their bands?

CB: Well, they tried, but being a female horn player and not a vocalist, per se, they ran into a lot of resistance from the fellas in the band, as well as from the wives, agents, and managers. See, in the case with Dizzy—who was my mentor; he was my friend, we loved each other—he had gone through a thing where he'd been accused of being a father of a baby, so he had to be very careful of what he did with a female. Basie had gone through the same with the singers, you know, and his wife had found out about it. There were so many things that Dizzy had wanted to do, but he could not do them because he was married. Ours was a platonic relationship. I don't know what would've happened had we been lovers, but I don't think it could have been any better, because Dizzy would do what he could. He'd put my name out there. He wouldn't give people money. All the guys would tell you that Dizzy was very stingy because his wife took care of the money situation. Count Basie and Duke Ellington, they could only do so much for a female unless you were their lover. They could sneak around and do it, but I wasn't going for that. I thought too much of myself.

WE: As you were coming up, did you hear comments like "She plays good for a girl"?

CB: That was the usual comment from men about all-girl bands. It was during the '40s and '50s, because the war was on and girl bands were in. At that time the women were just beginning to get a toehold in the big time. I tell the girls today they're walking on our backs because we paved the way for them. I didn't mind those comments at the time, but I don't like to hear it now. You don't go up to a man and say, "You play good for a man." But you know what? *I* didn't have that problem. See, Diz and those guys never said, "You play good for a girl." They'd just say, "Damn, girl, you're good." I never had a problem with that because I *wanted* to be defined as a female. I always wanted to play like they *say* a man plays. I wanted to play like that, but I didn't want it to be something different because I was a female and I was able to do it. I just wanted to do it because that's the way you played. Most of them think that *women are too weak* to play the trumpet. So when they say you play good for a girl, I think that's the old left-field compliment, but it is still a compliment, as far as I'm concerned.

WE: Have you lost out on jobs because of your gender?

CB: Oh, sure. *And* my color. I got a call to do Ada Leonard's All-Girl Band on TV. I did one week, and then they got calls to get that n-i-g-g-e-r off that show. I was the only black on there. This was somewhere around 1951 or 1952.

JS: During the beginning stages of your career, you sat in with a lot of groups. How many female horn players were sitting in at bebop jam sessions in the late '40s and early '50s?[7]

CB: I would be the only one there.

JS: I bet it took courage to go out and play under that circumstance.

CB: That was the main thing: *nerve.* I never ran into any interference with the guys, you know. There was never any intimidation; they were never trying to put me down. All they would say is, "Here comes Clora with her widdle trumpet." Instead of "little," they'd say "widdle" trumpet. They'd let me call the tunes that I wanted to play. They would never try to show me up or play something like "Cherokee" at a fast tempo. At first I was trying to play the bebop. Then it dawned on me: "Clora, you'll never be able to play like Dizzy." To me that was the epitome of bebop.

I was the next generation after Dizzy. To come to grips with that, I would sit at home and practice. I'd get some bebop records and I'd play note for note. That's the way you really woodshedded and learned. You'd learn how to play somebody's solo, and then you'd pick it apart and take what you want out of it and try to build on that. I learned that by just sitting and listening to the guys. I noticed that they'd learn a solo, like a Charlie Parker solo, and then I'd hear them trying to get away from it, trying to insert some of what *they* felt. I got so my ears became like antennas because I listened so hard. And I'd keep time. You know, my foot would be going, and if somebody would get off, they'd check *my* foot to see if they were on the beat. They said, "Clora, don't you ever get off?" And that has a lot to do with the way that the guys accepted me, because I was so intent in listening to the music and trying to learn.

JS: With regard to your place in the generation after Dizzy Gillespie, do you feel that you contributed something new to the trumpet lineage?

CB: No. I don't think so. I don't know of any female that's been an innovator. I mean, Mary Lou Williams was there, you know, but she didn't bring anything new. She came out of somebody else. We have not created anything. I am speaking strictly of instrumentalists. Women singers were out there doing it before the men instrumentalists. Singers like Bessie

Smith brought the instrumentalists into the recording industry. They initiated a lot of things. But instrumentally, I think, we've been smothered a lot. A lot of women would get intimidated by some of the actions of the guys, but that never bothered me. I knew what I wanted to do. I never had any desire to try to start something new because I loved what was going on at the time. I loved swing music and I love bebop.

WE: What was the biggest musical difference between swing and bop?

CB: Well, for one thing it was the rhythms. You see, Dizzy brought in the conga drums; that gave it a different rhythm. They were playing a lot of different rhythms against each other like the Africans did. With swing it was just one, two, three, four. But the bop drummers changed the bass drum beat—"Klooke"[8] changed the bass drum beat—they'd drop bombs. That, to me, was the difference from swing. It was the rhythm that set bebop apart from swing along with all the other harmonies. I also began to become interested in the drums, which I ended up playing later on. In the '40s I played the trumpet with one hand and the drums with the other hand.

WE: Did you study drums?

CB: No, I was with a girls' group, and we needed a drummer. So I said, "Okay." And I went downtown to this music store and rented a set of drums and started playing.

WE: How did you know the proper way to hold the sticks?

CB: I watched. I watched everybody. A lot of trumpet players play the drums. Dizzy, Charlie Shavers played the drums. Most trumpet players have good rhythm. Roy Eldridge played drums. Roy was telling about one time that he'd taken a job playing some big rich person's party, you know, and he got loaded. He got ready to leave, and everybody was gone and he couldn't take the drums down. So he had to put the drum set already set up in the station wagon. I thought that was hysterical. He was so drunk he couldn't take his own drums down. Now, that was really drunk. (*Laughter.*)

JS: Is it harder to play bebop than it is to play swing?

CB: Oh, yeah! That's my opinion.

WE: Were there social as well as musical reasons for the development of bebop?

CB: Dizzy was just looking to do something different. There were so many things that Roy and other swing trumpeters had done. Critics will credit Louis and Buddy Bolden and Freddie Keppard and all those guys. Their glory had been stolen away from them by the Original Dixieland Jazz Band simply because they recorded first. But they had been coming over to the black part of New Orleans, listening and stealing the music. So they got the glory, and they got to use the name the Original Dixieland Jazz Band. But how could you be *original* if you didn't create anything? The same way with hanging the king title on Paul Whiteman, the "King of Jazz." Lord knows that Paul Whiteman wasn't the King of Jazz. He didn't know jazz if you hung it around his neck. And hanging the title of "King of Swing" on Benny Goodman and the title of "King of Rock and Roll" on Elvis Presley. Because, you see, we were rocking and rolling in the '30s. Ella Fitzgerald had this song out called "Rock It for Me" in 1938. The music we were doing, they ended up calling it first rhythm and blues. Then out of rhythm and blues, when Elvis came along, it was rock and roll. It's the same thing with the Original Dixieland Jazz Band.

JS: Was it a common perception among your generation that white musicians stole music from black musicians?

CB: Yes, from my point of view, and from just sitting backstage and listening to the ones that were creating, like Duke Ellington and Count Basie and Louis. Louis was not happy with what had happened, but he said, "There is nothing you can do about it." I hear that so much. But how long will we have to settle for "That's just the way it is"? It was the same thing that happened when Freddie Keppard didn't want to record. He played with a handkerchief over his hand because he didn't want the white guys stealing his music. But he didn't realize that they weren't watching his fingers; the music was coming out of his horn. You could write it down, so you could play it. But Dizzy and the beboppers felt that they had gone as far as they could go, and everything they played, the white guys would steal. Nobody probably has come right out and said that, but that was the way Dizzy laid it on me.

Dizzy and the beboppers wanted to get something new. Yet the music had to swing. See, that's where a lot of guys miss it with bop. Dizzy came through the rhythm and blues scene and swing, so he knew what swung. Most of the white guys were imitating Dizzy, like a lot of Stan Kenton's guys used to come over and listen to him when he was playing on the east side on Central Avenue. They would listen, but, see, they couldn't really get it. You can listen and you can steal, but there's some little something that you are missing.

WE: The rhythmic drive?

CB: Yeah, and a feel. That's what Dizzy said. "When I play, I'm just not playing the notes. It's the feeling." It's the same way with bop and with New Orleans music.

JS: When you just linked bop with music from New Orleans, it reminded me that prior to taping you said that true New Orleans music is different from Dixieland music.

CB: Yes. It's the rhythm and the time. There are certain songs they play at the same tempo, but it's *not* the same tempo. They could have the same tempo set by a metronome, but New Orleans music, when they play it at that same tempo, you're going to hear another little feel. You have to be listening for it; you just can't go with the flow. I worked with Dixieland bands and I played with a New Orleans band, and that's when I really found out the difference. Trummy Young and Barney Bigard had told me that there is a difference. When I played "When the Saints Go Marching In" with a Dixieland band, I knew it would be the same tempo I'd played it in with the New Orleans group, but with the Dixieland group I squared it up. Whereas with the New Orleans group I could play some Roy Eldridge and still have the New Orleans feel to it. You understand what I'm saying? With the Dixieland you have to stick to what they *think* the music is supposed to sound like. All the guys from New Orleans will tell you that there is a difference.

WE: Is the certain feel you've spoken of something that comes solely out of the African-American tradition?

CB: No, I don't think it comes out of that, but it's something that the white guys had to learn to feel because they had never felt or played with that feeling. A fact that is documented from the beginning with the Original Dixieland Jazz Band's recordings.

JS: You mentioned that members of Stan Kenton's band were some of the white players who were trying to imitate Dizzy. Didn't you sit in with Kenton's band?

CB: Yeah, I sat in with him in Chicago at the Blue Note. I only sat in because my manager in Chicago asked if I could. I did that one day. It wasn't a thing where I was sitting there just going crazy with the beat or anything, because it seems like Stan wrote his music where it didn't have that kind of swing. One time he had the nerve to come out on stage and tell Dizzy that he could play his music better than Dizzy could. But he was drunk. (*Laughs.*) So the next time he saw Dizzy, he crawled out on the stage on his knees and apologized. But Stan was so egotistical, he probably really thought he could play Dizzy's music better.

JS: During the '50s and '60s you were around some legendary players in Los Angeles, for example, trumpeter Lee Morgan.[9]

CB: We called him "Howdy Doody," Dizzy and I, 'cause of his ears. I met him when he was with Dizzy. We hung out together. I had just gotten a Grundig record player/radio. Lee Morgan and Charli Persip would come over to my house, and I'd fix breakfast and we'd be sittin' there listening to Clifford Brown's records. Or Miles Davis. We never listened to their records with Dizzy. They didn't want to listen to their music because they were playing it every night, you know. We'd listen to Clifford Brown and we'd sit there and say, "Man, how did he do that?" They'd get *very* technical. My antennas would go up so I'd know how to talk like that, too. That's the way I learned the ins and outs of the music, listening to all those guys that had been there and had been doin' it.

WE: Did you meet Ornette Coleman when he was on the LA scene?

CB: He used to come into the place where I was doing jam sessions.[10] At my jam sessions would be Ben Webster or Coleman Hawkins, and Max Roach or Kenny Dorham. Everybody that was in town came to my jam sessions. I was the leader. I had Carl Perkins on piano—that was the one true love of my life. I had a lot of boyfriends and lovers, but I was in love with Carl Perkins. We had a thing going on for about a year. What broke us up, he got loaded one night and he got off work and came over to my house. We were sitting there listening to some records, and then all of a sudden he went in the kitchen and came back with a butcher knife. My kids were in the bedrooms asleep, and I had to talk him down. I don't know what he was going to do with that knife, but I had to make him put the knife down. And I said, "It's best we don't see each other anymore." He was out of his head 'cause he would drop pills, too. I don't know what set him off. Boy, it scared me. I still love him. He was the only one that I ever felt that way about, dope or no dope. But he couldn't read a note the size of this room.

WE: Getting back to Ornette, would he participate in your jam sessions?

CB: Yes. Ornette had this little white plastic horn at the time. He and trumpet player Don Cherry, they would come in. Don would sit there with his little pocket trumpet. He wouldn't play in the jam session. But Ornette would come up, and then everybody would get off the bandstand. They didn't want to hear that noise. This was before he got his thing together—before he got with Billy Higgins. He was one of those I didn't do my usual thing and listen to. What came out turned me off. To me, it's just a little bit too much. He's not my type of player. I'm from the swing era. You gotta have some kind of rhythmic thing going where I can pop my fingers and tap my foot. But I give him credit for what he's doing.

JS: Looking at your career in later years, you had a serious car accident in 1972. Did that keep you from playing?

CB: It was a hit-and-run accident. A truck hit me; I had a little Toyota. It turned over twice, slid down the freeway, and threw me out. I had a compound fracture of the left leg, and I lost a half inch of bone, so the left leg is shorter than the right. But I never stopped working. When I came out of the hospital, I went to work in a wheelchair. I had just bought a house; I couldn't stop working. This band that I played in was really a swing-dance band. We played for a lot of swing-dance contests. I played in bands like that through the '70s.

JS: Did you play regularly into the '80s?

CB: Yes, and into the '90s, until I had my operation.[11]

JS: Tell us about your trip to Moscow in 1989.

CB: Oh, man! Getting there was something because I did it through my own initiative.

I wrote to Arts America in Washington, D.C., and I wrote to President Reagan trying to get some backing to go. After I wrote the letter to Gorbachev and got permission to go, I had to pay my own way, and I wanted to take my two sons. I couldn't get any help. So there was a Russian-American Communist organization at the time, and they paid my way. I know that during all that, my phone in Los Angeles must have been tapped, and they were checkin' on me because this Communist organization helped me get to Russia. But anyway, we had benefits, and I got money to take my two sons: my son Kevin, the drummer, and my son Darrin, a singer.

WE: Why did you want to go to Russia?

CB: When I wrote to Gorbachev, I wanted to be the first female *horn* player to play Russia. That was my hook.

JS: Aside from your sons, did you bring other American musicians along?

CB: We used Russian guys. All the hotels had big concert halls, and the first thing we did was at a hotel outside of Moscow. But when we got there, there was nobody there. A few musicians straggling around. We go downstairs to the dressing room—nice, big, pretty dressing room—and I pick up my horn and start playing. My son gets the sticks out, and we're having a good time. The next thing you know, the dressing room's full of people. We get upstairs and the auditorium is full. Just that quick. They have a network system over there that you wouldn't believe. The next night we played at the only jazz club that they had at the time, the Bluebird. We get there and the place is empty. Pretty soon the other musicians come in, and nobody's there. We started playing. We hadn't even finished one number, and the place filled up. TV cameras, newspaper reporters were there. We had a ball. [Our first piece of music was "Tight Like This," from *The Louis Armstrong Collection, Volume 4: Louis Armstrong and Earl Hines,* 1928; Columbia Records.]

CB: (*While the music is playing*) You know what's amazing? Louis, he didn't come through all these universities, he didn't have all these records like I did, so he couldn't listen and listen and listen. There were places where he could go and play, after he got out of that school he was in, and he could hear King Oliver and all those guys playing. But it's *amazing* how *he* turned the music around from where he came from. (*The music ends.*) He came from the *streets* of New Orleans. How did he do that? How did he take his upbringing and turn it into something where everybody all over the world loves and respects him? I mean, in Moscow I started doing Louis's things, and boy, I could get anything I wanted. They loved Louis just that much over there. This man with his lack of education, how was he able to create? I mean, people hadn't been phrasing like that. There hadn't been the syncopations like that in solos. Before, everything went straight up and down.

[The next selection was "Up Jumped Spring," from *Frank Morgan/Mood Indigo,* 1989; Antilles Records.]

JS: (*Before the music starts*) You know Frank Morgan personally, don't you?

CB: That's my boy. He was like my little brother. In l951, when Frank was still in high school, we were both playing in the house band at the (Club) Alabam. His dad would trust me to drive him to work six days a week because he was too young. He was in love with me! He'll tell you. (*Laughs.*)

[The music begins.]

WE: Frank Morgan had such a promising career. Why would he throw it all away to do drugs?

CB: Well, he was one of those that believed that if he did heroin he'd play like Charlie

Parker. There's a *very* funny story. This happened in 1951, when Frank and I we were working at the Alabam together. Anyway, Charlie Parker had been by the club and invited us to this party. Someone rich over in Pasadena was having a party for him. Like I said, I was bringing Frank to work, so we went over to Pasadena, and we get in there and it's packed. It was a big mansion with a pool and everything. Charlie is walking around, and people would be going up into these bedrooms. I don't know what they were doing in there. (*Laughs.*) We were sitting in kind of a den-like room that leads out to the pool. So then Charlie starts taking his jacket and his shirt off. He didn't stop. He took everything off and said, "Everybody who wants to stay here, you gotta take your clothes off." (*Laughs.*) David Bryant was there, too, a bass player, but my main witness was Frank, 'cause everybody took their clothes off but me. See, Charlie, he knew I wasn't going to do that. I didn't *leave,* either! The saxophone player, Donald Wilkerson, who worked with us on the show at the Alabam, would play "Flying Home" note for note the way Illinois Jacquet recorded it with Lionel Hampton in the '40s. When he'd do "Flying Home," he'd play the solo while doing a backbend. He'd go all the way back to the floor while blowing away. And he did that bucky naked. (*Laughter.*) Charlie Parker laughed so, he fell in the pool. That was a funny sight. I've seen some funny stuff in my life, but *that* was funny.

WE: What was Charlie Parker like?

CB: To me, he was like a little teddy bear. A lot of people said that when he was doin' his dope, he would get evil or he'd con you out of money. But I didn't meet him under those circumstances. Around '49 or '50, my first husband, he and Charlie used to shoot up. My husband would take me over when Charlie was staying in the garage. Charlie had met me, but he would be loaded. Their main thing was to get the dope and shoot it up, and I just happened to be there. I would sit in the car when they would shoot up, and Charlie would come out to the car afterwards. He knew that I was Joe Stone's wife, but it wasn't where we had a conversation about this and that.

WE: Were those the only times you met him?

CB: No. I was playing in Hermosa Beach in the early '50s when the Lighthouse was jumpin'. They had Shorty Rogers, Jim Giuffre, Bill Cooper, and Frank Rosolino, with Marty Paich on piano and Shelly Manne on the drums. I was playing next door at a place called the High Seas, where on Sundays they'd have jam sessions. You worked starting at two o'clock in the afternoon until two o'clock in the morning. On my intermission I'd go over to the Lighthouse, and there would be Marlon Brando, Jimmy Dean, all these people. I wasn't going to miss that, but my boss told me, "Clora, I'm paying you to work here." I said, "Yeah, but the union says I have fifteen minutes that I can do what I want to do. If I can go over there in fifteen minutes and come back and not interrupt my job, there's nothing you can do about it." And away I went. That paid off, because one Sunday Charlie Parker was at the Lighthouse. He came down to hear Max Roach; he had been up in 'Frisco playing with somebody and came back through here. This was just before Charlie died. Max was playing with the Lighthouse All Stars. The people in the audience and Howard Rumsey[12] tried to get Charlie to play, and he wouldn't do it. When I walked in, Charlie came over to me to say hi. As I said, Charlie Parker already knew me from when he and my first husband would shoot up. Dizzy had also told him about me; Dizzy told most of the guys about my playing. When Charlie found out I was playing next door, he came over there. As soon as he came in, he asked the tenor saxophone player [13] to let him play his horn. He played it and emptied the Lighthouse! He played a long time. Simply by me having gone over there all the time, I'd opened up a little rapport with everybody over there, so Charlie came over and brought the man some business. I said, "Now is it all right for me to go over there?" My boss said, "Go, go, go."

[The last song was "Honky Tonk," from *Miles Davis/Get Up with It,* 1974; Columbia Records.]

CB: (*While music is playing*) I wouldn't call that jazz.

WE: What would you call it?

CB: Punk rock. (*Laughs.*) That sounds like any rock band. (*Miles solos.*) See, all that undercurrent takes away from what he's playing. It doesn't enhance what he's doing. It made him break up his phrases. He's changed his whole way of playing. His playing changed like somebody turning your clothes inside out. The way he phrased, the notes that he picked. 'Cause, see, I always said when Miles played, he'd take notes that we'd throw away and just make them sound so pretty. They would fit, notes that we wouldn't think about using. But when he changed his style of playing, I don't know where he went. It seems like the rhythm section is taking him wherever. If he'd had a jazz rhythm section playing what he's playing, it would have made more sense to me.

WE: When he came back in the '80s, do you think his chops were blown?

CB: I know he was having problems with them, like Dizzy did before he died. But Dizzy would never tell people. One time Dizzy came backstage and his tongue was cut. He had a partial, and it was cutting his tongue. His tongue was bleeding. He took my fingernail file and filed it down. (*Chuckles.*) He was missing notes. I said, "Why don't you let me tell them what's wrong? They think you're just messing up." (*Laughs.*) He said, "I don't care what they think."

WE: Did you know Miles personally?

CB: (*Chuckles.*) I could never get close to Miles. I remember one time in the '50s he was playing at the It Club in LA over on Washington, and Dizzy was playing at a jazz club that had been Strip City. I was sitting right down front listening to Dizzy. Miles came in, and he sat down beside me. He wanted me to go back over to the It Club with him to hear him play. He was driving, so I went over there. He started playing, and he never announced anything. He'd turn his back, walk off, and go to the bar. I couldn't get it. I got somebody to take me back over to Dizzy, and Miles didn't speak to me for ten years. (*Chuckles.*) I wasn't used to that. I remember in Nice in 1987, I was there with the Cheathams,[14] and Dizzy had played—he had Moody and all those guys with him. And Miles Davis was there. So Dizzy and I went over to see Miles on the stage. Miles started playing his new music with all the amplification. Finally Dizzy looks at me and I look at him. He says, "You ready?" I said, "Yeah." (*Laughs.*) And we walked out. He didn't like what Miles was doing, either.

WE: What is your opinion of the current state of jazz?

CB: There are more young people coming to it, but to me, it's not healthy. See, nobody's telling them where they *came* from. They have all these schools, like Berklee School of Music, and they have all these teachers telling them how to play the notes, but they don't tell them who was playing the notes before and how they played them and why they were playin' them. My dad always said—this is one of his daddyisms—"You gotta know where you been to get where you're goin'." Out here in California, these kids don't know where they came from *or* where they're going. These people are writing notey, bad arrangements, and it all sounds like it's coming out of the same machine. All their arrangements sound alike, all the music sounds alike, all the kids taking solos sound alike, 'cause they get these books with all these jazz licks in it and they're playin' the same licks. They're not being creative themselves. That's where I think jazz is going astray.

Selected Discography

Clora Bryant . . . Gal with a Horn. V.S.O.P. #42 CD (1957, reissued 1995).

Notes

1. Nickname for a series of clubs for blacks only.
2. Mode Records, 1957. Reissued as a CD in 1995; V.S.O.P. Records.
3. Linda Dahl, *Stormy Weather: The Music and Lives of a Century of Jazzwomen* (New York: Limelight Editions, 1992), p. 215.
4. Sally Placksin, *American Women in Jazz, 1900 to the Present* (New York: Seaview Books, 1982), p. 154.
5. For more information on the Prairie View Co-Eds, see Sherrie Tucker, *Swing Shift: "All-Girl" Bands of the 1940s* (Durham, N.C.: Duke University Press, 2000).
6. Dahl, *Stormy Weather,* p. 213.
7. Ibid., pp. 213–214.
8. Kenny Clarke.
9. Placksin, *American Women in Jazz,* p. 154.
10. The Milamo.
11. Open-heart surgery in 1996.
12. Bassist who played in the Stan Kenton band in the early 1940s, he originated the Lighthouse All-Stars in 1951.
13. Sigmond (Sig) Calloway, spouse of Mahalia Jackson. He evidently had a brand new tenor saxophone, but after Parker played it that night, he never played it again.
14. Jeannie Cheatham (pianist and vocalist) and Jimmy Cheatham (bass trombonist and vocalist).

Terri Lyne Carrington

Terri Lyne Carrington

Drummer Terri Lyne Carrington has been turning heads with her playing since she was old enough to peer over the ride cymbal. A child prodigy, at age eleven she was the youngest student to be awarded a scholarship to the Berklee School of Music.

Born in Medford, Massachusetts, in 1965, Carrington was seven when she first picked up the drumsticks. Studying with esteemed drummer and master teacher Alan Dawson, she improved so quickly that she soon was sitting in and jamming at Boston area jazz clubs. This sensational young bebopper cut her first record while still in high school.[1]

Taking drummer Jack DeJohnette's advice, she moved to New York City in 1983 and found work with veterans Stan Getz and Lester Bowie, and younger musicians Mulgrew Miller and Steve Coleman. In 1986, she was invited to play in Wayne Shorter's band with whom she stayed for a year and a half. Carrington's New York period culminated with her major label debut, *Real Life Story*,[2] which includes her vocals and a dream lineup of featured guests.[3] This recording brought her a Grammy nomination.

After moving to Los Angeles in 1989, Carrington was the house drummer on *The Arsenio Hall Show* for four months. Succeeding in the pressure-filled world of television, she later spent one year on the TV show *VIBE*, where the bill of fare was R&B, funk, and rap.

Carrington is a swinging drummer who can bash and burn with the best, and then effortlessly downshift into exquisite, masterful brushwork. While her solos are thoughtful and well constructed, it is her ability to lay down a serious groove, no matter what the style, that serves as a distinguishing trademark. All of these elements are showcased in her 2002 release, *Jazz Is a Spirit*,[4] including a heartwarming tribute to one of her primary mentors, Papa Jo Jones.

Recently she has crossed boundaries in the music industry, assuming responsibilities in record production. She has produced or co-produced albums for many jazz and pop performers, including Diane Reeves and David Sanborn. Nevertheless, Carrington's calling card is that of a polystylist drummer, whose eclectic background is particularly suited to fusing jazz traditions with contemporary popular music.

Recorded July 29, 1997

WE: In its purest form, African-American culture is communally based. By extension, do you view the jazz world as a community, and do community values influence your professional practice?

TLC: Yeah, I do think of the jazz world as a community. One of many communities that I feel involved with to some degree, but it's definitely the one that's closest to my heart. Even with that, though, my sole purpose is not to feed the community. I mean, I will always be a jazz musician, because those are my roots. But I don't feel an alignment with that any more than I do to some other areas of the music business.

I like what you said as far as jazz being a community-based art form, which is very true. With that in mind, it's like some people *stay* in that community, either by choice or by necessity. And some people tend to get outside of that community and move to the suburbs (*chuckles*), if you will. Which is what I feel that I've done. I'm talking about other styles of music. For example, I'm not playing any jazz on this television show that I will be doing five days a week for however long it will last.

WE: You're speaking of the *VIBE* show?

TLC: Yeah. I guess it's supposed to be the television version of the magazine *VIBE,* which is a hip-hop magazine. It will be a lot of R&B. It's interesting, because R&B and hip-hop are subcultures, really of the same community. In the real sense of community, R&B might be more for and of the people. I think that jazz has been supported by an elite group of listeners. The core of the black community is not listening to jazz. That doesn't mean a whole lot to me, other than it's too bad that a lot of the black community is not aware of some of what jazz has to offer culturally—the richness and, traditionally speaking, how it's been a part of the community for so long. It's too bad that these younger generations—I'd say people from their forties on down—didn't grow up listening to traditional jazz. I mean, there's a lot of people today that *think* they're listening to jazz, but they're listening to smooth jazz. It's instrumental and there's improvisation, so, technically, some people would call it jazz. But you know, rhythmically and harmonically it's not as advanced, in the traditional sense. But if that will lead them to jazz, it would be great. I mean, people ask me about Erykah Badu all the time now. She's a hip-hop singer who has some jazz inflections, so people compare her to Billie Holiday, which is an outrage. I mean, there's a whole history, a whole legacy of Billie Holiday that this woman, who I believe was a schoolteacher and now has her first record out, obviously can't be compared to. I'm guessing she doesn't know most of the standard repertoire. But if that gets people to listen to Billie Holiday, then I think it's a good thing.

WE: Why doesn't the African-American community embrace jazz?

TLC: Well, it's kind of like the higher education scenario, you know. The common people since the beginning of time have not had the same resources at their disposal that the upper-class people have had, so they are not as exposed to high art. They've only had access to what's been on the radio stations that are based in their community. The thing that's crazy is that it has continued in that direction for so long. You see, in the '50s and '60s, they played jazz on these community-based stations. That's when R&B was great, in its inception. In the beginning of R&B, jazz was integrated on these stations and it was more musical. But a terrible thing happened since that time period, because the business managers of the radio stations realized that R&B is the type of music that makes people move. So in order to sell commercials, they went for what they thought people were responding to most: the beat. And maybe R&B *was* closer than jazz to the African tradition as far as rhythmic structure and groove. I don't know for sure if that's a reason why these people gravitated to this music, but the other *biggest* reason is vocally. I mean, now you have people talkin' to black people in their community about what's goin' on with them. Jazz didn't do that. In jazz they're singin' standards, *and* there's more concentration on great instrumentalists and so-loists. So you've *totally* cut out the spoken-word aspect of music. At some point, at least in Africa, music was for their society.

WE: It bonded them together.

TLC: Yeah. You have the debate between "art for art's sake" or "art for social con-sciousness." There's a place for both, but when you're dealing with a whole group of people that are mostly poor, they're wanting to hear you talk to them on a *real* level. And that's where the singing part comes in. Especially love songs; that's the main thing that people talk about. That's what they relate to as escapism from their daily struggles. The commercial idiom had some politically conscious black music that was coming out, especially in the '60s, that spoke to black people. And that's more than what jazz was doing, from their perspective. The jazz community was and is very socially and politically conscious, but you have to be in the midst of the culture to get this. A combination of all those factors is *why* the African-American community is not listening to jazz. This is something I'm really passionate about. We, the entire structure of jazz, need to figure out a way to make it more accessible.

JS: Let's change the subject and talk about your personal history. Why did your father take such an intense interest in encouraging you musically during your early childhood years?[5]

TLC: I was fortunate because he and my grandfather played. My grandfather passed away six months before I was born, and he played drums. My grandfather had actually been roommates in college with Chu Berry and had played with him. But he started a family and worked at General Electric. He was a musician at night and on the weekends. When people like Duke Ellington and Sammy Davis Jr. would come to town, which was the Boston area, and had pickup bands, he would play with them. My grandfather's drums were in the house, and my father occasionally would play them; my father also played saxophone. He went to college, and the same thing happened to him that happened to my grandfather. While in school, my father played in horn sections for bands like Ruth Brown and James Brown when they came through the area. He thought he was going to make music a full-time career. But he came home, got married, and got a regular job, though he continued to play a lot locally in the Boston area. So when I came along and showed musical interest, he wanted this family tradition to continue. And because my father played saxophone, when I was five I wanted to play the saxophone. The story goes that I put the alto in my mouth and kind of bent notes in tune, like a riff or something, with a record that was playing. My father immediately assessed that I had some type of musical inclination, and he wanted to cultivate it, because he was quite disappointed that he didn't have a son. He took me to Sunday afternoon jam sessions, and I played a little saxophone for a couple of years. When I took an interest in music, he was very excited that maybe, finally, there will be a Carrington who will make an important statement in the music world. I'm really thankful that my father didn't just dismiss it; some people would not have encouraged their daughters to do that.

JS: What was it like being a child prodigy?

TLC: I never really knew what the "child prodigy" term meant, or how it made me any different from anyone else. I just happened to do what I do. I did realize I had a special talent, I guess, because no one else was doing it, but I did not feel like a virtuoso. We look at that description more in classical terms. We can call a prodigious concert pianist or violinist a virtuoso because that music is based so much on technique. Jazz is more subtle in some ways, though improvisation is harder in many respects. And swing either is or isn't. It's not something you can teach a kid, really. So I guess the prodigy part came into place because I could swing at such a young age and mimic what I heard well. And somehow I understood the vocabulary of jazz without studying it. Just by listening. Some people may not consider that the working of a prodigy. Maybe that's why I was never one hundred percent comfortable with that term. A lot of the other little drum wizards that came along disappeared eventually. So I would say staying power is what makes you in the end.

JS: Buddy Rich played a role in your very early career. When did you first meet him?

TLC: I first met Buddy Rich when I was ten. I was performing at the Wichita Jazz Festival with Clark Terry and his East Coast/West Coast Jazz Giants. Buddy was there, but he had a rough travel day, so everyone warned me to stay away from him. But I wanted to meet him anyway, so I marched over to him, and someone told him who I was. He snapped at me, "Oh, yeah, well you better not be good." And I said, "Who's gonna stop me?" He was quite outdone at my quick comeback and asked me if I wanted to sit in with his band. Of course I wanted to, but out of loyalty to Clark I declined. Then Buddy came to Boston and asked me to sit in. We played Chicago. He asked Zildjian and Slingerland[6] to give me endorsements, which they did, and I became the youngest endorsee that Zildjian ever had.

WE: As that anecdote indicates, you had the spectacular opportunity as a youngster to meet and sit in with an array of jazz luminaries. Another example is when you were eleven and you played with Oscar Peterson. Can you describe the circumstances?

TLC: It was at the Globe Jazz Festival in Boston, where he was playing. My father took me, and afterwards we were backstage saying hi to Keter Betts and Bobby Durham, who were playing with Oscar Peterson. I had just played two nights before with the Clark Terry Quartet down in Cape Cod. Something happened to Clark's drummer—I think he was late, a snowstorm or something; anyway, he didn't get there on time. So, I played two sets with Clark. When I met Oscar, I said, "Oh, Clark Terry told me to tell you hello. I played a couple of sets with him." And Oscar said, "What? You played two sets with Clark Terry? Well, I've *got* to hear this." (*Laughter.*) Keter Betts was packing up his bass, and people were walking out of the auditorium. The drums were sitting there. Oscar told Keter, "Wait, don't put your bass away yet." We played a song, and the people who weren't all the way out yet came back. I don't remember what we played, but the important thing about it was that Lawrence and Alma Berk were there. They were founders of the Berklee College of Music. They heard me play and offered me a scholarship.

JS: What classes did you take at Berklee?

TLC: I took piano lessons and theory. I studied drums, and I went to ensemble classes where I played in a combo.

JS: Were you playing in your school bands at the same time that you went to Berklee?

TLC: No. (*Chuckles.*) It didn't interest me.

JS: What was it like playing in those combos at Berklee with people several years older than you?

TLC: Well, you know, most of them weren't that good. They were college students who were still learning how to get it together. I mean, at fourteen I was doing professional gigs of my own with Frank Foster, Kenny Barron, Buster Williams, George Coleman, and Junior Cook. The older students had maybe more technique than I did, 'cause some of them at that age played fast, but it didn't mean a whole lot because when they'd go to these ensembles and try to *swing,* they just didn't have a clue. But it was good in one sense just to be around some peers, and there would be a *few* good musicians.

WE: Did any of those good musicians rise to fame?

TLC: Definitely. Once at Berklee I was walking by the practice rooms and heard someone really playing the alto. I thought he was *bad,* so I ran and got my dad and told him I had just heard a new guy that was killing, and that the Boston Jazz Society should give him a scholarship. Dad checked him out, and they did award him a scholarship. We became friends. He would come over to our house to eat and play basketball. And I even remember one night when he was nervous to sit in with a group I had at Sandy's Jazz Revival[7] that included Kenny Barron, Buster Williams, and Frank Foster. We pushed him to do it, and he played "No Greater Love" with us. He then went on the road with Clark Terry and sent me road-weary postcards. This person was Branford Marsalis.

JS: You cut a record when you were sixteen called *TLC and Friends.* Can you tell us more about it and who the friends were?

TLC: Well, Max Roach had been trying to get Blue Note to record me, but then they didn't come through. So my father decided we would record it ourselves, print some, and maybe get a record company to buy it later.[8] I fell in love with Alan Dawson's style, and at sixteen I was in good shape from studying with him. The friends were George Coleman, Kenny Barron, and Buster Williams. My father played on one tune as well. We pressed five hundred copies ourselves and sent them to people, one of them being Illinois Jacquet, a friend of my dad's. Here is a funny story. The tune my father played on was "Sonnymoon for Two," a blues by Sonny Rollins, and the only medium-groove song on the album to capture a real nice pocket. Maybe six months after the mailing, in the middle of the night, the phone rings and it was Illinois Jacquet. "Sonnymoon for Two" was playing in the background, and it seemed he had had a few cocktails. He said to my father, "Man, she's just not supposed to be able to play like that. Do you hear that swing on this blues?" It was funny because people seemed to always be surprised at what I did not think was much of a big deal. I get it more now because I believe I innately understood and could capture the spirit of jazz, and that was quite uncommon for an adolescent girl.

WE: You've told us about playing with Oscar Peterson and Clark Terry when you were young. Are there any other memorable experiences with jazz musicians in your early history that come to mind?

TLC: When I was about five, I met and sat in with Rahsaan Roland Kirk. I shook a tambourine. The next time I may have blown into a sax, playing an easy riff or something. Then around age seven or eight, I started to sit in with him on drums. He would go into a long dissertation on how I was real and Karen Carpenter was not because she played jive pop beats on the drums. That is how my eight-year-old mind interpreted it. He would say,

"Terri Lyne, set it up," which meant give them four or eight bars out front on the drums to go into the tune. Steve Turre was in the band, and he always reminds me of that. Rahsaan used to come over to the house to eat and hang out, and I was so amazed at how he functioned as a blind person, how he would eat and walk and stuff like that. I was very inquisitive and asked a lot of questions, so my mother spent a lot of time doing damage control. The most amazing thing was watching him play basketball. Someone would have to hit the rim with a key or something. He would hear the distance, shoot the ball, and get it in! When he passed, I heard that at the wake the little bouquet of flowers I sent were in the casket with him, in his arms or hands, I believe.

WE: Before we began taping, you described Dizzy Gillespie as a legendary musician. Did you have occasion to interact with him?

TLC: I sat in with Dizzy Gillespie one evening when I was about eleven or twelve. My dad had asked if I could play a tune with him. Dizzy did not believe I could play and was quite hesitant, but agreed. When I got up there, he asked me what I wanted to play, and I said, "Straight No Chaser," trying to pick something he played. He said, "Ah, I'm sorry. I don't remember how that goes. Can you hum it to me?" So I started to, and he cut me off after a couple of bars and said, "Oh, oh, I remember now." And we played it. I did not realize until later that it was a test. I thought maybe he just forgot it.

I also remember hanging out with Dizzy in Boston and taking him to the train station because the weather was so bad; he wanted to get home and could not fly. He needed to make a stop first at Legal Seafood for its world-famous clam and fish chowders. We got close to South Station, and I could not even get all the way to the door because the weather was so bad. He got out and trudged through the snow in these unbelievably gorgeous boots that were now ruined. I just was happy to be helping him out and talking to him in the car. When I got home, I realized that he had left these two huge containers of chowder in the back seat by mistake. I felt so bad because I knew how much he wanted it, but not bad enough not to eat it.

JS: How about Clark Terry? You alluded to playing with him, but you have not made any observations about him personally.

TLC: First and foremost, I love Clark madly, in the words of Ellington. One of my greatest lessons in responsibility came from him. He was the first person to take me on the road with him, and it was a great learning experience, musically and personally. He would say that there were three things that should be in everyone's vocabulary: "Please," "Thank you," and "I'm sorry." Now, that sounds simple enough, but there are many occasions when I experience a void in those words from others and I think about Clark. But my lesson came one night when we were playing Chicago at Rick's Cafe, a jazz club at the top of a Holiday Inn. In between sets I would go to my room. Well, this was when they first experimented with a pro women's basketball league that did not last long, but it paved the way for the WNBA. I was befriended by Deborah Rodman that week. I think she played for the Dallas team. More recently I discovered that she is Dennis Rodman's sister. I believe I was talking with her and so I was late getting back down to the second set, but only by a few minutes. When I walked in, Clark was playing the drums. My heart sank, but I noticed he was grinning, so I thought maybe he's not mad. I walked onstage hesitantly, and coming out of his smiling mouth was a very soft-in-volume curse-out, telling me to get behind the drums. I have rarely, if ever, been late to a set or concert again.

WE: Nat Adderley, who played a role in your formative years, recently lost a leg to diabetes.

TLC: Get out of town! Really? I didn't know that. Oh my God!

WE: I believe he's out of mortal danger, but in view of this close call, do you have memories of times spent with Nat that you could relate?

TLC: Nat used to come over to our house and encourage me early on. Then by the time I was fourteen I played with him a few nights at a club in Boston. His regular drummer, Jimmy Cobb, could not make it. It was one of my first experiences playing with the New York cats several nights in a row. Nat is a beautiful person.[9] I did not know Cannonball, because I was too young, but my folks did, and they really loved him. They spoke more highly of him than almost any other musician they knew. When my father heard the news that he had passed, I think he cried.

But for me, this question brings up the death, in general, of so many of the musicians I knew and that were so encouraging to me. People I played with and people that I just met and had the honor of hanging with. Like Ella Fitzgerald, for example. I never played with her, but I hung out with her backstage a lot of times when she came to Boston. My fondest memory of Ella was one night I said to her that I had heard her on the Grammys with Carmen, Sarah, and I believe Betty was the fourth. And they got into a scatting routine, trading and whatnot. I told Ella my opinion, that basically she blew the others out of the ballpark when the scatting came around. I mean, it seemed common knowledge not to mess with Ella in any kind of cutting session. She said, "Oh, no, I'm just a rhythm singer. Those other women are real singers." I was blown away by her humility.

JS: You sat in with Betty Carter when you were about fourteen. Do you have lasting impressions of her?

TLC: You know, Betty Carter could be an intimidating type of woman, especially for someone at my young age. I was pretty precocious, though. I didn't intimidate easily, but I would get nervous before playing with somebody of that stature. When my dad took me to see Betty Carter, apparently she had just won the *Down Beat* Critics Poll or Readers Poll, and my dad was congratulating her on this. She said, "Finally they gave it to someone other than Ella." I felt the need to stand up for Ella; Ella was, like, the nicest woman in the world that you'll ever meet. So I emphatically said, "I like Ella." And she snapped at me, "But she's won every year. Let someone else have a chance." At that moment I understood better that sometimes children should hang out and listen and not always speak. But all these people were great to me. I mean, you'd have a few people that were *dry,* but most jazz musicians are very colorful types of individuals.

WE: What do you mean by the comment that some musicians are "dry"?

TLC: Dry is more of a personality description than a musical description. But I never found the MJQ, for instance, to be extremely exciting, so I may use the term "dry" to describe them. I must add, though, that at their level of musicianship there would be times when I would not find them dry. Having played with Percy and having been in the company of Milt Jackson, their personalities were definitely not dry. And their playing outside of the MJQ was not. Sometimes, when a certain combination of musicians get together, the overall sound is quite different than the individual sound.

Saying that last sentence reminds me of another story, when it landed me in a bit of, not hot, but warm water. I did a tribute once to Chick Corea in Boston. This was part of the Boston Globe Jazz Fest, and the evening was produced by the local jazz DJ. He put all the musicians together for it, including myself, and had me on his radio show to promote it. I was around seventeen. On the show, he got into a bit of a rampage about how he had heard that Dizzy Gillespie had in his band at one point Chick, bassist Eddie Gomez, drummer Steve Gadd, and how Diz called them the "staccato trio."[10] This DJ tried to get me involved in agreeing that they were stiff, but I didn't agree. Well, at the concert Chick's mother was backstage and was not pleased to meet me at all. She said, "You were the one talking about my Chicky on the radio. You said he was stiff." I tried to explain to her that I did NOT say that. At this point, Chick's wife tried to smooth it over by saying, "You have the right to your opinion regarding Chick. She's being a protective mom." That, of course, made it feel even worse, because it was not my opinion at all about Chick. I love the playing of all those guys, especially Chick, and would love to play with him. But, I never have played with him, and may never!

JS: Getting back to your chronology, you moved to New York City, as you said, at age eighteen after only one and one-half years at Berklee. What prompted you to leave midyear, and without completing your degree?

TLC: I think I was just burnt out a little on Boston because I had grown up there and was going to Berklee for many years once a week through junior high and high school. I was ready to play with the cats and not be a local drummer. Went right on the road with Clark Terry to Europe and never looked back. I went to New York with a good friend of mine from Berklee, Niels Lan Doky, and we decided to be roommates. Also my good friend Greg Osby had just moved to Brooklyn and was staying with friends. After a year in Spanish Harlem with Niels, I moved to Brooklyn, and Greg and I got a place together and were roommates for four years. I knew so many musicians, and they all said they would look out for me and promised my folks that as well, so I was cool. The jazz community is kind of like an extended family, even with its little offshoots and sub-communities. There's a lot of love among the musicians, even though it can be a bit cutthroat as well. The real deal is that no one wants any harm to come to anyone else, even though they may want their gig.

JS: Give us a description of the New York jazz scene when you first entered it.

TLC: Sometimes I feel like I caught the end of an era. In the early '80s, there were a lot of "greats" around. I was fortunate to have firsthand experiences with the masters. More recently it seems they have been dropping faster. I feel bad for the young people today. You barely have any great jazz singers left. Ella, Carmen, Sarah, and Betty all left in a short amount of time. Anyway, the scene was more vibrant to me in a way, because people still really had a seeking spirit about it all. It seems to me that today there are more and more young players that are more and more traditional, going further back in time, rather than progressing. I feel this started around the time Wynton Marsalis came on the scene. He really helped to resurrect jazz in a way, which has been important, but also something was lost in the process. Young people used to stretch the limits and still respect where they came from. Now it seems like they have less respect for the people that came before who were not purist or engulfed in the tradition. That is very sad to me. For the first time, I have started to feel old. And when that happens, the last thing you want is for a young whippersnapper, if I may, to look at you like you don't know about the cats or the tradition.

JS: Did you suffer through some lean times in the City? Were you forced to take a day job?

TLC: I've never had a day job in my life, and I know that I am very fortunate to be able to say that. Sometimes people think that someone like myself has not suffered, but you cannot judge a person until you walk a mile in their moccasins. Even then, you still can't judge them or their life. I never had too much financial suffering. I have always been a sensitive soul, and my suffering came more from my heart than anything else. I could get hurt by people. I was a strange blend of tough and way too soft at the same time. I used to not really be able to watch much of the news without breaking down, but I have become a lot more balanced in my life, so my capacity to deal with things is greater. I feel in harmony with most things, in large part because of my beliefs in Buddhist philosophy, the spiritual world, and nature in general.

JS: Your development in New York ended when you relocated to Los Angeles in 1988, at age twenty-three. Was that a smooth transition?

TLC: Most definitely. 1988 was a great year for me. I played tours with Wayne Shorter, Stan Getz, and David Sanborn; I made my record *Real Life Story;* then I moved to LA and got *The Arsenio Hall Show.* A lot of changes in that one year. It felt good, and exactly what I was supposed to be doing at the time. I still played with New York cats, but mainly in Europe. So in a way, my New York development never ended, just slowed down a bit. Getting the gig with Wayne was definitely one of my bigger life-changing and defining moments. My world musically and personally opened up. Wayne introduced me to a spiritual path that I have tried to maintain, and he was instrumental in my moving to LA.

WE: To get the gig with Wayne Shorter, did you audition?

TLC: He had ten drummers audition, and he did the same thing with everyone. He started off playing while facing them. As he played he eventually turned his back, to see if he felt safe. (*Laughter.*) He said I was the first one he felt safe with. Everybody played the same drum kit, and he also said that I was the first one who seemed to get more of a personal sound out of the kit. Then he said that when I played, he got this feeling in his stomach that he used to feel when he drank cognac. So those were the reasons he hired me. Wayne is a champion for women. He's into science fiction, and you know, in all the science-fiction books women and children are in the forefront of making change. He likes to employ that science-fiction philosophy in his life.

JS: Let's talk about your second album, *Real Life Story.* What was your reaction when the recording received mixed reviews in the music press?

TLC: The bottom line for me is that the record was good. The songs were good, and it was well executed. It was a good representation of where I was then. You know, I'm a traditional jazz musician in some aspects, but I'm into contemporary jazz and electronics as well. I wasn't interested in doing a "spangalang" record at that point in my career.

WE: Translate "spangalang," please.

TLC: Swing. (*Chuckles.*) The pattern on the ride cymbal—some people say "titty boom." I wasn't interested in doing that because it's been done so much. Plus, the five or ten thousand people that may have bought that kind of record couldn't compare to the one hundred thousand people that bought *Real Life Story.* This is a business as well. I wanted to do something of quality, but something that more people would be able to check out than just traditional jazz fans. I'm interested in a career. You know, you do a jazz record and if it doesn't sell well, if it doesn't recoup, then you don't know if you're gonna do another one. So if I do that, who did I do the record for? Myself and for jazz fans, and for critics and some musicians, you know what I mean? (*Laughs.*) Although I would do a jazz record now, I would still do it differently. I don't want to do a record where it's just this intense drumming and, you know, "Here I am, let me demonstrate what I can do." I'm *not* interested in showing off, and maybe I should be. I don't need a solo when I perform. A great soloist in a rhythm section is secondary to how well he or she accompanies, unless you are the bandleader and this is why people are coming to hear you. The people that are hiring you want you to make them look good and respect the music, so showboating has never been my thing. Maybe to a fault. Anyway, I have always wanted to blend and be a part of the whole. That is stronger to me. Let me add, however, that with quality interactive playing, I am using the same skills as when soloing. It's kind of like soloing with, or at the same time as, the soloist.

WE: At the time you recorded *Real Life Story*, other musicians were drawing on musics outside of jazz. You roomed with Greg Osby; he and Steve Coleman with M-Base were using a variety of contemporary sources with the aim, I believe, of transforming those materials into serious music.

TLC: Okay, this is true. Let me tell you, I came up with Steve and Greg. I was there when Steve made up the word "M-Base." Macro-Basic Array of Structural Extemporizations is what M-Base means. It was mainly an effort to label our own music. Something intelligent and something that can be explained. I think it is important to take the ball and run, to make decisions that shape your own destiny rather than let others do it for you. This is what Steve and all the others were trying to do. Progressive thinking and a take-action approach. Steve and Greg were very dedicated to innovation. That was their goal.

WE: So in addition to the learning environment embodied by the old masters who were still around in New York, you were also caught up in the new music excitement of the '80s?

TLC: It was an interesting time in the '80s in New York, as far as the surge of energy from younger musicians that were trying to take the music somewhere else. I really respect the purists and the young musicians that decide to play the tradition as it was laid out. But it is more like classical music to me when done that way, when you play from a set repertoire or use the vocabulary that the innovators of jazz and bebop created. It is important to do so, but it's just as important to stretch the boundaries, find a new sense of freedom within those boundaries, create a new repertoire, and expand the vocabulary. That is what Steve and others were all about. Steve can play Charlie Parker note for note, but he decided not to make his life's work based on that kind of vocabulary. Greg Osby used to play a lot more like Cannonball, but then went for his own thing. Gary Thomas, Geri Allen, Cassandra Wilson, Robin Eubanks, Graham Haynes—these were the people who were hanging out during this time, reaching and trying to explore new territory. Then there were all the people that started working with Steve: David Gilmore, Kevin Harris, and the list goes on. I lost touch with that crew because that is about the time I split. I was always more interested, I think, in popular music. I was writing little pop songs with lyrics and enjoyed playing that stuff occasionally. So my move to LA and playing a TV show made sense for me. Maybe if I had not done that, I would have developed differently in New York. Probably I would have still moved out here, but I may have had more time to let my own sound out and grow from there. Don't get me wrong, I have no regrets about the direction of my career, though sometimes I get a little pissed when others, especially record company executives, question me as a jazz musician or think I lost something from moving out here. I still know about the essence of what it is more than any person on the business end will ever know. They have not lived it. I take it personally and very seriously. It is my life.

WE: It puzzles me that you made *Real Life Story* only a short time after your experiences with M-Base, and yet your conception seems markedly unfazed by the passion for change you say defined the work of Coleman and Osby.

TLC: As I said, I was never a traditionalist. So I had no ambitions to be an innovator as far as jazz drumming. Steve and Greg put a lot of time into developing their style of playing. When I spoke about Steve and Greg, I meant innovative in the traditional sense of jazz. They're reaching for things on their instruments that have not been done before. That's not what I'm interested in. My goal was to have my technique and my coordination as a drummer together enough so that I could play whatever I felt, at any given moment. As far as playing, I'm out of the mindset of a guy like Wayne who would rather play something new and different, meaning the music, the style. The record for me was more of a presentation of who I was as a total artist, including my writing, as opposed to who I was as a drummer. This was true even though I played with Wayne Shorter, who came from Miles Davis. Davis is a person who isn't going to do something that's been done before. Guys like Miles and Wayne would do something awful before they would do something that's been done before. They'd rather do that than play a standard.

Miles, for instance, would have some bands—back about twenty years ago—that were tryin' to play on this fusion stuff. Sometimes it wasn't great; some of the musicians just weren't good. Maybe it was because of the way he went about hiring people. He didn't go hear them himself. He didn't necessarily hold auditions. He'd go by recommendations. "This guy's the funkiest musician in the world." So he'd get this funky guy to come play guitar. Well, the funky guy playing guitar had no real knowledge of any of the places that Miles had been, so he couldn't meet Miles on equal ground. He could only do what he does. Miles might go someplace else, and it might clash. It created a stage environment where he had a band full of people that couldn't go to the places he wanted to go even within that fusion format. So what I'm sayin' is that Miles would rather have had those guys onstage than, say, a George Benson on guitar—I'm just using the guitar as an example—who could hang more with him. Because that's not what he wanted. He did not want something that had already happened. He was reaching for something else in his presentation and in his music. I'm not saying it's a bad thing; I'm saying sometimes you sacrifice to break new ground, new territory.[11]

JS: Continuing with your recorded history, you cut a second session for Verve that was never released.

TLC: Yeah. It was much more commercial than the first one, and it wasn't released for a combination of reasons. I had management at the time that did not get along with Richard Seidel,[12] who signed me. My managers handled large acts, so they treated their relationship with the record company as if I was a larger act than I was. They were maybe a little more hard-core than they needed to be, and I'm the one who suffered. Also, Seidel was really a jazz guy. That's where his heart was, so when I did the first record, I didn't get the feeling that he was much into it. But when it sold well, he was very happy. So it's like "Okay, we'll just do another one." But since it wasn't where his heart was, he was not really behind me. So I got lost in the shuffle when the other departments at the label didn't embrace it.

JS: Shifting to your current activities, what attracted you to producing records?

TLC: It's something that I always wanted to do. When I did my own record I liked it, 'cause it's like painting—the closest thing I'll ever have to painting. You're shaping things; you turn something like an embryo into something tangible.

WE: Would you give up producing if you could have your own working band?

TLC: The only way to do that is to have an album out, but that doesn't guarantee gigging as a leader. I mean, the last time I gigged as a leader—when I made *Real Life*

Story—it cost me money. You have overhead, and if a gig falls through, you still have the musicians out there. I mean, I lost, like, ten thousand dollars. So I'm not going to do that unless it makes sense financially. And the only way I'd make money touring as a leader is if I've built a following and tour consistently, which is easier to do with an established recording career. So I'm not concentrating on touring as a leader right now.

JS: With reference to more recent recordings, you had the chance to back James Moody during his seventieth-birthday week at the Blue Note in 1995.[13] Was that a special gig for you?

TLC: (*Laughs.*) Actually it was a frustrating gig musically, but a great party! I was frustrated because Telarc was recording, and I was told that the drums were too loud. Or that stylistically I was playing too much for the Telarc recording. Al Grey was also playing at the Blue Note, and he was recording, too, and I know they weren't saying anything to his drummer, Bobby Durham. I think they actually may have tried, but he probably wasn't very polite to them. The record people asked Moody, and he told them that I was playing the way he wanted me to and that they should stay out of it. Then they went to his wife, who handles all his day-to-day business, and to his manager. They asked them specifically to try to get me to play more subtle, because Telarc likes a certain style record. Moody's wife came to me and she said, "You know, Moody really needs to get this record out. I know it's a drag, but could you just do whatever you can?" That is why I was frustrated, and I don't really like my performance. It is too bad, because normally my gigs with Moody are very hip.

JS: How would you have preferred to play in that context?

TLC: I like playing more like Jack DeJohnette's style of drumming. It's looser, and time can expand; you know, it's more freeing. No strict traditional bebop vocabulary is being utilized. Now, Moody may not call Jack DeJohnette. It's not what he probably is used to hearing behind him.

WE: I understand that you have had a steady gig with Herbie Hancock. When did you first meet him?

TLC: When I was a kid in junior high school, I attended a Herbie Hancock concert. I went backstage afterward to meet him. I remember his energy was the same as it is now. He is quite consistent as a human being. He gave me an orange, and I took it to school the next day to share with my music teacher, a young guy who played the guitar. We ate it and swore it was the sweetest orange we had ever had, mostly 'cause it was from Herbie. Then about five years later, Eddie Henderson, the trumpet player who had been working with Herbie over the years and was in the Mwandishi Band, told me to call Herbie because he was looking for a drummer. Eddie had recommended me. Well, that was weird. I thought, how do I call Herbie and say, "I heard you were looking for a drummer and I'm your girl!" But I managed to gather the courage to call him, and he picked up the phone himself. I guess I did not expect that. I was quite nervous, and I told him that Eddie told me to call him. He said, "Oh, yeah, I heard you're bad." So I think I sent him a tape. I never heard anything from him, but now that I have seen the inner workings of his office and his timing to getting around to things, I'm not sure if he ever really heard it, at least not before he needed a drummer.

JS: How did your current work with him get started?

TLC: Herbie Hancock lives out here, too. Wayne has a long relationship with him, and because of this I started doing little gigs with them occasionally. The time they actually called me to go on the road for a European tour, I was working with Al Jarreau and could not do it, but who wants to flat-out turn down going out with Herbie and Wayne? So I recommended an old friend from college, Gene Jackson. Basically, I thought he was subbing for me and I would get asked the next time, but Gene stayed for six or seven years, and I still waited for the chance to play jazz with Herbie. I say "jazz" because I played a funk tour with him, but it is not the same. Finally he asked me to play on his recording *Gershwin's World*,[14] because Gene was in New York, and I guess they were being budget-conscious. I ended up on the only four tracks on the CD that had trap drums. After that, I did three tours with him to support the record, and I've been playing with him ever since.

WE: Let's change our focus to your experiences as a woman in jazz. Since drumming has traditionally been thought of as a man's medium, do you meet with resistance?

TLC: Some people still think that way. There are a lot of women playing drums right now, and some of them are definitely meeting that type of resistance. It depends on your surroundings and who you're dealing with. I don't feel that I meet it as much as a lot of other women, because I feel respected. And I don't invite it, you know. Not only do I not invite it, I don't accept it. Occasionally I hear stories of what other musicians or drummers say. For example, a drummer said, "Why didn't Herbie call one of 'the cats' for *Gershwin's World*?" And a bass player said, "Why did they call her for *The Arsenio Hall Show*? There are a lot of brothers that need the work." And for a moment this kind of thing bothers me, but I get over it. I don't think about it anymore, because I'm making a living and I know my limitations and my strengths. As long as I'm secure with that it doesn't really matter what other people think.

JS: Does the perception persist that a woman instrumentalist playing jazz is not feminine? And on the flip side, that a woman isn't strong enough to compete on horns and drums?

TLC: I think it is still perceived as somewhat not feminine to some people, but they are in the dark ages. It was probably a man or group of men that decided what "feminine" means in the social context. If a man cooks a meal or cleans up, is he considered effeminate? We must release these dangerous stereotypes. Women have done things that men do for years, and there was a time when women were more dominant, as history teaches us. On the second question, there is still a large imbalance of male/female horn players or instrumentalists in general, though I hear women play horns and drums in college bands, and they sound strong to me. I know I'm strong. If I were playing more rock—a style that requires more strength—maybe I would have developed stronger. I can't bench-press much at all. But for the strength needed to play an instrument, I think women can physically handle it. I also think social conditioning plays more of a role as to why less women do it.

JS: Do women bring an aesthetic to jazz that differs from what men contribute?

TLC: I used to feel that I naturally bring things to the table that would be considered more feminine, like a higher sensitivity, softer approach, less ego, less competitive spirit. But I have heard too many men that possess as much or more of those qualities than I to believe that anymore. Elvin Jones is the epitome of strength, but when I hear him play ballads, it is some of the most sensitive and beautiful playing I have ever heard. He plays a ballad more beautifully, I feel, than me. Obviously, he smacks the hell out of the drums as well in a very male way. (*Chuckles.*) On the other hand, I know women drummers who are very abrasive, and I don't feel as much sensitivity from them, which, stereotypically, one would think should come easy. I think both men and women have a female and a male aspect, so it's a matter of tapping into each side, the yin and the yang.

[To conclude the interview, we listened to "Drums Unlimited," from *Max Roach—To the Max!*, recorded 1990, 1991; Max Roach Production Inc./Blue Moon Records.]

TLC: I did something with Max where we all played solo drums. It was called "Rise and

Fly." It's something he does a lot, especially when there are a bunch of drummers on the bill, like either at a club or festival. You play a little bit, you rise and you fly, and somebody else sits down at the drums and plays a little bit, they rise and they fly. I did it once with just me and him at a club in the middle of one of his sets. We just kept exchanging back and forth on one drum set. Max likes to do that 'cause he's very much into solo drumming. He has a very strong, innovative voice doing solo drum stuff out of the bebop tradition. But one thing I find interesting is that there's an underlying funkiness to how he plays. Even when you put that piece on, the first thing I heard was a backbeat, like a funk beat underneath what he's playing. We have to think it's tribal of sorts. It goes back to what we were saying about why black people like certain R&B-type rhythms. Maybe the average person can't hear it (*chuckles*), but I always hear it in Max's playing. I mean, even if he's swinging, it always has that funk undertone.

WE: Was "Papa" Jo Jones a major influence on Max Roach?

TLC: Yeah. Jo was the first one to use a hi-hat, and Max got that stuff from Papa Jo. I haven't listened to Papa Jo in recent years very much. I used to more. I had a great relationship with him, and I would go hear him whenever he came to town and played with his band. One time he came to my parents' house for dinner and stayed overnight. My mother prepared a huge meal, like she often used to do when musicians were in town, and he declined to eat. He sat up and told stories, and we had a grand time. When it was time to go to sleep, he pulled a piece of tin foil out of his overcoat and proceeded to unwrap a pork chop. My dad looked at him as if to say, "Man, we just prepared all this food for you and you did not eat." He simply stated, "I don't eat other people's cooking."

Selected Discography

*Jazz Is a Spirit. ACT Music 9408-2 (2002).
Moody's Party: Live at the Blue Note. Telarc 83382 (1995). (With James Moody.)
Gershwin's World. Verve 557797-2 (1998). (With Herbie Hancock.)

Notes

1. *TLC and Friends,* 1972 (privately issued).
2. 1989; Verve Forecast.
3. They include Patrice Rushen, Greg Osby, Carlos Santana, Wayne Shorter, and John Scofield.
4. ACT Music.
5. Richard Brown, "Terri Lyne Carrington," *Down Beat,* March 22, 1979, pp. 32–34.
6. Zildjian is a cymbal company; Slingerland is a drum company.
7. A Boston club.
8. This record was never commercially released.
9. Nat Adderly died on January 2, 2000, of complications from diabetes.
10. "Staccato trio" is a term typically used to describe playing that is too crisp. David Baker, noted jazz performer and educator, proclaims jazz to be a legato art form.
11. Ms. Carrington adds: "I want to clarify that I did not have a personal relationship with Miles at all. Any influence taken from him is by way of Wayne and Herbie."
12. Executive producer at Verve Records.
13. *Moody's Party; Live at the Blue Note,* 1995; Telarc.
14. *Gershwin's World,* 1998; Verve.

Regina Carter

Regina Carter

A fiddler who can make her four strings sing, swing, and cry the blues, Regina Carter is the most significant violinist to emerge on the jazz scene in decades. Powered by major-label marketing muscle, this five-foot-tall Detroit native has created her niche playing improvised music on an instrument usually limited to the concert hall. Carter has solidified her international reputation by winning the *Down Beat* Critics Poll as best jazz violinist for five straight years.

Daughter of a Ford autoworker and a schoolteacher, Carter was born on August 6, 1966. She took violin lessons via the Suzuki method at age four and later performed in the Detroit Youth Symphony. Steeped in local melting-pot sounds, Carter played with professional popular music groups from the age of fifteen. After graduating from college with a Bachelor of Arts in violin performance, she spent the next two years in Europe listening, woodshedding, and finally settling on a career in jazz.

After returning home, Carter initially gained media attention by playing electric violin with the all-female Detroit-based combo, Straight Ahead, which served as a springboard for her solo career. She relocated to New York in the early '90s, where she played with Mary J. Blige, the Black Rock Coalition, and the cutting-edge String Trio of New York.

In 1997 she toured with Wynton Marsalis's *Blood on the Fields.* The two-hour oratorio featured Carter briefly, but prominently, as a show-stopping soloist depicting a slave's cry for freedom. Signing with Verve in 1998, Carter released three breakthrough albums in succession: *Rhythms of the Heart,*[1] *Motor City Moments,*[2] and *Freefall.*[3] The latter recording, a duo with pianist Kenny Barron, allowed Carter's eclectic virtuosity to shine in a pared-down setting.

With a dark Hungarian-like tone that slips occasionally into the timbre of a viola, Carter combines whirlwind technique with a fiery, unrelenting sense of swing. She possesses a puckish wit, and one of her trademarks is the shameless use of musical quotations within her careening improvisations. When performing, she twists, arches, bends, and whirls, using her violin to dynamically interact both with the musicians onstage and with her audience.

Regina Carter was recently awarded an honor not previously bestowed on a jazz musician: she was invited to play the 250-year-old Guarneri violin, once owned by Nicolo Paganini. This treasured instrument, insured for $40 million, is played just once per year, traditionally by a classical virtuoso. However, in December 2001, the people of Genoa, Italy, chose New York's jazz violinist to play at their annual festival, and then donated the proceeds to the 9/11 Fund. Carter's magnetic performance won over the skeptics, earned two standing ovations, and led to her 2003 recording *Paganini: After a Dream.*[4]

Recorded March 25, 1997

WE: In your early years you were schooled as a classical musician. How did that training advance your jazz playing?

RC: Well, first of all, it gave me training for my instrument. The necessary tools I needed to get around on the instrument. Being able to read. When you're studying jazz, you're studying the music and the theory. When you're studying classical music, you have to first learn the instrument. The scales and the arpeggios, all of that. Then there are some things that are different in jazz—alterations. But, basically, once you know the scales, you're gonna be set for whatever kind of music you want to do.

WE: I don't expect that too many first-class symphony violinists could have ripped off that solo you play in Marsalis's *Blood on the Fields.* Is improvisation a gift, or can it be learned?

RC: I think you can learn it, but I definitely think that it is a gift as well. I think I was given a gift to be able to improvise. I was given a gift of having an ear to be able to hear and to repeat what I hear—that's how you learn jazz. To learn from a record. You don't learn jazz by going into school and reading a book and taking a class. Although that's how it's presented now in these institutions. You know, the people who go in and learn—I can hear it in their playing.

WE: What do you hear? Stiffness?

RC: Yeah, stiffness, and they all get these same patterns in institutional jazz. They're playing patterns, they're not playing thoughts and ideas. Jazz is a language, and once you get the grammar down, then you learn to form sentences and to express yourself. A lot of people take words out of the book. They just go through the book and cut out some words, and then put it together. Well, that's not a sentence. That's you cutting out someone else's words and just putting them in an order. I've been studying recently with Mike Longo—he used to play piano with Dizzy. He was the one that hipped me to that, 'cause I learned jazz basically by listening to records and imitating. I have no theory background for that. I don't read chord changes per se. I read notes, but I don't read chord changes. So I hear everything, which I think is a definite good. All my teachers in the past, and even Mike has said to me, "Be happy with that because that's where most jazz musicians are tryin' to get to."

So I'm doin' it all backwards. But I said, "Well, I listen to this and I listen to that, and I take this pattern, and I put it with this." And Mike said, "Well, you're not playing your own solo, you're just putting other people's words together. I have to show you how you can use all those notes and create." When he said that, it opened up a whole new thing for me as far as how to hear and what to play.

WE: Overall, do you think there is any benefit to studying jazz at a university?

RC: I don't really believe in goin' to school to be a jazz musician. I think you definitely still have to find that on the street. The music comes from the people.

WE: Let's talk more about your playing. When, for example, Lester Young, Wes Montgomery, or Milt Jackson play, their solos have the naturalness of a good conversationalist, including taking breaths. Is that a quality you aspire to?

RC: Yes. And it's something that I try and think about. Especially being a string player, 'cause you don't have to breathe. I can just play and play and play—run-on sentences, you know. (*Laughter.*) I have to really make a conscious effort to breathe, and it's *so easy* to forget that. You just jump in and start playing *at* people instead of playing *for* people.

WE: Do you prime yourself about breathing before you take a solo, or is that something you concentrate on as you're playing?

RC: As I play. Maybe I'm not consciously saying, "Okay, now you're gonna breathe." (*Laughter.*) But I know it's going on, and it depends on what's happened before me. Maybe if I heard the piano player's solo end with something really nice, I can grab on to what he just finished saying and use that to continue. Or maybe just let some space go by and say, "Okay, now I'm gonna say something completely different." Sometimes a whole flow of ideas just come to me; the idea is already there, and it just comes out. But I have to think about it more if I'm not feeling anything, if I don't have anything to really say. That's when I really become aware of it. I'm still very young in this music, so I only have a limited amount of things I can say right now. I have to really listen and understand *how* to tell a story. I'm learning by listening all the time.

WE: You're honest about your limitations. Regardless, your generation of players is often described by critics and older jazz musicians as technically proficient, but lacking in heart. Is that label fair or unfair?

RC: I think it's unfair. We have a lot of heart, but I think at our ages, you know, we haven't lived as long as they've lived. You know, if you season a piece of meat and let the seasoning stay on for three hours instead of just putting it in a pan, it's definitely going to taste better. But I would say that the musicians who are being talked about as having no soul or no emotion, maybe those are the ones that try to run after the stardom thing—"Let me give them what they want right now: surface music."

WE: While we're speaking about younger musicians, should we believe the reported disputes between the Marsalis neo-boppers and segments of the elder community? Is that a press phenomenon, or is there truth to it?

RC: I think there's some truth to it. Definitely, yeah, I think there *are* a whole group of musicians who are not taking the music further. They want to preserve the music. But I think Wynton was put into a position at a very early age, and it's funny to watch how we build someone up and then when they get to a certain spot we tear them back down. (*Laughs.*) I think he was pretty young and he was very headstrong. He was very opinionated, and I think he has this whole school of thought, and that's fine. I think there always have been schools of thought. A lot of older musicians, and rightfully so, are saying that the music is not being taken further. But Wynton and the Lincoln Center musicians are not the only school of thought out here. I think they're the ones that are getting the press. There's a whole group of musicians out here that are experimenting. So I think that people need not be afraid that everyone is getting caught up into the Wynton vibe, 'cause there are a lot of musicians that are not interested in that school at all.

WE: Who are some of the newer musicians trying to advance the music?

RC: Who do I think? Rodney Whitaker, Stefon Harris, Carlos McKinney, Lewis Nash, Don Byron.

WE: Is there resentment because Wynton gets so much press coverage?

RC: Yeah, there are some musicians that feel that way. You know, rightfully so. But I mean, this is a business, and that's just the way it works. And they need Wynton. I always call him the chosen one. But it's really funny being on the road with Wynton, and to see the press come. Really, they're just *ready* for him before he can even say anything. Basically they know what they're going to write before they even interview him. I think they're just ready to keep the controversy going. They're holding on to his thoughts from ten years ago. And sometimes I think musicians use the press. Like, they'll badmouth Wynton because he is such a huge figure. They badmouth him because they know that it creates controversy for them. If I can get a gig at Lincoln Center against his band, I'll say something, too. (*Laughs.*) Not saying that everyone doesn't believe what they're saying, but I think that some people are using it as a tool.

WE: In addition to the media, another behemoth musicians have to deal with is the music industry. How are relations these days between jazz musicians and the industry?

RC: I think from the point of view of the industry, it's definitely every man for himself. It's definitely not a community thing; it's about what's gonna sell right now. I think musicians have gotten farther away from it being a very community-based type of music because the industry has forced us to be very competitive with one another. You know what was lost in the '70s? Musicians getting together and just playing all day at one another's homes or loft spaces. It's still not back, and it'll never be like that. We can't afford to do that, economically, these days. And because of the economics now, it's almost impossible to make a living at being a jazz musician. So the industry has almost forced some people to think, "Well, if you want to make money, this is what you have to do." It's not about a group effort anymore. I think musicians have to be very careful.

On the other hand, I see a small group of musicians that are fighting against that. They are saying no, this has still got to be a community effort, we have to help each other out, and you can't really get caught up in what the industry is tryin' to put on you because you're not gonna stay there for long. You know, you'll be the big name for this year, and then they won't return your phone calls next year. It seems like more younger musicians are coming back to playing what they love and holding on to the tradition, instead of buying into what the industry is pushing. I think more and more younger musicians are saying it's almost like it's us against the industry.

WE: Maybe there are too many musicians. Why is it necessary for so many of you to have careers and be full-time working musicians?

RC: Well, first of all, I don't think that a lot of us chose to be musicians. I didn't; it chose me. I think it's my job. I consider myself, in a way, to be a healer or to deliver a message. I definitely think it was a gift, and I don't believe in slamming the door on a gift. And what other jobs are we gonna get? If you look at the economics of it (*laughs*), I'm better off being a musician. My mom, she was always so scared when I was growing up. She goes, "I want you to teach, I want you to get a real job so you can have Blue Cross and an old-age pension and blah, blah, blah." I'm like, "Right, Mom, now look what's happening." There's so many people that are losing their jobs before they can even get those benefits. People that've been in universities for years and years, studying their special craft that they were going to do, and now they're out of a job. What are they gonna do? You know, I can always create some kind of job, like strolling in a restaurant somewhere.

WE: Perhaps another factor for jazz musicians to negotiate is audience retention, especially the African-American community. In my experience, most of the people who attend jazz concerts are white. It makes me wonder why more black people don't support the music. Or do you think what I'm saying isn't true?

RC: No, it's true, unfortunately. I think the music is really not getting to them. I think, first of all, if you look at radio, some of these stations are not playing traditional jazz, they're playing what is labeled "smooth jazz." And they're playing what the record labels are saying is gonna sell this year. People are at work and they hear these stations all day long, and they don't hear any Miles Davis, they don't hear any of the more traditional music, so they're very uninformed. And it's not being played in homes. Some people grew up with their parents listening to jazz. I didn't; my parents didn't listen to jazz, which is really interesting. In fact, I've schooled my mother on jazz. (*Laughs.*) But I think the majority are listening to what they're hearing on the radio. The popular radio stations are cramming down their throats one type of music that excludes blues and traditional jazz. They don't understand the music because they're not exposed to it. It seems very intimidating. And I think that we had a history of rejecting things that have a negative label. Like jazz music, at one time, was thought of—I hate this word—but it was very attached to maybe slavery or "nigger" music, which you still hear said in Germany and some other parts of Europe on some of the Bavarian stations. I was living there for a while, and they'd play some jazz and they'd say, "Turn that nigger music off."

WE: Some Bavarian people would say that?

RC: Yeah. They'd call in to the radio station. I think basically they just want to hear "oompah" music. I have a lot of German friends. In fact, I was with a friend of mine when we were listening to the radio one night and that happened. He said the Bavarian people are very closed-minded, and they hate the music.

WE: Europe has long been a haven for expatriate jazz musicians. From your experience, does it remain so?

RC: Yeah, I think there are still a few Americans over there that are able to make a better living than they are here. But the Europeans are really upset with the fact that Americans can come over there and make all this money, but they can't come over here. So now they're enforcing the foreign musician's tax. I forgot what percentage the presenter has to pay on top of what he's paying the groups to come over, but it's a huge percentage. So much so that unless you're a really, really big name, they're not bringing as many groups over from the States as they used to.

WE: Before we began recording, you intimated that in Europe there is also a changing view of what jazz is.

RC: Right. I was saying that in Europe, the definition of jazz is very different from what I grew up learning. It's not music that comes from African-American roots. That's not jazz anymore in Europe. The real jazz of today is more a mixing of European classical music—

composers like Anthony Davis or Anthony Braxton. And the French believe in the French School of jazz, separating it from American jazz as well.

WE: Let's turn the clock back to your early years. What prompted your interest in music when you were a youngster?

RC: Well, I have two older brothers. One played piano and trumpet, the other piano and clarinet. And they took tap-dance lessons. My mom is a retired schoolteacher, and her idea was that we should be involved in as many activities as possible to keep us off the streets and out of trouble. And just to give us a very well-rounded education so we'd have a lot of career moves to pick from when we got older. So there was a piano in our house. My mother says when I was about two years old, I walked up to the piano one day and played my brother's piano lesson. His teacher was at the house and said, "Who taught her that?" My mother said, "No one, she's just been doing that." So my mother enrolled me in a school, the Heritage House, with a woman, Mrs. Love. She's still around today. She taught me, but she told my mother that I was stubborn. I didn't want to learn out of the book; I wanted to create my own songs. Every week I'd say, "Listen to my song I just wrote." (*Laughs.*)

WE: At two, how did you manage to write a song down?

RC: In Detroit they had this green paper with these huge lines when you're first learning how to write your name. It's not like regular writing paper. I would make that my music paper, and I would draw these huge dinosaur eggs on it. That would be my music. My mom showed it to me this year; my teacher sent it to my mom. My mom made a book out of it. It was the most hilarious thing to look at. (*Laughs.*)

WE: Did you continue with Mrs. Love?

RC: She told my mom she thought I was too young to study, and that she should just let me continue to play at home. Then when I was about four, she called my mother about a method called Suzuki, where they taught children how to play by ear. She thought it would be really good for me, and it was on violin. My mom enrolled me in that, and I just had a great time. I would go to this school about two or three times a week—once for theory, once for a private lesson. On Saturdays I'd be there all day. I'd have master class in the morning, where you had to play as much of a piece as you could remember; it didn't matter how many bars. And my teacher did something very experimental. She would line us up, maybe six of us in a class, and she would play something off the top of her head, in a classical setting. When she tapped you on the shoulder, you had to take up on violin where she left off, and continue to create until you heard the next person start to pick up from where you left off. So I think she really helped introduce me to what we call improvisation today. I mean, I didn't know what that was about, but I'm not afraid to leave the music as most classical players are. I think if more people learned that way, they wouldn't be as afraid.

WE: My understanding is that many classical composers in the past left openings in their scores for musicians to spontaneously create variations.

RC: Right. Like Bach. If you look at his manuscripts, there are certain areas that are not written. That was for whoever was playing at the time to improvise. You find that especially in Baroque music, but we got further and further away from that. And it's funny, because in college a lot of teachers will say, "Well, you have to play this piece this way because this is what this composer meant." How do you know unless you were sitting down and talking to him? I just don't feel that way. That kind of started to turn me off to classical music, because I didn't want to necessarily play it like fifty other people have already played it. To be so strict turns it into a museum type of music.

WE: When did jazz first get your attention?

RC: When I was in high school. Someone actually brought me a record of Jean-Luc Ponty and said, "Listen to this." And I was *so* elated. It just turned me on to think, "Wow, here's someone improvising, here's someone playing something that's not written down, and it sounds like it's so much fun." It just really grabbed me, and I said, "This is what I'm gonna do."

WE: Did you have your sights set on being a musician before that?

RC: Yeah, when I was about twelve I decided that I was gonna play violin. At the time I was doing violin, piano, and dance, and it got to be way too much. So I said, "Okay, I'm going to be a violinist." But I planned on being a soloist, traveling around with the major symphony orchestras. (*Laughs.*)

WE: Tell me about your experience playing in the Detroit Youth Symphony.

RC: It was set up by the Detroit Symphony. When I joined, I was the youngest member; I was still in junior high, I think. Everyone else was at the end of high school. The symphony members would come in and sit sometimes on the rehearsal and play. My teacher actually got me in it, and sometimes she would come and be my stand partner. It was really interesting to see how an orchestra worked, because we were there every Saturday from ten o'clock in the morning until four in the afternoon, just like the real symphony's rehearsals. We rehearsed these hard pieces and had many concerts per year.

WE: How many years did you do this?

RC: I was about twelve when I joined, and I stopped maybe at sixteen.

WE: Growing up in Detroit, was there a time when you were seduced by, let's say, the Motown sound, or local rock bands?

RC: Yeah, definitely. The funk thing with George Clinton and Parliament and the Fun-kadelics was out of Detroit. Motown, definitely. In fact, in high school, when I was sixteen, I started to travel with a rock/funk group that was really big, called Brainstorm. I traveled on the weekends with them. I would fly out wherever they were and do opening gigs. We'd open up for other major acts like Michael Jackson and Mother's Finest, which was another rock group.

WE: Were you also drawn to ethnic musics in Detroit?

RC: There's a lot of Greek music, in the restaurants especially. In Detroit we have a section where a lot of Chaldeans live; there's a Chaldean-American Center. I hooked up with musicians there, and we had a huge band mixed with Chaldeans, Americans, and East Indians. We'd do rock tunes—we did "Wild Thing," where one guy sang the first verse in Arabic, and then the second guy did it in English, and the opening might have been someone playing the sitar. That was a lot of fun. Then we have a *huge* Latin community, and I love Latin music. In Detroit, there doesn't seem to be the divisions that there are in a lot of other cities.

WE: The musics you referred to are heavily rhythmic, and I have a tendency to think of the violin as a more melodic instrument. How do you manage to get the violin heard in strong rhythmic settings? Do you amplify?

RC: Yeah, with most groups I do amplify. But the thing is, my playing, which I never realized until people started to point it out, is more rhythmic than melodic. I'm able to play very melodic, but when I solo I tend to definitely be drawn to the drums and to play more like a drummer.

WE: Could you become part of a rhythm section?

RC: Yes. In the String Trio [of New York], in fact, we would trade roles. Sometimes I would be the rhythm section or the drummer. There's all kinds of things you can do with the violin besides just put the bow on the strings and play it. You can use it as a percussive instrument, which I tend to do.

WE: What jazz violinists do you listen to?

RC: You know, it's funny, I don't really listen to violin players. Not my peers, anyway. Once in a while I'll put on Stuff Smith. I really like his playing; but that's once in a while. I listen to horn players. (*Laughs.*)

WE: It seems sometimes that all non-horn-playing jazz musicians listen to horn players. There's a lot of pressure on horn players! (*Laughter.*)

RC: Well, that's definitely an instrument in the idiom, where violin really is not. I mean, there were cats who were doubling on horn and violin, but basically they were horn players. The phrasing, you gotta get that from the horn players. If I'm playing more of a ballad, or if I'm playing a piece that has words to it, then I'll listen to a vocalist, because you have to understand the words and the phrasing. When I do a Billie Holiday tune, I definitely listen to her sing it to understand. But if I'm trying to play bebop, I'm I definitely putting some Charlie Parker on, to understand the phrasing and the breathing.

WE: You've cited Itzhak Perlman as an influence. Why?

RC: Well, at the school where I studied when I was quite young, he came in and gave master classes several times. It was just amazing to be that close to talk to him, and to see him be human and say things about practicing. I also had a master class with Yehudi Menuhin when I was in high school. My teacher at the time hated the fact that I wanted to play jazz. He said, "You can't do both. You're only gonna do one." And Yehudi Menuhin said, "Why?" He told my teacher, "Leave her alone, it's great music."

WE: Both those players have beautiful tones. Don't you have to sacrifice tonal quality to play jazz?

RC: I've been told that one thing people tend to like about my playing is that it's not abrasive.

WE: So tone is important to you?

RC: Yes. Especially on violin. (*Laughs.*) People are already afraid of it 'cause they think it's going to sound like a cat screechin'. (*Laughs.*)

WE: You studied at the New England Conservatory. Was that an enjoyable period of your life?

RC: I hated it. (*Laughs.*) I hated Boston. I still hate Boston. I think it's such an uptight city. When I was at the Conservatory, I felt a definite split between the classical and the jazz departments. I definitely felt tensions. I got some of that from some of the symphony players, or people on the board, when I wanted to do both classical and jazz. You know, like, "Why do you want to do that music?" I don't think the two departments were very supportive of one another. Now I hear it's completely different.

WE: Was the violin considered strictly a classical instrument at the Conservatory?

RC: Yeah. No one was writing, and saying, "Okay, I'm gonna use violin in this." Not in the jazz department. In the third stream department there were people doing that, but not really in the jazz department. So I was just acting as a horn player, which is cool, you know.

WE: After the Conservatory, you went to Oakland University. Was that a better experience?

RC: Yes. It was better for me because it was a university. I was surrounded by people other than musicians, which I definitely needed to get a balance. And I played in a big band. I played the lead alto charts on violin. A lot of musicians that graduated from Oakland still played in the band, and a lot of the cats from the scene in Detroit would come up. So we'd have band rehearsal, and you were sitting next to someone who was a professional already. I was forty-five minutes away from Detroit, so I could always go and hear music and sit in and play. And I actually was working with some Detroit bands at the same time I was in school.

WE: What did you do after you graduated from Oakland University in the mid-'80s?

RC: I taught in Detroit public schools. I was a string specialist. The symphony hired me to go to so many schools a day and per week, to help out with instruction, 'cause a lot of the schools didn't have an orchestra teacher. I would go into some of these schools and tutor the kids so that they did get some string instruction during the week. I did that for about a year. Then I took off for Europe for supposedly three months. I came back two years later. (*Laughs.*)

WE: Why did you go to Europe?

RC: At that point I wasn't really sure if I wanted to play violin anymore, or what I wanted to do. I had been in school, it seemed like forever, and I was just tired. I said, "Okay, I'm gonna go to a foreign country where no one knows me, I can't speak the language, and see what happens." It was sort of a weird thing. I just needed to travel and be around some other people and learn that way, instead of everything coming out of a book. I did have to work over there, so the thing was to figure out how to work. You start to be creative and find out things about yourself.

WE: Did you work day jobs or play music?

RC: Whatever. I found a German-American funk band over there that I played with for a little while. On Sundays I'd play in an American church. And then I was an au pair girl, a nanny, for about a year and a half.

WE: That was your main source of income?

RC: Yeah. That was a trip. (*Laughs.*)

WE: Did you advance in your music over there?

RC: I think I did. The first year music was kinda like on the side, or behind me. I didn't really worry about it; I didn't care. I didn't practice a lot. I just, like, discovered things. In the second year I said, "Okay, now you have to really decide what you're gonna do. You just can't keep flailin' around here." 'Cause it was so funny, I started to meet so many musicians coming over. They'd say, "So, what are you doin' over here?" I'd tell them and they'd kinda look at me strange. (*Laughs.*) You know, they just didn't get it. So the second year I moved to a small cow town where no one spoke English. I met a guy, actually, and we were gonna get married. We lived together in this little tiny town, Kassel, in Germany. He worked all day. I couldn't get a job 'cause my German wasn't up to par at the time, and so I was home all day. My thing was I felt really guilty when he got up. I said to myself, "You just can't lay in bed all day." So when he would get up in the morning, I would get up with him. And when he left for work, I would practice until he came home for lunch. We'd eat lunch, and then I'd practice again. That was my job then, to practice, and I learned a whole bunch of Charlie Parker's solos. (*Laughter.*)

When I came home to Detroit, I started hanging out with Marcus Belgrave. He would have rehearsals at his house every day, and everyone noticed the difference in my playing.

Then they were really into what I was trying to do, and seeing that I was more serious. Then *I* got more serious. Like I said, I was goin' to his house every day for rehearsals. Anybody could come by and play. We'd play for hours. Marcus would teach us about phrasing or soloing. For me, it was the thing then to open up my ears to some different sounds that I wasn't used to as far as the way chord structures happen. Just to do that every day, weeks on end.

WE: What did you soak up from Parker's solos?

RC: An introduction to what jazz was. Up until then, I didn't really know. I didn't really know what it entailed to just play the music. When you listen to him, you know that you got a whole lot of work to do. It opened me up to hearing other people on his records and saying, "Oh, then I can check this person out, and this person." It got all this information in front of me, whereas before I just didn't know. I thought, "Oh, I learned all of Jean-Luc Ponty's solos. I'm done." You know, where's my record deal? (*Laughs.*)

WE: Did your study of Parker urge you toward the blues?

RC: You know, it didn't take me into that direction. I didn't really get into the blues until maybe about a year or two ago. Well, I shouldn't say that; I mean I heard it all the time. And it's funny, because some people say that that's what they hear in my playing. Maybe that's the thing that comes from home. Detroit. Up south, you know.

WE: Did free jazz have an impact on you?

RC: No. 'Cause I didn't really hear that stuff growin' up. It wasn't until maybe '88, '89 that I started to hear that a little bit. And playing with the String Trio for the last six years, they were more into that. It was really new to me. It took me a minute, and I didn't always feel very comfortable in that. It's not something that I really enjoy immensely. I mean, too much of it just really gets on my nerves. It's like all right already, can I hear a melody somewhere just for a hot second? (*Laughs.*) You know, I need that. I need a little structure. It doesn't have to be extremely structured, but I do need some. Maybe it's 'cause I don't really understand it, but it doesn't touch me so I don't care to understand it. So I don't care.

WE: You've also played with Muhal Richard Abrams, a prominent free player. Does his work offer something that other free music doesn't?

RC: Yes. For me, Muhal's music has a groove in there, some kind of way. It's not just open. Sometimes I feel, like some of that music, people just kinda, without thinking about it, took their pencil and wrote a bunch of dots, you know, and then they try and get really abstract about it. (*Chuckles.*) But his music still has a soul and a groove to it. He wrote a piece for the String Trio—it was so happenin', 'cause the three instruments, although they seemed to be really separate, they weren't. The rhythms would lock up. It was more like polyrhythms locking up. That was really hip.

WE: After Belgrave, you linked up with the all-woman fusion group Straight Ahead. How did that come about?

RC: Well, they had been together years before that, and they were lookin' for a horn player. I guess they couldn't find one. They wanted a woman. So the original leader of the group, Miche Braden, said, "Let's call Regina, she's back in town." So I said, "Okay, I'll give it a shot, but I have to warn you, I'm not gonna be here long. I'm moving to New York this year." Which took me like until six years ago to do. (*Laughs.*)

WE: What finally precipitated your move to New York?

RC: I knew that if I wanted to play music for a living, it wasn't gonna happen in Detroit. The scene was just dryin' up. You'll be hard pressed to find a place to play there now, and you're gonna play the same clubs over and over and over. I wouldn't have gotten the opportunity to play with Wynton if I'd still been livin' in Detroit. You know, there are a whole lot of opportunities I just would not have had. So I moved, and a lot of people that I wanted to play with, I'm playing with now. And other people that I hadn't even thought about, I'm getting an opportunity to play with. So it was definitely the right move to make.

WE: Are you able to make a living playing music?

RC: Yes. I don't know how I'm doin' it. (*Laughs.*) I'm afraid to sit down and figure it out. (*Laughs.*) The first year I moved into this apartment—three or four years ago—I sat down on the floor and I said, "I'm gonna figure out how much money I need to make every month to live here and to have whatever I wanna have." When I did it, I just freaked out and I said, "Never do that again. Never." Some kind of way, you make it. It happens.

WE: Do you often have to play music you'd prefer not doing, to make ends meet?

RC: You know, I haven't had to do that lately. Praise God. I work enough with my group—I could definitely work some more, that's still pretty new—and I worked with the String Trio for the last six years until the Wynton tour. Now, this year, new things are coming in. It's always scary when you lose something that's been very steady in your life. I thought, "Oh my God, what's gonna happen to me?" But it's great. Kenny Barron called me; I'm playin' with him. He wants to do some duo work together as well. Then I've been playing with Steve Turre's band, and I'm getting ready to do some work with Lewis Nash.

WE: I've listened to your eponymous debut as a leader,[5] and although I enjoy your playing, what surrounds you often reminds me of commercial fusion.

RC: That's where I was then. On this first record I thought about "Is this going to get radio play?" On this new record,[6] I didn't think about it all. There's only one tune in this new record that has the machinery. The rest is live playing, whereas on the first record a lot of it was done by machines. Or *if* there were other players, they weren't necessarily there when I was there, which makes a big difference. When you have your band there and you lay the tune down, you're not going to overdub. It is what it is. There are things on the new record where, like my A&R guy from Atlantic would say, "Well, don't you want to fix that? There's a little squeak in the violin." I just said, "No, I want to leave it alone. I don't care." When I play, sometimes that happens. But this whole thing with Wynton is really funny now. I like the record that I've done this time, but that whole experience made me know that my next record will be a lot different still.

WE: How will the third recording be different?

RC: The band I use is pretty big. That's because I grew up in a city where there's so much different music, and because I've had the opportunity to play with Oliver Lake, a string trio, Wynton, Dolly Parton, Patti LaBelle, like every kind of thing. So I want to calm the music down. Even this second record is very energetic—just fire all the time. Now I'm takin' a breath. I want to scale the band way down, and work with an upright player who plays standard jazz, but who understands funk music.

WE: Is it fair to say that you're wanting to move further away from commercial endeavors toward more ambitious music?

RC: Yes, I am. And to strip away some of my surroundings. To be a little bit more naked, not padded with things around me. Like the percussion and the drums and the vocal groups. Instead of, like, giving the nine-course meal, we're just gonna have meat, beans, and potatoes now.

WE: You're on a diet.

RC: Yeah. (*Laughs.*) I think, in a way, I felt like I needed all those things for people to enjoy it. But now I'm getting to the point of saying, "Okay, here's another part of me, let's just go to the barest essentials." No electronics—just play the violin. Those five minutes every night with Wynton just really did something to me. (*Laughs.*) I kinda almost feel like I'm getting ready to move maybe to a more conservative place, which is very odd, you know, considering what's going on. But that's just how I'm feeling right now.

WE: The ready cure for that is to move back to Boston.

RC: No way!!! (*Laughs.*)

WE: What's your diagnosis of jazz today? Where do you see the music heading?

RC: Well, I think more young people are gonna be forced to really look at the music for what it is, why they're playing it and what they're going to do with it. The industry's forcing us, you know. Maybe I say that 'cause I have a deal, and you know, in the beginning you might think a deal is really gonna make your life a lot better. A lot of times it kinda complicates things, 'cause you get so worried about selling records that you lose sight of the music. Now I'm having to see, okay, when you don't have this deal anymore, what are you gonna do to be a part of history and to take the music forward? I think maybe more and more people are seeing that. It's funny, there are not that many people that are being innovative. Not like before.

WE: Do you think it's no longer possible to be an innovator?

RC: I think it's possible; I think that we have a lot of work to do to get to that. I think we have to wake up to that fact. Those people that are out here, that are tryin' to be innovators and take the music on, really aren't getting paid any attention to. So we tend to say there's no one out here doin' that. There *are*, we just don't know about 'em because the industry isn't putting them out. They're not on a major label, or they're not on a label at all. And a lot of people don't spend enough time perfecting their craft on their instrument. People who are doing that, they're being innovators as well because they're taking their instrument further, the vocabulary or the use of the instrument itself.

WE: Let's switch to gender issues. Have you had to endure any obstacles to your career due to sexual discrimination?

RC: Just an incident which wasn't gonna affect my career at all. When I first moved here, I experienced that from an older musician. I signed up on this list to sit in, and they never got to my name. I noticed two women vocalists—I wouldn't call them vocalists, 'cause they were singers. For me there's a definite difference. To me, a vocalist is a serious singer who knows about the music. They were, like, really sidled up to him. He introduced them as studying with Barry Harris. I thought we're gonna hear this great stuff, and basically, they couldn't sing their way out of an open paper bag. (*Chuckles.*) I saw then what was goin' on. I said, okay, if that's what it takes, forget it, I just won't be sittin' in here. And I left. But that was just one incident. I think people know that I'm serious. I'm not just out here trying to get over being a girl or playing the cute thing. It's funny, I don't usually get it from musicians, I get a vibe from people that maybe I'm gonna work for—promoters.

WE: Some promoters have been less than convinced that you could do the job because you're a woman?

RC: Yeah. Or I could tell by the way they treat me when I get there. They're not sure what's gonna happen. Silly stuff; it doesn't bother me, it doesn't stop me. I gotta do what I gotta do. It's funny, if they're not quite sure, if the band is there and they go and talk to one of the guys about something, the guys will always say, "You gotta talk to her, she's the boss." (*Laughs.*) And it's my band! I always have to prove myself. After we play, then it's a different story.

WE: I'd like to focus on the way you've been packaged. On this first record, the cover has you naked to the waist with your back turned to the viewer. Other images in the insert catch you with a sultry look on your face. How do you feel about your sexuality being marketed?

RC: Actually, I love the cover. It was the photographer's idea. It comes from the painter Man Ray. In that picture, I am the instrument. Of course, people are gonna look at it and say, "Oh, she's naked." It didn't help my record sales much, you know. (*Laughs.*) I didn't sell one hundred thousand units, so I wasn't doin' it for that. I'm very comfortable with my sexuality and being a woman. I know what I stand for. I don't really have a problem when women are posing nude in men's magazines. But I'm not saying, "Okay, sex sells; let's put it on here." If that were the case, I probably would have posed full naked frontwards. (*Laughs.*)

WE: Do you think that women represent a different aesthetic than men?

RC: Yes. We can't help it, 'cause we're women. We are nurturers. We just bring a different energy, totally. When you have men and women, there's gonna be a different kind of balance and energy happening. I like it when there's a mixture of both.

[We turned to the first piece of music: "Bugle Blues," from *Swingin' Stuff,* recorded 1965; EmArcy Records, Stuff Smith on violin.]

RC: (*As the music is playing*) I love to hear music like this, that has this intensity to it. A lot of times you don't hear that intensity. You know, players have the technical ability, but the raw energy's just not there. There's just such an energy that he had that you don't get from violin players. Stuff Smith was a real bebop player on the instrument. And he swings. He's the epitome of jazz violin to me. I think sometimes we get too academic about the music. You know, it's good to know that stuff, but, like, you have to forget it once you learn it. That's the trick: can you forget all that stuff once you learn it?

WE: Did you find Smith's tone beautiful?

RC: Yeah, for what he's doin'. He doesn't have what people now consider the perfect tone for violins, which is very clear. But for the music that he's playing, that raunchy tone is needed. That's what's makin' it, almost as much as the notes he's playin', is that sound. It reaches in and grabs you. I can't see anybody listening to that tape and not moving. They'd be dead. (*Laughs.*)

WE: It didn't sound like he had such a great violin, either.

RC: No. Not at all. Those cats back then were playin'—they called them fiddles—just a box. And that's what's really funny today, like when I go into a violin shop, or if I'm playin' with other string players, or even on this tour with Wynton. Other violinists will come up and say, "Oh, what kind of violin do you have?" I'm like, *please.* You know? It's not going to be what you wanna hear. It's not some grand name, nowhere near it. And "Oh, what kind of bow, and what kind of—." It's like, for me, none of that matters. It's just a certain sound I'm tryin' to get.

WE: You don't wish for a world-class instrument?

RC: Yeah, one day I would like to. Just to have it. But it's still gonna have to have the tone. You know, I like a very dark, gypsyish-sounding violin, which most classical players don't like. They like a very feminine-sounding violin. I think the Italians are the ones that make the very dark-sounding violins. You know, the tone is the first important thing. Like the violin is supposed to have this very clear tone, and because I was schooled for a long time in the classical world, that, for me, is more important to have. That's what I strive for first. And it's really funny sometimes when I play; if I get that more raucous sound, I tend to get away from it really fast. And sometimes I'll be playing and people will say, "No, stay there." It's very odd for me because I'm so used to the other world of "No, it's got to be this perfect, sweet tone."

WE: Another question about "Bugle Blues." Was the arrangement designed for the violin, or could, say, Dexter Gordon just as easily have played it?

RC: Dexter, anybody could have played that. It is not a violin piece, but that's what's so incredible about Stuff Smith. He's not approaching it, I don't think, from the standpoint of: Is it violinistic? No matter what you would have been playing, he was going to make it fit that instrument.

[The second selection was "Lay-By," from *Suite Thursday, Duke Ellington, The Great Paris Concert,* recorded 1963; Atlantic Records, Ray Nance on violin.]

RC: I love it. (*Laughs.*) There's just so much humor in it, too. His tone is much different than Stuff's; his tone is more sweet.

WE: Is his playing more violinistic?

RC: Yeah.

WE: Did Ellington's arrangement support and complement Nance?

RC: Oh, yeah. Even the way that he arranged the horns around it. He kept them basically out of the range of the violin. Some of it was in the same range as the lowest string of the violin in G, but because of the different timbre it wouldn't get in the way. Sometimes horns and violins can sound so much alike that it just gets in the way. Especially if you're soloing, you just feel like too many people are in your space. The way everything was arranged gave him the opportunity to take his time and really say something.

WE: Let's see how you respond to the tone of the violin in this next piece ["King Kong," from *Jean-Luc Ponty, Cantaloupe Island,* recorded 1969; Blue Note Records, Jean-Luc Ponty, violin].

RC: I mean, his tone is nice, it's the electric violin. When they're acoustic, they're okay. But the electric violins themselves, I hate. I think they sound horrible.

[We turn to the last selection: "Snowflakes and Sunshine," *Ornette Coleman at the Golden Circle, Volume Two,* recorded 1965; Blue Note Records, Ornette Coleman on violin.]

RC: (*Laughs.*) Oh, God! That's about all I can handle. My mother would say, "They make money, too?" (*Laughs uproariously.*) The intensity is great, but I can't handle a whole night of that; I just can't. I'd go out and shoot someone. (*Laughs.*) It's just not my bag.

WE: How do you respond to *his* tone?

RC: You know, for what he's playing, for that type of music, I can respond to it. For the energy purposes, okay, you know, it was great, but it just grates on my nerves.

WE: Did you hear in Ornette's playing a background of academic training on the instrument?

RC: No. Not for the violin, I don't. It's definitely great to let the academics of it go. Just to get at what you're trying to get at, and not worry about it. But this is almost like not trying to *get* at something, and so not worrying about the sound. Maybe he thought that the sound was needed for that.

WE: Is it valid for a musician who only has the rudiments of an instrument down to use those basics for expressive purposes?

RC: Hmmm. That's a very interesting question. I don't think that he has the rudiments for the violin down. That's for sure. (*Laughs.*) Sorry, Ornette! (*Laughter.*)

WE: What does he have?

RC: On the violin? He just has the energy. But for that piece it was valid.

WE: Would the piece have suffered if you had done it with all your technique?

RC: Yeah.

WE: A final question. In addition to the String Trio of New York, you've played with several other professional string groups. Since your main influences come from horn players, is it interesting for you to play with other strings?

RC: No. (*Laughs.*) I'm not interested in doing a lot of string work, and I usually don't know a lot of string players. 'Cause the thing is, a whole lot of string players don't really know anything. They don't listen to horn players and don't really know the phrasing, and so then it becomes very corny and it's not fun for me. I enjoy cellist Akua Dixon's[7] group. Akua has a lot of interesting arrangements. And with the Uptown,[8] some of that string stuff was just phenomenal. Like they did some stuff that Max [Roach] did back with Bird with strings. It's incredibly difficult; you really gotta know the phrasing for that. But all in all, I don't really like playing with string players. I'd rather play in a saxophone section, you know, or just play when I'm the string section. (*Laughs.*) If I were gonna really aspire to play with a string group, I want to swing with a string group. I think you're gonna be hard-pressed to find that.

Selected Discography

Rhythms of the Heart. Verve 314 547 177-2 (1999). (Vocal by Cassandra Wilson on one selection.)
*Motor City Moments. Verve 314 543 927-2 (2000).
Freefall. Verve 314 549 706-2 (2001). (Duets with pianist Kenny Barron)

Notes

1. 1985; Atlantic.
2. 1999; Verve.
3. 2001; Verve.
4. 2003; Verve.
5. *Regina Carter,* Atlantic Jazz; recorded 1995.
6. *Something for Grace,* Atlantic Jazz; 1997.
7. Jazz trombonist Steve Turre's wife.
8. Uptown String Quartet.

Marilyn Crispell

Marilyn Crispell

Marilyn Crispell has been visible as an important pianist since 1983 when she began a decade-long association with saxophonist Anthony Braxton. Originally pigeon-holed within the fold of so-called free players, a longer view of her work reveals a style that defies strict categorization. Career highlights include a recent affiliation with the jazz label ECM and thirty recordings as a leader.

Born in Philadelphia in 1947, at age seven Crispell began classical piano study, later augmented by weekly lessons at the Peabody Music School in Baltimore. As a teen, she was fascinated by the music of twentieth-century composers Arnold Schoenberg and Karlheinz Stockhausen, and under their influence she improvised her own pieces. After earning degrees in classical piano and composition from the New England Conservatory of Music, Crispell spent the next six years searching for a direction.

Her musical epiphany occurred at age twenty-eight, when she discovered jazz. Following two years of concentrated study in Boston, she moved to Woodstock, New York, to continue her apprenticeship at Karl Berger's Creative Music Studio.

Her tenure at Woodstock led to the long musical partnership with Anthony Braxton. In quartet and duo settings, her virtuosic piano style and insistent rhythmic counterpoint served as an ideal foil to his abstract playing. Their critically acclaimed concerts, recordings, and world tours propelled Crispell to the forefront of the avant-garde. Trademarks of her early period (1976–1992) included the tactical use of tone clusters and crossovers, leapfrog phrasing, and even two-fisted thunderous pounding that heightened the expressive force of her music through the sheer magnitude of her physical involvement. Throughout, Crispell's classical background and training in twelve-tone row composition remained evident in her playing.

Her more recent work has belied the facile dubbing of her as a "female Cecil Taylor." A student of Buddhism and Tibetan culture, she fully shows her rhapsodic and contemplative sides on a recent ECM release, *Nothing ever was, anyway.*[1] Crispell's crystalline interpretations of the haiku-like song structures of Annette Peacock were met with widespread acclaim, and the recording placed among the best jazz records for 1997. Her 2001 release for ECM, *Amaryllis,* rated critical praise in *Jazz Times, New Yorker, Schwann,* and the *BBC Magazine.*

Marilyn Crispell maintains an active international performing and recording schedule with such ensembles as the Barry Guy New Orchestra[2] and the Evan Parker Trio[3] in England, an all-female trio led by Denmark's Lotte Ankur, and the Europe-based Quartet Noir.[4] She will be featured in an upcoming documentary film about New Zealand's improvised music scene and Maori culture by jazz filmmaker Burill Crohn. In addition to playing, she has taught improvisation workshops and presented lecture/demonstrations at universities and art centers around the globe.

Recorded June 26, 1998

WE: Do you consider yourself to be an avant-garde musician?

MC: I think the term "avant-garde" is a fairly useless term. Most of the stuff that people refer to as avant-garde is at least fifty years old. To me, my stuff sounds fairly accessible. (*Laughs.*) I've been studying classical music since I was seven and I have studied traditional jazz, so what I do is very heavily informed by things that went before. I think in the free-jazz movement in the '60s, there may have been a lot of times when that was not the case, and a lot of people got up on the bandwagon and then fell off when it wasn't hip anymore. People were dealing with sounds without maybe knowing what they were doing.

WE: Average listeners might euphemistically refer to your music as "abstract," meaning they can't understand it. How would you respond to them?

MC: When people ask me how should they listen to my music, I usually say, "Don't try to figure out what it is or compare it to something. Just listen and let something happen." It's the same as looking at a so-called abstract painting: it's a way of seeing. People always want to relate it to something figurative—"Oh, that looks like a tree"—rather than appreciating the composition just for what it is. It's similar to saying, "Do you see images when you play, or do you think about particular images or ideas if you compose something?" And my answer would be no. It's a really pure abstract musical thing. And yet, when you say "abstract," that for me is even a problem, because to me, my music is not abstract. To me, it's using very specific elements and developing them in very specific ways.

When I first started listening to music—I had never studied it, I'd never analyzed it—it had a very emotional, magical quality for me. Then I started going to classes when I was about fourteen—you know, harmony, theory, composition, and analyzing everything. I felt like the magic was completely destroyed. It had just become this technical exercise. Then at a certain point, when things that I'd studied became part of my understanding without actually having to think about them and analyze them consciously, I found it was like going back to the first thing, but on a new level. It's like being very primitive at first, then learning about something, and then going *back* to that primitive thing, but with what you've learned being incorporated as this total part of who you are. You're not separate from it, analyzing it; you just understand it. So if somebody's listening to this for the first time, I don't think they can possibly understand it the way I would, or somebody who's really familiar with that kind of music would. And I don't think it's necessary. I'm sure that a lot of people think it's coming from nowhere, you know. It's just an outpouring of emotion or whatever. The first time I heard Cecil Taylor, I remember thinking to myself, "Oh, this is really similar to the music I've been interested in since I was a teenager—contemporary classical music. But I'm not really sure what he's doing." And it took years and years of listening to hear the themes and what they were related to and how they developed. Things didn't become apparent all that quickly even to me, you know, someone who was really more familiar with these things. Actually I've always believed if you do something with conviction, that people will be able to relate to it, and indeed they seem to, particularly in a live concert situation.

WE: I used the term "abstract" to refer to the way art is separate from, and a distillation of, everyday reality. How do we differ on that?

MC: If we're going to use the word "abstract" in that sense, music is, I think, the most abstract art of all the arts. It's something that's very ephemeral unless you're putting it down on tape or something. In fact, for a long time I didn't want to record. I didn't like the idea of recording. I liked the idea of playing music, and it floats out into the cosmos and disappears. To this day I have trouble committing music to paper because of that feeling. I really work from intuition and inspiration.

WE: Although you assert that your music is accessible, isn't its existence marginal in relation to mass culture?

MC: I think that's because the mass culture hasn't had any exposure to it. I don't think that it's inaccessible. You know, I used to wonder about that, and then I've played in places in the United States where people basically are not familiar with this kind of music at all because it's not played on the radio, it's not pushed by the big record companies. And the response has just been fantastic. People are often *wildly* enthusiastic. But I don't think you're going to get the same kind of audiences that Michael Jackson's gonna get. I don't think that really matters. I think what matters is that you say what you have to say, and the people who are going to hear it, hear it. If it were pushed by the big record companies, it's possible it could get an audience like Michael Jackson. But so much of the top forty, so much of what's popular, has nothing to do with music. It has to do with marketing, and, you know, money. It has to do with record companies creating stars so that they can make money. When I was in Copenhagen recently, saxophonist John Tchicai was leading a musical parade down the streets. Like the Pied Piper, he picked up people as he went along. Hundreds of people were walking along behind him, and there's no reason something like that couldn't happen here. It's just that it hasn't been part of the culture. Maybe it's been part of the culture in other ways: Sousa and July 4th parades, and stuff like that.

WE: To put a finer point on this, I've spoken with well-known jazz musicians, and even they have problems with so-called free music. Their identities might surprise you.

MC: Oh, no, I don't think I would be surprised. I think some of the musicians you may be talking about probably have a lot invested politically and historically in maintaining that their music is jazz and our music is not. And frankly, I don't think it *matters* what you call it. Oliver Lake has a poetry and music piece that he does where he says, "Put all my food on one plate." And he's talking about music. He said, "I play this, this, this, and that. It's just music. I play what I feel." I mean, I've been going through a fair amount of hell dealing with the whole category thing. Like if I play this more lyrical thing, are the people who like the other stuff I did years ago going to think I'm selling out?

WE: What's the basis for your concern about categories—fan mail?

MC: No, I'm basing it on what I know—the way people think. You know, you're supposed to be in a category. You're supposed to be a certain thing. It's not a flexible dance. You're supposed to get put into a box—this is who you are—and, okay, this is an avant-garde festival, so we'll call them, them, and them. This is a real jazz festival, so we won't call them, them, and them. Well, I think those lines shouldn't be there. It's scary to people to allow you the freedom to not have those walls around you. I guess it's the human thing to want to do, to classify something. You know, to classify it so that you can stand back and look at it and think that you understand it, whereas actually I don't think you can really classify what's happening now that way.

WE: You observed that some musicians have a stake in certain forms of jazz. Can you give an example of what you meant by that?

MC: This whole thing that's happening with Lincoln Center and the jazz wars.

WE: You're referring to Wynton Marsalis and his sphere of influence?

MC: Yeah. I mean, those people have a lot invested for their personal careers and their sense of history of black music. What is jazz? What is not jazz, you know? "It's only jazz if it comes from the blues," "The blues is black music," and so on and so on and so on. Okay, a person would have to be *stupid* not to realize the fact that if there had not been black people here, jazz would not exist. *They* were responsible for creating this brilliant synthesis. They brought their own thing with them, took what they found in a new culture, and put it together. And yet what it's become since then has such a large history with so many people, and it's incorporated a lot of world music. I think that the term "jazz" is almost obsolete now, you know. It's like what these people are trying to do is put it in a *museum* where they can look at it and control it and have it be safe and respected. I mean, I think it's fine in a *certain* way to do that, and yet to me, jazz has always denoted freedom, creativity, and exploration. Why should that stop now? Why should it suddenly be put into a museum?

WE: But what's wrong with Marsalis wanting to revivify past musics and extend their traditions?

MC: There's nothing wrong with that. What's wrong is that he's not open to anything else, *and* he's in a position of tremendous power. He has *a lot* of power, and he's used that power in very destructive ways towards people who are very sincerely trying to do something they believe in. I think he has no right to do that.

WE: Let's discuss some of your history. Can you remember an early, watershed experience with music?

MC: That would have to be in so-called Western classical music, when I was about fourteen years old. I went to a small music camp in northern Vermont. It was run by this very incredible woman who taught at Peabody Conservatory in Baltimore. Her name was Grace Cushman. She was very poor, you know. She basically devoted her whole life to teaching kids. She had this small camp with maybe thirty kids and ten to fifteen people on the staff. Every Monday night there would be a composers' forum. Kids who had composed something would have it played. We would listen, then they'd play it again. If it was really weird, the first time people might laugh a little bit, which is often a response if you don't understand something. That's why the pieces were played twice—to give people a chance to get over their nervous first reaction. On Saturdays we went mountain climbing in the Green Mountains of Vermont or the White Mountains of New Hampshire. It was just this very beautiful, idealistic experience, and for the next five years I *lived* to go back to this place for six weeks every summer. And it wasn't only about music. I mean, up to that point in Baltimore I would say the social structure of my life had not been very happy. First of all, being uprooted from Philadelphia at the age of ten was very difficult. It was very difficult for me to fit into the new social structure in Baltimore, which was much more based around little junior sororities and things like that.

WE: You found yourself in a more gentrified situation?

MC: It was just a different cultural situation. Where I grew up in Philadelphia was pretty much an Irish Catholic working-class neighborhood, and all the kids would put on these little fairy-tale theater pieces. It was a very creative kind of life there. And then all of a sudden moving to this other place where all people thought about was, you know, lipstick (*chuckles*) and high heels and who was the prettiest and who had the best personality—it was very shocking. I didn't fit in *at all* until I went to this music camp. People there were kind, and they were good people. It was a whole different kind of aesthetic, and I remember bursting into tears and crying for hours because it was such a relief. Then that became my life—this whole thing became my life.

WE: Define "whole thing."

MC: This camp and the people and the whole life aesthetic there. Music was a part of that, and a lot of what went on there was what you would call avant-garde classical music. So I guess my taste for that music began at about that time. Also, I was always, kind of in my own quiet way, a very offbeat person, and so these so-called offbeat things just appealed to my nature. I think you get attracted to things because they reflect part of what's already in your own nature.

WE: When did you get serious about music?

MC: I didn't seriously get into music as a life's work until I was about twenty-eight years old and I heard John Coltrane. I heard *A Love Supreme*,[5] and that was the real awakening. I had gone to New England Conservatory, mostly because my parents wanted me to go to school. I wanted to graduate from high school, go to Paris, and get a job at the American Library. You know, I had this romantic illusion of living in Paris. But they didn't like that idea. They wanted me to go to school, and I thought, "Okay, I'll go to school and be a composition major." Kind of do what comes naturally, and, you know, maybe not have to work too hard. Of course, that was a joke because I could never ever get caught up with my work there. I ended up abandoning being a composition major and became a piano major instead.

WE: You graduated from the Conservatory and married in 1967. Did your creative momentum continue during that period?

MC: No. It took a sabbatical. (*Laughs.*) I was mostly working in psychiatric and medical hospitals with my husband for the six years we were married.

WE: Was he a medical professional?

MC: No. He was also a musician, just working in these hospitals. He was a talented composer and trumpet player. We were very young and inexperienced when we got married. I was not really into getting married, but for one reason or another—not to be hassled by our parents or whatever—we did it, you know. I mean, he's a wonderful person; I don't regret that at all. We're still friends thirty years later. But after about six years, I was feeling really suffocated and stifled and remember sitting in a chair in the living room thinking, "I wish something would happen." And what happened is that my husband met someone else. (*Laughs.*) I sent him back to school to learn the cello because he had these great cello hands and it was my favorite instrument. I didn't *send* him back, but I said what a great idea it would be. He liked the idea, and when he was there he met someone else. Gradually things just eroded. In a sense it was very devastating for me. And I would say the *only* thing that got me through that was returning to music. The *only* thing. It was like this lifeline that I was holding on to, without which I felt that I would have died.

WE: When the marriage ended, what was the first musical milestone for you?

MC: Actually, I was in a band as a singer for a few years. I had kind of given up playing the piano. And then at a certain point in this band, they wanted me to play piano. I said, "I can't; I've never played this kind of music." They said, "Well, you have a good ear. Just try." So I did. Then I met a guy who was a jazz and blues pianist. I was working in a bookstore, and he was working in the record store across the hall in the mall. We got together, and he had this great record collection. One night I was alone in our apartment and I heard *A Love Supreme.* That was the big eye-opener.

WE: It's been reported that you sensed John Coltrane was in the room as you listened to *A Love Supreme.*[6] Is that accurate?

MC: Yes.

WE: That may sound a bit cosmic to readers. Do you really think he was there, or was it the rush of a self-affirming moment?

MC: Hard to say. I felt a presence. A very loving, powerful presence. It could just have been what came through in his music. But it was strong enough that it changed my life and set me on the path that I'm now on.

WE: Can you be more specific about what struck you in his music?

MC: It was total inspiration. I would even say love, recognition. Coltrane was like a loosening of the spirit. I felt like with Coltrane there was an intensity, almost—I don't want to use the word "desperation," but he was going into different, uncharted territory. There was a passionate emotion, a powerful spirituality.

WE: Did you relate with equal intensity to Coltrane's later music?

MC: To tell you the truth, I have not listened to a tremendous amount of music. I tend to find a particular thing, and I'll listen to that a lot and really get it in my blood. But I won't listen to everything that a person has ever done. I probably have not even heard that much Coltrane. That particular thing hit me; that's what I got into, and that's what I studied really hard. What Coltrane did after that, I probably heard more from the different musicians I've been involved with. I've probably heard the results of what Coltrane did more than what he actually did.

WE: After you heard *A Love Supreme,* you moved to Boston and worked with Charlie Banacos. What did you study with him?

MC: I studied traditional jazz. I had to, like, really go from scratch. I had to do everything in twelve keys. I had to write out seven solos in every key on every piece. I had to listen to tons of stuff and transcribe it to be able to hear and understand what was happening, you know, within the confines of these time cycles and chord changes. How were people using the chords and the notes and the chords and the scales? Where did they go outside of them?

WE: Who were some of the people you studied?

MC: Charlie Parker, Charlie Mariano, McCoy Tyner, Wes Montgomery, Keith Jarrett, Bud Powell. I had a thick book of transcriptions which I ended up throwing in the garbage several years later, because, as my friend Karl Berger said, "The solos are better on the record than on the paper." It was very good for studying, but I didn't think it was something that should become an icon that you would try to imitate.

WE: After studying with Charlie Banacos, what prompted you to seek out Karl Berger's Creative Music Studio here in Woodstock?

MC: When I was in Boston I met Charlie Mariano, and he told me about it. He said, "You're ready to play, and there's this place up in Woodstock where people are doing things similar to what you're interested in doing." I went up to meet people and have experience playing in ensembles, playing different people's music. I hadn't really had a lot of ensemble experience.

WE: Describe how learning was structured at the Studio.

MC: Workshops. Classes. Performing. Some people would come, and things would be written down. Don Cherry would come, and he would do everything by memory. He'd play or sing thirty pieces, and then that night you were supposed to be able to remember them all and play them at a concert. And he would switch without any notice between one and the other. People were going crazy, like, you know, trying to write the stuff down, and "Oh, what'll we do?" In other words, they were having to use their ears.

WE: Was that an effective teaching method?

MC: Oh, I thought it was the best thing there.

WE: You met a number of prominent musicians there, including Anthony Braxton, Roscoe Mitchell, and Cecil Taylor. Would you relate in your own words your first meeting with Taylor, when you took the opportunity to play for him?

MC: Yeah. I mean I felt like he was a kind of musical soulmate. And I really wanted him to hear me play. It was like I was wanting to talk with him on a deep soul level. The main building was this old motel complex. In the main building there was a concert room where classes were also held. Then you'd walk out into a room where there was a bar, and there were little practice rooms all around with upright pianos in them. Cecil was out there in that barroom with some friends. So I went into one of the little practice rooms, and I played a whole concert knowing that he was out there listening. When I came out he kissed my hand. After this, I was very shy just talking with him for about four years. I used to give him flowers and write him poetry. He's one of the few people I've ever, ever been really awestruck by. Usually I'll go up and talk to anybody.

WE: How was his conduct toward you?

MC: To me, he has always been incredibly warm and open and appreciative. I just *adore* him. At one point he said, "You know, we're both just human beings." And I said, "Yeah, but I can't forget who you are." Because I think that he and Braxton are two of the greatest innovators of this century in music. They really took all these different influences and did something incredibly original.

WE: You rank them alongside Armstrong and Parker?

MC: Well, I'm just talking about the people I'm most familiar with. Because that's where my main interest lies, and that's what influenced me mostly. And of course Ornette Coleman was important to me. But Ornette was not as big a part of my friend's record collection, so I wasn't as exposed to him. (*Laughs.*) Cecil was a *large* part of it.

WE: Let's dig a bit deeper into that topic. Considering the span of jazz history, what musical resources do you most relate to?

MC: I'd say pretty much the contemporary stuff is what I relate to. I felt it was important to study the other things because I thought it would be arrogant to go into something called jazz not knowing anything about them. But it's not where my main interest lies. Where my heart really lies is starting around Cecil and Ornette Coleman, Paul Bley and Keith Jarrett,

McCoy Tyner, Coltrane, Albert Ayler, Don Pullen, Dollar Brand [Abdullah Ibrahim]. Lots of African music. Bach. I guess I'm just not that interested in some of the more traditional stuff.

WE: Now that I have your sources in perspective, can you describe in more depth why you think Taylor and Braxton are such major innovators?

MC: Because they made the greatest changes, the greatest crossovers. I think they made a true synthesis between the Western classical tradition and the jazz tradition. I mean, Cecil abandoned—and he was maybe the only one at that time—traditional rhythmic structures. Ornette abandoned the idea of having to play on the changes. There'd be a tune, and then you'd play on the feeling of the tune. But it was still in a certain time concept. Whereas Cecil abandoned that time concept, and Braxton, too.

WE: While you were studying and then teaching in Berger's organization, you began doing some work for Braxton. Didn't he record a gargantuan project at Oberlin College about that time?[7]

MC: I was involved in that. That was kind of a disaster, actually, because Braxton lived in Woodstock at the time, and he had a lot of students from the school doing transcriptions and proofreading. I was proofreading, and it was like Santa's workshop: huge score pages draped over the balconies, and everybody working like busy little bees. I was about to do my first tour with him—my first tour ever. My first trip to Europe; my first real professional gig.

WE: With the Creative Music Orchestra?

MC: Yes. And I wanted some time to practice. I was getting nervous because the deadline for this other thing kept getting moved up; it seemed to be, like, never ending. So at a certain point, I remember asking him if he would be able to find someone to take my place in this, because I was really nervous that I wouldn't have enough time to prepare for the tour. Well, he was very offended by that and fired me on the spot. I still did the tour, but we didn't speak for about a year after that.

WE: Were there any memorable incidents on the tour that you'd care to relate?

MC: Yeah. (*Laughs.*). At one point, Braxton took [trombonist] George Lewis and me backstage and said, "Don't play those blues licks. These people can really hear the music." And I remember being really flattered that he thought I had played blues licks. (*Laughter.*) And also during the rehearsal he told me to have a beer so that I would slow down and not play so many notes. I learned a lot from him about space and breathing. Because when I first got into serious improvisation,[8] it was like jumping off a cliff. The person who was playing with me at that time said, "Just start playing and don't stop." So I got in the habit of playing *lots* of notes really fast all the time.

WE: Who was this person playing with you?

MC: A guitarist named Baird Hersey, who actually now lives up here in Woodstock. He had a band called Year of the Ear, and they were doing really creative stuff. He took it upon himself to help me 'cause he thought there was something there, you know. So he came over to the place where I was living. I had a piano and he brought his guitar, and he said, "Just start playing." And that was my first real experience of just letting go and improvising with someone. Later, working with Braxton, it was like having this big piece of stone, and he helped me sculpt something out of it. Before I was just playing every piece of the stone, and he kind of showed me how to use space and silence to define different facets of the sculpture. You know, not just play the whole thing all the time.

WE: In 1983, you began your decade-long association in Braxton's "classic quartet."

Since, as you commented earlier, you have trouble committing music to paper, were you at all hesitant in dealing with his heavily annotated structures?

MC: No, not at all. You see, I love working with structures. I'm not closed off to anything. I mean, I don't want to spend months and months and months learning a heavily notated piece. I'm just not interested in that. But, you know, his pieces had a lot of room for interpretation. He was never fanatical about playing something *exactly* the way it was written. He didn't even want that. He has something in one of his books where he says, "If it's too perfect, then you haven't understood." In fact, half an hour before the quartet would go onstage, he would often bring in a new, very complex piece that we couldn't possibly play right the first time. We'd have a quick backstage rehearsal where we'd sing through our lines. But he wasn't after it being played, exactly. He was trying to give you a road sign, but it wasn't like somebody holding a knife over your head if you miss a note or something.

WE: Just prior to joining Braxton's quartet, you made your recording debut on Cadence Records. In the early stages of your career, were you anxious to get in a studio and document your work?

MC: Well, at the beginning, *before* I did that Cadence recording,[9] I wasn't interested in recording until I realized that I had to record in order to go out and perform. I had to have this product, you know. At the time, it felt to me like an unfortunate necessity. But since then I've enjoyed recording. My favorite recordings are the ones I've structured in the studio, where I've had a lot of control over the production. Earlier on, it was more live recordings. It would usually be at a festival, a one-shot deal. In the studio you can stop and say, "Let's try that again." At this point, it's fun to structure projects more. I mean, things are coming a little more into focus, whereas at the beginning it was kind of like a universe is being born, you know, stars exploding and stuff. Now things are cooling off and planets are forming. (*Laughs.*)

WE: You've moved into a different league by signing with ECM. What will you do if yet a larger label calls, especially if it should mean some level of compromise on your part?

MC: I'm not interested in working with any company that's going to try to commercialize what I do; that doesn't have respect for what I do; that's going to try to package me in some way, to sell me. I mean, if they're interested in my music, that's one thing. The whole reason I approached ECM is because they are the antithesis of that. I don't care if I don't become a big commercial success. To me, it's never been about quantity, it's always been about quality. As far as I'm concerned, I'd be happy recording for ECM permanently. I mean, I really don't care if Columbia calls me or Blue Note calls me.

When I say it doesn't matter to me if Columbia or Blue Note call, the idea of success to me doesn't mean how many records you made, or how many you've sold, or how many people know your name, or anything like that. That is not my idea of success. In a certain sense it almost wouldn't matter to me—and even as I'm saying this I'm biting my fingers— but it almost wouldn't matter to me if I did nothing else with music. I mean, I could conceive of having a life that was accomplishing what I'm trying to accomplish without playing music, if I couldn't play the music I want to play and in the way I want to. My idea of success is to go into yourself and find your own truth in your life. Music happens to be an important part of that to me, but I could also conceive of doing it without music.

WE: At the beginning of the interview, you mentioned that you've been exploring a more lyrical expression in your music. That seems in keeping with your reflective nature.

MC: I always have had a lyrical quality; it's something I've been exploring *a lot* more since about 1992.

WE: What happened in 1992?

MC: What happened is there was something changing in *me* going that way. All these years I've been writing these romantic, beautiful pieces, and then I kept them in the closet. And in November 1992, I was at a festival in Stockholm where I heard a Swedish bass player—his name is Anders Jormin—and something just clicked. I said, "This is someone I can go in both directions with. You know, I can go up to Sweden and safely explore this lyrical side of myself, away from where people know me and will make judgments."

WE: Why was safety an issue?

MC: Well, I was nervous about it because I had such a reputation for being a Cecil Taylor clone in a sense, you know. So I wanted a safe space to do my thing, away from the prying eyes of whoever. It was very scary at first because, for one thing, I was kind of learning it—it was so new—and I wasn't that good at it at first. And also, I admit, because I was worried about what people would think. I'm trying to be less worried about what people will think in spite of my desire to express myself unapologetically at all times. But it was somewhere I wanted to go.

WE: So a need to open up a more romantic side of your sensibility had been brewing for quite awhile?

MC: Yes, definitely. It was allowing something to come out that I had stuffed down before. This certain part of me started to want to emerge, and it was like what I said before about being attracted towards things that already are similar to something in your nature. As well as being attracted to more contemporary styles, I had always been attracted to classically beautiful things. Like, I loved a lot of Keith Jarrett's music. His melodies, the way they just spin off. Paul Bley, and those beautiful Coltrane ballads. That just suddenly wanted to come out. Manfred[10] said, "People don't realize what you do. They just have you classified as a certain thing." Like Marian McPartland, she was *so* surprised that I played these traditional things and that I learned her music.[11] I called her that night to thank her and she said, "Yeah, it was great and everything that you learned that stuff, but next time we should just do your music." I didn't know whether she was trying to say in a polite way, "It really wasn't great; you should just do your own music," or what. But why not do it all? I had a great time learning "All the Things You Are," you know.

WE: Since you broached the topic, allow me to ask the inevitable question: How do you feel about being thought of as a "Cecil Taylor clone"?

MC: Well, I was always very flattered to be mentioned in the same breath with him, to begin with. People would say "The female Cecil Taylor." He's been a *huge* influence on me. Hearing what he was doing—the context that he did it in—was an eye-opener for me. I was doing it in a context of classical music, and he was doing it with a rhythm section and horns and in a very extended way. Because we had this similar aesthetic sensibility, I grasped onto what he was doing, and he became, like, a teacher for me. You know, "Okay, this is where I can actually go with this." Hearing him was a stepping stone for me to get into improvisation. But I would also like people to hear where my music has diverged. I think there's a similarity in the aesthetics, but the actual vocabulary that we use is different. And my stuff is lyrical in a different way from his and uses different tonalities.

WE: Perhaps it's superficial, but would a conspicuous similarity be the way you both employ tonal clusters?

MC: I'm not doing many clusters these days. What I do tends to be single note lines more, and when I was doing clusters, I was exploring different rhythmic things or using clusters as lines, in the shapes of lines. I think of it as my bebop thing, almost. Similar to what Don Pullen does, which I didn't discover until much later. People also compare him a lot to Cecil, and he didn't like that because he wanted people to hear the difference.

WE: During this interview, you've cited your attraction to beautiful music. Are you interested in your own work having a romantic bent, but without sentiment?

MC: I think I'm trying to let what I feel come out, and I don't think one *has* to cancel out the other. I think you can have irony *and* romanticism together. Yeah, I think there's some sentimentality in what I'm doing. I don't think it's necessarily a bad thing. I'm not talking about soupy, maudlin, supermarket, Muzak-type stuff.

WE: Isn't there a danger you may cross over the line?

MC: Sure, it's dangerous. I mean, I like danger. I like living on the edge. I like not quite knowing where my next step is gonna take me.

WE: Is part of the danger exposing your more vulnerable, emotional side?

MC: Yeah, and maybe exposing my feminine side, which I was very reluctant to do for many years, you know, because I wanted to be taken seriously. It always was a great compliment to me when people would say, "You play like a man" or "I thought that was a man. I couldn't believe that was a woman playing." If somebody relates to what I do, on any level, I'm happy.

WE: I think many women players dislike having gender tied to their music.

MC: Well, I think a lot of people have a lot of hang-ups. I think there *are* a lot of people who use political issues having to do with gender or race as an excuse for their own shortcomings, frankly. And, you know, I've never been that interested in playing on women's festivals, women's this, women's that. I think it's not necessary to say that if it's a woman playing, it's women's music. Certainly if it is a woman playing, it's a woman's music. That just seems kind of stupid to me. I don't think there is a women's music. When you hear Marian McPartland play, do you think *that's* a woman playing? I think it's a bunch of baloney, I really do. I mean, look at Bill Evans. He had a very feminine energy in his playing. Keith Jarrett has some of that. People always want to separate. I think you can't separate. Everyone has masculine and feminine energy. There are definitely issues that have to be dealt with, like women getting paid less than men, and women not getting hired because they're women. Discrimination on any level has to be dealt with. But to say a women's music or a women's art—to me it's meaningless.

WE: Have you faced career obstacles because you're a woman?

MC: Generally that has not been a problem for me. However, there was one instance where a journalist came backstage to invite me out after a concert. I declined because of an early departure the next day and subsequently found out that he wrote a personally vicious and devastating review of my concert, which had received a standing ovation and enthusiastic response from the audience and promoters—including an invitation to return again. But I think wherever I've gotten to, I've gotten to because I was absolutely driven to go there. Actually, being a woman might have contributed to my visibility. Yeah, in some ways it's probably worked for me, not against me.

WE: Let's talk more in depth about your music. You have used the phrase "points in space" to describe your playing.[12] Yet in some of your recordings I hear space compacting rather than gesturing out.

MC: I may actually have been talking about a kind of pointillistic counterpoint—i.e., fragmented rather than connected lines in counterpoint. But to address your question, I think as I've gotten older—as I've changed—there's more space. I think one of the reasons I don't like my early recordings as much as some of the later ones is specifically because of that.

WE: Clearly, many jazz musicians, as well as their fans, put a premium on swing. Do you swing?

MC: To me, it's kind of like the question "Is what you play jazz or not?" What is swing? I mean, if it has a rhythmic propulsion? If it swings in relation to traditional blues? Sometimes my playing does, sometimes it doesn't, and it doesn't matter.

WE: Is inciting involuntary body movement in the listener important to you as a performer?

MC: For me, the most important relationship is between music and dance. I've always been very involved with dance—playing for dancers, watching dance, and dancing myself. I *always* feel and see movement when I play. Braxton talks about a thing called rhythmic pulse, where it's not necessarily a thing where you're going to snap your fingers in 4/4. It's more the pulse of your own breathing, your own heartbeat. People have their own pulses, and phrases tend to fit into those kinds of pulses. It's not traditional swing. But does it swing? For me it does. Little kids, before they know that they're not supposed to like it, they dance to it.

WE: Your piano technique has been called unorthodox. Is that description warranted?

MC: Well, for one thing, when you play classical piano you play these nice legato lines, Chopin etudes, whatever. One of the things that Charlie Banacos made me do was practice playing melodies with two fingers to try to get into a different kind of touch, different phrasing, a different feeling. What happened is that I realized you could get a much more percussive sound that way. If you were playing a line, and there were a lot of other instruments playing, the piano often just doesn't come through. But if you're playing it with two fingers percussively, it *will* come through. So I started doing a lot of that, playing lines with two fingers.

WE: You're not talking about two fingers on one hand?

MC: No. Although that, too. I do whatever I need to do to get the sound to come out. Sometimes I just play with my whole hand in the bass like a bass drum, and get some percussive rhythm going. Not to be weird or out or something, but just because if I play it with my whole hand, it'll make more sound. It'll sound like a drum.

WE: You used the word "out" a moment ago. "Free music," "playing outside," "the new thing" are some of the terms to designate the genre you work in. Do you have a preference for what to call your music?

MC: I actually kind of like the term "progressive jazz." It just has a nice ring to it.

WE: So long as it doesn't blur into a "contemporary" jazz category and the likes of Kenny G.

MC: Kenny G.—I've heard him a few times on the radio. I think he has a nice sound, and he plays with a lot of feeling.

WE: You probably lost more people with that comment than with your stance on women's music.

MC: (*Laughs.*) Bill Clinton likes him.

WE: I can't help but notice how modest your apartment is, with its spare furnishings. I take it that the apparent absence of material things is by choice so you can focus on the non-material?

MC: Yep. I don't want to accumulate a lot of stuff. I want to be free to maybe move to Europe, or do whatever I want to do. When I moved into this apartment eight years ago, part of the purpose was—I mean, it's a very kind of private apartment; you can see there are hardly any windows, there are those thermal windows way up high, and one little window above the bed, and then those kitchen doors—part of it was to put myself into a kind of enforced seclusion to really just get down to business. To get down to the core issue of my life. That was partially successful. There are just too many distractions. You know, I've a lot of friends, and I'm traveling a lot, and my cat, and daily life. It wasn't quite the retreat I had planned it to be. It's very difficult to seclude yourself unless you go off to a cabin somewhere and don't tell anybody where you're going. And don't have a telephone. If it weren't for my cat, I might do that. (*Chuckles.*)

[We turned to the first music selection: "The Piano Piece," by Henry Cowell; 1924.]

MC: I know this was written in 1924, which is extraordinary. To me, this is like a similar kind of language that Cecil would use—it has the same kind of breath and phrasing, but it doesn't swing. Cecil could play that and it would swing.

[The next selection was intended to be Dave Brubeck's "Blue Rondo a la Turk." The tape was miscued, however, and "Take Five"[13] inadvertently came on. We listened briefly to it.]

MC: "Take Five" is the very first jazz piece I ever heard, and I fell totally in love with it. The next thing I heard after that was when I went to buy a jazz record, knowing nothing about it, and I got Horace Silver live at the Village Gate[14]—a lucky choice! When I was still at that music camp, I heard "Take Five" and I adored it. Kind of neat that that came on.

[We turned to "Blue Rondo a la Turk," *Time Out,* Dave Brubeck Quartet, Columbia Records; 1959. "Take Five" is also included on this album.]

MC: (*While the music is playing*) It'd be a great dance piece. I remember loving it. It was my second favorite piece on the record. It's even better than I remembered. (*Chuckles.*) It's great the way he goes in between those four-bar phrases and changes tempos so dramatically.

WE: Critics have pointed to this piece as a prime example of how Brubeck doesn't swing.

MC: Oh, it's baloney. I think they just like to hear themselves talk. They have to figure out something to say. (*Laughs.*) They don't really know what they are talking about.

WE: Are there enduring progressive elements in it, or is the work firmly rooted in an earlier era?

MC: Well, I think there are definitely some progressive elements in it—the way he switches back and forth between the different phrases and tempos. It still sounds fairly modern to me.

[We listened to "Turn Out the Stars," *Highlights from Turn Out the Stars: Bill Evans Trio,* Warner Brothers Records, Inc.; recorded 1980.]

MC: Beautiful—this is my favorite Bill Evans composition.

WE: Was Evans an influence on you?

MC: Bill Evans was definitely an influence. He was in my friend's record collection, too. (*Laughs.*)

WE: Did you get to hear him in person?

MC: I did. There was a place in Boston at the time, in the mid-'70s, called the Jazz

Workshop. The first *live* jazz concert I ever heard was Pharaoh Sanders, when he was still dressing up in African clothes and he had all these African instruments lying around. Leon Thomas was with him singing. I was *extremely* taken by it. If there was somebody I liked, I would go back night after night and stay the whole night. Bill Evans was one person I did that with.

WE: Were you able to strike up a friendship with either Bill Evans or Pharaoh Sanders?

MC: Actually, I became friends with Pharaoh when I went back to hear him a year later at the same club. I wanted to give him something in return for the beautiful music he'd played, so I bought him a small African thumb piano. As he passed my table after the first set, I handed it to him in a brown paper bag. I think he was quite touched. He has always been very supportive of young jazz musicians, and he invited me to a jam session at the Jazz Workshop the next afternoon. I went, although I was too shy to play very much—I'd had no real experience at that point.

[The next selection was "Money Jungle," *Money Jungle,* Duke Ellington, Blue Note Records; recorded 1962, Duke Ellington, piano, Charles Mingus, bass, and Max Roach, drums.]

MC: (*As the music is playing*) See, I can tell Cecil listened to him. I heard a recording of Ellington playing "Summertime," and I thought it was Cecil. I mean it's out, what he's playing. If you just took that part right there and played it for somebody, they wouldn't guess Ellington. It's amazing. This is not traditional stuff, what they're playing now. It's very creative. (*After the music ends*) That's why he's such a great musician. You know, I never listen to much Ellington, but every time someone plays me Ellington I go, "Whoa!" (*Laughs.*)

WE: As you said, Ellington goes "out" in places, but then he comes back to the theme. How does that compare with Cecil?

MC: I think Cecil just took it one step further. Cecil had his own themes. He might take those moments and use them as the theme.

WE: Thelonious Monk and Cecil Taylor both cited Ellington as an influence. Are they primary sources for you?

MC: Well, Monk was definitely a source for me. I think one of the reasons so many contemporary pianists play his stuff is that it's very angular, kind of minimal, and the harmonies he uses can really almost go anywhere. There's a real kind of openness there—rhythmically and every other way. It's the same with Bach—his music travels well into modern times.

[The last piece of music was "Reap the Whirlwind," *New Beginnings,* Don Pullen, Blue Note Records; 1989, Gary Peacock on bass, Tony Williams on drums.]

MC: This piece in a way reminds me of the Henry Cowell. It has almost a static rhythmic thing happening. I don't know, I would be tempted to play more loosely *around* that rhythm. I would still have the bass and drums playing regular figures, but I would be doing more rhythmic variations, and not so much, like, playing the same pattern along with them. I love Don Pullen. I played after him one night at the Knitting Factory, and I heard a comment he made to someone: "Oh, I feel so bad for Marilyn." There was blood all over the keys after his set. He played that hard.

WE: Thanks for the interview.

MC: Oh, it's been inspiring to me. Actually, it's just what I needed to kind of get the fire under me to start working on the stuff for my tour. I've been just "futzing" around reading *Women Who Run with the Wolves*[15] and hanging out with my cat, and now I'm going to really start working.

Selected Discography

Live in San Francisco. Music & Arts Programs of America CD 633 (1990). (Solo recording that ranges from abstract works by Crispell to gorgeous interpretations of compositions by Monk and Coltrane.)

Gaia. Leo Records CD LR 152 (1994).

Santuerio. Leo CD LR 191 (1993).

Nothing ever was, anyway: The Music of Annette Peacock. ECM 537222-2 2-CD (1997).

Amarylis. ECM 1742013400-2 (2001).

Notes

1. *Nothing ever was, anyway: The Music of Annette Peacock,* 1997; ECM, including bassist Gary Peacock and drummer Paul Motian.

2. *Inscape—Tableaux,* 2001; Intakt.

3. *After Appleby,* 2000; Leo.

4. *Quartet Noir,* 1999; Victo.

5. Impulse Records; 1964.

6. Howard Mandell, "Profile/Marilyn Crispell," *Down Beat,* September 1984, p. 42.

7. (*For Four Orchestras*), 1978; Arista Records.

8. When she was in Boston, studying with Charlie Banacos.

9. *Spirit Music;* 1982.

10. Manfred Eicher, owner of ECM Records.

11. This is in reference to Crispell's appearance on *Piano Jazz.*

12. Mandell, "Profile/Marilyn Crispell."

13. From *Time Out,* the Dave Brubeck Quartet, Columbia Records; 1959.

14. *Doin' the Thing: The Horace Silver Quintet at the Village Gate,* Blue Note Records; 1961.

15. Clarissa Pinkola Estes, *Women Who Run with the Wolves: Myths and Stories of the Wild Woman Archetype* (New York: Ballantine Books, 1992).

Barbara Dennerlein

Barbara Dennerlein

Although the jazz organ lapsed from public consciousness for two decades after its heyday in the 1950s, the '80s saw a revival of this so-called miscellaneous instrument spurred by a coterie of new practitioners. Among the most exciting to emerge was the German organist Barbara Dennerlein. Taking on the pure physicality and vociferousness of the Hammond organ, the mostly self-taught Dennerlein developed a unique boppish modern style that is one of the highlights of this period of resurgence for the behemoth B3.

Born in 1964, the Munich native's first and only choice of musical instruments was the organ. Musically gifted as a child, Dennerlein advanced quickly and by age fifteen was performing in local jazz clubs. After high school, she embarked on her professional career, soon becoming one of Germany's top jazz artists, as well as one of the leading organ players on both sides of the Atlantic.

Dedicated to the development of the Hammond B3 within the jazz idiom, Dennerlein has made numerous modifications to the instrument. She was the first person to radically alter the sound of the foot pedals by sampling an acoustic bass. Although uninterested in playing an actual synthesizer, she combines this new technology and samplers with the B3 keyboard to create exuberant soundscapes that are in stark contrast to the often lugubrious European organ tradition.

Dennerlein uses these new techniques to good advantage in her own compositions. Written specifically on the organ, her rollicking tunes exploit a multitude of timbres, rhythms, and harmonies that move to a serious groove. A veritable Houdini at her instrument, the tall, slender Dennerlein plays on two organ manuals while pushing and sliding the controls, and using both feet to tap dance precisely across the pedals.

A canny businesswoman, Dennerlein founded her own record company, BEBAB, which has released seven of her studio dates. Additionally, she has a total of ten recordings under her leadership on the Enja and Verve labels. Barbara Dennerlein has won the *Down Beat* "Talent Deserving of Wider Recognition" title five times, and is a three-time recipient of the prestigious German Critics Award.

Recorded October 18, 1996

WE: At what age did you own your first organ?

BD: When I was eleven. It was a small Hohner electronic organ. It was a present from my grandfather for Christmas. It had just one keyboard, and no foot pedals. Immediately I played "Silent Night" by ear. I played it with two voices, you know, just out of what I heard. It was really my absolute start, no other instrument before. I couldn't play any note.

WE: Let me see if I understand what you just said. You got the Hohner on Christmas Day, at age eleven, and although you'd never played an instrument before, you played "Silent Night" that evening by ear?

BD: Yes. Exactly at that evening I played it. I played it with two lines going on. (*Laughs.*)

WE: Did you have an interest in music before you received the organ at Christmas?

BD: No. Nothing. I didn't have the interest because I never had the idea that I could do something like that, you know. It just didn't come up to my mind. Before I started playing that instrument, I had never thought about whether I could play an instrument, or that I would have such a talent to play music. I was very good at school, and that was my work. And then finally there was this instrument at Christmas, totally unexpected for me. It fascinated me so much even if it was not yet the Hammond organ.

WE: What prompted your grandfather to buy you the Hohner?

BD: Because my grandfather said a child should play an instrument. My parents, especially my father, always loved the organ. Both of my parents always loved jazz music.

WE: When did you first encounter the B3?

BD: The first time I heard the Hammond B3 was when I had this teacher, Paul Greisl. Mostly I had no teacher. I'm an autodidact, as we say in German; I learned it by myself. But I had this teacher for about two years, and he had the B3. I remember I heard the B3 the first time at his house, not knowing at all what this is, and it really touched me. I always say it was love with the first tone. From that time it was my dream to be able to play such an instrument. For me it was something sacred, really holy to me. And when I was allowed by my teacher to also play on that organ, it was, you know, like a small child being allowed to do what she is really dreaming of.

WE: After playing the B3, did you remain satisfied with your smaller Hohner?

BD: When I was at Paul Greisl's home to get these instructions, I saw that you also play with your feet on the B3 organ, you know, and that it has two keyboards. I went home to my parents and I said, "I can't practice on this; I need to play foot pedals." And so it started. They presented me a bigger organ, and another bigger organ, until I had two or three different organs before the Hammond B3. The B3 was really something which could not be reached for me because it was so far away. Also, this teacher I had, he made a big secret out of the Hammond B3. He said, "Oh, it's hard to get them and they're very expensive." So my father really tried hard to find out where you can get it in Germany. Because if you are not in this subject, you do not know how to get such an instrument, as they are not built anymore. My teacher didn't give us a hint about it, but he let me play on it because I was his best pupil and he was very proud of me. I don't remember when it actually was, but after some detective work (*chuckles*), my father found out where he could get the Hammond organ. And my first Hammond organ my parents presented to me, maybe when I was thirteen. This was like in heaven for me!

WE: In addition to your parents, did Paul Greisl encourage you to play jazz?

BD: I think it was very important that he felt the love for jazz I had and that he did not say, "You have to practice only this and that," you know, stupid exercises. He allowed me also to start playing jazz music. That's what I really wanted to do, because the first time I heard jazz music, real conscious, was when he played a concert in a club in Munich— Columbus Club, I think it was called. It was an American club there. I said to my parents, "Please, let's go, he is playing a concert there with a drummer, and I want to hear him." I remember we went there, and I was so fascinated. I never heard anybody playing jazz music before. So that was my dream from that point on. Also, I listened a lot to radio. I remember laying in bed at night, because in Germany jazz on radio was always quite late. When I heard interesting things—jazz music—I remember being really excited and starting to sweat. (*Laughs.*) It was really touching me.

WE: Do you still have that sense of excitement about the music?

BD: It depends. I mean, it's becoming more difficult, because what I expect from music I think goes more higher. If something's really touching me, then I get goose bumps. (*Laughs.*)

WE: That's your test?

BD: Yes. For example, we recorded one tune called "Nightowls" on my new CD[1] where David Murray played a great solo. There's a special part of his solo where he goes up and modulates the tone, and I always get goose bumps when I hear that. (*Laughs.*)

WE: Was Paul Greisl the only person in Germany who could have taught you to play the B3?

BD: I guess so. Anyway, still today there are not many people who can teach the organ, and there are not *any* who can teach jazz organ. I was really lucky that my parents found that person and that he played the jazz music. It was just by chance; I could have been with a teacher who didn't understand jazz. Sometimes you get chances in your life, and that helps you do something special.

WE: Why was no one else teaching jazz organ, given the love Europeans have for both organ music and jazz?

BD: Well, I started at a time when the jazz organ was not so popular. And I think because there are not so many organ players around. I mean, you have thousands of great piano players, but you have only a little part from that amount of good players who play jazz organ. It is just a rare instrument in jazz. I mean, right now there is a big boom for the organ, and everyone is suddenly playing the B3 organ. But you know, that's going up and down; these are just waves. So I think that's one reason. The second reason is that it's an instrument coming from the States. It was developed in the States and built in the States, and to bring it over is a big hassle, you know. You have to convert it to our electricity, to the 220 volt, and it needs a new motor inside. And there's only one company in Germany who does that, so it's really hard to buy these organs. That's the reason you can't hear it so often. Following that, people just don't have the idea to play the instrument. Because it's not so popular, they don't hear it so often, you know. Also in jazz music, it's quite in front through people like Jimmy Smith, Jimmy McGriff, and Wild Bill Davis. But in pop or rock music the organ was always used as a background instrument. It's very rare that you hear it really as a leading instrument.

WE: Were people surprised at the sight of you playing it?

BD: People looked at me in a very strange way. This young girl with that old instrument. Why does she like that? Very often people asked me about that.

WE: Did the European tradition of the church organ have any influence on you?

BD: You know, as I didn't think about music before I had this instrument, I was really "clean," if I may use that expression. I was not corrupted. (*Laughs.*) And since my parents listened to a lot of jazz music, I was up with that music without being conscious about it. But I was not so much interested in listening to my parents' recordings. I was just interested in that instrument and to play music. That was what basically interested me. I never got in touch with a church or a church organ, so it was not my tradition at all. I was really a clean slate. My first contact with music was the organ, and with jazz it was through the teacher I had. There was nothing else which could distract me, you know. This music was important for me, and I was never interested in other things. I mean, I did not very often go, like other children in my age, to parties—you know, that stuff. I remember at that time *any* written music I could get, I took it and I made photocopies. I have a huge collection of standards, because everything I could get I just went into the copy shop and copied and copied. It's not allowed, but that's what I did.

WE: Did you copy the sheet music for popular songs or jazz standards?

BD: Basically more jazzy stuff, and I had the ability to play these things when it was written. I learned a lot with the drill-book stuff, you know, where you have just the melody and chords. I really had the ability without knowing the tunes, because I didn't have the background at that time. I didn't know all these jazz standards, but I played them the right way. I don't know why. You could give me some paper with the melody and the chords, and I just played it, and it was mostly in the right interpretation, even if I never heard it before. So my teacher at the time gave me a nickname, which is in English, I think you would say, "music killer." (*Laughter.*) It means that I could read everything.

WE: When did you first play in public?

BD: I started already during these two years with my teacher because he played concerts showing his pupils. I had my first concerts after one year or something, where I played to a small public. My first gig, I think already at thirteen or fourteen, was in a senior center. Then I was in touch with organ companies. You know, we have Böhm and Wersi in Germany. They are making organs, and they were interested about me. I loved to go where other organ players show the organs to the public for the German organ companies. I remember once when I went there and this guy was playing. I was really a young girl, and I asked if I'm allowed to try the organ. He said, "Yeah, of course, you can." And it was always very funny because these people, you could really watch them, like, "What is she doing!!?" (*Laughter.*) I remember this one guy, when he saw how I played the pedals already at that time—which is something not used by many organ players—he just made the bass very soft. As I didn't know the organ, you know, because I didn't know how to make registration, I could not find where to make it louder. (*Laughs.*)

WE: Were you improvising at this stage of your development?

BD: Yes.

WE: How did you learn?

BD: I saw that with my teacher and I said, "How do you do that?" And so he said, "Try to play over the chords." I tried, and in the beginning I thought, "Oh, God, I never will be able to." Then there was a period of time where I almost *only* improvised. (*Laughs.*) I didn't want to play themes anymore because it was so much fun. I improvised after one and a half years.

WE: Were you still studying with Paul Greisl at this point?

BE: After these two years I had this teacher, I split. There were some personal reasons, and it was not so easy anymore. He really couldn't show me a lot of new things, and so I went away from him. From that point onwards, I taught myself.

WE: Using the drill-books?

BD: Yeah, books. When I saw some books about theory, I just got them and, you know, tried to learn by that. Also I discovered a lot by myself. And from time to time there were people—like there was a piano player who showed me how to play a chord properly on the organ. Not to play the basic note. You should play the basic note on the pedals, and then you play the third, for example, and the seventh and the ninth or something, you know on the keyboards. Simple things, but they were enough that I could develop. That helped me quite a lot.

WE: During these formative years, was there a particular jazz musician who had an impact on you?

BD: I never in my life had an idol. Never. And I don't have one so far, because I think music is such a complex thing. I love so much about it that it would be hard to focus on just one musician, or a few. I mean, there are so many I like and it can be out of different directions, and almost no musician where I say I love everything from him. I'm very open.

WE: Did you go through stylistic shifts based on the musicians that you heard?

BD: No. (*Laughs.*) I was just interested in the music. The funny thing is, I did not so early think about developing my own style, but I think that's what I did. I was never interested in copying someone, and finding out what he's really doing. This might sound strange to you, but I was just interested to play what I feel. I was never interested so much in other persons. Of course, I happened to listen to Jimmy Smith and Shirley Scott and all these people, because my teacher had these recordings. I liked them very much, there's no question. I also liked my teacher's playing very much at that time. I think he was my first, well, influence, you can say, because I was near to him and I could see him play. You know, it's much more important than only listening to records. I remember quite often that people came to me and told me, "You're sounding like so and so." Or, "You sound exactly like Rhoda Scott."[2] I said, "Oh, that's interesting; who is that?" (*Laughs.*)

WE: Were you influenced by periods or schools of jazz?

BD: I played a lot of swing music at that time, but there was a period when I played a lot of bebop tunes. That came after the swing period. I also discovered very soon the Latin things, you know, the bossa nova and all that. And, of course, blues is always there. I developed basically by myself going in different directions. I mean, I never said now I play bebop and I don't play swing anymore, or Latin. I was always open to all that. After these two years with my teacher, I met with his drummer and guitar player every week at least one evening. We played at my parents' home. My father started to make a studio for me, you know, where I had my organ, and my father recorded us. This drummer and the guitar player started to compose, and so I was involved in composing. I was thirteen when I started composing with them. We worked a lot on special tunes, old tunes. That was nice, but we also played, for example, "Samba Pa Ti" from Santana.

WE: Let me ask you about the sources of your music. It may be said that jazz, particularly when played by African Americans, reflects the black experience in this country. Looking back, what aspects of Western culture shaped your playing?

BD: You know, it's a common thing that people say, okay, someone plays like that, you can really feel that he comes from that. I'm not sure that that's right all the time. I think very often that's just the person who is listening; that person has a special feeling for where it comes from. Except if the musician who's playing, he says that's from that background or that's what influenced me. I think today very often we have to deal with opinions in public about how this kind of music comes from that, and if someone plays like that, he has to come from there. But you see, for example in my case, I come from somewhere totally different, because at that time I never knew about the States, or about, you know, black musicians or white musicians or about the history. I just played that music coming out of myself.

WE: Can you describe this "totally different" place you came from?

BD: My parents took very much care about me. I was very safe growing up, and so I didn't experience all that what people think jazz musicians have experienced, like suffering and feeling the blues. What I think was important is I heard the music without thinking about it, because as a child I didn't think about music. It just was there through what my parents listened to, and that's how I think I got in touch with it. I didn't know at that time, but when I came up to the point where I played the instrument, it just came out. I guess that's the influence, because I grew up in a very safe neighborhood, and there was nothing what you would say is typical jazzy. (*Laughs.*) All the children in my age, nobody listened to jazz music. They listened to only rock musicians. They all had their idols they admired. I never understood that anyway, because that was not my music so much.

WE: Identification with a media superstar was not part of your teenage years?

BD: No. I never understood that people can go crazy about one person being onstage, like the children do today about their rock star. You know, they faint. Or they take the pictures out of the newspaper or the magazine and put them on the wall. These things were not what I did. It was not what I felt.

WE: Now, as an adult, do you have favorite musicians in the popular music world?

BD: There are a lot of people I like. Barbra Streisand is my favorite singer, *if* there's one favorite. (*Chuckles.*) I just like her voice very much, and how she's expressing her feelings. It's just great for me. Her voice is just touching me.

WE: Does she give you goose bumps as well?

BD: Yeah. It depends; not always. I like musicians who are going in a little more jazz context, like, for example, Sting. And I also can like rock bands. It depends; sometimes it's a special tune I really like. I mean, there are many things I like about rock music, so I'm not at all narrow-minded in music. I hate it if jazz is taken in that kind of a narrow way. I hate if people say, "This is our music, and we don't care if you like it." Or, you know, "We don't want to spread out" or "We don't like to get other influences in our music." I hate that. I think that jazz is expressing freedom of your thoughts, of how your life is, how you live. Because you can only play jazz music if you're free.

WE: When you associate jazz with freedom of thought, are you speaking of political freedom, or simply a liberal point of view?

BD: Both. Improvisation is something which is free because you can play anything what touches you at that moment, or what comes in your mind. If you go for jazz music, you go against the masses, you know, against most people's opinion. You always belong to a kind of minority, and so you go in another direction than most other people go. So I think that's the kind of freedom to do that, and to have your individuality grow.

WE: You indicated that jazz also expressed political freedom. An obvious example would be the oppression suffered by black people.

BD: It was their freedom, their possibility to break out of their situation. Maybe it was in another sense for me, because maybe I wanted to break out from my safe home. That could be because I was a very nice girl and I did always what my parents told me. They said I was really obedient. I never made them troubles, not at all. They could rely on me, and so I was really in very clean surroundings. I led a very clean life; you know, I never smoked, I never drank alcohol. I did nothing; I went to school, I had great notes. So maybe that music is my kind of getting out of that, you know. Not being too normal or whatever.

WE: Although no one musician or type of music influenced your approach, did you focus your listening during your formative years on organ players?

BD: I was not orientating too much with organ players. I listened also to saxophone players, guitar players. There was a time where I discovered a lot of bebop, and especially Charlie Parker. He's a musician whom I still really admire. The great tone he has.

WE: When you're listening and learning from a musician like Parker, how do you process the information? Do you copy licks from his improvisations?

BD: No, it doesn't show up that way. A lot of young musicians listen to the solos of their heroes and then they write it down. They play their phrases in all keys and all that stuff. Something I never did. I mean, I think it would have been good to do it, just technical-wise and for interest. But I never had the time to do it. I had other things which I thought were more important for me, and so the way I learned was not at all copying. Because the danger is, if you start to analyze another person's solo, that you take their vocabulary in your own and then you just play the phrases from another person. I just tried to play my own way. And I think my own way is very different from how other players, especially organ players, play.

WE: In terms of your own identity on the organ, I've read that you identified, on some level, with Larry Young's work.[3]

BD: Only in that what I hated very much was that everyone in the beginning said, "Oh, you sound like Jimmy Smith." It doesn't mean that I don't like his playing. It's very good and I like it and I listen to it, but I don't play like him. Very often people who are not so much used to the Hammond organ sound, the one organ player they know is Jimmy Smith. So they say, "Oh, you sound like Jimmy Smith." I read that in articles about me very often, and I hate that. I'm sure Jimmy Smith wouldn't like it if someone says you play like Wild Bill Davis. I just said Larry Young because Larry Young went away from this typical Jimmy Smith style. I think a lot of organ players copied a lot from Jimmy Smith.

WE: What are the characteristics of the Jimmy Smith style?

BD: Oh, his special phrases. His registration, of course. I use that, too, but I play it different. But basically, he was the first person who used the percussion thing. Wild Bill Davis played more this other registration, which was a softer sound, I think. Not so percussive. And because also when Wild Bill Davis played organ, the Hammond organ didn't have the percussion. It was invented a little bit later. But Jimmy Smith was one of the first who played the organ like that and made it popular like that. And he has developed special organ phrases he's using, and, of course, sometimes I also play some typical organ phrases. I think nobody's free of that. But still, I really have my own style. Of course, you can't get around what Jimmy Smith played, because there are some phrases which occur in every organ player's playing, because they just sound great on the organ, you know. Maybe without Jimmy Smith it would have happened anyway, because it's just good at the organ. But Larry Young is one of the rare organ players who really went away from these typical organ phrases and the typical playing, like Jimmy Smith's, and that's why I say I feel more related to Larry Young. He was a very modern player at that time. But I don't play like Larry Young.

WE: Can you be more specific about how your playing is distinguished from Jimmy Smith's?

BD: First of all, Jimmy Smith plays a lot of blues and tunes with simple harmonies. I use, for example, chords he would never use. He's basically into this blues thing, and I'm playing, for example, suspended chords with major seventh. Or I just play a G chord over an A flat, things like that, which are really going away from those simpler chords. But I'm also living in another time, you know. I don't know how I would've played if I would have grown up when Jimmy Smith grew up. When you are a young musician from today, you can listen to much more different kinds of music than the older musicians could listen to.

WE: As an ambitious musician, what do you hope to achieve in jazz?

BD: What I want to do is really to show what an organ can make. I want to go in other directions than people have done before. I have such a love for the organ. I'm very often asked, "Do you also play piano?" I say, "Yeah, I play piano sometimes." It's like if you ask a trumpet player, "Why don't you play a saxophone?" You know, that's how far away, I think, the piano is from the organ. It's a totally different instrument. I'm talking soundwise now. It's also a keyboard, but you can't compare it. It's really like a trumpet is not a saxophone, so an organ is not a piano.

WE: Is it important, then, to start on the organ instead of learning first on the piano and switching later on?

BD: I think it's important to start with the organ, because I think I developed a very special style, including the foot pedal work. You know, what I play on my foot pedals and the timing I have with what I play on the keyboard. It's something very special. I think for anybody who starts with piano and goes to play the organ later, he has problems with that because it's like playing two instruments. For me, bass pedal playing's very important, even from time to time when I play with a bass player. I try to explain it like it's a special feeling of your body, you know. For example, very often when I'm composing, I never think, "Can I play what I'm composing technically?" Sometimes, to improve my ability to play, I'm composing quite difficult rhythmical things, or bass lines together with the organ, which are very hard to play. Since I have a computer, I'm playing the single lines on the computer and playing the bass separate. Then I can hear my whole arrangement. And that tempts me to compose more complicated bass lines because I just play them separate with my hands. And after that, I have to start to practice that. Everything I record on my CDs with a bass player, I also can play it by myself, which is sometimes hard if it is difficult in rhythm. The easiest thing to do is playing a walking bass. It's not easy to play fast in all these lines. It's easier to play a bass in a rock groove than to play a piece in 7/4, for example. It's very difficult to have these different rhythms going on.

WE: You've been stressing the use of foot pedals on the organ. Yet, when you were very young, didn't you have problems with your feet?

BD: When I was born, my feet were not in the right position. I had to wear a cast. I had that when I was a baby growing up. I had to do a lot of exercises with my mother to get them straight. But they're all right now.

WE: Is that early condition the reason why you play the pedals with your toes?

BD: I think the main reason why I learned it like that was that my teacher did it like that. I didn't know the classical technique like they do with church organs, where they use both the heel and the toe. Now I do it sometimes because I also play a little bit of church organ from time to time.

WE: To me, as a layperson, it seems incredible that you can coordinate all your limbs, up and down on the organ, with such precision.

BD: It's like a drummer, you know, playing different rhythms with his arms and his feet. And I also have to play the right notes, too, which makes it even more difficult. In the beginning, when you start to practice things like that, you just start on your pedals, or just play on your keyboard. Then you try a combination, or then you try to improvise over it. You know, different methods of just getting the groove right in the hands and the feet. In the beginning it's kind of stiff, and you really think about when to play what, you know. Then there comes a point when suddenly you stop thinking about it and it's a feeling of your body. Your body is the groove, maybe like a dancer who's feeling his music. I think it's the phenomenon of swing, for example, not the style of swing, but the right timing to swing. To groove. I think I have developed a special groove with my pedal playing.

WE: Once you've mastered the pedals and the keyboard on a complex piece, what would be the reason for having a bass player?

BD: Because I want to have a different sound. You know, I can't play a slap bass or the nice sound a contrabass has. A bass player can pitch the tone and do things I just can't do on my foot pedal. And it gives another color to my music. For example, on my new CD I play about half of the tunes with my foot, and half of the tunes are played by Lonnie Plaxico on bass.

WE: You also use a synthesizer and a sampler, correct?

BD: Yeah. But only to make it more interesting as background for the organ, or to combine sounds. The main thing for me is my foot pedals, because the original Hammond organ foot pedal sound is a sound without any sustain. So if you hit a key, it makes "pop" and not "pahh" like a string, where there's a delay after you hit it. So, if you play a walking bass line on that pedal, it sounds not so good. Especially if you play just with your toe, then it's short. You can't play really legato with one foot and using your toe. So I started very early to get string bass; these are electronic basses which produce a sound like a bass. I tried to go in the direction of a real contrabass. Suddenly when all this media was invented—samplers and all that stuff—you had the possibility to take a real bass and sample the sound, and have those sounds when you play on your instrument. That changed the possibilities; that was when I started to get the MIDI[4] system for my foot pedals. MIDI means that you have new contacts for the keys. When you press a key, then you get the sound from your source like a synthesizer or a sampler, whatever you use. So you can use other sounds.

WE: You took this odyssey through new technology because you wanted a more authentic bass sound?

BD: First it was to be able to have a sound like a real contrabass, like a real upright bass. That was the intention. I was, of course, the first one who had that. There's one person in Germany who makes all that for the Hammond organ. Then I thought, "Why not have the same thing on the keyboard?" You know, being able to use other sounds. So I got him to make this also for my keyboards, having the MIDI technique inside, and that means a totally independent technique inside of the organ. It has nothing to do with the real organ sound. I can just play MIDI sound—you know, a synthesizer sound on my Hammond without playing the Hammond organ sound. It happened only one time in a concert that my Hammond organ didn't work anymore, because there was a contact not right and we didn't find what it was. So what I did (*chuckles*), I programmed an organ sound on my synthesizer. And I played the synthesizer sound on my Hammond organ—you know, having a piano on the lower keyboard and the organ on the upper, and having the sampler bass sound on my foot pedals. Most people didn't even realize. (*Laughs.*)

WE: The jazz purist would ask why you're tampering with the gorgeous B3 sound.

BD: I hate purists. (*Laughs.*)

WE: But what's your response to those who would say you're denaturing the organ?

BD: They're stupid. Because still the organ sound is my sound, and the other thing is, it's like I have a horn player with the organ. It's just another element added, but I don't substitute the organ sound. I use it more when I play solo because it gives me more sound possibilities, and sometimes it shows the Hammond B3 sound in another context. But it's always the Hammond sound which is important. If I have a band like I have on *Take Off!*,[5] or on my new CD where I have many musical colors, then I don't need so much the synthesizer sound because I can create so many musical colors by the real instruments.

WE: Let me see if I can sum up your ambitions. You're attempting to enlarge the organ's vocabulary of sound, and to advance a holistic approach to the instrument by mastering the relationship between pedals and keyboard?

BD: And also bringing the organ into other contexts. I mean, I'm composing a lot of stuff which is in other beats—not 4/4. Or using other chords than organ players often use. You know, I just go my way, and it sounds very often different from what you are used to hearing from an organ, in harmonical ways or groove ways. I just want to explore the whole area, because organ basically has been used as a blues instrument, playing standards, playing rhythm and blues. As Larry Young did, going in another direction, I also want to explore other directions. Being maybe a bridge between the traditional and the modern. I think that's an important role for me.

WE: Do you compose with certain instrumentalists in mind?

BD: No, sometimes it's the other way. What I do is, I compose the tunes which just come out of me. Then I think about the instrumentation in terms of how would I best be able to arrange that tune and the intention that I want to reach with that tune. What instruments, what players? And that's only possible if you know that afterwards you can get almost whoever you want. Of course, it's not totally possible, but I'm with a very good record label, and I have a good budget to be able to afford many musicians. Of course, if it comes out I will only have a trio for the recording, then I have to rearrange the tunes and see how I can get them in a trio setting. That's what I do anyway for my live playing, because it's almost impossible to get such a band onstage like I have on my recording.

WE: Do you take breaks from touring to compose and arrange?

BD: Yeah, I have to. On this new CD I composed and arranged all the tunes, and I have about fifteen recordings made. That's a lot of originals for me to write, so that takes time. I mean, composing is not that long, but arranging for such a group takes quite a while.

WE: Typically speaking, how long does it take you to compose a tune?

BD: Totally different. I'll just show you an example, it's better for you to understand. I played the tunes which I wanted to do on my new CD for my husband. And he said, "Yeah, but you know, you don't have a tune like 'Give It Up' on the last CD. You know, such a groovy thing." I said, "Yeah, maybe you're right." And I sat down and I had a tune like that in two minutes. That was "Walk on Air," which is on my new CD. So these are tunes which really happen in a few minutes. Arranging lasts longer, because it's so complex. And then there are tunes like the title song on the *Hot Stuff* [6] or "Green Paradise" on *Take Off!* [7] which took me a little longer to compose.

WE: What's a little longer—five minutes? (*Laughter.*)

BD: It depends. It can be an hour or two hours. Or it can be a few days if you just feel that you are at the point where there's nothing new coming anymore. Then I say, "Okay, I'll look at it tomorrow again." You can't know beforehand how it goes. Very often ideas just come to me. I try to practice, and suddenly I can't practice because I have the idea for a new tune. I have to write that on a paper or record that so that I don't forget it.

WE: I'd like to change the topic and get your views on gender politics. Can you speak about professional obstacles you've had to overcome because you are a woman?

BD: Difficulties which appear from time to time is, for example, if a woman knows what she wants and she goes her way, then she's very easily called, it's a very bad expression, but you know, like a "bitch." But if a *man* is doing the same thing, everyone has respect and says, "Oh, he's a great guy. He's knowing what he wants." So that's the difference, which is *always* appearing. Also, it's very often you have the problem that the ego from the man is hurt if you tell a man what to do as a woman. Because it's still the old rule that the man should be the leading person and the woman should more or less do what the man wants. I say it a little bit more exaggerated, but that's in a way how it still is. I love to be a woman, and I'm not a militant feminist. I like it if a man helps me with my coat or opens the door for me, you know, in the ways of having good manners. I like to be protected by a man, for example, but I also want to be respected like a person on the same level; I want to be able to go my way and do my thing and develop what I want to do with the same chances a man has.

WE: Do you have to contend with gender politics as a bandleader?

BD: Yeah, I had that very often. It's becoming less the more famous you become and the more respect people have for you. But it still happens, and also not only in the band. It's also when you do negotiations with promoters or record companies. Women who go their way, who have no manager, who do everything by themselves and also try to do the negotiations and all that, they make many men afraid. Men think they're strange, suspicious, maybe; it makes them insecure. So, to reach the same thing like a man, sometimes it takes much more effort, more power. Because you can get problems a man would not have, just because you're a women.

WE: Like what?

BD: If you want to do a project and you tell it to another person who is important for the project, this person might not want to contribute to this project, or help you, just because you're a woman. If a man makes a suggestion, for example, another man would maybe think about it and say, "Oh, yeah, that's a good idea." But if a woman does that, sometimes he might just not be so open to think about it. I don't say that everyone is like that, but it happens from time to time. It's a question of personality. And to be able to work with a man on the same level, this man has to have a strong personality by himself. If he doesn't have that, then he might have problems with his ego.

WE: Are you asked to play in women's jazz festivals?

BD: Not often. I guess people know how I think about it, so they don't ask me so much anymore. (*Laughs.*)

WE: You're not interested in that type of format?

BD: Well, you know, I think it's kind of stupid if people come up to you as a woman and say, "We're doing a women's festival and we want you to play there, but you're only allowed to have women in your band." That doesn't help their purposes. They want to show that women are good musicians, but it doesn't make sense to choose your musicians just on the basis of sex. For me that's childish, and it doesn't say anything. That's why I never do that. It's more important to choose the musicians on how they play. So it makes sense to me if they say, okay, we just want to have women in our festival, but if they invite me I can bring my band with good musicians how I want. Because that's enough to show that, as a woman, I do a good thing if I have a great band, when I'm the leader with a lot of men doing what I want.

WE: Let's discuss entrepreneurial matters. How did you start your record label?

BD: Well, the very first record I did was with an organ company in Germany. They financed my first two records just to promote their organs, because I am the only one who was already quite famous in Germany and could represent this organ. I played my music; it's just that I played their organ. After that I was not so much interested in them anymore, because the Hammond is my organ, and Hammond, as a company, was never interested in giving me any support. That is because I play the old Hammond, and they wanted to advertise for the new Hammond. And I don't make compromises in that way. After that I wanted to do a CD with my quintet, but I didn't have a label that was interested. So I decided I'd produce it by myself. It was not a stupid way I did it because before I produced it, I had already sold some amounts of my CDs to two distributors. I had it already guaranteed, before I made it, that they would take a special amount of the finished product and sell it. I organized the recording session, I made contracts with the musicians, and I organized the recording people. And founded my own label. Yeah, I found out how that works, and I did my first CD. My former boyfriend—he's from the film business—he helped me with the cover. So I financed it totally myself. It was not very expensive because it was a live recording; I didn't have to pay for a studio. I did a lot of promotion for it. I sent the CD to all the stations and to the newspapers. It was a lot of work, I tell you. But it was quite successful. I got a prize for it; it's a prize from the German critics who write record reviews.[8] They decide every quarter of the year who is getting that prize.

WE: What was the name of the CD?

BD: *Bebab,* like my label. It was a mixture between my name, Barbara, and bebop. That was the period when I really played a lot of bebop. Then I did another one together with an airplane company. (*Chuckles.*) They financed my next CD. I was quite successful with all of that, so one day another label came up to me, Koala Records. It's a German label; they produced most of Peter Herbolzheimer's recordings. Peter Herbolzheimer is very famous in

Germany with his big band. He asked me if I would be interested to do a big band recording with him, and of course I was happy to do that. That was also successful; it received that prize, too. I also received it for *Take Off!* so I have had it three times up to now.

WE: Did those earlier successes set the stage for your contract with Enja?

BD: I mean, I was in touch with Enja before, but they were not so much interested. But suddenly one day Matthias[9] called me and said, "Yeah, I think the time is right now. I want to ask you if you would be interested to come to my label and record with the American musicians." I said, "Yes, of course." That's when the CD *Straight Ahead*[10] was produced.

WE: More recently you made the jump to Verve. Was that calculated to get you wider visibility and distribution?

BD: Yeah. I was very satisfied working with Matthias Winckelmann of Enja Records. I think we have done three nice CDs, and I had a very good communication with him because he understands very much about jazz music. And he has a good nose for putting the right musicians together, or finding new musicians. He loves the music very much. It's a very important label, but they don't have many people, and they don't have distribution in all the countries. He doesn't have the time and, I guess, also not the budget to make a real big promotion tour. And that's something what Verve has. When I talked with Matthias about going to Verve, I also talked with him about another CD. I told him that I really would like to, but on the other hand, it's very tempting to get a very big budget to be able to work with all of these musicians and to get more promotion than I could with him. It was a hard decision for me to make because I really liked the way we worked together, and I like him personally. So I didn't really want to say, "Okay, now I go." But on the other hand, I think the promotion they did for my new CDs also helped him sell the old ones.

WE: On the face of it, though, it would appear that smaller, independent labels give jazz musicians more freedom to record what they want.

BD: Basically, that's right. I found out that the American record companies take much more influence on the musicians than, for example, German labels do. So basically what you say is right, but it depends on the personality you are. I had long negotiations with Verve about a contract, and I made the point about my freedom very clear. I was even so far that I said no. (*Laughs.*) I said no, I don't make it. So it was really long until we found a way of making a contract which gives me the possibility to really develop my music.

WE: How important are good reviews in jazz magazines for you or your recording company?

BD: Oh, I think it's success to get that. I feel very honored if they give me such a good rating, you know, in *Down Beat.* But, I mean, even if I would be number one, I would not think that I'm the best musician. Gosh, I never will be, and nobody will be because it's always a question of taste. I mean, everyone has something special which only this person can give. So I think the expression "the best musician" is nonsense. There is no best musician in the world.

Let me just point out another thing about the critics. In the *Down Beat* there is one part where a few critics write about the same CD, and it's interesting to see sometime how different their rating is. That's one thing which is almost unfair for a musician. Because if your CD is criticized by someone who just doesn't like the style or the kind of music you play, you get a much worse rating than another person who liked the music and would write about it. I think a lot of readers just read that and they think, "Oh, it's written there, he must know about it." And they are not conscious of it's also very much a question of taste of that person. So it's sometimes hard, you know, to be criticized. It's always a subjective thing.

Selected Discography

Straight Ahead. Enja R2 79608 (1988).
Hot Stuff. Enja R2 79654 (1990). (Includes catchy renditions of "Killer Joe" and "Seven Steps to Heaven.")
**Take Off!* Verve 314 527 664-2 (1995).
Outhipped. Verve 314547503-2 (2000).

Notes

1. *Junkanoo,* Verve; 1997.
2. Rhoda Scott is a French organist.
3. Steve Futterman, "Jazzing It Up," *Harper's Bazaar,* May 1993, p. 55.
4. Modular Interface Digital Interconnect.
5. 1996; Verve.
6. 1990; Enja.
7. 1995; Verve.
8. *Preis der Deutschen Schallplattenkritik.*
9. Matthias Winckelmann, owner of Enja Records.
10. 1988; Enja.

Dottie Dodgion

Dottie Dodgion

The sight of an attractive female behind the drums locking in with bass legends such as Eugene Wright, Ron Carter, Bob Cranshaw, and Milt Hinton turned many a head in the 1960s. With a career spanning six decades, jazz drummer Dottie Dodgion has lived a life populated by dozens of well-known jazz musicians, and she has a story about every one of them. Although living in the musical shadows of these luminaries, she has relished her supporting role as the drummer who makes it comfortable for others to swing.

Born in Brea, California, in 1929, Dorothy Giaimo, a Sicilian, grew up in the world of show business. Her father was a professional drummer, so when little Dottie showed a similar interest, he bought a drum set for her. As a youth, she also had a passion for dancing, but after she was stricken with polio at age fifteen, the decision to pursue music was inevitable.

In the late 1940s, Dodgion began her music career in the San Francisco area with a young Charles Mingus. She married bassist Monty Budwig in 1950, and two years later they had a daughter, Deborah. After divorcing Budwig, she married alto saxophonist Jerry Dodgion. Undeterred by the demands of family life, she pursued her career in jazz and by the mid-'50s emerged as a solid drummer. The Dodgions moved to New York in 1961, where she joined the Benny Goodman Band and was also a regular with the Marian McPartland Trio.

Highlights of Dodgion's mid-career include performing and recording with Ruby Braff in the early '70s, television appearances on the *Today Show* and the *Dick Cavett Show*, touring with Tony Bennett, and, in 1978, serving as house drummer for the very first Women's Jazz Festival, held in Kansas City. From 1976 to 1978, she was musical director for the Rogue and Jar, a popular jazz club in Washington, D.C., booking and playing with such notable jazz figures as Thad Jones, Tommy Flanagan, and the Brecker Brothers.

Approaching the drum set with a traditional handgrip, Dodgion lays down an ageless swing that is peppered with savory accents and subtle colors which are encouraging to the soloist. Her solos, though infrequent, are often compact gems that demonstrate her relaxed touch and her ingenuity (e.g., seamlessly layering 6/8 figures with 4/4). In talking about how she swings, Dodgion has long claimed that it's all in the wrist and where you place the beat. Her attitude toward the challenge of performing in a world dominated by men is simply that the drums are not male *or* female. When asked about Buddy Rich, her tongue-in-cheek reply was, "He plays good for a man."[1]

The native Californian returned to her home state in 1984, and embarked on a new and unusual dual career as drummer/vocalist. Her first album as a leader,[2] released late in her life, features Dodgion not as a fixture behind the drum kit but out front as a jazz singer. The manner in which she phrases is accentuated by her knowing interpretation of a lyric and its melodic essence. Subsequent recordings find her back at the drum set; these recent dates[3] showcase a rare combination of voice and percussion as Dottie Dodgion sings, scats, and swings her way through standards with impeccable taste and timing, a reflection of her affinity for the drums.

Recorded July 30, 1997

WE: Dottie, how has your career been proceeding in recent years?

DD: (*Laughs.*) I've gone a long time without having the pros that I was used to playing with. I was so privileged. I didn't know how difficult it was to play until I played with people who didn't know how to play. After I'd turned fifty, I thought, "Oh my God, nobody will hire an old drummer; I've had it." And then things started happening again. I got a call from someone who decided that I was worthy and I was still valid, and so that got me all excited. Then there's a long period where nothing happens again. I mean, that's the jazz musician's life. But the older you get, the *longer* the periods are, it seems, in between. And there is no gimmick for selling an old lady. If you're a young woman and you have a decent figure, they can sell you like mad.

I just started singing again after years and years. You must understand that when I was playing drums, when I was first married to Monty Budwig, I was singing. He loved my singing, but the guys knew my dad had been a drummer, so they wanted me to play a little brushes on a magazine. When the drummer would be late, I'd want to oblige. Monty was, oh! he was just furious; he was very ashamed about a woman drummer. He didn't care for that at all. So later on I met Jerry Dodgion, and the drummer that was with the band that Jerry and I was with, he liked to sing, and Jerry hated his drums. Jerry loved my drumming. He didn't want me to sing; he wanted me to play drums. So my famous saying is I divorced both of them, and now I do what I want to do. (*Laughter.*)

WE: Why didn't Jerry Dodgion want you to sing?

DD: All musicians hate girl singers. That's been a joke with Bill Berry and I. I said, "I want to be loved so I took up drums." (*Laughs.*) Well, I can understand, because most of the time the girl singer couldn't sing. She had a nice body, she looked cute, and she was going with the bandleader or somebody else in the band. That's the reason she was on the stand. Not because she was a good singer. So girl singers got a *bad* name. That's why Jerry didn't want me to be known as a "girl singer"; he was afraid they wouldn't take me serious. (*Laughs.*) He used to say, "They'll either call you a drummer who sings a little or a singer who plays a little drums." And I'm sure he was right, you know, 'cause I had to fight my way up the hard way. I'd sit in the corner, my hair cut short, and wear black so they wouldn't know I was really a girl. (*Laughs.*)

WE: The description you gave of your appearance, wearing black and with a very manageable hairstyle, almost sounds like the "feminist uniform" many women wear today. Did you think of yourself as a pioneer?

DD: I was a pioneer, definitely, as far as women playing drums. But not the way I cut my hair or anything. That was my own personal way of staying out of the spotlight, because, you see, if you were glamorous, or if you were up there being cutesy, you were not a jazz person. If you *smiled,* you weren't jazz. It took me a long time to really relax a smile (*laughs*) while I was playing. Too afraid that I'd be "show biz," I'd be "on," and I would be misinterpreted.

WE: Do you consider yourself an early feminist?

DD: That word had *never* entered my mind until the feminists started coming after me. I really wasn't very good material for them, because I was in love with my husband. (*Laughs.*) He helped me with dishes. I mean, you know, they wanted a *juicy* story about how Jerry was holding me back, but he wasn't holding me back. He was encouraging me. So they let me go real quick when that came out. Because a couple of them said, "Ahh, we don't want to hear about *this.* We don't want to hear about a happy girl." (*Laughs.*)

WE: If things worked out ideally from this point forward, what would you like to see happen with your career?

DD: I'd like to play up and down the coast. You know, Santa Barbara, maybe LA. I'm really not too fond of Los Angeles. It's "Death Valley" to me. I've been there twice and I tried to kill myself both times. I got very suicidal in Los Angeles. I think it's the weather; it eats up your brain. Nothing seems very sincere there—it's movieland all the time with everybody. There are very few contractors. Mel Lewis one time said he moved to New York because he got tired of having to cater to three contractors. Imagine, three contractors! They manage the whole thing in Hollywood. In New York it's three thousand contractors!

WE: In this ideal scenario would you continue playing drums?

DD: No. That's another era of my life. I'd love to just get in the melodic end and let all of that out.

JS: When you perform as a vocalist, do you tell stories to the audience between numbers?

DD: Yes, sometimes. I've got some pretty funny things that've happened to me. (*Laughs.*) Especially being a woman drummer.

WE: Regale us with one.

DD: I love this one. Jerry and I were in Perugia. He was with the Thad Jones/Mel Lewis Band, and I had gone along because we were going to play in Munich together with our own quartet. Perugia was the last stop for the band, and then we were gonna drive to Munich for our gig. Anyway, we're in a brand new hotel in Perugia and Victorio DeSica's son comes up and says (*Dottie mimics a male Italian voice*), "Jerry, Jerry, how are you?" Jerry says, "I want you to meet my wife." And DeSica's son says, "Jerry, I want you to meet this drummer." Jerry says, "Oh, my wife is a drummer." And the son looked at me and said, "No, this guy's a real drummer." (*Dottie laughs uproariously.*) Jerry and I just howled. You see, I can't get indignant about people's ignorance; that's where I was a pioneer—a woman just didn't play drums. It threatened the guys' balls because they felt the band drummer was the backbone, and he had to be (*chuckles*)—he had to be a *he.*

I understood where the guys were comin' from, too. So many women were not serious about playing, it was just a gimmick. And believe me, the promoters would jump on that like crazy. Promoters or club owners always want an all-woman band. Virginia Mayhew, a wonderful saxophone player, was out here a few months ago. I had Dena DaRose, a lady piano player, and I said, "I'd like to bring in my group." The club owner says, "Who's on bass?" I said, "Well, I have to get a male bass player." And he said, "Oh, no, no." And I said, "Oh, for Christ's sake, what do you mean, no, no, no." He said, "Well, there's no hook." I said, "Forget it." Never mind you're a musician. You happen to be female, you gotta have the "hook": all women—TA-DA! Freako, freako, you know. I've gotten very discouraged and disgusted about that kind of stuff, to tell you the truth.

WE: I want to return to your comment about the protocol of being a jazz musician. You said that smiling wasn't condoned, but was there also a stigma attached to a jazz musician singing?

DD: You see, in New York, if you *sang,* they'd say that was very commercial. If a jazz player sang, naughty, naughty. That didn't happen. Grady Tate got by with it later, but not when I was comin' up.

WE: How about Louis, or Teagarden?

DD: I'm talking about the hard-core men. You didn't see Miles Davis singing, you didn't see John Coltrane singing.

WE: So that kind of conduct—what it meant to be a "pro"—filtered down from the most visible players to affect jazz musicians across the board?

DD: Yes, that's right; and it was hard—I mean, talk about the yardstick. In a way, it was great training for later on, because you had to be such a perfectionist, and I am to a certain extent anyway. It's like if you survive New York you can survive anywhere, you know, and I did. Ruby Braff is not an easy person. He would *never* hire you just because you were a girl. God! Somebody said that one time. I played the Concord Jazz Festival with Ruby, Milt Hinton, and Hank Jones. We'd been playin' all over for about two years. Philip Elwood of the *San Francisco Chronicle* said, "Well, it's obvious to see why Dottie's there, it's for visual effects." Well, Ruby was *furious!* He called him up and he says, "How dare you say that I would hire somebody for any other reason than music!!" Ruby gave it to him good. (*Laughs.*)

JS: Let's make a U-turn and change the subject to your formative beginnings. At what age did you start singing?

DD: When I was about five years old. My dad was a drummer. He played with, gee, I think Bing Crosby a long time ago, when Crosby was married to Dixie. They were on the road, and I remember being sat on the piano and I'd sing "Three Little Fishes" or something. And then later on, when I was about ten, they hired me to sing with Vincent Lopez at the Coconut Grove in LA. I'd do the dinner show. I was, you know, a child prodigy.

JS: How long did you work for Lopez?

DD: One year, and that was that. I grew up in one year so fast that I lost that job. (*Laughs.*) They said I didn't look like a kid anymore. I vaguely remember that era. I felt like I was being pushed around pretty much, manipulated at that time. I kinda blocked that out. It wasn't a very happy time in my life. I don't know how long I lasted, but I know it didn't work. I felt rejected about that, too, because I didn't understand about the media. I just thought I wasn't doing a good job. Probably 'cause I wasn't good enough. So that was another thing that set me back.

JS: Did you want to be a singer?

DD: I wanted to be a dancer. I wanted to be a dancer so badly and my dad said, "Nah, gypsies never make any money, they're always broke." Dancers were gypsies. He said, "You be a singer." I said, "Okay, I'll be a singer." I didn't know that I actually could make a choice, or that I didn't have a choice. I thought when Daddy said I have to be a singer, I'll be a singer. I didn't know if I *could* sing or not. Anyway, I said okay. Daddy had a good jazz band in San Francisco then; Pete Rugolo was doing arrangements for him. My father played the strip joints in San Francisco.

JS: How did you learn to sing?

DD: I lived in Berkeley, El Cerrito, or Albany, all across the bay from San Francisco. My dad was living in a hotel next door to the Union. When I would spend weekends with him, you know, after he'd finish the strip places, he would take me downstairs, sneak me in the back, and the girls would make me up, put powder all over me. And here they'd be nude and everything, and my dad used to say, "Don't ever be a snob. Those women have children, and they have to do this business to make a living for their kids. But it doesn't make them bad people." I'll never forget that. That was the greatest lesson he could have ever given me.

So anyway, when we'd finish we'd go to Original Joe's and we'd have something to eat, you know, like at two o'clock in the morning. Then we'd go back to the hotel, and there's the two beds. We'd sit in between them, and Daddy would play me Duke Ellington, Count Basie, Billie Holiday, and we wouldn't talk. He'd say, "Listen to this, honey." He never played me anything bad. They were all these great people. They had so much soul, it used to just reach right down deep inside of me. My dad gave me a marvelous start on music. He was *so* serious about it. I'm nine years old, you know, and he's telling me the facts of life. (*Laughs.*) "When you're a girl singer on the bandstand, you got three strikes against you." He says, "Everybody in that band is gonna try to get to you. You keep your business *off* the bandstand, your boyfriends *off* the bandstand." I'm saying, "Right, Daddy." I'm nine years old. (*Laughter.*) But I remembered it later on, I'll tell you, whenever the guys made their move. The leaders were protecting me, too. When I was about sixteen, I was singing with Nick Esposito's group. We were doing phonetics before the Jackie Cain–Roy Kral thing. I didn't hardly sing any lyrics. Nick had to take out guardianship papers on me to take me across state lines. At night, after the job, he'd truck me up the street and almost lock me in. (*Laughs.*) He'd tell the guys, "jail bait"—forget this.

WE: What were the second and third strikes?

DD: Oh, well, the three strikes were that, one, you're a girl singer; two, that every guy's gonna try and get to you; and three, once they do you'll be out of a job, because then you'll cause friction on the stand. Then everybody hates you, nobody loves you. It's true. Boy, I've seen it happen too many times. That was the smartest thing he told me.

JS: Was your father a full-time musician?

DD: Oh, yes. He wouldn't do anything else. He used to give me twenty dollars and say, "Don't get a day gig." He said, "If you get a day gig, you'll get caught in that money trap and you'll never become a full-time musician."

JS: He wanted you to follow in his footsteps?

DD: Oh, yeah. And I loved it. I *wanted* to do it.

WE: Was your mother supportive?

DD: Oh, yes. Mom was.

WE: Was she a dancer?

DD: She danced with DeMarcos,[4] I think, in her early years. They were ballroom dancers. She never got her dream, so she was very supportive of me getting mine.

JS: When did you get back to singing professionally?

DD: When I was in my teens, I was singing with Daddy's band or with different groups. I worked with Merle Howard's band up at Russian River in the summertime. That was the first time, when I was fifteen, that I really sang with a big band. Now, I went to Catholic school when I was young, and my mother used to tell me, "You can go on the road when you graduate." So I hit the books, skipped grades, and graduated when I was fifteen, almost sixteen years old. I wanted to do that so badly; I got straight As. But right in the same year as graduation, see, here I am all set to go, and I come down with polio. I got it at a lake. Oh, boy, I wanted that job so bad. I got about sixteen spinals because they couldn't figure out if I had it or I didn't. It was proof positive and negative, positive and negative. So my grandparents flew up some serum. It was about one thousand dollars a shot. I must of had six or seven of 'em, and it worked.

WE: Was this during the early development of the polio vaccine?

DD: I think this was when it was first coming out. This was not Dr. Salk, of course.

WE: Was the serum treatment a risky thing to be doing?

DD: Yeah, it was. But they had tried it on my aunt. I had an aunt who had polio. She was stricken with it when she was two years old. Of course, she was already stricken with it so much that it didn't work, but they were having really great results on it. I'm in the textbooks on this one (*laughs*), because I proved positive-negative so many times.

WE: Did your illness sour the summer gig?

DD: No. What happened is, I had this job and the doctor said, "Well, she's all right, but we can't get her to walk. It's mental because everything has worked." I said, "I wanna go on the road!" So the doctor told my mother, "It would be the best thing in the world if you could find some way to do it." So Mom let me go on the job. Lou Gillioni, this male singer on the band, he carried me from the cabin down to the bandstand. I'd pull myself up to the mike, I'd sing my little heart out and sit down again. I was doing "Exactly Like You" and "It Had to Be You." The band was a swing band—Howard Fredericks, he was the swing band around this area for a long time. I stayed with him for about a year and a half, I guess.

JS: Did you have any formal instruction in singing?

DD: No. I went to one vocal coach in my life when I was seventeen, and he taught me something very valuable. He taught me to speak when I'm singing, just like I'm talking. And don't worry about the diaphragm. He said when you talk you breathe right, so when you're singing, talk. And it helped me *tell* the story. Here's how I sing (*sings "don't blame me" with short notes for each word*), instead of (*sings the same words again, holding the notes longer*). I didn't have the chops for that, you know. So I would shorten things and say the story. That kind of helped me develop my style—isn't that funny, something like that—'cause I had to get around not having any chops.

WE: Anita O'Day uses a clipped style of phrasing.

DD: Right. That's why I liked her, too.

WE: Did the vocal coach help you before you heard Anita?

DD: No. I had been listening to Anita. But, see, I didn't have any one favorite. Except Billie. She'd say "is," and it meant something. (*Laughs.*) I loved Ella Fitzgerald, of course, for her bebopping, but I never even thought about bebopping. I did phonetics. Like with Charlie Mingus. I went to work with Charlie Mingus when I was eighteen. Just singing and doing phonetics, you know. But I never scatted. Scatting means freely off the top of your head. But what I did was rehearsed. I rehearsed five hours a day with Charlie Mingus, and I loved every minute of it. I never learned so much as I did with him. He was here on the West Coast trying to get into the symphony, and they weren't hiring black musicians at that time. We were rehearsing 'cause we had this job over in Oakland, and he wanted it to be perfect, of course, because he was a perfectionist.

WE: When was this?

DD: 1947. He had this band, and he didn't like the drummer. On New Year's Eve he took and threw him off the bandstand. (*Laughs.*) He kept warning him. "If you don't concentrate, quit lookin' at the bitches, I'm gonna throw you off the stand." God, I thought he'd killed the guy, 'cause he was behind the bar and there were some steps, you know. But he loved me because I have good ears.

WE: How did you first meet Mingus?

DD: Oh, a session. You know, somebody said, "Come up and sing" and I sang something. His time and my time agreed. That's why he thought about hiring me to do that other voice. You know, Chazz was always inventing, and I was one of his inventions. He would bow, and I would sing with the bowing. That just knocked me out to be able to do that. But, see, because I didn't read, I had to remember. I had to memorize all that stuff, so that's why the five hours. But, you know, those five hours—by the time the rest of the guys had it, I had it down.

WE: How long did the job in Oakland last?

DD: Oh, I guess we were there for about pretty close to six months.

WE: Did you have an option to continue working with him?

DD: No, because Chazz left. He got very discouraged. He was determined he was going to get into that symphony, that he was good enough. And he could've. But they didn't do it, and it was racial. It definitely was racial. It was like he was hiding out or just biding his time with us, and while he was doin' it he was gonna take these kids and do somethin' with them. But we weren't any great part of his life later on. The cute part was that *years and years later,* Charlie comes into the Half Note, where I'm playing with Zoot [Sims]. Chazz, he's starin' at me. I could see him staring at me. He never knew I played drums; he never knew anything about that. (*Laughs.*) He comes over and he says, "Is that you?" (*Laughter.*) I says, "Yeah." And he says, "Zoot, I wanna play, I wanna play, I wanna play." Zoot says, "Sure, of course." So we played a number together, and he said, "Damn, Dottie, damn." (*Laughter.*)

JS: You got to meet Billie Holiday, your favorite vocalist, in the 1950s. What was she like?

DD: She didn't have much to say to anybody. She'd come out, get in the crooks of the piano, and sing her little heart out. She wouldn't talk to the audience, she wouldn't tell them one tune or nothing, she'd just open her mouth. I wish to hell I could do that. I would *love* that, just go out there, do your thing, and get off.

JS: That would be a loss, since I'm sure audiences love your engaging personality.

DD: It takes away from it. It's almost like they're expecting something from you, and what I really wanna do is just sing my songs. But Billie got away with it. There's this one story about Billie—Jerry was working with her. It was intermission, and she had these two little Chihuahuas, you know, and the lady, Helen, who ran this club, she was always bitching about the musicians. If there wasn't any business, it was the musicians' fault. I don't know how many times we heard that. So one night she's bitching and bitching, and Billie has her two little Chihuahuas up on the bar, you know, and she's really been drinking quite a bit. She looks at Helen and she goes, "Sic her!" (*Laughter.*) And the little dogs go "yip, yip, yip, yip, yip." And Helen pulls back in horror. (*Laughs.*)

JS: Getting back to the drums, did your father school you in basic techniques?

DD: No. Isn't that something? I used to go to all his jobs and I'd watch him, but I never really thought about playing drums. I was so used to sitting and listening and keeping my mouth shut, because if you wanted to succeed as a woman in this business, that's *exactly* what you did. You observed, you listened, you didn't say dumb-ass silly things that women usually say, trying to get attention. You did not do any of those things if you were a really serious musician. So I learned how to listen, and I didn't even know that it was happening to me. My father was a very good drummer. His time was excellent. When I told you he had worked the strip joints, he had the best jazz musicians in the world. They were playing behind Lenny Bruce, you know, comics who were just beginning out. So the fact that I was listening to that all the time—it was going in my ears—I think that that's why, when somebody asked me to play some brushes on a magazine the first time I ever did it, that I think it came so natural to me.

JS: This seems like the perfect time for your Omaha, Nebraska, story.[5]

DD: That's how I learned to play drums. In Omaha I was with this stuttering comedian who was also a singer. I left LA with this guy. I was a straight woman, and then I'd sing a couple of tunes. There was a couple of other local guys in the band. But this comedian took everybody's bread and went across the state line. Blew it on gambling, and then he split. We were owed two weeks back salary and hotel, too. So I was stranded at the hotel. The Mary Kay Trio was working the sister club to this club where we were in Omaha, and we became really good friends. Gee, I was only seventeen then. Anyway, they [the trio] bailed me out of the hotel, and they took me to Springfield, Illinois, with them because that was their next job. They said, "We can't send you home." You know, it took all their money to get me out of the hotel, and then they were broke, too. So they said, "You go to Springfield with us and we'll figure out something." So I get to Springfield, and they got the owner, Matt, of the Orchid Club in Springfield, Illinois, to hire me to play with them. Trying to get me enough money to get home. So, Frank[6] said, "You can play standup drums." I said, "No, I've never played drums." He said, "Sure you can, easy." He gets this standup tall tom-tom. It didn't have a pedal on the bottom, it just was one drum. Frank said, "It's easy. Take the brushes and say apple pie, apple pie, apple pie, apple pie, apple pie, apple pie." To this day when women come up to me and say, "I want to learn how to play," I say, "Get yourself a pair of brushes and learn apple pie, apple pie, apple pie."[7] That was the beginning of me playing drums.

WE: Let me get this straight. Before your father bought you a set of drums, before you'd even picked up a pair of drumsticks, you stood up and did this apple pie routine?

DD: Yeah. See, that's the dancer in me that probably came out, you know, the coordination stuff; I was very good in basketball, too. (*Laughs.*) I was just singing and doing it and didn't think anything about it. Then my appendix burst in Springfield, Illinois.

WE: During the period when you were performing with the Mary Kay Trio?

DD: Right. I'll never forget it; I'll always be indebted to them. It was terrible. They took me to this Catholic hospital, where they wanted to remove my ovaries. They said that gangrene had set in. So they called my mother three thousand miles away and asked her permission. My mother said no. My mother had been a nurse's aide, and she used to read a lot of medical books. She had the doctor tell her everything and she said, "No, I won't give you my permission. I don't believe it's necessary." So they didn't, and I lived anyway. I had a scar you can't believe, a fourteen-inch scar. When I was in the hospital, Frank would come in with pencils in his hat (*laughs*) and bells on his shoes, you know. I said, "Don't make me laugh, Frank." I'm holding my stomach, you know. Tryin' to cheer me up, and I've got a fourteen-inch scar. (*Laughter.*) So, anyway, that's why I didn't go right back home. I had to work my way back. I had to take care of myself since I was young, but when I was seventeen and out on the road, I really had to do it. So now I get back to Los Angeles, 'cause that's where I had been living, and I get adhesions. I pass out on Hollywood and Vine.

WE: What are adhesions?

DD: When they open you up, it's the tissues, and with me they closed over the bowel, so it just took all the air out of me. I was knocked out, and I woke up in the hospital again. I had died that time. I actually died. They brought me back. They told me I was dead for so many seconds. My mother had to come and get me then, you know. She drove down, and they took me back 'cause I survived that. I went back to singing when I got well. I just kind of forgot about the drums until later on when I married Monty Budwig. I started doing it, I'm tellin' you, 'cause the drummer was always late. And I remembered that I could play apple pie on a magazine, and that's all the guys wanted. They didn't want a soloist. You know, musicians hate soloist drummers. They want rhythm.

WE: How do you personally feel about soloing?

DD: I'm not really a soloist. I play the melody. I'm not a paradiddle Joe—Josephine. (*Laughs.*) Actually, I used to say I'm not a real drummer, I don't like solos. (*Laughs.*) It doesn't excite me to play a lot of stick with my fingers. It's the swing, the division, the flow that excites me.

JS: When did you marry Monty Budwig?

DD: 1950. My daughter was born in 1952, and we split in 1953. It was a lot of pressure.

JS: Did you continue your singing career when you were married to Monty?

DD: Oh, yes. In fact, I was holding down three jobs. I was working as a film cutter for Columbia in San Francisco; I was working as a legal secretary in the afternoon for a few hours, and singing with a terrible girls' group in San Raphael three nights a week. Tryin' to make it. I had to get baby sitters and I'd come home and they didn't take care of her.

JS: It sounds as if you were overworked and unhappy.

DD: Really, really. So Monty was unhappy too. It just didn't work, and that was that. I went to work right after that with this little trio out in San Raphael, and that's where I met Jerry Dodgion. He was the alto player on it, and he lied to me. I was twenty-three and he said he was, too, and he was twenty-one. (*Laughs.*) But, anyway, that went on for about a year and a half, just us working together. Nothing serious, it just kind of grew and we became friends. We were married twenty-seven years, and I think that's why. We really became friends before we got married, and trusted each other and no lies and all of that stuff. You know, musicians' wives and everything—they can't tell their wife this, they can't tell their wife that. So they live vicariously or, you know, cheat on their old ladies and stuff. It was a great lesson, and I wasn't about to get married again *ever*, but Jerry's mama was dying of breast cancer, and she said, "I'll give you a Volkswagen and five hundred dollars." So, he says, "What's a piece of paper!" (*Laughter.*)

JS: After your marriage to Jerry, when did your drumming apprenticeship begin?

DD: Like I said, we were working with a band with a drummer who used to like to sing. And so I would play drums while he sang, and Jerry got to like my drums so much that he would encourage this guy to sing all the time. And then shortly after Jerry and I were married, Eugene Wright[8] came into my life. You see, Jerry was playing with Billie Holiday at a place in San Francisco, and Buddy DeFranco came in right after. Buddy DeFranco had Kenny Drew and Art Blakey and Eugene Wright. And, I mean, when he brought me in to hear that group, my mouth dropped open. I heard those tempos, boy, fourteen choruses like nothing, just flying by, *swinging.* I'd never heard a small-group rhythm section play in person like that. That group just thrilled me to death. Eugene saw that I was interested, so every time he came to town we'd invite him to the house. He and I would play and he'd say, "Come on, Dot, yeah, Dot, yeah! Whoa, cookin! Wow!" Just encourage me, you know. He taught me the most wonderful things, the little nuances of jazz in a rhythm section. If a piano player plays on top, a little tight, we'd be playing and he'd say, "Okay, Dot, let's widen out on him." He meant the stroke, my stroke, my division on the cymbal and his stroke on the bass. He'd widen out a little bit because the piano player's already playing tight. You don't want to play tight with him because then there's no spacing and there's no swinging. So to swing you widen out. We'd played with a piano player who used to lay back on the tempo. Then Eugene would say, "Okay, Dot, let's tip on him" (*demonstrates a more crisp, on-the-beat attack*), in order to make it work, you see. This was invaluable information for me. One time when Joe Morello got sick, Dave [Brubeck] said, "What drummer do you want?" Joe said, "Dottie Dodgion." And Dave said, "What!" (*Laughs.*) So I played about eight days with them.

WE: Brubeck has such a percussive style. Does it leave much room for a drummer?

DD: Oh, it's all right with me. The drummer's supposed to play a supportive, underneath tempo that makes them wanna just go to heaven. That's how Eugene is; he said, "We're just goin' to swing him out of this world." He said, "You know, it's so wonderful to be swingin' a horn player when they don't even know it." That's where you listen to the music and you don't let your ego come in; you just are part of whoever kicks off the tempo. If you don't like that tempo, too bad, that's where it was kicked off. There's many tunes that don't lay right at certain tempos that you kick off, you know. But you gotta make that tempo swing, 'cause that's where the overall sound is.

WE: With reference to swinging a band, let's listen to some Chick Webb.
["Congo," Chick Webb and His Orchestra, from *Chick Webb, King of the Savoy, Volume Two,* recorded 1937; Decca Records.]

DD: (*During Webb's solo*) See, even though Chick was the leader, he was a supportive player. I hear him soloing in the background all by himself. He's driving the band. Man, he's using a loose drum, too. (*Chuckles.*) (*During Webb's solo*) See, Buddy Rich listened to him. (*At the conclusion*) That was a wonderful solo. But notice how he was driving the band all the other times. He wasn't doing any of that lickety-split stuff while the soloists were playing. That's what I mean, a really supportive player.

JS: Can you describe in laymen's terms how you make the music swing?

DD: Swing? It's pretty hard to say, it's so intangible, you know. It really is.

JS: Is it harder on two and four?

DD: No. That has nothing to do with it. It's where your division[9] is. Like the "apple pie." All right, it's dah-dah-dah, apple pie. Or as some drummers will play, bah-dah-dah, bah-bah-dah, bop-BA-dup, bop-BA-dup. You know, their division, wherever they place those three notes.

WE: Is it also a matter of accent?

DD: Yeah, in a way it is the accent, I guess. But no, actually, it's the stroke. With me, it's even.

WE: An equal emphasis?

DD: Yes. Now the more modern drummers would go (*scats with an emphasis on ONE-two-three*). One would be it. Or one and three. That's their division. Whatever the right hand does, or if they're left-handed, you know, that's their division. This is where you find some rhythm sections work and some don't. They don't divide in the same place. Of course, you hardly ever find anybody where you're really that compatible. So it's up to the drummer and the bass player to adjust, and that's what Eugene taught me: adjusting. That guy plays a little bit more back, so you've gotta adjust your division so that you're not in the way and you're not taking over. That's what's so intangible. You hear and feel it more than anything.

WE: Can a steadily working band still have those division problems?

DD: Oh, yes. And the funny part of it is, instead of the bandleader asking the bass player or the drummer who they want, *bandleaders* hire who they want, and then they put them together. Maybe it's the trumpet player who hires the band, and he likes the way that drummer swings. So he'll hire him. But he won't ask that drummer what bass player he wants, and that's what they should do. He might hire a bass player just because he has a good name and has worked with a lot of other stars, but that doesn't mean that those two are going to get along, or that their division is that close.

JS: In 1961, your husband, Jerry, got a job in Benny Goodman's band. Tell us how that developed into an opportunity for you.

DD: Jerry was with five different bands that Benny Goodman had. (*Laughs.*) You know, Benny was always gettin' a band together for one thing or another. One time he had this band, I think it was at the Sahara. Jack Sheldon was on it, Flip Phillips, and we were jammin' afterwards; I was playing drums. Benny walks in and he says, "Hey, can I play?" The guys said, "Sure, Benny." So he took a couple of choruses, and we just had a ball, man. And so our first day in New York, the band had a rehearsal at Basin Street East. I went out, bought myself a beautiful coat, and came back after rehearsal. I always carried my playing shoes, my flats, in my purse. I came in, and Benny looks at me and he says, "Dottie, do you have your shoes?" I said, "Sure." And he goes, "Come on up here." So I thought, "Great, man, I'm gonna jam; rehearsal's all over with." So I go up there and there's a band book, and he takes that book and he closes it. He knew I couldn't read. But what he didn't know is that since I was a little girl, my daddy had been playing Benny Goodman tunes for me. And Benny hadn't changed a chart. He was still wearing buttons on his fly, for cryin' out loud. (*Laughter.*) He thought I was a *genius* 'cause I knew all the breaks, and he said, "You're hired." And I went to work that night. Now, he tried about fourteen drummers that day, and he didn't like any of 'em. I got the gig, and it was because that time that we jammed and we divided right. So Zoot takes me around the corner to one of those Irish bars—boy, I was throwing scotches, and I'm not feelin' a thing.

JS: Because you were nervous?

DD: Oh! Nervous was not the word. So Benny says to Jay, the manager, "Okay, go and get her a blazer and skirt." I said, "Benny, I can't wear a skirt." He said, "No, no, no." So he got me a skirt. Well, that night I had the photographer take a picture of me, and I'm sitting on the chair so you could see my thigh. I showed it to Benny. He said, "Okay, culottes." (*Laughter.*)

JS: How long did that gig last?

DD: Ten days. That was a hard gig for me. Naturally, I'm pretty excited, but at the same time, we had Jimmy Rushing, we had a girl singer, and then we had a ten-piece band playing bright tempos. Now he's going to do the sextet thing. Well, boy, my hands are gettin' like mops, you know. And then the last song is "Sing, Sing, Sing." Well, Jesus, you know, I'm not a soloist, either. But I got through it, and, boy, everybody was happy. Everything was going along fine until one night he didn't introduce me. Now, Benny was very forgetful; he'd forget to introduce guys all the time. Well, he forgot to introduce me that night, and I'm the only woman on the band. So the people in the audience said, "The drummer, the drummer." He said, "Huh? Oh, yeah—Dottie Dodgion." Well, they brought the house down. When I walked off the stand, Jay said, "Bye." I got my notice the next night.

WE: An example of Benny's ego?

DD: Yes. The King was the King, man. I got the heat. He didn't know I was a girl before that. (*Laughs.*) He only knew that I answered his ad. Yeah, that was a drag. But that's all right. He went on to do a date with Morton Gould, and I could never have read those charts anyway. (*Laughs.*)

WE: Did you experience Goodman's infamous "ray"?

DD: Oh! Oh! He used to have this thing, you know. When it was cookin' too much, I mean really swinging, and he wasn't playing, he'd turn around to motion you down. Like if Zoot was takin' a solo and swingin', and he wasn't playing, he would look at me and he'd take his hands like to come down in volume. John Markham, who worked with Benny Goodman also, and a couple of other drummers I knew, too, they said, "Whenever he starts looking at you, gives you the look, don't let him catch your eye." So, man, when we were cookin', I could almost feel that he was going to do it, and I'd start fixin' my drums. I'd look down, man, I'd fix somethin', and I just kept playin' and everything, you know, until I got off. (*Laughs.*) There's so many Benny Goodman stories, mine are just lightweight compared to the horror stories a lot of people have to tell about Benny. (*Laughs.*)

WE: Did musicians love him, nonetheless?

DD: Nobody loved Benny. I mean, I'm sorry, but he wouldn't allow it. He wouldn't let you get that close. He really was remote. I mean, you respected the hell out of him. He could really swing, and, Jesus, you know, Benny was somethin'. I felt honored to do it. But he never hung out with the guys or anything, and he never had any money. I mean, if you ever took a cab, everybody else always had to pay the cab. He never had any cigarettes, he was always bummin'. Oh, I gotta tell you this. When I was with Benny Goodman, Gene Krupa sent me roses. And he says, "Just remember, he's fired the best. Don't let him get to you, baby."

WE: It seems appropriate to play a Benny Goodman piece.

[We played "I Got Rhythm," from *Benny Goodman Live at Carnegie Hall,* Columbia Records; recorded 1937, Gene Krupa on drums.]

DD: He liked hi-hat a lot, too, Gene did. He plays hi-hat with a stick. Notice the difference between Chick Webb and Gene? Chick's way of swinging was different. Gene accented every beat; it was almost like on two all the time. Where Chick's was 4/4; it was actually smoother. You didn't hear that division, did you?

WE: No. Actually, to me, Krupa's attack is unrelenting. It reminds me of a maniacal metronome.

DD: Yes, yes. Well, of course, in those days that was really looked upon favorably in some circles, for those who liked flashy drummers. By flashy I mean he'd throw drumsticks in the air, wave his arms about—he was very animated, but still swinging. Then there was Jo Jones, who was really different. He barely moved his shoulders, his arms were close to his side, and his wrists and fingers—that's where the smoothness and the swing came out. And Jo Jones was so, oh! what a gentleman, and what a beautiful player.

JS: During the '60s you played with a variety of prominent New York musicians. Do you have any anecdotes from that time that you care to relate?

DD: I got one: how I got my job with Billy Mitchell. He was playing at the Gordian Knot on the East Side, and Grady Tate was playing drums with him. Jerry and I wanted to go over and hear them. The place was packed. There were only two seats—right next to the drummer, up against the wall. So I said, "Great for me, right next to Grady! Let's go sit there." Grady turns around and smiles and says, "Hi, what's happening?" So he's playing along, and he hits his finger and it starts to bleed. He goes, "My God." And he said, "Come here" to me. So without changing a beat (*laughs*), I get up and we change, you know. And, boy, I tried to cook Billy the best way I knew how. So Billy turns around and he said, "Damn! Grady, that was . . . You're not Grady! You wanna go to Chicago?" (*Laughs.*) And that's how I got the gig with him.

JS: How did Grady feel about this?

DD: Well, Grady was busy. He wouldn't have gone to Chicago. Billy had to get a drummer anyway to go out of town. Grady was happy for me, but I'll never forget Grady, God love him for doing that, man. But see, I was needed, so I wasn't frightened. If I would have said, "Oh, no, not me," where was Grady going to get a drummer without making a big thing about it and interrupting Billy's solos? Number one, you've got to be professional. You don't do anything to take away from the star.

WE: Another interesting character you played with was Joe Venuti, known for his practical jokes. Do you recall a particularly memorable episode with him?

DD: Yeah, I do. (*Laughs.*) We were in Toronto, and Mule [Major Holly] was playing bass, and Mike Longo [pianist], he had just finished doing something with Dizzy, but Joe had never played with him. So we're going to have rehearsal, and Joe says, "Nah, nah, just see you on the stand tonight." That's Joe. So Mike is getting his music out and he says, "We'll be outta here early tonight, huh?" I said, "What'd ya mean?" He says, "Well, this old man, Joe, we'll probably just play a few tunes." I didn't say anything. (*Laughs.*) That night we get up and Joe says, "Okay, we'll do so-and-so tune." One, two, and then a furious tempo. And Mike, when we finished the tune, he said, "*Jesus*! That old man knocked me into bad health." (*Laughs.*) Well, I just laughed, because Joe, he surprised everybody. Boy, he had chops that he hadn't even used yet himself. Anyway, he took me to LaScala for dinner. He says (*she imitates Venuti's gruff voice*), "Have you ever eaten in LaScala?" I said, "No, I never have." He said, "They're good there; they treat me good there, too." Boy, did they ever. As soon as the doors opened, "Maestro, maestro, maestro, maestro; yes, yes, this way." So we sit down. He said, "Shall I order for us?" I said, "Yeah, Joe, go ahead." So he orders some stuff. He's ordering in Italian most of the time. Then he does this on purpose so I'll hear him: he orders a bottle of red wine and he says, "Chill it." My eyebrows must have gone up a little bit because he says, "You think I'm crazy, huh, chilling red wine, right? Let me tell you somethin', if the friggin' Italians ever had any ice, we would've always had chilled red wine!" (*Laughter.*)

JS: Earlier you mentioned Jerry's tenure with the Thad Jones/Mel Lewis band. What did you think of the co-leader's drumming?

DD: Oh, God, man, talk about a workhorse and a stalwart drummer. I mean, Jesus, I used to see a lot of drummers sit in with that band. They thought that they would outplay Mel, you know. Mel was what we call a down-the-middle drummer. Mel was very consistent, and he *read* so well. So there'd be a lot of drummers—I'd see Elvin, Mickey Roker, Grady. I saw 'em all come in, man, and step all over it, as far as I was concerned. They wouldn't appreciate me saying that, but what I'm really tryin' to get across is that Thad's and Mel's band was such a perfectly knitted band. As soon as Thad stepped on that stand, whoever was on that bandstand gave him their full attention. Because during the time you'd be playin' the tune, he might wave the trombones out and give 'em another chord. So the thing is that you had to give it up. As a drummer, you had to give it up to Thad, and a lot of drummers can't give it up.

JS: Mel was equally good with small groups, and with brushes as well as sticks, don't you think?

DD: Yeah, he was all-round. But he didn't have an edge. There was no excitement to Mel's playing. In fact, Mraz used to tell him (*chuckles*), "Come on outside, I want to have a car hit you." (*Laughter.*) I mean, you should have heard what the cats used to say to him. Because he didn't have that edge, so that meant everybody else had to produce it. (*Laughs.*) Mel would just laugh, you know, he just took it; he knew Mraz[10] was crazy anyway.

JS: Do you feel you were similarly versatile, able to play in small groups as well as subbing in big bands?

DD: Oh, no. Not at all. No, I felt I was a small group drummer. I always used to say, "Give me a Nat King Cole room and I'll be happy the rest of my life." I love the intimate room. And big band is a workhorse. Everybody plays different. You know, we talked about the division. Everybody has their own little spot to play. Trumpet player gets up and the drummer's supposed to fit. Tenor player gets up and he plays his solo, the drummer's supposed to fit. You really have to lay the wood down all the time. Bass solo, you're still supposed to play a little bit underneath the bass. You never get time off. One time I got to sit in with Lionel Hampton (*laughs*), and boy, that was fun. That was my first time I ever played with a big band. It was in Las Vegas.

WE: In the 1960s?

DD: Yeah. Maybe this was mid-'60s. Jerry and I, and Benny Powell and Frank Wess of Count Basie's band, we were all out partying, and we went to see Hamp. Hamp came off intermission, came over to the table, and said hello to the guys. And Frank says, "This is Dottie Dodgion. Man, you oughta hear her play drums." Hamp says, "Yeah? She play drums? Wanna play with us?" And Jerry's goin' like this, "No, no, no, no." And Benny's goin' like this, "Yeah, yeah, yeah." (*Laughs.*) So I said, "Okay." (*Laughter.*) And Jerry's dying. Oh, he thinks I'm going to make a fool of myself. After the intermission, Hamp says, "Okay, come on up." I *am* nervous, but I'm determined to do this because Eugene used to tell me, "Jump in the water when it's the deepest or you'll never learn how to swim." I had to know if I could do it or not. Frank Wess says to me, "Just listen to the lead trumpet player, baby, that's your cue." So Hamp, he'd turn around, and I'd do solos and we did fours and we traded eights, and, oh, God! he was so happy. Man, he was just havin' a ball and he said,

"Gee, baby, would you like to go on the road?" And his wife, Gladys, is standing down at the bottom of the stage, and she said, "Uh-uh!" (*Laughs uproariously.*) And that was the end of that.

JS: The number of women in jazz seems to be increasing geometrically with the last few generations. To what do you attribute this increase?

DD: Well, education. It's been a learning process, I think, for the people. Also it opened up for the women so much more. Again, I think money and the media entered this. It was a gimmick and they took the gimmick, and then out of the gimmicks some good came because there were some very serious lady musicians who benefited by it. As far as acceptance, I don't think it just opened up all of a sudden. I think it's been a long, slow process; I think it's still going on in a lot of cases.

JS: Do you think that by virtue of their gender women contribute a different aesthetic to jazz?

DD: No. I've always said there isn't any gender to music.

JS: You don't think that because you're female you are perhaps more sensitive?

DD: No. I smile at that. I definitely don't think music has a gender at all. It's your heart and it's what you hear. Your heart and your ears—you have to connect those two, and it has to be so powerful that it will come out of your embouchure or your hands. But it's gotta be powerful. It's gotta be all-consuming. I don't think that you can be a real pro unless you put in the time. You've got to put in the time to get the rewards.

Selected Discography

Dottie Dodgion Sings. Arbors Records ARCD 19128 (1994).
*Live at the Elkhorn Slough Yacht Club. Monterey Mattress Marquee (2000). (Dodgion on vocals and
　　at the drums.)
This Is What I'm Here For. Envirophonic Records EPR-0302 (2003).

Notes

1. Carol Sloane, "A Drummer Is a Woman," *Down Beat,* May 1969.
2. *Dottie Dodgion Sings,* 1994; Arbors Records.
3. *Live at the Elkhorn Slough Yacht Club,* Monterey Mattress Marquee; 2000.
4. The DeMarco Dance Team.
5. Linda Dahl, *Stormy Weather: The Music and Lives of a Century of Jazzwomen* (New York: Limelight Editions, 1984), p. 219.
6. Frank Ross of the Mary Kay Trio.
7. "Apple pie" refers to the drummer's subdivision of the beat when playing triplets on a ride cymbal, or brushes on a snare drum.
8. Jazz bass player who was part of the classic Dave Brubeck Quartet.
9. Dottie Dodgion's use of the word "division" refers to how the drummer plays the triplets on his or her ride cymbal. It's the space between the triplets that she calls division.
10. Bassist George Mraz.

Shirley Horn

Shirley Horn

From a local D.C. phenom to one of the grande dames of jazz, Shirley Horn has, for fifty years, captured audiences with a mesmerizing blend of voice and piano that has redefined the standard for dual performers. Fashioning a career built on love songs, her 1992 Verve release, *Here's to Life,* was the most popular jazz recording that year, and it remains one of the best-selling albums in the music's history. With thirty recordings as a leader, many of them issued within the past decade, she is among today's most popular jazz figures.

Born on May 1, 1934, Shirley Horn was a child prodigy. Groomed for a career as a classical pianist, as a youngster she began private lessons at the junior division of Howard University. Her musical course veered, however, when she discovered the recordings of Erroll Garner and Oscar Peterson. By eighteen, she was working her way through the Washington, D.C., club scene, honing her skills as a jazz pianist and vocalist.

Horn's first record, *Embers and Ashes,*[1] opened the door for her to appear in the best clubs in New York, and brought her to the attention of the jazz elite, including Miles Davis. She released several additional albums on the Mercury label, including *Travelin' Light*[2] and, with producer/arranger Quincy Jones, *Shirley Horn with Horns.*[3] In 1965, while perched on the edge of stardom, she took a self-imposed hiatus from the national recording scene to raise her daughter, Rainy.

Horn performed sporadically in the Washington area during this period. Nonetheless, she gradually built a reputation as the city's jazz matriarch. In the '70s and '80s, with her longtime bandmates bassist Charles Ables and drummer Steve Williams, she toured Denmark and Paris, where she cultivated a large following and recorded for the European-based Steeplechase label.

As a vocalist, she holds her audiences rapt with a vaporous timbre, a particularly well-controlled vibrato, and, most important, a warmth and conviction in delivering the lyric. At the piano Horn is strikingly adept at sparse, in-the-pocket playing during the slow—very slow—ballads that remain her trademark. On up-tempo tunes, her classical training is in evidence by virtue of dazzling octave runs and complex chords highlighting her often overlooked prowess as a straight-ahead swinger.

Signing with Verve/Polygram in 1987 elevated her career to a new level of commercial viability and was the first step toward achieving the near-classic status of her reputation today. Her 1991 issue, *You Won't Forget Me,*[4] underscored her musical symbiosis with Miles Davis and was one of his final recordings. Their empathic bond was reprised on record seven years after his death in her Grammy-winning tribute *I Remember Miles.*[5]

In 2003, quite possibly at the apex of her extraordinary career, the sixty-nine-year old Horn will release her twelfth recording on Verve, aptly titled *May the Music Never End.*[6] The virtues that impressed Miles Davis and Quincy Jones in the early '60s have been affirmed by the awards[7] and accolades she has collected over the years, including seven consecutive Grammy nominations and several command performances at the White House.

Recorded November 23, 1996, and March 23, 1999

WE: Shirley, who influenced you as a piano player/vocalist?

SH: I heard such a wide range of music as a child. My mother was very musical—she didn't study. I had one uncle who whistled like a bird. It was beautiful. And my grandmother, untaught, she played piano and organ. I respect particularly Dinah Washington; you could understand every word she said. Billie Holiday swings. Peggy Lee's swingin'. The way they held a note. I can't really put my finger on it, but I do believe we take somethin' from each other. I did somethin' on a recent record that Sarah Vaughan did all the time.

WE: What did you take from Sarah?

SH: Sarah sometimes sways into a note. I don't know what you even call that. It's one of her "cutesy" sounds, purring sounds, you know. Sarah is very cutesy, even in speaking. She came over here once and she said, "I'm starvin' to death, you got some food for me?" It was really hot; I don't use air conditioning, but I had the fans going. She said (*Shirley mimics a high-pitched swooning voice*), "Oh, it's so hot in here." Jayne Mansfield used to say "devoon" instead of divine. So, I said, "Sarah's just devoon." Yeah, she's sassy, but she came and she's just purrin' all over the house. And I'm lookin' at her, you know, "You're not on stage." But this is Sarah; she's devoon. (*Laughs.*)

WE: Was there no one early on who provided you a role model as both a vocalist *and* a pianist?

SH: There's one thing I remember, but this is so many years ago. There was an after-hours spot in Washington called Lindsey's. At a very young age, I wanted to go into Lindsey's. Well, Lindsey was a little short old man and he'd say (*she mimics a husky voice*), "You too young, you can't come in here." 'Cause this was after hours. I used to bug him all the time. Finally he started lettin' me in with my band. Actually, I put my age up two years so I could play in the nightclub. That's the only way you come in, you gotta play. One night I was there and we were foolin' around playing, trying to buy a drink. Lindsey's sister ran the bar, so she knew we were all underage. In walks Nat King Cole—ohhh! He was hot then. Boy, he was always hot. He came in and he looked around, and he went all the way back where there was a huge kitchen where Lindsey cooked all kinda soul food and stuff. He went back there eating. Such a gentleman. He was so quiet. In comes Dinah Washington. (*Laughs.*) She had on a great big gorgeous full-length white fur. We were just kind of sittin' around; I was ticklin' the piano. She said, "I'm the queen and there's my king." She and Nat Cole started huggin', then they went on to eat. So I said, "Let's play somethin'," so we did. Later, when it was gettin' to be about four o'clock in the morning, she came in. She said, "Move over, move over." So I got right on up off the stool, and she sat down and played the piano. Now, Dinah is the more forceful of the singers that I heard. She played some rough piano. Years ago, when I was really a child, there was some woman called Nellie Lutcher. She had a song, a hit record, called "In the Dark." I think I recorded one of her songs. I remember onstage she played the piano and sang. That's the only one, I'm thinkin'. She was a woman who accompanied herself.

WE: What about Fats Waller?

SH: He was a helluva musician. I just remember hearing tales that he had a dirty mouth. My grandmother wanted to see him at the theater, and my mother didn't want to take her because he was pretty foul. I saw him on television. I think they play it every February, Black History Month; I hate it. One hank of his is hanging off the stool. I heard about him as a child, but you don't pay too much attention. Then when I saw him on the television he was a joke to me. But then again, he played a lot of piano and he sang.

WE: Let's talk about you in live performance. Does your audience have a responsibility when you perform?

SH: Oh, yeah. I can tell after maybe three minutes just what kind of audience it's gonna be. I must refer to the European audience—wonderful, passionate. We did an album in Paris, and they had oversold the concert. The place was jammed, people were double-seated on the steps. When we walked out to sit down, everything just went shhhh.

WE: Like a big hush?

SH: That's right. I mean a big hush you could hear. It was that way through the whole thing; the audience was just hangin' on every word I said. It was such a quiet concert. The recording is called *I Love You, Paris.*[8] Someone way in the background coughed, and I told the engineer, "Leave it on there, they'll know it's a live performance." Nobody said a word until it was over, and then they just went *crazy!* They had come to listen to the music, you know. I've had some great moments with a European audience, and then I discovered, you know, they study this music, this art form, in the school system.

JS: In performance, you seem to have the ability to make each member of your audience feel as though you were singing for him or her.

SH: That's what I try to do every time I sit down and sing to you.

JS: How do you do that?

SH: It just happens. I don't know. I'm a very emotional person. Like on that *Paris* thing—I was backstage, and I was a little excited. People were tryin' to get backstage and I said, "I'm not going to talk to anyone until *after* it's over." I was told, "There's a surprise for you." I said, "Fine. When I'm done, then I'll get the surprise." And I wasn't very happy with the dressing room. It was too big and it was kind of chilly. I was sitting there writing down just what I think I'm gonna feel like doing when I go out there. I forgot and left the note on the dressing table. I walked out, and it's a huge stage. I met this hush, and I sat down and I said, "Damn, I left my list in the dressing room. What am I going to do?" I got a stupid smile on my face (*laughs*), and the guys are wondering: "What's going on?" When I don't have a little piece of paper that has at least five songs on it, or if I don't have the first song in mind to go on with, I lose it. So I said, "No, I'm not gonna stop," and I just smiled and smiled. (*Laughs.*) I wasn't in such a good mood, but I got lost in the music. For one thing, the piano was one of the greatest I've ever played on, one of those old Steinways. The sound was so fantastic; you know, I thought I'd have the booming back, like in Carnegie Hall: when you play and it comes back and knocks you down. But the sound was just *great.* We got into "Here Comes the Honey Man"/"I Loves You, Porgy." I think Miles came across my mind. I don't know where that "I Loves You, Porgy" came from, but it just came, and I don't think the three of us can do that rendition again. We've tried, but we can't get it. We were like in a trance. I had goose pimples, and it was hard to get out of it. This wasn't planned. It just happened. I've had a lot of people ask me, "Who taught you this?" I had never had a voice lesson in my life, and I don't know how to plan. I just know that the lyric, if it affects me, that's what I'm gonna lay out on you, and I'm going to sing that song to you.

WE: Have you had some bad moments with audiences?

SH: Oh, earlier, when I was younger. In Washington, D.C., you know, people came out to have a good time. I guess I was about twenty-one or so before people would start to really listen to me. Before that it was all fun because I knew absolutely nothing about jazz piano. I was right out of school, and I'm trying to learn how. It was fun, it was *exciting.* And then I learned a little bit and I said, "Well, I want somebody to listen." I don't have problems with audiences now. You know, my audience is ninety percent white. All over the United States.

WE: Why wouldn't American blacks be coming out to your concerts?

SH: Well, maybe it's 'cause I'm not funky enough. Whatever that is supposed to mean.

WE: Maybe black audiences in general don't respond well to jazz?

SH: I think the young people coming along don't know anything about jazz. In Europe, the kids grow up with it. They study this thing called jazz music in school, and it's respected like in Japan. I have two grandsons. When I go to visit, I hear the little one say, "Take off that stuff; Grandmother's coming in the house." Because I don't like what I hear them listening to, you know. Unfortunately, they haven't been exposed to jazz music. These are trying times for children. Some of this stuff I see on the television totally disgusts me.

JS: You began piano at age four, actual instruction at age five. Did you ask for lessons?

SH: Yes. My grandmother played piano and organ. She had a corner house, and the parlor with the piano was right when you come in the door. The doors were kept closed. The parlor was where company sat. That parlor was always cold. And I remember having trouble getting up on the stool, 'cause she had one of those round stools. But I remember the piano very, very well. I wouldn't go out and play with the kids, even in the summertime, till my grandmother told my mother, "Give her piano lessons." 'Cause that's all I wanted to do: I wanted to go to my grandmother's. She would give me pound cake, and I would play the piano. I was four. Before four I was trying to get up on that stool and pick on that piano.

JS: Who was your first piano teacher?

SH: Mr. Murphy; I'll never forget him. Oh, he was a nice man. I don't know how he taught me. I was four years old; I couldn't read or write. I was with him until I was eleven years old, and then he told my mother he wanted to recommend somebody else 'cause he taught me all he knew. And I got Dr. Frances Hughes. She was a rough teacher—oh, she was rough. But I respected her; today I just adore her. I was a good student and I wanted it. I was thinking concert stage, classics. My mother and father weren't well-to-do, but as it so happened there was a special school at Howard University. My uncle, I. B. Horn, is a prominent physician here in Washington. Between him and Dr. Hughes they developed the Junior School of Music at Howard University. Frank Wess was in the class. He was comin' back to take some postgraduate courses. I mean, they were the old guys. And I was in there. This teacher, Dr. Hughes, she got me a scholarship to Juilliard, but my people couldn't afford it—and they didn't want me to go to New York, you know; I wasn't ready. But I remember music and the piano, like I don't remember havin' a puppy dog or somethin' like that. As a child, I loved it. My mother used to get so upset with me 'cause I practiced *all* the time. I'd go to school, go to Howard, come home, and practice. "Shirley, you've got to do some homework." (*Laughs.*) "Will you please play with the other kids?" And I didn't want to. I didn't want to play with the other kids. I wanted to play that piano.

JS: Did you have a role model for a career in classical music?

SH: My mother took me to see Phillipa Skylar[9] over at Constitutional Hall. I said, "That's what I want to do." I wanted to play classical music, that's what I knew. But I wanted to play the piano, too. Maybe I wanted to go up on the stage and do it like she did. Young girl, you know. She came out in this long gown and sat at the piano.

JS: How old were you then?

SH: Thirteen or fourteen. My father worked two jobs 'cause my piano lessons cost as much as the house, new. I studied till I was eighteen, but then I heard Erroll Garner. In school, I loved Rachmaninoff and Debussy. But I heard Erroll Garner and all that beautiful stuff he wrote. I was about thirteen years old when he came up with that "Penthouse Serenade."

JS: That's the one you learned note for note?

SH: That's right. I met him once; I think that was about 1965. He came to where I was playin'. My fingers wouldn't act right, they just started crumbling. He was a sweetheart, though. But I heard him and I said, "I think that's the route I want to go." Then I heard Ahmad Jamal on records. Then I heard Oscar Peterson. So Oscar Peterson is my Rachmaninoff, and Ahmad Jamal is my Debussy. I love both of them. They are right today my number one pianists. I just did a tribute to Oscar. In fact, I'm gonna sing with his trio; that's gonna be my next record project.

JS: Tell us about the tribute for Oscar Peterson.

SH: Oh, I was so nervous. I was so nervous. They wanted me to do two songs, so I was really thrilled. You know, at Town Hall, the stage entrance is long. So I was standing out there because I was smoking, and they were moving things around. Tony Bennett came up and we were talkin'. He said, "What's wrong?" I said, "I'm so nervous; I'm gonna sing with Oscar Peterson." I said, "Will you hold my hand?" (*Laughs.*) So Tony stood with me at the piano and held my hand while I sang just running over this song. Even though Oscar has had some health problems with his hand, I didn't really look at his hands. Years ago, before he had the stroke, I said, "He just needs *one* hand."

WE: Where did you first hear Oscar Peterson perform?

SH: First time I heard him, it was at the Village Vanguard. They had this funny-looking red upright piano there. That was his favorite piano. I was right in the front. The Vanguard carpet, I know this from playing there many times through the years, is the same, they don't vacuum it, and there was a newspaper from 1920-somethin' in back behind the curtain. Well, when Oscar Peterson got through playing, all that dust was in the air, and I felt like I didn't want to hear any more music for a long time. I was just spent! I felt like the top of my head was gonna come off. John Levy[10] said, "Do you want to go someplace?" I said, "No. I want to go right to the hotel, get into bed, and hold on to this music."

WE: So you're as much a fan as the rest of us.

SH: Oh, *yeah.* Yes, indeed! (*Laughs.*)

JS: How about a duo piano record with Peterson or Jamal?

SH: Are you kiddin'? I wouldn't be able to do that. I would be too nervous. They're my idols. I just finished building a room, closing my new piano in, and I said, "The first person who's gonna play that piano is Ahmad Jamal." He called me that very night and he said, "I heard you got your damn piano." I said, "How did you know?" Well, he knew the room was finished because we were both signed with Steinway Artists. He was comin' here to play at Blues Alley and he had talked with Emma Hillis. Emma's in Washington; she takes care of the piano. She knows all the Steinway people. And she knew what was happening 'cause I had ordered my piano from New York and it was coming. And she said, "Are you excited?" I said, "Emma I can't talk to you now." That was because the whole back of that room was open so they could bring the piano in. I was sitting in this other room, and there were nine or ten men and I said, "I'm not gonna look." But I could not leave that area. I'm sitting there. It was like I was having a baby: one, two, three; they didn't say "push," but I was sayin' it. (*Laughs.*) They were raisin' it up, you know, and it got in. I had a couple of girlfriends who are both pianists. They said, "What are you gonna do now?" I said, "I don't know, but the first person to play this piano would be Ahmad Jamal." Well, I got that phone call that evening and I said, "Ahmad, are you coming by here when you get done?" He said, "I'll be by there." And he came by and played. I have one girlfriend who *loves* music. She got on the rug under the piano. He played for about an hour and a half, so beautifully.

WE: You mentioned building a room. Did your dad teach you carpentry?

SH: No. My dad was not into that. My uncles, you know, they all loved me 'cause I was little and I played the piano, so I was kinda the favorite. All the little cousins didn't like me. I mean, I wanted to go to piano lessons. They would cry; they didn't want to go, you know. No, when I was little, my mother used to send me out with my uncles, who were builders. I had an apron with a little hammer and nails, and they would take me out on their jobs with them and get me out of the house away from the piano. I learned a lot from my uncles, and I'm always doing something with my hands. Just in recent years I got some problems, so I don't take to the hammer too often. But I built a lot of stuff in this house.

JS: What was your earliest experience performing for the public?

SH: I sang Sunday School in church. I was just the musical kid around town. (*Laughs.*)

JS: And after that?

SH: When I was thirteen years old, I went on a radio show. I was on for thirteen weeks, and they held me over for another thirteen weeks. Then I started getting calls to do this and that. People didn't believe I was the age I was. I was thirteen, but I was singing like an older woman. 'Cause I sang the songs that I heard at home. I heard a lot of Billie Holiday. I was singin' "Lover Man." I don't think I knew what it meant, but my interpretation was good enough for them to think I was a full-grown woman.

WE: When you were a little older, wasn't there an incident in a club involving a teddy bear?[11]

SH: One day this woman called me. Her name was Clara Bow. She played and sang—she was good. She'd heard me around when I was in school. So Clara helped me—I'd leave Howard University and go to this club, where she had asked this man to give me a job. I was cuttin' school—not too often, but I did—and sneakin' a job at this Bill Thompson's—that was the name of that place. It was beautiful. It was a dining room. He'd have women playing piano during dinner, and then they had somebody else playin' for the cocktail hours. I fit perfectly, playin' the classics and all that.

Anyway, it was getting close to Christmas time, and there was a little man who used to come in every night, have his dinner, tip his hat, and leave. Okay. So this night he came in and there was a teddy bear as tall as I. Somehow I knew that was my teddy bear. He sent a note up to me—he never said anything to me before—sent a note that said, "If you sing 'Melancholy Baby,' the teddy bear is yours." Well, of course, I knew "Melancholy Baby," 'cause my mother had sung these songs. She wasn't a professional vocalist or anything, but she sang at home all the time. And I got the teddy bear.

So Clara Bow went to the owner and said, "Well, she can sing; she's gotta get more money." And then I discovered that with singing you get more money, 'cause I was a very quiet child. I was very shy. I mean, I was scared to death every time I would open my mouth to sing. My hands used to sweat and all. It took me a long time to get over that nervousness. See, at the radio show I didn't have a live audience, but at Bill Thompson's I did. It was a little hard for me to do. On that first job I think I was making $125 'cause I worked Tuesday, Wednesday, Thursday, and Friday, two hours in the evening. And then I started making $175 for those days. I said, "Okay!" That was a lot of money then. You know, that teddy bear made a statement: If you can make more money singin', singing is what you got to do.

WE: How old were you when you were working at Thompson's club?

SH: I was right under eighteen. And it's against the law, see. Clara lied about my age 'cause I had to say I was eighteen. I didn't belong in there where they were selling liquor. So it went on. It was pretty good for, I guess, about four months. And one night my mother and father came in—well, I figured this is the end of my career. (*Laughs.*)

WE: How did they find out you were there?

SH: Well, the word got around. You know, Washington is a small place. I never asked because I just got my coat and I said, "Goodbye, Miss Bow." (*Laughs.*) I went home, and my mother didn't speak to me for about a week.

WE: Before that happened, weren't you worried about your parents getting suspicious, since you weren't coming right home after your studies at Howard?

SH: See, my father caught me one time, but he didn't tell. My father was my partner. But he said, "You are going to have to stop because your mother's gonna find out." Oh, my mother, she was a very strict lady. My mother actually didn't hear me sing until I was freshly married, and I'm singing at a joint, the Seventh and T club. It was around the corner from the Howard Theater. Very famous. She knew I was doing a trio. It's not the kind of place that you want to see your daughter, you know. Anyway, she came up the steps at this cocktail lounge, and all these men and musicians were there from the Howard Theater. When my mother rounded that corner, I was singing "Love for Sale." I didn't know she was coming. My father said there was nothing he could do about it. She sat down, and I just ran that song on and on and on, and I played the break tune a long time. I said, "I got to come down off this stage sometime" (*laughs*), and I did. I said, "Hi, Mother." She said "Hello,

Shirley; Ernest, I think we should be going." And she walked out. I said, "Oh, boy." (*Laughs.*) It was rough.

JS: Back to the Bill Thompson episode—did you play there at about the same time as when you got the scholarship to Juilliard?

SH: That was around the same time.

JS: Were you really shattered when you couldn't attend Juilliard to study classical music?

SH: No. I don't think I've ever really been shattered. My grandmother used to say, "What's for you, you'll get," and I kind of believe that. I've never been a pusher. I'd go around to the clubs and sit in with the guys. They used to just call me a pest. But I tried anyway. You know, I wanted to learn how to play this thing called "jazz" music. And nobody would give me a chance. I said, "One day you gonna come to me." (*Laughs.*) The nicest person to me was Buck Hill. You know, Buck is my favorite; I just love him. He'd say, "Let her sit in, let her sit in." And I would sit in, and I learned a lot. I caught on to tryin' to swing. Yeah, I was pretty then, I was cute. (*Laughs.*) A lot of jobs I got because the guy liked the way I looked. And then I got my own band. That was funny. I think I could play "How High the Moon" and the blues. I had a vibes player and bass and drums. I could sing some songs, you know, sing it when I didn't think anybody was listening.

JS: But classical music was still your primary interest?

SH: Yes.

JS: And you really had to work at learning to swing?

SH: Yeah. I guess I had a little rhythm in me, but I didn't know where to put it. I always knew to pat my foot on two and four (*laughs*), but it's really hard to come out of the classics right into jazz. You know, that's a gradual thing.

WE: Did this period of learning occur around 1954 when you formed your first band?

SH: Wait a minute—I'll think about cars. I had a white convertible in '58. So it was about '57. My husband worked in the day and I worked the nights, so that worked fine. I was in and out of places right here in town; I played all the government buildings, all the theaters. I was just busy doing all kinds of things. I can't say I was confused, but one day I was doing Chopin, and the next day I played at a Dixieland club where I did a single. I think I worked maybe an hour a night. I used to fool around trying to play the Dixieland stuff.

WE: I take it that when the musicians called you a pest, it was a friendly remark.

SH: Yeah.

WE: Did you have any tough times with men in the business because you are a woman?

SH: Well, the only problem I had was with the club owners. And I had nothin' to sell but the music. I never had trouble with my band members because I'm a very positive person. I know what I want to do, and I know what I want you to do. We're going in this direction; I make all the arrangements. Be there.

WE: Did club owners try to tell you what kind of music to play or how to dress?

SH: No. They wanted to get in my pants.

WE: Really?

SH: Yeah. I always dressed respectfully. I dressed well. Just enough. My mother gave me that. You know, there was no low down and all this kinda showing everything. But my husband used to have to go with me at pay time, because that's the only time I'd have to go in the office with a club owner. I had one in a *very* popular club in town, and he was actually trying to attack me right there. Then my band came in, and that was the end of that. I ran into a lot of that, but otherwise I had no problems.

WE: What led up to your first record, *Embers and Ashes,* in 1960?

SH: That's when I had my first job. I worked at the Bohemian Caverns in Washington for a year and a half. Then they go famous, and they put me out. They booked John Coltrane and they booked Miles. You know, they were booking the big folks. Angelo Alvino and Tony Taylor were involved in this venue. Angelo had the money, and Tony was—you know, the big mustached man who knows all the musicians (*she mimics a deep voice*): "Man, you oughta do this, you oughta do that." I used to look at him and laugh, the funniest mustache I've ever seen. But he wanted me to go to New York. He says, "You ought to be recording." I said, "I'm not going to do anything. Whoever wants to see me will come to Washington." And I really didn't think about recording 'cause I was happy playing the music. I was learning, and during those times I had a great trio. Eventually I recorded *Embers and Ashes* in New York. Tony went up with me.

JS: Could you tell us something about composer Curtis Lewis and his relationship to the *Embers and Ashes* date?

SH: When I was in the studio recording *Embers and Ashes,* they wanted me to play the politics and use no slouch musicians. So I had completely new musicians. But see, I already had my own guys, and we were playing every night. I was really upset about it. I'm in the middle of this thing and I said, "Oh, what am I gonna do?" I didn't want to do it. John Levy was there. He said, "We gotta go through this door." I said, "Never again." The first day of the recording—well, naturally I'm very nervous, my first recording. I'm away from home, I'm feelin' like a motherless child, and these other two strange musicians are there. I don't want to have a jam session record. Then Curtis Lewis came in.

JS: Lewis just appeared at your recording session?

SH: Yes.

JS: How did he gain access to you?

SH: Well, he knew somebody in the band who told him that this chick Shirley Horn is gonna record tomorrow, and he should bring her some stuff. So there he was in the studio with all his music. John didn't push me. He said, "Look at it and see if you like it. He thinks you can do the whole suite." I looked at that music—the ink was still wet—and I liked it. So I turned the whole thing around. I think I did ten songs, and it turned out to be the majority of the music I'm just hearing, you know. But I wasn't very happy with that. I got disgusted, and I got very depressed and I started cryin'. John said, "What do you want to do?" I said, "I want to go back to the hotel." I just walked in and locked my door. It was a bit much.

WE: You met Miles Davis around this time, opening for him in 1960 at the Vanguard. Tell us about your first encounter with him.

SH: I was with my husband at my mother-in-law's house, and I got a phone call. To this day I don't know how he got ahold of me. He said (*imitates his voice*), "This is Miles Davis, I want you to come to New York." This is early in the morning; I'm at my mother-in-law's house with all this gorgeous food. I said, "Okay, right." And I said to myself, "Who is this?" I thought it was a friend of mine playing a joke. Then he says, "I think you should come to New York because there's some people you should meet." I said, "Okay." I went on back to finish eating all that good food. As we were driving home, I said, "I think I better go to New York." You know, it kind of bugged me a bit. Anyway, I went right to his address, and sure enough, there was Teo Macero, Gil Evans, and a lot of important people that I just read about. And to let me know that he knew about my music—you know, Miles has five or six boys and each one of those boys sang a song on *Embers and Ashes.* I knew it was no lie. Oh, and he said, "Come here, I want to sing something." And he sang it. I was just lookin'. I mean, I was thrilled; I was very proud.

WE: Let me see if I understand. Miles actually sang a tune from *Embers and Ashes*?

SH: Yep.

WE: Did he have a good voice?

SH: (*Laughter.*) No. After that we talked a lot. He told me I was too fat, and he took me downstairs to the gym. It was all in fun, but he meant it. He was a very caring person. See, then again, Miles knew my people. The Horns lived in East St. Louis. My aunt taught Miles. He was the biggest pest in East St. Louis High School. My people knew his people; they were traditional people. And he wasn't. (*Laughs.*) He kinda clued me in to New York and New York musicians. Don't hang with this person, it's not good; be into that, and I don't want to hear about you being involved with that. You know, it really wasn't a problem, but he didn't know that, 'cause I don't hang out much in New York anyway. Whenever I would go to New York, he'd always want me to come up. I said, "I'm not gonna go down in that gym anymore." (*Laughs.*) And he'd have fixed me something special to eat—like, don't eat beef, pork; eat veal.

JS: We understand he put restrictions on you when you opened for him at the Village Vanguard?

SH: I couldn't smoke but one cigarette. He'd always be on me about smoking. When he first saw I smoked a cigarette, oh, he went off. (*Imitates Davis's voice*) "You smokin' that cigarette?" And we drank champagne. Not beer. I love beer; even as a child I loved beer. And I had to sit in the back with the rest of the guys, which was fun because there was so much cuttin' up and joke tellin'. Wynton Kelly used to take his teeth out and hand them to you, all that kind of stuff. It was fun. But I liked to sit at the bar, you know, to appear sophisticated and grown-up.

JS: Miles didn't want you to sit at the bar?

SH: No, indeed. Because it didn't look like a lady. So (*laughs*) I didn't sit at the bar.

JS: How did the Vanguard gig happen?

SH: He called me and said, "Do you want to play at the Vanguard with me?" I said, "Oh, no." 'Cause I thought he meant sittin' down and playin' with him, right? He said, "No, with *your* group." So I said, "Okay, you talk to John Levy." So he called John, and John set it up.

JS: What was the arrangement?

SH: In the beginning, I guess I thought things would go like things are supposed to go. (*Laughs.*) Miles wanted me to do twenty minutes, and then we came offstage. Whenever Miles showed up, he took over. Well, I'd get there on time at 9:15, ready to go onstage. Miles came in any time he felt like it. As Max Gordon[12] got to know me, he'd say, "No, no, wait a little while. Maybe Miles will be comin' in pretty soon." Sometimes Max would say, "Would you mind going up now?" It would be quarter to ten. Then Miles would come in whenever he got ready to. One night he came in and he was pretty mad about somethin'. The guys went onstage, they wound it up and got it together, and Miles played one note. I have that note right here in my head. Then he put his horn down and walked out. The band played on and on. (*Laughs.*) They finally took a break, and no Miles.

WE: Do you remember the first night of the gig?

SH: That was a thrilling time in my life because the opening night was the opening night for *A Raisin in the Sun.* That night in that audience, Lena Horne was there, Claudia McNeil, and I had gone up to the bar and Sidney Poitier came and said, "I really enjoyed your music, Miss Horn." I almost fainted. Who's the bass player—who's the crazy bass player?

WE: Charles Mingus?

SH: Yeah. He was standing there by the bar in a fur coat. Well, he was frightenin'; I got away from him.

WE: Why were you afraid of Mingus?

SH: Because he was strange lookin'. Now, it was hot as Hades. Great big man in a big fur coat and a big hat. I was a little girl, I was little then; and I didn't know who he was. I looked at him and he scared me. (*Laughs.*) I finally got around back to where the musicians sat, and I said, "Who is that with the fur coat?" The guys started laughing, "It's Charlie Mingus." I didn't hear much of him growin' up. But it was so thrilling, just being there and hearing Miles and all those guys. Oh, God, it was just like being in a dream.

WE: You said that originally you thought Miles wanted you to play piano in his band. Why couldn't you do that?

SH: Are you *kiddin'*?!!

WE: Didn't you have confidence in your playing?

SH: No. And I wasn't real strong. No, I couldn't do that. But one night, there were a lot of people in there, and Wynton was tryin' to get me to play. I adored him, too. He said, "Come on and sit in." I said, "I'll play if you sit on the stool with me." So he sat up on the stool with me. I started playin', and he slipped away. He said, "I'm gonna get a drink, I'll be right back." And he left me.

WE: This was an actual set, or in between sets?

SH: This was the set. Miles was there. They was playin' blues. I look around, there was Paul Chambers and there was Jimmy Cobb. Everybody's lookin' at me and I said, "Don't blow it, don't blow it." (*Laughs.*)

WE: Did you back Miles?

SH: Yeah. I was scared to death. I was just scared, that's all there is to it. But Philly Joe came in, and I stopped playing because I didn't understand what he was doin'. He came and took the sticks away from Jimmy Cobb. It was kind of a little fight at that time, 'cause Miles loved Philly Joe and Jimmy Cobb had the gig.

WE: It seems to me that Miles didn't make a display of his virtuosity, and neither do you. Could that have been a feature of your work he appreciated?

SH: Yes, I think so. I told him one time, "You know, when you make corn liquor, you're the last drop that comes out of the corn liquor funnel." He said, "Say what?" Yeah, a little jewel; I call him "Jewel."

WE: In print, Miles has often been portrayed as an unsavory character. Could you give us your impression of him?

SH: Of course, I'd read all those things they said about him. You know, how he turns his back on people and stuff. Well, when you're tryin' to play and concentrate, you don't want candles on the table, you don't want nobody's flash taking your picture, right? So that's a good reason to turn your back. That makes sense to me. But from the day I met him, I found him to be a loving, caring person who *really* cared about people. A lot of people he didn't like, he didn't bother with. But he cared about me, and I knew that. He was one of my favorite people in all the world.

WE: Did you visit a lot with each other as the years passed?

SH: We didn't see that much of each other. In recent years we had a lot of bookings together in France, but we couldn't be together because there was always a mob. I saw some terrible things happen right in Philadelphia, and it frightened me. The mob scene. They were rockin' the limo and stuff, and I said, "Whoa, wait a minute." I see why he's gotta have bodyguards and all that kind of stuff.

WE: He had a tough image, in part, to protect himself?

SH: Oh, yeah. You can imagine, you know, somebody always in your face. We had a minute or two at the Hague in the '80s—all the musicians stayed in the same hotel. Well, it was so crowded and loud downstairs that I couldn't stay there; I couldn't even hear the music. Blakey was playing on one end of the joint, and somebody else was playing at the other end. And I said, "Nah, it's too much." So I went upstairs. I called room service to get a Coke. I wanted a Coca-Cola with ice. It was hot. But I couldn't get a Coke. Well, I put on my robe and my house shoes and I went downstairs (*chuckles*) to the front desk to see if I could get someone to give me a Coke and take it back upstairs myself. And Miles was comin' in. He said (*imitating Davis's voice*), "Whatcha doin' in your night clothes?" I said, "I was just trying to get a Coke." He said, "Don't you know it's dangerous?" I said, "I wouldn't think, 'cause everybody is downstairs." "Nah," he said, "I'm gonna take you to your room." So he took me to my room, and we talked about forty-five minutes with bodyguards at the door. He had three big dudes standing outside the door when he was in my room. (*Laughs.*) Then he had people callin' for him and stuff. It was too much. He told me, "You know, sometime I just want to go someplace and hide." But there were no hiding places for him. He was loved all over the world.

WE: How do you respond to the music he made in the '80s and '90s?

SH: I used to joke with him about that space music he was playin'. He was in Washington at this place and I went there, and there were so many people—I mean, Georgetown was loaded. Everybody's tryin' to get in this one little joint. I *finally* got backstage, and I couldn't stand it. He started playing this stuff, and everybody was angry because everybody wanted to get a seat. I said, "I'm not in the right place right now." So I went out the back door, down the back steps, with people tryin' to get in the back door and up the steps. He calls me and says, "Why'd you split?" I said, "I couldn't handle that space music you were playin'." He laughed.

WE: Where were you when Miles died?

SH: I had seen him in New York. Then I went to California and from there to Tokyo, Japan, and I was *so* tired. I was concerned, and I said once I chill out I'm gonna try to get in touch with him, get a call through. I laid down; I stretched out on the bed and I went *out*. Then the phone rang and it was daylight. I'd slept all night. The curtains were open and I said, "Where the hell am I?" This must have been about eight o'clock in the morning. The caller asks (*she imitates a high-pitched Asian voice*), "Is Miss Shirley Horn?" I said, "Who is this?" Again the caller asks, "Miss Shirley Horn?" I said, "What do you want?" She said, "I want to talk to you about Miles Davis." I said, "I can't comment; the only thing I know is that Miles is not well in the hospital." "Oh, no, Miss Shirley Horn, Miles Davis died." That was rough.

JS: Let's turn back to your mid-career. How did you first get signed to the Steeplechase label in the late 1970s?

SH: Well, I was sittin' in the house, very comfortable, a beautiful Sunday evening, and the phone rang. It was a guy called Nils Winther. Well, I couldn't understand him, his English was very poor. Then Billy Hart called me: "Hey, man, don't you want to record? Nils Winther wants you to record for Steeplechase." Billy Hart, I took him on the road with me when he was seventeen years old, and his mama said, "Take good care of my baby." He lived around the corner from me.

JS: How did Billy Hart know that Nils Winther had called you?

SH: 'Cause Billy had put Nils up to calling me. He had done a lot of recording with Nils Winther.

JS: What did you say to Billy Hart about doing the recording?

SH: I said, "You gonna play with me?" He said, "Yeah." I said, "Okay, get that old boy Buster Williams." That was Friday; Sunday we got in the car, and I don't know what I'm gonna play. I said, "If you're drivin' me, then I can think on the way." Well, we went on to the studio in New York. I met this Nils Winther, and we did an album with Steeplechase. Then I got word from somebody at the North Sea that wanted to book me, that Nils wanted to record me. At that point I didn't have any representation; I really wasn't interested in any. And I didn't think to call John [Levy]. Anyway, I went there and Nils Winther recorded me three nights.[13] So the records came out, and I'm not happy with but a couple of songs on those records. And there's one record cover where I look like I'm dead because the photographer came at seven o'clock in the morning to take a picture. Who comes at seven o'clock in the morning to take a picture? I look like I'm dead; I'm white and I have these flowers on me, and I'm looking terrible. Anyway, it didn't cost him any money—this is Steeplechase.[14] I'm naming names on this dog. I didn't get any money, and I think that's eight, nine, or ten years ago. I still get a report from him. I think I'm at $280,000 and some odd cents.

JS: That you're supposed to get?

SH: That's what I owe.

JS: That's what you owe?!! Why do you owe any money?

SH: Oh, there's somethin' in the contract. It was my fault for even being bothered with him. He said it cost this much to record that album. It didn't cost him anything because he recorded a concert that I got paid for. I was stupid.

WE: You started recording for Steeplechase in 1978 after a fifteen-year dry spell. Wasn't your visibility fairly low during that period?

SH: Yes. I was raisin' my daughter. But I have no regrets. Not at all. A lot of people said, "Oh, you know, you stopped all that time raisin' your child." Well, my child was important to me. She came first. About ten years. But I wasn't just sittin' round the house. I was busy. I was building rooms. (*Laughs.*) I did a lot of things during that time. I get that question all the time: "Why would you stay home to take care of your child?" When someone asks me this, especially a woman, I just look at the person. I'm glad I did that.

JS: When you signed your contract with Verve eight years ago or so, was it your idea or did they contact you?

SH: No, indeed, they came to me and bugged me. I was working this joint in New York called the Circle Bar, and I didn't want to work there. It was rainin' and cold; my foot was killing me. The monitor was about two by six, the piano was the smallest piano I'd seen in my life, and no sound system. And no one to set up the stuff. The first night it's rainin' cats and dogs; I was *so* disgusted. Why did I say I want to do this? So I asked for some more sound, and the waiter set his tray down and went and adjusted the thing. That was what I was into. About Friday night this man came in and asked if I wanted to record for PolyGram. I said to my band, "What is a polygram?" (*Laughter.*) He gave me his card. About six months later, the same person called asking me to do it. I said, "All right, I'll do it." I signed with them and that was PolyGram. Then they wanted me to do more, and I'm on Verve now. PolyGram, Verve, I don't understand the difference.

JS: Did the Verve people think you were crazy to want to record *The Main Ingredient*[15] in your own house?

SH: Well, they kinda think I'm a little nuts anyway. I'm very determined. "You want to do it in your house?" "Sure." 'Cause I was tryin' to get a little taste of yesteryear, you know. But they didn't want any audience. And I got a little angry because this is my house. I would have liked to have had some of my friends to be like old times. But, phew! There was enough recording equipment in there. I mean, these big black boxes came in my house. They moved my plants, they moved my drapes. I was a little uptight but I said, "I'm not going to let this throw me." 'Cause I also had all these musicians coming and goin', flyin' from here and there. The guys rehearsed a little, but see, I had told them this is what I want you to play, so they knew the songs. Elvin Jones—I hadn't seen him in thirty years, I guess. Oh, boy, I know why they call him the "drum machine." That room was built for that piano in there. Elvin set up the drums and he hit a rim shot that I think jarred the floor. God! It was great, though; it was fun. (*Laughs.*) Elvin had earphones on, right? And the earphones fell down on his eyes like the guy on *Star Trek*. We were laughing. He was facing us. Everybody else was looking at him. Wow!

JS: You talked about fried chicken and mustard greens at the beginning of that recording. Were they on a menu that was served at the sessions?

SH: No. I didn't have fried chicken and mustard greens, but I had all other kinds of food. 'Cause I cooked every night when the guys left. And on the first break, then I served. But years ago—this was when I was working the gig at the Caverns—I worked for a year and a half, and we worked hard. I mean a lot of hours. But it was good for me because I was strong. And my daughter was a little girl. But every night before I'd leave home, I'd fix three meals a day. I'd go to work and there was always somethin' left over. When the guys would come by my house, there was some greens on the table, pie, some fried chicken left over, whatever. We'd come in, been playing all night long—three shows a night—but we'd stay, eatin' and drinkin' and playin' the music, until a lot of times my husband would leave at six.

WE: Would it be correct to say that *Here's to Life* was a special project, but *The Main Ingredient* is more like what you're about most of the time?

SH: I'm like both, but I think I'm more like *Here's to Life* than *The Main Ingredient*. I think it tells a story about me. During' that time I had some deaths that affected me, and I think I was singin' my pain out in *Here's to Life*. *The Main Ingredient*—I was just havin' fun.

WE: Let's talk more about *Here's to Life*. How did you first come across the title song?

SH: I had just gotten to California. Turned the television on, and Joe Williams was singing a part of this song. I was half asleep, and it woke me right up. I called John Levy and said, "I've got to have that song right now, in my suite, tonight." He had it there in a couple of hours. I said, "This is my song." It was like somethin' just came all over me. I wanted that to be the title of my new album, and also I wanted Johnny Mandel. Well, it turned out to be kind of a mess, because Joe Williams had been holding onto it for four or five years. I said, "I will go to the Supreme Court." I called Verve, and I said, "The next recording is *Here's to Life*, that's the title song and that's it." Joe recorded it twice after I recorded it. It was kind of a nasty scene. But, you know, that song just hit me like somebody slapped me with a wet towel and woke me up and said, "That's your song."

JS: How did you get hooked up with Mandel to do *Here's to Life*?

SH: I was playing in this club, the Cine Grill, in Hollywood; we play there about three times a year. He came in, and I didn't know who he was, really. We met and I said, "I want you to do the music for *Here's to Life.*" I told him there are two songs I want you to do: "Where Do You Start" and "Here's to Life." We shook hands and we hugged. We met in New York. I went to the studio, and my trio put down the foundation, you might as well say. He took the tape to California and put in all the rest of the stuff. See, what a lot of people don't understand is the foundation is the Shirley Horn Trio on *Here's to Life.* All the sweeteners and the decorations, that's Johnny Mandel *on top.* We were in the studio together for the songs "Here's to Life" and "Where Do You Start"?

JS: Was recording with the large ensemble a good experience?

SH: I don't like to go in the booth, you know. I always need to be where I can touch a piano. There were so many musicians; they couldn't put a little spinet piano in there for me to be able to touch like they always did in New York whenever I stood up. But I felt a little uncomfortable. Then when I heard what Johnny had done, I was just in heaven. Oh!

WE: Touching a piano, that's a security thing?

SH: Yeah. That's what they call it. (*Laughs.*) You know, when I did a thing with the Boston Pops, they wanted to know was I gonna stand or sit. And I said, "Well, I'll have to have a stool and be somewhat close so I can touch that piano." You know, just to be able to put my hands somewhere. It's kind of strange, isn't it?

[At this point, we listened to "Am I Blue," Billie Holiday and Her Orchestra, *The Quintessential Billie Holiday, Vol. 9,* Columbia Records, recorded 1941.]

WE: Were you influenced by her phrasing?

SH: Oh, no. I've been influenced by everybody, but as far as phrasing that's definitely me. You notice I kinda speak in long meter. (*Laughs.*)

WE: Did you ever get to meet Billie?

SH: Yes, one time. I was in my ninth month—my baby was ten and a half pounds. Billie was in Baltimore.[16] That Sunday I found out about it, I said to my husband, "I'm going to see Billie Holiday." He said, "I'm not takin' you." Well, I said, "I'm goin' and I'm gonna drive." He called my mother and everybody said, "Don't go out of this house; you're about to have the baby." I started to have labor pains, but I went and I saw her. I wanted to go back in the dressing room, and nobody argues with anybody who's pregnant, right? But she didn't know me from Adam. I went back there, and they wouldn't let me in at that time. I got a seat right in front. My husband was sitting there with two of my friends waitin' for me to have this baby at any time. And she came out and she sang. But she was so sick. God, she was sooo sick. She was holdin' on to the chair 'cause she was gonna fall, you know. She managed somehow to make it. Then after that they let me come backstage and she was very nice. "Baby, you better sit down, like somethin' is gonna happen to you right now." But she was so out of it.

WE: I noticed you have *Lady in Satin*[17] in your collection. Is it a travesty that she was recorded at that time, or do you think she was even more powerful at that stage?

SH: She was more powerful. It's hard for me to listen to it. Every time I listen, it's her life just laid out there raw. Carmen[18] and I listened to it once together. She cried and I cried.

WE: Do you think a musician has to have a tough life to be able to sing like that?

SH: (*Laughs.*) No. No. It's pure emotion. Some people are just emotional. *I'm* very emotional. Oh, boy, some of these interviewers want to know about my tragic life. I had a very good life. You know, I didn't have to pound the pavement and all that in the streets of New York. Stuff was just handed to me. And I thank God for that. On *Here's to Life,* I'm singing my hurt for the people that died right before I recorded it. Special people to me. Pure emotion takes the moment.

Selected Discography

*Close Enough for Love. Verve 837933-2 (1988) (with Buck Hill).
You Won't Forget Me. Verve 847482 (1990). (Miles Davis plays on the title track.)
Light Out of Darkness. Verve 314 519 703-2 (1993). (Tribute to Ray Charles that includes Horn playing organ on several selections.)
The Main Ingredient. Verve 314 52 955-2 (1995).
I Remember Miles. Verve 314 557 199-2 (1998).

Notes

1. *Embers and Ashes/Songs of Lost Love Sung by Shirley Horn,*1960; Hi-Life Records.
2. 1965.
3. 1963.
4. 1991; Verve/Polygram.
5. 1998; Verve.
6. 2003.
7. She was awarded an Honorary Doctorate from the Berklee College of Music in 2002.
8. 1994; PolyGram/Verve.
9. Phillipa Skylar was a classical pianist.
10. Ms. Horn's manager.
11. Leslie Gourse, *Madam Jazz* (New York: Oxford University Press, 1995), pp. 175–176.
12. Owner of the Village Vanguard.
13. *At North Sea;* 1981.
14. *A Lazy Afternoon;* 1978.
15. Released 1996, Verve/PolyGram Records.
16. Billie Holiday was appearing at the Tijuana Club, in 1958.
17. 1958; Columbia Records.
18. Carmen McRae.

Ingrid Jensen

Ingrid Jensen

A bold voice in the vanguard of young female instrumentalists, trumpeter Ingrid Jensen has all the characteristics of a major talent. Playing with a sound devoid of vibrato and possessing technique and musical ability to burn, she has an authoritative delivery of advanced hard-bop improvisation that has earned sensational reviews from the critics. Defying categories and stereotypes, the blond, athletic Jensen exploded onto the recording scene with her first CD, securing a place among the leading lights of younger jazz musicians.

Jensen was born in 1967 in Cedar-by-the-Sea, a small town in British Columbia. She and her siblings grew up listening to jazz. She found her way to the brass family and held the trumpet chair in her high school's award-winning jazz combos. As a youth she also gained valuable experience by playing regularly in a first-class local big band.

After earning degrees from Malaspina College (Namaimo, B.C.) and Berklee College of Music, Jensen moved to Europe in search of a fresh start. Settling in Vienna in 1992, she befriended expatriate flumpeter[1] Art Farmer, whose reminiscences about earlier jazz eras and anecdotes about Clifford Brown inspired Jensen to recommit all her energies to becoming a serious jazz trumpeter.

While in Europe, Ingrid Jensen caught the ear of Matthias Winckelmann. Her debut recording on his Enja label, *Vernal Fields,* merited a four-star rating from *Down Beat* and earned Canada's Juno Award as "Best Mainstream Album of 1995." That same year, Jensen received the "Best Newcomer Award" at the Cork Jazz Festival in Ireland. Weeks later, she won the second annual Carmine Caruso International Jazz Solo Trumpet Competition.

Admittedly influenced by the Freddie Hubbard/Woody Shaw mold, Jensen has none-theless fashioned her own identifiable voice. Capable of performing with bruising intensity, she bends and coils her body while hunching her shoulders on her way to unleashing a blistering array of pyrotechnical trumpet lines. Jensen also applies her distinctive matte finish sound to languid explorations on the flugelhorn. Her venturesome solos are well conceived as she deftly shifts between playing inside and outside the chord changes.

Since *Vernal Fields,* Jensen's career has been in high gear, with three more CDs as a leader and numerous others on which she plays a key supporting role. Sought after as a soloist, she has been featured with the Maria Schneider Jazz Orchestra, the Mingus Big Band, and the all-female big band DIVA. Currently on faculty at the Peabody Conservatory of Music in Baltimore, Jensen travels and performs extensively, conducting clinics and workshops with a variety of ensembles from around the world.

Recorded September 8, 1999

JS: Was the trumpet your preferred instrument as a youngster?

IJ: Actually, no! Originally I wanted to play the trombone because my voice is more in the low alto range, and I was hearing things there as opposed to the soprano register. I was raised on a lot of trombone music, like Jack Teagarden, so I really was gravitating toward the trombone as a kid. Unbeknownst to me, though, my family had been talking with the band director of the school I was about to go into, saying that I had the right attitude and spunk to play the trumpet. I got the trumpet, and I sounded terrible for years. I couldn't stand it! I thought my trumpet sound was the worst, so I started playing long tones and learning how to get my voice through the instrument and how to channel my own expression in *one note,* let alone playing jazz or playing chords. I'm glad I had a problem with the instrument when I was young, because now I've learned to love it and to find a way to feel comfortable with it. The people who inspired me to go for that were Clark Terry, Freddie Hubbard, Miles, and Clifford Brown. I heard the sounds of *every one* of these guys as a completely different character. It was not a trumpet to me anymore. It wasn't like one generic brassy sound. It was really voices of people oozing out like the instrument didn't matter.

WE: Were there other players who were significant influences on you?

IJ: The truly original voices are the ones who got my attention. People like Miles, Freddie Hubbard, Harry "Sweets" Edison, Clark Terry, Booker Little, Thad Jones, Don Cherry, Kenny Wheeler, Woody Shaw, Lester Bowie, Bix Beiderbecke, and, of course, Louis! These are personalities whose daring attitudes transcend all "traditional sounds" and dig deep into momentary experiences where what they play is more like a heartfelt, improvised composition than a "trumpet solo." The "lifting" and "jamming" phase during my teen years had a pretty heavy effect on me as well, as far as my sound, my phrasing, and my articulation. I'd play along with records and transcribe a lot and try to get inside the minds of the players, sort of an osmosis kind of thing. Like I'd transcribe a Freddie Hubbard solo and pretend in my mind that I *actually* was Freddie playing the trumpet. But there comes a point in time when you have to say, "Wait a minute, I'm not Freddie Hubbard, and I don't want to be." I think that a lot of times musicians forget to go beyond what it is they already know and search into the unknown, which is yourself. One of the most effective ways to get to your own voice is to let go of all those things that you know. A player can transcribe, memorize, and copy a whole lot of other people's ideas and play them back in solos forever, almost a kind of plagiarizing thing. But until that player lets all that go, nothing new or revolutionary will take place. I think there's a lot of self-conscious playing where people play safely knowing what notes and what approach will work.

In that regard, I don't hear a lot of trumpet players these days looking for their own voices. I hear a lot of people who are sticking to a formulated way of improvising and are following in the path of greats, kind of sampling and regurgitating what's already been done really well. It's a kind of historical preservation scene, I guess, but it isn't anything new or groundbreaking, just safe and economical.

WE: How do you defeat the self-consciousness you referred to?

IJ: There's a point when, if you practice—or live—in a way that balances your conscious with your unconscious development, then when it comes time to play live and you're in the moment, it's just like having a good conversation with friends. That's challenging, but it's the most rewarding because you're not thinking of everything ahead of time. You didn't plan everything before you left the house, so that when you hang out with your friends you're not going to say everything in a preconceived order. Music has a tendency to sound like that sometimes when people play safely. I worked to go against the grain of all that. I never practiced exactly in many of the ways my teachers told me. I took it all and I figured out what part of it was the best for me.

WE: So I take it you have worked to achieve a particular sound on the trumpet?

IJ: Yeah, anything that didn't sound like a typical trumpet. (*Laughs.*) I was trying to get as far away from the actual sound that the metal instrument makes when people blow through it, to a vocal sound. You know, it's metal, it barely moves; it's not like a saxophone with the reed vibrating all over the place. It's a little heavier than that.

WE: Please elaborate on your comment that you wanted to get closer to a vocal sound on the trumpet.

IJ: One of the beauties about the trumpet is that it's such an expressive instrument. The more control you get over it and the more control you get physically and mentally over your body, the more those emotions come through. I mean, Miles was a boxer not just because he loved to box, but because it *really* affected his playing. And Woody Shaw was a Tai Chi/Chi Quong master. I'm sure he experienced much deeper control over his music as he got deeper into his practice. Those things are very related to the voice and very related to the resonance and energy you get from within when you're in tune with not only the music, but with the physical, spiritual, emotional, and mental parts which really have to be taken care of and synched up. And I think, just as a small aside, that the demise of many people is that they don't take care of a huge part of the work that art is about. That's your self-respect. For me the development of self-respect is a lifelong project: from the food I choose to eat, to the amount of exercise I get, to how much time I spend on my music, to whom I choose to play with, and so on.

WE: Does music, for you, have powers that transcend entertainment, or even art? Could it be a healing force, for example?

IJ: Good question! Definitely, music can heal! One thing I was weaned on, because of my mother, was music as a form of meditation. My mother was raising three girls by herself with very little support and working a nine-to-five job teaching every day for quite a few years. What I believe kept her sane through a really horrible divorce was the piano. She could sit down at the end of the night, kids in bed, and she'd start playing. That was her form of meditation and healing. Then she could get up in the morning and be ready to deal with whatever crap might come her way. For me, I'm sure it's the same thing. Now, more than ever, I try to incorporate a meditational state when I'm practicing, because it really connects the instrument with my body. So that when I'm playing—and this is the major bonus of it all—I'll open my eyes and look at my fingers and hands and think, "Oh my God, who's doing this? Wow! Who would have thought!"

JS: Do you remember at what age you decided to become a jazz musician?

IJ: Oh, I still don't know if I want to become a jazz musician. (*Laughs.*) I never decided. Apparently, it was decided for me. That's what Hal Galper said to me once. I was going through my, you know, really insecure college years because I was the only female trumpet player at Berklee who was improvising. Nobody at Berklee had ever seen a woman play like that on trumpet. There were no role models on trumpet at all. I was the first female jazz trumpeter, at least as far as I know. And there were only a handful of other women instrumentalists who could play pentatonic, altered, outness kind of things, let alone swing through some changes. It was trippy because I felt a lot of people also weren't able to accept the fact that someone who didn't look like the normal jazz-trumpet person was playing all this fairly advanced stuff. I felt it the most from some of the black students, who probably weren't used to seeing a white girl playing a bunch of Freddie Hubbard licks.

Anyway, I went to see Hal Galper at a club in Boston one night, and I was, like, "You know, this school thing's freaking me out. I don't know about playing jazz. I think I should try and figure out what else I can do in life, 'cause I don't think I'm really cut out for this." He said, "Don't be talking to me about this bullshit; you have no choice but to do this. You have no choice at all." I was, like, "Oh, okay, you're right. Guess I better go practice then." (*Laughs.*) That was kind of a cool thing to say to someone who had no clue whether or not she should commit to being a jazz musician. I don't think there is even a commitment to be made to being a *jazz* musician. I mean, there's a commitment to doing what you love. And when you do it, things happen; good things happen. But being a jazz musician is more than just knowing all the language involved; it's a way of life and a really unorthodox type of mindset.

JS: Good things might have happened, but it sounds as if your early stay at Berklee had its rough edges.

IJ: That was a very heavy transitional time for me. I probably went through three phases. I came in from Nanaimo, B.C., which is Vancouver Island, which is the most *harmless* place you could ever choose to live. Full of wonderful people and a really supportive community. It didn't matter if a dog was playing bass trombone, as long as it was into it. (*Laughs.*) I mean, everyone played music. It's like, "Oh, we got old Fred Miller's dog on fourth trombone tonight in the big band. Is that okay? Oh, yeah! He's not very in tune, but it'll work." (*Laughter.*) It wasn't about what you looked like. If you showed *any* interest whatsoever in jazz, there were a whole bunch of people that would jump up and make you tapes and records and fill you in on what was goin' on.

JS: What big band in Nanaimo are you referring to?

IJ: It was the Nanaimo Musicians Association Big Band. NMA we called it, and I probably got more experience there than I did in all of my early school-band years. At the time, I probably took it totally for granted. Now I look back and I'm just, like, amazed that out of ten schools there was only one band director who could not play. They were all players; they were all gigging; they were all screaming musicians. They put together a band with all their friends and then the youngsters. So through that I gained a lot of valuable experience and never thought once about being a chick. Never once, because that wasn't the issue. The issue was whether or not I was working on the trumpet and checking out music.

So being at Berklee was a huge shock to my system because, first of all, I'd never been *really* in that level of competition. I never understood a music school would have to have, you know, good, medium, and bad. I thought everyone was just there to learn. I was very naïve, and the first phase I went through was culture shock. The second phase was that I felt like I had to prove that I could play. I already knew I could play, but I forgot that because I was so busy trying to show people that I could play as good as them. In a way, it was the first time the competition factor crept into my playing. I felt like a lot of guys were getting more opportunities to play in challenging ensembles and getting more solo features than me, and only because they were in "the club" girls weren't allowed to join. A lot of times teachers would give the guys all the solos and not even give me a chance to try. It was frustrating, for sure, but I realize now that it was no different than the real world—a world where people that I know I play just as well as get all the opportunities to do great gigs and get experience I could really use. Meanwhile, I'm stuck in a rehearsal band or some crummy gig situation. So there was a combination of that proving attitude and a little bit of bitterness, and probably some frustration and anger that started to form in my mind, thanks to a lot of my Boston experience.

WE: You said that when you were playing in the NMA, it didn't matter what you looked like. Were there other women players sitting alongside you and Fred Miller's dog?

IJ: Well, that's a good point, because, you know, Diana Krall was one of our biggest inspirations. She was a piano player and not singing at all back then. She was probably the first woman live I saw really hitting and playing with a trio. I said, "Wow, that's really cool, I could do that." The thing that was very unique is that most of the bands *I* played with when I was growing up were all-female bands. All of the bands and combos I was in from grade eight through grade ten, we would go to these national finals and *kick butt.* We'd get all these medals and wipe everybody out. These guys would come from schools with 2,000 people—we had about 250 people in our school—and they'd be like, "I don't get it. These little girls from Cedar-by-the-Sea, and we're from, you know, like a city!"

JS: You discussed two phases of your development at Berklee. What about the third phase?

IJ: The third phase was after the Berklee experience. I just wanted to get out, but I didn't want to go home. So when I graduated I got on a plane and went to Copenhagen, Denmark, because I'd fallen in love with Thad Jones through listening to his music. I had this dream in my mind that I would hang out with Thad Jones. But he died a year before I graduated. I still felt this kind of need to go to Europe, though, since I had family there, and I'd been there when I was a kid and had always wanted to go back. So, I said, "Bye, parents," and flew over to Denmark and stayed there for a couple of months. *That* was a place where I finally settled back down into what I originally had fallen in love with in the music, which was to get out and play and communicate and have fun. I took boxes and boxes of tapes and transcribed them all. Learned tunes and really spent a lot of time just thinking about music. I kind of got my head back in shape again.

JS: So the European trip was a time when you rediscovered your roots and developed a refreshed excitement for the music?

IJ: Well, that was the beginning. After that were the dark journey years—the Darth Vader days. I moved back to New York about four months later because I had a boyfriend in New York. At least I thought I did. I got off the plane and I *didn't* have a boyfriend in New York. So, that was a nice way to be welcomed into the City, staying in somebody's apartment who didn't really want me there. And having no money and just kind of not knowing what I was doing, except that I wanted to study trumpet and be around the New York scene. So I got a job in a hotel, the Waldorf Astoria, doing audio-visual technical servicing. I schlepped around carts full of VCRs and TVs for doctors' meetings and recorded the most fascinating conventions you ever could imagine. (*Laughter.*) It was probably the most challenging time of my life because I wasn't able to play music every day. I was only able to practice, like, an hour a day. I was up at 6:30 in the morning, on the train with the nine-to-fivers, going (*screams*) "AAAAH! How did I get here?" (*Laughs.*) I eventually had to quit my job because the visa I was on expired. When I quit the job, I just really was beyond convinced that the only thing I could do in life was music because without it I was a *total* wreck. I was completely miserable and dark and cynical and couldn't laugh. I really understood that hell for me is a life without playing music.

So I joined a band called the Jazz Rainbow Coalition, which included a former heroin addict, an African-American drummer, a Jewish piano player, a Japanese bass player, and a Canadian trumpet player—me. We played gigs in the subway. We had this little sign, "Jazz Under New York." We'd go home with eleven dollars or fourteen dollars and on a good day thirty-five dollars. We really cleaned up sometimes. But I started playing again. I took trumpet lessons with Laurie Frink, who teaches the Carmine Caruso method. Laurie really helped me, because up until then I felt like if I couldn't get the trumpet together, then I had to figure out another way to play music. It was continually messing me up because I'd want to play something I could hear, but I couldn't because I didn't know how to play the trumpet. It was frustrating me beyond belief.

JS: How old were you at this point?

IJ: Twenty-six. I feel I really didn't start practicing until I was twenty-six.

JS: Didn't you practice at Berklee?

IJ: At Berklee I kind of practiced, but I didn't know how to play the trumpet. That was the problem. There were great music teachers at Berklee, but there weren't great trumpet teachers. I was very limited on my instrument. So Laurie Frink helped me to really figure out how to play the trumpet.

JS: Did your frustrations diminish in proportion to your improvement on the trumpet?

IJ: At that time the Gulf War was going on, and being a Canadian without a visa and not being able to get a job and having to play with all-woman club-date bands and wearing push-up bras and high-heeled shoes and short skirts was really a drag. It really sucked, and it really was a horrible way to make a living, but it paid the rent. A lot of club dates where you don't get fed and come home at three A.M. and wonder, "Why do I play music?"

JS: Did you also have some good playing experiences, or make important contacts, during your dues-paying years?

IJ: Well, besides the club dates that I didn't necessarily want to do and the day job, I got pretty involved in the all-women band scene. It's almost like New York causes people to create their own networks so certain groups can support one another's survival. A lot of the women I've met over the years are living proof of this survival instinct; they look out for one another and create work that helps keep them in demand. DIVA and the Kit McClure Band were two I played in which did some pretty "show biz"–oriented music in order to stay in business. It paid my rent, for sure, and I learned a lot from some of the great players in the bands, but the artistic element was almost nonexistent. I was usually left feeling pretty bummed out after my usual two solos a night on a few up-tempo choruses on "Caravan." Fortunately, I got offered a gig in Austria at that time, which bailed me out completely because it was a tour and it paid a couple thousand dollars.

JS: What was the name of the group that you toured with in Europe?

IJ: The Vienna Art Orchestra. It was a project called "Fe and Males." Of course, I had a little crush on this trombone player, so that worked to my advantage. He was teaching at a conservatory in Linz, Austria. I stayed a few days after the tour, and one day I went and hung out with him. On a whim, I ended up doing a partial audition for a job there. And the director of the conservatory said, "You know, we really want to hire a new trumpet professor, so we're going to fly you back in a couple of weeks to audition in front of the panel." They offered me a thousand bucks just to do the audition. I was, like, "Cool, I'll take it." The flights were cheap—with the Gulf War nobody wanted to fly—so I got a flight for 250 bucks and flew to Austria. I didn't even *consider* that I'd get the job.

I did the audition, and the day I was leaving to come back to New York, they called me up and said, "You got the job." I was like, "Really! I'm twenty-six years old and I'm going to be a professor in a conservatory? Wow!" I didn't really decide right away to do it, because it just didn't occur to me that it would be a good idea. I went back to New York, and my roommates in the East Village said, "You are *nuts* if you don't take this opportunity." They were completely right. I ended up moving to Austria for two and a half years and taught in the school and played all over Europe with different types of bands, from avant-garde free to funk and a lot of jazz. That time was really important for me, and I got a lot of recording experience in Europe.[2]

JS: As I understand it, you made a guest appearance in Munich with an act called the Golden Men of Jazz,[3] which indirectly led to your signing with the Enja label. Detail that episode for us.

IJ: Alex, the road manager of the Golden Men of Jazz, really liked me, and so he wanted to help me out. He made a bunch of tapes and sent them to all these record labels, but I don't think he put whether or not I was a woman on it. I think he just wrote that I was a new, emerging trumpet player on the scene. The only one who really responded was Matthias Winckelmann of Enja. He said, "Well, this is really good. I'd like to hear some more of this guy's playing." Then Alex said, "Actually, you know, she's a woman. I thought that might be interesting." And Matthias said, "That's very interesting." Because obviously, that's going to work for publicity purposes.

JS: You now have three recordings[4] under your leadership. Were you in complete control at each of those sessions?

IJ: Yeah, I was. That's the great thing about being on Enja. Matthias Winckelmann really lets his artists decide what they want to do. He doesn't force anybody to do anything. He just gave me the budget and the studio. We talked about musicians a little bit, but for the most part I put the date together and gathered the tunes. The last CD to me is the most satisfying, because the first two were such a new experience, and I was still shedding that old baggage of "I have to prove I can play."

WE: In view of your reservations about the first two recordings, do you think that nowadays young players are being recorded prematurely to feed the appetite of the market-place?

IJ: No, I think that the experience we get as young developing players is crucial to our development. It's the ultimate proving ground to go into the studio and then hear back what you sound like. For me it was a gift. It resulted in more personal and musical growth than any school could ever give me. Before I made it I thought, "Man, I'm probably not going to record until I'm thirty." And there I was in the studio, twenty-seven years old, still feeling like I was *way* too inexperienced and *way* too young, and I was only getting the opportunity 'cause I'm a girl. It was pretty weak thinking on my part. Even though I couldn't listen to it for months, it's *such* a beautiful documentation of where I was in my life at that time. On one hand, I probably should have been working for another ten years and writing and paying dues. But on the other hand, I got an opportunity to document my work, and the topper of it all is that a whole bunch of people *love* it. (*Laughs.*) It won a Juno[5] award, which is that phallic piece of plastic up there (*points to a statuette*).

Of course, record companies do put out records by twelve-year-olds that play a great piano, but where are they now? I'm *so* glad that I never took any of the opportunities that I was approached with when I was younger, because many people wanted to produce me and do a pop record. You know, dress me up, make me look nice with makeup and stuff. I could've done it but there was something deep in my gut saying, "No, don't, you'll screw it all up. Just keep playing and learning and practicing and discovering things about life that you love."

WE: Do you ever wonder whether, if you had recorded when you were younger, you would have been a teenage sensation with an MTV-like mass audience?

IJ: I guess I'm not totally concerned about winning over the mass audience. That's clear by the choice of material that I'm playing. I'm concerned about showing off all the facets of my personality in relationship to the musicians I choose to work with. The marketing thing, I think, is really secondary, because I have faith in the audiences that when they actually hear a cut on the radio, they'll create their own image in their mind of what the music is about. The whole MTV glam generation is fine. There's an audience for that, but I'm not honestly interested in that audience because I don't think that they're the deep ones who truly can appreciate what's going on. Maybe I'm underestimating their listening abilities, but for me, one of the most disappointing performance scenarios is when I play badly and people still say, "Oh, that was great. You look so good. Oh, it was so great to see a woman play." That's when I have to try hard not to get too dark, because then I know that people aren't listening. The most rewarding scenario is when people walk away with the feeling of a message that came across. When there was all this interplay and communication, and I played who I was and they don't really care about what it looked like. There are not comments about it being cool or not cool.

JS: Let's talk about more recent events in your life. Since you've moved to New York, how much time do you get to spend in a day practicing your craft without interruption?

IJ: Without interruptions? Ha, ha! Well, that's why I moved to this Brooklyn space on my own about seven months ago from a loft in Chelsea where I lived with three other musicians. Unfortunately, when you're going through the dues phase you can't have everything you want. I was definitely going through the dues phase my first five years of living in New York. So only recently have I found what I call my ideal space, where I have pretty well free rein on my time.

WE: What for you is an ideal day?

IJ: An *ideal* day would start with my morning tea, followed by some Chi Quong, a form of Chinese movement that I learned from my acupuncturist. Or I do some yoga. I write in a journal in the morning to clear my brain of whatever thoughts and strange things might be going on. Sometimes I'll be studying books. I'm reading Erich Fromm right now. I'll read a chapter and write my thoughts on it. *Then* I usually go to the piano and start playing anything that comes to mind, and record it. Just spontaneously composing. Or maybe I'll pick up the trumpet and do the same thing, without really thinking about anything at all, like, "Oh, I want to write a straight-eighth tune" or "I want to write a 3/4 ballad." I just play freely.

The biggest reason I moved here, and invested in a more expensive lifestyle, was to really concentrate on getting my voice on paper, because that's an area of my life which doesn't come as easily for me as it does for some people. Then there's the trumpet. It is my good excuse for not composing, because the trumpet is *so* demanding to play consistently well. Especially if there's not a lot of gigs going on and I'm not traveling a lot. At a time like that, I'll spend a couple of hours doing a physical routine starting from basically long tones, then expanding the long tone into harmonic studies, melodic studies, rhythmic studies, and articulation. Then I'll take a break and do some business, the part of the day which is most frustrating because you think it'll take an hour and it takes three. I have to take care of details like hiring bands and getting the music together.

WE: Do you have any time to get around to clubs and check out other musicians' gigs?

IJ: Oh, I definitely do that, but not as much as I used to. When I first lived in New York, I used to go out a lot. Then I went through a phase where I found myself being pretty disappointed with a lot of the music I was hearing. Maybe I got spoiled? I would go on tour with lesser-known musicians that would come together as a band and really make a statement. Then I'd come back and hear a band that had been at a club for a week, and they sounded tired. They didn't sound like they were there for the right reasons. It became a little frustrating and a little disillusioning. I'm not saying everything sucked that I went out to hear, but there was a period where every time I'd go out it was, like, wow! This could be so good, but there are all of these disappointing elements.

WE: Were any of your idols knocked off their pedestals?

IJ: Or allowing themselves to be knocked off by hiring the wrong people? I don't even want to go there. Now when I go out, I choose to hear music that, even if it's going to be bad, will have someone in there that I hope will touch me. And I'm usually not disappointed. I went out the other night and heard a band, and Lew Soloff was playing. I hadn't heard him in a long time, and his chops were down. He'd been playing a lot and he had a big blister. But everything he played was golden. It reminded me of hearing Dizzy when he was really old—not that Lew is old! (*Laughs.*) The last time I heard Diz, in Vienna, he had a lot less endurance, less mastery over his high chops, but it didn't matter because *what* he played he played with such total mind, body, and soul conviction that I just loved it. His playing was as great as always, but not as flashy. You know, "Message came across; thank you, Diz." Maybe now that I'm a bit older, I'm more open to hearing what is happening in the "gray" areas of music, as opposed to the slick, rangy, impressive stuff that I see a lot of kids getting off on when I am adjudicating at jazz festivals.

WE: I'd like to explore your thoughts about music in more detail. Earlier you said that you're not so concerned about being a jazz player. With that in mind, can you conceive that in the future you might forgo improvisation and swing?

IJ: Well, in so many ways, my roots are actually as down home as anyone from New Orleans. I mean, swing is in my blood. I remember a day when a friend of mine—he played the alto, tenor, and piano equally well and was just burning—he said, "Oh, but you know what they say, 'white people can't swing.' " I'm, like, "Well, that's your problem, because I'm a white woman and I *can* swing." In fact, one of the main reasons I never pursued the classical route was because every time I took a lesson, the trumpet teacher would spend the whole hour trying to get me to play my eighth notes straight, which I couldn't do, and we would both end up totally frustrated! When I play along with a record, I know I'm not outside of what jazz is. That whole thing—that you can tell the difference between a white person swinging and a black person—I never bought that for a second. I guess it didn't hurt either that a lot of my early idols and teachers were people coming from all over the planet with all kinds of influences. White, Indian, black, Asian, the list goes on, and it would never occur to me that you had to look a certain way to sell your music, until I was confronted by the marketing of it all. Like Bobby Shew said after he heard me playing while he was backstage at a band festival, "Damn girl, I thought you were an old black guy playin' like that up there. What a surprise to see a young white chick!" I blushed and took it as a real compliment at the time, being fourteen years old and all that. I don't know if that answers your question.

WE: You've answered half of it. The other half of my question concerned the premium you place on improvisation.

IJ: Improvised music was an extension of my childhood environment. It was the way I was brought up. Playing music and communing with nature. Communing with nature may not have much to do with jazz, but the fact that my sisters and I were constantly being sent outside to create our own games rather than drain our brains sitting in front of the TV had a profound effect on the way we perceived life. The natural environment I grew up in was unbelievable. It was on an island on the ocean. I was playing street hockey with the guys and climbing trees as a kid. I had a horse as well. I would fill my pockets with tapes and slap on a Walkman and ride. If I wasn't listening to music on my Walkman, I'd be inspired by the birds and the sounds I'd hear from the ocean as well as the incredible visual atmosphere of it all. Being a country girl was a big part of the imagery that I get to carry in my mind through my life. Not just stealing licks from the warbling brook or the chatty birds (*laughs*), but the real inner peace of the environment and its effect on me. In a way, it was almost an upbringing in meditation that I now am so thankful for.

JS: Are you pleased to be called a jazz musician? Or is that term immaterial to you?

IJ: It doesn't mean much to me anymore, because jazz has become such a *huge* umbrella. Jazz could be a German Dixie band. It could be Maria Schneider, but it's not. Wynton Marsalis has a good definition of jazz, but I don't agree with it. Maybe it's a word that should be given a break, given a vacation. But it's hard to come up with anything else to describe it. I like to say improvised music with groove elements based on a jazz/blues tradition. Because all folk music and world music has also got the elements of jazz. It's really an exciting world when you think about it, but at the same time it's very overwhelming to try and put it into one package. And that's something I want to avoid as much as anything.

WE: You just made two provocative statements that beg questions. First, what did you mean by saying that jazz could be Maria Schneider, but it's not?

IJ: Well, Maria Schneider is a brilliant composer and arranger who is able to step into an event, absorb all that is taking place, document it according to her own perception, and leave the audience with a feeling of that moment. She even takes this process one step further and gives space to her soloists to add more layers to that story she has set up. It's an amazing thing when you think about it, but is it jazz? It seems to me that "jazz" in its truest description was a reflection of a time period that America experienced at a point in its history. It was a style of music that reflected what was going on in certain people's lives, and they expressed it in a certain way, with music, fashion, and language.

WE: Second, elaborate on the point that Wynton Marsalis has a good definition of jazz but it's not one that you agree with.

IJ: I guess I should eat a bit of that statement, since I can't quote him directly on his definition of jazz, but I will elaborate on some of the impressions I get from him. I think he is more about the image of jazz and preserving the historical side of it than actually doing something new or in the moment. I have no problem with historians except when they wield so much power that the real art of the day gets covered up or doesn't receive the attention it deserves. For there to be a balance in all of this, I think we need leaders who care about the world on a larger scale and see things beyond their own limited views.

WE: Is all the ink Marsalis and this issue are getting relevant to the jazz community?

IJ: It's a drag. I'm not gonna say it's not relevant or it's not real. Obviously there are a lot of musicians who I wish I could have played with, but I'm not willing to schmooze into that scene because I know the price I would have to pay.

WE: What do you mean by "schmooze into that scene"?

IJ: To hang out at the clubs, kind of be cool with the guys and play whatever games just so you can get closer to Mr. X, who you've always wanted to play with. To me, it's not really why I moved to New York or why I got into music. I think certain musicians don't get the experience and the mentorship that they deserve *because* of the politics. That's something that I maybe have argued with other people about, but it's a pretty tough argument for them to win. Because as a white woman, there are many gigs that I would never, ever even be called to audition for.

WE: Gigs that a white male would be called for?

IJ: I think a white male would have a better chance because, you know, it's the male bonding thing. They have a friend who knows a friend. I guess that's anywhere in life. People like to be with people who are the same because it gives them confidence. If they're not so secure with who they are, then they can have their club. And there's clubs on both sides. You see all these all-white big bands. They're great. They're killing! They're wonderful musicians, but I wonder why is there not a black musician in there? Why is it so unbalanced? I honestly don't know. I'm open to playing with anybody.

WE: The imbalance puzzles me, too. From the standpoint of a bandleader, why wouldn't it just be good business to mix things up? If a woman can play and contribute to a band, and if her uniqueness will draw an audience, doesn't it make sense to hire her?

IJ: You mean like a freak show? I think that's why all-women bands come together, because they want to put all these great players together and capitalize on the image. But in the end it doesn't sound like a band to me.

WE: I didn't have a "freak show" in mind when I asked the question. Can you explain why you used that terminology?

IJ: I use the term "freak show" loosely, in reference to a couple of gigs I've done. One image this phrase stirs up is when a band's selling point is not based entirely on the music. In fact, the music becomes secondary, and the image is the "hook." Some of the all-women projects I've been involved with fall into this category. They are bands in theory, but the main focus is not geared toward featuring and supporting individual voices as much as it is to prove to the audience that women can play, too.

WE: On this subject of diversity, and at the risk of sounding naïve, aren't jazz musicians eager to have different voices in their bands to shake up patterns that have become habits?

IJ: (*Laughs mockingly.*) One would hope! One would definitely hope. But unfortunately, in my own experience, a lot of men are *extremely* threatened by me when they hear me play. I'm sorry that it brings out a negative quality. But I've been told by other musicians whom I really respect that I just have to follow my voice, and be aware that some men are extremely insecure and extremely unable to give it up. The negative experiences *I've* had in my life—and I don't mind if it goes on record—are when musicians of *both* colors, but unfortunately more black, will refuse to acknowledge my presence because it is such an unnatural thing for them to accept in their world. So I'll play and it'll be strong, and the audience will go nuts, and I won't get as much as an eye contact, let alone "Hey, yeah, that was cool" or "Great to hear you." Unfortunately, there is something that is really unhealthy in the whole industry in that sense.

JS: Do you think that the form of the music we call jazz will change as more women get their voices into its mainstream?

IJ: Hal Galper said something that was interesting. We were talking at the bar at Sweet Basil's once and somebody said, "So, Hal, you know, jazz has pretty well gone as far as it can go, right? I mean, what's left to change? We've had the free stuff, we've had the funk." Hal looked at me and he goes, "I guess the only thing left to change is women. More women." (*Laughter.*) I was like, "Really? That's cool!" 'Cause I kind of feel the same way. I think it's definitely a given if you would talk to some of the guys who have been under my leadership or who I've worked with in Maria's band. They would all say that there's a unique element that is new to the music, that it's a nice change and is adding another color.

JS: Do you get much feedback on your playing?

IJ: When I started playing, and I first was getting the exposure I'd been waiting so long for, I had musicians in the band and in the audience give me feedback like "It's very sexy." Not sexy in a dirty way, but sexy in a way that it makes sense because there's this energy going on. I think one of the things that I've found over the years is that I love men. I flirt with men. I love the energy that I get from them. I've always played mostly with men, except for the DIVA experience, and some all-women things which were usually not that satisfying in comparison, mostly because the chemistry is never really right. If you want a band to be really great, you have to cast people into it based on their chemistry as well as their playing ability. As far as the whole feminine side of being a player goes, I think for a long time I was quite deluded by the fact that my idols were black men. Most people who I thought played the trumpet were black men, and so I thought that I looked as cool as they did in pictures. Then I got pictures of me playing from some concerts and I freaked out. It was, like, "That's disgusting."

JS: What didn't you like?

IJ: Oh, I just thought I looked absolutely horrible. My face was all swollen up, everything was puffy, and I was all serious. Now I look back on those pictures and I think they're absolutely beautiful because I'm just playing music. I think the way girls are brought up in general is way too focused on a certain image; we have all the Barbies, we have all the magazines, this is how you're supposed to look. It's a pretty freaky thing to start playing and not care about how you look—to just close your eyes and get into the music. So I went through a long period of definitely being one of the *guys.* I was proud to be one of the guys because I was playing as good as them anyway, so it was a little like membership into the exclusive club of greatness. That's fun. You know, you're a kid, you're growing up.

I think there came a point, though, when I recognized there was a larger world out there. I remember a guy—I think he was either Turkish or French—he came up to me after I had done a concert at Berklee and he said, "Do you have any idea how sexy you look when you play?" I thought he was hitting on me. It turned out that wasn't at all where he was coming from. It took me a minute for his message to sink in, but it was basically that he thought that my music was sexy and beautiful, and his compliment was meant to go much deeper than what I was perceiving from the outside. In my mind I didn't want to be sexy as much as I wanted to be cool, like Freddie or Miles. Thanks to this guy's enlightened European upbringing, he didn't see me so much as an odd-looking "jazz trumpeter." He saw and heard me on a much deeper level than anyone had ever said to me up until that point. Again, this is where having no real role model made things pretty difficult and confusing at times. I was pretty hung up on my male role models and in my mind was convinced that I looked like them when I was playing. The way this man explained how I was coming across made me reevaluate what it was I was doing.

JS: It's interesting that you remember so vividly when you shed your subconscious dependency on role models.

IJ: Well, that's a whole other area, too—talking about the unconscious or the subconscious coming into play—since I'm a dominantly left-handed person, and a trumpet is designed to be played with your right hand. A lot of the movements that I make, and a lot of pictures where I'm all gimped up, those are completely unconscious things because my body's actually reacting to the creative energy that wants to come out of my left hand; it wants to be involved. So, when I talk about doing yoga and Chi Quong and meditating, those have a direct relationship on me overcoming that movement. Because ideally one should be completely focused and centered, and playing straight through the horn is the most logical because you're not changing anything—any of your settings, any of the muscles, or causing any interference between the ears and the sound and the music. So, it's really been a challenge for me to get all of the facility together in my right hand and to develop that part of my brain which was not planning on being developed. (*Laughs.*)

[Our first music selection was "Rahsaan's Run," from *Woody Shaw/Rosewood,* 1978; Columbia Records.]

IJ: (*During Shaw's solo*) Wow! Yeah, Woody. Angular perfection. [Music stops.]

JS: Can you explain what you meant by "angular perfection"?

IJ: I mean, he just is so incredible as far as what the melodies are that underlie his way of approaching the changes. A lot of people say, "Oh, it's all pentatonics," which is in reference to a five-note scale that gives the improviser a chance to develop ideas based on the interval of the fourth. But it's much deeper than that, because it's all based on inner harmonies. He's playing off of all that. Instead of producing flowing lines or little melodies and stuff, it creates a much more kind of hexagonic vibe, with oddly shaped motifs and quirky leaps and turns in his lines that all make perfect sense compositionally. Yeah, he's a master.

WE: When I heard Shaw for the first time I was impressed by the conversational nature of his playing. Is that a quality that is important to you?

IJ: Totally. Totally. Absolutely. My mission in life is to make it all relate, and to make sure that everything I'm playing is something that comes from deep inside, and there's not a lick or a pattern that I practiced. I find myself completely disappointed when I have to rely on things that I know. That's why music is so exciting—I can get into the inside structures, which are everything. Inside structures are the rhythm that happens from the time-feeling of the tune; they can also be the harmony and the extensions off the harmony, depending on how deep you're willing to go. And for me, that's usually more than a blues scale. What I practice is *so* thorough, yet at the same time I feel like I'm only practicing my basics. It's really kind of a double-edged sword, because on one side I *am* practicing and hearing things on a whole other extended level, but at the same time I'm practicing and ingraining the basics, so that when I'm playing with people I have that strength to maintain the conversation. Yeah, that's a goal. That's a deep one.

[The final selection was "Interplanetary Travelers," from *Sonny Simmons/Staying on the Watch,* 1966; ESP-Disk, Barbara Donald on trumpet.]

IJ: Wow! That's incredible. I know I have a sampler that has, like, one tune of her playing. I think it's something along these lines. I mean, what a *sound*! Gosh! Fat! That sound would scare Freddie. Talk about someone's voice coming through. A very, very advanced mentality. Her playing is very through-composed and very meaningful. Very passionate and done with absolute conviction. There's no show biz in any of this stuff. Screw show biz; and I kind of feel the same way when I play. I'm not trying to please anybody anymore. I'm trying to get to the core of what the moment is. Are there recordings of her playing more straight ahead, just playing tunes?

WE: Yes, I believe there are a few later recordings that fit that description, but why do you ask?

IJ: Because I'd like to hear her play in a mellower setting. I mean, that recording is really intense, and everything I've heard from her is really intense. I can hear the femininity, I can hear the *angry* woman in there, but I'd like to also hear the other parts. I'm curious if the other parts were recorded.

WE: Are you in a position with your career where, if you were so moved, you could make a recording in the more free mode of the Simmons/Donald session we just heard?

IJ: That's a hard question because now I have a little pressure from management to follow along the lines of the music I've already recorded. But not a lot. I stay more independent so that I can choose what I want to do. If I decide I want to start playing funk or electric or commercial or free, I think I *could* do it, actually. There are some CDs of me playing some *really* free, freaky out stuff with some bands in Paris. There's a band called Machination.[6] In France, we did a live recording and a bunch of tours. It made me feel really good at the time, and was a healing thing in many ways after getting so caught up in the New York "survival" scene. Thankfully, I am now a lot freer in my career to say no to the type of gigs that are more work than play. It's a great feeling to be playing creative music for a living; I feel like a child in many ways. Like a kid with a huge box of Legos and a million possible plans to construct an entire universe. It's the coolest, from workshops and concerts with high school and college big bands, to playing at festivals or recording with my own groups or being a side girl with various leaders, or just hanging out in New York writing and playing sessions. It's all a blast, and it makes the grueling travel crap make sense.

Here on Earth. Enja ENJ-9313 (1997).
Higher Grounds. Enja ENJ-9353 (1999).
* *Project O, Now and Then.* Jig Records JIG3704 (2003). (Ingrid Jensen, leader, with Jon Wikan and Gary
Versace.)

Notes

1. Conceived by Art Farmer, it is a cross between a flugelhorn and a trumpet. Flumpets are now commercially available.

2. Recordings include *The Vienna Art Orchestra,* Fe and Males Production, Amadao/EMI; and *Wheelz Around the World;* ACT Records.

3. This package included Clark Terry, Al Grey, Harry "Sweets" Edison, and Lionel Hampton.

4. *Vernal Fields,* 1995; *Here on Earth,* 1997; *Higher Grounds,* 1999.

5. Canadian music award, similar to the Grammy. *Vernal Fields* won the Juno for "Best Mainstream Album" in 1995.

6. *Machination,* led by Héléne LaBarriére, 1994; Deux 2 (French label).

Sheila Jordan

Sheila Jordan

A singer's singer who is comfortable with risky flights of improvisation, Sheila Jordan is one of the most innovative vocalists in jazz history. Her signature child-like sound remains unmistakable in a recording career that encompasses five decades. Jordan's novel approach was shaped by her immersion in bebop, and especially by her close study of the modernist virtuoso Charlie "Yardbird" Parker.

Born in 1928, Jordan was raised by her grandparents in impoverished Pennsylvania coal-mining country. Singing in public at the age of three, as a youth she appeared in a variety of talent and radio shows to escape the hardships of home life. At fourteen she moved to Detroit, discovered the recordings of Parker, and had a close working rapport with some of the best jazz musicians Detroit had to offer. Singing in solo and trio contexts, she developed a local reputation before moving to New York in search of "Bird."

Settling in Greenwich Village, as part of the first crowd to live in newly available loft spaces, Jordan took work as a typist. With her warm, vivacious personality serving as a magnet, Jordan's cozy apartment was soon the scene of spirited all-night jam sessions. She became close friends with Parker (their bond is symbolized by a conspicuous street sign, Charlie Parker Place, affixed to a barn on her sylvan property in the Catskills), and in 1955 she married his pianist, Duke Jordan. Ironically, during this same period she studied with Lennie Tristano, who was forging an alternative to the Parker school.

In 1962, Jordan received critical praise for her unnerving rendition of "You Are My Sunshine" on George Russell's recording *The Outer View*.[1] Subsequently, Russell brought Jordan to the attention of Blue Note's Alfred Lion. Her recording debut as a leader, *Portrait of Sheila*, was widely acclaimed, and in the 1963 *Down Beat* Critics Poll she was ranked first among "Talent Deserving Wider Recognition" in the vocal category.[2] Despite this auspicious beginning, she made very few recordings between

1962 and 1975. As a single mother with a daughter to raise, Jordan is the quintessential example of a musician who takes day jobs to subsidize her art.

In the late '60s, Jordan's uncompromising experimental style precluded commercial success. She found modest performing opportunities within the sphere of free music, however, and this association with the avant-garde solidified her underground reputation. However, with *The Crossing,*[3] featuring a stellar supporting cast, her visibility moved beyond insider status and brought her to the cusp of a more consistent recording career. Also in demand as a sidewoman, Jordan has appeared on more than thirty recordings since 1979.

Sheila Jordan's vocal style is more properly compared to a horn player than to a singer. She scoops[4] in and out of phrases as a saxophonist might, and the variety of colors she can produce ranges from throaty, to pure and cool, to stratospheric. She is a pioneer of the bass/voice duo, and her authority as a soloist and penchant for dissonant note choice are highlighted in this transparent setting.

At this late stage of Jordan's career, her standing as a unique, influential, and richly nuanced jazz vocalist is unimpeachable. As confirmation, she was recently profiled in *Jazz Times* and *Coda* magazines, she received Detroit's Lifetime Achievement in Jazz Award in 1995, and, most notably, in 1997 she was honored as a "National Treasure" by the U.S. Congress.

Recorded June 21, 1996

JS: Sheila, do you call yourself a jazz singer?

SJ: Oh, yes!

JS: Can you elaborate on what that means?

SJ: It's taking freedom with the song. Knowing the song well enough, feeling it strongly enough, to be able to take liberties with it. Which a lot of singers in other types of music kind of shy away from. They usually stick to what's there and leave it at that. Me, I hear other ideas. I hear a song, I hear the way it's written, I learn everything about the song, and then I recompose it, so to speak.

WE: Is your conception prepared before you go onstage?

SJ: No. Everything is spur of the moment. I like to surprise myself. If I'm going to improvise, I want it to be a natural improv; I don't want to work it out or think about it. It's the spontaneity—that's what jazz singing is. I might set up head arrangements for songs. I might say I'd like to do this out of time and then go into time at the B section or the bridge. But I don't set it up. There are certain little things that I've been singing in songs that were never there in the beginning which I still might reflect back on. Maybe I'll improvise on that original improv, but I always treat a song as the first time I'm singing it. I keep it fresh, and when it becomes unfresh I don't do it for a while.

WE: When you're performing, are you always in the moment, or are you thinking several measures ahead?

SJ: No. No. It's right at the moment. The farthest I'm thinking is that chord change, and if I don't hear it, I hear it in my head. So when I hear it in my head, it's there regardless—

hopefully I'll hear it on the piano, but when I'm singing with bass and voice, I'm not hearing the changes. (*Laughs.*) We're talking about something totally different here, and that's something I've been doing since the early '50s. I would say I'm the pioneer of bass and voice.[5]

WE: Is the bass for you like the drum is for Anita O'Day?

SJ: Yes. I love the sound of the bass. I love the sound of the strings. I love the sound of the wood. I really identify with that sound. It's the freedom. It's the space. I like space when I sing. I don't like a lot going on underneath me. I like it really open and free. I don't like a lot of chords and fills. I don't like a lot of melody, and I don't like a lot of overplaying underneath me because that's what I do. If you're going to do all of that, then I don't need to do that. And then it's not me anymore, you know. I like to be played for like you would play for a horn player.

WE: So are you a jazz vocalist or a horn player?

SJ: (*Laughter.*) I don't know. I don't deliberately try to sound like a horn, and I don't deliberately try to be an instrumentalist. That's the way I hear the music. There have been certain critics who have said that I have no regard for lyrics. That's false, because I have *total* regard for lyrics. I think that reshaping lyrics, reshaping phrasing, is a whole different ballgame from scat singing, and that's what I try to teach. You can't just jump into scatting. You really have to know how to sing and phrase. This is a whole other language. We're talking about getting your own syllables, getting your own sound. You get your own sound through singing lyrics. People usually can tell me, because I don't sound like anybody else. That's because I didn't study singers while I was coming up. So I think that in order to scat, it's almost the way that you say a word; it's almost the syllable that you'll use. It becomes your way of phrasing. Your way of making a syllable sound the way it does. I have my own syllables that I use. They just happened. They were natural.

JS: I listened to your 1962 recording *Portrait of Sheila,*[6] on which you did basically no scat singing or improvisation. Then I heard your 1989 recording, *Lost and Found,*[7] where you do at least two numbers with significant improvised solos. Is that difference a result of your evolution or the result of directions they gave you back in 1962?

SJ: They never told me what to do in 1962, but strangely enough, if you know the original melodies on these tunes, you'll find that I improvise a lot on there. But if you're talking about improvising as far as . . .

JS: Taking a chorus.

SJ: No, I was not doing that then. I could do it, but I wasn't sure that it was what I wanted to do yet. When I started to sing this music, I didn't sing songs. I scatted. Because my guru was Charlie Parker. I was listening to his records and singing his solos, or trying to sing them. And singing everybody else's for that matter: drums, bass, whatever. I just copied whole records, that's how I learned.

So, yes, I was evolving. I think what happened was when I started to do jazz, I was so enthralled with Charlie Parker and the beboppers, that's the only thing I did. And then I just sort of let that go for a while and went back to the lyric, per se. Improvising lyrically with the song, like second choruses. Now I've just started taking more than one chorus and one and a half choruses. That's evolved since my first recording. Very clever you noticed that. Most people don't ever notice that. Maybe that's why they liked that record so much—I sang less. (*Laughs.*)

WE: Are you analytic about your performances?

SJ: I've never been able to sit down and analyze what I do or how I do it or why I do it. I do it because I feel it. The music is the most important thing in my life, except for my daughter. When she was first growing up, she came first. That's probably why I didn't work a lot when she was growing up. I don't know what I'd do if I couldn't do this music. It saved my life. I'm sure I would be dead right now if I didn't have this music.

WE: Has that always been the case?

SJ: Always! Always! I grew up poverty stricken. Very, very heavy alcoholism in my family. I grew up in a small coal-mining town in Pennsylvania, and most of the boys in my family were coal miners.

JS: How many in your family?

SJ: There were ten of us altogether, including me. My grandmother raised me, so the kids in the family were my aunts and uncles. But the fact that my mother was so young when she had me, and since my grandmother raised me, I considered them my brothers and sisters. When I was growing up, I guess there were seven of us at home. That was rough. My grandfather was a house painter, and he had the disease of alcoholism. My grandfather spent what he made on alcohol. Eventually all the boys had it. My mother died from it. Her liver was gone. So growing up at that time, in that kind of an environment when you are at the ridicule of everybody in the town, it was very, very difficult for me. And music brought me out of it. My pain was expressed in music.

WE: What were your sources for music? Were you glued to the radio?

SJ: We didn't always have lights in our house. If the bill wasn't paid, the lights were taken off. But when we had the lights, then we had a radio, and we had pretty good tunes in those days. As a young person, I did a lot of work for people in the town, cleaning, scrubbing floors. I made money, and I'd hitchhike to town on Saturday and see a movie. They were all Fred Astaire movies. That's where I got the music. They had these wonderful scores; I'd sit through them two times just to listen to the music and try to learn the songs.

WE: Did you like Astaire's singing?

SJ: Oh, I *loved* his singing! I think he's a great singer. He was my idol when I was a little tiny kid before I heard Bird.

WE: Why do jazz musicians respond well to Astaire? He didn't have a great voice.

SJ: No. It has nothing to do with voice. It has to do with the feeling, the intensity, the conviction, and the way he phrased. He really believed in what he sang. I think in jazz singing people can have beautiful voices and wonderful instruments, but they don't always touch you emotionally. Astaire touched me emotionally. I didn't know it as a little kid. I didn't know what it was about his singing that I liked. I just knew that he was a fabulous dancer, and the way he sang was an extension of his dancing to me.

JS: When did you get into jazz?

SJ: I moved to Detroit to live with my mother when I was fourteen. And that's where I really got into jazz. I was going to Cass Tech. They had a jukebox downstairs, and that's the first time I heard Charlie Parker. Charlie Parker and his Reboppers was on the jukebox. Very hip school, very hip records. Unbelievable. Prez, everybody was on the jukebox. But I heard Bird, and from that moment on I was hooked. I never knew what kind of music I wanted to sing growing up, and then I heard Bird and I said, "That's it! That's what I want to sing." I wanted to just devote my life to that music. I began trying to find out where can I find this music. And I happened to meet a wonderful young woman who was also going to Cass

Tech at the time, Jackie Berkhoff. She was into this music like I was, and we were the same age, so that was somebody for me to hang with. Between the two of us we found out where these places were, and we went and heard this music anyplace we could in Detroit.

WE: When you were about sixteen, didn't you and your friend stand in an alley behind a Detroit club to try and hear Charlie Parker?

SJ: That's because we couldn't get in the club. I forged my mother's birth certificate, dyed my hair, pancake makeup, I wore a hat with a veil and high-heeled shoes. I was smoking Lucky Strike cigarettes. I was gonna get in the door to hear Charlie Parker, and the guy said, "Go home and do your homework. What, are you kidding me? You want to get me in trouble?" We're talking about a city that had a lot of racism. We're not talking about me living in some Afro-American community down south somewhere or up north somewhere where there's less prejudice. We're talkin' about the hotbed of racism, Detroit, Michigan, and here's this kid dressed up looking like Halloween trying to get in to hear Charlie Parker.

JS: Was the problem that you were white or that you were too young?

SJ: *All* of the above! I was white, I was underage. And was I kidding? So we went around in the alley. We're sitting on garbage cans, and Bird opened up the door. He knew we were there. He saw these kids at the door trying to get in. Somebody opened up the back door; I'm not sure it was Bird. But somebody opened up the door and he played. He knew we were in the alley and that we couldn't hear him unless we sat out there in the alley with the door open. Luckily it was summer.

JS: When did you first sit in with Charlie Parker?

SJ: At the Club Sudan. I don't remember how old I was. You didn't have to be twenty-one. A lot of kids hung out there. That's where I met Tommy Flanagan and Barry Harris and Kenny Burrell. We were all around the same age, and we were just learning the music together. The Club Sudan was owned by this couple from Canada—a white couple from Windsor. They didn't sell alcohol there; they just sold soft drinks, "pop," as we called it. It was a place for kids to play and sing. The police ran the owners out of town eventually because they didn't want the mixing.

JS: How did you have the guts to approach Charlie Parker?

SJ: I didn't ask Charlie Parker. The kids and all the musicians said, "You should hear her sing." Me? I was so shy. Are you kidding? I was so shy and scared, it was unbelievable.

WE: Did Parker comment on your singing?

SJ: Yes. He always told me I had million-dollar ears. I could listen to a Charlie Parker record and know when they were playing "I Got Rhythm." I didn't know they were called rhythm changes at the time. It's very easy for me to remember and memorize. That's why it's hard for me technically to read music. I can hear it quicker than I can read it. I mean, I was supposed to sing. I don't know how I did it. It's amazing. It amazes me today.

WE: Did Parker back you up?

SJ: Sure. But I didn't work with him. He didn't give me jobs, call me up and say, "I want you to do this gig" or anything. That's a misquote. I usually don't like to say that I sat in with Bird, because immediately it's taken out of context, and then the next thing you know you're working with him, which is not true. But every time he saw me in a club, he asked me to get up and sing with him.

JS: Did the racial tensions in Detroit affect you personally?

SJ: I had a hard time when I was growing up, constantly being stopped on the street by the cops, constantly being asked where I was going, constantly asked what I was doing with these "niggers." It was very degrading. It got to the point where I told them that I was Afro-American.

JS: They believed you?

SJ: They had no choice. In their sick minds, they would say, "Well, what person would want to be black? You couldn't possibly want to be that." So it must be true, right? In their sick minds. I was very happy. (*Laughs.*) The people thought I was Afro-American, or at least part, because I *wanted* to be Afro-American. I wanted the freedom, and I wanted to be able to *relax* and be with the people I wanted to be with, and around the music I wanted. I didn't want to be hassled like I was some kind of a criminal. Nobody was doing anything wrong. But it was hard growing up there. I made a decision that I was going to go to New York for two reasons: to hear Charlie Parker—I knew he lived in New York—and I was tired of the racial prejudice. I knew that New York was a little bit more open and a little bit more cosmopolitan. The last time I got busted, I was with Frank Foster, and I wasn't a kid anymore. We were going out to Belle Isle and have a nice little picnic. I was going with Frank at the time, you know? Even to the point where I threw a cigarette out of the car and they picked it up and smelled it because they thought we were smoking dope. They took us down to the station and separated us. They asked me all kinds of unbelievable questions. You know what this plainclothesman said to me? He said, "You know, I have a nine-year-old daughter. If I caught my daughter the way I did you tonight, I'd take this gun and shoot her brains out." Now, isn't that a nice thing to say? I just looked at that guy and said to myself, "This guy is sick."

WE: Were you singing with your African-American friends?

SJ: Oh, yes. Whenever there were opportunities and sessions, I sat in and sang. I've been singing jazz since I was fifteen.

WE: Did you have any formal training?

SJ: I'd had no voice training whatsoever. What happened was, my great-aunt who was a piano teacher taught me piano a little bit when I was young. But she was rough. She used to beat you over your knuckles if you didn't place your hands on the right keys. Oh, that was real fun. That really makes a good piano player out of you!! You just want to get the hell out of there. If this is what learning music is about—they're going to beat you up—I mean, who needs it? But I stopped going to her, too, because she got in a fight with my grandfather. She was very upset that he drank the way he did. He had all these kids to support, and we were on welfare. That was, like, disgraceful. Once she stopped talking to my grandfather, the piano lessons stopped.

Then I started taking piano with a teacher in South Fork in the first year of high school, just before I moved to Detroit. He was the one who got me singing again. I was on the radio a lot as a young kid, in Johnstown and Altoona. But there for a while I stopped singing because the kids in my town made fun of the way I sang. I think they were probably jealous. But it's one thing to be made fun of because of your background and another thing to be made fun of because of something that saved your ass as a little kid. Kids can be very cruel. They don't mean to be, but they can be. So I just stopped singing from the time I was in about the seventh or eighth grade until my first year of high school. Professor Rushing was the one who encouraged me to sing again. He had some kind of an assembly, and I sang for it.

WE: I want to refer back to your desire to be African-American. Does that seem unusual, especially in view of your love for the Astaire-Rogers films, which were the epitome of white culture at that time?

SJ: Music was colorless to me.

WE: Was there a black community where you grew up in Pennsylvania?

SJ: No.

WE: So when you moved to Detroit . . .

SJ: That was my first encounter.

WE: I understand that you were seeking out people who were involved with the music you loved, but were there other things about black culture that attracted you?

SJ: I think I identified with that culture because of being put down a lot and being sort of ostracized in a small town like Summerhill, Pennsylvania. We were made fun of as kids because we didn't dress the way everybody else did; we didn't have what everybody else had, being one of the poorest families in the town. The word "half-breed" was thrown around a bit once in a while—my maternal grandfather was from Native American background, and, even though I did not know my father, my paternal grandfather was part Cherokee Indian. And my grandfather was one of the town drunks. So it was a combination of *all* of that. I felt that the only people that could know the suffering that I went through, that I could identify with, was the Afro-Americans, because I knew that they had been ridiculed and ostracized in the same kind of way. I wasn't as bad off: at least I was able to go in places and not be refused because I was Afro-American. But basically the taunting and the ridicule was the same. It doesn't matter whether they're calling you a nasty name because of your color, or whether they're calling you a nasty name because your mother is a drunk and a runaround. I mean, it's the same shit. Maybe that's why I generated my feelings and my friendships more toward Afro-American people, because I really felt that they understood what I was feeling. They knew the minute I started singing that there was something in my sound that must have come from a very painful existence as a younger person. They said, "Where did you get that soul? You must have really lived as a kid, and you must have been really pushed around a lot." I don't know whether that's how you get soul or feeling; I have never been able to figure it out.

JS: Do you think struggling against oppression is a factor?

SJ: Well, I think people who have been oppressed, whether they are white or Afro-American, when they finally get a chance to come out and be who they want to be and do what they want to do, regardless of all the obstacles that might stand in their way—it's the determination. I mean, you've really fought a battle to be able to overcome all that's happened. To be able to overcome all the obstacles that stand in your way and still come out, in my case, singing, is something. Because by all rights, from the time I was a baby up until now at sixty-seven years old, almost sixty-eight, with the obstacles in my way, it's *amazing* that I sing today. So, obviously, there's something much more important than myself looking out for me. I have to believe that. Because by all rights, I should not be singing. I was a full-blown alcoholic, which took about fifteen years out of my life.

JS: When was that?

SJ: I started drinking when I was in high school in Detroit because I was so distraught; I had so much pain in my life. I remember when I first met these two young guys, Skeeter Spight and Mitch [Leroy Mitchell], who I sang with in Detroit. I said, "Oh, I want to sing what you guys are singing." And they said, "If you want to sing, then you've gotta stop drinking." And I did stop for a while. I was going through my high school fling, you know.

I got into very heavy cocaine usage in the 1980s. But I wasn't an everyday drunk, and I wasn't an everyday cocaine user. I tried most all drugs except heroin. I didn't do it every day, but the thing is, when I did it I was unmanageable. I was out of control. That had a lot to do with the background, the growing up, the pain that I felt and not being able to express this pain. Maybe if I'd sung more at that time to express this pain, I wouldn't have drank as much.

JS: When did you stop drinking?

SJ: I stopped drinking in 1978, and I finally went for help in the beginning of 1986. The reason I went for help is that I started to use cocaine after I stopped drinking. Because I said, "Well, I'm not a drug addict, and you can't get addicted to cocaine." It was so new at that time. OH MY GOD! Did I find out quick.

So what happened to me is somewhere down the line I had what is called a spiritual awakening. I was told from a voice in my head, "If you don't stop drinking, if you don't stop destroying yourself, I'm taking this gift away from you." And that's what stopped me from destroying myself. Because I had a choice to make between the alcohol and the drugs, and the music. Was it more important to me to be passed out drunk half the time, or was it more important that I do the music?

JS: Let's talk about moving to New York. You just bravely picked up your roots?

SJ: Yes. Don't forget I'd been on my own since I was seventeen, so it didn't matter to me where I lived. But that's why I changed from Cass Tech to Commerce High.[8] I changed my studies into something that I knew I could make a living at so I could support this wonderful music. So when I came to New York in the early '50s, I immediately went to an agency that was hiring secretaries.

JS: Did you go to New York with a particular goal in mind?

SJ: I wanted to be closer to Bird. He was my teacher and I wanted to be where he played. Of course, a lot of times he didn't show up. But then we got friendly. He remembered me from Detroit, and eventually he used to come to my loft. I stayed in a furnished room for a while, and then I married Duke Jordan. I met him through Bird. I used to joke and tell people I married Duke Jordan just to be close to Charlie Parker. I was with Duke Jordan for seven years.

WE: Did you learn about music from Duke Jordan?

SJ: No. Duke was too messed up. He had his own problems. No, the person that taught me was Bird. He didn't sit me down and say this is how it goes and this is what you do. He taught me from listening to him, from buying his records and asking him a few questions. He spent many, many hours at my loft years later, and he talked to me at great length about music. Through Charlie Parker I learned more about music in four years than I ever thought possible in my life. He turned me on to everybody. Not only to the jazz people, but he turned me on to contemporary composers: he turned me on to Bela Bartók, he turned me on to Stravinsky. He brought records to my house. He never came on to me sexually. He never hit on me. He was like a scholar to me. Obviously, whatever our relationship was, my higher power put Bird in my life to show me the way.

JS: Considering all the racial problems you encountered in Detroit, was New York a welcome change?

SJ: This is an amazing story. I went through all of that racial tension in Detroit, Michigan, and I'm going to New York, where it's cosmopolitan and cool. I came to New York and I had a loft on Twenty-Sixth Street, and Charlie Parker and Monk and Sonny Rollins and everybody came up there to play. I had an old piano, and I had sessions up there, and it was before the in thing was to have loft sessions. Bird was *always* at my loft. He practically lived there. There were always very artistic people around. Allen Ginsberg came a few times, and I used to have painters up there.

One time I went out with two painters, when there was a session going on at my loft, to get some Chinese food. And the two painters happened to be Afro-American. We went, we got food. I hadn't been in New York that long yet. This had to be like 1953, before my daughter was born. I was studying with Lennie Tristano at the time. I'm walking back to my loft, and on the corner four white guys jumped out of a bar, grabbed the two painters, held them, grabbed me, threw me down on the street, kicked me, and knocked my eyetooth out, or loosened it—it was a cap. They were ready to bash my head in, kick me to death. I looked up, and I saw a guy walkin' across the street in a suit. He had a gun out. I said, "Well, this is it." Here I am, laying on a street in New York about two doors from my loft, and I know I'm gonna get killed. And there's a big session going on—probably Sonny Rollins is up there blowin', or Jackie McLean, and I'm down here getting killed." (*Laughs.*) That's all I could think of—I'm missing all this great music. The guy comes over, and he happens to be a plainclothesman; so there's a plainclothesman in Detroit who totally disrespected me and my beliefs, and here's a plainclothesman in New York who saved my life. He was off duty. He just happened to have his gun. He said, "Do you know these guys?" I said, "No, I don't know these guys. I never saw them in my life." So there you are. I mean, it wasn't my time to go.

WE: You said you were studying with Lennie Tristano at the time of the incident you just described.

SJ: Yeah. Lennie Tristano was the first free player I ever heard.

WE: What did he teach you?

SJ: He taught me to get out there and do what I have to do and be original at it.

WE: How do you teach somebody that?

SJ: Just by letting them get up and sing and express themselves. We had wonderful sessions at night. He went through a lot of things like theory; he taught me timing and harmony. When he first started to teach me, he wanted me to learn a Bird solo. I said, "I know that." He said, "Oh, yeah? Sing it." So I sang it and he said, "Oh, you do know it. Do you know a Prez solo?" I said, "No." He said, "Well, then, learn a Prez solo." But I think it was just giving me encouragement as a woman musician. He made me believe that I was not just a "chick" singer. He made me believe that I was a musician, and that I was an improviser, and that I should continue doing what I was doing. He showed me ways just by what he played, by letting me experience the feeling of improvising with other musicians— improvising with bass, which he knew I loved to do. He taught me how to respect myself and gain respect as a musician.

JS: As a white woman performer trying to break in by singing jazz like a horn, were you taken seriously?

SJ: No, they thought I was crazy. I wasn't your run-of-the-mill dress sexy and singin' songs that they could understand—what the hell is this woman doin'? I got fired from more gigs than I can even tell you trying to get out there to do the music, but I *always* found a place to sing. The musicians understood. I started singing in a club when I came to New York a couple a nights a week to keep the music alive. I was doing it for the emotional release. It was basically a gay club, the Page Three, in the Village. There were a lot of gay people coming in, and I wasn't hassled there. They let me sing the way I sang. A "New Note in Jazz" they called me. It was great. I was really workin' my butt off, though. By that time Duke Jordan left me, and I had this little girl to raise by myself. I was workin' there at night and a half a day in the office. Then I had to have some time with my kid, you know. It was a struggle for me financially and physically, but I got the strength somewhere because I really wanted to do the music.

WE: Were you building an audience at that time?

SJ: That waited until after the Blue Note recording. And I still didn't get that many gigs, and I didn't have a manager. The person who helped me very much in my life was George Russell. He came into the Page Three. The piano player at the time was studying with George, and George came down to hear him, and in so doing heard me among six other singers. He was very impressed. He said, "Where do you come from to sing like that?" And I told him I come from the coal mines in Pennsylvania. He said, "I would like to go back there to see what it's like." So he took me back and we went into this bar, including my grandmother, who loved to drink her beer. The miners were out of work at the time—there was a union strike, and then, by this time, heating by coal was sort of starting to die out. There was an old miner in there who said, "Do you still sing 'You Are My Sunshine'?" I said, "Nah, I don't sing that anymore." So George said, "Come on, let's play it and sing it." So George started to play it, and my Grandmother literally knocked him off the bench and said, "That's not the way you play that." George said she sounded like Thelonious Monk. So she played and I sang, and then we went home. He called me up about a month or so later and said, "I've got somethin' that I want you to hear. I'd like you to sing it." So that's how "Sunshine" came to be. It was a musical documentary dedicated to the coal miners of Pennsylvania.

WE: Were you prepared for Russell's arrangement?

SJ: No. When I heard it for the first time, it really shocked me. I said, "Whoa! What is that?" He said, "Well, start to sing it." I said, "By myself?" He said, "Well, didn't you sing by yourself when you were little?" I said, "Yeah." He said, "So why can't you do it again?" I understand it was quite a surprise when it came out because the jazz world had never heard that. I was singing totally alone, nothing but the naked voice, and then he brings in all these weird sounds, which were beautiful. That's what I mean about jazz; what other music could you express this through? The miners being out of work. The mines closing up. These people back on the welfare roll again.

WE: I want to change the subject to get your perspective on certain vocalists who have become pop icons. Let's start with Sinatra. In your mind, is he a jazz singer?

SJ: No. Not in my mind. Oh, I think he's a nice singer. I think he's a wonderful, warm singer with lots of feeling, but I've never been a big Sinatra fan.

WE: So you're not knocked out when he phrases a ballad?

SJ: Nah. (*Laughter.*) I'm sorry to say. I'm knocked out when Mark Murphy sings a ballad. I think he's a great jazz singer. Very underrated. I'm not putting Sinatra down. I think it's great that he's reached people, and he's maintained his integrity. He's done a lot for popular music, but I would never consider him a jazz singer. A guy that really to me is a jazz singer when he sings ballads is Joe Williams. I *love* Joe Williams. I don't know how many people are aware of how well Joe Williams can sing a ballad and swing just a straight-ahead swinging tune. I mean, I prefer Bob Dylan to Frank Sinatra.

WE: Why?

SJ: Because of the rawness. And what he's singin'. He's a helluva poet. And I love the way Sting sings. He moves me when he sings. I mean, I'm not saying he's a jazz singer, I just think he's a special singer.

WE: There are some pop singers who have tried more overtly to make a jazz crossover. For instance, Tony Bennett sang with Bill Evans.

SJ: Well, I never thought of Tony Bennett as a jazz singer, either.

WE: Are you saying this because neither Sinatra nor Bennett improvise?

SJ: Yeah, they're really safe. I'm not putting them down, but I don't know that I'd go and buy their records. But then again, I don't buy many singers' recordings; most of the singers' records I have were given to me. If I had money to buy a record when I was a kid, I never went and bought Sarah Vaughan or Ella records. I went and bought Bird records or Bud Powell or Thelonious Monk. That is the music that I heard first and foremost as opposed to singers. And that's weird, being a singer *myself*. I don't know whether it was something that I decided when I was very young—I don't want to listen to singers too much, because I don't want to get inspired to the point where I start rippin' them off trying to do their thing. I don't know, maybe subconsciously that's what I thought.

[We listened to "Get Happy," from *Ella Fitzgerald, The Harold Arlen Songbook, Volume 2,* Verve Records; recorded 1961.]

SJ: Ella's number one for me. Her scatting is unbelievable. I mean, I love her syllables; I love her sense of swing. And I never realized how much she knocked me out until I saw a video that she did in 1987 from—I think it was the Berlin Jazz Festival. It was just unbelievable the way she improvised on lyrics; the simplicity and the ease with which she sang this whole concert with Joe Pass on guitar.

WE: How do you think she managed to be so commercially successful at the same time? Was it the series of songbooks that had less jazz content?

SJ: But I think that got to your general audience. It seems that if an audience hears something that they can identify with, they'll go back or forward with that artist. After that artist has touched them. And Ella had the ability to touch the ordinary layman, much more than a lot of the other singers. Did Ella scat on that tune you just played?

WE: No.

SJ: That's what I like. See, she could just sing lyrics, improvising, not have to scat on everything. Although she could if she wanted to. And, getting back to that appeal, I think that was also very prominent in her acceptance by non-jazzers. In other words, sometimes non-jazzers are turned off by scat singing. Like if they hear too much scat singing, they don't understand, and they get uptight because they say "I'm supposed to know what this is about." They don't go by the feeling; okay, just feel the damn music, you don't have to know every chord change. Scat singing is a little bit more popular now, but in those days I think a general audience was a little afraid of scat singing. So I think Ella was very smart in the fact that she didn't scat sing on everything. She did it in another way where she sang lyrics and she still improvised on them, and I think that got to the public. The same as Billie.

Billie was an unbelievable improviser. Did you ever hear her scat? I had a record of her at a party, scatting, and I tell you she sounded damn good. Everybody was stoned, and they said, "Billie, go ahead and scat," and she did. It was unbelievable. But I just want to say how natural Billie Holiday improvised. She improvised so natural that until I went to the sheet music and knew how the song went, I didn't realize that a lot of that was improvisation. Just the way she'd inflect, just the way she'd turn a note around, or just the way she would phrase differently. Just a little melody change here and there without deliberately doing it. It was just her own natural way of singing. I never realized *what* an improviser this woman was until I learned the melody of the song and saw where that laid in response to what she sang. And that blew my mind. I have to say, emotionally, the singer that reached me the most was Billie, because she just says one word and it thrills you. Hearing her was like hearing Bird, you know.

[The second selection was "Droppin' Things," from *Betty Carter, Droppin' Things,* Verve Records; 1990.]

SJ: That was fantastic. Great band. Betty Carter has her own sense of who she is, what she does; she's never sacrificed. She waited until her turn came, until they finally discovered who Betty Carter was, and that was a long time. She never changed what she believed in. And I admire that. And she was such an individual sound—there are no influences at all from other singers. A lot of times she's way behind the beat and I'm just, like, holding my breath. But she always makes it, and it's just wonderful to hear that happen. The other thing I love about her is her choice of syllables. She's definitely got her own syllables goin'.

WE: It seems to me that I've read critics lament certain mannerisms that occasionally surface in Betty Carter's work. Do you do a self-check from time to time to detect self-conscious patterns?

SJ: I don't hear it in Betty Carter. I think I know immediately when I'm being mannered. I know I would know it, because it would be leaving that spontaneity. The minute I leave that, I know I'm getting into something that in the beginning was very different, and then I'm overkilling it. And that would not be an honest way for me to deliver a song.

WE: Isn't the temptation great, though, to turn a successful approach into a formula?

SJ: It's safety. It's getting somewhere and being safe. You want to be safe because you've got all these people who adore you, and God forbid that you should try something and it didn't work and they would be disappointed. Maybe that's why I try to keep what I do pure. If you loved me then and I'm going somewhere else—I'm gonna be taking other chances or I'm gonna feel other emotions—then you'll have to love that, too. I don't want to get to a point where I sing a song and everybody who has studied my records sings it along with me and it comes out the same way.

JS: What if the audience wants to hear in performance what you put on record?

SJ: Well, I don't care about an audience. I know they pay the way and they help make it happen, but I think my creativity has to come first. It goes back to that thing I said earlier. If you must keep that improv in, then improvise on that improv. Sometimes it's very hard to remember if you've repeated something, especially if you're treating it like the first time you've ever sung it. And especially if you're somebody like me who never listens to their records.

WE: You never listen to your records?

SJ: No. God, no. Why would I want to?

WE: You look like you just sucked on a lemon.

SJ: Yeah, I did. It's gone, it's over, it's past. I just don't want to hear myself. If I go to a party, hey, you're not doin' me a favor by playing me when I'm walkin' in, because you are ruining my evening. I know the feeling that I get when I am communicating with the rhythm section, and that's a greet feeling. But I don't want to hear that record. I have broadcasts I never listen to. I don't want to be discouraged. Because I know what I do; I'm sitting there and I say, "Oh, I could have done that there. Why didn't I hear that?" (*Laughs.*)

Oh, God! And then I'm, like, reinventing the whole song again. I heard *Portrait of Sheila*
once a few years ago.

JS: What was the occasion?

SJ: It came out on a CD. It was originally recorded on monaural, then they put it through stereo somehow. I just wanted to hear the sound quality. Then when I heard it I said, "Gee, you were beating yourself up all those thirty years, and it's not so bad."

WE: Considering your firsthand experience with the development of modern jazz, do you agree, as some pundits claim, that today's rap is an extension of bebop?

SJ: Well, it has a nice rhythm to it. I don't think it's as intricate or as musical as bop, but I think it's got its place. If somebody asked me to do hip-hop, if I liked the music, I'd do it. On the *Lost and Found* album, I did "The Water Is Wide," which is an old Scottish ballad. I mean, I do music if I feel it. So if something appeals to me—that's what I love about what Cassandra Wilson is doing. Strangely enough, one song that she did I'd been seriously thinking of doing. She did it and I said, "My God, then it's not me; I'm not crazy." That was the Hank Williams tune "I'm So Lonesome I Could Cry." I *love* that song. And I thought, why can't I sing that? So, it was great to hear that she did that song, because that means that music is music. But I have to like something. I'm very, very strong in what I will and will not sing. A lot of times I've heard songs and I've said, "Ah, I don't really like that song so well." Then, after I've heard them a few times, I've thought, "Hey, that's a nice tune; I think I really like that song." So I have to be able to be a little bit more open.

JS: Name a song you changed your mind about.

SJ: "The Caterpillar Song."[9] I said "Oh, well, that's okay," but it got to me. And doing Kuhn songs.

WE: How about "The Zoo"[10] from Steve Kuhn's *Playground* recording?

SJ: (*Sings*) "Send twenty dollars to me." I *love* to do "The Zoo." That's a great tune! (*Laughs.*) And I love to do "The Saga of Harrison Crabfeathers." Those are some weird lyrics, but I like that. They made sense to me. I have to picture in my mind: What are these lyrics about? What is this story about? It's whatever I want to make it. Some people used to think that "The Saga of Harrison Crabfeathers" was about a child who died at an early age. Actually, it was originally named after a piano player who was advertised in the back of a *Down Beat* magazine. Steve saw the name and liked it. He never knew the guy, but he was intrigued with his name. After the death of the great ballplayer Thurman Munson, Steve renamed the composition in memory of him. Fifteen was Thurman's number. The song became known as "Poem for #15."[11]

WE: One final question: When did you last see Charlie Parker?

SJ: The early part of '55. I was pregnant with my daughter. I went to Detroit to visit, and Bird happened to be playin' there at the Graystone Ballroom. He didn't know I was gonna be there. He was up there playing; he happened to look down and he saw me. He finished out the chorus and put his horn down. He came off the stage, took me in the back, and he said, "What are you doin' here?" I said "Well, I came to see my mother, and you just happened to be in town." He hugged me, and he was so glad to see me. We hung out. I think we had some food or something, and he was running around, trying to get some dope, I'm sure. The point was that when he saw me, he had such love in his eyes, such a joy at seeing me. It was the last I saw him. That was in January, and he died in March. March 12th. I went to the funeral and he looked very old. I was surprised because he was only thirty-four, but he looked so much older. My biggest thing in life was to be able to visit his grave one day. So I did, in about the early '80s, at the Kansas City Women's Jazz Festival. On the way to the airport they took me by Bird's grave, and I put the flowers that they gave me on his grave. That was the end, but I feel Bird's still around.

Selected Discography

Portrait of Sheila. Blue Note CDP 7 89002 2 (1962, reissued 1989).
Lost and Found. Muse Records MCD 5390 (1990).
**Heart Strings.* Muse MCD 5468 (1993). (Beautiful recording with rhythm section and string quartet.)
I've Grown Accustomed to the Bass. Highnote Records HCD 7042 (2000). (Duets with bassist Cameron Brown.)

Notes

1. 1962; Milestone Records.
2. Sheila Jordan won *Down Beat's* TDWR vocal category a record nine times.
3. 1984; Black Saint. (Features Tom Harrell, Kenny Barron, Harvie Swartz, and Ben Riley.)
4. "Scoop" is an instrumental musician's term for approaching a note from below its actual pitch.
5. In 1997, Ms. Jordan released *I've Grown Accustomed to the Bass,* recorded in duet with Cameron Brown on bass; Highnote Records.
6. Blue Note Records.
7. Muse Records.
8. Commerce High was adjacent to the Cass Tech campus.
9. Included as part of a medley on *Sheila Jordan, Heart Strings,* 1994; Muse Records.
10. "The Zoo" appears on *Playground* (The Steve Kuhn Band), 1979; ECM Records, and on *Sheila Jordan/Jazz Child,* 1997; High Note Records.
11. Also appears on *Playground.*

Diana Krall

Diana Krall

Canadian-born Diana Krall enjoys a superstar status attained by few jazz musicians. Trained as a jazz pianist, she added singing to her resume when the demand for dual performers became too lucrative to ignore. Her stunning good looks, record-breaking album sales, and fierce media attention have made Krall's performances among the hottest tickets on today's jazz and pop scenes.

Born in 1968 in Nanaimo, British Columbia, the young Krall was absorbed in vintage recordings and the classic comedy of bygone eras. A rich local music scene accelerated her growth as a pianist. After winning the Vancouver Jazz Festival Scholarship, she ventured east to Boston's Berklee College of Music to begin her formal education in jazz, but returned home a year and a half later.

Encouragement from bassist Ray Brown and financial support from a Canada Arts Council Grant allowed Krall to move to Los Angeles to study with pianist and occasional vocalist Jimmy Rowles. Ten years of learning her craft, with schooling from proven musical elders, preceded her "overnight success."

Although she released two distinguished trio recordings in the early 1990s, including her undervalued sophomore effort, *Only Trust Your Heart,*[1] Krall's commercial breakthrough came in 1996 with her tribute to Nat King Cole, *All for You.*[2] It spent seventy weeks on the Billboard Top Ten Traditional Jazz Charts and received a Grammy nomination. She recorded three more successful studio dates leading up to *Live in Paris* (2002),[3] which won the Grammy and Canadian Juno Awards for Best Jazz Vocal Album of the year.

With her aesthetic firmly positioned within the optimism of the swing-based mainstream, Krall attracts jazz fans across generations. Comping with a keenly developed sense of timing and harmonic variety, she can switch gears and unleash a finger-popping piano solo filled with spirited displays of fluid technique. Onstage, her manner is unpretentious, with a hint of cockiness that gives her persona an edge that coincides with the punchy rhythmic vamps she favors. Krall's vocal work contains an almost postfeminist air; indeed, her feminine seductiveness, coupled with a veneer of masculine toughness, is capable of evoking a powerful response. (When she is performing, her physiognomy, including the occasional snarl, might be described as Presley-like.)

Questions of image versus substance surface whenever a jazz figure is wildly popular, and Krall is no stranger to controversy of this sort. Commanding the type of media coverage usually reserved for rock music icons, she has compiled an impressive list of television, magazine, and even film music credits to date. Regardless, Diana Krall maintains that she is a jazz pianist first and foremost, who is committed to interpreting the treasury of the Great American Songbook.

Recorded May 5, 1999

WE: Diana, I'd like you to free-associate on a question that's philosophically important for our culture: "Why a duck?"[4]

DK: (*Chuckles.*) Viaduct? Are you talking about the Groucho Marx thing?

WE: Yes. The mischievousness I sense at times in your music and stage demeanor reminds me of the Marx Brothers.

DK: In eighth grade I used to dress up as Groucho Marx on Halloween. I think it puzzled the librarian. (*Laughter.*) I don't know if I want to print this; I don't care anymore—you don't work for the *Inquirer,* do you?

WE: I'm with the *Star.*

DK: I'm influenced by Jack Benny and by the Marx Brothers. Jack Benny for timing, for his use of silence, his self-deprecating humor. I think the ability to laugh at yourself is important; I find that a challenge. I always remember that episode with Fred McMurray, Tony Martin, and Kirk Douglas. They all came to his house for a band rehearsal. They ask him, "Can I have a soda, Jack?" He said, "Sure, help yourself." He'd open up the cabinet, and there would be an automat—you know, put a quarter in. (*Laughter.*) I go home and I still watch the *same* Jack Benny episode with my dad, and we laugh like hell. It gives you great joy to see somebody so talented who'd make fun of himself, like that whole thing that he was cheap, when really he was a very generous man who did great things.

WE: I take it that you place much value on tapping sources that are outside music.

DK: I think the most important thing is that we're not only influenced by the musical art form. Everything affects me—paintings, everything. The old man sitting across the street on the park bench—riding in a cab yesterday, I was trying to figure out what his story is. It all goes into music, not just transcribing Art Tatum. The study of dance, for instance; I've read a lot about Martha Graham and how she approached the art form, and it's pretty much the same. I've always loved that Martha Graham quote about how there's only a divine dissatisfaction in being an artist. That it's not your place to judge how good or not good it is. It's your place to just do it.

WE: You mentioned the act of transcribing music. Have you had a history of studying the work of your predecessors in jazz?

DK: Yeah, but not by necessarily writing things down. I played along with records. I'm very spontaneous. All my arrangements are usually done on the spot. They're so quick because otherwise I would forget things.

WE: Could spontaneity imply a lack of control?

DK: Spontaneity can still be controlled. Sometimes I'll get a little overexcited, and I'll vocally do things that make me think "Why did I do that? I didn't need to do that."

WE: Maybe your treatment was excessive?

DK: Yeah. I'll get back to my old Ernestine Anderson days—I used to practice piano along with Ernestine Anderson records with Monty Alexander. Try to play with Monty and sing like Ernestine. And it just doesn't sound like me. It can sound affected because I'm not Ernestine. I think I'm talking about oversinging. I've really worked hard on not doing that.

WE: When you do arrangements in the studio, does your band have enough time to rehearse?

DK: We rehearse. At the same time, I'm not very specific about "I want you to play this here, this way." I always say, "What're you gonna bring to the party?" We had a rehearsal yesterday, and I was working with the guitarists. I said, "Look, we just have to play it, and we'll get to the point where it feels comfortable." I usually show by example what the feeling I want is, rather than try to verbalize it. I don't want to have musicians around me over-analyzing, *thinking* too much about what they have to do. I don't like structure, structure, structure. It's about music. Just go out there and play it, have the freedom to let things evolve. You know, it's just inexplicable. It's trust more than anything. I tell them, "I trust you; I know you're gonna go with me." I went to Bermuda last night for a minute on one tune, and they were right there with me. And it was okay (*chuckles*), you know; the weather was nice.

WE: Has your study of artists in other mediums, and the original body of work they produced, inspired you toward writing your own compositions?

DK: I would like to compose, but I'm studying really hard the art of the great composers and the great interpreters. I loved listening to my dad's 78 RPM records; I loved Bing Crosby, I loved Frank Sinatra, and I loved good songs. I knew how the songs sounded originally; I knew what the composers wrote. I sometimes knew the first recordings. It was just something I liked to do, and I would sing with my grandmother. You know, I couldn't tell you when "Hard Hearted Hannah" was written, but I could tell you that I first heard Ella Fitzgerald singing it in *Pete Kelly's Blues* with Jack Webb and Peggy Lee. Then I heard other interpretations of it, like what Shirley Horn did with it. Or how Ahmad Jamal made "But Not for Me" his own; everybody knows that bass line. I've always found that really exciting. To take "I've Got You Under My Skin" from Frank Sinatra in 4/4, break it down, and it means something completely different. Something maybe even sad, like a more tragic kind of feeling. So I've found the great art of interpreting a lyric very fulfilling. Singing the songs simply, and not *trying* to be a jazz singer.

WE: Let's focus on your early years. Instead of music as a career, is it accurate to say that you had your sights set on becoming an astronaut?

DK: Yup.

WE: Were you a science buff?

DK: Yes. When I got the right teachers, I got straight A's in science.

WE: When did the first spark of interest in jazz occur?

DK: We had a talent day in fourth grade. I played Henry Mancini's "Baby Elephant

Walk." I found it in my dad's sheet music. I liked the left hand, but it was too hard for me to read the second part of the tune. So I made the rest of it up. And I had my piano teacher play Albert Ammons[5] for me; it was something I liked. The high school band came to my elementary school and played when I was in fourth grade, and I thought "That's what I want to do." But as far as a career—I don't think I'm still realizing this is my career. (*Laughter.*) I'm still thinking I'd better go to law school or something, and get my university degree. Then I'll be legitimate. That's how I was raised.

WE: Allow me to summarize some of your interests when you were young: you studied piano since the age of four and enjoyed boogie-woogie; you were very interested in science; you loved aspects of popular culture that occurred generations before you. If I were your friend in high school, would I know all these things?

DK: Nope. Unless you were Blair What's-His-Face, who I met. I thought he was great. I had a crush on him, and he was building rockets like I was. Then he told me he put gerbils in them. (*Laughter.*) I wasn't quite that wacky. Nobody else pretty much knew about it. You'd know me on the swim team, and as a skier. I was very athletic, rode horses. I was into clothes, just like I am now. I had a Peter Frampton poster on the wall—the whole bare chest. I was listening to Elton John, playing Supertramp and Genesis and Phil Collins and Marvin Gaye. I was listening to rock and roll just like anybody else. A very sociable, normal, adjusted, good kid. I wasn't, like, this nerdy recluse; people try to make me out like that.

WE: What people?

DK: Some journalists, based on impressions. I used to come home and play the piano by myself. I spent a lot of time with my grandparents, but I had my best friends. Then I got involved in the band program and had to give up the swim team, but still went skiing on weekends. I'd hang out with my family. That's a very important thing. I've never put my work before my family. Well, sometimes I *have* to do that, being far away from home. I also was a big fan of "Prairie Home Companion" with Garrison Keillor, which some people sort of pooh-pooh aside as corny. And it is! But I grew up among the Lutherans and the Catholics, and so we listened to it every Saturday. My mother and I, we'd lie on the couch and listen to the monologue and totally relate to it. I just *loved* the show. It was comforting to me on the road. I listened to the tapes when I was lonely in LA. I listened to the show every morning, and it was a sense of home when I was away by myself.

Years and years later, maybe four years ago, I was playing at a great jazz club called the Dakota in St. Paul. I walked in and I saw this big, tall guy. I went, "Oh my God." I *got* to the pay phone (*laughs*), and I called mother. I said, "Garrison Keillor's here." He came to my show, and he wrote me a note on a napkin. It said, "I really enjoyed it; come do the show." I've done the show four times, and I've been to his home. When he calls me—"Hi, Diana, it's Garrison"—I'm, like, "Save the message!" (*Laughs.*) It's freaky that I meet people I admire, and I meet them very naturally. I met an astronaut. Somebody called me and said, "Your music's in space." I got the paper, and it was the Canadian astronaut Bob Thirsk who had my CD *Only Trust Your Heart* in the space shuttle. He sent me a picture of him in weightlessness, and some space shuttle patches. He didn't have any idea that I had that dream as a kid. I got off the phone in tears, calling my friend Bill, who helped me build the rockets. I said to him, "I finally got up in space, but it was just my CD."

WE: Your description of growing up in Canada makes you sound like a transplanted Minnesotan. Did American society dominate your environment, or was there a vital Canadian culture?

DK: Canadians are stuck between the Americans and the British. Mike Myers is a perfect example of that, and Martin Short. Like, I also have all the scripts of *Fawlty Towers,* and *Monty Python*, and George Formby—Gene Lees[6] and I were talking about George Formby[7] the other day. I was, like, "I am finally talking to somebody who knows who George Formby is." I'm sure the waiter thought we were nuts, singing all these George Formby tunes. He was more popular than the Beatles. So I had this, like, British influence as well, with Marty Feldman and Peter Sellers—all the British shows that I loved to watch.

WE: As a youth in Canada, who was your role model for jazz?

DK: My band teacher, Bryan Stovall. He was a professional musician before he became a teacher, which doesn't happen so often anymore. He went to Berklee College of Music and then became a teacher. He had an extra special thing about him because he was one of the "cats." This incredible man, who was picking me up for school every morning for early band program, was my mentor. I'd spend summers over at his house, and he'd give me a Bill Evans record. He introduced me to all the guys he used to play with: David McMurdo, Rob McConnell and the Boss Brass; took me to Toronto on a band trip, got me a lesson with Don Thompson.[8] So all it takes is one person in a small town who is a good teacher. I just ran into him in the airport when I was home, and I got the biggest hug from him. He inspired me, and my grandmother inspired me.

WE: After high school, you won a jazz festival contest. Was that the launching pad to go to the Berklee College of Music?

DK: Yes, it was. It was a two thousand dollar scholarship. I still remember crying and telling my mother, "I got a scholarship." 'Cause I got to go to the "Big City."

WE: You hadn't been to a big city before?

DK: Well, Vancouver, sure, and Seattle, yeah, but not an East Coast city with Harvard and MIT. I didn't realize it then, but it was very hard for me when I went to Berklee. I was *so* homesick. I was far away, and I was lonely, and I was scared. Then I really got into it. I didn't want to stay in the classroom. I had another teacher, named Greg Battlelotto, who understood that. I'd come in late for class and he'd go, "Diana, go across the street, get coffee, a donut, and come back." (*Laughter.*) I used to go to Symphony Hall by myself and get rush tickets, go home and get dressed up, enjoy the symphony by myself. Even the pizza was different. That was really neat, you know—putting garlic on pizza. Who'd have thought? I went to the museum almost every weekend and saw, for the first time, original Monets. At that age, I was into the Impressionists; that was the first time I'd ever seen the cathedrals.[9] And Degas' sculpture, which is still burned in my brain. I used to hang out there a lot.

WE: You've mentioned twice that painting is important to you. Obviously, visual form inspires you?

DK: Yeah. I'm very careful about talking about it, though, because that insecurity about not having a university degree comes out. I think, "God, I don't know what I'm talking about." I won't be able to describe it, or maybe I won't know the exact painting, but I'll remember things. And, when I rationalize it, I know it's not necessary for me to know what it is, it's necessary for me to be moved.

WE: Have you indulged your interest by actually trying to draw or paint?

DK: I've been trying to sketch, badly. I'm reading *Drawing on the Right Side of the Brain.*[10] I don't tell anybody. I started sketching on hotel stationery.

WE: Are you also delighted by architecture?

DK: Oh, I have this wonderful friend who's an ophthalmologist, a glaucoma specialist, and he's fascinated with buildings. When we walk around New York, or wherever we go, he'll say, "Look at that building there." I never really looked at buildings as much as I do now. I took thirty-six pictures of this hotel room I stayed in in Italy. (*Laughs.*) In case, when I have my house someday, I wanted to do stuff like that.

WE: A few moments ago you referred to some of the wonderful experiences you had *outside* of the Berklee School of Music. Generally speaking, were you restless when it came to learning in a classroom setting?

DK: In school I used to drive my teachers crazy. I'd walk in and say, "I'm taking two weeks off," or "I'm taking a week off to practice for the festival." They'd be like, "You're telling us this?" I was always *very* impatient. Still am. It's a *fault,* because as I can pick up things very fast, I wish I had the discipline to work harder.

WE: You seem to have contradictory impulses in that one part of you feels illegitimate academically, but another part pursues knowledge outside an academic environment.

DK: Well, I know that there's just things that I wish I'd gone through and taken—like a whole English literature course. I now have on a list to read all the things that I haven't read and the things I don't know about, like history. Things that I think when I skipped time in school to practice or put into music I should've taken that slower route. So now I'm trying to catch up. That's something that's also very personal, which I don't know if I want everybody in the world to know. Nor do I want parents coming to me and saying, "You discouraged my kid to go to school." But a lot of great people didn't have university degrees. I talk about this with Tommy LiPuma[11] all the time, and he says, "Hey, all you gotta do is read. You have a curiosity and a hunger for knowledge."

I always look at what I don't know instead of—I can talk about Bill Challis or Billy Murray.[12] When I was seventeen, I took a train to Williamsburg, Massachusetts, to see the Paul Whiteman archives so I could look at the original Bill Challis arrangements. The curator there, Carl Johnson I think was his name, showed me the original little piano that the Rhythm Boys[13] used, and he showed me the scores where Bix played. I was fascinated with Bix Beiderbecke, so I wanted to see those scores. Then I went to visit this Finnish trumpet player, Sylvester Ahola, who played next to Bix Beiderbecke. He's ninety years old. I had tea and sandwiches with him and his wife. I think part of the fun is discovering things that we might not when we're told in a class "Here it is, learn it." My father's like this, and I'm like this, too, with tunes. I'll just sit there at my father's bookcase and go through all the sheet music trying to find tunes. I'll go, "Oh my gosh, I've discovered this great tune." A lot of that is just the satisfaction of discovering something on your own.

WE: Getting back to your college days, you left Berklee without finishing your degree. Was that because you were in a rush to get on with your life?

DK: Well, I couldn't afford it! And I wasn't sure what I wanted to do. I left because I didn't want to be at Berklee. I lived at home for a year and just did local gigs; played solo piano places, and had a lot of work, actually. Then I met Jeff Hamilton and Ray Brown in my hometown. They encouraged me to come to LA. I studied with Alan Broadbent first, and then Jimmy Rowles.

WE: What did you study with Alan Broadbent and Jimmy Rowles?

DK: Well, I'd like more time with Alan, because at that time I think I was not emotionally ready to work with him. And I was not familiar with Alan's work. But he is probably one of my most important teachers, and I have tremendous respect for him. I was actually working on trying to transcribe some of his voicings yesterday. "When I Look in Your Eyes"[14] is directly from Alan Broadbent and Irene Kral—I learned it from that record.[15] Alan had me singing solos. I can still sing them (*scats a few bars of "Pound Cake" by Count Basie*). And listening to Billie Holiday. I was also studying the music of Bill Evans, but I was really into Jimmy Rowles. Jimmy Rowles was a whole different ball of wax. That was: go over to the house, sit down, and see what you can see. I think it is as important to hang out with somebody and listen to their stories as it is to have a piano lesson. I've had that recently with Ray Brown. I was on the road with him for three weeks, and we're very, very close. Even closer than ever. He's says I'm like his daughter, which is a great honor. We'd sit at dinner and I'd ask, "Ray, what was Charlie Parker like?" And four hours later . . .

WE: In one article about you, it says that Ray Brown taught you the Zen of swing.[16]

DK: That's some quote somebody made up. Nobody taught me swing. I swung when I was four years old. My sister's got it, too. As does my grandmother. I got it from my grandmother, I guess. I'm not saying that, like, boastingly, that I swung when I was four years old. It's just something that I never analyzed or studied. It's something that I felt and was told that I could do. To me, it's the most important thing. The only thing I have to think about is *relaxing*. Sometimes things can sound nervous. Whenever I listen to a musician, I always listen if they swing or not. That's why I like Ray Brown so much. If you told me when I was seventeen that I was going to play with Ray Brown, I would have thought you were out of your mind. Just to sit next to him; I live for that. Christian McBride, too.

WE: Returning to the subject of Jimmy Rowles, can you add any more dimension to his image, particularly since he was a musician who was not well known?

DK: Yeah, it makes me very sad. I think Jimmy was also someone who was *full* of contradictions. I think that may be why we related so well to each other. The first Jimmy Rowles piece I ever heard, when I was sixteen, was "My Buddy."[17] I knew the song. It was something that my grandfather sang. But what interested me about Jimmy was that he took the "My Buddy" that I knew from my grandfather and made it into *that*.

I used to give him Louis L'Amour books for his birthday—that was his favorite writer—because he was a cowboy. You know, who could write a song called "The Ballad of Thelonious Monk" as a cowboy song? You gotta be not too tightly wrapped (*laughs*), as Carmen McRae says on that record.[18] I wish I could have been there at that Great American Songbook at Donte's with Joe Pass and Jimmy and Carmen McRae. Those were the days when they were singing songs, and they weren't into worrying about whether you scat sang or not. You knew you were a jazz singer by the way you approached things. It wasn't about, you know, "You're not a jazz singer unless you're singing 'Giant Steps.' "[19] I was teasing the band that I'm going to write lyrics to that. (*Laughs.*) And I'm not putting down people who do, but I'm a singer, whether I'm a jazz singer or not, and a piano player. I'm definitely a jazz piano player—I improvise, no question. I sing songs, but I'm not going to try to be a horn player with my vocals. I'm trying to be an interpreter of lyrics. And that's what Jimmy was, as well. He sang great songs and he sang them in his own way, and it was gravelly. He was a piano player who loved to play Wayne Shorter tunes. "CHECK THIS OUT!" I can still hear him saying that to me about Wayne Shorter's stuff, and listening to "Daphnis and Chloe," conducted by Ernest Ansermet.[20] He loved Billie Holiday, Duke Ellington, Thelonious Monk, and he loved to play tennis. He was very funny, a cartoonist. But then he had all the scores to Ravel. He was a very deep cat.

WE: You just seemed to cast your own doubts on whether you are a jazz singer. I seem to remember that you've been quoted elsewhere making a similar statement.

DK: Yeah, but that just got totally taken out of context. *Billboard* printed, "I don't want to be a jazz diva." And it pissed me off because print is so difficult. It's so difficult for me to verbalize anyway, but print, the interpretation of print, is toughest. My first influence as a jazz singer, or as a musician, was Betty Carter's "Seems Like Old Times." (*Sings a few bars, then dramatically modulates a key change like Carter.*) You know, it was, like, "Wow, what is this?" This is another place where I know this song the way it was, and this is where it went, and I was completely fascinated with that. But I choose not to scat sing. I choose to focus on the lyric. But in *no* way, and I have to be very clear on this, does that negate the other side of doing things. Or to say that I'm not influenced by Betty Carter, Sarah Vaughan, or my peers, Cassandra [Wilson] or Dee Dee Bridgewater. I love what they do. But I don't scat sing really well. I haven't worked hard on it. I'm working on piano improvisations; that's where it's coming from, rather than the vocals. I've got a lot of stuff to do, you know; I've got two different instruments.

WE: You recently formed a new band, changing from a trio format to a quartet. Is that a difficult, perhaps even risky, proposition?

DK: Risk is everything. I found that I could make *All for You* ten times over, or *Love Scenes.* But you have to take a risk and do something different. You know, I'm not going to tell the band, "Okay, I want you to do exactly what we did before." Bringing the drums in has changed the tunes. Take "Peel Me a Grape," it's just changed. I'm enjoying it, so it's healthy to bring new influences in. That's why you can play the same tune for years and years and years, and it keeps ever evolving. At the same time I get this lump in my throat like, "Will they still like me 'cause I'm changing? Maybe I should stay the way I was before?" If I'm going to be honest—"Will I still make people happy?" But that's getting away from what the music is all about. That's about what people think; that's not about music. I've never made a record thinking, "Gosh, will they like it, will it sell?" Not that I want to print that either, but it's important to know that everybody's not perfect. The temptation with success is to say, "Okay, I've got this and I don't want to lose it now." And that's when music goes out the window. As long as you think about the music, the music, the music, then I don't care. I said to Tommy LiPuma, "I don't care if this record sells two. I don't care if the two people who buy it are my mom and my dad." I know I've made an honest and beautiful record. That's all I could be expected to do. Not just to sit back and say, "Okay, I'd better make another trio record." 'Cause people are asking me, "Why did you do this, why all of a sudden strings and drums?" I'm, like, "Because I'm growing, you know?" I'm getting upset! (*Laughs.*) This is intense stuff. It's personal, a lot of it.

WE: Earlier, you described the way musicians transform songs. With respect to "Peel Me a Grape," was your approach to that song based on hearing something that Blossom Dearie didn't bring to it?

DK: It's like, why decide to do "I've Got You Under My Skin" slowly instead of fast. It's just, "Let's try this." My sister typed up the lyrics for me. When my mom had cancer and we were alone—she was going through a bone marrow transplant—we'd crank it up in my mother's kitchen and we'd be singing "Peel Me a Grape." It cheered us up. She typed all the lyrics for me, and four years ago for her birthday I sang the tune for her. And people went nuts. Now I'm stuck with it! (*Laughter.*) They just come to hear that one tune. I took the tempo down, and it made it somewhat cheekier.

WE: Did you get a response from Blossom Dearie about your version of "Peel Me a Grape"?[21]

DK: It's hilarious what happened. I don't know if I should tell the story, but I went to hear Blossom Dearie at Danny's Skylight Room[22] with a journalist who's doing a piece on me in *GQ*. I'd never heard her. I guess some people told her that I was in the audience, because she said, "Ladies and gentlemen, we have a very special person in the audience tonight, the wonderful Irene Kral." (*Laughter.*) I went, "She's dead." Then Blossom Dearie goes, "Oh, Diana Krall!" She's just kinda like "Whatever." I adore her.

WE: A little while ago you said that you've got a lot to do, working with two different instruments. Is it difficult, even frustrating, to try and find your voice on the piano when you also have the vocals, not to mention the band's interaction, to address?

DK: Yes, but I'm having a helluva lot of fun in the process. It's almost that silly thing, like, "Oh my God, I had too much fun last night." I've been saying for the last few years, "My goal is to be a better piano player, I want to work on my piano playing." I said to a friend, "Maybe I'm just playing too much piano. Maybe people don't want to hear me playing the piano; I'm not the greatest piano player in the world, but I love to play." And one band member said, "You're *crazy*! What are you talkin' about?" It's not like I played twenty-five choruses. Playing the piano with this band, I'm having so much *fun* and it feels so good. As Jeff Hamilton has told me since I was nineteen, "Every time you sit down to play you should have the excitement of the red sparkle drum set or the purple bike with tassels on the handlebars Christmas morning." So I always think of a red sparkle drum set.

WE: Nice image.

DK: You should have a can that says five cents on it; I could put a nickel in that can for therapy. This is better than my therapist. (*Laughs.*) Why, as artists, are we hard on ourselves if something comes easy to us? "Oh, we must not have worked hard enough—it was too easy." Or why do we beat ourselves up because we're having a *great* time—"Uh-oh, I gotta be serious. Having too much fun here." I had such a good time that I was thinking, "I didn't even know there was an audience."

WE: Do you envision doing a piano record?

DK: Yes. I want to do a solo piano and vocal record. I would like to tour by myself for a while. I haven't told anybody that, 'cause maybe it won't happen. I want to do a quartet for four months—work this band—then I'd like to do two weeks with Christian McBride, just as a duo. I'd like to go out with Ray Brown. I'd like to maybe study theater or acting. I'd like to work with a personal trainer for six months. Get a killer body. (*Laughs.*) I'd like to do Lilith Fair. You know, I went to the Grammys this year for fun; you're supposed to always go for fun, but the last two times I was nominated it was like, ahhhh. (*Laughs.*) I went with Tommy [LiPuma], and we had just a blast. I felt like I was a kid at a rock concert. It was, like, "Yeah! That's such and such." Tommy's going, "Hey Babe, if you weren't here, I wouldn't even know who some of these people were." I was like, "Rock and roll, light my Bic lighter." (*Laughs.*) Not really, but, you know, I felt like that. I went to this Universal after-party and I met Bono. I associate his music with my sister playing U2 upstairs all the time, and I used to play those things in the piano bars. I said to him, "I really admire you," and he goes, "I've got this great song for you, Diana." I was, like, "Huh?" And Erykah Badu came up to me and said, "You are so dope. I love your music." I was like "Oh my God!" I was shocked that they even knew who I was. I've had a chance to talk to a lot of, like, pop artists—like Sarah McLachlan—and we've talked about getting together. I don't know if that will ever happen, but I'd love to play piano on a D'Angelo record. Do something, not for the sake of doing something different, but because it interests me.

WE: When did you first sing professionally in public?

DK: In LA. I got this gig in Long Beach, and it was a piano bar. They wanted me to sing, and they had no PA system. It was, like, my voice would come over on the speakers that were above us, but not the piano, and it was piped through the whole restaurant. (*Laughter.*) Ray Brown came to hear me once. He went to the men's room and he goes, "I'm in the men's room and all I hear is your voice and no piano." (*Laughs.*) Those were not exactly the easiest times for me, because I spent a lot of time traveling and touring in Europe and thinking that I could just sing standards. I was frantically learning Beatles tunes and pop tunes, and I did not like playing a six-hour piano-bar gig. I tell you, piano bar people who sing and play piano, they work their butts off. And it's a thankless job sometimes. I always have respect for musicians that I see in hotel lobbies. Sometimes they're happy and they're really good at it. I just wasn't good at it. I wasn't good at being the entertainer.

WE: Let's talk about gender politics. As a woman in jazz, have you been discouraged due to sexist behavior?

DK: If I did, I probably wouldn't notice it. I probably just would've thought that the person had a problem. Lately, I've had a problem (*chuckles sardonically*), because you're not supposed to be attractive. "You're only successful 'cause you're a white, blond, girl-next-door type." "Girl next door meets sex kitten," was one quote in the paper. A put-down. I'm frustrated because my photographs in some instances are too glamorous for certain publications. I can't be a serious artist because of my looks; or I'm only successful because of my looks. Because of that, there's a prejudice against digging a little deeper. I don't feel comfortable talking about this because I think that it's nothing that I can't deal with. And it's not a big deal—look at prejudices that people—I mean, uhh.

WE: You're speaking about people of color?

DK: Yeah, and it seems somewhat even silly of me saying that. I won't even use that word, "prejudice," because I think that it's mostly misunderstood. Women are just as guilty of it. I have a lot of women friends—lawyers, dentists—who are very powerful professional people, and women friends who are involved in family. Each is equally legitimate. And the women who have chosen to stay with their children are treated badly by the professionals. Like, "Housewife, oh my God." Maybe that's because my mother stayed at home with us because she could afford to. Then when we were in school, she taught so she had the same hours as us. When we were fifteen and sixteen, she went away to summer school and finished her degree. When we were in our late twenties, she went off to San Diego by herself and got her master's. So, you know, I have a *really* together mom and a *really* together dad. Like I said this joke last night: "That's why my sister and I are so mixed up." And I thought, "Oh, no, they're gonna think that I meant it." But I think it's hard for us in our relationships, because we have such a good example in our parents that it's almost unreal in every aspect. We always say, "That's why we're still single, because we just have too high expectations."

My father had to learn how to work the washing machine. But he did it. (*Laughs.*) I had hot dogs for two weeks—it's like, "You make great hot dogs, Dad." But, you know, he didn't hold my mother back from anything. So we had that great role model of what women can do. We laugh because my sister was a police officer for a long time, an undercover drug cop. We've got a teacher for a mother and an accountant for a father, and they'd be asked, "You've got two daughters. How did you get a cop and the other's a jazz pianist?" We just always said, "One's a cop and the other has a record." (*Laughter.*) So we were really strong kids and we were never discouraged. I still don't believe that anybody's going to look at me differently because I'm a woman, or hold me back. I just won't believe it. If you don't believe it, you won't look for it; it's not there. The only thing is, like, I can find on the Internet that they're talking about the size of my breasts, you know, or that I looked tired today. That has nothing to do with being a woman, that has just to do with being a public person. The only thing is that sometimes—women *and* men who look at my photograph on an album cover say, "Credibility is out the window."

WE: How do you feel about that?

DK: It pisses me off! (*Laughs.*)

WE: But it's hard to deny, it seems to me, the seductiveness of the cover and liner photos for *Love Scenes.*

DK: Look, you know, I gave the most athletic wind-blown pictures, like in the pouring rain, for some magazine, and it was *still* too pretty for people. I thought, "Okay, let me get a cigarette and I won't shave my armpits (*laughs*), and then I'll have more credibility as an artist." Screw 'em. I'm not coming to concerts with boobs hanging out or with over makeup. That photograph[23] was something I chose because I like those old movie-glam photos. Do they ever talk about men's covers like that?

WE: In this context, I just listened to "Popsicle Toes,"[24] which may be a sensational item for you.

DK: Oh, no. Why did I do it?

WE: I was pleased to hear it. My interpretation was that you decided to meet the challenge head-on and sing a bawdy song. Why shouldn't you celebrate things that are sexual and sensuous?

DK: I know, I know. See, I went to that place. I went to defend myself. Instead it's the old worry about what people think, kind of Lutheran guilt. My mother and I talk about it all the time: "Oh my God, what are they gonna say about me?" I played "Popsicle Toes" for her, and she was reading things into it that I didn't even know. I was, like, "Really?" She goes (*chidingly*), "Lower your Pentax." I was going, "Well, I never thought of that." (*Laughter.*) My mom has the same kind of filthy mind that I do.

You know, I'm starting to think now I *love* to dress up in great clothes. I love to be a girl. I love to be in my raincoat and my old sneakers and no makeup and this stupid barrette in my hair. (*Laughs.*)[25] It's a contradiction again. I'm not the kind of person who's going to get dressed up to go in an airplane, and that's where people have sometimes talked to me. "I saw Diana Krall, and I wouldn't like to wake up next to her without her Revlon kit." *That's* what somebody said! On the Internet! I was, like, laughing. Because I was exhausted flying on a plane, and I don't care. I don't assume that people can recognize me. I don't dress up like that. I don't want to waste my time. When I perform, I like to dress up. But when I'm out in the day, I'm myself. I get on the plane and I think, "I should probably dress up a little better." But I'm traveling, and I'm not living my life to be recognized. I have great passion about what I do, and I'm very serious about the music. I know that. Maybe someday they'll find out.

WE: Do you think that women make a special contribution to the aesthetic of jazz?

DK: I don't think it has anything to do with being a woman. Sometimes men have said, "Playing with a woman is different because they bring that sort of sensitivity." I don't believe that.

WE: Are there certain women in the history of jazz whom you would single out for their contributions?

DK: Mary Lou Williams.

WE: Do you consider her an innovator?

DK: She could have been. It's a hard question to answer. Miles Davis, is he an innovator? Yes, everybody's influenced by him because they're aware of him. Is Mary Lou Williams an innovator? She should be because of her compositions, because of her style, because of her uniqueness. I'm starting to study her music, so I'm not really as familiar with her as I should be. But when I was a kid, that's one of the first records I bought *because* she was a woman. Cool. But did she innovate? Ask Marian McPartland. She's someone who, I think, has also been a role model to me. I called her up from my home when I was sixteen. My dad says, "What the hell you doin' callin' Marian McPartland?" (*Laughter.*) I said, "Well, I wanted to ask her advice on what I should do with my life." I called Marian McPartland because she was a woman. I was calling men, too, but I called her because I thought that I could relate to her. We sat up last year at a festival and talked. There's someone who's very, very elegant and obviously concerned about looking like a lady and loves clothes and always has makeup on and takes care of herself. Anyhow, it's nice sitting there with someone like that and then we've both got mouths like sailors. (*Laughs.*) There's still that jazz musician, you know, in there. Not always like sailors, but, you know, we're ladies and we're elegant, but we can hang.

[We turned to the first piece of music: "I Ain't Got Nobody," *'34/'35 Fats Waller,* 1935; RCA Victor, Al Casey, guitar.]

DK: Fats Waller was my first big influence. I mean, sometimes this stuff brings tears to my eyes because it reminds me of being at home. Al Casey on guitar. I met Al Casey for the first time a few weeks ago when Russell Malone and I went to this place called Louisiana Grill where they had the Harlem All Stars. And there's Al Casey still playing. That sound—you cannot capture that kind of sound—and the humor. I liked Fats Waller because I could relate to him as a kid; I loved humor. Some people will criticize his use of humor. But he was a funny guy. I remember at the top of the sheet music for "This Joint Is Jumpin' " it said, "Tempo: disturb de neighbors." (*Laughter.*) Mom and dad took me to see *Ain't Misbehavin'* in Vancouver. I played the soundtrack over and over again, learned everything. Tried to learn "Handful of Keys"—still tryin' to learn "Handful of Keys"—but just got immersed in Fats Waller. I loved his singing and his piano playing. He's very underrated. I used to practice saxophone along with the records. All those expressions, even, that he used—"Make it sweat." Musicians in my bands will pick up on those things, and that'll be, like, the new band phrase, "Make it sweat." So now I'm gonna use that tonight. It makes me very happy for personal reasons and musical reasons. I always go back to it, and it's always fresh. It reminds me of my grandmother. (*Starts to cry.*)

[The second selection was "Wrap Your Troubles in Dreams," *Bing Crosby/Wrap Your Troubles in Dreams,* 1931; RCA Victor.]

DK: You can see what I'm talking about when I say I'm very emotionally connected to music? I mean, I could analyze this and tell you about very early Bing Crosby recordings—I listened to all of them because he's a favorite of my dad's. I mean, you can hear probably Al Jolson in that particular one; that's how early that is. So, yeah, that's a big influence on me. Huge. But without knowing about it. But all early, never late Bing Crosby; we never listened to that. It was mostly recordings with the Paul Whiteman Orchestra.

But what this does *to me* is make me very homesick. It affects me emotionally more than all the technical things or the influences, which is, I think, the most important thing. I'm motivated to do "A Ghost of a Chance" because of Bing Crosby. And the verses—he sang the verses, and there's a sweetness about it. And also because, for me, it's about home. At home, well, my dad will put a stack of 78s on, who knows what's in it, and we'll play cards and scream at each other. And then sing along with the 78s—not really even knowing what it is. I don't listen to Bing Crosby that much anymore 'cause I get so homesick. But I should, because that's not something that you should always push aside.

[The next piece of music was "I've Found a New Baby," *Lester Young Trio,* 1946; Verve Records, Nat Cole, piano.]

DK: Can you imagine if you were able to hear that live? He's comping very (*chuckles*)—I hate that word "progressive"—but very interesting harmonically. He was just an unbelievable piano player. I think he's the only singer/piano player that I know as two separate people, but you couldn't have one without the other. There was the Nat Cole singing "Pick Yourself Up," which is why I did that. It took me a long time to do it. That Nat Cole is, I think, my favorite. For me, it's Nat, Frank [Sinatra]—probably Nat first. The most important, for me as a piano player, is Nat and the trio. It just embodies everything that I would strive to be.

WE: As we know, Cole eventually left the piano. Can you envision yourself as a standup vocalist?

DK: I think I over-emote when I don't play the piano. When I'm singing out front it's, like, "Well, what am I doin'; I'm not doin' anything. I've got to do something. I've got to sing more." Bobby Short was the same way. They said when Bobby Short first started singing out front without playing, he used to gesticulate all the time. So now I sing, I don't like to move. It's not comfortable for me. I'm not comfortable standing up anyway; I feel like an awkward teenager. So I tend to fiddle. Now I just try to stand up straight and sing, rather than try to fake moving around. Because I'm not good at it.

[The last selection was "Tulip or Turnip" from *Carmen McRae/Any Old Time,* 1987; Nippon Columbia.]

WE: You're often compared to Carmen McRae.

DK: I know, it's so funny. I don't want to be compared to her. I think, well, it's the association with Jimmy Rowles, and that she plays piano.

WE: Another basis for comparison seems to be the way you both approach phrasing, but I don't fully subscribe to that since her attack has more bite and irony.

DK: Oh, I've gone there and Russell Malone said, "Okay, Carmen Krall." I was, like, "Okay, I won't do it." (*Laughs.*) She had a very—I can't use barnyard epithets, as somebody told me I can't swear. But sometimes it's hard not to, to describe something. She had a "don't mess with me" attitude. I wouldn't want to cross her.

WE: But you do feel an identification with her?

DK: Yeah, strong. I've got every recording that I can find on LP. I usually go to Japan and clean up, you know. She did a solo piano record of her own, live at the Dug.[26] That record *kills* me. Apparently she didn't like it. Not a perfect voice, either. Got it from Billie Holiday, but not sounding like Billie Holiday. Plus she wasn't safe, you know. She brought some of her personal views in her music. Wasn't afraid to state her opinions. It took courage to do that at that time. If you look at Frank and Nat, they're entertainers. But if you're gonna say jazz singer, I always think of Carmen McRae.

Only Trust Your Heart. GPR 059810-2 (1994). (With Stanley Turrentine, Ray Brown, and Christian McBride.)

All for You (A Dedication to the Nat King Cole Trio). Impulse IMPD-182 (1996).

*Live In Paris. Verve 440 065 109-2 (2002). (Krall stretches out at the piano on several selections.)

Notes

1. 1995; GRP.
2. 1996; Impulse.
3. Verve.
4. This refers to the famous comedy sequence "viaduct/why a duck?" in the Marx Brothers' film *Coconuts,* 1929; Paramount Pictures.
5. One of the principal, early boogie-woogie pianists.
6. Noted American jazz writer.
7. British entertainer who was also a popular movie comedian in English cinema during the 1930s and early 1940s.
8. Canadian jazz pianist.
9. Monet's paintings of the Rouen Cathedral façades.
10. Betty Edwards (Los Angeles: J. P. Tarcher, 1989).
11. Producer at Verve Records.
12. A dialect comedian and vaudeville vocalist.
13. Vaudeville singing trio that included Bing Crosby.
14. *Irene Kral/Where Is Love?,* 1975; Choice Records.
15. From *Diana Krall/When I Look in Your Eyes,* 1999; GRP Records.
16. David E. Thigpen, *Time,* June 10, 1996, p. 82.
17. From *Stan Getz Presents Jimmy Rowles,* 1994 (originally released 1977); Columbia Jazz Masters Series.
18. Carmen McRae, *The Great American Songbook,* live at Donte's in Los Angeles, 1972; Atlantic Jazz.
19. Composed by John Coltrane.
20. Important French School conductor known for his interpretations of Ravel.
21. Included on *Love Scenes,* 1997; GRP Records.
22. Cabaret in New York's theater district.
23. The *Love Scenes* images.
24. Included on *When I Look in Your Eyes.*
25. Ms. Krall was dressed in her raincoat and sneakers, wore no makeup, and had a barrette in her hair during our interview.
26. *As Time Goes By,* recorded at the Dug in Tokyo, November 21, 1973; Japanese Victor Records.

Abbey Lincoln

Abbey Lincoln

A preeminent survivor, singer, poet, composer, painter, actress, and social critic, Abbey Lincoln has led one of the more extraordinary lives in jazz. Beginning as a popular vocalist and early African-American sex symbol, Lincoln appeared on the cover of *Ebony* magazine in 1956 and had starring roles in two films of the 1960s.[1] Determined to carve her own destiny, this wily individualist was in her sixties when she signed with a major record label and traded her cult-like stature for that of a celebrated jazz vocalist.

Born Anna Marie Wooldridge in 1930, she grew up in rural Michigan as the tenth of twelve children. Naturally inclined toward music, she relished her starring roles in annual school musical productions. After winning an amateur talent contest at nineteen, Anna Marie moved west to Los Angeles.

She became a favorite entertainer at supper clubs along the coast until the chance arrived to perform in Hawaii, where she crossed paths with her mentor, Billie Holiday. Two years at high-class Honolulu clubs proved to be an important formative period; after her return to Los Angeles, the youthful Anna Marie was offered a job singing at the famous Moulin Rouge. Wearing sophisticated costumes with feathers and strategic side slits, she was given the French name Gabby Lee and became a popular headliner. This role led to a fortuitous meeting with drummer Max Roach.

She and Roach struck up a friendship, and the newly named Abbey Lincoln headed to New York in 1957 for the promise of greater opportunities. Roach introduced her to some of the city's leading musicians, and produced her first album[2] for Riverside, which launched her newfound jazz career.

Abbey Lincoln and Max Roach were married in 1962 and together recorded eleven LPs. On one album, *We Insist! Freedom Now Suite*,[3] her uninhibited vocal interpretations elicited clamorous responses from critical as well as political arenas. In 1969,

Maxwell House Coffee featured Lincoln and Roach as the first real-life black couple to appear in a television commercial. When the marriage ended in 1970, Lincoln moved back to Los Angeles and maintained a fairly low profile while immersing herself in books and research about African culture.

Lincoln returned from a trip to Africa in 1972 with a deeper understanding of her roots, a firm resolution to share her philosophy of life, and a new name, Aminata Moseka. Encouraged by Miles Davis and others to continue singing through the 1970s and 1980s, Lincoln began to resurface when Enja records released her two-volume tribute to Lady Day.[4] Sounding uncannily similar to Billie Holiday, Lincoln sings with a quavery vibrato, meticulous diction, and trademark laid-back timing.

A prolific composer, Lincoln pens thought-provoking lyrics that are like distilled poems set to music. The melodies she creates have an easy familiarity leavened by unexpected harmonic leaps and resolutions that craftily bridge minor and major passages. As a performer, Lincoln has a dramatic, penetrating delivery that reaches into an emotional space rarely ventured by other singers. With pliant phrasing, this worldly-wise songstress uses her earthy alto voice to stretch syllables and nuzzle notes into tonal crevices.

Lincoln's visibility as a significant jazz singer was enhanced when, in the 1990s, she was signed by Verve. Lincoln has executed eleven consistently successful recordings for that label. In March 2002, a gala celebration of her multifaceted career took place at New York City's Lincoln Center. This musical retrospective featured Abbey, accompanied by special guests, performing a full program of her own compositions for three consecutive evenings. A musical iconoclast and charismatic figure who ably summons up visions of her African ancestry, Abbey Lincoln ranks among the premier storytellers in jazz.

Recorded September 5, 1998

WE: Abbey, you've been honored with the name Aminata Moseka. Describe for me the powers possessed by the two gods Aminata and Moseka.

AL: They're African gods. Miriam Makeba took me for a vacation to Africa at the end of '72 and the beginning of '73; I was there for two months with her. I had come to a realization before I went to Africa that God was male and female. Miriam introduced to me the president of Guinea, took me to the People's Palace, where we had breakfast. He named me Aminata at the breakfast table. It was his wife's name and his daughter's name. Then she took me to Zaire, which is no more. The Minister of Information added Moseka. He said, "I give you this name." They spoke French, and I didn't know how to communicate with them, but Miriam translated for me. He told her to tell me that it was a god of love in the form of a maiden. He didn't say it was a goddess, and I knew I had come home, because I always knew that the African gods were male and female. It really helps me in my life to look to myself to the god that is mine, and not outside myself for anything I need.

WE: If Moseka is a god of love, what does Aminata embody?

AL: It's a great African god—Amen. He's Egyptian, Tutankhamen. That's what they say at the end of a chapter in the Bible: Amen. Aminata: it's the female amen. A lot of Africans are named Amen, even though we don't remember our gods anymore. For me, I took it like this: The female is a god and her power is in love. She brings the children here, and she gives them a spirit and tells them how to feel. They get it from her. If she does not see herself as God, if he's the only one who can be God and she brings them here, it's confusing to everybody. Because how does that work? He can't make anybody. He can bring the thing that she uses to make it, but she makes it—the baby—out of her body. And she's not God? So it doesn't have to be either/or. God is male and female. We're the only ones who say there's a God. The other animals don't talk about it.

WE: Do you feel that the jazz world would be better off if these gods were recognized?

AL: Yes. We have inherited a great music, but as a people we are not great anymore. There was a time when we were. This music is a holdover. It comes with us like the skin, the texture of our hair. Our ancestors practiced the arts and the sciences to a *fare-thee-well*. It's our memory banks. That's why the athletes are efficient and can do the things they do. And we don't remember anybody. We look to Europe for our lives. This music walks the water. Everywhere in the world they send for it.

WE: Jazz?

AL: What they *call* jazz. What they *call* rock. What they *call* rap. All of this stuff. It's the African muse transplanted to America, transplanted and transformed. There's a lot that's been added to it. We never played four in Africa. I think we got that from the Irish jig. We adapted other forms, but this spirit of the music is an African spirit or muse, and it's all about the drum. It's a blessing, because without it I don't know what we would do as a people. It's not right to have all of this and see yourself as underprivileged and poor. You have to be a real nut (*laughs*) to go for that and to express that. You know, we're a long ways from home. A long, long, long ways from home.

WE: Why did you say that African Americans are no longer a great people?

AL: Because we have forgotten our gods. We're the only people on the planet who try to live without our gods. They are in Egypt. And the people here tell us that these are not our ancestors. That North Africa was not Africa. This is the way the story goes today. That's not supposed to be my relative? He looks *just* like me. My father and my brother. Am I a vampire that I don't know my image in the mirror? This is what we're going through. You can kill somebody dead through slander. Just curse their ancestors and tell them they're a bunch of savages. After a while they learn to believe it.

I live for the vindication of my ancestors who were said to be savages. I want them to stop lying on us! You know, the way you live is through your ancestors. Can you imagine what kind of people the Italians would be if they didn't know Rome was built by their ancestors? Italy is not a good country anymore, but it was once. Greece? I've been to Greece. What would Greece be like if they didn't know that their ancestors made these contributions? Well, Egypt is mine! And whatever happened to the Egyptians? The same thing that happened to the Italians and the Greeks and the Spanish. You can be great today and nothin' tomorrow. But if somebody kills your ancestors off, then they have taken your life.

We were ripped off. We were not allowed to keep our names here, and our gods went with our names and our ancestors went with our names. We've done pretty good, but I think it finally got the best of us. That's why the kids are lost; they don't know who they are.

WE: What is the role of art in the vindication of your ancestors?

AL: It's the way of our ancestors. They always practiced the arts. That's why all Negroes can sing and dance. (*Laughs.*) When I was a kid, they used to say that "All Negroes can sing and dance." It would make some people really angry. And they'd say, "That's a lie, I can't dance." But it's true. All Negroes can sing and dance because this is what they do. That's what they did, and they're still doin' it. It's as natural as swallowing.

WE: Are you dedicated to social advancement?

AL: No, I'm not interested in social advancement. I don't know about anybody else, I'm not trying to change anything. I'm only expressing myself. If I couldn't speak my mind, I would die. I'd choke on my breath. I'm like my mother. (*Laughs.*) She told us who we were and where we came from. So I'm doin' that on the stage. I sing about my life.

WE: Let's turn to your personal history. As a youngster, when did you begin performing?

AL: I used to perform in school when I was, like, seven and eight. I started out at home. I'm one of twelve children. My father, Alexander Wooldridge, built the house I grew up in, in Michigan. We had a piano, an upright, and I was the one who went to the piano when I was going on five. I wasn't really conscious of what I was doing, either. Here is a story about one of my brothers, Melvin. We were visiting the Smith family in Calvin Center. There were quite a few people there—the Smiths and Alvin Steel and us, the Wooldridges—and I heard my brother say—he wanted me to hear it, too—"You know, Anna Marie plays the piano." And Alvin said, "You're lying; she's too little to play the piano." He said, "Yes, but she does. She picks out melodies at the piano." Well, after that, I know I was conscious of doing it. I didn't get opposition at home. My relatives were first generation from slavery, and they knew how to treat somebody. I didn't have to fight for my space. It was my little space. Yeah, my very own.

WE: When did you become career-minded?

AL: I didn't know there was a career until I was nineteen. It wasn't anything I went for or wished for. I didn't really know anything about the arts. I didn't know what I'd become. I played records on the Victrola. I grew up before television. I saw television the first time when I was nineteen. I was working as a mother's helper in Kalamazoo, and Jackson, too. I learned how to take care of a pretty house. We took care of our house, but Mama didn't have silver. They sacrificed everything for us. When I was fourteen, I got my first job. Then when I was seventeen and eighteen, like that, I would work—domestic work. If it hadn't been for music, that's probably what I'd be doing. Because I tried out as a chiropractor's assistant, and I tried to be a secretary for a minute, for a lawyer. I couldn't handle it.

WE: You grew up in a pastoral setting. As a result, were you isolated from the world at large when you were a youngster?

AL: Yeah, we all were. The next neighbor was a mile up the road, and the other one was maybe two miles. The school was three miles away if we went one direction, and five miles if we went the other direction to have company. We didn't have radios. I learned how to entertain myself. We used to play in the grape orchard in Calvin Center. We'd pick berries and hunt for frogs in the pond.

WE: As an African-American family in rural Michigan, did you suffer from racism?

AL: We all had some African blood, but our neighbors had a standard. You had to be a pale-skin yellow, and with dark, straight hair. Our neighbors had mixed with Indians and with the Europeans. There was a Hoffman family who owned the lake. Mr. Hoffman and his kids went to the same school we went to. There was just one school. The teachers were always African-American. I went there till the eighth grade. They did not teach us racism, so

I didn't learn to have a complex about who I was. My mother taught me how to be a lady. (*Laughs.*) A queen, you understand?

WE: Was there a strong religious undercurrent in the community of Calvin Center?

AL: No. They had two churches, though—the Baptist church and the Methodist church. We went to the Methodist church 'cause they were more laid-back. (*Laughs.*) It was really a social thing, because Mama didn't tell us Jesus was God or nobody else. She gave us the Psalms to read. She studied Christian Science.

WE: How did she handle illnesses in the family?

AL: She healed herself and she healed us. My father would go to the forest. Our land was clear, but he'd go across the way into the forest and bring sassafras bark. Mama would boil it; it would be a wonderful red color that would cleanse our system for the summer, in the spring.

WE: You drank this as a matter of course?

AL: Yeah. You know people who were slaves couldn't afford to be ignorant of medicine. Who's going to take care of them? We ate dandelion greens that cleans your system. They sell them now in capsule form. I developed arthritis when I was forty-three, and I couldn't get up the stairs. My sister brought some herbs home and introduced me to this herbalist. I was really relieved, because I knew that they would cleanse my system and heal me. It took me about six weeks to be cleansed.

WE: Was your family self-sufficient in other ways?

AL: Mama made our clothes, and as the girls got older, they learned how to make their own clothes. I learned how to make my clothes when I was around ten. There was a sewing machine with a foot pedal. I made my first dirndl skirt by the time I was fourteen, because we couldn't afford to go to the stores and buy those things. I made a skirt out of my brother's pants that he had thrown away. By the last year in high school, I was a dandy. (*Laughs.*)

But the thing that hurt me the most, that got on my nerves the most, is that my siblings and school peers said my hair wasn't any good. My hair wasn't any good! They called it nappy and bad. Everybody who's black, this is what we suffer from. You learn this at home. Not at school. You learn it at home that your hair is nappy and your nose is too big (*laughs*) and your mouth, black, ugly. We're going through this. It would give somebody a terrible complex. I'm glad to be able to talk about it. Maybe it will help to exorcise these demons. They told me that my hair wasn't any good (*laughs*), and then they told me that a woman's crowning glory was her hair! Around the same time, I heard this. So by the time I was fourteen or fifteen, I'd brush it and put oils 'cause it's dry. And tie these big black grosgrain ribbons—I'd put the ribbon up, and it would frame my face just like I had long hair. (*Laughs.*) The boys loved it, because it was imaginative, probably. I started wearing my hair in an Afro around 1959, and I found my last place where I wasn't supposed to be beautiful, 'cause they used to say my shoulder bones were too bony, my feet were too big.

WE: Your family said this?

AL: Yeah, you know how they do ya? (*Laughs.*) I finally lifted every curse there was on my body. That was the last place—my hair!

WE: So you were a pioneer when it came to wearing your hair natural?

AL: Yes. I started wearing my hair natural after I made *The Girl Can't Help It.*[5] In '57 I started living in New York, hanging with the hip intellectual crowd. It was really wonderful for me, because I'd never met these kind of people before who had a hold on what's going down in the society. And I would watch these black men look at a white woman with lust and complain about this white man who's keeping him back. So I asked somebody one day, "What is that look on your face for a European woman? What is that all about?" He told me, "Well, since a lot of times a black woman was a poor imitation of a white woman— she straightened her hair and everything—some men just thought they ought to have the real thing." I said, "Wow, is that what it is?" (*Chuckles.*) So I went to the barber the next day, and he cut it. I didn't know I could wear it long and natural.

WE: Tell me more about this hip crowd you began moving with in 1957.

AL: I met all these wonderful people. I had been hanging with Maya Angelou for a while; Oscar Brown Jr., Max Roach. I got another sense of myself. For the first time, I was beginning to understand what the music was about. I heard it on the radio, but I didn't know of its serious nature. I didn't know who Charlie Parker was. Not really. I didn't know there was Thelonious Monk or John Coltrane. Roach introduced me to that particular crowd of musicians. I was newly famous. I had a movie, I had my own recording with Benny Carter.[6] I was working in supper clubs—in Miami, in Las Vegas—with musicians who didn't care about any music. It just was a job for them, you know. I worked Las Vegas twice. The first time I was at a little joint, and I worked there for a couple weeks. The second time was at Caesar's Palace after I made *For Love Of Ivy*.[7] And they *fired* me in the lobby because I was singing John Coltrane's "Africa." I had written a lyric to John Coltrane's "Africa." I had all this material; they couldn't handle it.

WE: Returning to your earlier history, you had such a wonderful life in Calvin Center, why did your family move to Kalamazoo?

AL: Mama and Dad got a divorce when I was ten. They were great, both of them, but he needed his space and she needed hers. They got tired of one another, you know what I mean? So Mama said, "Okay, you got it." My father went to Chicago to live. We went to Chicago because she had a lot of respect for him. My father wasn't the kind of man you could really mess over. In Chicago's where she told him she was going back to the country, and he better not come back out there. And he didn't. My father gave her the house. He was glad to finally have some time to himself; he'd given his whole life to his children. Nobody really appreciated him as much as they should have. They didn't appreciate Mama, neither.

When we went back to the country, I was ten. There were five of us. Mama didn't know anything about being the breadwinner. My father had taken care of everything, always. But she meant to do this. She gave me a lot of courage. She said, "I'm not going to do this anymore." She told the judge—'cause I was there when she got the divorce—that she was afraid of him and she didn't want any money from him. Because my father, if he had to work and support his family and couldn't come home, he might of come out there and "did" everybody. (*Laughs.*) And she knew it. So we did the best we could. We couldn't get relief because the people in the community were angry with her. It was a black community [Calvin Center], but they didn't think that she should leave this man. Who did she think she was? We'd been away for about six months. They said that since she'd been away too long, she couldn't get any benefits. So we almost starved to death. It was in the country, in the winter, and my brother Kenneth brought these people to our house in a big truck. They were European-American, and they had about twenty rabbits that they gave us. We kept them in the snow. They brought us rabbits a couple of other times. That's how we survived the winter. Then when I was fourteen, she sold the house and moved us to Kalamazoo.

WE: Since you weren't taught about racism in Calvin Center, did you first experience it while in high school in Kalamazoo?

AL: You're right; it was my first time to encounter racism in school. I went to Kalamazoo Central High School. That was the school that was built for the wealthy kids that lived on top of the hill. We lived at the bottom of the hill. This is where the servants lived and took care of the people on the hill. So we went to the same school. The teachers, they'd find an excuse or reason to laugh at my ancestors. They said we were a bunch of savages, practiced cannibalism. You'd go to the movies and you'd see these newsreels, and the Africans would be naked, with their ears pierced, with costumes, dancing. In the sun you don't need clothes. They laughed at us. But look at these children today. We're putting earrings in our tongues, in our clitorises; it's *disgusting.*

WE: Was there a time in these formative years when you decided that you wanted to be a performer?

AL: Yeah, well, I hated school. If Mama had wanted me to go to university I would've left home. It was all I could do to get through high school, and I was *never going to a university.* And I don't miss it! I don't care for them, the atmosphere or anything. The only way I could stay in high school was Mr. Chenery put me on the band follies once a year.[8] I had learned to love to perform. I didn't know how to be excellent, or great, but it was what I wanted to do. Mr. Chenery made it possible. There was always a way made for me, is what I'm saying. I didn't have to go out of my way for a career. Somebody always brought me something.

WE: Did you receive any formal training in music when you were young?

AL: Mama sent me to a piano teacher. I walked up the road about five miles. It was the only lesson I took; she may have been arthritic. But anyway, she had a style—you know the way they teach you how to play the scales—and I was already playing songs. I didn't want to go through that, but Mama offered me some lessons anyway. I always remember that. I didn't start to study until I was about twenty-four.

WE: After working your first professional gigs in Jackson and Battle Creek, Michigan, your brother took you to Los Angeles. Why did you go way out west rather than make the shorter trip to New York?

AL: I'd never heard of New York.

WE: Was it the lure of Hollywood that took you to Los Angeles?

AL: No, I wasn't thinking about *none of that*!

WE: Why, then, did you go to Los Angeles?

AL: So I could get away from Kalamazoo and Jackson! (*Laughter.*) I don't like little towns.

WE: Did you find work quickly?

AL: No, I had to go and hang until I was twenty-one. They didn't let you work in clubs if you weren't twenty-one.

WE: What did you do for that year?

AL: I hung around my auntie's house, my brother's house, and a liquor store and restaurant in Watts. Watts wasn't supposed to be a slum then. There was a red car that went from downtown all the way to Watts, and the houses were beautiful. They were pink and green and blue like everywhere else in Los Angeles. It was before the freeways, and everything was pristine. It was a paradise. So I was there for a little while. Then a friend of the liquor store owner, a liquor salesman, brought me an agent, Johnny Robinson. John had big dimples and walked on his tiptoes. He was as crazy as a loon. (*Laughs.*) When I got to be twenty-one, I went to work in San Diego, and the soldiers and the sailors liked me. I went to Salt Lake City and Roseburg, Oregon. Then he sent me to Honolulu, and I stayed there for two years. First at the Trade Winds and then at the Brown Derby. I went to Honolulu in 1951; for two years I lived over there and sang. And escaped street life. You know what I mean, street life? Dope and pimps and whores. They always did gather around the music. They came to get me and the musicians. I didn't give up *nothin'*. (*Laughs.*) They used to call me "the square broad that works at the Brown Derby."

WE: Is Honolulu where you got your professional act together, so to speak?

AL: Yeah, with these guys called the Rampart Streeters. They were brilliant, but not motivated, you know. The saxophone player would lay on his back on the bar. They called him "Backman." He would blow his horn and sing "Love for Sale." After the band would do their thing, they'd call Anna Marie, and I'd close the show.

WE: Were you studying music at that point?

AL: No. I wasn't studying anything; I was making a living, and I was relieved I didn't have to scrub anybody else's floor. I could stand on the stage and sing, and I was making $99 and change a week. I had never made that much money in my life. In a year I was making, like, $150 a week. I thought that I was really well off.

WE: Did your return to Los Angeles coincide with a change of your name?

AL: Yes. When I worked at the Moulin Rouge in Hollywood, Bob Lilly, the producer, wanted me to have a French name. He didn't know I already had a French name, and I didn't either. Neither did the woman who was the other producer. (*Laughs.*) They didn't know I had a French name, and they gave me Gabby. That's German! They kept Wooldridge. (*Laughs.*) I was like a Sadie Thompson character. For the first time in my career, they started making over me. They were messing me around, pretending that there was value in the way I looked. You know, "Oh, she's gorgeous, she's sexy."

WE: Couldn't you see a way to capitalize on that image and still do the singing you wanted to do?

AL: They don't go together. You're either sincere on the stage or you're not. I tried for a while to be insincere. I never felt sexy, and I said to my manager, Bob Russell[9]—he was the one who changed my name to Abbey Lincoln—I said, "I have the feeling you people are robbing me of my individuality." He said, "You don't *have* any individuality, but you will if you learn to take directions." And I knew he was a foolish person to *say* that to *me*! It's too late for somebody to tell me I didn't have individuality. Eventually I fired everybody.

WE: You met Max Roach about this time in Los Angeles. How did that occur?

AL: He came to see me when I was working at the LaMadelon. After I'd come from Honolulu. Maury Dell was the piano player. Roach was in town at the Lighthouse or some-place. Millie, Maury Dell's wife, went to see him and told him that there was a wonderful singer working at the LaMadelon, and he came to see me. He had an ability for concentration; I checked that out. Anyway, we started to see each other. I probably knew he was married then.

WE: Did you hear him at the Lighthouse?

AL: No. I heard him at the Haig.[10] He sat in one night with some musicians. I think they were all white musicians. They knew who Max was. I didn't know who he was. But when I saw him on the drums, I knew who he was. When I heard him play, I knew who he was. I didn't know who he was, but I knew who he was. (*Laughs.*) When I came to New York, I started to see him again. For me, it was companionship I was looking for, because the only thing I really was frantic about was finding the right man. A man! A man! This is what the women all sang about, "this man." That had a lot to do with it.

WE: What prompted your move to New York in 1957?

AL: My manager, Bob Russell, sent me to New York with a press agent to star at the Village Vanguard. I sold fifty percent of myself to him. That's how I came to New York. I'd made [the movie] *The Girl Can't Help It.* In it I sang a song called "Spread the Word, Spread the Gospel, Speak the Truth," in Marilyn Monroe's dress. Bob Russell wrote this song.

WE: You were a pop star at that time. How did you get booked into a prime jazz club like the Vanguard?

AL: It wasn't a jazz club, then. It was a room for up-and-coming performers. It was before Max Gordon's[11] time with jazz. Back then he had a kitchen. Behind the stage there was a *wonderful* dressing room. When they decided it was a jazz room, he got rid of the dressing room, he got rid of the kitchen, because there is no respect for these men who play this music, and it's their fault because they allow it. When it became a jazz room, it became a joint. And I was never a pop singer. I've always been a serious singer.

WE: Speaking of *The Girl Can't Help It,* what happened to Marilyn Monroe's dress?

AL: I burned the dress that Marilyn wore in the incinerator where I lived in my house in New York. I wanted to make sure I never got caught in it again, you know. I sacrificed it. I knew that it was a famous dress. I burned it, and burned that part of my career.

WE: How did your first Riverside recording[12] come about?

AL: Roach said to me one day, "You want to make a jazz album?" I said, "I'm not a jazz singer." He said, "You're black, aren't you?" And he took me to Riverside. Sonny Rollins was a part of his band, Kenny Dorham was a part of his band—it was his band, really. Wynton Kelly had already been working with me. And Paul Chambers—he fell asleep at the session because somebody told him I wasn't no singer. He got drunk and fell asleep. That's how Wynton Kelly happened to pick up the bass and play "Hush, Now, Don't Explain." I didn't miss Paul. I sang "Tender Is the Rose" all by myself. I never had any complexes. I never looked at anybody awestruck. I'd already met Duke Ellington, and Louis Armstrong, and Benny Carter, and Frank Sinatra, and Nat King Cole. I wasn't impressed with any musicians. (*Laughs.*) I didn't come there for honor or for prestige. For the first time, I was introduced, really, to the arts. It was another world. The world of this music they call jazz. Thelonious Monk, John Coltrane, people who did not do things for *money.* I'd never experienced that before. It changed my life.

WE: At this point, when you'd discovered your calling in jazz, weren't you already a national figure?

AL: I was, but I didn't know what I was doing. I was a novice as far as the work was concerned. I was getting a lot of attention. I was in the papers every day. People believe what they read in the papers. Steve Allen had had me on his show a couple of times. I was a star.

WE: Exactly, you were a star. But then you decided to commit to an area that has much less . . .

AL: Fanfare? It was the only serious approach to the arts I'd ever met.

WE: You didn't feel that you were giving up a lot?

AL: I didn't give up anything. I gave up an insincere approach to the arts, and I'm thankful that I found a way to do that. Roach helped me live. He paid all the bills. (*Laughs.*)

WE: I'd like to talk about a famous recorded collaboration between you and Max Roach, *We Insist! Freedom Now Suite.*[13] Let's focus first on "Triptych."[14]

AL: My career survived that, too. My career survived it.

WE: What do you mean? You like that piece, don't you?

AL: No, I don't. It's brilliant and everything. It's not my song. I didn't write it; it's Roach's work. I was the voice that interpreted it. I have no need to scream. It makes people uncomfortable when they hear a woman scream. That's not music. I remember this great singer, Leontyne Price, she screamed a really controlled scream, but you knew it was onstage. I didn't know how to do that. Hollering and screaming, it's alarming. It's an approach I never used and never will use. I don't petition anybody. If I'm going to complain, it'll be to God. I'm glad that all is behind me.

WE: When you recorded those screams in the studio, were the other musicians at the session prepared for it?

AL: Yeah. We'd been doin' it in the clubs. The NAACP asked us to do a benefit for them. When I started screaming, the security guards ran in with their guns. They tried to put us out of the apartment on Central Park West, because they thought Roach was beating me after we recorded it and we would play it. It wasn't uneventful, believe me. I sang it all over Europe.

WE: How do you respond to other selections on the recording, like "Driva' Man"?

AL: I wrote none of that. That's Oscar Brown Jr. I don't care who the man's nanny is, you understand? "Driva' Man, he made a life, but the mammy ain't his wife." It may be somethin' to somebody, don't mean shit to me. I don't care who his mammy is. (*Laughs.*) His daddy, either.

WE: But you sang that piece with such conviction.

AL: I sang Paul Lawrence Dunbar's "When Malindy Sings"[15] with conviction, too. "You ain't got the natural organs for to make the sound come right."[16] That's racist! The fact that I did it doesn't make it right. I didn't know it was racist until I heard it and I changed it— "Well everybody's got some organs"—but I'm not changing this man's work. I write my own words.

WE: Why did you say your career "survived" the *Freedom Now Suite*?

AL: I got a reputation for being this weirdy broad because I had become socially conscious. People would say, "I guess I'll go hear Abbey scream tonight." They forgave Max Roach for pounding the drum while I screamed, but I was the one who took the weight. I didn't get any offers for records after that. *Down Beat* magazine—I don't like them, either— called me a "professional negro" with "When Malindy Sings" and all that. Yeah, I have enemies here.

WE: One of your early composing ventures was writing a lyric for "Blue Monk"[17] for your 1961 recording, *Straight Ahead.*[18] Tell me how that occurred.

AL: I had heard the song over and over on the radio, and I decided that I wanted to record it. So Max called Thelonious on the phone and told him that I had written this lyric, and would he come to the studio to hear it to see if we could use it. We'd already recorded it. He heard it and he listened to the next thing I did, and he danced a little bit. Before he left, he came over and whispered in my ear, "Don't be so perfect." I said to Max after he'd gone, "Thelonious said 'Don't be so perfect.' What does he mean?" Roach said, "He means make a mistake." I didn't know what either one of them were talking about. It was years later, when the album was re-released and Roach was doing the liner notes, that he asked

Thelonious for a quote. And Thelonious said on the back of my album cover, "Abbey Lincoln has to make it because she is not only a great singer and an actress, she's also a great composer." He said to me, "Abbey, you don't have to write lyrics to other people's songs; you can hear a melody yourself." So I started to believe. And I really am thankful, too, because I have about seventy-five songs in my publishing house, and they're all recorded.

WE: You said you didn't know what Monk or Roach were talking about when they said, "Don't be so perfect" and "Make a mistake." Do you know now?

AL: Yeah. It means that you reach for something. Go for broke. If you don't make it, you tried.

WE: Continuing our look at your documented work, I'm not aware of any recordings by you from roughly 1966 until the early 1970s.

AL: I wasn't being invited to do anything. I was somebody that they had resentment for. Who did I think I was? Wearing my hair natural, having too much to say and singing these freaky freedom songs. Weirdy, weirdy, weird. "Why don't you just sing some ballads?" They've always said this to me. If I told them, they wouldn't understand it. But I know who I am. (*Chuckles.*) Yeah.

WE: When did you seriously begin to write your own compositions?

AL: I saw myself as a composer after "People in Me."[19] I was in Africa, and I discovered I had not been bastardized after all. They knew I was African, only they just didn't know where to put me because of the way I was dressed. And I wore my hair in braids. I heard "People in Me" as a result of that trip. I recorded it in Japan the next month.

WE: In one of the cover photos for the album *People in Me,* you're pictured with Miles Davis. Was he a consultant for that recording?

AL: The people who produced that took full advantage of Miles and his generosity. Miles never said anything about it. He came to help me. He was working in Japan at the same time with this big band of youngsters. I went over there by myself. I was supposed to take a piano player. At the last minute this little cow said she couldn't go. So I went by myself and worked with a trio of Japanese musicians. There were two recording dates for me there. The drummer was not so strong, and we asked Miles for his drummer. He sent us his drummer, Al Foster, his percussionist, James Mtume, and his saxophonist, Dave Liebman. Miles set the tempo for "The Man with the Magic." He didn't seem to be well. That's when I heard "Bird Alone"; I wrote "Bird Alone" for Miles. He was with his band, but he was by himself. He came and set the tempo and befriended me.

WE: Despite not recording much, were you productive in other ways during the '70s and '80s?

AL: Yes. I taught for a year at a university theater.[20] I would go to other universities and do lectures. I wrote a lot during that time. I wrote scholarly papers and gave them as lectures. I'd write poems and recite them. Here's one: "Where are the African gods? Did they leave us on our journey over here? *Where are* the African gods? Will we know them when they suddenly appear? The ones dismissed with voodoo, rock and roll, and all that jazz, and jungle mumbo-jumbo and the razzmatazz. *Where are* the African gods who live within the skin? Within the skin. Without the skin and in the skin again. Do they hide among the shadows while we stumble on the way, or did they go with heaven to prepare another day? Where are the African gods who save us from this misery and shame? *Where are the African gods?* Will we find them while we pray in Jesus' name? Where are the African gods who live and set us free? We are the African gods. We are! You and me."

WE: One of your records from the '80s, *Talking to the Sun*,²¹ features Steve Coleman on tenor saxophone. Was that when he was with M-Base?

AL: No, before M-Base. He came to see me at Sweet Basil's. He was working on the street with the Johnson Brothers, and he was wearing big brogan shoes. He had a big Afro and a railroad workers' cap, and these coveralls. He looked like he was about nineteen. I said, "Are you a musician?" He said, "Yeah." I said, "What do you play?" "Saxophone." I asked him to sit in with us on a Saturday night. He tore the house down. I had a chance to work with him for a while. Didn't take him long. He was the one who created Cassandra Wilson. Steve Coleman is a brilliant musician.

WE: What prompted you to write "People on the Street" from that recording?

AL: I wrote that song in New York about people living on the street. I saw it in Los Angeles first. I was in Hollywood, and I was driving in my car. I saw this elderly woman who had rags around her feet. She couldn't afford shoes, I guess, but she lived in that neighborhood. She asked these kids who were in the car in front of me for a ride. Then she turned to me, and I indicated "Come here, I'll take you." When she got in the car with me she said, "Those kids said to me, 'Take a taxi.' Do you think if I had the money for a taxi, I'd be thumbing a ride?" I dropped her off at this big house where she lived. Maybe she still owned it, but I thought she must be really down on her luck. That's when the words to "People on the Street" came to me: "Lovely little child growing fast and wild. Lonely children living in despair. Left out in the cold with the love you hold, on a sidewalk, living anywhere." We're lost. You can't raise your children like this.

WE: Most recently you signed with Verve. Your first recording for that label as a leader was *The World Is Falling Down*.²² To me, you sounded different than you had on earlier dates.

AL: In 1969 I studied with a great teacher, whose name is David Collier. I met him in New York. He was a singer. He sang in the European classic tradition. He was eighty, and his voice was beautiful. He knew everything about the human voice. He taught me what my instrument was, how it worked. For the first time, I understood it. I'd had some other teachers in California and they'd say, "Reach for it." But David showed me exactly how to hold it. When I got to Los Angeles in 1970, I was a little scared because my sound was deepening. (*Laughs.*) It was wider, and I had a lot more control and a lot more power. My instrument is better than it ever was.

WE: Has the range of your voice changed?

AL: They say that I never had any range. That goes with this thing some people have on me. I just got a little paper, somebody faxed it to me, saying: "Even though, like Billie, her range is limited . . ." My instrument is a lot bigger than Billie's; but Billie wasn't limited, either. Singers have about two octaves, and I have *at least* two. Maria Callas, when you study that tradition, that's another thing. But in *this* music, it's a rare singer who has more than two octaves. An octave and a half, that's all you need.

WE: You have a very demonstrative sound.

AL: I sound like my mother. My mother had this sound. She was not in the choir; she wasn't supposed to have a beautiful voice. She would sing in the audience, and you could hear her over everybody else. A strident sound. I've got a sound like hers. It's not pretty. Sarah had a pretty sound.

WE: Do you think that your delivery over the years has become more percussive?

AL: Yeah. I was really influenced by Max. He taught me a lot about it. He said to me once, "Abbey, why do you sing everything legato?" To make his point, he'd be playing at the drums and I'd hear him saying to me while I was singing, "On the beat, on the beat, on the beat." But it helped me. I learned how to sing on the beat. He was my best teacher.

WE: Compared to many vocalists in the jazz idiom, you don't indulge in vocal acrobatics.

AL: You know, that's for horns. I don't sing like that; I sing in the tradition of Billie Holiday and Bessie Smith. Musicians don't have words, so they have to get through without the words, and they improvise. I always think that the singers are in competition with the musicians. Musicians are the ones who know how to do that. Why bother with musicians at all? Just come to the stage by yourself. I don't care for that approach. Tell us a story. If you're using words, tell us what you're talkin' about. Don't hide behind scatting—you're anonymous. I mean, who are you? You're telling me something, and I can't understand what you're saying? I'm the singer. I have words, and sometimes the words can get lost if you're hung up trying to compete with the musicians. I don't do anything they do.

WE: The content of the lyric is paramount?

AL: Yes. Otherwise why sing it?

WE: Well, there's another tradition, with Betty Carter at the helm, where vocalists take choruses like a horn player.

AL: I know. I disagree with that. It's not anything I aspire to. In the first place, the vocal instrument is not as great as the piano or the horns. They have a lot more range. Every once in a while I do some scatting. Sometimes it's corny. (*Laughs.*) But for the most part, I don't scat. Why would I compete with a horn? A horn can't talk. It can't say a word. I don't want to be like the musicians. I'm a singer, and I tell a story. I wouldn't have it any other way.

WE: Do you plan out your approach to a song ahead of time?

AL: No, no, no. It's a happening. I learn the song; I learn how to play it on the piano. I live with the song—usually I write it. I know the changes, everything! Then the muse sings. I don't try to direct it. I sing with my throat clear. It's not full of fog. Sometimes it is.

WE: Who does your arrangements?

AL: They're all head arrangements. I haven't had an arranger in a long time because they make it oppressive. The arrangement is oppressive. You gotta live with the daggone thing, you know.

WE: What, for you, is the bedrock description of your work?

AL: I'm a storyteller. I don't have any confusion about it in my mind at all. I tell stories on the stage set to music. The audience says to me, "I heard that!" (*Laughs.*) I am an actress; I'm a singer; I'm a poet. And I get a chance to get it all off on the stage. You can't do that any better than that way.

WE: The poetry of your lyrics is a hallmark of your compositions. Did you have a love for words as you matured?

AL: Yeah. I loved English. In the one-room schoolhouse there was a dictionary in the back of the room, and I'd spend a little time there. English was always my best subject. Later on, Bob Russell introduced me to a book on semantics by a Japanese writer. And another book on how to increase your vocabulary by one thousand words.

WE: Another aspect of your compositions that appeals to me is that you write about unusual subject matter, not just the boy-girl genre.

AL: I know, because it's a structured life we live. When I came to the stage, the women were singing about unrequited love. Love in spite of love! You know, this is all they had. And I thought, "Listen, I'm not gonna sing this stuff, because if he's nothin' then that means that she ain't nothin' either." How could I have a man that he ain't nothin' and I am? So I just took that out of my mouth. I don't sing the praises of somebody I don't respect. I sang all those songs, you know, following after Billie and Sarah and Dinah. I don't sing that stuff anymore.

WE: It strikes me that the lyrics of commercial pop songs are so often literal, whereas your material depends upon powerful imagery that acts metaphorically.

AL: You're right. I get a lot of my direction from the writers in the Bible. The approach they use to a story. The way they describe something. Metaphor, that's what I use.

WE: I am particularly fond of your second Verve date,[23] with Stan Getz backing you so beautifully.

AL: That was my first one-hundred-thousand seller. I always talk about Stan. Yeah, he blessed me before he left here. It took us all that time. He pulled my coat. (*Laughter.*) He did, he pulled my coat and told me, "Well, it's all about being black, right? *Black. Black. Black.*" (*Laughter.*) If I had waited to ask him to be on my album, I never would have had a chance to record with him. He died about three months later. I met him when he was a youngster. When we were young, in Los Angeles, when my name was Anna Marie. He was hanging with Shorty Rogers and that crowd.

WE: Speaking about Getz prompts me to ask you about the debate these days concerning black innovators and whether white musicians really can play jazz. Where do you figure in on this?

AL: Well, the African musicians are the river for the music. They are the ones who decide which direction the music is going to go. So far we haven't had a white musician who said, "Okay, we're goin' this way." There are a few people who are the ones who bring innovation. The women don't do this, either. You know who does this? The black man! Nobody says to them stop and go. They come to the music without anybody's permission. They're not guaranteed any money, *nothin'*! It's like a pregnancy. And they have to deliver this child. This is a music like the European classic form. Anybody can play it, but you have to really go for it. It takes practice and understanding. It's an approach to something.

WE: When you say that women don't deliver innovation, isn't it likely that the difference rests on the fact that women in jazz haven't had the same opportunities?

AL: The men didn't have the opportunity either, but they made it. Women are made to bring children here! She brings the human being, imbues it with her spirit and everything. He builds the outside world, and she makes the people. Now, you gonna change that? I'm sayin', how's anybody gonna change that? Nobody gives the men permission to go to the stage with this music. It's what they have to do. And the women do it if they have to do it. But nobody's trying to play like Hazel Scott. Nobody's trying to play like Mary Lou Williams. They were wonderful and famous, but nobody is trying to play like any of them. They're not the rivers. The men are the ones. The rivers are Thelonious Monk, Bud Powell—these are the ones that people are trying to play like.

WE: The number of women who have entered the jazz world has increased dramatically over the last ten years. Don't you think that will make a difference in terms of future contributions?

AL: When she learns to play this instrument. It's a lot to ask. It's a lot like playing football. When she can stand on the stage with Charlie Parker and John Coltrane (*laughs*), it'd be fine with everybody. But this is a lusty music, and it's hard for anybody to hang there. These men, it's all they have, really, in this world. It's *all* they have. If the women want to attack something, let them go and find out why it is the women are not the conductors for the big symphony orchestras. Why it is they are not the composers? Why aren't they wagging that tail? What did they come here for, pretending that somebody is disinheriting them?

WE: Do women make an important contribution to this music?

AL: The women sing. There's no greater singer than the female. She stands in front of the men. Sometimes she doesn't know B flat from A minor chord. It's true. A lot of times it's like that. Sarah played the piano. Dinah played the piano. But most of them don't know anything. I remember the first time in Kalamazoo the piano player asked me what key I sang the song in. I didn't know what he was talking about. (*Laughs.*) I didn't know there was such a thing as a key, though I'd been playing with the piano. The singer gets her instrument free, gratis. But the musician has to go out and buy an instrument and sit and learn how to play it. And he's dedicated. There's some great young musicians out here right now. They work with me.

WE: You're referring to men?

AL: Yes, I'm talking about men. If I was dependent on the women, I wouldn't have nobody to call. Who am I gonna call? There's a couple of girls who play the drum. (*Laughs.*) I wouldn't hire anybody because of their gender. But if the women were really a part of this music like they say they want to be, they would have done it a long time ago. This music has been here as long as we've been here. The women don't play the drum. They don't play the saxophone. The musicians made this a special instrument. It wasn't theirs.

WE: You mean the saxophone was a European instrument and jazz musicians made it their own?

AL: Yes. Didn't nobody give them permission to do this. They did it. If the women want to make a contribution to the music as musicians, they should do it.

WE: Do you deny the possibility that it might happen?

AL: We'll see. It'll be interesting the day that we see somebody who can play the drum like Elvin Jones, or Art Blakey, or Max Roach. Who can play a horn like Lester Young, Coleman Hawkins? All you have to do is do it. The men love anybody who can bring it, even though they have their prejudices and everything. They loved Billie Holiday and they love me. I've never had any trouble with musicians.

WE: Would the prospect of performing with an all-woman band be appealing to you?

AL: No. I'm not interested in any feminist thing. I have a friend named Cobi Narita[24] and I told her more than once, "Don't include me. Go somewhere else." Feminists have nothing to do with this music, and I don't want to be someplace where there're not any men around. I don't get it. I really don't get it. If I could find a way for all the singers to come to the stage and jam like the horns do—we don't know how to do that yet—I'd like to. It's something I can hear; I dream of it sometimes. *Talkin' to the Sun,* I was experimenting with it.

WE: Have you experienced difficulties professionally due to your race?

AL: No, because the greatest thing in this world is to be a singer if you have African ancestors. Yeah, everybody expects that you can do it. Movies, that's something else; but in this music, if you're a black woman, you're supposed to be able to sing. They expect that you can, anyway.

[The first music selection was "The End of a Love Affair" from *Billie Holiday/Lady In Satin,* 1958; Columbia Records.]

AL: (*As the music is playing*) When I heard her sing "For All We Know" on this album, I wept. (*She cries.*) I'm surprised at myself. (*Laughs.*) She died in jail, arrested in the hospital.

With $250 strapped to her leg. (*The music concludes.*) She had just come from Europe. I remember reading that in the paper. They've been livin' on her blood ever since she died. She was a great queen. The greatest singer of *her* time—probably of any time. She looks like a relative of mine; she looks like my older sister, Eleanor. She might be a relative anyway. I wouldn't have known which way to go if it hadn't been for Billie. It's the same feeling I had the first time I heard her on the Victrola, in the country.

[Next, we listened to "Like Someone in Love" from *Sarah Vaughan Recorded Live,* 1958; EmArcy Jazz Series.]

AL: (*As the music is playing*) I wouldn't have recognized this as Sarah. She's obviously from Billie.

WE: In what way?

AL: Well, in a way she's show biz—impressing other people. She was great, but Billie Holiday was somebody who really evolved. That's why she's still with us. She was an evolved spirit. It was painful for her to witness all this. So she used things to dull the pain. She was a queen without her court, without her king. She was out here by herself and lived with a man who would beat her. Sarah lived through that. Dinah. Men who beat women. Singers seem to attract them.

WE: In comparison to Sarah, don't you think Billie Holiday lived a tragic life?

AL: I don't see Billie's life as tragic. She didn't die of any dread disease.

WE: How about the social injustice she suffered?

AL: (*The music concludes.*) She was a victim, yes. The difference between Billie and me was Billie's mother was thirteen when she carried. My mother was thirty-eight. She had a lot of information that Billie's mother never had—you know, she was a kid. Billie was working in brothels. Changing things, cleaning up behind the prostitutes, and she fell in love with the music there. So, she was born to street life. If Billie had been given the same kind of circumstances I had, I believe her life would have been totally different.

[We listened to "Hellhound on My Trail" from *Cassandra Wilson/Blue Light 'Til Dawn,* 1993; Blue Note Records.]

AL: (*As the music is playing*) I have a hard time sometimes understanding what the story is, because I don't always understand the words she uses. She has a wonderful sound, got her own sound. But I never can get lost in the story that she's telling, because it's hard for me to hear what she's saying. It's her sound more than the words that you hear. I don't know what she's talkin' about. The queens would tell you a story, and you understand every word they said. I think Cassandra should fix that.

[The last piece of music was "Drop Me Off in Harlem" from *Ella Fitzgerald Sings the Duke Ellington Songbook,* 1957; Verve Records.]

AL: (*As the music is playing*) Yeah. You can understand every word she says. The great Ella Fitzgerald, no doubt about it. (*As Ella scats*) All the singers—Sarah, everybody—were tryin' to do it the way that Ella could do it. It's really brilliant. I wouldn't want to try and do that. (*The music stops.*)

WE: Is she the exception to the rule about scatting that you were talking about earlier?

AL: For me she is. Ella was really good at it. Sarah was a great scatter; so was Carmen. But Ella was the one who led the way. Everybody scatted after Ella. She's the original for the singers. That's my understanding, anyway. She's a great musician, I believe.

WE: What about Louis Armstrong?

AL: Yes. You're right. Louis Armstrong precedes her, but she took scatting to another place. Billie comes from Louis. I heard Louis one day on the radio; he was younger, and I thought it was Billie Holiday. Yeah, Louis Armstrong. I met him in Honolulu. He would do the show and then receive his guests in his shorts and tee shirt with a handkerchief tied around his head to absorb the sweat. And there was nothing unseemly about it. There wasn't an evil bone in his body. He didn't look at women's behinds. There was no bitch in his mouth. A *gentleman.* Yeah.

WE: It's a shame, don't you think, that Louis Armstrong was accused of being an Uncle Tom later in his life?

AL: That's what people said. It's just a lie. Anyway, Uncle Tom was a heroic character. They're just lying on him. He was a great man, Uncle Tom. So was Louis Armstrong. I remember hearing that he was supposed to be some Uncle Tom. Because, allegedly, he ingratiated himself while entertaining white people. He entertained everybody. He wasn't doing that for whites. It was his style of music.

Selected Discography

Straight Ahead. Candid CCD 79015 (1961, reissued 1989). (With Coleman Hawkins, Eric Dolphy, and Max Roach.)
People in Me. Verve 515246-2 (1973).
Talkin' to the Sun. Enja ENJ4060 (1983).
**The World Is Falling Down.* Verve 843 476-2 (1990).
You Gotta Pay the Band. Verve 314511110-2 (1991). (This was one of Stan Getz's last recordings. He is featured extensively.)
A Turtle's Dream. Verve 314 527 382-2 (1994).

Notes

1. *Nothin' but a Man,* DuArt Film Laboratories, 1964, and *For Love of Ivy* (opposite Sidney Poitier), Anchor Bay Entertainment, 1968.
2. *That's Him,* 1957.
3. 1960; Candid Records (lyrics by Oscar Brown Jr.)
4. *Abbey Sings Billie*, 1987; Enja and *Abbey Sings Billie, Volume 2*, 1987; Enja.
5. 1956; 20th Century Fox.
6. 1956; Liberty Records.
7. 1968; Palomar Pictures International.
8. Mr. Chenery produced the band follies each year at Kalamazoo Central High School.
9. A songwriter, Bob Russell wrote the lyrics for Duke Ellington's standards "Do Nothing 'til You Hear from Me" and "Don't Get Around Much Anymore."
10. Jazz club in Los Angeles.
11. Max Gordon was the owner of the Village Vanguard.
12. *That's Him,* 1957.
13. 1960; Candid records (lyrics by Oscar Brown Jr.).
14. The full title of the work is *Triptych: Prayer, Protest and Peace.*
15. From *Straight Ahead,* 1961; Candid Recordings.
16. From Paul Lawrence Dunbar, *When Malindy Sings* (New York: Dodd Mead and Co., 1903). The original stanzas read, "You ain't got de nachel o'gans Fu' to make de soun' come right. . . ."
17. Composed by Thelonious Monk.
18. Interview with Dan Morgenstern, from *Abbey Lincoln/You Gotta Pay the Band,* Verve/Polygram video; 1991.
19. From the album *People in Me,* 1973; Inner City Records.

20. University of California at Northridge.

21. 1983; Enja Records.

22. 1990.

23. *You Gotta Pay the Band,* 1991.

24. Founder and President, Jazz Center of New York, Inc., and Universal Jazz Coalition, Inc.; Founder and Past President, International Women in Jazz, Inc.

Virginia Mayhew

Virginia Mayhew

Among the new crop of jazz musicians to emerge in the 1990s, saxophonist Virginia Mayhew is one of the players to watch. An incisive mainstream stylist and a gifted composer, the former classical clarinetist opted in mid-career to redirect her professional ambitions toward the jazz life. During the 1993 and 1995 Floating Jazz Festivals,[1] Mayhew's playing caught the attention of Chiaroscuro Records producer Hank O'Neal, who offered to issue her debut recording on his independent label.

Born May 14, 1959, Mayhew was raised in the San Francisco area. She moved to New York in 1987 after receiving the first Zoot Sims Memorial Scholarship to study jazz at the New School. A charter member of the all-female big band DIVA, Mayhew was a featured soloist on their first two recordings. From 1990 to 1998, she worked and recorded with veteran trombonist Al Grey, while cultivating her arranging skills.

Mayhew's visibility took a quantum leap with the 1997 release of *Nini Green,*[2] which was chosen "Best New Release" by both *Cadence* and *Jazziz* magazines. The success of this CD can be attributed to Mayhew's sinewy improvisations on tenor and soprano, her memorable compositions, and the telepathic stoking that comes from a regular working band.[3] Her next album, *No Walls,*[4] recorded in 1999 and featuring similar personnel, was also well received.

With a surfeit of young saxophonists flooding the jazz scene, Mayhew's robust sound elevates her above the pack. She employs a straight-ahead boppish style to deliver solos that are harmonically advanced and driven by an engaging rhythmic propulsion. Never relying on gimmicks or trickery, she displays her technical prowess and organic note choice as she demonstrates uncanny instincts for mixing hot and cool phrases.

Mayhew enjoys high praise for her saxophone playing and reaps even more plaudits for her skills as a writer. Her compositions range from pristine melodies superimposed over nonconventional time feels, to hard-hitting tunes ideally suited for Mayhew and trumpeter Ingrid Jensen to play furious bop-like lines in tight harmony. Her 2003 release, *Phantoms*,[5] features her most definitive writing yet, highlighted by demiurgic treatments of several jazz standards.

Since establishing herself in New York, Mayhew has worked with renowned musicians such as Clark Terry, Joe Williams, Toshiko Akiyoshi, and Chico O'Farrill. She has appeared as a leader at many of the city's major jazz clubs, while also performing throughout the United States, Europe, the Caribbean, and Australia. Recently, she has traveled to the Newly Independent States (formerly the USSR) and Southeast Asia as a Jazz Ambassador for the U.S. State Department.

Recorded August 1, 2000

JS: You began studies at the New School for Social Research shortly after moving from the West Coast to New York. Is there a particularly memorable encounter with one of the jazz faculty that you'd care to relate?

VM: When I was at the New School, Jaki Byard was teaching piano there. I was in his class, and we were playing some tune. I shouldn't say this on tape, but I guess I'll confess. I had already played my solo and I was sitting, trying to figure something out on my horn, really softly. I don't know how anyone could hear it, but he jumps up, slams downs the piano, reaches in his bag on the piano, and pulls out a fourteen-inch machete. He glares at us all and says, "Who's playing!?!" Everybody's petrified. He said, "Don't play while I'm playing my solo, God damn it." (*Laughter.*) That was probably the most memorable.

WE: Certainly he was just teasing.

VM: He was crazy enough, you never know. But I don't think he really would have stabbed anybody.

WE: Did he ever find out who was playing?

VM: No. I didn't confess until now, when he's safely in his grave.

JS: Let's switch our focus to your formative years. Were there other musicians in your family?

VM: Three of my four grandparents were musicians. My maternal grandmother was a classical singer—not professional, but very fine. My grandfather, until the time he was twenty-five, he was gearing up for a career as a classical pianist. My paternal grandfather and father both played piano by ear. That grandfather died when my father was twelve, and my father died when I was seven, so I didn't really get to reap the benefits. But the *love* of music was definitely around. And my mother studied piano for sixteen years.

JS: Did you follow suit and start on piano?

VM: No. When I was ten I started on clarinet. I wanted to play the saxophone, but they didn't let girls play the saxophone at that school at that time.

WE: When did you first encounter jazz?

VM: Not until I was sixteen. I was doing well on the clarinet, and the Sequoia High School jazz band needed a saxophone. So, the band director, Ed Harris, asked me if I wanted to play saxophone in the jazz band, and I said, "Yeah, sure." I went to my private clarinet teacher, and I said, "Look, I'm going to be playing saxophone in the jazz band. Can you give me a couple of lessons to get me started?" He was *really* excited. Much more excited than he had ever been for the clarinet. The truth turned out to be that he was really a jazz saxophone player trying to make a living, and he was teaching clarinet. I mean, he could play the clarinet and everything, but his passion was jazz saxophone. Once that started, then he really became, you know, a much more intense teacher. He told my mother to buy me certain records, and I was almost old enough to start going to the Keystone Korner in San Francisco. And so he'd tell me, "Okay, you gotta go this week, you know, Dexter Gordon's there," or "Art Blakey's there, you gotta come up."

JS: What were your ambitions after high school?

VM: I decided I wanted to be a music major. I went to the University of Colorado as a clarinet major because I couldn't make up my mind what to do.

WE: Despite your newfound interest in the saxophone, your focus was still on the clarinet?

VM: Yes. I wasn't very good at saxophone for a long time. I mean, I was playing lead alto in the jazz band, but I'd hate to hear a tape of it. I'm sure it was dreadful.

WE: The clarinet is such a beautiful instrument, yet it's seldom heard in jazz.

VM: I don't really like it in jazz. I played classical clarinet and jazz saxophone—never the two shall meet! Unfortunately, the time I spent on each instrument didn't particularly help the other. In classical clarinet playing, the emphasis is on a pure, perfect tone, being able to articulate rapidly, and other technical aspects, as well as interpreting the music in an appropriate way. With jazz saxophone, the main emphasis is on improvisation, something that is rarely done in the classical music I played. Compared to classical clarinet tone, the desired tone in jazz is a reedy, sometimes airy sound, and finding your personal "voice" is very important. Although the technique one develops from practicing the clarinet is helpful, the main emphases are very different.

WE: What is it about jazz clarinet that you object to?

VM: I don't *object* to it; I don't like it. I mean, I love Lester Young on the clarinet.

WE: How about the Barney Bigard, New Orleans–type clarinet sound?

VM: I like *that* kind of jazz clarinet playing much better than the modern bebop, or swing kinds of clarinet playing. It might be just because I was raised with, you know, classical music. I really don't care for any of the jazz clarinet players. To me, they don't swing. Those old guys, yes, but most of the modern guys, to me, they articulate a lot, and it doesn't really swing.

JS: How long were you at the University of Colorado?

VM: I was there two years. Clarinet was my major, but I also studied saxophone. Then I realized that if I really wanted to be serious, I needed to go somewhere more serious. And I didn't feel like I was ready to go to New York. So I went to San Francisco State for one year, and I met Johnny Coppola, great trumpet player. He became my first mentor. He played lead trumpet with Stan Kenton and Woody Herman. He took me under his wing and lent me records, all different types of jazz. I would come back and say, "I loved this; I hated this; I didn't understand this." And it turned out that he and I had almost exactly the same taste. He started putting me on gigs. He introduced me to my teacher, Kirt Bradford; his given name was Mustapha Hashim. He had played lead alto with Jimmy Lunceford after Willie Smith left the band. He had a *great* sound. He was very old school, and he had his method for practicing and learning how to improvise. It was great for me because I really needed it. So then I had two mentors, and the better I got, the more gigs John put me on. I really learned how to play lead alto because I played in a band with Kirt Bradford every week for years. When he left, I played lead. Then John would hire me to play lead alto in his big band. So that was really lucky.

WE: What was Kirt Bradford's method for teaching you how to improvise?

VM: He had a whole program he called Applied Modern Harmony, which was an approach to learn all the notes that are in each chord. I don't know; I mean, every year I'm improving. I'm sure I was really terrible back then, but I just kept going.

WE: When did you have fully the realization that you wanted to be a jazz musician?

VM: Two or three years before I came to New York, I met with a friend of a friend of mine in San Francisco, who was an older professional musician. My friend said, "This guy'll give you the straight scoop on New York." I trusted him, so I met with this guy. He was really nice. We talked awhile, and he said, "Listen, you're white, you're female"—I mean, he's saying this to me like a big brother—"the music business is never going to let you in. You already play clarinet; I would suggest you start working on the flute really hard, and when you get a grip on that, start on the double reeds, and you can do shows." He said it in such a way that I felt grateful. I went home, and I started taking flute lessons and began switching my emphasis from the saxophone. I did that for a year or so. Then all of a sudden one day I realized, "This is not what I want to do." Because I was getting up every morning practicing the clarinet, practicing the flute; I wasn't getting any better at improvising, which was the thing that I loved the most. One day around this time, John Coppola said to me, "Look, you love the saxophone, you love jazz. Why don't you be a jazz musician and quit torturing yourself?" That moment is frozen in time for me. It was like a fog in my brain lifted, and everything became very clear. I should follow my heart and become a jazz musician.

WE: What finally precipitated your move to New York?

VM: I had a band of my own. A Latin jazz group. I was a co-leader, and I worked really hard to get us gigs. One night this club owner came by to hear the band. I was *so glad,* because I'd been trying to get him to come by for months. I went to one of the other leaders of the band and I said, "Okay, the guy from the Montmarte is here; we should start." And she was, as usual, drunk, and she wouldn't get back on. I tried to talk her into coming back on, and she got really mad. She went up to the mike and started saying, "Well, Miss Virginia Mayhew says it's time for us to start playing, . . . and she's the boss . . . I don't know who she thinks she is, but . . ." She was staggering and really drunk and obnoxious, slurring her words. I was so frustrated and disappointed and disgusted, and embarrassed. I had worked so hard to write charts for the band, rehearse the band, get gigs for the band. That was the last straw. And another thing before the last straw was that there was one good bass player in town at the time. I had one of my first gigs I had arranged, and I think the day before the gig he called me up and said he'd been offered an eighty-dollar gig instead of my seventy-five-dollar gig, so he'd taken it. It was stuff like that—I just didn't want to be around it any more. There were some *great, great* jazz musicians in the Bay area, but I just wanted to be around more.

The next day I opened up the Musicians' Union paper, and there was an ad for the New School. Two weeks later I flew to New York to check out the program. That was in the middle of November 1986. I moved to New York at the beginning of January 1987.

JS: Were you playing a lot at that time in the San Francisco area?

VM: I was playing *a lot.*

JS: Making a decent living?

VM: Yes, I was making a lot of money then. I was doing all sorts of music: classical music, jazz big band, shows, Latin. I played clarinet with the Oakland Ballet Orchestra, and I played saxophone with the Berkeley Symphony Orchestra when it did Frank Zappa's symphony. Things were going well, but I could see that in ten years I'd be doing about the same gigs. I saw what the best players were doing workwise, and it wasn't that different from what I was doing. I saw very few musicians who were driven, and I was definitely driven. It was really hard to get people together to play jam sessions. For the most part, people weren't passionate about jazz. It was like a job to them. It's a nice life out in San Francisco, but I wanted to be in the heart of the jazz world, surrounded by people who were passionate about the music.

JS: Once you arrived in New York, how long was it before you were working?

VM: Well, I started working pretty soon after I got here; somehow I met people and I started getting Latin gigs. But it was pretty brutal. Low money, coming home on the train at four in the morning. When I first moved here, I also worked with the Kit McClure Big Band for a little while.

WE: Have you yet gotten close to the income you achieved in San Francisco?

VM: It goes up and down. The more I want to do my own thing, the less it is. Well, that's not true, either. Last year I had a great year. I did some major festivals as a leader, and I made some nice money. This year's been really, really slow, but I hope when my new CD[6] comes out, then it'll be another good year.

JS: After your first CD, *Nini Green*, how long was it before you started thinking about the new one?

VM: *Nini Green* was recorded in August of '96, and it came out in August of '97. In '99 I contacted Chiaroscuro to see if they wanted to do a new one. They hadn't recorded anybody in the studio since me. They do a lot of jazz cruises; they record people on those and release them. We're on good terms, but they just couldn't do it at that point. I couldn't find anybody else to do it, so I took my life savings out of the bank and did this. My life is a constant series of investments in my future. Someday I'll get the payoff.

WE: Your CDs emphasize originals. Do you include a few standards to appease the buying public?

VM: I am conscious of having a couple standards on there, so there'll be something that people will recognize. When I get a little more established, or secure, I might not do that anymore—if I have enough of my own material that I like. Because I don't write a lot. I mean, basically on both of these CDs I used all of my tunes that I'm happy with. Then it's just a matter of filling in the other stuff.

WE: Is composing difficult for you?

VM: No, it's really easy. I don't work on it; it just comes, and I have to write it down. When I try to write something and I'm not in the mood, it just never works out. For me, composing is emotional and it's spontaneous. Everything is sort of in me already. Arranging is also easy for me. I love that.

JS: Let's talk about what you meant to convey in particular compositions. What was the inspiration behind the title tune of your first recording, "Nini Green"?

VM: I was in Italy on tour. I was sitting in the back of this car, looking out the window and thinking of how much I love my grandmother,[7] and it came to me. The *whole* tune just came to me. I didn't have a keyboard or anything, but I managed to somehow write it down enough so that I could remember it.

WE: How about "The Visit We Missed" from *No Walls*?

VM: Well, my mother was supposed to come visit me—-I don't remember what happened. I think it ended up I was going to be working every night. I'd done this big band gig that I do every Monday with the Howard Williams Big Band, and it's almost *all* 4/4. So I'm sitting in a car on my way home, and I'm thinking about my mom and too bad that it didn't work out. All of a sudden this bass line comes in my head, and "Oh, I should figure out what that is so I can write it down." Then I realized it's in five, which was sort of ironic 'cause I'd been playing four all night.

WE: So, a fair amount of your composing has autobiographical overtones?

VM: Absolutely. That's where I get my inspiration.

WE: Do you ever draw upon particularly unpleasant experiences, and as a result write an ugly piece?

VM: I did write something that was ugly. It's called "Time Alone,"[8] which I wrote after I'd been spending too much time alone. It's very fast and intense and harsh. That was what I was feeling, and that's what I wanted to write. I achieved my goal, but "Time Alone" is an exception. Beauty is very important to me. I'm always striving for a good tone, for instance, and to play with a singing quality. I've learned a lot listening to great singers of all styles of music. The saxophone can be a lot like the voice, and that's something I strive for. I also use rhythm to make the music more interesting. I love the drums, the "feel" of the music. I appreciate the more complex aspects of harmony and polyrhythms, but it's the beat that thrills me. Beauty and the beat! There are so many shades of beauty. My palette is always growing. I love to listen to Billie Holiday and Shirley Horn. They are the masters of the bittersweet—perhaps the most common deep feeling. But beauty is the most important thing.

JS: Returning to your chronology, how did you first get the call from DIVA?

VM: I already knew Sherrie Maricle[9] when they started putting the band together, so she called me and asked me if I wanted to audition. I said, "Sure, I'd love to." At that point, I was strictly a lead alto player. So I went down there, and I was the best lead alto that auditioned. I mean, I'm not egocentric, but one thing I know is how to play lead alto. But something happened, and they offered me the first tenor chair instead. They said, "If you want to be in the band, you'll have to play tenor." I really wanted to be in the band, and I always wanted to play tenor, which is the instrument I've been in love with since I first heard jazz. But I was too insecure; you know, there are a million great tenor players. But I said, "Okay, if you're going to pay me to do it, sure, I'll play tenor."

JS: Did you own a tenor?

VM: I owned a tenor, but I never played it. I was working for Al Grey then, too, and he wanted me to play tenor in his sextet. So I was like, "Okay." So I started hauling around both of them to my gigs. Tenor was what I always listened to, and what I always wanted to play.

WE: It was a blessing in disguise?

VM: It was absolutely a blessing. The solos that were on the tenor books were much better—much more to my taste than the solos that were on the alto books, for the most part. So it worked out great. I was with DIVA for about three years. I left the band in '96.

JS: Characterize for us the early years of DIVA.

VM: When DIVA started out, it was *very* exciting. The musicians were really good, plus we had Mike Abene and other quality writers doing the arrangements. We understood that the all-female angle was a necessary hook to get work, but the original mission was about this band playing great jazz. You know, here's a burnin' band, and they happen to all be women! That was the priority. Now it's really changed. I mean, every band has its problems, but the first couple years it was really exciting because we all still believed that it was going to be a jazz band.

JS: What do you mean by "it was going to be a jazz band"? Wasn't DIVA a jazz band from the start?

VM: It was, but now it seems like the female part, the show business aspect, is getting the emphasis instead of the jazz part. The musicians in the band are still good, but the music the band is playing is more "commercial" jazz. It's too bad, because there are some great players who could really tear it up if they were given more than thirty seconds to play.

JS: Overall, do you think the existence of DIVA has been a benefit?

VM: Absolutely. The DIVA big band has given a lot of female jazz musicians experience and connections, and even provided help with immigration papers for some. Being employed in the band has made it easier for members to survive financially in New York City. DIVA is fulfilling a valuable function by providing female role models, even if they're not playing as much on the cutting edge as I and others would like to see. Hopefully someday bands like DIVA won't be necessary.

WE: As you survey the jazz world, do you feel that the chances are good that women horn players will finally gain major recognition?

VM: I'm a little burnt out on it. It's so far past due. I just try to be encouraged by the progress that is being made. There are *so* many more really good women horn players, specifically—but every instrument now—than there were ten years ago when I moved here. There's no comparison. But it's still a matter of "You hoo, we're here."

WE: Do critics attend your performances?

VM: Almost never. Stuart Troup of *Newsday* was in my corner until he died. Since then, it's rare for a critic to attend one of my shows.

WE: How do you view your options at this point?

VM: At this point, I try not to think about it. I just keep going. I recognize it for what it is, and I try to talk to the younger women that I know if they start getting bummed out. It happens all the time that a young woman is at a certain level and she'll go out and see what's happening. She'll go to four or five different places, and there'll be four or five guys on her instrument that are not as good as she is. They're all workin', and her phone isn't ringing.

JS: What's the source of the problem?

VM: I don't know what it is. If there's a woman in the band, she's going to get extra attention. Just because a lot of people won't have ever seen a woman in the band before. Maybe bandleaders don't want somebody in their band getting attention. They want the attention, or they want the attention to be strictly on the music. It's not that this woman is *asking* for the attention, but you get extra attention. It's not an old-boy network, but people call their buddies a lot. If you need a sub, you'll call your buddy. The women don't usually hang out with the men as much, because the guys, you know, finish the gig and go hang out until five in the morning.

WE: So for women players, the camaraderie isn't there with the men who sit in the driver's seat?

VM: Yeah, and plus sexual dynamics, I think. If I hang out with a bunch of guys, you know, it can't just be about the music. There's always an undercurrent of, well, maybe, you know, something else is happening here. But I think the real problem isn't with the musicians, because I think the musicians are pretty cool. I think it's with the club owners, the critics, and the labels, because they're the ones who have all the power, really.

JS: Have you suffered overt sexual discrimination in your career?

VM: Oh, yeah. Once I was trying to get into this show. A friend of mine talked to the contractor. He told my friend that he would never hire a woman to play in the show. That was in the late '80s. You know, people weren't so sophisticated yet; today they wouldn't actually say it. But you run into it all the time. At the very least what you get is, "Oh, we're so glad to have a woman in the band." Women are just looking forward to the day that it's a non-issue. You know, that we're there because of how we play and that we're a nice person. Because that has something to do with it. You know, you don't want to hang out with people that are jerks.

JS: Are professionals in the jazz world condescending toward you because you're female?

VM: That's what I run into the most: the condescension. The people with power not taking you seriously, talking to you like you're eighteen years old. It's really aggravating when that happens, and you know, you still have to be polite. You still want the gig. If I had to pick one word, "condescending" would be it, because they just don't take you seriously. "Oh, you play the saxophone. How cute. Oh, that's nice." I mean, I did a rehearsal last Wednesday night, and I got the business from this bandleader. He came up, I held out my hand, and he kissed me on the cheek. I never met this guy before. I mean, I could have shoved him away, but I just let it go. But it was definitely not something that I had encouraged. Then he made a big announcement: "Isn't it nice to have a woman in the band." You know, I've heard it so many times. Then he comes over and says, "Okay, stand up. I want to see what size you are to measure you for a jacket." It was really awful. Then he tried to give me another big kiss when I left. This is 2000, you know, and I have to put up with this stuff. We're sophisticated and we live in a sophisticated world, but I think the majority of the population is still really way behind. For instance, almost every time I play, somebody comes up and says, "Oh, I've never seen a girl saxophone player before." It's amazing that this still even exists, but, in fact, most people have never seen a woman saxophone player.

JS: Given the increase in the number of women jazz players in recent years, do you anticipate any impact on the aesthetics of the music with their arrival?

VM: Well, first of all, although there's been a *huge* increase proportionately in the number of women in the jazz scene, it's still a very small number. So I don't know if there are enough of us to make a change like that. But I think it is possible, and it might be happening on a *very* small scale. I mean, for instance, Maria Schneider, her band has a completely different sound than anybody else's band. She comes out of the Gil Evans thing, which is already softer, but she's taken it her own direction. It's current, and I'm sure that's affecting the big band sound. Specifically, where I see it possibly happening is getting rid of that extreme outer edge of machismo playing.

JS: Define "machismo" playing for us.

VM: Muscular, showy technique for technique's sake. "Mine's bigger than yours" kind of playing. There are a couple of women I know who play like that, and there are men who don't play like that, too; it's not gender-specific. I see myself as sort of in the middle. I mean, I play with a big sound and I play loud, but I don't play on that extreme edge; you know, I'm not competing every time I play. I mean, Lester Young played very gently and beautifully at times, and Lee Konitz. It's not like it's something new, but I think proportionately the more women are like that and the more it makes it okay for men to play like that, it might have the effect of getting the emphasis back on music and off a sort of "sports" mentality. Talking to young and not-so-young women that I know on the scene, I see that they are disgusted with that whole machismo, jam-session mentality. It's as if music is about competition, which is not what's happening. Like when you're first starting out, you know, you want to be in the club and you try to do all that kind of stuff. But as we're getting older and more mature and our taste is refining—and I'm sure most guys as they get older feel like this, too—we see, well, that's not really where it's at.

JS: Have you been witness to other women jazz players suffering career inequities?

VM: I think it's hard for everybody unless you have some sort of financial help. Or you're willing to do weddings, and things like that. If you just want to play jazz, unless you're Wynton Marsalis or a handful of other people, it's going to be a financial struggle. Especially in New York, because there are, what, four or five big clubs—the Vanguard, Sweet Basil, the Blue Note, the Jazz Standard—and they don't pay a lot for sidemen. Even if they did, you can't work in those clubs every week, even if you're a rhythm section player who plays in numerous bands. The rest of the gigs are fifty-dollar gigs, and if you have to take a cab home, that's twenty bucks. You make more of your money traveling. But it's hard for everybody, you know. And, like, some people don't want whites in the band, some people don't want blacks in the band, some people don't want women in the band, some people don't want anybody over thirty in the band. I mean, there are so many problems; the female issue isn't the only one.

WE: Your comment that some bands have racial preferences surprised me. I thought integrated groups were the rule.

VM: You don't see it that much. It seems to me when I go out to hear music, a lot of times it's either a black band or a white band.

WE: How does it happen that many bands are divided by race?

VM: I think it might be the same thing as when I said that musicians hang out with their buddies, and how that has to do with who you call to sub for you. Also, the black bands generally have a different style than the white bands of today. A lot of the white bands are further from the roots of jazz. They're less groove-oriented. They're into more complicated harmonic and rhythmic stuff. And I would imagine that the black people probably would think that—and, I mean, they wouldn't be alone in this—it doesn't swing, or it's not jazz, and it doesn't have any feeling. The people that like one kind of music or the other will gravitate to that crowd. You know, like white-boy jazz—you don't see a lot of black people playing that.

WE: How do you respond to the notion that white players have not innovated in the idiom and as stylists they are far less compelling?

VM: I think it's bull. I think that there are gross generalizations which *are* true on both sides, which I don't really want to go into.

WE: Generalizations are not helpful. Can you provide any specifics on that point?

VM: "White men can't swing." Some white people don't swing, I agree. But I've heard black people that can't swing, too. I don't like to get into the politics of it because I'm really just into the music. I think that the music rises above the politics. I've known a lot of black masters, and they're about the music. I mean, they do have their personal history, and I'm sure that if you sat down and started talking to them about it, they'd have a lot to say. But the important thing is the music.

JS: Does jazz in the year 2000 have a color?

VM: I think that it has more colors than it's ever had. I'm a little curious to see where it's going to go—not just jazz, but all the different musics—because with the easy access, they're taking on so many different flavors. I mean, it used to be you could pigeonhole pretty easily what was jazz. Now there's so much music that jazz musicians are playing that, you know, if you played it twenty or thirty years ago, there's no way it would have been considered jazz. Plus all the white intellectual side that's coming in.

WE: There's a black intellectual side as well, isn't there, with musicians like Anthony Davis and Anthony Braxton?

VM: Absolutely. That's a really good point. I'm glad you said that. But the black avant-garde has been around for decades. When I was saying the white intellectual side, I sort of mean what's happening now—this white thing that's happening, that's coming out of all these white kids that are going to the schools.

JS: There's a "white thing" out there now?

VM: To me there is. It's like, I'd say, the under-fortyish, jazz college–educated, white male intellectual thing.

JS: Is it a negative force?

VM: It's negative to me. I really don't like it. These guys, you probably haven't heard of them. They're not on major labels, but there are a *lot* of them, and they're all over. They're very highly trained, incredible technicians. They can play anything, read amazingly, play really fast in odd meters, play all this really complicated harmonic stuff, and cut through all sorts of hard changes. But they've lost, or they didn't get, the *essence* of jazz.

JS: Are they attracting a jazz audience?

VM: I don't know if there will be an audience for it, but there certainly is a large number of people in that category, and it's growing. I think it's changing the sound of, like, a lot of big band sections. You're seeing more and more of these players in the big bands because they *are* great readers and they play all the doubles. It's really different than the days when you had Frank Wess playing lead alto. He plays his doubles very well and he's got his own voice. There are bunches of these kids that don't play half as well as Frank, as far as *music* goes, but they've got gobs of technique. I think they're really changing the sound of jazz. I think it might be the natural evolution of where jazz is going to go next.

WE: The way you're describing them, it sounds like an infestation in the city. Are these people bumping jazz masters from gigs?

VM: No. They don't even get that many gigs, and they certainly don't get most of the good gigs. "Infestation" is a good word, because they're growing and they're creating movement just by their sheer number. It's really different from jazz as we've known it. It's much more technically oriented, as opposed to emotionally oriented. But the world is changing, because the older masters that are still alive, they probably can't play half the stuff that these kids can play, *but* they can play music and they have their own voice and they have their style. But that is the competition these days. These kids can be anywhere and learn how to play all that burning stuff. Somebody just gave me a CD of a guy in Pittsburgh. He's never lived in New York, but he sounds just like a hundred other burning white tenor players that are in New York. And he lives in Timbuktu.

WE: I don't want to cultivate paranoia, but isn't there concern in the jazz community that younger, more callow players are being promoted by the record industry at the expense of documenting current masters of the music?

VM: Well, all those things that you said are true. But I mean, we're spending a lot of time talking about this, and I just want to make sure that you understand that for me, the *important* thing is the music. All this other stuff is incidental. I surround myself with people that care about the music, and by definition, they don't care about a person's color, they don't care about a person's sex, they don't care about a person's age; they care about the music.

WE: It seems to me we've explored this topic for two reasons. First is the provocative picture you've painted of this horde of under-forty white technicians influencing the music. Second, if your ability to get gigs is compromised by politics, then your voice is to some degree muffled.

VM: You're absolutely right, because my ability to get gigs *is* affected by politics, every day. But I can't do anything about it. Politics are politics, and I try just to steer clear of them, and that's why I'm getting a little nervous, because I don't want too much emphasis to be on me saying something negative. My main thing is the music, the music, the music. That's what I'm into. That's why I'm in this field. The BS exists everywhere. There are musicians that are racists and sexists, and most of the club owners, the record labels, the promoters, you know, they don't really care about the music. They care about making money, and they assume that to make money they need to have a certain-looking group and a certain-sounding group. I try not to let any of that affect me. I just try to be sincere in my music, surround myself with like-minded people, and keep growing and exploring and learning and improving.

WE: In relation to growth and exploration, what's your position with regard to the debate that rages around Wynton Marsalis, his so-called neo-bop approach, and the Lincoln Center Jazz Repertory Orchestra?

VM: Well, I'd like to say that it's risky to respond in an honest way to that question because Wynton Marsalis has so much power. I remember sometime within the last year or two, a very famous piano player[10] wrote a letter to the *New York Times* about Wynton, and he said everything that everybody wants to say but is too afraid to say because Wynton Marsalis has so much power. And he has all the other people with power in the palm of his hands—the clubs, the labels, all the people we were talking about earlier. And so, you know, to say something negative about him is sort of like slashing your own wrist. I'm sure you heard that he said he didn't want anybody over thirty in the band. A friend of mine was at a press conference and raised her hand and asked the question, "Why don't you have any women in your band?" He just laughed. That was his response. I don't like him anyway; he's so arrogant and pompous.

JS: This is the man whose life is about jazz education, and saving the legacy of jazz through his outreach program.

VM: I think he's done a lot for getting jazz out there, but he also has a very close-minded approach. And *he* is very close-minded, like: "This is the way it is." There's no *one* thing that is jazz. Jazz is hundreds of different people over the time that it's been in existence, and he is so close-minded and rigid about "*the way jazz is.*" And if you argue with him, you're wrong. I don't think that's a good thing to put in kids' minds. I think it's good to expose them to jazz, and he's done a lot of wonderful things. But with his attitude, that's anti-jazz to me—close-minded, rigid, conformist. But it's really risky to say negative things about him. I mean, I'm not in that world, but he works at the same clubs I'd like to work at. I mean, I'd love to have a gig at Lincoln Center. The sidemen make eighty grand a year. You know, there are hundreds of musicians in New York that could play circles around some of the people in that band, people that you'd never heard of before they were in the Lincoln Center Band. They're young, gifted, and black. And I'm happy for them that they are getting this great opportunity, but it seems like something that's sponsored by the city shouldn't be a racist institution. Well, there I went and said it all. (*Laughs.*)

[We played our first piece of music: "Soy Califa," from *Dexter Gordon; A Swingin' Affair,* 1962; Blue Note Records.]

VM: I haven't listened to this album in ten years, and it sounds so great. I still love him, Dexter Gordon. What a sound!

WE: Were you particularly attracted to Gordon's Blue Note period?

VM: Yeah. That was the stuff. Like the album *One Flight Up.*[11] I mean, I had some of his earlier recordings, and I have some of his later ones that sounded really tense and harsh to me. But that Blue Note period with Billy Higgins—I just love that stuff. I hear a lot of his tone in my sound, especially in the throat register, and sometimes his vibrato creeps into my playing. Coming out of the Lester Young tradition, Dexter didn't play a lot of notes. He really improvises in sentences, which is something I try to do, also. He's relaxed-sounding when he plays, as opposed to many of the younger players of today, who play a lot more on top of the beat, and play lots of notes. Even though I haven't listened to Dexter much in recent years, his concepts still affect my approach.

WE: With regard to improvising, when you're playing a solo, how much of it is truly extemporaneous?

VM: The slower stuff is usually extemporaneous. The faster stuff is usually some version of something I've worked on at some time.

JS: So the more you play a work, the more your approach takes a final shape?

VM: There are two different ways, that I'm aware of, that people approach improvisation. One of them is that people practice a bunch of licks, and then they try to squeeze them into their solo. I don't usually practice licks, but sometimes I'll play something through the keys; I might practice some sort of pattern or something, then I'll use parts of it in my solo. But when it comes to my solo, I have no preconceived licks that I'm going to use. Musically, it seems normal usually to start off sort of slow, you know, and build it up and go somewhere. But I never know where I'm going to go, because it depends how I feel. It depends what the rhythm section is doing. The drummer may play something I like, and I make a left and go out there—somewhere I've never been before. That's what's so exciting.

WE: I suspect most listeners have their attention riveted on the soloist during a performance. As the soloist, are you, on the other hand, very attentive to what your band members are doing?

VM: Oh, yeah. I mean, it's so ironic. The whole concept of listening to the rhythm section, I never even heard that until I moved to New York. My band is an interactive band, meaning that we are all listening and responding to each other at all times. Some of my music calls for an ostinato bass line, or a steady groove, but even then we are listening. Harvie[12] might pull a little harder on a certain note, or change up the pattern while still keeping the feeling. Allison[13] often adds colors and tasty fills to a steady groove, enhancing what's going on. Especially when we're playing something up-tempo, we take a lot of chances, breaking up the time, using polyrhythmic ideas, playing other feels over the top of the time. Harvie might go into a pedal, or a syncopated Latin bass line, or he and Allison might start playing some hits together. It's really fun and exciting! I prefer to play with a rhythm section that is listening to me and responding to me, and giving me something to listen to and respond to other than 1-2-3-4, 1-2-3-4. Keep the groove happening, but make it interesting at the same time.

[The next selection was "It's Easy to Remember" from *Ballads,* the John Coltrane Quartet, 1962; Impulse Records.]

VM: God, that's beautiful. I haven't listened to that one in a while, either. I remember when I first heard that it bothered me that his intonation was a little bit funny. But now, I mean, I notice it, but it just doesn't matter! The music so far outweighs the intonation problems. Sometimes playing a little sharp adds to the intensity of a note—makes you feel it even more.

WE: Coltrane didn't embark on an extended solo on that piece. He ornamented the melody. I haven't heard you take that deceptively simple, more "straight" approach to a tune on your CDs.

VM: Yeah, I should do that. To play the melody. The fills he plays are so perfect, tasteful. And he played a few little runs. That's basically what he does on the whole record. I do that occasionally. I haven't done it on any of my CDs, but sometimes I'll do it if I want to play a ballad on a set and we're running out of time. Or if I'm in a mood to just play a certain thing and don't want to go off on a long excursion. I think it takes maturity to play a ballad well. Whether you improvise or just play the melody. If you don't know the words, chances are you're going to play something really wrong in the phrasing of the melody, or destroy the spirit. He just gets you with the feeling of the song. It's a very sad song. What he did was perfect.

WE: Coltrane's tone is so intense and penetrating. I believe he used a hard reed. Have you followed his example?

VM: I use a pretty hard reed, but I have a different setup than he had.

JS: Does a hard reed enable you to achieve a more pure tone? More free of the influence of the reed?

VM: Yeah. There is less reediness. The sound is more like a brass instrument.

JS: Does a harder reed make the instrument more difficult to play?

VM: There are at least three factors that affect how hard it is to play. If the tip of the mouthpiece is *very* close to the reed, that won't be hard to play. But if you have a mouthpiece that's what we call open—which means that the tip opening is bigger—the bigger it gets, the harder it is to get a sound. Because it takes more air to get the reed to vibrate. The reed doesn't have to vibrate very much if the mouthpiece is closed. What I have is a very open mouthpiece with about a medium hard to hard reed. Because I like to work. I blow hard when I play, so I have to work hard to get it to vibrate. But I like that sound. Some people like a soft reed so that they don't have to work very hard.

WE: Clearly, then, the type of mouthpiece and grade of reed you use are expressive choices.

VM: Yes. Absolutely. And the reeds are the biggest pain in the world for saxophone players.

WE: Why is that?

VM: They're not very good. You have to really work on them a lot with a reed knife and keep adjusting them. And the air conditioner has one effect and heat has another effect. That's a big challenge to being a saxophone player.

[The final piece of music was "Balm in Gilead" from *I, Eye, Aye, Rahsaan Roland Kirk, Live at the Montreux Jazz Festival; Switzerland, 1972;* Rhino Records.]

VM: I really didn't like that at all, aside from the fact that he was playing two instruments at once—which is a nice gimmick, but they were out of tune! And I don't like that style where the tone breaks up, you know, that screaming. I mean, I really like Coltrane's stuff—he worked his way there, and it made sense.

JS: Are you a fan of Rahsaan otherwise?

VM: No.

JS: Didn't you hear him at the Keystone Korner?

VM: Yeah, I heard him. I didn't like him then, either.

WE: You used the term "gimmick," so I take it you're not impressed with Kirk's command of the instruments or the musical values connected with playing several instruments at once?

VM: Well, I'm impressed that anybody could do it, but it's not like he's playing them well. Let's leave the fact that he's playing two or three instruments at the same time—other than that, it's the same old stuff. I mean, that music he's playing is like eighty years old. He didn't really do anything to make it any better or any fresher; he just played two or three instruments out of tune. I don't like that style of playing where it's all raspy and notes are cracking and squeaking and slipping from one register to the other, whether unintentionally or not.

JS: Did you respond any better to his sound on the clarinet in this piece?

VM: He could have been a good clarinet player. He had a good tone. But then it was like he must not have wanted to make that tiny little bit of effort that would have kept it in focus and not distorting. I mean, he must have wanted a distorted sound. I think he probably achieved what he was after, because he definitely could play the clarinet. I don't know his playing. I heard him that one time at the Keystone Korner, and then I heard this. I haven't really even checked him out.

JS: Do you have a goal to extend your instrument's sound potential into uncharted areas?

VM: I don't really think about going places that are uncharted. Pretty much everything's been done. There are some people these days that are really mastering the altissimo register. It's a lot more common for people to play lines way up there in the altissimo register. It doesn't appeal to me, so I haven't worked on that at all. I like the sound of harmonics, sort of a distorted sound that I like, and I use that a lot. But people have done that before.

WE: What's the distinction between the distortion in Kirk's clarinet work and the distorted sound that you like?

VM: They are really two different things. Kirk has a sound that is unfocused, and distorted, throughout the instrument. What I'm talking about is using harmonics, which create a distorted sound on specific notes. It's a choice I make when I'm looking for a more intense sound.

WE: Now that we've finished listening to music, I have a final question. Earlier in this interview you talked about making investments in your future, and that someday you'll get the payoff. You've been in New York for thirteen years. How long do you wait with your dream deferred?

VM: Well, I'm in for the long haul. I won't sell out or play anything that I will be embarrassed about later. Playing jazz and writing music are two of my main passions in life, and I don't plan on that changing anytime soon.

Nini Green. Chiaroscuro CR(D) 351 (1997).
No Walls. Foxhaven FX-10010 (1999).
Phantoms. Renma 6397 CD (2003).

Notes

1. These are annual events conducted aboard cruise ships produced by HOSS, Inc.

2. Chiaroscuro Records.

3. Ingrid Jensen (trumpet), Kenny Barron (piano), Harvie Swartz (bass), Adam Cruz (drums), and Leon Parker (percussion).

4. Foxhaven Records.

5. Renma Recordings.

6. *No Walls,* recorded 1999.

7. Her grandmother's name is Nini Green.

8. From *Nini Green.*

9. Drummer and leader of DIVA.

10. Keith Jarrett.

11. 1964; Blue Note Records.

12. Harvie Swartz is a bassist who works regularly with Mayhew.

13. Allison Miller is a drummer who works regularly with Mayhew.

Marian McPartland

Marian McPartland

Pianist, bandleader, composer, educator, radio personality, and author, Marian McPartland is aptly dubbed "The First Lady of Jazz." With a long and storied career that has outlived numerous stylistic changes in jazz, the classically trained McPartland has released more than one hundred recordings as a leader. Her integrity and acumen on both the artistic and entrepreneurial fronts of the music business have made her a role model for men and women alike in the jazz idiom.

Margaret Marian Turner was born on March 20, 1918, in a small English village near Windsor. She displayed an early deftness at the piano, and at age fifteen began classical studies at London's Guildhall School of Music, where, in her off time, she discovered the music of Duke Ellington. Under the spell of jazz, McPartland eventually left the Guildhall to travel the United Kingdom in a four-piano vaudeville act, only to have her fledgling career interrupted by World War II.

Touring with ENSA[1] and later in the USO,[2] she met and performed with her future husband, the Bix Beiderbecke–influenced cornetist Jimmy McPartland. After the war, they moved to the United States, and for the next three years she honed her craft in her husband's Chicago-based Dixieland band.

In 1949 the McPartlands moved to New York, where they were welcomed into the local jazz scene. Encouraged by Jimmy to form her own group, Marian began her career as a leader at the Embers, an upscale club on the west side. Her big break came in 1952, when her trio played the legendary Hickory House on Fifty-Second Street for a two-week gig that extended into a year, followed by return engagements over the next decade. Featuring Joe Morello on drums and Bill Crow on bass, her trio was named "Small Group of the Year" in 1955 by *Metronome* magazine.

In 1969, McPartland, frustrated with the slumping jazz recording market, founded her own label, Halcyon, which flourished through the '70s. Since 1978, she has been recording on a regular basis for the Concord label, primarily in a piano trio format.

With a timeless elegance, McPartland blends bebop, modal, and occasional dissonance into a mainstream style that has proven appeal for a cross-section of the jazz audience. Her work at the keyboard is highlighted by thick chords, rich harmonies, and sensitive melodic lines, all of which are reminiscent of one of her major influences, the late pianist Bill Evans. When performing, she typically employs her well-bred English civility and charismatic bearing to capture the listeners' attention prior to enveloping them in her bewitching pianism.

McPartland has been showered with accolades. Her recent awards include induction into the IAJE[3] Hall of Fame, recognition as one of the American Jazz Masters in 2000 by the National Endowment for the Arts, and winning the 2001 Gracie Allen Award.[4] She is also eloquent with the written word: Her book *Marian McPartland's Jazz World* was reprinted in 2003 by the University of Illinois Press. But she has perhaps been most honored for her role as hostess of *Piano Jazz,* which is the longest-running cultural program on National Public Radio. Winner of the George Peabody Award for excellence in broadcasting as well as the ASCAP–Deems Taylor Lifetime Achievement Award, the show reaches audiences in forty-five states and twenty-four foreign countries and has its slate of guests lined up for the next two years. It is noteworthy that the successful run of *Piano Jazz* has coincided with the gradual resurgence of jazz over the last three decades. In her role as an advocate for the music, McPartland is the prime forerunner for other activist musicians who have championed the art form, most significantly Wynton Marsalis.

In March 2003, Marian McPartland celebrated her eighty-fifth birthday in royal fashion, as the jazz world's doyenne performed alongside her court members at a sold-out party at New York's Birdland.

Recorded November 24, 1996

WE: Marian, some sources list your birthplace as Windsor. Is that correct?

MM: I was actually born in Slough, but Windsor sounds better. It's next to Slough. I used to be on the *Steve Allen Show* when he had the original *Tonight Show* in the '50s. He used to have all the jazz people, whoever was around. I was always in town at the Hickory House, so I would be on the show periodically. He would make jokes about coming from Slough—or "Sluff," he called it. I got sick of all this, so I would just say, "Well, I live near Windsor." It sounded much better. All my mother's relatives live in Windsor. Some of them were quite well known in the area. I get lost in the family tree here. I think they were my mother's uncles and cousins. You see, they were all named Dyson. Mummy's cousin Cyril Dyson became the mayor of Windsor. He had a beautiful jewelry shop right in Windsor and he had the Coat of Arms on the shop front. He was the jeweler to the royal family. Big stuff. Later on, Queen Elizabeth knighted him. One of those things you read about, kneeling in the streets, you know: "Arise, Sir Cyril." Terribly romantic to me.

WE: So were you upper-crust, so to speak?

MM: I suppose so. I like to think I was sort of medium-upper-crust.

WE: What first inspired you toward jazz?

MM: Hearing a lot of it. On the BBC there was *a lot* of jazz. First thing is, I always played. I actually started hearing my mother play the piano. I remember her playing a Chopin waltz. I guess I was two or three. I think I tried to play what she was playing. It just seems to me I was *always* at the piano trying to play. I remember going to Windsor for visits to one of these great-uncles. This particular one, Uncle Harry, he was one of my favorites, and Aunt Frances. They had probably, by today's standards, a very ancient piano in the living room. In fact, it had that fluting and candelabra on it, you know. I remember playing that thing and having them just so knocked out and admiring. I was probably five. Those early years I remember being in kindergarten and playing and learning the tunes. We were in kind of a one-room schoolhouse situation, and I loved the teacher. I guess she must have played these songs, because I learned them and I could play them for the kids to sing. That's always been my claim to fame.

JS: When did you start formal piano lessons?

MM: When I was maybe twelve or thirteen. I had a sort of interim piano teacher who would come to the house. Her name was Gwen Massey. I guess the best thing she did for me was to get me to learn some pieces, and I would perform in the local music festival in town. I did win a few things in different competitions, small stuff. During all this time, of course, I went to several different schools, because we kept moving. We had moved to Woolwich because my father was a civil engineer. Woolwich is kind of a suburb of London, really, not a beautiful spot at all. I was born in Slough, but we went almost immediately to live in Woolwich. Then we moved to a place called Bromley; that's when I was in kindergarten. And then another school. Then I went to a convent, which I enjoyed a lot. By then, I guess, I must have been fifteen or sixteen.

My mother was getting complaints from the nuns that I was hard to handle. I mean, when I think of what kids do nowadays, I can't believe I was hard to handle. I was just sort of a cutup, I suppose; a lot of us were, you know. Anyway, Mummy kept saying, "Well, if you don't behave, we're going to send you to boarding school." So lo and behold, this happened, that I was sent to this girls' school called Stratford House. It was probably a good school, but I couldn't take being in boarding school, and I developed terrible sick headaches. The doctor apparently said to Mummy, "Oh, you've got to take her away from there."

So then I became a day student, and that was fine. But then my penchant for leaving a place before I was finished took over. I left there to go to the Guildhall to start taking piano lessons, because my father had said to a teacher at Stratford House, "What shall we *do* with her?" She apparently said to Daddy something like, "Well, you should have her go to a music academy; she has talent." She made very complimentary remarks about my playing. Anyway, I auditioned for the Guildhall and was accepted. So I left Stratford House before I actually graduated. They call it the school certificate, which I did not get. Nobody seemed to care. I left and went to the Guildhall and plunged into all the things I hadn't done at all, like really practicing and learning the repertoire.

I mean, my whole teenage life was taken up with doing this. I really wanted to catch up and do all these things that I hadn't done while I was fiddling around playing by ear. I thought that I wanted to do it right, so I was taking piano, of course, and composition, and sight-singing, believe it or not. And as a second instrument, violin, but that didn't last long. I didn't like the teacher, so I quit. I think he wanted to look up my dress.

JS: Did you catch up?

MM: Well, to a certain extent. I mean, I can look back on having a pretty good repertoire of Beethoven and Bach, and a lot of short pieces by various composers, known and unknown, and doing concerts at the Guildhall. Meanwhile, I really was into jazz, even though I was going to the Guildhall, because by this time I had a boyfriend who was really a jazz nut, and he had records by everybody—Bud Freeman, Muggsy Spanier, Sidney Bechet, Benny Goodman, Duke Ellington. A whole polyglot mixture of styles. I listened to everything with an equal sense of how exciting it all was and how wonderful it was—especially the Benny Goodman group—and trying to play like Teddy Wilson, and trying to play like Fats Waller, and trying to play like Art Tatum. Just really getting into all that stuff—meanwhile learning tunes, and then having another boyfriend who was a fair jazz piano player. We would get together at his house, talk about tunes, and play them.

In the back of my mind, I just enjoyed playing jazz so much, even though I was supposed to be having a classical career. I was training to be a concert pianist. One day I was supposed to be practicing something for a lesson, instead of which I was trying to play some Teddy Wilson runs, and my piano professor heard me. He opened the door and said, "Stop playing that trash!" I think that might have been the thing that really made me know that I was going to leave there and do something else. I went to see this pianist, Billy Mayerl, very well known. He was like a British Frankie Carle, maybe. He composed very pretty pieces. They were sort of quasi-jazz. They had a lot of jazz about them in the rhythm. Anyway, I went to see Billy, thinking I would learn something about how to improve my jazz playing. He promptly offered me a job, saying they were going out with this piano quartet. I got all excited, rushed home, and my family didn't want me to go, needless to say. My father came rushing up to London to see Billy Mayerl. "What's this, you're wanting to take my daughter on the road? Are you going to treat her properly? How much money is she going to make?" Well, he wasn't a good negotiator, because I think the money I made was very little.

JS: What year of study were you in at the Guildhall when you decided to leave?

MM: End of the third; I don't know. I left before I had really finished everything. I did get one degree, which is called LGSM Licentiate. It sounds kind of vulgar, doesn't it? Licentiate of the Guildhall School of Music. It's a teaching degree. I have the certificate on the wall downstairs, but I never did get the concert degree, because I left.

JS: How long were you on the road with Mayerl?

MM: Oh, maybe a year or two. We played every vaudeville theater in the country, good and bad. Some of them were wonderful, with velvet seats and velvet curtains. They've probably all been torn down and made into parking lots. I have a pretty good memory of where I went, but I regret that I didn't keep a diary. You don't think of that at the time. I always promised that I would go back to the Guildhall. I made all these rash promises. I feel sorry about it now, but I'm not sorry that I went on the road. My father would have liked for me to be a nurse, something I had no desire to be, or work in a bank, or probably he could have accepted me as a music *teacher*. Oh, God! But as long as it was "something *nice.*" What I was doing was not nice. I was mingling with people he considered below my station in life. People that he wouldn't consider I should be hobnobbing with. He would say, "They're not top drawer."

WE: Do you think he would have thought that way if you had been his son? Or did he want you in a decorous profession because you were his daughter?

MM: It's funny, you know. I've always thought that he probably would have liked a son.

He was great, but I've often wondered if it was a psychological slip with him—he would always call me "old chap." (*Laughter.*) He did so many great things for me. He really made me love gardening and all the things that people think obnoxious, like cutting hedges and planting cuttings and weeding. I loved doing that. I never found that onerous. He was a great gardener, and he got me interested in that, but I was always the apprentice. I was always standing around while he did something. I would get very impatient, and then I would go away, and he would say, "Come back here, I need you right away." I have very good memories about that, but I know that he and my mother were terribly afraid that I would blot the family's escutcheon by going into vaudeville, of all things.

WE: What happened after your tour with Billy Mayerl ended?

MM: At one point there were a lot of theater groups in England, and I played a show with another woman pianist, named Roma Clarke. We played some Gershwin tunes in the pit, instead of an orchestra. That's one job I had. Then I had another job, in the summertime, something they would call "Concert Party." There would be people who played on the pier, like at Blackpool, or some seaside town where they'd have a hall at the end of the pier, and there would be a group made up of a girl singer, a juggler, two comedians, and various assorted acts. I would be the piano player for that kind of date. That's probably the most sight-reading I ever did, playing for those kind of gigs.

WE: Did you continue to work as World War II approached?

MM: The war started in 1939, and I was doing a Concert Party engagement right then in a town called Felixstowe. My sister, Joyce, was there, and she remembers how everything suddenly became very ominous and they put up barbed wire on the beach—you knew something terrible was going to happen. Some time after the war had started, I joined a group called "Carroll Levis's Discoveries." This was again a variety show, similar to the one run here by Major Bowes, except I was not a "discovery." I was the piano player for the group. I had to do things like having all the music and rehearsing it with the pit band. I don't know how I did this, but I must have been all right because the show went on okay. We would have a girl singer, a tap dancer, different acts, and I would play their music and tell the orchestra where to come in.

Then, I guess, after that I went with ENSA,[5] because it got to be that I had to join some entertainment group like that, or be conscripted into the women's army, which I definitely couldn't see myself doing. So I promptly joined ENSA. That was the same kind of a group, you know, singer, dancer, juggler, comedian, except we would be playing for the troops. It really was a lot of fun, and one of the girls who had been with Carroll Levis, that I was very friendly with, joined USO Camp Shows, and she said, "Oh, you'll make more money if you join USO. You'll meet all these great American guys." She made it sound very glamorous, so I went to USO headquarters and said that I'd like to join USO, but I thought they were crazy! They would come over from the States bringing a bunch of acts and expect to find piano players all ready for them in England. I thought that that was rather rash.

JS: Did you play the same kind of dates with the USO that you did with ENSA?

MM: We started playing the same kind of dates, but with American acts, comedians, singers, and dancers. Then every so often some big wheel would come over and be a guest with our show. We did a show with James Cagney, and then we had Edward G. Robinson. Eventually we learned that we were going to France with the first group after the invasion, which was about a month afterwards. We had to learn how to put up a pup tent in case we had to live in it. And we had all the GI equipment, the boots and the helmets, everything except the guns. We waded ashore like MacArthur, out of a small boat. Here again, I'm so sorry I never kept a diary. It's kind of sinful to say you had a good time when you're driving through villages that were razed to the ground and there was a smell of death. You knew that behind the hedge something or someone was dead there, and you could go through where there were houses standing, and you could see that people had just jumped up from the table and run for their lives. I mean, it was really tragic, but somehow I didn't feel it as much then as I did afterwards. We were having such a jolly time enjoying playing everywhere we played, 'cause naturally the GIs were thrilled to have this entertainment. They would either build a stage or we would perform on the back of a flatbed truck. At one point we had Fred Astaire as a guest, and he did his show in combat boots on a makeshift stage.

JS: When did you first meet Jimmy McPartland?

MM: Well, this was in Belgium, and I guess we were attached to the First Army. We were going up through these battered towns, and eventually arrived at a rest center which was a town in Belgium, called Eupen. We were put in this nice hotel, the Schmitzroth Hotel. Then I started to hear this rumor going through the camp: "Jimmy McPartland's coming; Jimmy McPartland's coming." It's funny, but Jimmy was one musician I had *not* listened to in all my days of hearing Bud Freeman, Sidney Bechet, and all those other people. Somehow I missed getting a record that had Jimmy on it.

JS: Had you heard of Jimmy McPartland?

MM: No, sad to say. But everybody was saying how great he was, and then they gave this party in a tent—they were going to have a jam session—and of course I wanted to be in on it. I probably was really pushy. Anyway, Jimmy says he could see me from across the tent, and when I got up to the piano he said to himself, "Oh, God, there's a woman musician who wants to sit in, and I expect she'll be terrible." "And you *were,*" he said. (*Laughter.*) Which was really unkind, because I wasn't that bad. But I'm sure I didn't have a good sense of rhythm at that time. He told me that I would rush the beat. I probably did, as I think about it. But anyway, that's how I got to meet Jimmy. He was part of a Triple-A unit, a gun group. He wasn't performing, but somebody said, "Oh, this man should be in Special Service; he shouldn't be in combat." So someone pulled strings, or did whatever they had to do, to get Jimmy into Special Service. And we worked together in this little group, Jimmy and myself, a GI bass player and drummer, and a singer and dancer from the USO group. We would go out every day in a weapons carrier, which was very uncomfortable, and play for the troops in the front lines.

JS: Were you in jeopardy at times?

MM: There were one or two occasions. I remember having lunch—you know, you'd have the same food as the GIs: a mess kit with a big piece of meat in it, and then if it's pineapple for dessert, they slap the pineapple on top of the meat. I remember this because I was eating and we suddenly got strafed—planes went over very low. But this happened so fast that by the time you knew what was going on, it was over. Nobody got hurt, and I finished the pineapple. This would happen once in a while, but we were all enjoying ourselves even with all the hardships, like sleeping in a tent and washing our hair in the river. That was part of it. But at this point we were in this nice hotel, and all USO members were receiving an officer's liquor ration. God, there was an awful lot of drinking going on. Of course, with Jimmy, I didn't know what a problem he had with alcohol, but I always told him that he liked me because I had a liquor ration. (*Laughter.*)

WE: How serious was Jimmy's alcohol problem?

MM: Well, Jimmy was an alcoholic, but I didn't really know what it was until we got back to the States. Jimmy always said, "Oh, well, this is war time. I don't drink like this when we're in the States. I drink like a gentleman." Which was totally untrue. But I was sure I could do something about it. I was sure that knowing me was going to make everything all right. I guess women think they can change somebody, but that is such a crock—as I found out later. But Jimmy did join AA, and it was great that he did.

WE: Digressing for a moment, Jimmy McParland knew Bix Biederbecke and eventually replaced him in the Wolverines. Were you familiar with Bix's work before you met Jimmy?

MM: I had listened to him. Then at one point Jimmy and I had a little group together in the late '40s. We were working in Moline, and I put together a really nice little arrangement of "In a Mist"[6] that we played and recorded on probably what might have been the earliest of the homemade labels called Unison. We only put out about four sides, and then we went to England and leased or sold these records to a guy named Dick Auty, who had a record company. They're all floating around somewhere.

JS: What happened after the end of the war, prior to your going to the States?

MM: Well, I felt that I was getting to be a better jazz musician. When we still were in Belgium, Jimmy got to be in charge of the band at the hotel that'd play for dancing. It was a rest area. I would play with the band and as a result I just got better by doing. In the midst of all this excitement we got married in Aachen, Germany. Before the war ended, Jimmy got his discharge in Paris, then he joined the USO. We had another show with a different group of people, but there were problems with Jimmy drinking too much. Actually, they were funny, but I don't know if you want to hear about them.

JS: Sure.

MM: One of them *was* funny. I was always complaining to this one woman in the group about Jimmy drinking. She said, "Well, why don't you just drink as much as he does and show him how awful it looks." Silly advice. So I did that and started to flirt with some officer—we were in this club where all the USO people were staying—and I did get quite drunk. I think I must have passed out in the ladies' room on the floor, and remember some old French lady coming in to sweep up, who couldn't speak English, and looking at me like "What are you doing here?" I struggled to my feet, and oh, God, then it all came back to me. I got out of there, and I ran up the hill, got in the hotel, and then Jimmy bopped me in the face. He thought I was flirting with this guy. So then I had a cut lip. He apologized, and he quit drinking for three days. Then once we couldn't get out of this party. Some jazz fans wanted to talk to him, and it was the same thing—these two guys were drinking and he's drinking, and finally when we got out of there I was so mad that I bopped him on the head with the heel of my shoe. All he said was, "What'd you wanna do that for?"

WE: Despite your divorce it, seems that you and Jimmy had a special romance within the jazz world.

MM: It was. But I feel that I was so unfair to him a lot of times. It did seem like I was always pushing him into things, because he was still playing at least a couple of years, maybe a year, before he got sick. But you would have to really drive him to practice, and then when he'd done the job he'd be all enthusiastic: "Oh, I must practice more, I should keep practicing." Of course, he didn't, because what he wanted to do was sit in a chair and watch the fights or baseball and smoke cigarettes, which he never quit, and is what finally killed him. I always used to say the divorce was a failure, not the marriage. Really, the divorce *was* a failure. I don't know, we probably shouldn't have gotten the divorce.

JS: Let's return to your chronology. What happened when you first hit these shores?

MM: I guess I haven't got to the point of coming back on the ship with Jimmy to New York, which was a big thrill. Making the rounds of the clubs, going to Eddie Condon's and sitting in, seeing Louis Armstrong, meeting Gene Krupa and staying at his house. He and Jimmy were very friendly.

JS: Did they let you sit in because you were Marian McPartland, or because you were Jimmy's wife?

MM: Probably because I was Jimmy's wife. I was Marian Nobody. I think once, while we were still in New York, I subbed for Ralph Sutton, who was doing solo piano at the club. And I was so nervous that I said to the manager, "Don't put a light on the piano; let me just sit there and be in the dark." I was a nervous wreck. Although I didn't mind getting up and playing with the band, because then I was sort of showing off. I knew all the tunes. Wild Bill Davison, George Wettling, Pee Wee Russell, and George Brunis were in the band. A bunch of hard drinkers if you ever saw them. Every one of those guys had problems with alcoholism. It's a shame. All such nice guys when they were sober.

Anyway, we were in New York and going around, and I met Louis Armstrong. He was such a down-to-earth guy, and he and Jimmy had grown up together. They were great friends. And then the guys at Condon's greeted Jimmy like a long-lost buddy. Actually, I guess Wild Bill was going to go on tour, and Eddie wanted Jimmy to work there. He offered him a job, but Jimmy refused and said he wanted to go back to Chicago and see his family. I felt that that was such a wrong move. He should have stayed and worked at Condon's, and I tried to persuade him. "No, I'm not ready to work. I just got back from the war. I want to relax." Things would have probably turned out differently, but he was set on going to Chicago.

So that's what we did. Stayed at his sister's house, and there was really some heavy drinking going on there, but we eventually did start working with a little group. We moved downtown to the Croydon Hotel, a real musicians' hotel. And I was starting to worry about money. Then we moved to this little apartment. My mother always said, "Oh! You'll marry a musician and live in an attic; you'll come to no good." So I always tell people that's exactly what happened. (*Laughter.*) It was a one-room apartment on Dearborn Street, and we started working at a place on the south side called the Rose Bowl, which was a bar next to a bowling alley. A glorified bar that had music. I remember that in this particular place, the Rose Bowl, I would play a classical solo in the set, which was *dumb,* as I think about it now. Jimmy would give me a big buildup, and in the middle of the piece somebody in the bowling alley got a strike and this cheering would come from the bowling alley. This always happened. (*Laughter.*) The scene was just terribly funny. It still is, though at the time I was distraught; my solo was always spoiled. Of course, later I stopped playing those things. I got into bebop.

JS: In the late 1940s, you and Jimmy moved to Long Island. What prompted that decision?

MM: I don't know why we decided to go there; I think it was Jimmy's idea. We stayed in an apartment hotel in Long Beach. I remember we actually walked on the beach on Christmas Day. Jimmy no longer had his New York 802 Union card; he had to wait six months to get back in. I'm sure there must have been strings he could have pulled, but he didn't. You couldn't work on a steady job, you had to take one-nighters for about three months, or something like that. I was trying to get my card as well. I already had my Chicago card. When I went to apply for it, the union guys would say, "Have you filed the papers to become a citizen?" And I would say, "Yes, I'm working on it." But I never did, and I didn't do it in

New York, either. I'm still not a citizen. There was a clause in the papers you had to fill out that says, "If war was declared, would you take up arms against your country?" When I read that, I just put the paper back in the drawer, and I never did become a citizen. But, anyway, we were living there in Long Beach and working at some one-night places in New York. Then I guess we moved into New York. We got an apartment on the West Side—West Eighty-First Street—which was a little bigger and better.

JS: Around that time your trio opened at the Embers. That must have made you feel good.

MM: I really didn't. It was really my first job with a trio, and I was a nervous wreck. I was wondering how I was ever going to make it. Oh, I was sort of pleased, I guess, and I went out and bought some great-looking clothes, which were quite expensive. Eddie Heywood and his trio were the other act. Jimmy and I had been going there a lot because Joe Bushkin had been performing there. He had people falling at his feet because, at that time, he was really popular. People like Tallulah Bankhead would come to hear him, and the club was always packed. Well, when he left and Eddie Heywood became the headliner and I led the other group, business fell off. Of course, I felt bad about that.

JS: Were bassist Eddie Safranski and drummer Don Lamond with you from the beginning?

MM: Actually, I had had another bass player in the beginning, who was a very obnoxious guy; I can't even remember his name. Anyway, I had to fire him. This was my first bad experience as a leader. I didn't know how to handle it, so I put up with him for quite a while. I finally talked to Jimmy about it, so Jimmy said, "Well, there's nothing to that; for Christ's sake, fire the guy." So I did. Then, apropos of that incident, Jimmy was working in the afternoon somewhere at a club, and the same guy was in the band, on bass. I don't know who else was in the band, but this bass player lasted about ten minutes with Jimmy. He said, "Take your fucking bass and get the fuck out of here." Anyway, after *I* fired the guy, I got Eddie Safranski, and he and Don Lamond were very nice to me. But business still wasn't very good, so the owner, Ralph Watkins, brought in some guest stars who would build up the business in the room. The guests were Coleman Hawkins and Roy Eldridge. Can you imagine that?

JS: To play with your trio?

MM: Yes. Well, Eddie Heywood didn't want them to play with him, so I was only too thrilled to have them play with me. I was delighted. I mean, they were fantastic musicians, and they were very kind. They never told me what to play, so I guess I must have been playing quite well by that time. We also had a remote broadcast from the club on station WNEW.

WE: Let's jump ahead to 1952 and your stint at the Hickory House. After you formed your trio with Bill Crow and Joe Morello, how long were you all together?

MM: Three years. I was in the Hickory House on and off for ten years. But then Bill left to go with Gerry Mulligan. He left before Joe did. Joe was getting offers from the Dorsey Brothers and Benny Goodman, but they didn't hire him because they didn't think he could read the charts. Joe had bad eyesight, but he had such an intuitive sense. He could have done well with any band, but of course I was glad he didn't go. Then we got a bass player named Bill Britto.

WE: For Morello, those were pre-Brubeck days.

MM: Yes, but Dave and Paul Desmond would come to the Hickory House a lot to hear the trio. They were working close by at Basin Street. This was just off Broadway, and sometimes Joe and I would run over there between sets to hear them. This was really the start of the Dave Brubeck era. Every time Dave and Paul would come into the Hickory House, I would think, "How nice that they came to hear our trio," but of course they were really listening to Joe, thinking they would hire him away from me. And then I went to England on a trip, so this actually happened while I was gone. I guess Joe thought that would be a good time to split, so he did. Actually he had more dates to do with me after I came back, but by that time he had made the commitment to Dave, which I had to go along with because Joe was great. It really was time for him to join a bigger group than mine. Nevertheless, I had always envisioned him going with somebody like Dizzy Gillespie, who always had a really hot, hard, swinging group, where he could cut loose. Whereas playing with Dave got him involved with all these different time signatures.

WE: Kind of restrained him a bit?

MM: Well, restrained him as far as uninhibited jazz playing. But Dave could never have done those time-signature things without Joe. And he admits it. Joe was fantastic in being able to play not only 5/4 but 7/8, 7/4, 15 over 3, and all these weird things. So, I mean, that was the place for him and he did very well with Dave, of course. But I always felt that Joe really never worked enough with black groups, because they do play in a different way.

WE: It's interesting that you say, that because I was noting as you were talking that you cut your teeth on Waller and Tatum.

MM: Many of my heroes were black people.

WE: With that in mind, did you find yourself at times yearning to sit in with groups of black players?

MM: Well, black *and* white. When Duke Ellington was at Birdland, I would go over there between sets from the Hickory House, and he would ask me to sit in. Actually, he spent a lot of time in the Hickory House. His press agent was the press agent for the Hickory House, so he would go there to have dinner. Occasionally he would actually sit in with *my* group. Sometimes he would invite me over to the table—he was always so charming—and would flirt with me. I was so green and callow, I just didn't know how to act. Sometimes he would play at the Rainbow Grill, and I would get to sit in there as well. I also used to go down to the Half Note a lot and play with Zoot Sims and his group. I enjoyed sitting in with lots of different people.

WE: You joined Benny Goodman in 1963. Did Goodman want you to tour with him as his piano player?

MM: Yes. I forget what money I asked for—some very nominal sum like five hundred dollars a week, and he said, "Oh, you want all that money, when you go down and play at the Half Note for nothing?" Anyway, I went over to his apartment; he wanted to rehearse. I found out later on that this is a Benny Goodman gambit, just to try somebody out and perhaps put a little band together. I would go to the house and we just played tunes. He never said, "Well, you sound fine," or anything like that. I guess I really *wanted* to work with him, so we started with a gig in York, Pennsylvania. He had Steve Swallow on bass, and a drummer named Ron Lundberg. Benny was playing a concerto with the York Symphony, but then when he played with the trio, it was really good. Steve Swallow knew how to play for him, and Benny seemed quite happy. Then later on it got to be a bigger group, with [cornetist] Bobby Hackett, [vibist] Red Norvo, and a saxophone player whose name I can't recall.

Anyway, now we're rehearsing, ready to go on the road with this group, and I got this funny feeling because things just didn't seem as cool as they were with the trio. Bobby Hackett kept coming up to me and saying, "Oh, Benny wishes you'd do so and so." I was so insecure that I just let him tell me. Now I think I'd say, "Why doesn't *Benny* tell me? What are *you* telling me for?" I never quite knew what was happening; what I wasn't doing right. In any event, we went on the road and we played a lot of dates, and Benny kept giving me the famous "ray."

WE: Did you know why he was giving you the ray?

MM: No. You couldn't ask him. One day we played a tune, "Rose Room," or something. He said, "Do you know that tune?" I said, "Well, we just played it, didn't we?" And he said, "Ha ha," or something like that. So, anyway, one night we were at this party, and I had a few drinks and I was sitting next to Benny. I said, "Benny, I know you don't like my playing. Why did you ever hire me?" And he said, "I'm damned if I know." So I said, "Well, why don't you get somebody else, and I'll just play my trio numbers with the rhythm section?" He said, "Oh, do you mind? That would be great." Then he became very charming, and he hired John Bunch. So John Bunch came to join us, and we were out in the west somewhere. On the night of the concert, Benny said, "Oh, let Marian play the show; you can play it tomorrow." So I played the show, and at the end he called up John Bunch to play a duet with me—four hands! We were a sensation! People absolutely loved it, so, of course, we never did it again!

WE: Because it took the spotlight away from Benny?

MM: Yes, of course. So then for the rest of the tour, I just did my trio numbers and John played with the band. And then the president got shot just as we were driving towards Dallas. So we sat around moping in the motel for about five days, and then we finished up the tour in Topeka, Kansas. I had already thought about going to the Menninger Clinic, while we were in Topeka, because I was feeling really unhappy. I thought it would be a good idea to go there and see if some of their doctors could straighten my head out. So I went, and, actually, I had a wonderful time. It is a fantastic place.

WE: Did you leave the band at that point?

MM: Well, the tour ended in Topeka. We played one date and that was it. Everyone went their separate ways, but I stayed in Topeka at the Jayhawk Hotel and was an outpatient at the clinic for two weeks. It was hard to get away from there because everybody was so wonderful, and they had a great piano and all the music magazines, *Down Beat,* etc. I thought the patients were a lot hipper than those of us on the outside. It turned out to be a very good experience, because the doctors recommended an analyst for me to go to in Long Island. I was in analysis for a long time after that.

WE: Why did you feel the need for help on a protracted basis?

MM: Oh, I don't know. I just felt as if I wasn't getting anywhere—that I was stepping all over myself, and not really being happy with my marriage. That was the only way I could sum it up. I always tell people as a joke, "Benny Goodman drove me to the Menninger Clinic." I think even before I went with Benny, I felt I wasn't improving, job-wise. I wasn't getting any good recording dates. In fact, that's what led me to start Halcyon later on—trying to get a recording. I think rock had pretty much taken over, and I was doing a lot of school concerts and workshops.

JS: Your commitment to exposing young people to jazz is noteworthy. How did you start playing in schools?

MM: I got into doing concerts in schools in the early '50s. We were on the road playing at a place called Joe Squeezer's Bar in Rochester, New York—Joe Morello, Bill Britto, and myself. A disc jockey there in town, Will Moyle, came and begged me to take the trio and play in the school where his son was. "Oh, the kids will love it." I had never done anything like that, and I said that they won't like what we're doing. You know, playing "Stomping at the Savoy" and tunes like that. Anyway we went, and these were teenagers—thirteen, fourteen. We played "Lullaby of Birdland" and tunes I'm sure they didn't know. They were all applauding a lot. Finally, I said, "What would you kids like to hear?" They all hollered out, "You Ain't Nothin' but a Hound Dog." That made me realize they didn't know anything about jazz. So that really started me on a crusade of going to schools and playing jazz and trying to get them interested. I did that for a long time with no attempt to get paid; I would just offer my services in any town I was in by asking a teacher, "Would you like to have us come and play in your school?" "Oh, yes, we would love it." And we'd go and play a concert.

JS: As an educator you've perhaps been most broadly influential with *Piano Jazz*. Was that show your idea?

MM: No. Actually, Alec Wilder had a show on NPR in Columbia, South Carolina, where my show is produced on South Carolina Educational Radio. When his series ended, he recommended me. I was asked whether I could do something that would be entertaining and educational, similar to the show that Alec had been doing. I thought of having two pianos, that that would be the easiest way of doing it. The people in South Carolina didn't have much money, so we started doing the show in the Baldwin Piano showroom. There were about twenty pianos in there; we'd just pick out two that we liked, pull them up side by side, and do the show right there. The engineer would set up his equipment in a broom closet or something, and that's how we started *Piano Jazz*. I had no idea that it was going to be such a success.

JS: Do you think *Piano Jazz* represents an important contribution to jazz literature?

MM: I do now. That's actually the thing I feel most good about, is having managed to get all these people that jazz scholars would be interested in. You know, like Teddy Wilson, Mary Lou Williams, Oscar Peterson, Bill Evans, and actually have them talking and playing and describing what they do. I think that is kind of important. The Smithsonian wants to have all the tapes. The Library of Congress already has them.

WE: Let's change topics to explore your experience as a woman in the jazz world. Have there been obstacles to overcome because of your gender?

MM: When did they start calling it "gender" and they wouldn't say "your sex"? It's so wrong, somehow, isn't it? I know they do it, but it always strikes me funny.

WE: Gender is a cultural thing, whereas sex is physiological. I think that's the usual distinction.

MM: Oh, is that it? They talk about the gender gap and all those things. Now you'll have to say the question again. Sorry, I got carried away with gender.

WE: I was asking whether your sex has caused obstacles in your professional life?

MM: When I started my long-term engagement at the Hickory House, one of the first reviews I had was from Leonard Feather. It followed Leonard around all his life. He said, "Oh, she has three strikes against her. She's English, white, and a woman." Leonard was sort of embarrassed and he would say, "Well, I was really only kidding." I said, "No, I don't think you were kidding." But it never bothered me. Actually, I was pleased to be written about, and I just sort of took it as an accolade. I just was somebody who kind of went barging ahead no matter what.

JS: Did you ever have to endure statements like, "You play good for a girl"?

MM: Oh, yes, I had a lot of that. I mean, I think I really came to grips with that at the Hickory House. People would say, "Well, you play good for a girl." "You play just like a man" was the other one. For a long time, I sort of took everything that was said as a compliment, and then I started to think, "Why did somebody say I played aggressively?" I think you can play strong without being aggressive. I just started to take these things apart and say to some guy, "Why do you think I play like a man? Do you expect me to have my pinkie stuck up in the air?" I guess I got more confidence so that I could sort of argue with people about that. Be humorous about it.

JS: Did any of those situations ever change the way you thought about your work?

MM: Oh, no. I might get a little depressed once in a while. I recall something that happened, and yet at the time I don't remember being upset about it. Maybe I would suppress certain things. There was a big article about me in a Canadian magazine called *Mayfair,* and the writer had asked Bill Crow to say something about my playing. Bill implied that, because of my upbringing and where I came from, I didn't swing very much. It wasn't exactly uncomplimentary, but I always remember him talking about my "time." I never said anything to him about it. I just let it go, but it must still have been in the back of my mind, because just recently they had a program on NPR called *Portraits.* Nancy Wilson is the moderator, and I was one of the guests on it. They had Bill Crow being interviewed about me, so I said to the producer of the show, "Ask Bill Crow if he thinks my time is better now." I guess that incident has been in my head all these years. I must be weirder than I thought to remember a thing like that.

WE: Do you often play at women's jazz festivals?

MM: Well, they're still viable. I played several times in Kansas City because at that time it was a new thing. They were wonderful, and I felt it was a very popular thing because we just can't get away from it. They just keep calling us "women musicians," and it was a chance to have a group of people together who can really play. They had Toshiko Akyioshi and her band. She was picketed by women outside because they said there were too many men in the band. It was just her and all men in the band. She said, "The men are playing my music; I am the band. I'm the composer, not them."

WE: There certainly are narrow conceptions about what women are capable of doing.

MM: Well, when you think of what average women have to do in their lives, like give birth, do laundry, make beds, and carry kids around, who should judge them as not strong enough to play a horn? When I think about the International Sweethearts of Rhythm Band, some of those women were really powerhouses. In 1977 we did a recording with Vi Redd, Mary Osborne, Dottie Dodgion, and Lynn Milano for Halcyon.[7] It was a pretty interesting session.

JS: Were you responsible for that recording date?

MM: Yes. What happened was, I was trying to get a women's group together around the New York Festival time, and I thought it would be fun to have a women's group on TV. I'm very friendly with Gene Shalit, and he was with the *Today Show* at that time. He thought it was a great idea to have us on the show, so then I had to get this band together. I got Mary Osborne and Vi Redd from California; Lynn Milano lives in the area; and Dottie Dodgion lived here at that time. So we did the *Today Show,* and then it seemed like a good idea to try to do a recording date with this group, so I booked a club in Rochester called the Rountowner. Actually we did three things, all at the same time. We did the club date, which was recorded, and we did a taping for PBS.

WE: Is there an urgent need for a scholarly study of women's contributions to jazz?

MM: I guess all of us women would like to see that. I guess we all still feel like the underdog. Maybe it'll always be that way, because a lot of the women had this family thing to think about. Like Vi Redd was working with Earl Hines, or some big band, and she was trying to raise a family. Her kids said to her, "Oh, Mommy, we don't like you being on the road." So she left the band and maybe sabotaged part of her career, or maybe all of it. I've known a lot of women who've done that. Mary Osborne was one, and she was such a fabulous player. She was married to this guy, who I always felt was a nice guy, but who didn't do very well money-wise. He got a job in Bakersfield, California, and they moved. So she was right out of the scene, and raised her two sons there, who turned out to be great young men. But when she came back to New York and tried to do something, nobody knew about her anymore.

WE: Let's talk more in depth about your music and your views on the jazz world. First, do you think that you have an immediately recognizable sound?

MM: No. I don't feel as if I ever really got a style of my own. Probably the best thing I do is a ballad, but I don't think my general playing is all that different.

WE: When you play someone else's composition, say, for instance, a Monk tune, do you conceive of your approach as if it were a vessel for the composer?

MM: Well, if I do a Thelonious Monk tune, I will do my own thing with it. The same with a John Coltrane tune. Of course—"a vessel for the composer," that's good!—I want to try to stay in the idiom to a certain extent, but try to play my own ideas at the same time. Like playing "Red Planet"[8] and not getting all flowery.

JS: Or Ornette Coleman's "Turnaround"?

MM: Oh, that's a tune I love to play, but it's basically a blues. Then I do "Ramblin'," which is another of his. I suppose I *do* play them in the style they were written in, but not really aggressively so, or saying I must try to play this lick because Ornette played it. But maybe playing in that idiom. I guess one thing I've always liked to do—and I probably got this from Mary Lou—is to kind of keep up with things. I mean, I couldn't imagine Teddy Wilson ever wanting to play a Coltrane tune. I remember talking to Teddy about the Beatles and saying, "Some of those tunes are wonderful. Do you know any Beatle tunes?" He said, "No." I mean, Teddy played the same repertoire of tunes. I thought he was fantastic, but then he did sort of level off. He just wanted to play what he was known for. It's a challenge. I'm not an old fuddy-duddy, after all. I certainly do like to play different kinds of music.

JS: In addition to your virtuosity as a pianist, you're a composer. How long have you been composing?

MM: Since the '50s, but I had no confidence. I really didn't want to write something, because I was afraid somebody would criticize it unfavorably.

JS: Did you show your writing to Jimmy?

MM: Jimmy was not a good critic. He always thought everything I did was great, and I certainly miss that! A big-time music publisher, Jack Robbins, used to come into the Hickory House a lot, and he was a big fan. "Marian, you've got to write something." So I wrote a tune and played it on the job, not knowing what the result would be, and he liked it. He took this tune to Irving Caesar to write a lyric. Of course, Irving was a great lyric writer, having written millions of things, including "Tea for Two." But I wasn't too thrilled with the lyric. Nobody has ever sung this tune, and I look at it now and it doesn't seem too bad. It's called "Stranger in a Dream." I wrote a song that I called "With You in Mind." Mayfair Music was the publisher, and Carolyn Leigh started to write a lyric for it. She was such a great lyricist, as you may remember. She got about the first eight bars done, and I could see that it was gonna be really terrific, but then she called me up and said, "Oh, Marian, I can't work with you anymore. I'm going with Harold Arlen. We're going to do 'House of Flowers.' " So that was that. I was so disappointed. And Mayfair didn't find me anybody else to work with. I got very depressed about that. So the tune still doesn't have a lyric.

JS: How many tunes do you figure you've written?

MM: Maybe about fifty. Some of them have never seen the light of day. Some have, like "Ambiance" and "Twilight World," with a lyric by Johnny Mercer, and "In the Days of Our Love," with a lyric by Peggy Lee. I wrote "Ambiance" in Norman, Oklahoma, while doing some stage-band clinics with kids. I always felt a little more ambitious around a bunch of music students. You had to prove yourself to show them you could do something. So I sat down and wrote that tune one afternoon, and one of the band directors made an arrangement of it.

WE: From your perspective, is jazz progressing?

MM: I do think it's progressing, no matter what some of the pessimistic musicians say. I think it has to be, because there are a lot of new, good young players. And I say good; I don't actually know yet how many people are coming up who are gonna be great. There's such a variety of music. You can take some of the better elements of rock—I mean, there's a lot of it that I don't like—and there's all the Brazilian music, and music from Africa. There are so many different places to draw from, I don't see how it can *not* keep going. There's some people, Milt Jackson for one, who is saying, "When we're gone there isn't gonna be any more." I hate to think that way because, you know, there are a lot of wonderful young players who've listened to Milt—Gary Burton and Bobby Hutcherson. Then there's this young guy, Joe Locke—fantastic player with all the enthusiasm and ideas. You just hope that it will all continue.

JS: When you were a young, aspiring musician, did you hear the opinion expressed that jazz had nowhere left to go?

MM: You know what? I have a real feeling of regret. Of course, you've seen that movie *A Great Day in Harlem*?[9] At that particular time it seemed to me that jazz was in a good position, that there was a lot happening, and people were very enthusiastic. There was a lot more of a general good spirit. There was all this talent. There was Bud Powell and Phineas Newborn and all these wonderful horn players. And, of course, Miles. I did love Miles, except at the end.

JS: You were a big jazz family?

MM: Yes, and I didn't really know too much about the prejudice against blacks until I went on my first road trip to somewhere in South Carolina, and seeing signs on the buildings saying, "colored only" or "white only"—that kind of thing. But I never really knew what was going on in the South till then. I went to Atlanta to play at a place called At the Top of the Stairs. This must have been in the '60s. Willie Ruff and Dwike Mitchell were playing in the club opposite my trio, and the manager told me, "Now that you're working with colored people, you're not at any time to be on the stage with them." Needless to say, we immediately got very friendly (*laughter*), and both of them are fantastic musicians. Anyway, during one of my sets I played a tune of my own that Willie liked, and he wanted to play it on the French horn, so I invited him up on the stage, and we played it together. Surprisingly, nothing was ever said.

WE: Where do you think jazz can go? Some people say the form is used up. You're saying it can absorb other musics. It's always been eclectic, but has it reached a saturation point?

MM: Well, you say the form is used up. Yet people still play Bach and Mozart, and nobody says *that* form is used up.

WE: They might. People continue to interpret Bach and Beethoven, but contemporary composers don't write in those styles. Do you think that jazz as we know it can still attract ambitious musicians, or are hip-hop and rap the future?

MM: God, I hope not. I regard hip-hop and rap and all this stuff as transitory, including much of rock. To me, rock is sort of like theater, with Klieg lights and Mick Jagger prancing up and down the stage in his long underwear, and ear-splitting volume. To me, it's not really music as I think of it. Rap in a certain form was around long ago—I mean, Cab Calloway did rap. It just wasn't called rap. It was sort of like rhyming slang or funny verses. But today's youth has made it into something obnoxious, hostile, and vicious. Things it doesn't need to be.

WE: Since you mentioned one film, *A Great Day in Harlem,* I would be remiss not to ask you about the inspiration for that movie. Were you knocked out that all those musicians showed up for the Art Kane photograph?

MM: I was knocked out to be *included in the photo!* I thought, "My God, this is a great thing." And I feel so sorry that Jimmy wasn't in it.

WE: Why wasn't he?

MM: Well, it's kind of a shame. Some newspaperman put in the paper that Jimmy was probably hung over, but he wasn't. He had joined AA, and wasn't even drinking at all. He was just too lazy to get up! It was too early for him.

WE: How early was it?

MM: We had to be there at ten o'clock. Jimmy's exact words were "That's too fuckin' early." I didn't know what it was going to be, but I was sort of anxious for publicity, you know, liking to be on the scene. So I went. It was a jolly atmosphere there. It was like a social event, everybody shaking hands and hugging, and saying, "Hey, baby." Some guy had a jug in a brown paper bag. (*Laughter.*) I think after the picture half of them went over to this bar on Broadway. I mean, the photo really took up a whole day. We were there for hours. Art Kane couldn't get everybody to stand still, or to come together, because they were all too busy saying hello.

WE: Recently, *Life* published a photo at the same spot[10] with just a few of you left standing. That must have been tough to do.

MM: It *was* kind of tough. And seeing how the whole place had deteriorated in the past years. The house that we stood in front of was boarded up. There was graffiti all over it, and the other houses weren't well kept. The first time that we were there, they were really quite well kept. The street was neat, but now everything seemed run down. Milt Hinton said, "Gee, I've lasted longer than this street has!" (*Laughter.*)

WE: Gerry Mulligan died not long after that.

MM: I know, and you could see that he was in bad shape at the time. He had a cane. He really couldn't walk. They took the cane away from him to let them take the picture. That is rather a poignant picture, in fact. They told us to look sad. Gordon Parks—he was very good; he's a wonderful photographer. But, you know, we certainly had no trouble looking sad. We *were* sad.

WE: One of the most enigmatic figures in that photograph is Thelonious Monk.

MM: I never quite could figure what Monk was about. I mean, now everybody's hailing him as a genius. Some of the things he's done are so wonderful, but sometimes I wonder whether he would play some really bad chords and put people on, and then everybody would imitate them years later. I sometimes wondered whether he was poking fun, or really being serious.

JS: What was he like on a personal level?

MM: I didn't know him that well—but I did tell this to Jean Bach; she thought it was funny. I was at the Hickory House, and everybody was playing Monk tunes, and talking about Monk. I had been down to the Five Spot a lot to hear him play, and watch him do his little dance around the piano. I really wanted to hear what he was doing. Anyway, the first tune I learned was " 'Round Midnight." I'd met Monk on the street—he was talkative in those days; he was quite verbal. He said hello, and I must have been so callow because I said to him, "Gee I love your tune 'Round Midnight.' I wish you'd come by the Hickory House some night, I'd like you to hear what I'm doing with it." God, he must have laughed. Maybe I didn't say it that way, maybe I was a little more humble than that. He said, "Okay." So about a week later, on a pouring wet night, he came by with another guy. They looked like two black crows, in raincoats from head to foot and black berets. They looked very sinister. They went to a back table. He didn't say hello or anything. They sat opposite each other and talked very earnestly for the entire set. I looked to see if there was any kind of interest there. Of course, I was hoping he'd pay me a compliment, but they got up and walked out and left me with the bill. (*Laughs.*) I thought that was wonderful. I mean, it was poetic justice. I don't think he meant any harm; I think that was just typical Monk.

JS: Turning to your entrepreneurial side, tell us about the creation of the Halcyon label.

MM: I think I started my own record company in about 1970, because I was frustrated that I didn't have a record date. I guess the only people who *were* recording were Miles Davis and Thelonious Monk. Once I called up Teo Macero and asked him, "Do you think I could do a record of Beatle tunes?" He said, "Oh, it's been done. Nobody would buy that." And then a composer named Sam Coslow came along, who wrote a lot of music for movies, and tunes like "My Old Flame" and "Cocktails for Two." Sam Coslow did a very nice thing; he said he wanted me to make an album of his tunes, and he would underwrite it. So I did, but I was a little disappointed with the way the company [Dot Records] put the LP together, because they had a vocal group behind some of the tunes. They were going "doo-wah, doo-wah," and, you know, I had no say in this. But I had a wonderful rhythm section—Grady Tate and Ron Carter. Then they packaged the thing for the adult pop market. It had a great picture of a beautiful girl on the cover, obviously not me, and on the back it had some sort of amorphous kind of liner notes, with no mention of the rhythm section, as if it would be lovely music for you to cuddle up to. I just didn't like the way it was marketed.

Anyway, I think I said something like "Fuck it, I'm going to put out my own damn records." And that's where Sherman Fairchild came into the picture. Sherman Fairchild owned Fairchild Cameras and Fairchild Aviation, and he was a great jazz fan. He had two pianos in his apartment, and he would give parties at which people like Hoagy Carmichael and Joe Bushkin, and movie stars like Jeanne Crain, would come. It would be sort of expected that you would play, so I would get to do duets with Hoagy or whoever was there. And Lee Wiley would sing. Anyway, Sherman was interested in helping me start Halcyon as a mail order business, which we did. Hank O'Neal, who now has his own record company, Chiaroscuro, got involved, and that's how the whole thing started.

Meanwhile, Sherman got ill and died, which was really a shame. I was very sad about that, because he had just been a wonderful friend to me. At that point Hank and I divided up everything that we had recorded and agreed to go our separate ways. He started his Chiaroscuro label, and I kept going with Halcyon.

JS: Is the label still going?

MM: No, it isn't, but I still occasionally get requests for something from the Halcyon catalogue. I refer them to Jazz Alliance, because they've got several of them out on their label, and I think they're going to put them *all* out, which means they'll still be available. So I've really been lucky. When I think back how these things got done, I can't believe it. Because I was doing club dates at the same time. I remember working at the Riverboat and having to go and meet Hank O'Neal to discuss what was going to be on the back of an album. Running over there in a cab between sets—I mean, crazy things. But I guess I would still do it if I had to. It's nice to still see these really good products, that they are not going to die.

[We turned to our selections of music, beginning with "Nightlife," a piano solo by Mary Lou Williams, Brunswick Records; recorded in 1930.]

MM: It's amazing how sharp all her stride playing is. It's very accurate, very strong. I can't get over how perfect it is as opposed to things she did later. I never heard her play like that. Not in person. I mean, she had really developed, gone into bebop and beyond. I think a lot of her music is very blues-oriented. Even that one is basically a blues-type thing. The way she played it, she was really in good shape.

WE: I was struck by all the changes in dynamics and tempo.

MM: Well, she didn't really change tempo; she just turned the beat around with those bass notes, which a lot of piano players like Eubie Blake did. I don't mean turning the beat around, but putting the emphasis in another place. She didn't exactly change tempo. She changed key, and then she went into another figure like that D minor thing, and then she went back to the stride piano. It was certainly a formalized kind of beat.

WE: There was a little section that all of a sudden got very dark.

MM: Yes, well, that's where she changed key and did the bass line. That's something that she did a lot. She would have some line going in the bass. She always liked to have a kind of Afro-Cuban or Latin kind of feeling going on.

JS: You commented on the strength of her playing.

MM: That's one of the things I liked about her. When she had the trio, she would take a handful of notes—kind of stabbing the chords in the bass with her left hand. There's one called "Free Spirits"[11] with Mickey Roker and Buster Williams, one of my favorite ones. It's much later. I guess when I was trying to find stuff of hers to play, I mostly went to the later things. I identify with them more. It seems to me that every time I hear a radio program of Mary Lou's, they're always playing something that's really old and has a bad sound. They did a whole series of her music on WBGO,[12] and it was all taken from various archives. It was so old that I didn't feel it was representative of what she did in her later life. But I thought the things with the band[13] stood up well after all these years. She wrote one that I recorded, "Walkin' and Swingin'," which is one of her real early ones done with the band.

[Our next selection was "Georgia on My Mind," solo piano by Art Tatum, from *God Is in the House,* recorded 1940; Onyx Records.]

MM: Oh, well, anything by Tatum! (*As the tune is playing*) Things like that, going through chord changes like that. Maybe he'll do it again. Now, that's ridiculous! I don't know how to describe that, but it's amazing.

JS: Taking the original chord changes and making it more complex with substitutions and dramatic readings?

MM: Thanks. Spoken like a true music educator. Exactly. I couldn't express it better myself. He puts in a lot more changes than are there originally.

JS: Would that performance scare people today?

MM: It would *impress* people today. I think even Oscar Peterson admits that nobody could carry off those runs. He did some two-octave things, and scales. It was like three guys playing. It had a lot of humor in it, too—to me, a lot of those chord substitutions have a kind of humorous quality to them. Once in a while he would interpolate part of another tune. I feel that all those runs he did were such a part of him; it was almost like a reflex action, he just couldn't help doing them. I remember once in England I saw a book of his transcriptions in a music shop, and I bought it. I looked at it—it was ridiculous. There's no way I could play those pieces. I just never tried. I put the book away.

[We listened to "While We're Young," by Alec Wilder, from *7X Wilder, The Bob Brookmeyer 4*, 1961; Verve Records. Bob Brookmeyer, trombone and piano; Jim Hall, guitar; Bill Crow, bass; Mel Lewis, drums.]

MM: They're really not playing it correctly. Alec would get mad. I think I'm getting more like Alec every day. I can't stand to hear the melody played wrong the first time around. It's a funny arrangement.

JS: It's kind of a halting arrangement.

MM: Well, Bob is having Bill play in two on the bass, and it's kind of an up-tempo for this particular tune. And Mel is just going whish, whish, whish on the drums.

JS: We used this recording to open up the subject of Alec Wilder. Could you put him in perspective as a composer, and as a champion of the American popular song?

MM: Well, he didn't have a tremendous output of songs, but some of the ones he did write were landmark songs. A lot of people don't know Alec Wilder. Then you say, well, he wrote songs like (*hums the melody of "I'll Be Around"*), then they immediately know *that* song. I defy anybody not to know that tune or love it; I think that *is* a great song. He wrote the words and the music. And I think this one, "While We're Young," was a really good song. Peggy Lee did the definitive arrangement of that one. But he couldn't get it published at first. He was always talking about people in the Brill Building that didn't like the song because it had long pauses where nothing was happening. There was four bars of holding a long note and they would say, "Oh, you can't have a song that's so empty in there." And, for a while, nobody took the song. Alec got very bitter about different things, and that was one of them. But then Peggy recorded it and made a hit out of it. Then Alec got mad at her because he said she changed the melody on the bridge. I mean, he could just be awfully rude. It's alleged—I don't know how true it is—that during one of his drunken times at the Algonquin bar, when he met Peggy, he said, "When you get to the bridge, jump off." He was such a mass of contradictions. Alec was his own worst enemy. When you think that Peggy took a song that he couldn't get accepted, and she made a hit out of it, and all he could do was get mad at her! The Mills Brothers had a big hit with "I'll Be Around." I heard from some friends of Alec that somebody played him the record and he took it and broke it in half, because he didn't like the Mills Brothers. He didn't like their music. He didn't like the arrangement.

Alec was really weird, really strange. He wrote a lot of pieces for me, which I was totally thrilled about—nobody'd ever written anything for me—and I recorded some of them. I seem to be talking about the bad things about him, but he was very generous and kind and terribly funny. He had a fantastic sense of humor—a kind of black humor. He was a very funny guy. Very vulgar, low-down humor. Yet he had the nerve to tell me *I* was the most vulgar person he'd ever met!

[We began playing "Lena," from *Live! Cecil Taylor at the Cafe Montmartre,* 1962; Fantasy Records.]

MM: I wonder what year this was.

WE: 1962.

MM: Oh, he was fairly understandable in those days. He's actually playing chords! This is funny: JoAnne Brackeen and I once went to the Blue Note because JoAnne wanted me to hear Cecil and his group. She likes Cecil—I hadn't heard him for a long time—and I thought I would like it, too. He had two or three horns, drums, and bass, and it was such total cacophony. I think I was there about a half-hour, and I said to JoAnne, "I'm sorry, I just can't take it." We were sitting behind the piano, and Cecil had on his usual knit cap and I got hysterical. I got up, and I just fell all over people to get out fast. "Let me out of here." He never even knew; he was still playing away. I mean, that was the first and last time I ever made a commotion. The club owner said, "Marian, Marian, what's the matter?" I said, "I'm sorry, I've got to go; I can't stand it."

WE: How did JoAnne react?

MM: Oh, she laughed. She stayed. She's more into that music than I am. She can see something I couldn't. I mean, it was okay with piano alone—I enjoyed playing piano with Cecil[14]—but to hear the sounds they played on the horns, I couldn't figure what they were trying to do.

WE: You're saying that as a jazz musician you were unable to tolerate what another jazz musician was playing? Why couldn't you decipher what he was doing and respect it on an intellectual level?

MM: Oh, that's ridiculous! To be sitting in a nightclub, hearing a lot of honking and total cacophony. To me, that's not music, and I certainly wouldn't expect to have to stay there and have my ears assaulted. If people play that way to get some sort of reaction, they certainly got it from me, and I don't think that I should be judged as an intolerant person because I didn't appreciate what was going on. I sometimes think people in the audience pretend to like it because they think it's the thing to do.

[We skipped ahead to Taylor's solo.]

MM: You know, I could like it more, or I could be persuaded to listen to it, if I was given something for my mind's eye, like "We're going to do a piece which has to do with rocks and rivers." Maybe whitewater rafting would go with something like that.

JS: Program notes?

MM: Yes, if it was for a TV show or something, where you could say I want to hear music for this kind of a scene.

JS: Why don't you respond well to this piece of music?

MM: Well, I guess maybe it's just being old-fashioned. I don't like to hear so much what to me is disruptive stuff. They probably never played this before, and I don't know what they have in their minds. So to me it's kind of an ugly noise on the horns, and I just don't hear any sort of melodic lines or order.

WE: How do you react to Cecil's piano work on this recording?

MM: Well, I don't hear a strong melodic line. It's just fascinating, especially going to hear him once at Town Hall—he was running around the piano. He had on tennis shoes, and he'd get up and go down to the end of the piano and pluck the strings, and then he'd run back to the keyboard and play some more. This was years ago. I remember I went to this concert with Patti Bown. I enjoyed it in a strange kind of way. I mean, it's something so different. I can't say it's not good. It's just me having difficulty understanding it.

Selected Discography

Plays the Music of Alec Wilder. Jazz Alliance TJA-10016 (recorded 1973, released 1992).
A Sentimental Journey. Jazz Alliance TJA-10025 (1973). (With Jimmy McPartland.)
Live at Maybeck Recital Hall, Vol. 9. Concord CCD 4460 (1991). (Solo piano.)
Live at Yoshi's Nitespot. Concord CCD-4712 (1996).
Just Friends. Concord CCD-4805-2 (1998). (Duets with Tommy Flanagan, Renee Rosnes, George Shearing, Geri Allen, Dave Brubeck, Gene Harris.)

Notes

1. Entertainment National Service Association.
2. United Service Organizations.
3. International Association of Jazz Education.
4. Presented annually by the American Women in Radio and Television.
5. ENSA was similar to the American USO.
6. "In a Mist" is one of Bix Beiderbecke's celebrated compositions.
7. *Now's the Time* is the recording that Marian refers to, with Vi Redd, alto saxophone; Mary Osborne, guitar; Dottie Dodgion, drums; and Lynn Milano, bass.
8. Composed by John Coltrane.
9. Produced by Jean Bach, 1995; ABC Video.
10. February 1996; pages 64 and 65.
11. From *Free Spirits,* 1975; Steeplechase.
12. Radio station based in Newark, New Jersey.
13. Andy Kirk's Clouds of Joy.
14. Cecil Taylor appeared twice as a guest on *Piano Jazz.* Unfortunately, neither date was recorded.

Helen Merrill

Helen Merrill

For the past half-century, rarified vocalist Helen Merrill has been steadfast in her refusal to sacrifice artistry for commercial success. She has nonetheless recorded a significant body of work on some of the best labels in the music business, collaborating with a long list of jazz icons. Although her fame shifted to expatriate status during the prime of her career, Merrill's ability to transmute her material into art song has made her a favorite of international critics and cognoscenti alike.

Born Jelena Ana Milcetic at home on July 21, 1930, in the Chelsea district of Manhattan, Merrill was the daughter of immigrants. As a teenager, she was singing in amateur hour club contests in Manhattan; at sixteen, she was hired as the featured vocalist for Reggie Childs's Big Band. On the side, she began sitting in on jam sessions with some of New York's best bop musicians.

In 1952, Merrill spent three months touring with pianist Earl "Fatha" Hines. Backed by cutting-edge arrangements that helped define her distinctive sound, she established a reputation as one of the premier small group vocalists of the period. In 1954, EmArcy/Mercury Records signed Helen Merrill as a solo artist. Preferring slower tunes over up-tempo numbers, this graceful stylist lent her luminous voice to a host of ballads, which became her trademark.

Her eponymous album in 1954[1] was a masterful freshman effort, featuring arrangements by Quincy Jones and the trumpet playing of Clifford Brown. Well-received by audiences and critics alike, it remains one of the best examples of jazz singing ever produced. Merrill went on to issue several other successful recordings in the '50s, including *The Nearness of You,*[2] with pianist Bill Evans. In 1957 she was part of the "Music for Moderns" tour, which also included Miles Davis and Cannonball Adderley. Between 1959 and 1972, she spent most of her time abroad.

Merrill stands out among the handful of vocalists christened as "cool" in the 1950s. This sophisticated singer developed a smoldering style combined with a clear-voiced dispassionate delivery of the lyric that, for the audience, puts her just out of reach. When performing ballads, her elongated phrase endings allow for very little space, intoxicating the listener as nuances of a lyric seemingly dissipate into the confidential atmosphere she creates. Merrill's bop roots furnished her a musical versatility, enabling her to be harmonically adventurous in the spontaneous environment of a jazz combo.

A Grammy-nominated album reignited her career in 1976,[3] and Merrill has been steadily recording ever since. Her 1980 release, *Chasin' the Bird*,[4] was also up for a Grammy. Recently signed by Verve, she continues to work with the cream of the jazz crop; her latest CD[5] features soprano saxophonist Steve Lacy and the late pianist Sir Roland Hanna. Helen Merrill currently has the luxury of selective touring and concertizing, with Japan and France her favorite stops. In 1996, the International Women in Jazz presented her with the Lifetime Achievement Award to a Living Legend.

Recorded March 24, 1997

WE: I have a sense from my research that you are an idealist when it comes to the aesthetics of your work, and that your idealism has made you a reluctant performer.[6] Are those descriptions accurate?

HM: I don't know if it's not true of *all* performers, but in my case the aesthetics of what I imagine ought to be has gotten in the way, because I've thought that the commercial end of the business—the managers and all that stuff—was not honest. It was kind of idealistic and crazy, but that has affected my performance until recently. Today I'm pretty cool and relaxed. I do a lot of concerts, which is good, because it keeps a distance. You don't have to entertain. You can do music in a more aesthetic way.

WE: What is it about entertaining that doesn't appeal to you?

HM: It interferes with the music. You have to appeal to another sense. You have to understand that when I first started singing, I worked in nightclubs, and all you could hear out there were glasses clinking together and men and women making comments about you personally. The music was second to the atmosphere of the club: cigarettes, martinis, and so forth. It was something that frightened me.

WE: When you began your professional career, did you play in dives or higher-class clubs?

HM: I started out pretty high, unfortunately. It was too much too soon. I couldn't handle it. I was very naïve because my exposure had been limited. I married very young, and I was taking care of a child. My first obligation was to my child. My family's very important to me; that female side of me is strong. I tried to perform at the same time, but it didn't always work out very easily. And I didn't have the background of a lot of small nightclubs. Generally speaking, it was rough. One of my first engagements after the release of the Quincy Jones album was at Birdland. I was so frightened that my knees were actually knocking together. (*Laughs.*) But I don't think it was the audience's fault. I think that my kind of sensitivity requires complete silence, and the atmosphere of those places was not like that. Today the clubs are very nice. They're quiet, no smoking. But in those days it was not like that.

WE: You said that the atmosphere of nightclubs frightened you. Did your upbringing shelter you or promote assertiveness?

HM: I didn't come from a show business–type background, or one with an aggressive kind of an interest in worldly things. My parents were immigrants from Croatia. We were poor, and our parents sacrificed a great deal. My sisters and I had to find a way to escape, in fact, from the kind of life that they endured as immigrants. It was our duty as children of immigrants to succeed.

WE: How poor was your family? Were you at times without food or the ability to pay the rent?

HM: Oh, no, we had all of that. My father was a tugboat captain; he always worked. But there was a lot of emotional poverty. My mother was sick when we were very young, and in effect, we didn't have a mother. We were deprived of her guidance and love as her illness became the dominant force. That is true poverty.

WE: How many siblings do you have?

HM: Three sisters, and a boy that we never knew. He died when he was very young, and tragically. It affected my mother deeply. We were four sisters, and we're very close to this day. And we're all successful in many respects.

WE: Is it true that your mother loved to sing?[7]

HM: Yes! My mother would express her feelings through music. Not to be noticed, nor for applause; singing was what she loved to do. At home, she would sing beautiful Croatian folk songs from her childhood. My mother's taste ran from folk music to devotional songs to Kern to Caruso, John McCormick, and, yes, Rudy Vallee. I remember as a very little girl listening to songs like "All the Things You Are," "The Object of My Affection," "The Way You Look Tonight," and so on. She'd sing them with such depth of feeling that she'd make your hair stand up. The most touching song was "I'll Take You Home Again, Kathleen."[8] It was apparent that the song was about herself, though in the third person. I learned from that song in particular that music was universal and that I could choose any song to convey the feelings that we all share.

WE: Was she your first role model?

HM: Absolutely. When we went to parties that were affiliated with my parents' Croatian background, my mother was the life of the party. There was folk dancing and group singing, and my mother was right in the middle of it all. Everyone loved her, and that was the time I saw true joy in her face. That was my early introduction to music.

WE: Did your mother have professional ambitions?

HM: My mother had absolutely no professional ambitions. From her background, it would have been a disgrace to be in show business. No, not even a thought.

WE: Was such strong opposition a matter of religious or cultural beliefs?

HM: Cultural. It would have been disgraceful for my father to have his wife working in any capacity other than mother, wife, and homemaker. And my mother fully agreed. It was unthinkable for a wife to work.

WE: How, then, did you make the leap into "show business"?

HM: A lot of chutzpa. I'll tell you something: I knew from childhood that I was going to be a singer. That's a lucky thing. I was determined that I was going to suffer anything to do that. And I did; with blinders on, I just kept marching straight ahead. That's really how it happened. I mean, it was marvelous fun, but I did a lot of stumbling along the way. I would change the way I did business, but I wouldn't change being a musician.

WE: Speaking of changes, where did the name Merrill come from?

HM: People were ashamed of their ethnic names in those days. And especially in show business. That was an era when you were ashamed of everything, and you dreamed of having blue eyes and blond hair. I'm sorry, but that was true. You certainly couldn't put a name like Helen Milcetic on a marquee. Anyway, I got the name Merrill like any teenager would. My girlfriend had a boyfriend who was a paratrooper, and his name was Merrill. And so I thought, "What a nice name." It had an "M," and that justified using it. Childish as that was, it stayed with me.

WE: Since you had a bead on becoming a singer from such an early age, did your family provide you with formal training?

HM: No. I tried to take singing lessons or piano lessons (*chuckles sardonically*), but I was punished severely. I used to see ads in magazines for singing lessons, I would send for the material, and on two occasions a salesman appeared at our door. I was about seven the first time. My mother reacted very angrily toward the idea, and I was punished. The second time I was about thirteen. This time it was my father who reacted angrily; he knew that these were scams. Luckily he directed the anger toward the salesperson, and I was scot-free.

As for piano, we did not have an instrument, and that was the last thing on my father's mind at that time. So, I took lessons at school and practiced on a cardboard keyboard. It was most unsatisfactory, and I soon gave up studying in a conventional manner. Undaunted, I turned my studying to listening. I developed "radar ears," which was perfect for jazz.

WE: Was your earlier punishment the result of another cultural taboo?

HM: No. My mother got very sick. I was nine years old when she entered the hospital for the last time. My father was taking care of us, and he thought that studying music was foolishness. And he thought that anybody singing in a nightclub was lowly. He'd never say that, but he (*laughs*) used to sing a song to hint to me that this was a bad profession: "There's a café in town where you're known as a clown, how happy you seem to be. Everyone's buddy but nobody's bride, you're the loneliest girl in town." (*Laughs heartily.*) No, the stage most certainly would have been a terrible thing to aspire to. However, that philosophy did not stop me from dreaming of how I could become a singer. I mean, against all odds, I just forged ahead. Had my mother been at home, I would never have entered this business at all. She was very adamant. You know, she left Catholicism to go to Seventh-day Adventism, so for two years we were part of that church. There was a lot of conflict at home about her religion—we were Roman Catholics for centuries. My father was *very* upset with this situation. Oh! That's a part of my childhood that's very difficult.

WE: Your mother didn't live to see you become a professional. Did your dad acknowledge your success?

HM: Yes, but he remained reserved about show business. That song he used to sing to me (*laughter*), he believed it until the end. I got a telegram to do a TV show opposite Mel Torme. The chance of a lifetime. My father did not tell me until weeks later; he did not believe the telegram, thought it was a hoax. I never did get over that; it would have changed my direction. No doubt about it.

WE: Nevertheless, was he proud of you?

HM: Sure he was proud, but he was trying to be protective. He had four girls, all good-looking, to bring up. Boy, there was no way he could speak to us directly about *anything.* He could never speak directly about things that a mother, in his mind, should have talked about with us, and so, as I said, he had to speak in songs or euphemisms. (*Chuckles.*) He'd leave little notes: "Don't do this, don't do that." He would sign his name as "Pop the Cop," as a joke, of course, but that would give us the message that he was watching us even though he was at work. "Pop the Cop is watching." My father was our hero. He took care of my mother and four children, sometimes working two shifts. He did things that very few men would undertake. He cooked for us before going to work, he cleaned our clothes—he even shopped for our clothes.

WE: Do you recall the first time you had the chance to sing in front of an audience?

HM: I started on *Amateur Hour.* There was a woman in my building who had the most glorious voice, but she could not become a singer because her husband wouldn't let her. He abused her, actually. I was about twelve, and she used to tell me all her troubles. I realized she was not a role model by any means, but I thought this poor woman might be able to give me a hint on how I could start my career. And she did. She said, "There's a man on Broadway in the Brill Building who books talent for the *Amateur Hour* at clubs. Why don't you go to see him?" I did, and he would escort a bunch of us on the subway to sing at various small nightclubs. We would pretend that we were part of the audience and volunteer to perform in the contest of the evening. Sometimes I won, and sometimes I didn't. We were all pretty good, and the audience loved it. We got about two dollars each, I guess. At fifteen, that's how I started performing. In retrospect, it was a riot.

WE: Aside from the *Amateur Hour* stints in 1945, what were some other highlights of your formative years?

HM: While I was still in high school, I used to go to a place called the 845 Club in New York; I'd hang out there and listen to the afternoon concerts. They'd have people like Don Byas, Dizzy, Ben Webster, Bud Powell. And somehow I had the audacity to talk the promoter, Johnny Johnson, into the thought that I was a great singer. I said, "Please let me sing at one of your jam sessions." He was such a sweet man, he said, "Okay." I had my real name on the marquee, Helen Milcetic. In any case, this guy let me sing, and the pianist accompanying me was Bud Powell. (*Laughs.*) I started to sing, and Bud apparently loved it and was very surprised to hear my unusual voice and approach to music. He stopped playing and looked at me with the most loving smile of approval I have ever experienced. I can picture that at any time; it has left a wonderful warmth that I can feel until today. But you must realize that at that time the musicians I was listening to—like Bird, Al Haig, John Lewis, Lester, Teddy Kotick—were the "ordinary" musicians that were in New York. And they were very, very supportive of young musicians; they helped each other.

WE: Did you hear Bird at the 845 Club?

HM: Yes. I heard him many times, and I sang with him more than once. But not on a professional basis. Just sitting in—he would encourage young people to sit in, not only me. Bird was very kind to young musicians. You don't hear nice things too much about him.

WE: He helped you musically, or with getting gigs?

HM: No, no, no. In those days, it was like a club of elitist musicians, and if you were gathered into the fold, that was it. You were made, you know. (*Laughs.*) You didn't make money, but you were a made musician. In that way, he helped me; like when he was in California and I was with Earl Hines. He was working in a Los Angeles nightclub, and I was in the audience. He got on the microphone and said (*imitating Parker's voice*), "Okay, Helen, get up here and show them how we sing in New York." I said, "Okay," and sang with him. You're full of courage when you're young.

WE: Speaking of Earl Hines, with whom you had your first real professional job, how was your experience working with him in the early 1950s when his career had been eclipsed by bop?

HM: He was great. My first husband, Aaron Sachs,[9] was with the band, too, along with [trombonist] Bennie Green—Bennie was responsible for my career, actually—[bassist] Tommy Potter, [trumpeter] Jonah Jones, [drummer] Osie Johnson, and [vocalist] Etta Jones. The band loved Earl. He was a bit pompous, but in everything he did he was very elegant. We called him "Major Hopple." (*Laughter.*)

WE: Was Hines tolerant of the bop inclinations of some of the members of the band?

HM: Although he was not entirely happy with the new music, he gave us all a lot of freedom. Jimmy Guiffre's arrangements were a bit modern for him, but he understood that the music was progressing, and he never tried to alter a group member's talent. He hired creative musicians and expected to hear jazz music. I had Jimmy Guiffre write me a couple of arrangements for the group. I sang them, and I thought I was being very modern. Jimmy did wonderful chords, you know; they were very modern changes at that time, and so I thought I was being *very, very* avant-garde and hip.

WE: With regard to the avant-garde, several of the musicians you were associated with at that time were changing the course of jazz.

HM: I was, too, in my own way. I was one of them. I was marching to my own drummer, musically. A "catch me if you can" sort of thing.

WE: Did that elite circle of modern players think of themselves as entertainers, as, I believe earlier musicians did when they were breaking new ground?

HM: Oh, no, no, no. We were rebels. We knew we were rebels. We were *proud* of it. In fact, that was a badge of honor, to be a rebel. I'm still that way in my music. I'm always looking for new things. Always. But we were rebellious and we were insistent upon our own way of doing it.

WE: Were you rebelling against certain musical forms?

HM: Absolutely, yes. I didn't like the old music too much; I never really liked swing music. I don't have a great deal of fun with it. I have more fun with introspective kinds of stuff. The first singer that really interested me was Sarah Vaughan. I mean, really and truly, in the sense of "Well, yeah, that's correct," in a musical sense. It was going where my thoughts were. To this day she remains for me a musician from a musician's point of view. She had it all. I recognized that as a kid. Leonard Feather did a blindfold test with Sarah, using "Daydream," from *The Feeling Is Mutual.*[10] She had never heard me before, and I was the only singer she gave five stars to. Leonard said she listened with great curiosity and then said, "That's five stars!" I was very, very proud of that, because it was like coming of age. I learned that kind of singing from Johnny Hodges. His version of "Daydream" was so elegant and so pure. That's what influenced *my* approach to that song.

WE: You had your first recording session in 1953, when you cut a single for Roost Records. How did that record date come about?

HM: I didn't record for Roost Records. What I did was I called Rudy Van Gelder[11] to book the studio time—as I recall, it cost practically nothing. I went there with [guitarist] Jimmy Raney. We recorded "The More I See You" and "My Funny Valentine." It was not done as a commercial, professional recording; it was done as a love project. We loved each other's musicianship. Then Roost Records purchased them; I got twenty-five dollars. They were very beautiful recordings, and unfortunately the factory burned, and I can't find any trace of that record.

WE: In 1954, you recorded on EmArcy with Clifford Brown.[12] What were the circumstances behind that major career step?

HM: That is really an amazing story. I was too shy to audition. It was ridiculous. I'd never auditioned; I was very, very retarded. This is where Bennie Green comes in: He called up Bob Shad[13] and said, "You've got to record this singer." In those days Bob used to put his ears to the ground, and musicians would talk about other musicians. That's how they got to be recorded and became famous. Remember, Clifford wasn't known at that time. Everybody asks, "How did you record with Clifford?" But how did he record with me? I mean, we were just together, that's all. Quincy [Jones] put that date together. I'd heard Clifford once in person. Quincy said, "You gotta have Clifford." I said, "Fine." It had nothing to do with a big thought process. I wanted [guitarist] Barry Galbraith 'cause he's like a security blanket, and so was [bassist] Oscar Pettiford. Those were my real supporters. And I was friendly with Quincy. He was struggling and living in a basement apartment with his wife and daughter. We were all "waiting to be discovered" musicians. But it was already becoming apparent that Quincy had something very special about him, and people listened when he talked about new talent. Both Quincy and Bennie strongly recommended me to Bob Shad. After Bennie Green called him, Bob Shad said, "Okay, let's record her." He'd never even heard me sing. (*Chuckles.*)

WE: Did you know what tunes you'd be doing before walking into the studio?

HM: Yes, I picked all the tunes for that date. But there was no rehearsal, no singing the tunes. In those days it was considered very courageous to just walk in and with your ears be able to do anything. I mean, it was ridiculous. You might not have the melody quite the way it should be, but you'd make something up, you know. It was very spontaneous music.

WE: Although the date may have been spontaneous, you must have been impressed by the way Clifford Brown complemented your vocals.

HM: If you listen to that album, Clifford never does anything but integrate or respond in the most appropriate way to what I'm doing. It's so sensitive; it isn't as though he's going BA DEEP BA DEEP BA DEEP while I'm singing, forcing me to sing the melody. I was never forced to be a melodist with him. He listened carefully. That music is quite complicated. It sounds easy, you know, but it really isn't. I don't know of anybody who could do it today. He just broke everybody's heart when he died.

I somehow could never believe that he was gone. We were young and thought that we would all live forever, and somewhere inside of me I kept looking for Clifford. I had to close that door. Clifford had an enormous effect on most people who got to know him or work with him. He was such a pure soul. He was so intelligent, and he was a wonderful husband and father. He was somebody that we all needed in the business, because there was just too much of the other stuff going on at that time—you know, a lot of drugs and ruining of lives. So to have a man like this come along was a breath of fresh air. When he died, something died in a lot of musicians. In fact, he died when I was recording with Gil [Evans].[14] They had to stop the session, and that was an expensive session to stop. Even Bob Shad, who should have been thinking about money, wasn't thinking about money. He ran into the studio and told the guys in the band that Clifford was gone. The session was aborted, and everyone left in depressed silence.

WE: Among your most celebrated recordings is "Dream of You," which, as you mentioned, was in session when you learned of Clifford Brown's death. Is it true that "Dream of You" was a catalyst of sorts for the subsequent Gil Evans/Miles Davis collaborations?[15]

HM: There's no question. I put that together. When we were on tour,[16] I said to Miles, "Listen, you know, I just did an album with Gil Evans. You should look him up again." He had done the other stuff with Gil.[17] Miles was very pensive on that tour. Now I realize I could hear his brain saying, "What am I doing here? This is too hard. I don't want to do this anymore." And it is very hard, one-nighters on the road with all sorts of problems. But, anyway, he thought about what I said, and the next thing you know he was working with Gil.

WE: You reprised "Dream of You" by making *Collaboration*[18] with Evans at a much later date. From today's perspective, what do you think of *Collaboration*?

HM: A lot of people think that *Collaboration* is better. I feel that the impact of the first record had something to do with my friends being on the date, such as Oscar Pettiford. When we did "Dream of You," Oscar was wearing earphones, and I was, in effect, singing to him. I could see his face and he was grinning broadly, and I was trying not to laugh. *Collaboration* was a nice idea; I think some of it worked; I would have preferred to do more new things with Gil, but he was not well at the time. He was starting to go, although you'd have never known it. I mean, he was active and flirtatious. He was a total gem. I'll give you an example. At the time of the *Collaboration* session, Steve Lacy was in town. He's one of the old-time guys, one of the gang. I said to Gil, "You know, it would be nice if we could have Steve on the album." He said, "Yeah, I see he's in town." I said, "Well, there's no more budget." Gil didn't say a word, but that night Steve appeared at the studio to join our session. There was no talk of money. Gil entered the room and took off one of his moccasins and pulled out three hundred dollars in cash. He handed it to Steve, paying him personally for the session. I was very moved. You know, it was always the music that counted for Steve and Gil. Gil gave up a very high-paying assignment to redo our old album. That's the kind of man Gil was; he was a really pure soul.

WE: He also had a pretty oblique sense of humor.

HM: Oh, God. He would say, "I'm going to a business meeting. I hate to talk about business; maybe I should smoke a little pot." (*Laughter.*) That's a good idea just before a business meeting, right? Everybody loved Gil. And, you know, Gil was Miles's surrogate father. He loved Gil. I mean, really loved him.

WE: And clearly, it seems to me, you were close to Miles.

HM: I loved Miles. We had a little flirt, but it didn't go anywhere. (*Laughs.*) As young as I was, I realized that Miles was too much for me. I skirted away, and then he was very funny. After our tour together, we joined a large table of friends at Birdland and someone asked me, "How's your son, Helen?" Miles looked at me and said, "How did you get *him*? Immaculate conception?" (*Laughter.*) I mean, he was so angry because, as Dick Katz[19] used to say, I had the biggest wall around me that no one could penetrate. So that was Miles; he was so funny. We remained very good friends, and we never consummated our crush. (*Chuckles.*)

WE: You've twice alluded to the "Music for Moderns" tour in 1957 that included Miles and his band. Do any memorable incidents from that tour come to mind?

HM: Well, one story. It was Thanksgiving, and Miles invited a few of us to his father's home in Missouri. (*Laughs.*) Dr. Davis picked us up in his car to drive us to his home. On the way, we stopped at his dental office. He took a bit of time to take care of some patient matters and then returned to the car. He entered on the passenger side, and we all waited for the trip to begin again. We were all too polite to say anything. After about fifteen minutes, Dr. Davis turned to Cannonball and asked, "Who is driving?" And Cannon said, "You are, Dr. Davis." "Oh," he said, without missing a beat, "of course." And he went to the driver's side and completed our trip to his farm. They had horses on the farm, and I'm a city girl.

Miles said, "Come on, let's take a look at the horses," and I go out into the mud. Well, as soon as the animals see me, they smell I'm afraid of them. A horse came galloping toward me, and I became so frightened, I started to run away in the deep mud. Miles thought it was the funniest thing he'd ever seen, because he was very comfortable with animals.

WE: From your description, it's fascinating how readily you were accepted by a black family in those days of segregation.

HM: Miles Davis's father inviting *me* out there to the farm was very, very open of him and very kind, because in those days his neighbors may not have liked it: a young blond woman. In retrospect, I think about how brave people were in the days when it wasn't very good to do things like that. That wasn't that long ago.

WE: Is it your experience that racial tensions have eased up in the music industry?

HM: Well, I'll tell you, they're a lot better than when I worked at Detroit with Charlie Mingus. Charlie, [vibist] Teddy Charles,[20] and myself were at a famous jazz club, and the owner, who hired us, called me over. He said, "How can you go on stage with a _____ "— you know, the "unsayable." I was shivering and stunned. I said, "You hired us. This is a jazz club, isn't it?" That's just one of the many incidents that did occur. But Charlie Mingus, he's very funny. I said to Charlie at the same job, "Let's do ' 'S Wonderful,' and play it as fast as you can." He looked at me and said, "As fast as I can?" In about four bars he's grinning, and I knew I'd made a big mistake. (*Laughter.*) We did have a lot of fun. But it wasn't a good time for integrated groups, especially with a young, attractive blond singer. That didn't fit very well with some people. Nothing could shake me, though, and it was not political. What was wrong was wrong, in my mind. I think I was a little bit banned from television because I worked with integrated bands. That was a no-no. They didn't even have black people on television very often unless they were using a lot of teeth. There had to be a lot of friendly smiling.

WE: When did you first notice a big change in racial attitudes?

HM: You know, [bassist] Henry Grimes was on the "Music for Moderns" tour, too. The law changed the week that we were booked into a very fancy hotel in Memphis. According to the new law, the hotel had to accept black and white. Most of the black musicians chose not to tackle the new law and stayed at a friendly motel that they were accustomed to. But Henry, being aware of the law change, and knowing that we had reservations at this famous hotel, walked up to the desk and checked in. He had a suitcase with a rope on it. The receptionist looked shocked. But we were booked as a group, and Henry was clearly on the list. He was a very, very courageous man. It touches my heart every time I think about that picture. It still goes on, as we all know, but there's quite a difference today.

WE: Returning to your chronology, you went to Brazil in 1957. What prompted the trip?

HM: *O Globo,* the largest Brazilian newspaper, voted me the Best American Singer— this weird career of mine. They gave me the Disco D'Oro, "The Golden Disk." It was kind of amazing to me; here comes this gold record in the mail. (*Laughs.*) Then I was invited to Brazil, but again, I really didn't have enough experience for any of that. I hadn't fallen off the tree in the sense of being in control. I can make the excuse of not wanting to be an entertainer, but it was more than that. It was a lack of confidence, you know, and the lack of knowing how to surround myself with the accoutrements of show business, like beautiful clothes and nice makeup and acting in a more connective way with the audience. I just didn't know how to do that so that I would be able to protect my music. I'd always been so torn between taking care of my son and my career that I never did "roll over my grandmother with my car," as one must do in order to be successful in this business. You must pay attention totally to yourself, and I didn't do that.

WE: Did you take your own group with you to Brazil?

HM: No, I didn't. I only took a pianist. Their rhythm sections didn't have much experience with jazz. Had I thought that samba music could become a part of jazz music—we're talking about the '50s, before people caught on to it—I would have sung all those songs.

WE: You could have preempted Stan Getz and Charlie Byrd.[21]

HM: That's right, I could have, but I was foolish. At that point, I was losing my interest in doing new stuff. I had done enough already. I don't know that I was doing anything important; I don't think I was working very much. I knew all about the samba, but I thought nobody's going to want to listen to this music outside of Brazil. Boy, was I wrong. (*Laughs.*)

WE: It sounds as though you were very conflicted in the mid-1950s about which direction to take your life.

HM: Let me just tell you: I was making choices, okay. I mean, I could have made female choices in the sense of marrying—there was a line that wouldn't quit of very wealthy men who were interested in me—but I could not go that way. So it was *my* choice to remain who I was, that's all. Maybe because I was brought up by a man, I didn't have a female mentality thinking that I had to marry. I didn't think that way, and I didn't want to. Because I realized, too, that I would become "Brunnhilde," and then (*chuckles*) there goes Helen Merrill.

WE: After Brazil, you began touring overseas more extensively, from Scandinavian countries to Lebanon. Was it difficult to leave behind your roots?

HM: I was also leaving behind a contract with Atlantic Records. I mean, I had a bad personal experience with someone that I was in love with—one of those silly things. I was a single mother, and I ran away to Europe. Leonard Feather was in England, and he invited me over to sing on the BBC with Dudley Moore on a radio show with an audience. After that I had my son in one hand and a suitcase in another, and off I went to find my way from there. I was invited to go to Comblain-La-Tour, which is in Belgium, to sing in a festival, and Romano Mussolini[22] was there. He invited me to come to Italy to sing. I did a lot of television and became quite a big name in Italy for about three years.

WE: You lived in Japan from 1967 to 1972. What was the status of your career during that span of time?

HM: It came to a halt. I got married in Tokyo to Donald Brydon, who was head of UPI[23] for all of Asia, and so I lived in Japan for that reason. I did some recordings, but, you know, I don't like being tied up. It stops who I am.

WE: Is being "tied up" synonymous with marriage?

HM: Yes, marriage. Some people impose things on you, like, you shouldn't work here, you shouldn't do that. I didn't work very much. I had a few assignments that my husband felt I shouldn't do, like working in nightclubs.

WE: He thought it was degrading?

HM: Yeah, but of course it isn't. Frankly, I didn't care much anymore. But I can't blame that on him, you know. I made choices, too, and I think the first time he said, "You shouldn't work those nightclubs"—they were very beautiful nightclubs—I sort of gave in too easily. So I gave up for a little while. Maybe I really didn't like the idea of doing it. I blame myself for giving up. But I guess I kept on trying, because I was able to produce a few records with Dick Katz.[24] While I was living in Japan I was sponsored by Trio Records;[25] they gave me the money to make records in the United States. The first one, however, *The Feeling Is Mutual,* which is really a classic album, Dick produced and financed totally.

WE: Aside from artistic doldrums, it sounds as if this was also a low point for you personally.

HM: I didn't like the kind of lifestyle that I was in. There were a lot of formal embassy functions. They became boring to me. When I married, I started to become part of the establishment. No question. I was a liberated woman in a sense—I worked, and I was very famous, actually, in Japan—and I think a lot of the women were a little jealous of me. They made sure that they gave me the shaft whenever they could. I couldn't believe it, you know. The first incident that occurred was when I joined the College Women's Association. I signed my name to become a member, and I put Mrs. Helen Brydon. The lady said, "Donald." So I knew right then and there: they're going to call me "Donald" now. (*Laughter.*) You sort of lose your identity in that. It was a hard time for me for many reasons. I enjoyed Japan very much, but to be Mrs. Somebody—he was very proud of me, but I was more like somebody to show. I couldn't live that kind of life. We stayed married for a long time, but it was not for me.

WE: Let's talk about your recording process. As you assemble the tunes for a recording, do you simultaneously work out your conception of how to sing them?

HM: No, no. There's always a spontaneous conversation. Always, always. My whole life has been like that. I'm probably the only one who has continued what I started—spontaneous music. Every single take is *always* very, very different. Just the way any jazz musician would be. I used that to advantage recently on a record. I said to the engineer, "You know, I think I sing in harmonies. Why don't you open up five pots in the front of this[26] and see what happens." I had the feeling that if he opened the pots, it would sound like a choir singing. And sure enough, the five voices were speaking to one another in harmony! (*Laughter.*) I thought, "Wow! That's probably how I improvise, and I don't know it." So we're using it on this record.[27]

WE: In contrast to the spontaneous process that you live by in your music, jazz these days has been academized. Is that okay by you?

HM: Look, it's not okay for the way I feel about music, but it's proper for the times. This is the time of technology. The kind of people I came from, most of them were not studied musicians. And their ability to play who they were inside was very coveted. Today it's more technique. I don't even think these people today understand what we were doing. And it's Mr. Clean today, with the exception of a very few people. That's another thing that kids have done today. They seem to all be very healthy. They don't drink; they're vegetarians; they don't eat too much cake like Jon Faddis. (*Laughter.*)

WE: In your opinion, are innovators operative in today's jazz?

HM: Of course they're there. But I think a lot of the musicians who potentially would be more interesting musically, from my point of view, have become so embroiled in management and lawyers. I mean, the art form itself is second to whether or not you can make a lot of money. Well, I have news for you: you can't make a lot of money in the world of jazz music.

WE: There are exceptions, of course, like Miles Davis.

HM: I know what Miles's highest price was toward the end of his life, and he was paid extremely well. Miles already was a wealthy person. He made a lot of money on royalties and concert fees because he finally became wise. I couldn't believe it; Miles and I were on the same concert tour somewhere in Switzerland not long ago. I met someone in the elevator and asked, "Oh, who are you with?" "Miles Davis," he said. I asked, "Oh, really, what do you play?" He said, "I'm in marketing." (*Laughter.*) I couldn't imagine—marketing? It took my breath away. He said, "We market Miles Davis T-shirts and Miles Davis key chains." This was like, hello, where have I been all these years? I mean, to me it was such a departure from the kind of jazz background where everybody was so into the art of it, and certainly not the monetary part of it. At that time it was shocking to me. It seemed so commercial.

WE: Turning to matters of aesthetics, is the breathy sensuality that you project a result of an uninhibited approach to singing?

HM: No. It isn't that. It's the honesty. I'm not ashamed to say that I have very deep feelings about things. Sensuality is a part of it that's normal. And very often it's in the ears of the listener. I think a lot of why I am offensive sometimes in this country is because I touch places you're not allowed to touch. The things that get me through to an audience in France or Japan are the unexpressed feelings that in the United States we're not supposed to feel very deeply. It's not very chic in this country, I think. You're supposed to entertain people. You're not supposed to touch their hearts, to make grown men and women feel like crying.

WE: Do you think that the sensual qualities of your singing style are akin to the "come hither" torchiness of some pop chanteuses?

HM: The word "sensual" implies sex, right? Now, that is the furthest thing from my mind when I'm singing. "Basta finito." "Sensual" perhaps is a word that I find offensive. Miles Davis, what do you think of his sound?

WE: Extremely sensual.

HM: Exactly. Okay, I'm going to clarify that. Miles used to come to watch me. We were very, very good friends. I used the close-mike technique to get this edgy sound, and then he started to use that. It's not that he copied me; it's that people listen to things. There's a sound that he heard that he liked, and he found it on his instrument.

WE: Although I used the word "sensual," I was not trying to imply a gross sexuality in your work. Rather, it seems to me that your vocal approach opens up a welter of emotional and sensual experiences.

HM: Longing, longing, longing, *longing*—a lot of longing. People maybe don't want to hear that. Maybe they want to hear something more superficial. But it's the unspoken that touches people. Not what's coming out of my mouth; it's what I don't say. It's the sound that I *don't* make that includes people. And that includes the audiences that don't speak English.

WE: Are the Europeans and Asians more relaxed about experiencing emotions?

HM: Well, it's such a generality; but when people come to hear me in Paris, for example, you can hear men sniffling in the audience. Maybe it's some experience they had with their own romance or some button I touched about loss or happiness. Sex, why not? Some people tell me they've made love to my record with Clifford Brown. You can't imagine how much that meant to me. (*Laughter.*) And I was such a dummy, you know, the last thing on my mind—I used to think a lot about it (*chuckles*), but remember the big wall around myself? (*Chuckles.*) But the thing is that inside, I, as most women are, have a lot of repressed sexuality, and perhaps it was coming out of there. But it's not something that I could say with my mouth or feel that I was saying with my songs. Yes, I hear sensuality in my singing, but it wasn't contrived.

WE: Let's talk about gender issues. Despite your close friendships with certain male musicians, have you been discriminated against because you're a woman?

HM: Of course. It's difficult to be a woman. But remember the wall that I learned to build? I mean, you couldn't come close to me too easily; you couldn't do it in terms of either sexual advances or trying to get to know me. I didn't like it when people assumed that they knew me, and I didn't like people being familiar. Now, you must remember that I remained a rather "pure" girl. I had no problems being a woman on the road; I controlled everything. No one ever approached me in any way that I did not want to be approached. That I'm going to make very, very clear.

But, yes, of course, it's different being a woman in the business than being a man. But, on the other hand, you probably get more help being a woman, too, if you're not playing it in a corny way. Men are very nice, especially musicians, and they're very, very sympathetic to a woman who is alone. So I think I used that to my advantage in the sense that musicians mostly protected me. The wall was really not for musicians; it was for the outside. The musicians were wonderful.

WE: Have you been in a leadership position, giving directions, and had men balk because you're a woman?

HM: I've never learned to do that properly. A woman has to be "feminine in her orders" for fear of alienating the musicians. The male-female interaction is very sensitive and can produce good music or no music. These things are instinctive to most women. Yeah, when you're a woman, it *is* different. You can't give orders as easily as you can when you're a man. They speak to each other in another way. But that's why I stopped working clubs, because I realized that I cannot handle dictating to people. If they can do it, that's fine. If they can't, I get *highly* nervous and I cannot sing.

WE: Did you have to suffer through condescending remarks? For instance, a female instrumentalist might hear "You did a good job for a woman."

HM: Oh, of course. I got plenty of that. They're just not giving you a chance as they would a guy. But I always thought of it as more a musical prejudice than it was a female prejudice. I understood, more or less, how to deal with being female. But "Good job for a woman" is a very interesting sentence. That's a sort of woman's cross to bear. I mean, the implication is *always* there that in order to be in a world where mostly men belong, there has to be something a little bit wrong with you. I think that women who are in the business, and especially in the time I was coming up, were considered a little different, you know. That you had to be strange to want to be on the road by yourself. You were always aware of being a woman.

WE: You said women didn't get chances that men did because of a "musical prejudice." Can you elaborate on that term?

HM: I think, in general, singers are discriminated against as opposed to being a player. Singers were always considered non-musicians; you had to do a lot of proving that you were a valuable addition to music. Singers are a little bit of a pain in the neck to a lot of musicians. We are, you know, "Wednesday's child"; we're not Monday or Tuesday. (*Chuckles.*) Sarah changed a lot of minds about singers. Roland Hanna said that working with her was rather like a religious experience, above and beyond all prejudice.

WE: On the other side of the coin, do you think that women bring something to jazz that men do not?

HM: Oh, sure, absolutely; as far as singing is concerned, I suspect there is. There is a softness that I think women brought to jazz music in the 1950s. At that time a great many musicians—Lester Young, all those people—used to listen to us to get material, to phrase, to understand the lyrics. They would listen to singers and get the sense of a song, and I think it was mostly women that they listened to. But I think even with instrumentalists there's a different touch. There's a different perspective. I think Marian's [McPartland] approach to the piano, for example, is very feminine. Although there are women pianists who are very aggressive and sound like men, which is supposed to be a compliment. But I would say in general, there *is* a difference.

WE: All in all, listening to your stories, it seems that your trials in the business were balanced by good times.

HM: Well, it was one big adventure. I just remember the good stuff, and when I think about those days, I have to laugh, I really do. For example, Oscar Pettiford, who used to love to drink, decided he was in love with me one night. I was afraid that Oscar would try to pursue me, and he was so HUGE that I had to take a dresser and push it against the door of my room. The next day he called me: (*imitates a meek voice*) "Did I do something wrong last night?" I said, "Nah! Yes!" (*Laughter.*) It was more funny than serious; but there were so many funny things. Oh my God, I don't know how I survived them all—by being quick-witted, I think. (*Laughs.*)

[We turned to the first piece of music: "Angel Eyes," from *Frank Sinatra Sings for Only the Lonely,* 1958; Capitol Records.]

HM: (*As the music starts*) Now I, as a kid, did not appreciate him, maybe because my older sister loved him so much. She was the bully, and as older sisters will be, she was in charge. She used to go to swoon at the Paramount Theatre. So of course I didn't like him; I wouldn't like what she liked. (*Laughs.*) But as an adult I realized what a wonderful singer he is, and I sure do appreciate him today. *He* is the best. Talk about knowing what he's singing about and speaking it. He's my hero. (*The music stops.*) Well, I'll tell you, that's perfect singing. His musicianship is impeccable. His pitch—he's always on top of it, and he did what a lot of us do; he hit it in other places. (*Chuckles.*) But "Angel Eyes" was an incredibly intelligent and emotional reading of lyrics. That kind of phrasing is a gift that very few singers have. He dealt with the music and the lyrics with simultaneous importance. He was able to speak to you in a natural way; it did not need explanation. That is true art.

[The next piece of music was "How Am I to Know," from *Shirley Horn/Here's to Life,* 1992; Verve Records.]

HM: (*As the music starts*) Shirley and Johnny Mandel did this recording apart from one another, you know. Johnny said it was the hardest arranging job he ever did in his life. Because the way she phrases sounds simple, right? It's not, she phrases all over the place. She is a very loose phraser. What she does is very subtle, very sophisticated, and *very* musical. Torrie,[28] after hearing her play the piano, said that if you could orchestrate what she plays, they'd make fabulous arrangements. (*The music stops.*) She's great. Not only do I love her musicianship, I just love her. She's very funny, too. She was riding in a taxi with Jean-Phillippe Allard, who's our producer with Polygram. They were passing a place called Slow Bar (*chuckles*) and she said, "I'm going to have to buy that place." (*Laughter.*) She can sing slower than anybody, you know. She's adorable, she really is.

WE: The two of you at times seem in a contest to see who can sing more slowly.

HM: (*Laughs.*) She wins. Shirley wins. Definitely Shirley wins. The Slow Bar will belong to her, and I'll be a customer. (*Laughter.*)

[The last selection was "If Dreams Come True," from *Billie Holiday/The Golden Years,* recorded 1938; Columbia Records.]

WE: Why do you think Billie Holiday was an important figure?

HM: Well, again, we're going to get back to musical phrasing; the very *personal* way that she expressed a song. You always had the feeling that Billie was singing about you. That's why it always kills me when people write about "the sorrow" in her singing—that she's singing from her personal childhood experiences. But there are many of us who can match equally sad childhoods. That doesn't make you Billie Holiday. What's important is how she turned all of that into music. I also don't like when writers have to talk about Billie Holiday getting stoned. That was the sad part of her life. And there was no difference in the singing; it didn't help. She had a lot of feelings, yes; but the reason she can project is because she's thinking about you. Her ability to speak to *you,* personally, to tell a story that you can be involved with, was incredible.

WE: You spoke much earlier about the importance of open spaces in music. To me, Holiday has a lot more space in her phrasing than does Sinatra.

HM: Yes, she does. She expresses it as a horn.

WE: Also, the way Sinatra's lines are connected to each other makes them seem more brittle to me. In contrast, Holiday's phrasing has a more organic and fluid feel.

HM: It slips and slides, yes. What you just said make sense. They're two different animals, both wonderful. Sinatra said that he learned a lot about phrasing from her, and I think he meant it. He came from another side of the tracks, musically. He was appealing to a more refined sense. I think Sinatra was aspiring to work with large string orchestras. Sinatra is urbanite, I guess you would say. Billie was down home. I mean, there's no pretense about her music. Billie Holiday succumbed to the music. I remember her at the Cafe Society downtown, where she sang a song I'd never heard before, "Strange Fruit." And, oh! the depth of her interpretation. Her voice wasn't important; it was the gravel that came in and the stoic way in which she interpreted the lyrics. It chilled me.

I am proud to say that Billie Holiday *loved* my singing. In fact, she hired me for her nightclub in Detroit; it was called the Holiday Room. We sang duets at Leonard Feather's house. Leonard used to have fabulous, fabulous parties. Everybody was there, from beginning musicians to Doris Duke. It was at one of those parties that Billie and I did duets together. They were great days in jazz.

Selected Discography

Helen Merrill. EmArcy 814 643-2 (1954). (With Clifford Brown.)
The Feeling Is Mutual. EmArcy 558849-2 (1965).
A Shade of Difference. EmArcy 558851-2 (1968).
*Clear Out of This World. EmArcy 510691-2 (1991).

Notes

1. This album was recently the highest-priced jazz LP on E-bay at $965.
2. 1957; EmArcy Records.
3. *Helen Merrill and John Lewis;* Mercury Records.
4. Inner City.
5. *Jelena Ana Milcetic, a.k.a. Helen Merrill,* 2000; Verve.

6. Don Gold, *Down Beat*, 1957.

7. Herb Nolan, "Helen Merrill," *Down Beat*, May 6, 1976, p. 36.

8. Appears on *Jelena*.

9. Clarinetist.

10. 1967; Milestone Records.

11. Well-known recording engineer.

12. *Helen Merrill*; EmArcy Records.

13. Record producer at EmArcy Records.

14. The *Dream of You* session, released in 1956 by EmArcy Records.

15. Postscript to "The Individualism of Gil Evans," in Francis Davis, *Outcats* (New York: Oxford University Press, 1990), p. 33.

16. The "Music for Moderns" tour in 1957.

17. *Birth of the Cool*, 1949–1950; Capitol Records.

18. 1987; Nippon Phonogram, a division of Polygram Records.

19. Contemporary jazz pianist.

20. Ms. Merrill related this interesting sidebar on Teddy Charles: "Teddy Charles loved my father and was influenced to give up music for the sea. He plays music today, but it is really the sea that he loves, and he is now a captain of his own boat."

21. *Jazz Samba*, 1962; Verve Records.

22. Italian jazz pianist and son of Benito Mussolini.

23. United Press International.

24. The other two recordings are *A Shade of Difference* and *Chasin' the Bird*.

25. Japanese label.

26. The recording process is done on many tracks and in several takes.

27. *You and The Night and The Music*; 1996, Verve Records.

28. Arranger conductor Torrie Zito, to whom Ms. Merrill has been married for twenty years.

Maria Schneider

Maria Schneider

Composer/arranger Maria Schneider is one of the freshest voices to emerge since the nonpareil orchestrator Gil Evans. Schneider's expansive compositions for big band tell personal stories in sound which unfold in arrangements that are the antithesis of the traditional theme and variations approach. Twice featured on the cover of *Jazz Times,* she is in demand around the world as a guest conductor, most notably with the finest European Jazz Radio orchestras.

Born November 27, 1960, in Windom, Minnesota, Schneider began studying piano at age five. She earned degrees in theory and composition from the University of Minnesota and the Eastman School of Music. After moving to New York in 1985, she received a National Endowment for the Arts grant to study composition with trombonist Bob Brookmeyer.

While studying and working as a music copyist, Schneider had a chance meeting with Tom Pierson that led to a three-year assistantship with her idol and mentor, Gil Evans. Initially charged with a variety of reorchestration projects, she graduated to work closely with Evans on the film score for *The Color of Money,*[1] and was invited to conduct his orchestra at the Spoleto Music Festival. As heir apparent, in 1993 she became the first recipient of the Gil Evans Scholarship established by trumpeter Herb Alpert.

Writing for other bands, including aggregations led by Mel Lewis and Woody Herman, only fueled her desire to hear her compositions exactly as she sonically envisioned them, played by an ensemble of handpicked musicians. With the help of her ex-husband John Fedchock, she formed the Maria Schneider Jazz Orchestra, which from 1993 to 1998 was a mainstay on Monday nights at the Greenwich Village club Visiones. *Evanescence,* the band's debut recording, was released in 1994 on Enja, followed by *Coming About* in 1996 on the same label. Both received Grammy nominations and top ratings from jazz critics.

Following in the footsteps of jazz composers Claude Thornhill and Evans, Schneider's music has the mark of exquisite craftsmanship, requiring the performers to play with subtlety and grace. Her unique method of composition unites conception with kinetics. During our interview, she demonstrated, with arms akimbo, how, when composing, she moves from scoresheet to scoresheet posted on her apartment walls.

Schneider's charts are decisively programmatic in character, each piece evolving through episodes of varying expressive values, from infectious gaiety to darker, menacing passages. Emotional intensity never spills into abandon in her work, however, but is contained by classical form. Superficially, although her work might be associated with so-called Third-Stream[2] music, her compositions avoid the bombast often associated with that genre by virtue of the delicacy of her melodies, the uneven time feels she employs, the unexpected colors of her voicings, and the manner in which ensemble sections seemingly float over the basic pulse of the music.

Evidence of her love for dance and movement can be felt in the propulsion and momentum of each musical phrase in her latest release, *Allegresse,*[3] included by both *Time* and *Billboard* in their "Top Ten recordings of 2000." At this writing, Maria Schneider has been named best arranger in the 2002 *Down Beat* Critics Poll, with her jazz orchestra finishing as runner-up in the Jazz Ensemble category.

Recorded October 28, 1995

JS: The rich delicacy of your scores is striking. Was your attraction to big bands the result of hearing a similar quality in certain established writers who preceded you?

MS: Yes. I was studying theory and classical composition at the University of Minnesota, and at the same time I was starting to listen a lot to composers that wrote in a jazz-orchestra medium. Those people mainly were Duke Ellington, Thad Jones, Gil Evans, Bob Brookmeyer, and George Russell. But the one that really I have to say most affected me right off the bat was Gil Evans, with Miles; and even some of his later things. To hear that much expression coming out of a big band, to hear jazz with a setting behind it that offered all these different hues, to me it gave a really beautiful backdrop for a soloist to play. It was so sound-oriented. Gil made the perfect setting for Miles's sound; he told me once that that's what really attracted him to Miles. And I think he even spoke in your book about sound, that people could hear Coltrane play forever and ever because Coltrane had such a personal and beautiful sound.[4] And it's the same thing, I think, sometimes with big bands. Sometimes they have a lot of power, but they don't have some sort of timbral beauty. So, it didn't surprise me years later when Gil actually told me that, because I kind of felt the same way. I was very sound-oriented, and at the same time I liked the power that you could get from a big band, you know, just that straight-on kind of energy and impact. To me, a big band can be such a dramatic device; you can get so much out of it.

JS: Clarify for me the distinction you're making between a sound-oriented band and the sound of a straight-ahead band.

MS: Unless the players have very distinctive sounds and a special way of phrasing, a big band can be rather impersonal. It might have impact and power, but it probably won't move and shake you in the way that I want. Big band music is usually orchestrated using three distinctive colors. You have your trumpets, you have your trombones, and you have your saxophones. So, using the ensemble in the typical way of brass against saxes, or everybody at once, kind of gives the sound that you're used to hearing in a big band. As opposed to the more unique sounds that you can get when you start cross-blending certain doublings and using the people more as individuals, mixing their sounds or using their individual sounds, rather than the typical orchestration. Ellington did that. Ellington was dealing with individual sounds in his orchestra and getting different mixes, and Gil certainly did that. And I'm attracted to their innovations, because I'm not that in love with most big band music. Actually, I don't really consider Gil Evans a big band writer at all, because the instrumentation, even the bands he wrote for, I mean, even when they were a sort of big band format, they never sounded like a big band in the typical sense. When I was in college, I started listening a lot to the big band composers like Thad Jones, Bob Brookmeyer, Gil Evans, and Ellington. I consider these men all writers of music for improvising musicians placed in the setting of a large ensemble.

WE: The powerhouse bands like Basie's have an immediate, visceral impact. How can your more nuanced style compete with that kind of raw power?

MS: There's many ways to create impact. It's more a matter of drawing someone into your world. Once you manage to do that, even silence can create impact. But you have to grab the people's attention in an instant at the beginning, and then you have to draw them through that piece, sort of coaxing them along with things that they desire. Or inversely, maybe by throwing in surprises, but surprises that feel inevitable, that make you say, "Oh, yeah! That had to happen, even though I didn't expect it. They set me up for it." And so there's that kind of dramatic element that I'm trying to get in my music that carries you through a piece.

Typical big band music, and actually jazz small-group music too, is more often than not theme and variations. You know, they play a tune, they play a head, and everybody improvises on it. I'm just getting a little bit tired of that. Form-wise, I feel like there's much more that can be done, but it's harder to do it in a small-group format, though certainly not impossible. I try to create all sorts of different color hues so it's like going into a room with lots of different little places. You know, places that feel warm and places that make you feel uncomfortable, like you gotta get out of there. But hopefully it kind of draws you along. Ellington's music did that, and I feel like Gil's music did that, too, in a very subtle way. The way he would have some passage moving along, inside there might be some descending line played by some very warm color passing behind a solo voice, and then, just when you take for granted that that line is going to keep going in the same way, suddenly it just stops on a tone and hangs there. That happens in "The Barbara Song."[5] It's one of my favorites. That moment is just mesmerizing! I mean, the impact that he can get with something so little, how he can just grab you and not lose you with the most minute little detail. To me, Gil's music is like looking inside a watch and seeing all the little gears and then watching it go around making the big hand sweep.

If you study Gil's music, you can't miss the intricacy of its planning. There's not a note that doesn't follow through melodically. I like the impact of BLAH! in your face and rhythm and time and power, but I also like the detail thing that's much more intimate and on the inside. I remember one of my first orchestration teachers referred to a voicing, a vertical structure, and he said, "Well, you could throw in one of these boys—BAM!" And there he slammed his hands on the piano on some kind of Thad [Jones]-style ensemble voicing. And to me, I just don't think in terms of "one of these boys" when I'm writing chords. I'm thinking of them as sonorities; I'm thinkin' about, "Ooh, how does this feel, where's it gotta go," you know, "what's the tension?" It's a much more inside kind of feeling as opposed to impact: "Ooh, that's solid." You know, all these catch words that you hear people use to describe big band music: "solid," "smokin'," and "kick." (*Laughs.*)

WE: I get the impression that your lineage is dominated by aural colorists, from Ellington to Evans, to perhaps Toshiko.

MS: The thing in their music that I was so attracted to was that subtle mixture of color, you know, as opposed to the big primary colors. Actually, it's interesting that there's three sections, just like the three primary colors, and I'm looking for the mix and all the subtle hues. I love going to art exhibits, and it very often inspires me to *paint sound.* Two of my pieces on my last album[6] were named after paintings. One was "Dance You Monster to my Soft Song," named after a favorite Paul Klee painting. His titles are wonderful. And then Kandinsky's "Some Circles."

I love to go to MOMA, which has these retrospectives. What I love is that I see the same development in the painter's expression as I hear in people's development as composers. Bob Brookmeyer is a really good example. The Miró retrospective that I went to—his paintings start out very intricate, not particularly abstract, but very beautiful. But somehow in the little inner shapes that make up the landscapes, or whatever he was painting, you can see what's going to be abstracted out of that later on. It becomes much more simple, kind of condensed, concise, and confident in later works. I've noticed it with Bob Brookmeyer. His first stuff was filled with clusters and intricacies, and his music is becoming more honed down to the bare elements that were in Brookmeyer's personality from the very beginning. I see Brookmeyer's music as big strokes, as *very* abstract, very modern, Kandinskian, you know, with the clean angles and the balance being precise. And he's thinking in terms of the long form. His music used to be more detailed, but it's become much more big-scheme now. The development is very clear. His playing is like that, too—taking three notes, maybe, and developing them so logically.

JS: You've discussed Gil Evans and Bob Brookmeyer individually. Can you contrast the two?

MS: Brookmeyer strikes me as more methodical. As a matter of fact, Gil actually told me that he was intimidated by Bob and by Bob's musical intellect. I think Bob can verbalize, or is willing to verbalize, his process more. Again, his music so deeply reflects his personality—the logic, the clarity, but also the warmth and humor. Bob has a very serious side that I hear, too. He was wonderful to study with, and I think he pulled me out of my crisis after I left Eastman. Bob was so full of questions. He would ask "why" again and again when looking at various aspects of my music. I started to realize that there were many aspects of my music that were simply hand-me-downs from the tradition. That there was much more room to formulate my own opinion.

Bob clearly forged his own path and made tremendous contributions to expanding form in orchestral jazz. He's still doing it. He and Gil were different that way. Gil did not really consider himself a composer as much as an orchestrator. And whether one is willing to agree with that or not, Bob's stamp on this music is surely compositional. His mind for development and form is absolutely amazing. When I heard the album *Make Me Smile*[7] for the first time, it struck me hard like Gil's music. In Gil's music I was inspired to hear so many subtle hues, instrumental and harmonic. In Bob's music I was inspired to hear music that dramatically could pass through so many places and still leave me with one deep impression. Both men, as far as I am concerned, brought elements of classical music deeper into the world of jazz and found their own new places with a very natural and organic mix of those elements. Gil's was more textural—using more airy orchestration and harmony. Bob's is more formal—through-composed composition.

JS: Changing the topic, I'd like to ask about some of the sociopolitical aspects of your profession. As a conductor, are you readily accepted by the male musicians under your leadership?

MS: You know, people always ask me what does it feel like being a woman composer in a man's world. And I really never gave it much thought until recently, and that's only because more and more people have been asking me about it. And then someone was trying to figure out why it is that I'm not really conscious about it. In talking to him, I realized—actually, he brought it to my attention, and I think it's true—my first mentor in my hometown, my teacher, who was *the* most respected artist in my community, a very small town, was a woman. She was very flamboyant and feminine and masculine all at once. She had red hair, and she was just like this incredible personality. She was very much a Dorothy Donegan type of player—classical, jazz, kind of this mix with this really bouncy, bubbly, entertaining kind of personality on top of it. So I think I grew up not really being conscious of the rarity of female artists in the working world. Also, she had the respect and admiration of everyone who heard her, so it never occurred to me that a woman artist would suffer some sort of discrimination. I think that's been a blessing because when I go and work with groups I never think about the fact that I'm a woman. Are they gonna not respect me, are they going to, you know, not follow me or work with me?

The only time something happened was with a group in Germany. There were a couple of trumpet players that looked at me the entire time as if they wanted to kill me. I don't know if they were just so unhappy in their job, if it was because I'm a female, if it was because they didn't like the music, or if they just had a bad day. I really didn't waste too much time trying to figure out what it was, but I know it kinda gets in the way of the music when that happens. It certainly wasn't a pleasant experience.

JS: Have you dealt with sexism in other professional circumstances?

MS: One thing happened, last year. Carnegie Hall had this concert of women composers in jazz. This was in November. The composers were me, Carla Bley, Toshiko, Mary Lou Williams, and Melba Liston. And to me there wasn't really anything that connected us too much as composers—a little bit, maybe me and Toshiko—except for the fact that we were women. There wasn't really a reason to put us all on the same concert for musical reasons, and it wasn't a very successful concert, I didn't feel. And they were criticized for it by the *New York Times*. Somebody said to me from the people that planned it, "Well, what else could we have called the concert?" I said, "Well, why don't you just hire your favorite composers?" I guess they feel that they have to come up with some sort of gimmick, something to give the concert a title, or something to make journalists want to write about it. Some people said, "Well, it's nice they're trying to give time to women, you know; they're trying to do a favor." But, at the same time, every woman on that concert, I would have to think that they're all respected. They don't need a bone thrown to them because they're women. I certainly don't feel that I do. I want people to hire me because they like the music.

JS: Since the jazz world is lagging behind other social domains in recognizing the contributions of women, do you think this type of concert is necessary in the short term? How about girls in the audience looking for role models?

MS: Well, maybe. I know when I saw Toshiko the first time, it had a big impact on me, but I wasn't thinking in terms of "Oh, there's a woman." It wasn't "Okay, we're having a *woman* composer at Orchestra Hall with her band." They were having Toshiko perform as an *artist* well worth programming. I was just so impressed with what she did, and, I don't know, I guess the fact that she was a woman kind of inspired me, because I didn't have too many female mentors in that way. One thing happened in Europe related to this subject. There was an article that came out after a concert I did there, and the headline was "Is she the next Carla Bley?" This is the only one that really bothered me. I thought what was disappointing about that is, first of all, Carla writes incredible music. She has a wonderful career, as well she should, and my music is really very different. Why on earth would anybody compare us just because we're female? It also seems like they wanted to pit us against each other, as if there's really only room for one woman. Like if the article was going to say "Maria's in, Carla's out" or "No, she's not the next Carla Bley. Carla's still the queen and Maria, well, she's flailing." That was the take I got from that, and I found that really disturbing.

I think that a lot of what's going on is people's paranoia about what they should do on these concert things. "God, maybe we don't have enough women!" I think that there's a lot of pressure to keep everything even. I think mentors are really an important thing for young women. The more women they see doing what they're doing, the more the thing's just gonna even itself out in kind of a natural way. Recently I was invited to work with an orchestra in the U.S. They called me and said they'd love to have me come out and direct their band [all men] for their "Women in Jazz" series. I decided to say something that I was nervous to say, but that they actually responded to very well. I told them that I'd love to work with them, but if the concert was billed as "Women in Jazz," I'd have to decline. I tried to make it very clear that I meant no disrespect to their series. I told the person who contacted me that there would be no hard feelings if he looked for someone else, but that I wished to be viewed only as a composer, I didn't want to fill a quota, and that if mentorship is truly important, it's important for young girls to see women working with no special fuss about them. They had a meeting, discussed it, and liked the idea. They played a beautiful concert.

WE: Let's plumb your music more deeply. Can you describe your writing process?

MS: Yeah. First of all, for me, writing is just a hell.

WE: Reminiscent of Beethoven?

MS: I don't know; yeah, maybe, I guess. My mother always calls me "Ludwig" whenever she calls me on the phone. (*Laughs.*) "You must eat, Ludwig." Like they did on that old *Saturday Night Live.* Because when I get writing, ugh! It's really pretty miserable. But somehow I keep doing it. In the moments where I get a flow going, I lose all track of time, and I feel like I could sit there forever. That's bliss, but anyway—the process. What I do is, I'll come up with some little idea, and I'll put up a big piece of score paper and then I'll just start manipulating that idea. I'll try to kind of play with it and see the different directions that I can go with it and start finding the things that inspire me about it. It'll be a mess— I'll have all these sheets with different manipulations of this idea or contrasting ideas, and then slowly relationships will start occurring to me. So it's kind of an improvisatory process, too. It's planning, and then it's improvisation, too. And I'll start drawing arrows and start realizing, okay, this really works with this if I transpose this to that. So I'll just write little notes like that, and slowly the thing starts coming together, like when you start seeing the big picture as you put together a puzzle. Then it becomes an existing picture that I'm reaching for through the fog. And then I'll dance. Because I want my music to have a feeling of motion getting inside of you and moving you in some way. To sit and write music like this, it's so intellectual, kind of. So I get up and I try to feel motion with my body, you know, resistance and movement. Also, dancing helps me to figure out the natural length certain sections should be. Sitting motionless gives me a distorted image of time somehow. My body can better judge timing.

Sometimes I'll sing and make comments into a tape recorder as I'm dancing. Or I'll dance to a tape I made at the piano to feel where it should go, how long it should go, or where I've gone wrong. So I'm dancing around, and sometimes I tape the paper up so that I can stand up and move and draw lines sort of graphically. That's the melodic manipulation, that's the harmonic thing, and I should also say that the color thing in my music, timbrally, isn't just instrumental color. I perceive colors as a mix of instrumental color with harmonic color. The different modes have different hues of dark and light, and so I kind of play those against one another, adding to that harmonic color instrumental color, color that kind of draws you along, you know. You can make it alive and really make it much deeper by adding the orchestration.

For me, the orchestration is the topping that makes the whole thing in living color. And then, with the orchestration, it isn't really like I have to sit down and think, "Now, what should this be?" In my ear I'm hearing this sound, so I just have to figure out, okay, now how do I get what I'm hearing with the instruments I have? Since the sounds I'm hearing aren't often typical big band sounds, this is where I really have to jump through some hoops. I think those things are separate for some composers. They come up with the whole scheme note-wise, and then they figure out what instruments should say it. For me, it's more of a simultaneous thing. Even though I don't immediately write down what instruments are playing particular passages until later, I'm already hearing the color in my imagination when I conceive the harmony and the melody.

WE: Laypeople have a tendency to think artists in any discipline work only when inspired and then dash things off. I hear you saying that, on the contrary, the process is arduous.

MS: Yes. Really arduous, because you have to work *so* hard to make something sound completely natural and seamless. I could probably whip something off in a certain way, but it wouldn't be something that was really attached to any part inside of me. Also, there's this process of knowing where you're going to go, and then having to figure out how you're going to get there so that it feels like that's the only thing that can happen. That it *has* to happen. So that means working your way backwards to get this natural flow. That sounds strange, doesn't it? When I listen to other composers' music and something just flows, I assume that they dashed it off and that I'm the only klutz in the world that has such a hard time. (*Laughs.*) I love to hear when other artists have a hard time, too.

When I was in Monterey, I had to give this talk about arranging to a lot of people who weren't arrangers. It wasn't a technical clinic or anything. I started talking about my writing process, and there was a woman there named Penny Vieregge. She said to me, "What you do sounds like chaos theory." She's doing a book on chaos theory in education. And I really didn't know anything about chaos theory. What I was describing was when I throw all these ideas on the paper, and that it's terrifying because it feels chaotic. But that you have to trust that there's a magical connection, a universal inevitability that will slowly draw this whole thing together and kind of have it take shape. And I think that phenomenon happens in different ways and at different steps of the process in composing and in performing.

JS: Earlier you mentioned an attraction to Bill Evans. As it was for him, is song form important in your work?

MS: Yeah. Although, in general, I think I'm writing more long-form composition, or I should say, through-composed. On my current album,[8] there are some things that are more like theme and variation writing, where somebody's blowing basically with the changes of what the tune is. So I do write that way sometimes, as opposed to other things that I write that are almost more orchestral in their sound. There isn't even any way you can have them blow on that kind of a piece, because the exposition might not really have harmony that can be reduced to changes. It has maybe more of an orchestral kind of through-composed content, so there's no way to solo on it.

JS: Do your pieces sometimes evolve from one intent to another?

MS: Sometimes I'll write a tune that, to me, is beautiful, kind of in a song or tune kind of way, but the changes aren't maybe quite so interesting on their own. So I'll alter the changes a little bit, extend them or add something to them that makes the changes something that, to me, is much more interesting to hear somebody improvise on, or maybe just for the reason that it offers contrast to what came before. I don't even think the listener is always aware that there's a difference between the changes and the form that the soloist is blowing on, because it might still have a similar character to it. It's pretty rare, actually, in my music that somebody's improvising on exactly the same chords as the beginning.

Sometimes I spend as much or more time working on the harmonic structure for a soloist as I do on a previous section that might be very intricately composed and orchestrated. It's like laying the groundwork for something to inspire spontaneity and variety from performance to performance, but at the same time, it must create a feeling of inevitability in the overall composition no matter how it's approached by the soloist. Let me tell you that that's difficult, and I spend many hours on those sections. In typical big band writing, the solo section is the easy part. You could use a Xerox machine and just copy out the previous changes. But I'm trying to do all sorts of things to try to make the solo section more interesting, to create an overall story in which the soloists play a unique part. There's so much detail.

One time I walked in Gil's apartment, and he was sitting at the piano in his underwear playing three little notes in a cluster, over and over again, and listening to it and then playing it again. This happened for a *really* long time, like fifteen to twenty minutes. And then I realized how much he, you know, sweats the details, and I was glad I saw that. That helped me, because I can sweat the details for a *long* time. Somethin' that goes by in a second and nobody even notices—and it takes me two days to decide. (*Laughs.*) And sometimes I feel like I'm throwing away more pages than I keep. That's the hardest: you write some section and you really like it, and then you realize it doesn't work for the good of the piece.

WE: You spoke before about paintings inspiring certain of your works. Are there other content sources for your writing?

MS: Most of my music is attached to some sort of childhood emotion or childhood image. You know how there are certain things that you recollect from your childhood and it just has a feel and smell and a color to it? I have to be in that hypnotic kind of place, usually, when I'm writing. Sometimes I turn off the light bulbs and turn on candles (*laughs*), so I get more of a light that has a movement to it. Then I kind of transport myself back into that feeling, into a place that I feel inspired to write. I'm just not inspired to write notes only for the sake of hearing sound.

WE: It'd be interesting to see what you did if we locked you up in an airport for two weeks.

MS: I'd be really depressed, I can tell you that. I hate fluorescent lights, except that's one of the childhood memories that I can draw on. (*Laughs.*) We just did the Monterey Jazz Festival, and I wrote this piece called "Scenes from Childhood." It's in three parts. The first piece is called "Bombshelter Beast," because my father had built this bomb shelter. In the Midwest, there was so much that I associated with the bomb shelter. First of all, the head-board of my bed was by the bomb shelter door, and of course my father, being an extraordinary engineer, builds everything stronger and deeper than anybody in the world. This thing went like to the center of the earth, these steep little steps. Then there's a long hallway that goes around a corner to a little room. At the top of the stairs there's a small, bare light bulb. But the next light didn't come until you went down and around the corner to the little room. Then you had to feel your way around the ceiling for the little chain on that light bulb. In every moment of feeling my way to the bottom, I could hear my heart beating, expecting some hand to grab me. To top it all off, my mother kept all our marionettes, puppets, costumes, and Halloween stuff down there, along with the full supply of canned soup and disaster supplies. There were just all these terrifying things that you're sure are going to come alive.

WE: Did your father build the bomb shelter around the time of the Cuban Missile Crisis?

MS: Yes. And so at the same time of just being scared of monsters from this dark hole in the ground, there was also this fear of nuclear war. So then I'd think about radiation and things. We lived on this hill next to this sort of a chemical plant and a flax plant. It was kind of barren, and every Wednesday that air-raid siren would go. Just in case somethin's gonna HAPPEN, you know! There were all these cold associations that I have attached to that time in my life, and a certain feel, and a certain smell. And that 1960s olive-green, mustard Naugahyde, chrome, and Formica thing. So I wrote this piece, "Bombshelter Beast," and I decided I wanted my bari player [Scott Robinson] to use a theremin. The theremin is like the first electronic instrument. It's from the 1920s; the guy who invented it was named Termen.[9] It's wild. When you put your hand next to its antenna, you get this whoooooooooooo. You know, like the old monster movies had those things. Scott can make an air-raid siren sound with this thing.

So when I wrote the music, all of a sudden I realized that it started to really feel in this one section like this hot summer afternoon when the air-raid siren went off. It captured the feeling that I wanted so much, and I knew that the air-raid siren with the theremin was the crowning touch that was going to transport me. So Scott does this thing where he moves his body in and out from the theremin, changing its pitch like the rise of a siren, and then he improvises simultaneously on his bari. It's incredible. When we premiered it at the Monterey Jazz Festival, when Scott played the theremin—this is the first time this ever really happened to me—I was up there conducting, but suddenly I was Maria in the '60s in Minnesota. I've never so effectively captured exactly what I wanted to capture enough that I actually felt like I'd just time-traveled. (*Laughs.*)

WE: What are the titles of the other two parts?

MS: The second one is called "Night Watchmen." The flax plant, which my father ran, had these night watchmen that would do their rounds.

WE: Why were night watchmen necessary at a flax plant?

MS: Well, I think it started when they had a problem with an arsonist. The company owned a huge field behind our house, where they would stack the flax bales. These flax stacks looked like gigantic hotels from Monopoly, you know. They were huge, and there were a lot of them spread throughout this big piece of barren land. One day, some crazy guy got the idea to shoot burning arrows into the dry stacks just to start these huge fires. From the window of our house, the whole sky would just be ablaze. So they began having night watchmen keep an eye on things through the night. As they'd do their rounds, you'd see their silhouette walk by the house. Some of these men were sort of tattooed; some of them almost had a little bit of that truck-driver kind of look, you know, that was kind of scary to me. But then at an age when I was kind of starting to be intrigued by the fact that I'm a woman and some people are men, there was like this strange sort of sexual tension about it—repulsion/attraction.

So "Night Watchmen" is about kind of mentally investigating your sexuality in strange, distorted, and confused ways. The first piece makes you feel trapped in tension and fear. The second piece is desire, but also with some resistance in it, too. It's basically a sexual piece. And then the third part is called "Coming About," and that's a sailing term. My parents had a small boat that we used to sail on a lake called Fish Lake. It's about moving ahead, and seeing the positive inside of the negative in your life. That's a piece about the magic of sailing, how it places you in the here and now. In that piece the momentum just races ahead and lifts you up.

WE: What do you think drives the need for much of your work to be autobiographical in its content?

MS: It isn't like I try to make it that way. I think it comes from the fact that when I was a child, the reason I did music was completely as fantasy and escape. Of course, I was studying, and I was intrigued about how music worked, and I had this incredible teacher that really got me thinking about theory and things. But at the same time, when I was playing, I was constantly fantasizing. Sometimes I was playing and fantasizing that there were talent scouts that were driving by the house, and that they had some sort of equipment that could hear inside people's homes. (*Laughs.*) I would always try to do my very best in case the talent scouts were considering taking me to New York. I lived in that kind of a fantasy world, and when I got to music school and suddenly was writing assignments—okay, now write in the style of this and that—it was interesting to a point. I liked doing it and I liked the learning, but when I left school I felt really cold. I didn't know what I wanted to write anymore. I remember I had my final meeting up at Eastman with Bill Dobbins and Ray Wright to discuss what I did during my master's studies. They felt like I did really well, but in that moment I just started crying. I said I didn't feel like anything in my writing really mattered. I didn't feel like my music was attached to *me.* So when I came to New York and I was working on my writing, I slowly found my way back, and music became more personal for me again.

WE: What's your own estimation of jazz in comparison to classical music? Will Ives, Stravinsky, and Copland always be ranked above Ellington, Monk, and Schneider in twentieth-century music?

MS: Well, they're always going to be above Schneider in my mind. (*Laughs.*) They're such different things, it's hard to compare. But in jazz, I think one thing that's happening—I don't know if this is on that subject exactly or not, but maybe it does tie in—is that we value another time as being more creative than this time. And to me, what music is about is an expression of now. We make a real mistake in looking back to something else as a golden age and imitating that. To me, a lot of the jazz musicians have kind of stunted what's really valuable and good and beautiful about this music by this hero worship. Granted, there were geniuses and heroes—I have my own that inspire me—but to me, the only thing you can do better than anybody else is to be yourself. Nobody can duplicate anybody else. And one thing that proves it is the bebop musicians: Charlie Parker and Dizzy Gillespie and Bud Powell. People for *decades* have been trying to play bop as well as or better than these men, and nobody's done it. You can't, because that was speaking of that time. And so much music doesn't really speak that deeply to people now necessarily, because everybody's surfacely hashing out this language of another time, rather than developing on it to say something about now. And I think that that's part of the reason why jazz doesn't speak to many people that much, because people aren't trying to speak their own mind.

WE: In the face of an ever more eclectic music scene, and the potency of rap and hip-hop with today's youth, can jazz still compete in the marketplace?

MS: Well, I think there's so many subdivisions of music now. And I see rap and hip-hop as being music that honestly does speak of culturally what's going on. But at the same time, it's music that causes people to want to ban it, because the music might have profanity or talk about violent acts, or killing cops. My feeling is, *that's* the real world. That's the reality that our society has created. Listen to what that says, because to me, music, it's the window to what's going on. That's very intense music whether you like to listen to it or not. I don't hear such intense expression coming from your average jazz player, if I'll be totally honest.

WE: Is jazz old hat?

MS: Well, I think jazz has kind of become that way because people are doing jazz for different reasons than they once did. It wasn't a matter of choice at that time; I think it was more a matter of necessity. It used to be music that came out of probably a very similar place as hip-hop. I mean, it was music out of the black community. And now people are learning jazz in schools, which is fine, but the whole circumstance of it has kind of changed. So it is only natural that it would be charged with an entirely different energy now. To look at jazz and expect that it's gonna have that same kind of feeling now, to me, is unrealistic. It's a different time, and jazz has a different role. Everybody admired jazz so much. So then everybody kind of tried to reproduce it, and I think that's the problem with it. I don't want to reproduce anything, and I don't hold an allegiance to any particular music. Of course I have my tastes, and I have my whole personal history that is infused with all the different music I've listened to. Jazz fills a rather large proportion of that. Just as your body becomes what you eat, one's music to a large extent will be infused with whatever that person has listened to. You know, Gil Evans spoke of his own music as being popular music. He said that to label it as classical, jazz, or whatever is simply a merchandiser's problem.[10] I know I don't really care to call my music jazz, even though sometimes it seems the simplest way to describe it. It's jazz-influenced, but to me it's American music. I think anybody who would listen to it would probably guess that I am an American composer.

WE: Do you view the Lincoln Center Repertory Band and all the young neo-boppers as obstacles to the music's natural flow?

MS: I don't know if it's obstacles. On a personal level, I find that when I go to those concerts, even though a lot of times the rhythm section is great and all sorts of nice things are happening, on some deep level it leaves me a little bit cold.

WE: Is it possible before jazz can go forward, it's necessary—perhaps even healthy— to go through a period when lessons of the past are assimilated?

MS: It could be. Although all that I would have to say about that is that musicians who I consider to be the innovators—like Charlie Parker and Miles Davis and Ellington—those people at the same age were in the business of creating something new. They were in the business of making music, and not imitating music. There were people they could have been imitating, too. I mean, they all certainly had predecessors that they loved, but they were building on that music, not doing concerts of playing transcriptions of things. Which, to me, is fine, but I'd rather hear an album of Ellington's band playing Ellington's music. That's what he wrote it for—those players. You know, to hear somebody play it, while it can be fun, and a pleasure to hear live, I'm not going to call it a deeply inspiring night of music. It's great to expose people to that music who might not have gone out and bought the Ellington albums. But on a different level, it isn't what I really wish was the biggest thing being offered.

WE: Speaking of Ellington, he is the prime example of composer as performer. What about you? I don't know you at all as a voice on your instrument.

MS: Yeah, I'm not a voice on my instrument. I started playing when I was five years old. We had a piano in our house. But this woman I told you about, she moved to Windom because her husband and her son had both died around the same time. She was this classical pianist and organist in Chicago, but she was also a stride player. She was devastated by the deaths, so she went to live with her daughter, who was married to a man in Windom. My parents invited her over for dinner, and after dinner she sat down at the piano and played for us. She played classical, she played jazz, and that was *it* for me. Like when Brookmeyer talks about hearing the Basie band,[11] or Miles talks of the Eckstine band, or Gil with hearing Louis Armstrong, for me, at age five, it was Mrs. Butler. I still see it—the flair with which she played. To me she looked like a white, female Dizzy Gillespie. I came to that analogy much later, obviously. Sounds crazy, but she had that same face and that *big* personality. That was the first introduction for me of somebody whose music was such a manifestation of their person. So I started studying with her. I told my parents, "I wanna be Mrs. Butler. I want lessons." She started teaching me classical and theory, enough theory to start playing chords right from the very beginning. Every piece that I played, starting from the very beginning, I had to analyze every chord in that piece, and account for every harmonic thing that happened.

JS: That's something that even some college theory majors can't do.

MS: Yeah. It was difficult. I was frustrated with those theory parts of our lessons. My very first lesson, I remember she taught me about the color of major and minor—bright and dark. She sang "Bright the day!" as she played one, three, five of the major triad. Then she sang "Dark the night!" as she sang one, three, five of the minor triad. First lesson. Then she taught me stride and she taught me chords. Every lesson we'd work out of a fake book, and I would do these little stride arrangements. At my recital I would play a stride thing that I arranged myself out of these fake books, and I'd always perform a classical piece. Sometimes I'd do an original composition. My parents had some records; they had a lot of classical. Mom liked Teddy Wilson, and she had some Ellington, and, you know, there were some different things.

But in general, my perception of jazz was that jazz was a music that stopped at a certain time. I just assumed that when pop music happened, jazz ended. And I remember once on *60 Minutes* they had a thing about the Basie band. But I saw them as these much older men and their day is gone. So it never occurred to me that there was anything for me to do with that music except maybe play some stride in a bar, but that I didn't really fit into the world of popular music, either. So I wanted to be a composer, I thought, but I wasn't *really* sure if I could compose. I knew I understood a lot about theory, and I knew I had to be a musician, but I really didn't know where I fit in. And I didn't have a good right hand as far as improvising. I didn't have very good technique; I was a good accompanist, but not to be, like, a concert pianist, nah. For me, the best thing about music was just kind of thinking things up and playing, sort of improvising in my own way and pulling new music off the shelf to play—my mom, luckily, she had tons of music. Every day I was sight-reading music, and I just loved to swallow new music. So when I went to college—and I'm sure that sometimes there's angels or something helping me—the first week in the dorm, some guy stopped by my room when he heard Ellington's music coming through my door. He said he had a big jazz record collection, and so he brought down Herbie Hancock's *Headhunters.*[12]

JS: What a first choice!

MS: Exactly! (*Laughter.*) And then he brought some McCoy Tyner and some different things, and I couldn't believe that these were *jazz* musicians. And McCoy with the chordal voicings in the left hand! I was in such shock.

JS: When was this?

MS: This is the fall of '79. I didn't even know about *bop.* (*Laughter.*) You know, I mean, we're talking that I'm seventeen years old, so I'd been really stunted back in this other time, yet I'd really gathered a lot of knowledge about theory and a big love of music. But there was this enormous world of music that had eluded me. So I just started listening to things and grabbing things and buying things. I heard Bill Evans on the radio, so I bought Bill Evans's Village Vanguard sessions.[13] It's still one of my favorites. And then I saw that at the University of Minnesota they had a big band, and I went and heard those guys. I remember the first time I heard them, they were backing up Bob Hope. Nothing' great, but because I didn't have a big band in my high school, it surprised me. So seeing these kids playing *swing*—I couldn't believe it was happening. I was so excited that this world that I had fantasized that I would have been a part of did still exist. Not only that, it had developed in so many ways that immediately resonated in me.

So then I discovered a Gil Evans album. I discovered Gil Evans because he was next to Bill Evans in the record store. I never told Gil that. He would have cracked up over that. The first Gil I got was Gil with Miles Davis, and *Svengali,*[14] which came later. I love *Svengali* as much as I loved the other stuff. And I was also amazed at how much his music had changed in between. I just went totally bonkers listening to music. So then I'm taking my classical lessons in composition, but I was discovering all this music, and the influence of it was, it was just like turning the faucet on high. My composition teacher couldn't really fight my enthusiasm, so he said, "Okay, write something for the jazz band if that's what you want to do." And so it just happened that even though I was a classical theory-comp major, that jazz kind of influenced me more.

JS: But how did you learn the roots, the standards?

MS: Through listening and practicing. I already knew lots of standards from my childhood—all those songbooks my mom had. I just hadn't heard them interpreted in such a modern way by jazz musicians. I was just like a sponge. I started studying jazz piano with a pianist named Manfredo Fest, a Brazilian pianist who lived in Minneapolis at the time. We would do transcriptions, like Bill Evans's things—and we always used a tape recorder at my lessons because Manfredo was blind. And so we would transcribe things, but not write them down. We transcribed the heads and solos of Bill Evans, and he helped me with my improvisation. But once more, I really gravitated to how the tunes worked and how Bill's inner voicing happened, and all the little compositional things. And I was still more writing-oriented than playing-oriented. I loved players, but I was so interested in what they were playing. I think maybe I listened to them in a different way than a real player would. I never really cared how well I executed things. I played with college bands and I played with friends, but my emphasis was never on playing. It was always on writing for improvising players. I still play at home a lot, but I've never been comfortable performing for other people. It's kind of a bizarre background, I suppose.

JS: Why do you stand in front of your band conducting instead of sitting at the piano?

MS: I conduct because most of the stuff that my band plays in concerts is the more developmental kind of music that has lots of expression of line swells and things. So I'm basically dancing in front. I feel like I'm improvising with the sound in a physical way, which is probably a bit unusual. I want my music played in a very expressive way. Also, no one in the band is hearing the full picture the way I am standing in front. The trumpets in the back can barely hear the reeds, so I think it's important to show them with my hands what I feel the music needs. Most big band music doesn't have the subtle dynamics that mine has. It seems natural to me that it has to be conducted.

JS: From all appearances, you enjoy conducting.

MS: It's really fun. It's really fun because I'm entitled. It's my music, I'm in front of the band, and I'm entitled to move however I feel inspired to move to make *them* do something. I wrote the music, and I alone know exactly what I want to hear. Also, sometimes I'm just reacting to what they do. And to be able to abandon what people are thinking of me and just be part of the music and get into this kind of thing with my group—it's just a ball. I feel so lucky. I feel *so* lucky.

JS: After all the arduous composing you do, are you apprehensive about hearing a piece for the first time?

MS: When I get to that point where I first hear my music—it's like these wordy little things that I've worked on so hard that I absolutely hate them. When I hear them the first time, I feel like somebody threw a brick in my face and it's scratching me. It's horrible. But as the group slowly brings their personality to it and it kind of gets all its hues and it starts to jell and become something, it isn't mine anymore. It's more like a child I had or something. And then I love them. They all have their personalities. They all depict another time— something that was going on for me. And then I can enjoy them myself.

WE: Is Visiones a testing ground for new works?

MS: Yes.

WE: Does your method in front of the band resemble Ellington, with you reworking parts or reassigning solos as a piece is being performed?

MS: Yeah, I change things, and we read things sometimes on the gig. It kind of makes me uptight. I get really nervous. I don't like exposing . . .

WE: The process?

MS: The process would be okay. It's just that I have such a low feeling about myself in each piece as I write it. I'm so terrified for what that piece sounds like. To strip it down in front of all those people for the first time is just so painful. I sweat. I really go through a living hell. It's hard, and it never gets easy. It's like Bob [Brookmeyer] said, you have to believe in a certain level that you're not going to drop below. But I always assume every time that the next piece could expose that I'd been a fraud the whole time. As if I didn't really write those other pieces. They were luck. And that the next one's gonna stink. It sounds kind of dramatic, but I do go through that. At the same time, I feel like I've been handed this opportunity to make my living as a composer. That doesn't happen to very many people. That's rare. And to have a group that plays only my music and that people want that and are willing to pay for it? Jeez, you know. That's a ball to run with, you know? Definitely.

Selected Discography

Evanescence. Enja ENJ 8048-2 (1994).
Coming About. Enja ENJ 9069-2 (1996).
*Allegresse. Enja ENJ 9393-2 (2000).

Notes

1. 1986; Touchstone Pictures.
2. Refers to a hybrid that merges elements of classical and jazz musics. The term "Third Stream" was originally coined by the composer, musician, and author Gunther Schuller.
3. 2000; Enja.
4. *Jazz Spoken Here,* p. 147.
5. *The Individualism of Gil Evans,* recorded 1963 and 1964; Verve Records.
6. *Evanescence,* 1993; Enja Records.
7. *Make Me Smile and Other New Works by Bob Brookmeyer,* Mel Lewis and the Jazz Orchestra, live at the Village Vanguard, January 7–11, 1982; Finesse Records.
8. *Coming About,* 1996; Enja Records.
9. Lev Sergeyevich Termen.
10. See liner notes, written by Gene Lees, for *The Individualism of Gil Evans,* p. 3.
11. Bob Brookmeyer said that hearing Count Basie live at about age ten "was the severest physical thrill I think I've ever had." *Jazz Spoken Here,* p. 66.
12. 1973; Columbia Records.
13. *At the Village Vanguard,* recorded 1961; Original Jazz Classics.
14. 1972; Atlantic Records.

Shirley Scott

Shirley Scott

"Queen of the Organ," Shirley Scott is among the earliest and most well-known women to conquer the Hammond B3. This hard-swinging organist was a prime mover in the popularization of the organ/tenor combination that was so integral to the soul jazz movement of the '50s and '60s. A spirited entertainer and a favorite with jazz audiences around the world, Scott had an illustrious career, as documented by her more than fifty albums.

Born March 14, 1934, Shirley Scott was raised in a Philadelphia neighborhood that boasted a surfeit of fine jazz musicians. Surrounded by music as a child, Shirley was first inspired to study the piano and then later, in school, the trumpet. In the early 1950s, when Jimmy Smith introduced the new jazz sound of the Hammond B3, Scott switched from piano to organ. In 1955, on the heels of that transition, she became a member of the Hi-Tones,[1] a local group which included a young John Coltrane as her bandmate.

The next year Scott was tapped to join the Eddie "Lockjaw" Davis Trio as his organist. They signed with the Prestige label in 1958, and after the release of *The Cookbook*,[2] her popularity soared. "Lockjaw" promoted her up front to a place in the spotlight as they began to share the billing. After leaving Davis in 1960, she began a decade-long association with veteran jazz stylist Stanley Turrentine, who became her second husband in 1961. In the midst of raising a family (they had three daughters), Scott and Turrentine maintained active musical careers, which included making eighteen LPs as joint leaders.

In 1971, Scott abandoned life on the road and returned home to Philadelphia to care for her mother. Remaining active, she made several recordings for the Chess label and then, in 1974, formed a bop trio with saxophonist Harold Vick. The '80s and '90s found Scott traveling again, this time as a sought-after guest on the European jazz festival circuit. In the early '90s she served as musical director for Bill Cosby's

TV show, *You Bet Your Life*, leading a house band that included trumpeter Terrell Stafford and saxophonist Bobby Watson. Meanwhile, she completed college degrees and joined the faculty of Cheyney University teaching piano and courses in jazz history.

Of all Jimmy Smith's organ offspring, Scott crafted the most alluring combination of jazz feeling and down-home blues. Her trademark at the organ was a biting, percussive attack while using a full, fast vibrato. An exceptional soloist, she skillfully combined the elements of complex bebop lines with soulful melodies to forge a fresh take on the hard-bop approach.

Her recordings from the '50s and '60s have recently had a resurgence of attention; some are currently marketed under the newly minted Acid Jazz label. Acknowledged by her peers, Scott was the recipient of the Mary Lou Williams Women in Jazz Award in 1999, as well as the 2000 Mid-Atlantic Arts Foundation's Living Legacy Jazz Award. Shirley Scott died on March 10, 2002, at the age of sixty-seven. This chapter consolidates two of her final interviews.

Recorded March 28, 1998, and July 31, 2000

WE: Shirley, what is the earliest experience you can remember when music had an impact on you?

SS: The earliest remembrances I have of being on this planet are, one, sitting in my mother's lap in a rocking chair, and, two, playing the piano. I could always play. I could play before I ever took a lesson. That was something, I guess, given to me by God. I came from a family who liked music, all kinds of music. My grandfather played the tuba; my mother played the piano. There was always some kind of music going in my house. The one thing about me is that I like music, period. My mother and I used to sit on the stoop of our house sometimes, singing duets. We'd sing anything, like "The Tennessee Waltz," or something by Jimmie Lunceford. You know, those records where the whole band would stand up and sing?

WE: "Four or Five Times"?

SS: Yes. "Four or Five Times." And "Yes, Indeed." We just liked music; it didn't matter what kind it was. It could have been music from the church, classical music, blues, bebop—I liked bebop. Bebop is the music that I heard every day, and it is my favorite music of all times.

WE: Did you play in church?

SS: I had played in church, and the polyrhythms and the call and response influenced me. But it's not exclusively from the church. It's part of whatever was laying in my bosom (*laughs*), from generations and generations and generations.

JS: Was there an event in your early life that piqued your interest in playing jazz?

SS: I have an older brother, T.L., who played saxophone. The way, I guess, I really got interested in becoming a jazz musician is that he was in a band. I was taking piano lessons when I was six years old. I studied for ten years, so I could read a little bit. By the time I was nine or ten years old, my brother would want to practice these pieces that they were going to play or rehearse. So he would sit at the piano and show me how to play the chords to the tunes. I liked doing that. But then the light bulb went on, and I wanted to play a solo. So he had to wait until I took a solo before I would play for him. (*Laughs.*) That's really the way I got to love the music. But I always thought that I would be a musician. That's what I thought when I was a little girl, and when I was big girl, and when I was a young woman and an old woman. (*Laughs.*)

JS: Were you also exposed to the music through records?

SS: Oh, yes. I used to love *Charlie Parker with Strings* and *Dizzy Gillespie with Strings.* I would play those records over and over and over and over. My parents—they were really great people—I know they were tired of listening. If I wore the record out, I'd get money and go and buy another. I liked Charlie Parker, Bud Powell, Thelonious Monk, Coleman Hawkins. I knew I liked the right people.

WE: Bebop was a shock for a lot of people when they first heard it.

SS: Maybe I didn't know enough not to like it! (*Laughs.*) It sounded great to me. And my brother liked that music, too. I guess I was just fortunate. When I was growing up as a young kid, about nine or ten, Philly Joe Jones and Red Garland used to live in the same block. Also a musician I don't know if you've ever heard of, but I thought he was one of the greatest musicians, a piano player named Fats Wright. He reminded me a lot of Art Tatum; he could play any tune, any tempo, any key.

WE: Did those musicians teach you to play?

SS: What would happen is my father had what he liked to call a private club. It was a political club—I mean a club where they had music, and my father had a license to sell liquor. It was really after hours, you know, and he had a band. The club was in the basement of our house, and there was always music there. So these people would come by, and maybe the piano player would be a little late. Then I'd sit down there. I got a chance to play with all these people, and somebody was *always* showing me something. "No, play that like this, this sounds better." I was just a lucky kid.

JS: You said your father had a *political* club?

SS: Yes. My father was a Republican; he was a ward leader or something. In our house he acquired what they call a charter. It was a chartered club; it was a legal club. You had to have a card to come in, and you had to be registered in the party. They did have some political meetings there, but that was during the day. Not at night. At night it turned into another thing. On the weekends he had music; he had jazz. (*Chuckles.*) A lot of good musicians were in Philadelphia at the time, and they would play in the club. They had not become well known. Like Philly Joe, he hadn't been out on the road where he'd gotten popular, although in Philadelphia we knew who he was. Just about anybody who was around used to come and play in the club. I was at the right place at the right time. I used to get a chance to hear them play. I couldn't go downstairs unless, as I said, a piano player was late and I had to fill in. I couldn't just go downstairs and be part of the audience, but I could sit at the top of the steps and listen to the music.

JS: Did local musicians tutor you outside the confines of the club?

SS: Oh, sure. They were nice to little kids who showed that they could play something. I used to go for piano lessons, and maybe Fats Wright or Red Garland would say, "Okay, let me hear it." I'd play for them and they would show me. I was lucky enough to grow up with these people, and it wasn't unusual to me. I thought, "Hey, you know, these are my friends." Of course, I never got a chance to play a gig with them. But I made some gigs, too, when I was about twelve. The piano player in my brother's group, he did something and he was on punishment. There was an Episcopal church—I think it was the Church of the Annunciation around the corner from us—and they used to let the young people have dances from six to eight. They would have live music. So this particular time the piano player was grounded, I got the gig. I made six dollars.

WE: At times, your block-chording technique is reminiscent of Red Garland.

SS: That's probably where I got that from. (*Laughs.*) I'm quite sure that's where I got it from. He used to do that so well. You might hear a little of him in my piano playing.

JS: What were the circumstances behind your taking up trumpet in high school?

SS: I was in ninth grade, and I was trying to win a scholarship.[3] The music teacher was—I'll never forget her name—Dorothy S. Weir. She was in charge of the band. She said to me, "Look, everybody in here that's applying for some kind of scholarship plays the piano. Why don't you pick another instrument?" I said, "But I don't want to play another instrument." She said, "Go get a small instrument, a flute or a trumpet or anything, and let's see how you do on it." And sure enough, I won a scholarship playing the trumpet. I was in All-City High Band with great people, like Lee Morgan. I'm a couple of years older than him, but he was in All-City High. Boy that was something. We marched in a place called Franklin Field one night; I'll never forget it. It was so cold that the mouthpiece stuck to your lips. (*Laughs.*) I even got to play first chair cornet and hang out with all the guys. It didn't matter to anybody else that I was a girl, so I have no complaints. But I won a scholarship to a school which is very prestigious now. It's called Felloman School, but when I went there it was called Germantown Settlement because it was situated in that section of the city called Germantown. I went there on Saturdays for three years. My trumpet teacher played with the Philadelphia Orchestra. I mean, I just came along at the right time. I had a few doors open for me.

JS: What was your first career step after you graduated from high school?

SS: Let's back up a little bit. I left high school when I was a senior. I went on the road with a guy named Coatsville Harris. He was a drummer.

JS: How did that association happen?

SS: Well, while I was in high school, I was working in the same club with him, a very popular club, then called Spider Kelly's. He lived around the corner—everybody lived around the corner! He said, "Well, what about your parents?" I said, "Don't tell them." (*Laughter.*)

WE: You were a rebellious sort.

SS: Oh, I was. And it was the funniest thing. I was young, but I looked younger than I was, and they didn't want to let me in the club to play. As it turned out, I could get on the bandstand and play, but then I had to go sit in the kitchen. (*Laughs.*)

WE: How long were you on the road?

SS: About a week. I think we were in a place called Allentown, Pennsylvania, and, of course, Coatsville Harris is from Coatsville, so we were in that area. Maybe it was longer than a week. It had to be, because I didn't go back to school. I missed all the finals. I missed the graduation and everything. But I was a musician and I didn't need that. What did I need to go to school for?

WE: What was your parents' response?

SS: They were heartbroken. They came and got me. I went to Lincoln Prep School and got a GED.

JS: After playing piano gigs around Philly for several years, you began on organ in 1955. Tell us the circumstances behind that switch.

SS: I was playing piano in Spider Kelly's. This is when Jimmy Smith and Bill Dogget, you know, they were making the organ very, very special. The gentleman that owned the club, he said, "Listen, I have a proposition for you. If I rent an organ for you to practice on for a week, could you play it?" I said, "Sure!" (*Laughs.*) Anybody knows that you don't learn to play any instrument within a week's time, but I was young. So he went to one of the local places in Philly where they sell the Hammonds, and sure enough, you could rent an organ in these little stalls in the basement. For two weeks I would go there every day for about an hour. Then he rented an organ and put it in the club. A Hammond B3.

JS: Did the club owner also pay for you to take lessons?

SS: No, he just rented the organ. I didn't even know how to turn it on. Someone had to show me how to turn it on. Jimmy Smith—God bless him—he showed me how to pull out some of the drawbars so I could get some tone.

JS: How much time did Jimmy Smith spend with you?

SS: Well, he was busy; he was hardly ever in town. But when he came in town and had a gig, I'd be all up underneath him. (*Laughs.*) Of course, I wasn't playing it properly, but I knew enough from the keyboard on the piano that I could make some little sounds. Eventually I learned how to play.

WE: In the early 1950s, you were impressed by organist Jackie Davis.[4] Why was he important to you?

SS: Well, Jackie Davis knew everything about the Hammond organ. He knew how to fix it if something went wrong. He knew how to go in the back of it to make the tones brighter or duller. And he could play. This man was a two-fisted organ player. I loved him. His orchestrations reminded me of a string section, or Count Basie's band; whatever you wanted to get out of it, he could get out of it. He, more than anybody, I think, made me really love that instrument. I had an idea of maybe I wanted to sound like him, do what he did, you know. He was the giant as far as I was concerned. And I had a chance to meet him, very, very, very soon after I played with Eddie "Lockjaw" Davis, because they were friends. All through the years we've stayed in contact with each other. A lot of people haven't heard of him. Once he was the organist on the *Howdy Doody Show.* (*Laughs.*)

WE: Were you influenced at all by earlier jazz musicians who played the organ? For example, Fats Waller and Count Basie?

SS: They didn't move me to play the organ. Not that there was anything wrong with what they did, but when I heard Jimmy Smith and Jackie Davis, Wild Bill Davis and Bill Dogget—what they were doing with that instrument—I wanted to play. It was more up to date. Jimmy Smith did so much to make that organ popular. *Down Beat* used to list it as miscellaneous until he started playing it.

WE: The same year as your conversion to the organ, you joined company with some future jazz heavyweights in the Hi-Tones.

SS: That was an experience, too. I got a chance to play with John Coltrane and Albert "Tootie" Heath. We used to have rehearsals at my mother's house. One thing about that group was I was playing an organ, but it was a white Wurlitzer. (*Laughs.*) It was a Wurlitzer, but it had a Leslie tone cabinet, which made it sound somewhat like a Hammond organ. I grew a little bit when I was in the Hi-Tones, because John Coltrane was in the group. He opened my ears a lot, harmonically and any other kind of way. (*Laughs.*) His concept was different from any other saxophone player I had ever worked with. Like, for instance, when he played a ballad. He didn't have to play but the melody. No one else could play an improvisation and make it any better. It was his tone and phrasing that made it work. He didn't have to fill up the bars with notes. And his harmonic concept—he'd play notes in places where I wouldn't think of putting them. But we didn't talk about music; I learned by playing with him. It was just the idea that I was able to be on the same bandstand, or rehearse, with him. I was fortunate.

JS: From a personal standpoint, how did you respond to John Coltrane's presence in the group?

SS: Oh, I loved John Coltrane. He was a neighbor, too. He lived about four blocks away from where my mother lived. That house now is an historic shrine, and his cousin Mary, for whom he named the tune,[5] still lives there. We're great friends. But I knew John Coltrane was a genius. And the *nicest* person. I never heard John say a harsh word; I never heard him raise his voice. He was just an ordinary person that was nice who happened to play the saxophone. All he did was practice. He practiced and then he played. He practiced and then he ate. When I first went with Eddie "Lockjaw" Davis, we played at Count Basie's club in New York for about a year. I had a small apartment there, and John and his wife at the time, Naima, lived about a block or so away. I used to go around to his home, but I hardly ever saw him, because if I got there nine o'clock in the morning John was in a room practicing. If I stayed from nine o'clock in the morning until nine o'clock at night, he came out to have lunch, or Naima went in and took his lunch, and (*laughs*) she went back in to take his dinner. He practiced from the time he got up until the time he had to get ready to go to work. As long as I knew him, he was like that.

WE: Your remarks describing how much John Coltrane practiced confirm the general impression about how serious he was. But did he also have a sense of humor?

SS: Yes, he had a heck of a sense of humor. You wouldn't think so, but he did. His sense of humor was not guffaw-like; it was more refined. When I say humor, maybe we would be looking at someone who did something stupid or funny, and without saying anything he would just get such an expression on his face that (*chuckles*) you didn't normally see there. I could give you his cousin's telephone number, and she probably would be able to give you some instances where he said something that would show a humorous side to him.

[Authors' aside: We took Shirley Scott's advice and called John Coltrane's cousin, Mary Alexander, who furnished us the following anecdotal information:

John had some sayings that he used all the time. If he was going out, he'd say, "I'll be black soon." Then, after he'd come back, he'd say, "I'm black." (*Laughs.*) He'd say these things with a straight face; he had a dry sense of humor. Another thing that he used to say all the time, he used to call the bathroom "toils-of-let," and, of course, that was the toilet. So he'd say, "Well, I guess I'll go to the toils-of-let." These things started at home, because John was really a homebody. And he would play with me a lot. Sometimes I would go out, and he would come downstairs to the door with me as if to say I was his wife. I'm going out the door, and he yells, "Get out and stay out!" People walking up and down the street, they're thinking that we're really arguing. He would stand with a little sly look on his face then. And his mother and my mother were sisters. My mother did most of the cooking; she used to make rolls. When he came home from a trip on the road, he'd run straight into the kitchen and say, "Aunt Betty, I want a hundred rolls."]

JS: My understanding is that John Coltrane and his cousin Mary were very close. Do you recall any incidents that illustrate their friendship?

SS: When they were young,[6] they used to go to the Academy of Music in Philadelphia. They had to buy the cheapest seats in the house, so they would have to walk *all* the way to the top of the theatre. And John would hold Mary's hand because she was scared.

[Authors' aside: During our above-cited phone conversation, Mary Alexander elaborated on the Academy of Music story:

We used to sit all the way up in the crow's nest. You had to walk outside, like on a fire escape or something, and then come inside the Academy up on the top floor. I was terrified. I would close my eyes (*chuckles*), and John would lead me out there on that fire escape, and then when we would get inside we had to walk down a little bit to our seats. Well, then I felt like I was going to fall right over on my face. But when they had "Jazz at the Philharmonic," we went to see almost every concert.]

WE: Did you identify with the content of John Coltrane's music and its purported relationship to black culture during the '60s?

SS: Well, there was one particular tune that I did. It was called "Alabama." It was a very moving, spiritual piece of music. It was about the little girls that were killed in a church. I could envision how he felt just by that piece of music. I guess if something like that situation in Alabama happened, I don't care how gentle you are, it must instill in you some sort of rage. He reacted through the music, and I think that's a great way to express yourself. Through expressing yourself, maybe somebody else can feel the same thing, or take notice, you know. Not necessarily to go and try to hurt someone, but just to know that these things exist, and they *shouldn't*. I think it's very important that he wrote those some say controversial pieces of music, because it brings a social injustice to the forefront.

WE: Was there a time, as you were growing up, when the facts of racial discrimination hit you particularly hard?

SS: No, I always knew that I was black, and being black, things were different. I didn't think I was anything other than a person whose race was not considered equal to the white race. When I grew up, I just knew those things. It wasn't that something happened in my life and I said, "Damn, I'm black!" (*Laughter.*) When I went to elementary school—you live in a black neighborhood, you go to a black school—most of the teachers were white. (*Chuckles.*) And when we used to say the Pledge of Allegiance, when we'd get to the part about "with liberty and justice for all," under our breath we'd say, "for everyone but me." The little music books that we used to sing out of, someone had gone through all of them in my class, and where it used to say *Old Black Joe* they crossed out "black" and put "white." So we knew.

JS: After the Hi-Tones, you played with Eddie Davis. How did that opportunity occur?

SS: During that time Eddie "Lockjaw" Davis had a group, and in his group was a very fine drummer from this area, whose name is Charlie Rice. The organist's name was Doc Bagby, also from Philadelphia. On a weekend this band came into town, and when they got here, Doc Bagby left Eddie Davis's group to form a group of his own. Davis's group had a gig to go to on Monday in Cleveland, Ohio, at a club called the Loop, and they were lookin' for an organ player. They looked high, they looked low; I was the only game in town. (*Laughs.*) Charlie had told him that he knew a girl who was playing the organ at Spider Kelly's. So he brought Eddie to hear me and I got the gig. We rehearsed that Sunday and went to Cleveland. That's how I got the job with Eddie Davis. Being in the right place at the right time.

JS: Do you recall any funny incidents on the road with Eddie Davis?

SS: I remember from that first road trip with Eddie "Lockjaw" Davis and Charlie Rice, when we pulled up in Cleveland, Eddie jumped out of the car and yelled, "Where the hos is?" This would happen just about everyplace we went. When we got in the town, in front of the club or wherever we were going to stay, and there was somebody he knew, he would say, "Where the hos is?" I couldn't figure it out. What was he going to do with water hoses? I was about nineteen or twenty years old, I didn't know anything. I said to Charles, "Charles, why does Eddie 'Lockjaw' Davis always want to know where the hoses are?" He said, "*Hoses!* He doesn't want to know where the hoses are, he wants to know where the 'hos is.' " When he referred to "hos," he was referring to the beautifully dressed women who always showed up when he played. It was his term of endearment for all those pretty ladies. (*Laughter.*)

JS: Is it true that Davis wasn't keen on having you in the group? It has been reported that you said, "I don't believe he really went for the idea of a girl, but he had no choice really, so I was hired out of desperation."[7]

SS: I never said that. Maybe he *didn't* want a girl, but he never told me that, and he never gave me that impression. He was quite a person to work for; he was a gentleman and maybe my best teacher. Where I really learned how to play the organ was with the Eddie "Lockjaw" Davis Trio. He taught me so much without my ever knowing. It's too bad that I didn't recognize it. I never got a chance to tell him what a great teacher he was, as far as I was concerned. He opened my ears up. His sense of harmonic half-steps was instrumental in the way that I play.

WE: In addition to his gifts as a musician, Eddie "Lockjaw" Davis was known to be an excellent road manager.

SS: He was. I had no problems on the road. He told my mother, "Mrs. Scott, if you let your daughter come with me, this is what I will do: she will send home money *every* week, because I'm not going to give it to her. (*Laughs.*) I'm going to send it to you." And he did that. He took good care of me. Between he and Charlie Rice, I didn't have any problems on the road. They were gentlemen who always made sure that after a gig I was home, wherever home was where we were staying. And Eddie Davis was a great musician. A lot of people used to call him an unorthodox musician because he would make sounds on the horn that weren't supposed to be on there. The fingering—you weren't supposed to be able to reach these particular notes. *Down Beat* used to talk pretty badly about him. He was self-taught. He made those sounds come out of that saxophone, that he wanted to come out of him, any kinda way that he could. Later on he learned how to read music.

JS: You signed with Prestige as a leader in your own right when you were in "Lockjaw" Davis's group. What prompted the Prestige people to come to you? Did they hear you someplace?

SS: At the Apollo Theater with Eddie "Lockjaw" Davis. Prestige came to me, before they came to Eddie, to ask me to record. I said, "I'm working with Eddie Davis, and I think he should record, too." So I did one[8] and he did one.[9]

WE: What was your format for that first recording?

SS: I think it was a trio. You're taking me back too far. You know how old I am? I'm old.

WE: Do you remember who was on bass?

SS: It was probably George Duvivier. They always—well, most always—made me use a bass player, which I detested. But the record company said that the organ didn't sound like a bass. And I said, "No, it sounds like an organ." (*Laughter.*) They wanted the bass line to sound like a bass, and of course the bass was so light compared to the forcefulness of the organ that I never liked it. Later on I got a chance to play without a bass.

JS: Working with a bass player, would you ever pop the pedal when you were playing a loud chord?

SS: No. That would be defeating the purpose of the bass player.

JS: When you were without a bass player, did you enjoy walking the bass lines?

SS: Yes.

JS: Are there recordings of you playing pedals?

SS: There's one called *One for Me.* It's on the Strata East label.[10]

WE: You mentioned working the Apollo Theater with Eddie Davis. Often the bill at the Apollo was loaded with star acts. Do you have good memories of performing there?

SC: I remember one time when there was such a bill, with Bobby Timmons, Lee Morgan, Wayne Shorter, and Jymie Merritt with Art Blakey and the Jazz Messengers. Before we would go on, the stagehands would have my organ on a dolly; they would turn it on before they rolled it on stage. This particular time (*chuckles*), it was time for Eddie Davis, Arthur Edghill, and myself to go on. Well, as they're opening the curtains we are supposed to start playing, but there's no electricity for the organ. I looked over to my left, and there's Bobby Timmons and Lee Morgan just cracking up; they were laughing to beat the band. They had unplugged the organ. Now I've got to think of something to get back at Bobby, because he was the one who did it. (*Chuckles.*) So before they went on, I took furniture polish and I rubbed it all over the piano keys. Anybody who knows anything about playing the piano knows that you do not oil the keys—you can't play. That's what I did to him. Everybody thought it was funny; we never got angry at each other. We were all kids, you know. It wasn't funny to Eddie Davis, and it wasn't funny to Art Blakey, but to us it was funny.

JS: As your fame began to build, did Eddie Davis feature you more prominently in the group?

SS: Oh, yes. Eddie used to put lights on the bottom of the organ—one red spot and one blue spot—and they were so darn hot. That was the most uncomfortable thing, to try to play with all that heat down there. Then I had to have these flashy high-heeled shoes, and they'd have to be special shoes. You couldn't wear the same pair of shoes if we were in a club for a week. (*Laughs.*) He used to dress me up like a kewpie doll. But yes, he gave me a chance. He didn't try to squelch or hold me back, or put himself, you know, in front of me.

WE: Do you remember a recording date you did with Eddie Davis that included Count Basie?[11] "Farouk" was one of the tunes.

SS: Yes. I was thrilled to be making the date with the great Count Basie. I think my Wild Bill Davis came out on that date with the block chords and everything. That's one of the things I used to like about him, the way that he would do that.

WE: You've cited a block-chord influence from both Red Garland and Wild Bill Davis.

SS: Different, though. On the piano you use two hands to play block chords; on the organ you usually just use one. I don't know how Wild Bill Davis would have done that on the piano, because the two instruments, although they each have a keyboard, are not alike.

WE: Let's listen to some Wild Bill Davis.

[We played "Satin Doll," from *Duke Ellington's 70th Birthday Concert,* recorded 1969; Solid State Records, Wild Bill Davis on organ.]

WE: As we started the music, you said you wondered why Wild Bill Davis would be playing organ with the Ellington orchestra.

SS: Oh, I see now—they have two orchestras: Wild Bill Davis and Duke Ellington. (*Laughs.*) One of the things I admired most about Wild Bill Davis was his ability to sound like a big band. If you noticed, he changed the registrations while he was playing to get the different colors. I mean, he didn't sound the same all the way through. It wasn't monotonous at all. It was like he had a horn section and a brass section, and then he combined them. It was just marvelous. Two big bands. (*Laughs.*)

WE: Is that one of the joys of playing the Instrument—using the organ's orchestral qualities in conjunction with a big band?

SS: I've never heard an organ with a big band before. Not like that. I recorded with a big band,[12] but that's not the same. I had a little space where I would play. But, you see, here the band and the organ were playing at the same time.

WE: Speaking of your playing, I notice that your solos follow a consistent narrative pattern.

SS: Are you taking about the organ or the piano? 'Cause they're different.

WE: The organ.

SS: It's the way I think when I'm playing. Since I have the organ, I like to use it. So I will play single lines for a while, then I will build. I'll play some chords and try to sound like a big band. But I think differently on the two instruments. The difference between the piano and the organ is that the piano is much harder for me to play than the organ.

JS: Why?

SS: Well, you have electricity going for you with the organ, for one thing. You can change the way the organ sounds with the drawbars; if you want the piano to sound differently, then you have to approach it differently. The way you strike it has to be different. There's only one way to play the organ, and that's to turn it on. You don't have to exert any energy to make it sound any louder, except to push your foot down on the pedal.

JS: Returning to aspects of your career, you had a family while touring with Jaws. Was your family life at all in conflict with your professional life?

SS: I was married and I had two little guys. It was kind of hard for my husband to see me go off on the road and he was there with the children. But I wanted to play, and my mother was there for my children. So I didn't worry about them. There was one time when we were in New York City at Count Basie's club[13] for about a year, and every Sunday night I would come home and go back every Tuesday. And in the summertime I would have my children there with me. It worked out. My mother would come with them to stay. That's before they started school. But I wasn't out there all the time then. We would go on the road, and I would come back. They were tiny, but they know about the road because I would drag them everywhere. (*Chuckles.*) Yes, it was hard on the marriage. No fault of their father.

JS: When you quit Davis's band in 1960, were you eager to return home and settle for a while?

SS: There was no "Okay, I'm coming home now and staying," like that. That didn't happen. I was young; I wanted to work. I was a musician; I wanted to play. I got a band of my own. I was the bandleader! I had Arthur Edghill on drums and Stanley Turrentine on tenor saxophone, and we went to Panama. That's when I met Stanley, on that first gig.

JS: You hadn't heard Stanley Turrentine before hiring him?

SS: I did not know him. I got the gig for Panama, and I needed a tenor player. Arthur Edghill, who had been the drummer with Eddie, too, he said, "I know this tenor player from Pittsburgh. He's living in Philadelphia, and I'm sure he'd be great." So I called him up on the telephone. We talked. We never had a rehearsal. We met in the airport—that was the first time I saw him—and we went off to Panama. That was the first time I'd ever been out of the country. I liked it. I liked being a bandleader.

JS: You played with Stanley Turrentine until 1971. What are some of your fondest memories of your professional union?

SS: The music, really. We had a wonderful musical marriage. I've never played with anybody that I enjoyed playing with more than I did with Stanley. Never, in all these years, have I heard another tenor player that sounds like Stanley. We were very compatible as far as playing the music is concerned. When we used to record, and even play, it was very important that we made eye contact. Why, I don't know. It was like a hand in a glove. It was really a nice experience. I wouldn't trade it for anything; I'm glad that happened.

JS: Among the recordings you did with Stanley, is there one that particularly stands out?

SS: There is a record that was recorded live at a place in Newark, New Jersey, called the Front Room.[14] I liked a lot of the albums that we did, but that one sorta kinda stands out because it was a live date. I didn't do too many of those; most of my recording sessions were in the studio. I enjoy live dates because you get caught up in the audience, and since you can't go back and do retakes, it's more authentic. I also liked that album because of the selection of tunes.

WE: You probably knew Stanley Turrentine better than anyone. Do you have any personal memories of him that you'd care to relate?

SS: Well, he was very devoted to his children. When we were working together in New York, we lived in New Jersey. We'd get off at four in the morning, but in the summertime he didn't mind getting up and taking the girls to the Bronx Zoo or to the playground. One of the things he liked to do was take pictures of them. For instance (*laughs*), when I would come home from the hospital with the babies, all they wanted to do is sleep, right? And here's Stanley with a flashbulb camera, being the proud daddy. He's trying to get them to smile, and they're jumping in their cribs trying to get away because of the flashbulbs. It was cruel. (*Laughs.*) The other thing was, when we would get ready to go on the road, the kids would get kind of tearful. When we'd go upstairs to get our suitcases, the kids would each grab a limb and just have a fit. Stanley would try to walk with kids hanging on his ankles. We were trying to go to the door dragging them. (*Laughs.*) We felt badly that we had to go to work, and it would take us at least five different times, for like an hour, before we could actually pull them away to go. No matter how many times we left, it never failed; this was the ritual we went through. It wasn't an easy thing to do—they'd say, "Oh, Mommy, oh, Daddy, please don't leave us!" But as soon as we were out the door, they were quiet.

WE: After the group with Stanley broke up, you signed with Chess. Do you feel that some of your recordings for that label tended to be more commercial?

SS: Yes, I think so. I did things that maybe the A&R man wrote. (*Laughs.*) I was playing tunes that I didn't want to play.

WE: Considering your stature at that time, why did you succumb to the pressure?

SS: Well, I mean, throughout there are things that I made concessions to that maybe I didn't want to do. (*Shirley takes out a Cadet record of hers, Mystical Lady.*[15]) Look, they dress me up in this stupid stuff. Who wrote "Mystical Lady"? I'm sure it was the A&R man, Esmond Edwards. He was the A&R man for Prestige, Chess, and Cadet. [We check the liner notes and confirm that Edwards wrote "Mystical Lady."] See what I mean? So, it wasn't easy.

WE: How long were you with Chess?

SS: I can't even remember. Some things I try to forget. I try to push that out so I can put something in that's worthwhile.

WE: You've recorded for a lot of labels over the years. Aside from Chess, how were your experiences with record companies in general?

SS: Early on I didn't know anything, so I tried to do whatever was asked of me. A lot of the A&R men would say to me, "Look, can't you play this like Jimmy Smith? Don't play so many flute stops, play some brass stops." They try to tell you what to play, and it wasn't always very nice. The record companies during the early part of my career made it seem as if you were working for them. They pulled all the strings. Well, when I was a young musician, what I wanted to do most was play. I didn't really know, or put it together, that they were working for me. But I survived it. I'm still here, and once in a while something nice got through the cracks and out, in spite of everything.

WE: Did you make decent money from record sales?

SS: I probably have millions of dollars floating around out there in royalties that are due me. I'd try to get as much money as I could up front, because in those days I didn't receive royalties for most of those things. But just the fact that the records were out and people were playing them on the radio would get us gigs, and that's the way I made most of the money. Not from the records, really.

WE: Wouldn't you sign a recording contract that guaranteed you a certain percentage of the royalties?

SS: Sure, you sign a contract. So what?

WE: Since you had contracts, couldn't you hire a lawyer and get your money?

SS: Find a lawyer for me, please. (*Laughs.*) I'll give you a percentage of what they collect. What used to happen—I don't know if they've changed tactics or not—but you pay for everything, you know. The record company pays for absolutely nothing. You know that, don't you?

WE: No. What do you mean you pay for everything? You pay the sidemen and all?

SS: Sure, that comes off the top. They don't give you a *dime.* If they have to remaster, you pay for the masters. You pay for the liner notes. They make all the decisions, but you pay all the money out of the royalties. And so they say, "Well, you know, we had to reprint, and I'm sorry there's just no money." That's what they *used* to do. They probably have a much more sophisticated way (*laughs*) of keeping your money away from you now.

[At this point we turned our attention to more music, beginning with "The Preacher," from *The Champ,* 1956; Blue Note Records, Jimmy Smith on organ.]

WE: How would you distinguish your playing from Jimmy Smith?

SS: Distinguish my playing? Ooh! I don't think I sound like Jimmy Smith at all. I admire him, but I don't play like him. Jimmy Smith was an innovator on the instrument. You have to have somebody to start it, you know, get us out there.

WE: When Smith takes a solo, he plays behind the beat a lot. In contrast, your attack is on the beat or ahead of it.

SS: He's kinda laid-back there. You know, you're right about that. You know these things. You're right; that's one of the things. (*Laughs.*) Also, the stops that we use, the registrations are different. There it sounded like a full organ, where he had pulled all of the stops out, and it also sounded like he was taking a solo with vibrato. Which is not what he does now. His use of vibrato there influenced my sound when I first started playing. I'm sure that's the case because he showed me how to pull the drawbars out. We may have used the same registrations, but the thoughts are different, the improvisation is different.

[The next recording was "The Broilers," from *The Eddie Lockjaw Davis Cookbook, Volume II*, recorded 1958; Prestige Records.]

WE: When you were with Davis, your approach to the organ was very assertive. Had you played the piano as percussively?

SS: I think it would be difficult for anyone to say, "Oh, that sounds like Shirley Scott playing the piano." It's like another side of my brain. I mean, I use one side to play one instrument and the other side to play the other. (*Laughs.*) But, no, I don't think the approaches are the same.

WE: Even when you comped behind Davis, you remained very busy.

SS: That's what he liked. You find out what they like and try to give it to 'em. Especially Eddie Davis, yes.

JS: I particularly enjoyed the way you growled behind Davis and urged him forward on that piece. Was that what he wanted you to do?

SS: Yes, but I was always underneath him. I didn't try to go over what he was doing— you know, to push the pedal down for the electricity? He liked playing in Basie's band because he used to like what was laid down behind him while he was playing. So I tried to emulate that as best I could.

JS: Among the records you made with "Lockjaw," do the two volumes of *The Cookbook*[16] stand out as the height of your achievement?

SS: That was probably the height. Numero uno.

WE: One jazz writer claims that the sterling qualities of *The Cookbook* are the result of what you and Eddie Davis play, and that "the other soloists are either competent or downright poor."[17]

SS: That is the most ridiculous thing I have ever heard! If that were the case, we wouldn't need them. But no way could we have produced something that sounded like that with just the two of us. Opinions are like, pardon my expression, assholes. Everybody has one. And that's as far as I will go with that.

[We turned to "Zoltan," from *Unity,* recorded 1965; Blue Note Records, Larry Young on organ.]

SS: I noticed that the registrations that Larry used were different from any of the other organ players up to that point. After that a lot of them were influenced by registrations that he used. I think he was really ahead of his time. The sound that he used is being used now a lot. Joey [DeFrancesco], I think, has some of those same registrations. He reminds me a lot of Larry. I've heard people say that Joey sounds a lot like Jimmy Smith. He likes Jimmy, and you can hear that—when you like a person, you're gonna hear something there—but I think that he liked Larry Young, too.

[The final selection was "Blues for J," from *All of Me,* 1989; Columbia Records, Joey De-Francesco, organ.]

JS: Is the Jimmy Smith influence apparent in DeFrancsco's playing on this piece?

SS: In a way. Some of the licks remind me of Jimmy Smith. Some of them remind me of Larry Young. And some of them remind me of Joey. I know that Joey admires Jimmy so much that he used to play a lot like him. Maybe that's where he gets a lot of his ideas from, or he used to. That's a tribute to Jimmy, I think. But Joey's maturing, and so is his playing. Joey's very fast. Jimmy may be fast for a little while, but Joey's consistent with his fluency. I like Joey. Joey sounds like a lot of people, and I'll tell you why. Since he was a little boy, he's been around organ players. And you know young minds are like sponges, and he soaked up a lot of stuff. I think it should flatter whoever he decides to let come out sometimes. That's a fine compliment to pay.

JS: Did Joey hang out with you?

SS: Yes. There's a club in Philadelphia called Gert's and all the local musicians would come in there. Gert's was not a large place, but there were two rooms. When you came in, there was a room with a little tiny bandstand with an organ and the drums on it, and a bar. In the back, there was another little room. What used to happen was, the tenor players and the trumpet players would line up and they would (*laughs*) wait to play. They would be on a big line all the way to the back of the second room. So the poor rhythm section never got a break unless an organ player or a drummer came in. Joey's father brought him into Gert's from the time he was about nine or ten. His father's an organist, too. We would set Joey up on the organ, and his little feet weren't even able to touch the pedals when he started playing.

WE: Shirley, before we close our discussion, I want to ask about your current state of health. We understand that your illness stems from a diet pill, fen/phen.

SS: When I was in Italy, I heard on television that it was dangerous. I stopped taking it and I came home. I have what they call primary pulmonary hypertension, which affects the lungs. That's why I'm using oxygen and medicine that I have to have twenty-four hours—it helps get the oxygen to the lungs and the heart. It's a pump, and it goes in my heart.

WE: Any chance you'll continue to perform?

SS: Oh, I can't perform.

WE: That's a tragedy.

SS: Well, it is, but I don't have to be here either, right? (*Chuckles.*) It depends on how you look at it. I can still write music, I can still enjoy music, and I can play. I just can't play for a long period of time. I don't think I'll make any gigs.

Selected Discography

Queen of the Organ: Shirley Scott Memorial Album. Prestige PRCD-11027-2 (2003). (Anthology of recordings, 1958–1964.)
*Queen of the Organ. Impulse GRD-123 (1964).
Blues Everywhere. Candid CCD 79525 (1992). (Scott at the piano with bass and drums.)
The Cookbook, Vol. 1. Original Jazz Classics OJC652 (1958). (With Eddie "Lockjaw" Davis.)

Notes

1. According to our research, the Hi-Tones was a jazz band led by vocalist Bill Carney. Other important musicians to pass through its ranks included organists Trudy Pitts and Richard "Groove" Holmes.

2. *In the Kitchen,* Eddie "Lockjaw" Davis Trio; Prestige.

3. She attended Philadelphia High School for Girls.

4. Barbara Gardner, "Shirley Scott/A Woman First," *Down Beat,* October 25, 1962, pp. 20–21.

5. "Cousin Mary," composed by John Coltrane, appears on *Giant Steps* (Atlantic Records; 1960).

6. Young adults, about eighteen years of age.

7. Barbara Gardner, p. 21.

8. *Great Scott!,* 1958; Prestige Records.

9. *Smokin',* 1958; Original Jazz Classics (previously released on Prestige Records).

10. Released 1974.

11. *Count Basie Presents The Eddie Davis Trio + Joe Newman,* 1957; Roulette Records. Also released as *Countin' with Basie;* Vogue Records.

12. For example, *Roll 'Em,* 1966; Impulse Records.

13. Count Basie's Bar in Harlem.

14. *Shirley Scott Queen of the Organ,* 1964; Impulse Records

15. Released 1972.

16. *The Cookbook, Volumes I and II,* recorded 1958; Original Jazz Classics (initially released on Prestige Records).

17. *The Blackwell Guide to Recorded Jazz: Second Edition,* edited by Barry Kernfeld (Oxford and Cambridge, Mass.: Blackwell, 1995), p. 323, contributed by Barry Kernfeld.

Carol Sloane

Carol Sloane

Vocalist Carol Sloane, often referred to as the "best-kept secret in jazz," entered the national music scene in 1961, lighting up the skies for a brief period. After a twenty-year dip in national prominence, New England's jazz diva was rediscovered by the Japanese record industry. Sloane's musical odyssey has come full circle since her 1991 signing with the major independent label Concord Records.

Born Carol Morvan, in 1937, she was raised in Providence, Rhode Island. She had her first professional singing gig at age fourteen with Ed Drew's dance band, and went on to earn her official musician's stripes during tours with the Larry Elgart Orchestra in the late 1950s.

Arriving in New York in 1958, she changed her surname to Sloane and frequented clubs on Fifty-Second Street. Her career received a boost in 1960 when she subbed in the popular trio of Lambert, Hendricks, & Ross. Sloane's career was truly launched, however, when she stunned concertgoers, critics, and fellow musicians in the summer of 1961 with her performance at the Music at Newport Festival. On the strength of that appearance, Columbia Records signed the new singer. Her 1962 recording debut[1] featured Sloane accompanied by stellar sidemen: trumpeter Clark Terry, trombonist Bob Brookmeyer, and guitarist Jim Hall.

In the early 1960s, she had regular bookings on the nightclub circuit, sharing the stage with Bill Cosby, Woody Allen, Lenny Bruce, and Richard Pryor. Her rising star landed her appearances on the *Tonight Show*. But as the decade waned, so did Sloane's visibility, and she relocated in North Carolina.

Singing regularly in Raleigh area nightclubs, Sloane was also busy booking acts, writing music reviews, and hosting a public radio show. During this period she befriended her mentor, Carmen McRae, and the two enjoyed a personal and professional camaraderie until McRae's death fifteen years later, in 1994. Sloane's admiration is reflected in her 1995 album tribute to the elder vocalist.

Now based in Boston, Carol Sloane has matured into a musician's singer. Her warm, sensual sound is reminiscent of lyrical qualities found in the early work of tenor men Ben Webster and Zoot Sims. Though she is rarely known to scat, her thirty-plus albums nonetheless carry the definitive stamp of jazz due to her keen understanding of a lyric, unerring sense of pitch, and feeling for jazz rhythms. Flawless diction and superb microphone technique serve to enhance her gift for musical intimacy, as she can shrink a concert hall down to a cozy jazz room.

Today, Sloane is in demand as a guest artist with some of the nation's finest symphony orchestras, including several appearances with her hometown Boston Pops. In the '90s, she made a series of finely crafted albums for the Concord label. More recently, Sloane signed with High Note, releasing *I Never Went Away* in 2001 and *Whisper Sweet* in 2003. An incandescent performer who embodies taste and control, Carol Sloane has long been on the short list of esteemed jazz vocalists among critics, musicians, and discerning audiences.

Recorded June 24, 1998

WE: Carol, have you struggled over the years to find your aesthetic direction?

CS: There hasn't been any struggle since the moment I heard Sarah Vaughan sing "Deep Purple" on the radio. I was, I think, maybe only twelve or thirteen. I made a decision that I wanted to be a part of that or explore that or get to know more about *what it was* that made her sing a song differently than other singers I'd heard. I asked some musician friends why it was different and they said, "She's improvising." I thought that was a much more interesting approach to singing.

WE: Were you raised in Providence?

CS: We lived about twelve miles north of Providence in a little town. I went to school on a school bus every day because my mother wanted me to go to the nuns. About sixth grade I began to see this sign on the road that said "Boston 40 miles, New York 125." And I mean the siren song was there every day. (*Laughs.*) I had to get to New York, and I did when I was sixteen. I made a record—there were some songwriters, a couple friends of mine in Rhode Island, who asked me to go with them to New York to sing their song. It's on a 78, and I still have it. It wasn't a demo, but it was done in a kind of factory. They had musicians who would sit all day in the studios. They would read the music that was put in front of them, they'd play it, and bang it was done. You'd pay for your hour in the recording studio, and you were gone. All of this was terribly, terribly interesting to me because Birdland still existed then, and a good many of the clubs around Fifty-Second Street. When I finally did move to New York in 1958, it was sort of at the very end of this era, but still there was lots of jazz and a lot of musicians, and a lot of recording. And the *hundreds,* it seemed, of jazz clubs. So the place was *shimmering* with the vibrations of creativity. So there you are. How far have I gone now? Up to 1958.

WE: Yeah, we're all done.

CS: Good. Thank you very much. It's been grand. (*Laughter.*)

WE: Growing up around Providence, listening to the radio and to recordings, did you distinguish generally between black performers and white performers?

CS: I began to distinguish that there was a way the Basie band sounded as opposed to the Dorsey band. There was a stronger emphasis on swing—I suddenly began to realize what swing was. I knew Benny Goodman's band was swinging, but Basie's band made more sense to me. It was laid-back, it had a bluesier feeling, it had more life to it. The melodies they played were more interesting to me, too. And black singers were singing songs that I heard white singers sing, and there was *no* comparison. I was much more intrigued by the way they [black singers] explored the tempos and the melodies. Now comes along Anita O'Day, who in her heyday could do exactly the same thing, and brilliantly. So I realized that I didn't just have to stand on the outside looking in, admiring these people. Possibly I could maybe even learn how to do some of that by studying them very carefully. And I began to do that. When I lived in New York, Carmen McRae was living there as well; whenever she sang in New York, I'd go to see her. I would stand in a corner or sit in the darkness and watch her, almost as if there was something she did with a hand or an eyebrow or a knee or a foot (*laughter*) that if I did it I would get the same thing, you know.

I must say that I have a personal tendency to like black singers more than I do white singers. Even white singers that are trying to sing jazz. I don't think that they quite understand; I don't think they quite get it. *I* think that the traditions established by Billie Holiday and Sarah Vaughan, and Carmen and Ella, too—they are the people we should emulate if we're gonna do some singing of this music. And I'm writing a book as well, by the way. The first chapter is "Do Not Scat Sing." The second chapter is "Don't Ever Scat Sing." The third chapter is "Please Don't Scat Sing." The fourth chapter is (*laughs*) "Don't Ever Scat Sing in My Presence." There's no reason in the world why that has to be a factor. It isn't necessary. Except for Louis Armstrong, 'cause he started it, and I would listen to him anytime. But I'd say to those who think they have to do it to prove they're a jazz singer, that's a mistake.

WE: Isn't it likely that some young vocalists will be more instrumentally inclined and, as a result, will be less interested in interpreting lyrics?

CS: Well, of course it is, but I don't want to hear that. I mean, if I'm going to listen to a singer, I don't want to hear an instrument. Bring a horn player along with you.

WE: How did you respond when you first heard Ella take a scat solo?

CS: I learned early on that I could not do so well what Ella Fitzgerald did, that incredible ability to improvise that she had. I tried it a few times, and of course I made a complete ass of myself. I don't like to be in that position, so I don't do it anymore. Here's a good example of what that's all about. My very first and important job in New York was at the Village Vanguard in August 1961. This was right after I'd been in Newport. Max Gordon [owner of the Village Vanguard] asked me to do this job before I went to Newport. He heard me sing one afternoon on a matinee show with Lambert, Hendricks, & Ross; Jon Hendricks asked me to sit in. So Max said, "In two weeks, you're opening for Oscar Peterson." I nearly fainted, of course. I'm going to get *paid* every night to listen to Oscar Peterson, Ray Brown, and Ed Thigpen. (*Laughs.*) Of course, the place is packed *every* night with musicians to hear Oscar. Well, I've got to prove that I'm a jazz singer, or what in the heck am I doin' there. So every night I would try to improvise on a beautiful song called "My Ship," which Oscar asked me to sing. So every night I would destroy "My Ship." I would take it apart; I would sing part of the melody, but mostly not.

WE: Were you scatting at this point?

CS: No, I wasn't scatting. But whatever the hell I was doing, it was all wrong. And every night when I'd look over at Oscar for approval, he would just sit there like a Buddha with his arms folded across his chest and his head lowered, and give me this kind of an odd look. The next night he'd say it again, "sing 'My Ship.'" Every night I would do the same damn thing, and every night the reaction was the same. Finally one night I got tired of this, and I sang it straight as a dime. I looked over at him, and he clapped with a big smile on his face. He had never said a word to me except, "sing 'My Ship,'" and I learned a lesson. I wasn't ready to do what I thought I should do, what I thought I had to do. I wasn't skilled enough to do it. What I was capable of doing was singing very clearly, with good diction, good intonation, and that was it. Only as I listened more and more to other singers, and began to latch on to one or two or three that I thought were *really* remarkable, did I begin to realize that there was a way of singing, like Carmen and like Anita O'Day, and still be true to the melody. Just to pull it back a little bit, to tell my own version of it.

WE: Sheila Jordan said that vocalists who were good at scatting developed their own "syllables."

CS: Sheila's absolutely right. I'm amazed that she never did take a horn, because she's able to make these wonderful sounds, and she certainly has the ability to improvise beautifully. If she had a horn, she'd be doing exactly what she's doing with her voice. She's one of the few I don't object to because it is so musical when Sheila does it. Furthermore, she has a nice little trick she does. It's pacing, which is another lovely lesson for people if they're seriously interested in jazz singing. She'll do one of her very, very, very complicated, I mean, absolutely astonishing improvisational pieces—maybe quite up-tempo or medium tempo. And after you've got yourself sort of pinned against the chair because you can't believe she's just done all that, she'll come with (*sings the opening line of "What'll I Do"*) and sing this thing just as straight as a die and make you breathe, because it's a way of lessening the tension. It goes into making a very successful performance over an hour and a half. Knowing the pacing takes a long time to learn. I used to listen to Carmen and write down everything she did, including modulations and what the tempos were. And then take a look at why I felt sorry when the set was over 'cause it didn't go on longer. I thought, "If everybody would feel that way about my singing—they didn't want me to get off, or they'd like me to sing at least one or two more—wouldn't that be the way to do it?" I mean, isn't that really it?

Decisions about pacing are getting a little bit easier for me, but still not where I want it to be. I hate making up a set; it makes me crazy 'cause it's really, really hard. I have so many songs, and I want them to be paced right, and I've got to figure in my head, "Did I do this song the last time I was in this club?" I keep copies of all the sets I ever do in a big bag marked "Used Sets," and where I did them, so then I know I'm not gonna go to that club and sing the same stuff over again. I've had to really work hard to get to a point where I could call just about any musician and be confident that they're not gonna turn me down. This is an accomplishment for me. I always call musicians that I admire and would like to sit down and listen to. And then when they agree to play for me, I'm still pretty much dazzled. I've had to really work hard on feeling confident enough when I walk out there that I don't think they're gonna throw tomatoes at me or something.

WE: Still today?

CS: No, a little bit less now. It's a lot easier now than it was, but it was really hard for the longest time. I really would question whether or not I deserve to be there. Now, that absolutely was the wrongest thing in the world, because I think it made my career not go in the right direction and not go as fast as it should have, perhaps. Because I didn't have the confidence in myself. I have always been unsure of whether I really deserve to be working in the clubs and working with musicians that I like a lot. Now I'm not quite so unsure. Which has really been a big help. Otherwise, you go out there terrified. You go out there not able to do your work because you can't relax.

WE: How many years have you suffered this anxiety?

CS: Twenty-five, thirty. (*Laughs.*)

WE: And how recently have you felt more relaxed?

CS: In the last year.

WE: What was the watershed that made you more relaxed?

CS: I lost a lot of weight.

WE: So it was a personal-image matter?

CS: Yup. Personal image. That's part of it. And, I think, when Clark Terry agreed as quickly as he did to the idea of us doing an album together.[2] He was just so up for it as soon as I mentioned it to him. I think the album has been a hit for Concord. It's the kind of album that I've always wanted to do, which is very relaxed and loose, and fun. The next one will be much more serious. (*Laughter.*)

WE: How did you first meet Carmen McRae?

CS: I tried to walk up to her a couple of times. But in those days she was working in clubs where there was no dressing room where she could go whenever she would come offstage. And Norman Simmons [McRae's pianist] said this about her: Whatever was bothering her in her personal life, she'd take it to the stage with her, and she didn't leave it there. When she came offstage she still had it, and so she would keep her head very up, her eyes lowered, and her whole body language would be "Don't come over here. Just leave me alone." So I was very reluctant ever to approach her.

Then she moved to California, and I lost track of her because I couldn't see her that much. I was buying her records and was aware of her that way. And then in 1981 I was booking a supper club in North Carolina in Chapel Hill. I booked Joe Williams, George Shearing, Shirley Horn, Anita O'Day, Jackie (Cain) and Roy (Kral). All my pals. Well, Carmen came, and I went to pick her up at the airport. I hadn't seen her in a very long time. I took her to the hotel, and I just made myself her lackey, if you will, for those days while she was there. She pretty much stayed in her hotel, and I never saw the inside of her room.

But one day during this week she said, "I've got to go buy shoes." I said, "I'll take you to the best shoe stores I know of." So we went. (*Laughs.*) This beautiful black lady in the very upscale shoe stores in Chapel Hill. She walks in and, picking up shoes, she says, "This is shit. These are all shit." And I'm tryin' to find the other side of the room. (*Chuckles.*) I'm not with this lady. She doesn't buy shoes. She buys me a pair of sandals which I still have— they're falling apart. I took her back to the place where I was living. I said, "Carmen, what would you like for lunch?" And she said, "Well, I want eggs"—and she started describing how to cook them. I said, "Here's the pan (*laughs*), there are the eggs, and there's the bacon and everything else. I'll make the toast." I said, "I'm not taking any chances making breakfast for you, or lunch or whatever. No. If you do it your way, then there's no mistake." We found out at that time that we also were watching the same soap operas, so we had a good afternoon. We became kind of good friends then. You know what she once said to me? That if Billie Holiday had told her to jump out the window on the fifteenth floor of a hotel, she'd have gone straight out the window. And I said to her, "You know, I feel the same way about you." (*Laughs.*) She pointed to the window. I said, "No, I don't think so." "I know you would," she said. And you know what was interesting? She said just like Lady Day never offered her any drugs of any kind, she said, "I wouldn't offer you any, either." I said, "I know it. Which is a pity, because you really ought to be offering some of that stuff."(*Laughs.*)

WE: Turning back to your career, you seem to have just hit your prime in the '90s. Is it correct to call you a reluctant star?

CS: No, I want to be a star. I want to make a lot of money. I wish I had a record company that would hype me the way they hype Diana Krall. Or Cassandra Wilson. I'd be pleased as punch if I had some record company willing to go around beating the drums for me. I think, in fact, it should've happened before this. I came at an odd time. In a way I resent it, but, I mean, if I allow myself to think about it too long, then I get bitter and dreadful and just not very happy. So I'm trying to focus on what I have to do and not what Cassandra Wilson is doing or Diana Krall, 'cause they're not focusing on what the heck I'm doing. Now, here's what I think I need to do: I need to do more symphonic work. Remember the recordings Sarah Vaughan made with Tilson Thomas and the Gershwin things she did? Some people may have thought it was odd for Sarah Vaughan, coming out of the bebop jazz thing, to be doing that. But it seemed very natural to me that she should be singing Gershwin with a big orchestra. That's where I am now, and it is something that I am going to make a serious effort to pursue with orchestras around the country. I'm *tired* of jazz clubs where the guy who runs the club doesn't care a damn about his piano, so they don't put the cover on. I'm tired of being in places where there's no serious commitment to the music. I'm tired of trying to fend for myself in what laughingly is called "the dressing room." When you get out of New York and Boston, you know, it gets pretty slim out there. Not a lot of places. And the young singers are taking over as well. I have to come to grips with that.

WE: The reason I used the term "reluctant star" is because of your disappearances from the jazz world.

CS: Yes. There was an explanation for that. When I was in New York the first time, from 1958 until '69, I think it was, I was doing pretty good. I was working a lot outside of New York at the best clubs—at Mr. Kelly's in Chicago, the Hungry I, all those good places. But then, right around the end of the '60s, the Beatles took over, and things really did get quite peculiar. Plus, you know, when you're a girl singer, you don't have the chance to get into clubs as often as an instrumentalist. They say, "Well, we had Carol Sloane two months ago; maybe we'll use her next year." Anyway, things started to get a little bit lean. I went to North Carolina in the beginning of 1969 to work in a club, and I was very reluctant to go because they used to hang black people down there. It turned out to be a very wonderful place. I stayed there for quite some time. I had a wonderful life and I was singing. I didn't have the pressures of New York. I didn't have the excitement, and I didn't have the challenges, either.

WE: Nor the visibility.

CS: That's right. I really disappeared.

WE: Didn't that cause you some anxiety?

CS: It was okay for a while. And then it wasn't okay, because the reason I went to North Carolina is because a man I met, with whom I fell madly in love, persuaded me to move there. So not only was I going to have a new, different life, a little less pressured, but I was also gonna have this wonderful love affair. When that ended, of course, that was when I looked around. So I got a call from Roland Hanna and he said, "Dee Dee Bridgewater is not able to go to Japan with us.[3] Would you be interested in going?" I said, "Yes. Of course."

This was 1977 when I went to Japan for the first time. So I went back to New York to work a gig with Roland and the guys as a warm-up.

One night George Mraz said to me, "I'm going to Bradley's." I said, "That's wonderful. Who's over there?" He said, "Jimmy Rowles." I said, "Oh, God, I'd love to go hear Jimmy." I'd never heard Jimmy play. So we went over to Bradley's, and the rest, as they say, is history. We moved in together in '77, and then Jimmy and I separated in '81. So I was back in New York. I thought things would be a little bit better, mainly because of my association with Jimmy, but it was just the opposite. People would call for Jimmy, and I wouldn't get the calls. I was kind of very unhappy. I got myself into a situation which I found almost intolerable, because Jimmy was *so* difficult. His drinking was *so* out of control and so hard to deal with. I lived with that for all those years.

WE: Did you drink heavily as well?

CS: Oh, yes. What the heck, if he's gonna have a double vodka before he can get his feet on the floor out of bed, I might as well have a Johnny Walker Black and water in the morning. Why not? Yeah, those were the days! Also, I tried to commit suicide one night while Jimmy was reading a book. I took all of his sleeping pills. He had just gotten a bottle of Dalman, and I took the whole bottle. The next thing I knew, Diana Flanagan[4] was standing over me and kinda roused me a bit and then got me to the hospital.

WE: Let's talk more about your early years. How did you join Larry Elgart's band?

CS: I was working in a little club in southern Massachusetts one night, and a beefy-looking guy walked in. He gave me his card and said he was the road manager for the Larry Elgart Orchestra. They were playing down the road at one of the amusement parks, and he said, "We really need a singer. Could you please come over and meet Larry? We've heard that you're a wonderful singer." So I went and I sang a couple of songs, and Larry said, "If we're gonna go out on the road in a couple of weeks, do you think you'd be interested?" I said, "One-nighters, I don't know." Somebody I was with said to me, "This is probably your golden opportunity. You've got a chance to go to New York and get this thing started. Take it, baby." Two weeks after Larry offered me the job, I went to New York. Two years on the road with these guys. I had a wonderful time and I learned a great deal. But when it was over, I was back in New York looking for a job as a secretary, because I didn't have any reputation beyond singing with a dance band for two years that was out in Minnesota and Iowa and North Carolina and wherever the hell we went.

WE: Were you headlined as Carol Sloane while performing with Elgart?

CS: I joined the band with the name Carol Vann, which was an abbreviation of my maiden name, Morvan. So when I met Larry Elgart, my singing name was Carol Vann, and he hated it. He said, "Why can't you be Carol Morvan?" I said, "I don't like it." Now I get with the band and we're going back and forth with names. So every night I'm Carol Smith, Carol Price, Carol Rogers, Smitty, Stinky, whatever. I never had a name. I had no identity, and I was really getting nervous because I just didn't know who I was. So one night in his studio we were goin' through names again. We hit Sloane and I said, "Stop. Just stop right there. With an e on the end, that's it. I don't want to go any further with this; I can't. I just have to get a new identity. I'm going to my lawyers and have my name changed."

WE: As Carol Sloane, what was your next big career step?

CS: The big beefy guy who came in with his card has gone from the Larry Elgart Band to Willard Alexander's office, which was a very big agency at the time. He was booking Benny Goodman and Basie, among others. So he said to me, "I've arranged for you to sing in a jazz festival in Pittsburgh. They don't know who you are, but I've managed to get them to agree that you can go on first on opening night." Jon Hendricks and Annie Ross and Dave Lambert were also on this bill that night. Jon heard me sing and he said, "Oh my gosh. Well, if Annie ever gets sick, blah, blah." I said, "Okay, if she gets sick, call me." I went back to New York and my little job, and I said to the man I worked for, "Mr. Halperin, the day may come when I can't even give you two weeks' notice because I have been asked to take a woman's place and she's a wonderful singer." He said, "Okay." Well, I listened to the records every night, and then pretty soon I was listening every other night, pretty soon once a week, because I wasn't getting the call. I finally *did* get the call. She was not able to work a job in Philadelphia, so I said to Mr. Halperin, "This is it." He shook my hand, the dear man, thanked me (*chuckles*), and I was out the door and on a train to Philadelphia to sit in for Annie Ross.

WE: Talk a bit about subbing for Annie Ross. Was it daunting having to join this red-hot, tight unit that had such complicated arrangements? And how about opening with a burner like "Cottontail"?[5]

CS: Yes, it was terrifying, but it seems to me I've spent all my life doing terrifying things. I'm out there thinking, "Oh, God, what am I doing here?" Both of them had my hands; I mean, they really both did. "Cottontail"—they did it really fast, so that even if I didn't have all the words, it didn't sort of matter. I had most of the notes, anyway. Once I got through that little bath of fire, though, the rest of it seemed even more difficult, because they did a lot of blues things where they'd each take about eighteen choruses scat singing, and then leave me out there. I said, "God, I don't know how to do this!!!" Dave wanted to go and have a glass of brandy, and this one wanted to go off and smoke a joint, and they want to leave you there. They used to do it to Annie, too, but Annie put her foot down, and I didn't know anything about this. I thought, "Well, you know, this is my responsibility; I guess Annie used to do this."

WE: So you would scat sing?

CS: Yes! And it would be dreadful. So after just, you know, getting as deep as I could and trying to extricate myself and trying to be as graceful about it as possible, I would just stop, turn around, and say, "C'mon, Jon, Dave, HELP!" (*Laughter.*) And they would come out and take over and "Ha, ha, ha, isn't it cute, ha, ha, ha." I mean, it was really amazing. There were times when Dave didn't show up, and Annie wasn't there, either. It'd be just Jon and myself trying to do all the things that they had done. But you learn that no matter what happens, you're gonna go out there, and you've got to do something. You just can't retreat.

WE: Didn't Jon Hendricks have a prominent role in getting you booked at Newport in 1961?

CS: Jon Hendricks went to Sid Bernstein, who was then in charge of the Newport Festival in 1961. There'd been a riot the year before. George Wein withdrew, and Sid Bernstein took it over. He was really a rock and roll promoter, but he was doing jazz anyway. Jon went to Sid Bernstein and said, "If you're going to do a 'new stars' thing, you've got to put this girl on here." And Jon had some resistance, I think, 'cause Sid didn't know who I was. But Jon told me that he told Sid, "If you don't put her on, we won't go on." (*Laughs.*) I said, "You didn't!" And he said, "Yeah, I did." I didn't know that until maybe a year ago.

WE: Tell me about your appearance at Newport.

CS: I got to sing on a Saturday afternoon: "New Stars of 1961." Who could ever forget? By the time I got out there, the audience had pretty much vanished. I remember the sun was setting; I put glasses on my face. I said to Gildo Mahones—I had the trio that played for Lambert, Hendricks, & Ross—"I want to do 'Little Girl Blue' in B flat. I'll do the verse." He said, "I don't know the verse." I said, "That's all right, just give me an arpeggio and I'll do the verse." So we did it that way, and when I came off the stage, George Simon from the *New York Herald Tribune* and John Wilson of the *New York Times,* those people had stayed and heard me sing. They were all over me about singing a verse a cappella and being in tune when I got to the chorus. So the press got all wild. I mean, the Providence paper, hometown girl—front page, mind you. My mother was going crazy. And John Wilson writing a beautiful review and George Simon writing a beautiful review and some guy from Columbia Records was there, too, and that's how *Out of the Blue* came.

WE: Your career was launched!

CS: That was how it started. I mean, I got to sing in a jazz festival, which is really where I wanted to be. I remember when I used to go as a spectator. I was there the night Mahalia Jackson sang "Didn't It Rain." We'd been sitting out there for hours waiting for her to come on. We all had the umbrellas. She came out and sang "Didn't it rain, children," and it stopped raining. We couldn't believe it. I would sit there and I'd think, "What must it be like to say hello to Oscar Peterson, have him know who you are?"

WE: Having the guts to realize a dream by singing at Newport demonstrates that you were assertive and did want to be known.

CS: Yes. I still want to be known. I feel like I'm a minor player; I really feel that that is the truth. When I think about the assistance some people have been getting from publicity machines, if I dwell on that, I start to become bitter and angry and frustrated, and I'm not a nice person.

WE: I'm impressed by the way Jon Hendricks helped you. Is that symptomatic of the kind of loyalty that exists among jazz people? Or was it unusual?

CS: I don't know. I thought it was very unusual. I didn't know that kind of generosity in the business because I just got there. I knew a certain tolerance from certain musicians. My perception was that they sort of tolerated me, 'cause I was cute, you know. But I'd never known anybody to make that kind of a commitment or expect me to then produce, which was even more frightening. However, I also knew, subconsciously probably, that I was actually going to stand on the stage that I had dreamed about and been looking at as a spectator for so long. So I'd better go out there and do the best I could. The microphone wouldn't come off the thing—I usually hold the microphone. But this is one of those mikes, and they had covered it with a condom as a wind protector. (*Laughter.*) It may not have been, but it looked just like a condom. They had maybe done it because that's all they had to keep the wind from making a sound if they were recording. Anyway, I did see this thing in front of me, and all these empty wooden chairs and the sun setting. I remember I couldn't take the mike, so what do I do with my hands? So I put them tightly against my waist, and I began to sing hanging on all the time. I mean, the audience saw this frightened little girl up there, and they heard her sing in tune, and they heard this lovely, sort of straightforward version of the song, and that was it. But I have to say this: the confidence never really was there. I've always been very unsure. I always believed I could do it, but I'd get out there and think, "God, what happens if I fail right here in front of everybody?" To be constantly badgered with your own sense of imminent doom doesn't make for a good performance.

WE: I have a question ready, but you seem like you want to make a point.

CS: I was going to get back to just making you understand one thing, because I haven't been very clear about it. I've always believed that I belong out there. I always believed that I'm a very, very good singer. I think I do what I do very well. I don't think any of the recordings reflect any of that. I can't listen to them.

WE: Why?

CS: I listen and I hear bad intonation, because I'd be nervous and I don't like to record. It's awful because you're stuck in this booth. They won't let me stand out in the studio with the musicians. *Out of the Blue* was done with just kind of a little thing that was open to the musicians, which was wonderful. I loved the freedom. To be able to breathe the air that the musicians were breathing and not be in this little confined space. But anyway, you see (*referring to the CDs of hers lying on the table between us*) I've got thirty-two of these things. This stuff represents the best it was at the time. When I look back on it now, I recognize it for that, but I don't think it really is as good as I want it to be. I still have to prove myself on a record. I did an album in Japan some years ago with a wonderful musician named Don Abney.[6] And I was out in the studio in this lovely big room with them. I like that album a lot. I said, "I just want to be out here." And they said, "Okay, Miss Sloane, you want to be out here, you can be." No argument.

WE: What prompted you to make the allusion to the film *Casablanca* in the title song for that recording?

CS: I was preparing to go to the record date, and I was in the bathroom. I remember I was putting eyeliner on, and all of a sudden the room got very, very hot. I thought, "Am I getting a really early hot flash?" In '82 it was just a wee bit premature. Or that thing in the ceiling that you turn on when you're taking a shower that keeps the room warm, I thought maybe that had gone on, somehow. But there was this terrific presence in this room, and I thought about Ingrid Bergman. I thought, "Oh, that's the reason; it's 'cause I'm gonna record 'As Time Goes By.' " I loved the film, and that makes sense. So I was gone for the rest of the day. Many hours later I got back to the room, and I turned the television on and it said, "Ingrid Bergman died today in Paris." I said, "Before she went, she came over to Japan. She had a quick stop in Tokyo." She was there, I swear.

WE: Focusing again on chronological milestones, why did your association with Columbia end after your second album?

CS: It was the end of a two-record deal, and they just didn't pick up the option. And remember, at that time—my timing's been really stupendously bad all these years—I think that's when Barbra Streisand was discovered. The whole company focused on promoting *her*. They made her a star. And so again, it's really a testament to what can happen if the mechanisms are in place. I'm not suggesting she's not a talent, she certainly is, but you can take some people with lesser ability and catapult them, shall we say.

WE: Let's flesh out the '60s a bit more. Columbia didn't renew your contract, but you played gigs until 1968. Did you have a working band?

CS: I don't remember actually having one trio of my own. When I was traveling, I usually wound up with the guys who were the house players, which in those days turned out to be wonderful musicians. And for a long time I was traveling without music, because I can't read music, and because it took a long time for me to get somebody who would take the time with me to go over a tune and tell me what key it was. I'd write it in a book. I used to travel with this little book. I still do, as a matter of fact. Like an address book. Under A you'll find "All of Me" and "After You've Gone" and the key I sing it in. So for a long time I had no music. Maybe I had some lead sheets, but certainly nothing was arranged. So I would get to these clubs and I would say to the guy, "Do you know this tune?" in whatever key. And he would say, "Oh, yeah, okay." Eventually the bass player would say to the piano player, "Are you playing B flat seventh on it? Well, no, I'd rather do this." So now they've gotta work all that out. They have no music in front of them.

WE: Wasn't that exasperating for the musicians?

CS: I'll tell you a story. Some years ago I was working in a club in Washington, D.C., called "Charlie's," which is a good club; Charlie Byrd had something to do with it. I'm working with two other singers, Susanna McCorkle and Maxine Sullivan. The three of us arrive for rehearsal. Susanna has arrangements that are color-coded. I mean, this is really serious stuff. She takes a long time to rehearse, because she does normally take a long time to rehearse. She's working with the house guys, with a piano player named Stef Scaggiari; that was my first time working with him. So Maxine and I are sittin' there in the club having our cigarettes, having a little gin and tonic, thank you very much, waiting for her to finish her work. Finally Maxine goes up to do hers. She has lead sheets, that's all she's got, but they're not color-coded. She's got lead sheets and I have nothing. I have no music. And by the time I'm going up there, anyway, it's time for them to go home and change clothes. I don't have any time for rehearsal, thank you, Susanna. So, I'll never forget, we went through all of this week, and it was interesting. At the end of the week, Stef came into the dressing room. He had Susanna's music all nicely assembled and put back in order. Then he said, "Here's all your music, Maxine," and handed her her stuff. Mine was written on the back of a cocktail napkin, and he just threw it. (*Laughter.*) But, I mean, we got along fine. And I was just fakin' tunes. I was fakin' it all the time because I never had the money to pay anybody. I don't know how anybody else does it. I always thought you had to pay people for their services. You should see the stuff. Bill Mays just last year said to me, "You know your reputation in this business is really flawless. Everybody knows that you sing great, but your book sucks." (*Laughs.*) So he's now taking to straightening out my book, which is a big accordion file full of lots of lead sheets. Some of them are tattered and torn and scotch-taped and held together with hairspray.

WE: Let's explore more deeply your thoughts about music. First, the perennial question: Do you have a definition of what it means to be a jazz singer?

CS: I know that a jazz singer has to have certain qualifications, but they also apply to people like Sinatra, who was not a jazz singer because he didn't improvise. That's the one thing. I think you have to be able to improvise. It doesn't mean scat singing. That means to be able to change the melody somewhat, to always use the words because that's your job, to sing the words. And you have to be able to swing. I mean, I can sing a song to you with a tempo in my head, but when I sing it to you, you should be able to hear it just as clearly as I hear it, it seems to me. There are some singers who really can't do it. Johnny Hartman wasn't very good at up-tempo stuff, by the way. Like Vic Damone isn't, but then he isn't supposed to be a jazz singer, anyway. But some singers who've made a lot of reputation over a long period of time don't have all these elements. Sinatra could do it all except he didn't improvise, and when he did, he'd do something stupid like "Ring-a-Ding-Ding." (*Laughs.*)

WE: Didn't Sinatra reharmonize some of his material?

CS: He was capable of doing it. He had the feeling for it, but he never really allowed himself to improvise. He really didn't have to, because when he sang a ballad he was singing as a jazz singer sings it. He sang as movingly as Carmen or Billie Holiday.

WE: Are you saying that one definition of jazz singing is expressing emotion?

CS: Oh, I think it has to do with the interpretation of those words. I mean, how many actors portrayed Hamlet or Macbeth, and how many have come up to Olivier's level? We all try to do it, and some of us don't get there. The script is there, it's already written. The American songbook is waiting for everybody to explore, and there's so much to explore, even if it's songs that we've known. It's very much like Shakespeare, as far as I'm concerned. It is that important. Not just to Americans, it's important to the world.

WE: Summarize for me, then, your definition of a jazz singer.

CS: It's improvisation, that's it. I think any singer who wants to sing ought to have basic things, like a good voice, decent range, some diction, know how to breathe properly to keep your sound up and get your intonation right, and then good material. And the material's sittin' right there. Improvise if you want to be a jazz singer, but you don't *have* to scat sing.

WE: Improvisation can be very subtle.

CS: Yes. Thank you. That's what it is. I always thought for a while that Sinatra came as close as any pop singer ever did to being a jazz singer. Because in the '60s when he was *absolutely* on top of it, God! He couldn't hit a bad note. I heard a story that he was having trouble one time with a couple of notes, and somebody, like Billy May or Gordon Jenkins, said, "Why are you having trouble with this? You're Sinatra." He went, "Oh, yeah, that's right. Why am I having trouble with this?" (*Laughter.*) He reminded himself of how good he was, and he didn't have any trouble with the note. (*Laughs.*) That's so weird. That's Sinatra! [We played Frank Sinatra's version of "Mood Indigo," from *In the Wee Small Hours,* 1955; Capitol Records.]

CS: (*A short way into the introduction*) I love this one. (*Sinatra sings a series of "no's" in a descending scale.*) I think he stole that from somebody. He may have gone over this with his piano player. It's not that spontaneous to me; it sounds like he rehearsed it. Yeah, I think that that was planned—that little improvisational thing.

WE: How about at the very end, where he strings many words together to lengthen the line?

CS: That's what he could do. He had great breath control. At this time in his career, his vibrato was still very tight. I mean, this was a flawless voice. This was just like Ella's. Ella's voice was so perfect.

WE: Lengthening a line isn't part of improvisation?

CS: Of course it is.

WE: So it's jazz-influenced?

CS: Well, yeah. I think *that* is. But what I'm saying is that "no, no, no, no, no" before that, I think at the beginning of the entrance of that chorus, it sounds to me as if he worked that out with his piano player. He would just change it slightly. But the very end, that was his own, I think. That just is my own feeling. How we're gonna string notes together, of course, that's all improvisation. And I've said he didn't do it. He *did* do this kind of thing and changed the phrasing of the song, which *was* improvisational, of course. He didn't scat sing. He didn't take a lot of liberties except for ring-a-ding-dings on up-tempo songs. But that phrasing, well, it is improvisational, yes, but not in the way we know it as it applies to a jazz singer who'd maybe do some little obligato or something else. I don't know what. Maybe I have to change my whole statement. Maybe I have to change everything now because I'm being confronted with my own words and have to eat them. (*Laughter.*) My favorite song of his is on *In the Wee Small Hours* when he sings "I see your face before me."[7]

[We listened to "Apricots on Their Wings" by Cassandra Wilson, from *New Air: Airshow No. 1*, 1986; Black Saint.]

CS: (*Midway through Wilson's first chorus*) I don't understand what she's saying anymore.

WE: (*Stopping the tape*) It's called "Apricots on Their Wings."

CS: Now, you see, you shouldn't have to tell me that. If the girl's doing it properly, then I should be able to understand what she's saying. I can't understand what she's saying, thank you.

WE: She wrote the piece.

CS: Good for her. That's an interesting, challenging piece of material, if that was all as written, the melody. I'm sure she does a little bit of improvising on it. I just feel sorry that I lost the words there. In an effort to be a horn, we lost the words. So what is the point of singing it? Why didn't she just go (*hums the tune*) without the words?

WE: Aside from enunciation, did you respond to the sound of her voice?

CS: Yeah, it sounds all right. It didn't sound like she's a bad singer. At one spot, where she lost her wind, did you hear her crack a bit?

WE: No.

CS: Yeah. She did. It was interesting, because she let it stay like a horn player would lose it. Maybe that's what she wants, doing real horn things with her voice. Which is fine. Betty Carter's been doing it for a long time. It just doesn't excite me enough. It doesn't make enough fire for me.

WE: The timbre of her voice, and its suggestion of intimacy, is reminiscent of yours. Both of you seem to come through the microphone on a recording, into the listener's space.

CS: That's one thing that I say to the engineer: "Please, I want presence on here." I've had some albums that I've listened to where I sound like I'm singing in Passaic, New Jersey. (*Laughter.*) I hear other recordings of other singers and think, "That's what I want; why can't I get that?" It's not so much what I'm doing, it is really then a mechanical process in the control room with the board. "Please keep the presence on the board."

[We turned to "These Foolish Things (Remind Me of You)," Billie Holiday with Oscar Peterson, piano; Barney Kessel, guitar; Ray Brown, bass; Alvin Stoller, drums; from *Billie Holiday/Lady in Autumn: The Best of the Verve Years*; Verve Records, recorded in 1952.]

CS: That was really a flawless performance. The voice was still intact, really; the vibrato's very pretty. She always had trouble with breathing, I think, because she was smoking the whole time, and drinking. So you put those two together, it's gonna take its toll on the voice. She had the horn quality; I hear a trumpet sound in her voice. And it was a perfect read. It'd tear your heart out.

WE: In what ways was she improvising on that song?

CS: Well, Lady Day never really hung behind the beginning of the phrase. She was usually right on it at the beginning of the phrase. It's when she got into the phrase itself that she'd start to pull back a little bit, or shorten a note here and there. But basically she was adhering to the melody most of the time. It was just a matter of bending something here, and adjusting this. She didn't hang behind the beat as much as other jazz singers.

I just always thought that she was the first one I ever heard who was singing from experience. This is when I began to understand that you can transmit personal pain to music and get people to understand what you've been through. When I heard Carmen, I realized that she obviously was doing the same thing. But when I first heard Lady Day, I was very young. I didn't understand Billie Holiday at fourteen. She made no sense to me at all; I didn't understand the pain. In fact, I was kind of astonished, because I knew there was pain but I didn't know that kind of pain, except maybe seeing it in a movie once in awhile. I'd never heard anybody sing it, and I'd never heard it be so intimate, and I never had received an invitation to bear witness, so I wasn't prepared for it. In fact, I just didn't want to hear her sing. It troubled me.

Also, I was the purist, and I remain one to this day, really. It meant the voice had to be flawless, the voice had to be beautiful-sounding. This wasn't beautiful-sounding. It sounded too cracked and broken and hurt and injured. So the other women had more appeal for me. When I finally began to realize her contribution, she was gone. I never got to see her. But I do feel that listening to Carmen as much as I did that I really got it very close to the original, and a lot of the songs that I sing come from Lady Day through Carmen to me. And that's okay by me.

[Next was Betty Carter's version of "The Trolley Song," from *The Audience with Betty Carter*, 1979; Verve Records.]

CS: (*Laughs along with the live audience at the dramatic tempo change early in the performance and at the exaggerated train sounds at the conclusion*) I hope she opened the set with that. It's great.

WE: Could she be described as a consummate jazz singer?

CS: Oh! Absolutely. She never had a big, big voice, you know. It's really, really almost tissue-thin, because she sings in the chest. But she's so unique and so special, and certainly her skills at improvisation are almost unparalleled, I think. I heard her a lot when she was just starting in New York, and I must say that what she's doing now is not very far from what she was doing then. So this is not something that's been developing. It's been finely tuned, but it was there from the beginning. She was doing some really out stuff, you know. Which is what she's doing now, compared to everybody else. And certainly compared to the likes of me, and people like me, who sing in this other sort of very straitlaced compartmentalized approach to the music.

When I first heard her in the late '50s in New York, it was fascinating that her body movements and her facial gestures were the same in order for her to get to where she needs to get. There's a parallel here with a young opera singer who just burst onto the scene a couple-a three years ago. She's a brilliant mezzo. Her name is Cecilia Bartoli. Now, when she first came out she had these *incredible* facial expressions. I mean, total distortion. Her face was all cockeyed and crazy, and the eyebrows up and really outrageous. And of course it distracted terrifically from the singing. Mind you, in order to sing Rossini, it's really hard as hell. I think Rossini must have hated singers. (*Laughter.*) But I've seen her since that time, and this has suddenly disappeared. I think if Betty Carter did that, we wouldn't want to go see her anymore. Half of the fun is watching Betty with her face and her great big wonderful mouth fly around. And she's hitting every note dead on. I always take my hat off to singers whose intonation stays intact. She's amazing.

WE: At times her pitch slides and gets indeterminate.

CS: I know, but Miles used to do that, too, sometimes. A lot of musicians do that, but they've established that that's their style. I think what happens to Betty when the tone stops is because the air is stopped. If the air's not coming out to support the sound, it's gonna drop. So she uses it. All of us have to live with our voices, and we're the only ones that really know how to make it do what we want it to do. I'm glad you played that for me from Betty, 'cause I haven't heard her in a while. I always thought she was an amazing woman. [The last selection was "I Don't Stand a Ghost of a Chance with You," by Diana Krall from *Love Scenes,* 1997; GRP Records.]

CS: (*After the second line*) Wrong. (*Laughs.*) (*Before Krall finishes the first chorus*) I'm gonna stop it for a minute because that's what I object to, and George Shearing and I feel the same way (*sings "I don't stand—a"*). It's the wrong spot to take the breath. Wish she wouldn't do that.

WE: You said "wrong" earlier.

CS: Well, because the note went down, and she ended her phrase on a very long note. No, she should sing the melody at the beginning the way it was written; that'd be nice. Musicians can get away with that sometimes. (*The music resumes.*)

CS: (*Parroting Krall's phrasing*) "I don't standa." It's like "What Kind of Fool I Yam!" I like your blindfold test. I've been trying to figure out who it is. Right now I don't have any idea. Basically, it's a pretentious read. I mean, c'mon, she's runnin' out of gas. I don't have a clue right now.

WE: It's not meant to be a blindfold test; I don't mind telling you who it is.

CS: Oh, I know, but I don't want you to tell me. I want to see if I can get it by just digging around here. Is she a new singer?

WE: Relatively, yes.

CS: But, I mean, one that I would not have heard?

WE: You've mentioned her several times during this interview.

CS: I did? Is this the young woman getting all the hype? Is this Diana?

WE: Yes.

CS: This young lady, when she was working here in Boston, I didn't hear about her much, because she was working on top of a hotel somewhere—I mean, it wasn't a jazz gig, it was a lounge gig, if you will. I was doin' this radio show then, and she called me one day to tell me that she'd studied with Jimmy [Rowles]. I said, "Well, that's very nice." A lot of people studied with Jimmy; it doesn't mean that you suddenly have credentials, really, except that Jimmy wouldn't just take anybody, that much we know. That's the only conversation I've ever had with this woman.

WE: You're not terribly impressed?

CS: I don't see what all the fuss is about, quite frankly, but of course she will become a big star. I'm not saying she isn't talented, but if you ask me, the best singer–piano player on the planet is still the one and only Shirley Horn. She's the real thing. We've known each other a very long time, and one of my favorite moments with her was one night at Carnegie Hall—the tribute to Ella in '96. Shirley came offstage, walked directly up to my face, paused, and said, "I love you." I was caught slightly off guard for a moment, but then said, "I love you, too." Another pause, and I added, "Let's get married," whereupon we fell over laughing. Les McCann took me to hear her sing when she hadn't even left Washington yet. Way back in the days when she was singing in this downstairs thing, and I was so astonished at what I heard. I thought, "God, that's the way a singer should sing. That's the sound I want to get, that's the vibrato, that's that beautiful intonation, that's that read of the lyric. Boy that's it!" Some years later in *Down Beat,* Anita [O'Day] had a blindfold test with Leonard Feather.

He played her a Shirley Horn record. She said, "Is that Carol Sloane?" (*Laughs.*) I said, "I've died and gone to heaven."

Selected Discography

Out of the Blue. Columbia (1962).

As Time Goes By. Fourstar Records 40049 (1990). (This one may be difficult to find, but it is worth the effort.)

*Heart's Desire. Concord CCD-4503 (1991).

I Never Went Away. High Note HCD 7085 (2001). (Includes versions of "Deep Purple" and "Cottontail.")

Notes

1. *Out of the Blue,* CBS/Sony.

2. *Carol Sloane and Clark Terry: The Songs Ella and Louis Sang,* 1997; Concord Records, Inc.

3. Roland Hanna was at that time a member of the New York Jazz Quartet, with Frank Wess, George Mraz, and Richie Pratt.

4. Jazz pianist Tommy Flanagan's wife.

5. Whitney Balliett, "Profiles/Carol Sloane and Julie Wilson," *New Yorker,* April 6, 1987, pp. 72–74.

6. *As Time Goes By,* Four Star Records. Recorded 1982 in Tokyo; released 1990.

7. From the song "I See Your Face Before Me" by Jimmy Van Hesuen and Eddie DeLange.

Teri Thornton

Teri Thornton

Jazz vocalist Teri Thornton's star shone briefly in the early 1960s. Her 1963 smash hit "Somewhere in the Night,"[1] a cover of the theme song from the television series *The Naked City*, skyrocketed her to the top of the popular music polls and earned her several guest appearances on Johnny Carson's *Tonight Show*. Soon after, Thornton plummeted from sight until 1998, when, rising like a phoenix, she won the Thelonious Monk International Jazz Competition.

Born Shirley Enid Avery in 1934, the Detroit native learned to play piano by ear. Three generations of the family—Shirley, her schoolteacher mother, and her grandmother, who was a traveling evangelist—often performed as a gospel vocal trio. While still in her teens, Shirley married Kenneth Thornton, changed her name, and at age eighteen went on the road with a vaudeville act.

Although an accomplished pianist, it was Teri Thornton's voice that attracted attention as she made her professional debut in the mid-'50s singing at jazz venues in Cleveland, Detroit, and the Midwest's music mecca, Chicago. Her success in Chicago set the stage for an auspicious start in New York City. In town for only eight hours, she was offered an appearance on national television, followed by a contract with Riverside Records.

Thornton recorded her first album, *Devil May Care*, in 1961 (this genial session received four stars from *Down Beat* when rereleased as a CD in 1999). The title track from her next album, the above-mentioned "Somewhere in the Night," reportedly sold over a million copies as a single in New York City alone. Despite these encouraging signs, personal trials and lack of good management led to three decades of professional oblivion.

Thornton's slow but determined rebound is a story about the triumph of the human spirit. In 1979, she began playing piano bars in Los Angeles, and in 1982 she moved back to Manhattan and worked in a variety of small rooms in an attempt to reestablish her name.

Manager Suzi Reynolds took Thornton under her wing in 1997, but by then a lifetime of substance abuse had taken its toll on Teri's health. While Thornton was in remission from a bout with cancer, Reynolds entered her in the 1998 Thelonious Monk International Jazz Competition. Weak from surgery, the valiant Thornton took the stage at the finals and began her performance by dedicating it to vocalist Betty Carter, who was herself battling cancer.

Backed by an impressive trio comprised of old friend, pianist Norman Simmons, bassist Michael Bowie, and Grady Tate at the drums, Thornton opened with a standard. For her second number she replaced Simmons at the piano. Beginning with an Afro-Cuban groove, she sang "I've Got You Under My Skin," all the while laughing with the audience as she played to them. Rewarded with thunderous applause, Thornton turned next to one of her own compositions, a raucous jump-blues tune titled "Salty Mama," which brought the crowd to its feet. Teri Thornton went home with a $20,000 cash prize, a recording contract with Verve, and the promise of tours and engagements around the world—the ultimate comeback.

The authors first interviewed Thornton at a small Manhattan jazz club when she was still an obscure figure attempting to rekindle her career. Our second interview was conducted at the Actors' Retirement Home in Englewood, New Jersey, following her triumph at the Monk Competition. Bedridden, Thornton remained upbeat, confident that she had beaten her illness. (It was not until the final five days of her life that she allowed the doctor to speak the word "terminal" in her presence.) Although she did live to see her new album released, Teri Thornton passed away from complications of bladder cancer on May 2, 2000.

Recorded October 28, 1995

WE: Teri, you haven't had a record released since 1963. Why have you had such a long dry spell?

TT: Well, there are a few reasons. Right around that time is when rock and roll came back, and Columbia Records did a whole housecleaning and hired A&R men who were more familiar with the pop market. So the people who could record a Teri Thornton were no longer. That's one reason. The second reason: I had two young children, and I couldn't devote *every* second of my life to my career. I never felt completely free to do that as long as they needed me. And also the fact that I'm kind of a hardhead; I won't compromise a great deal in order to do what I think should be done top-shelf. So I just took my time, raised my kids, kept honing my craft, working in out-of-the-way places, and finally they were grown and had their own kids. Then there was my parents. Being an only child, I had to make sure that they were all right until they were no longer here. So for the last year and a half, and *only* the last year and a half, I've been completely free to do what I want to do.

WE: Is there something in your temperament that has contributed to your relative obscurity?

TT: I don't know, except that I walk on the edge. I'm not a conventional person. And I do stay to myself; I'm a very private person. I was always afraid of being in a fishbowl. I don't mind now, 'cause I'm old. Who cares? Anybody who wants to see me now, please look at me. (*Laughs.*) Back then, you know, all the grappling and groping, I didn't want that. I kinda ran from the business itself to avoid the part that I didn't like.

JS: Let's talk about your early years. After your debut in Cleveland, what prompted your move to Chicago in 1956?

TT: A friend from Chicago, named Jessie Brooks, had heard me sing in one of the local clubs in Detroit. He said, "Let me take you to Chicago and introduce you to some of the people that I know." In Chicago, they called me the greatest microphone snatcher in the world. (*Laughs.*) Every time we'd go into a club, they'd say, "Let her sing." And once I'd sing, they'd hire me. And I was kinda like the Pied Piper, because all the local girls, they'd say, "Who is this chick coming in taking all the gigs?" So they started to kind of follow me around. I had my own little school of singers. (*Laughs.*) Everywhere I'd go they'd be there. "What's she gonna sing tonight?" (*Laughs.*) In Chicago I worked from one end to the other, all the way from the deep south side to Winnetka. I met a lot of great musicians, a lot of whom eventually came here to New York.

JS: Who were some of the musicians you met in Chicago?

TT: There was Johnny Griffin, who initiated my entry into Riverside Records. There was Norman Simmons, whose band I played with for years while I lived in Chicago. There was a young man named Leo Blevins, whom I'd met when I was fifteen. He was the guitar player with the Amos Milburn rock and roll band, and he eventually turned out to be my son's godfather and a great jazz bassist.

JS: With reference to Johnny Griffin, didn't you work with him in a small group setting?

TT: Yes. There was a small club called Swing Line. All the big musicians would pop in to do a set with Johnny. Some of Sun Ra's band were in Johnny's band at the time—Johnny Gilmore, Pat Patrick. They worked with Johnny before they went with Sun Ra. I guess I worked with Johnny for a good year. Steady, three nights a week—Thursday, Friday, and Saturday. Now, that was *great* experience, 'cause Johnny would let me do anything I wanted to do. In fact, Johnny recorded the first ditty I wrote, called "Teri's Tune." He had a band called the 63rd Street Jazz Band when he was in Chicago. He maintained this little band even after he went out with other people. They did an album on Riverside, and "Teri's Tune" is on that.[2]

WE: In 1959 you went to Canada. Why?

TT: I needed to go to Canada so I could make some money. I had been given the impression that one could surely starve to death in New York trying to pursue jazz. I just wanted to insulate myself as much as I could financially before I got here.

WE: How long did you spend in Canada?

TT: A year, off and on. I spent a great deal of time in Toronto as well as Montreal. I worked *many* clubs up there. I wasn't all that lucid in those years. Yeah, a lot of stuff was floatin' by me, because, you know (*laughs*), I was in the process of being a jazz musician.

WE: Are you talking about drugs and alcohol floating by you in Montreal?

TT: Not so much drugs as it was alcohol. But Chicago, there were drugs.

WE: You had a problem with drugs in Chicago?

TT: They weren't a problem. Let's put it this way: they were a problem by today's standards, certainly. Back then it was not a great big thing. I had a weight problem and I had a prescription for some amphetamines. The fact that they had a little speed in them (*laughs*) didn't matter to anybody.

WE: Was substance abuse a way at that time for you to cope?

TT: Yes. Just dealing with life, period. I thought I was pretty good, you know. I had all the dope I wanted. (*Laughs.*)

WE: Foreshadowing your alcohol use in Chicago and in Canada, wasn't drinking a problem even when you were a teenager?

TT: It was a problem probably the minute I picked the bottle up. But, you know, I was fifteen or sixteen. I was out of school; they'd taken me out when I was fourteen, and I'd never gone back. So I had a lot of time on my hands. And my dad drank. He didn't drink *often,* but he'd have his little crony parties, and I knew that their drinking was not condoned.

JS: Did your parents take you out of school?

TT: No. It was the educational system. It was one of those things where there were no schools for gifted children, and "You are a gifted child so we can't put you in the system because it's not going to do you any good. It's just gonna frustrate you and create a problem for the other students because you'll be bored." So, you go home at fourteen and find something to do with your life?

JS: Has drinking been a chronic problem throughout your career?

TT: No. Well, I shouldn't say that. After, you know, anything traumatic it would weaken my structure, and then, of course, the drink would be the next thing to lean on. But then when I got back with my fourteen-year-old son in the mid-'80s, I had to let it go. That's when I said, "Well, now, this kid has trusted me all up and down, bringin' him here, takin' him there, trust me, trust me, trust me." And then I'm gonna throw it in his face that I'm going to commit suicide in New York over a bottle? No way.

JS: Is alcohol a part of your life today?

TT: Yeah. Part of it.

JS: You mentioned that Johnny Griffin helped you when you first arrived in New York. Tell us about that.

TT: He came to New York at least a year before I did. I kept getting word: "When you comin' to New York? When you comin' to New York? We got you set up over here." He set up a great entrée for me with Riverside Records. He and Cannonball Adderley did that for me. So the minute I got here, I was able to record,[3] and that got the people aware of the fact that Teri Thornton was on the scene.

JS: With the album done, did you settle in New York?

TT: Things didn't really start to move right away, so I went back to Detroit. I did a one-woman concert at the Henry Ford Theater. There were some promoters there from Australia, and they asked if I would come over and sing on the same bill with Frank Sinatra. (*Chuckles.*) Going to Australia excited me because it was so far away and so exotic, so I said yes. I became part of an ongoing show, "Cavalcade of Stars," when I joined Chubby Checker and Bobby Rydell. I didn't know at the time that once I got to Australia, the whole scenario would be a lot different than I had expected. When I got there, Frank Sinatra had been long gone, and I didn't realize it but I had no fare back. When I was through with my ten-day performance with Chubby Checker and Bobby Rydell—totally, you know, out of my realm—I was looking for my paycheck like everybody else, and there was none coming. I said, "Well, what happened?" One of the promoters said, "Go over to the Peppermint Lounge and hang out with the girls. I'll deal with you later." I said, "Uh-oh." I came from a long line of warriors, and we don't sit still for that sort of thing. (*Laughs.*) So I raised plenty, plenty, plenty hell.

WE: What happened next?

TT: The first thing, I was evicted from the hotel in the middle of the day, and I don't know what to do. As I'm standing there, there's a man who was the editor of a nightlife magazine coming to probably talk about the next ad with the hotel. He looked at me and says, "I saw you at the Bayswater Stadium last night, and you were really great. What's going on?" I said, "I'm, being thrown out." He said, "Really? What happened?" And I said, "I can't explain it; I don't even know. I just wanted to get paid, and here I'm being thrown out of the hotel. (*Laughs.*) I have no fare back home and five pounds in my pocket." So he says, "Well, God, maybe I can help you." He gave me his card and asked me to call him. Which I did. He got me a job at the Quo Vadis club there.

This guy [Bruce McCrae, the club owner] had a contract. It was supposed to be mutually agreeable as to the termination point with a two-week notice. Well, a couple of weeks later a producer for the Brian Davies Show came in and offered me a spot on television. When I told McCrae that I was about to exercise this two-week mutual termination, he said, "Nope, I want ten percent of the television show, and you will remain here." I said, "Ohhh boy!" I went to the union and they said, "We can't help you, 'cause we have to live with these folks after you're gone." So I said, "What am I gonna do?" I still don't have any fare back, and I can't get along with this club owner. He's not going to let me do the television show, and he wants to take some of my money if I manage to do it. I felt that I was gonna really be taken to the cleaners.

Then I met a man named Sal Cianti, who was the head of Leeds Music Publishing in America. He was over there doing business because he had a couple of hot songs being done by Australian singers. We went to dinner one night. I told him my tale of woe, and he got a solicitor for me. The solicitor got a great barrister, and I went to court with this Bruce McCrae. He sued me, and I countersued and won. All of Australia thought I was their heroine. I had tackled these guys that everybody was afraid of, because a lot of the girls went over there and got done in. In the paper they had this great big write-up (*laughs*)—"She loves us in spite of ourselves," with this huge color picture—explaining that Australia hadn't been extremely kind to me, but that I had eventually lucked out. It was a *great* victory because I had no agent, so I had no ten percent to pay. There was no sponsoring club owner. I wasn't farmed out to all the clubs for one fee. I got paid by everybody, and once the news got out, everybody wanted Teri Thornton, this dusty maid from Detroit (*laughs*) that took on the powers that be. I stayed over six months and came back with fourteen bags, after having left with three, and a suitcase full of money. (*Laughs.*)

JS: Where did you work upon your return to the States?

TT: I came back to the new Playboy Club in Chicago. Now, Dick Gregory was *hot* then; he opened the Playboy Club. Dick and I worked the same club back in the beginning of my career, I guess in 1957, in Chicago. At that time, his jokes were so sophisticated they went over everybody's head. They thought he wasn't funny. Then in 1961, all of a sudden he was the thing. So the Playboy Club was jumpin' with Dick Gregory and Teri Thornton. That started to make me a little bit more viable on the American scene. So after having stayed in Chicago maybe six months, I came back to New York in 1962.

JS: Shortly thereafter you signed with Dauntless. How did that association occur?

TT: I had married my second husband, Gene Kinney, by this time. Gene's walking up the street and he saw a friend of his, Tom Wilson,[4] who said, "You know, we're looking for somebody to record. We got this new label [Dauntless], but we don't have any artists. Do you think that your wife would be interested?" So he told me about it and I said, "Yes, if I can do 'Somewhere in the Night.' I'd be happy to record 'cause I *love* the theme."

JS: Who was behind Dauntless?

TT: Sid Frye. He didn't have that much experience with jazz, so he hired Tom Wilson. Wilson hired Larry Wilcox to do the arrangements. Larry was with the Sal Salvador band at the time, just coming from Denver. A green kid, but he had such uncanny talent for arranging.

JS: Was "Somewhere in the Night" a national best-seller?

TT: Yes, it was. But basically in New York is where most of it was sold. Right out of the Colony Record Shop. You could go down the street and hear "Somewhere in the Night" blasting out of loudspeakers, with the album just plastered all over the front door. Then I got a lot more recognition because three young ladies who worked for the record company as publicity people went to Johnny Carson of the *Tonight Show* and set that up for me. Here's my "biggg" chance. I get on the Johnny Carson show and I forget the lyrics. (*Laughs.*) Well, the arrangement was strange to me, first of all. I hadn't done the song outside the studio, and Skitch Henderson's arrangement was different from Larry Wilcox's arrangement. So I got lost in there someplace and I was standing with my hands on my face and saying, "This is being taped. I'm sure they're going to stop the show and do it again." Forget it. I recovered the last eight bars and did a *big* finish. The crowd went wild, and I went backstage and broke down. I said, "My career is over."

WE: Why wouldn't they retape?

TT: They just didn't do it in those days. They had a time slot and that was it. Of course, they also liked the drama. Because on the show that night was Phil Foster, the comedian; David Merrick, Broadway producer; and Siobhan McKenna, the actress, who was ticked with David Merrick for making a derogatory statement about actors and actresses, saying they were basically inhuman, you know, they were just so much fluff. So after she came backstage to comfort me, she went out and said, "Okay, is this human or not?" Merrick sat there embarrassed, and the crowd's going wild. I came out, and Johnny put his arm around me—he never touches anybody; he has an aversion to people touching him—but he puts his arm around me like a great old warm uncle and says, "Look, not only is your career not over, you'll be back next Wednesday." And he had me on the show maybe five times in three months.

WE: So this seeming disaster actually boosted your career?

TT: I would've been just any other singer if I'd done the song all the way through. But forgetting the words did something to trigger a lot of sympathy from the people, a lot of compassion. So Carson, being a very gracious man, helped take advantage of that for both of our sakes.

JS: The extended exposure on the *Tonight Show* must have opened up other dates.

TT: It did. I was working Basin Street East with Duke Ellington and Woody Herman. I was just gettin' all sorts of star treatment, which I did not know how to handle. Then I saw the gleaming eyes of the exploitive promoters say, "Oh, look what we got here." You know, these gentle souls—young performers—would come and the promoters would say, "Okay, now we want to help you manage your career." Their teeth were sharpened.

JS: How did you react?

TT: I really got frightened. Because the one man that I really trusted, Sid Bernstein, had gotten involved with the Beatles. He started to do concert promotions and got out of the booking business. And my husband, Gene, wanted to be my manager; he didn't really know that much about the business. So as things were building up, they were also falling down. I didn't know how the business ran, so I said to myself at that time, "I'm going to find out how it goes, and then I'll get back into it." You know, I'll know how to protect myself even if I don't have management. So that began another whole series of ups and downs. In the meantime things had taken off with the other guys that Tom Wilson, my A&R man, had.

JS: What other guys?

TT: The musicians that Wilson had acquired since going to Columbia, like Dion, and Bob Dylan, and Simon and Garfunkel. This was his roster. Teri Thornton was suddenly another type of commodity. Anyway, the people from Columbia caught one of my performances at a nightclub called the Bonsua. But Streisand played the club, and we got hired out of there into other big situations. I was on the supper-club circuit, so to speak. Columbia approached me, and RCA Victor; a lot of big record companies were coming to me then. And Sid Frye, who put out "Somewhere in the Night," wanted to manage me. Now, Sid Frye had Audio Fidelity records, and he recorded stuff like the Grand Prix and Dukes of Dixieland and Roz Cronin, the "limbo queen." So with "Somewhere in the Night" we really had a hit on our hands, and Sid Frye *then* decided, "Well, no, I'm not going to let this go." Columbia wanted to buy it, RCA wanted to buy it. He says, "I'll sell it to you a dollar a copy."

JS: Which was an exorbitant amount to pay?

TT: Yeah. While all that was going on, I was just kinda in limbo waiting for them to figure out who was going to wind up with "Somewhere in the Night." Of course, the other companies had to pass on the product. In the meantime, Frye was pretty ticked, because I didn't feel that he would be a good manager for me. He never gave me any money. I never got a dime off "Somewhere in the Night." Not one.

JS: After the release of the album, wasn't "Somewhere in the Night" excerpted to become a single?

TT: Yes, it was a 45. The other side was my first rock and roll effort, called "You Gotta Have Heart." I like eight-to-the-bar music. The Beatles were coming in—that beat was coming in—and I used it against "You Gotta Have Heart" because I thought it fit. They didn't want to do it because it was so rock-and-roll-y, and so poppish, and "We're going for jazz here." But I did it anyway.

JS: You said "they" didn't want to do it. Who was "they"?

TT: Tom Wilson. But mainly Larry Wilcox, 'cause he didn't want to try and arrange for it. I mean, he could arrange anything in the world he wanted to, but he just thought "rock and roll's beneath Teri Thornton."

JS: You were trying to show that you were versatile?

TT: That's right. I'd been trying to show that for years, and they'd been snatching each opportunity from under me. So I finally got a little toehold there.

WE: *Open Highway*[5] was your last recording. It is a gorgeous session with exciting arrangements.

TT: Just great arrangements! That should have been a hit album—twenty-eight pieces and the New York Symphony string section. But then we ran into the managerial problem; Gene was still trying to struggle with it. Nobody to run with the ball. Promoters said, "Until you have management that we approve of, we're going to release your stuff regionally. We're not going to do the gung-ho production."

WE: Which promoters?

TT: The promoters at Columbia, who have been used to kind of a cushy life of organizing their promotions to suit their lunches.

WE: They told you that *Open Highway* was only going to get a regional push?

TT: Yes. So when they released it regionally, it was a hit in Nova Scotia. Guys came down from Nova Scotia and said, "Look, we will put ourselves up in a hotel here and help you promote this record." And you know what the Columbia promoters said? "No. Go back to Canada. We know what we're doing."

WE: I can understand your disillusionment with the recording industry, but why did you leave the New York club scene and move to Los Angeles in 1966?

TT: I was basically called out there. Sid Bernstein told me he had this friend named Bobby Burns who was acting as an agent for GAC [General Artists Corporation], the agency that I was with. He set up something through the Playboy Club and the Copacabana for me to come out there and do a little work. I wound up staying for three years. I was going out trying to get gigs and raising my little boy, my third child. He was born in 1968 in Santa Monica. Gene was gone. I hadn't divorced him, but I had left him. He was in New York, and I'm in California. Because I had the opportunity on the West Coast, I just let that be the fresh start. I was thinking in terms of becoming entrenched in California society, but it didn't work out. Because, first of all, I'd begun to see the holes in what was going on out there, and I never could make friends except for the people who were from the East Coast. I just couldn't get into Hollywood.

JS: What do you mean by becoming "entrenched in California society"?

TT: The Rolls-Royce brigade. You know, they don't care if you have talent or not, as long as you had an image.

JS: You were trying to fit in to further your career?

TT: Yeah, and there were people offering me things. Like maybe Pierre Cossette, the big-time specials producer, is gonna do a special. Bobby Burns, my agent, would send me over there and say, "See what you can do with Teri Thornton." Then they began to think in terms of—like the boys did at Columbia—"Let's see if we can't make the black Ann Margaret out of her." Pierre Cossette and those people would start thinkin' in terms of "Well, where would she fit in? In this special she would have to play this part, so we'll have to pattern her after so and so. She would wear these kinds of clothes, and she would portray this image, and this is the material she would sing." And create a little diva for the moment. Disposable diva! (*Laughs.*)

JS: It must have been disheartening.

TT: You know, I said I can't take this. Just let me be Teri Thornton, whoever that is. They never could figure out who Teri Thornton should be. I looked like everybody. "Well, you look a little like Dionne Warwick; you look a little like Diana Ross." I said, "These girls are younger than I am. I was here first, so I don't get the connection."

JS: Were there other times when people tried to make you more commercial?

TT: Yes. When I got to California, I met a man named H. B. Barnum, who's a very big arranger for pop singers and R&B. He hired me to do some background work for Lou Rawls, 'cause he was arranging for Lou. He wrote a song called "Green Power," which is really rock and roll. (*Laughs.*) He did a great arrangement on it. We recorded it on a label called Mother's Records, owned by Jay Ward, who's the owner and founder of Bullwinkle. It went nowhere. There were only two people on Mother's Records, Spanky Wilson and myself. We put this "Green Power" out, went to all the conventions, and it didn't mean a thing. I was still Teri Thornton the jazz singer, you know, the ballad singer.

JS: When you returned to New York in 1969, were you glad to be back?

TT: I couldn't stand it here. It was so gray and dingy, and the atmosphere was just so laden with fear and poverty and change. So in 1971 I went back to Detroit. Early in '72 I went back out west for a year or two. I was back and forth between California and Nevada trying to reconcile my differences with my third husband, Kerry, for my son's sake. And trying to pull out roots if I'm going to go back to New York and stay. It was sort of a chaotic time.

WE: In the mid-1970s, you were known as Enid Ebony. Why the name change? Were you tired of your image?

TT: Yeah. I thought the name Teri Thornton was so worn and insignificant that I had to take on a new identity in order to get in front of the public again. Lou Fugazy—you know, from the limousine people, who was introduced to me by Larry Wilcox—he thought so, too. He thought he could do something with me. He said, "Maybe we can get you back out there again." Not realizing that if you just wait long enough, it eventually comes back to you. Lou sent me to the health spa to slim me down. I took on this new image, and he gave me a new name. He changed my name to Enid Ebony and had me doing stone-cold rock and roll, which sold just zilch. (*Laughs.*) They were all my compositions. I had a great group of young white players playing rock and roll behind me. (*Laughs.*) My fans said, "Uh-uh, we're not buying this." So that dropped like a lead balloon.

JS: Let's shift our attention to some of the forces that early on shaped your talent. How old were you when you first started exploring the piano?

TT: Probably four or five. Before my fingers could reach, I was tryin' to play boogie-woogie. I banged away until I could find something that sounded pretty good. I came up with a tune and my mother said, "Well, maybe we won't get rid of the piano after all."

JS: Did you get exposed to live music as a youngster?

TT: I had a good basic exposure to music, because if somebody was in town that my mother wanted to see—Lena Horne, Lennie Jordan, Lionel Hampton—she'd snatch me right off the school grounds and say, "We're going, 'cause I won't be here when you get out of school and I don't trust you runnin' around by yourself." I got to see all the greats.

JS: Was your mother an important role model for you?

TT: My mother, Burniece—she spelled it differently than anybody else—was a genius who never left Detroit. She was a published author, a schoolteacher, a poet, a play director. She had her own radio show; she had a great voice, and she sang pop requests. Then she got married and I was born. That settled her down a little bit. But then she was always involved in drama clubs, repertory theater, civic organizations. All of that perked up my musical ears as a child.

JS: Did you have much formal training at the piano?

TT: Oh, I'd say half a year.

JS: Was your mother your first teacher?

TT: It was my godmother, Mary Oriole Doctor. She was a Juilliard graduate, and the one who influenced my mother. She was a real cultural influence. They were teens together. My mother stayed home, and my godmother went off to college. She came back with all this academic knowledge and she said to my mother, "I'm pullin' you out of this hole. (*Laughs.*) We're gonna put some polish on you and send you out there." She got my mother to sing opera. My mother was a young woman at the time.

JS: How did you respond to the piano lessons?

TT: I didn't want to know about the fingering, I didn't want to know about playing "The Spinning Song" and "Fur Elise." I wanted to play boogie-woogie, so the lessons went by the way of Sandusky—meaning, you know, "down the road," "in the circular file." (*Laughs.*) I just kept listening and playing. My mother used to throw books at me when I would play boogie. "That's lowlife music; can't you play anything else?" It was great.

JS: What sparked your interest in jazz?

TT: I really hadn't heard that much jazz until I got to be around fifteen. The first thing that really turned me on to jazz was I heard Woody Herman do "Four Brothers." That was it. I said, "This is the music that I want to be involved with." I ran out and started buying blues and jazz records and driving Mama crazy. When Erroll Garner was playing with Charlie Parker—that was great stuff. "Now's the Time," that was my theme song. (*Starts to scat.*)

WE: Who were some of your piano influences?

TT: Oscar Peterson, Nat Cole. Nat Cole was my mentor. I loved Frankie Carle, Meade Lux Lewis. Those were my guys, you know. Avery Parrish. Of course, my hometowners [Barry] Harris and [Tommy] Flanagan. They made me feel like I had webbed fingers and I didn't want to play at all after I got through listening to them. I was afraid I would *never*—I still feel I could *never*—achieve what they do in that bebop. And I *love* bebop. I reach for it and sometimes it comes. (*Laughs.*) When it does, then I work with it and try and hone that into something of my own.

WE: Did piano come first, before you started singing?

TT: Way before the singing. Singing was always easier.

WE: When did you begin supplying your own piano accompaniment?

TT: Well, I guess it was fairly early for a minute. When I was in Chicago, it was easier to get work if you played for yourself, but I hated my playing 'cause it was just so unprofessional, as far as I was concerned. I let it go when I got to New York because there was always a good trio around. I just didn't think I had enough together under my fingertips. I just kept listening and woodshedding. I'd work it out at home, but I would never play in public. Not until the mid-'70s.

WE: Are you accompanying yourself at present?

TT: Well, I've been doing it lately. I have my own trio, but when I can find a good piano player, I get right up. I sit down when I do some of my original stuff, because unless they live with it as long as I have, they won't play what I want to hear. When it comes to those good standards, I like to stand up and be free enough to improvise and not have to worry about my playing.

WE: Is there a difference in your approach depending upon whether you're standing or sitting?

TT: Different ballgame altogether. It's like being two different people.

WE: What's different when you're accompanying yourself?

TT: First of all, you're all bent up down there—the diaphragm—so you're using different dynamics. And there's got to be a rhythmic blend between what you're executing vocally and musically. You don't want them running over one another. You're kinda creating two things at the same time.

WE: Do you prefer standing up?

TT: Yeah. There's total freedom.

JS: Who were your early vocal influences?

TT: Dinah Washington and Little Louie Jordan. When I was in elementary school, Louie Jordan was singing "Run Joe" and "There Ain't Nobody Here but Us Chickens." That was great stuff for me. I liked the rhythm. I've always been a rhythm nut. I played bass in intermediate school; I was a frustrated bass player in high school, so I use my left hand a great deal. It's starting to be my trademark now.

JS: Did you have people who schooled you as a vocalist in your younger years?

TT: Not really. I listened to all the good singers, and I picked up all the stuff that I thought would be good for me. I listened to Ella first with "Lady Be Good." There was Judy Garland, and then along came Sarah. Sarah Vaughan had just impeccable taste in delivery and material. And Joan Sutherland, the opera singer—her resonance, tone quality, and use of vibrato.

JS: What did you get from Judy Garland?

TT: Her delivery, her sincerity. She could make you cry just about at will, and I like to bring out the emotions in people because I think when they come to see me they want to bare something that they can't talk about. Yeah, Judy Garland. She was jazz. I mean, she could sing Dixieland, she could sing anything.

JS: Did you listen to Billie Holiday?

TT: Not until later. Not until I had had the blues a few times; then I could listen to Billie Holiday. She was entirely too mournful and maudlin to me at the time, because I was out tryin' to have a good time. But once you've got the blues, then you can listen to Billie and understand where she was coming from. I was made more aware of her importance through other jazz musicians who really had followed her and knew what she was about. She was a storyteller with the greatest phrasing of anybody I've ever heard. I couldn't hear that way back then. I was too naïve.

WE: You're also a composer, as you noted when you mentioned "Teri's Tune" at the beginning of our conversation. More recently you've won awards for your song writing.

TT: Well, I won the Billboard Song Writing Contest for "Voyager II" in 1992. That was just a fluke. I sent in two songs; "Voyager II" won first prize, and "Kiss Me Where It Hurts" got honorable mention. It was just for the heck of it that I sent them in.

WE: Do your songs draw on personal experiences?

TT: Well, some of them are from experiences; most of them are from out of the blue, you know, scenarios. Like, a friend of mine was in court one day, and a man was getting put away for statutory rape. He was messing around with girls who were underage. His excuses were always that they wore their mama's shoes. "I didn't know she was sixteen; she had on her mama's shoes." (*Laughs.*) So I wrote a song called "Mama's Shoes," and it has nothing to do with my experience whatsoever. "Voyager II" is about the NASA space camera. I got "Kiss Me Where It Hurts" from a special on television. It was a hospital scene, and all the nurses were making out with all the doctors. They had a break one time, and a doctor pulled this nurse into a back room and says, "Kiss me where it hurts." (*Laughs.*) So I made a song out of it.

WE: Do you write out your own compositions and arrangements?

TT: I can't write a note. I can't read a note. I am not an academic musician; I didn't study. It's all ear. Well, I shouldn't say that; it's a lie. I can read and write music, but it's so slow it's not even practical to me anymore. I hear so much faster.

JS: Have you spent a lot of time developing your craft as a vocalist?

TT: I do all the time. I'm singing all the time. There was a time when I was in California, I was drivin' a cab⁶ and I never stopped singing. I was singin' in the cab. (*Laughs.*) I'm always reaching for better improvisational lines, for a better tone quality; to be very melodic and resonant. Those things are important to me. If it isn't pleasing to my ear, I won't sing it for anybody. I guess it's the musician in me responding to the singing, rather than just being a singer.

JS: Why were you driving a cab?

TT: I was running from somebody when I drove the cab. I didn't want to appear in any club because I didn't want my name to show up in the paper because I was afraid of him. This man was a master at what he did. He was a genius, but he could have been Hitler because of his particular bent as far as destruction and violence, you know. I eventually wound up having to defend myself against him physically, and I almost killed him. There was a court case and all that business. In the meantime, I was on probation for kidnapping my kid, because my husband, Kerry, had gone off the deep end and I couldn't stand it. And he had custody of my child. Between kidnapping and attempted murder, there was not a lot going for me. So I drove a cab.

WE: When you kidnapped your child in Los Angeles, where did you take him? To Detroit?

TT: Yes. It was totally intentional. I set it up. I took him on his visiting day, and I just didn't bring him back.

WE: Since you were on probation, did you see the inside of a jail?

TT: Sure.

WE: How long were you locked up?

TT: Ten days altogether, between county and state.

WE: Where did this happen?

TT: Detroit. I was extradited from Detroit back to California. And I allowed that to happen because my husband did come and get my child. Kidnapped him back off the schoolyard.

WE: You were in jail due to a kidnapping charge?

TT: Well, that was the result. It started out with a speeding ticket. It was the Fourth of July weekend, the roads were crowded, and I was tryin' to get to work. There was a warrant out. When they pulled me over for the ticket and found out I had a warrant, then they had to see if the warrant had been lifted. There was a lot of calling back and forth and me sitting around in jail. They finally found out that, yes, the warrant was still in effect. So they booked me. They wouldn't lift the warrant, so I was transferred from one jail to another, then onto the plane.

WE: Back to California?

TT: Yes. But they did it with so much dignity, you know. They didn't put me in cuffs—none of that stuff. I wore civilian clothes out; you wouldn't have known what was going on.

JS: You've had some difficult times, but let's look at adversity from a different angle. Have you had problems in the music business either because you're a woman or because you're an African-American woman?

TT: Not the African-American, just the woman. Because I'd say I'm selling my talent, not my body, you know. They couldn't see past the body, and I would be just running all the time. I had to stay married just to have somebody to protect me.

JS: Are you serious?

TT: I'm serious. They do it now. And I think, "Do I get too old? (*Laughter.*) Is there any such thing?" No.

JS: Have you ever had problems with male musicians?

TT: They always respect me as one of them. Once I started to show my musicianship through the piano, if I sat down just for a minute, then I went into the sacred realm. I was no longer the one up front taking all their money. (*Laughs.*) I was qualified because I played an instrument. No, I *never* had a problem with them. It was management.

JS: What kind of harassment did you suffer from management?

TT: Well, managers sometimes want to go beyond the managerial contract. Some of them would expect you to curry favor and become a paramour, of sorts. I wasn't interested in that end of it. I got passed on a lot.

WE: Did you know other singers who didn't play the piano who had a problem?

TT: Yessss. Because before I played, I had the problem.

WE: How intense was the problem for you?

TT: To the point where while you're performing they would play the wrong music on you. Just to see if they could throw you off. Take a bridge to another song, stick it up there while you're trying to sing. (*Laughs.*) They played the bridge to "Open Highway" on "Somewhere in the Night." I became independent and developed my ear so they could play anything they wanted to play, I always knew where I was.

JS: Do you think that women in jazz make an aesthetic contribution that differs from what the men create?

TT: Yes. Absolutely. The female touch; the mother element. That nurturing part of it. The seeing it through, you know. A new concept coming from motherhood; coming from the trials of the unwed, of the single, of the divorced. They bring all that to the arena. Men leave that stuff outside. Also, the turnaround of women executives in the recording industry, of managerial hands-on. They haven't been there before.

JS: As more women emerge in the jazz world, do you see the potential for major changes from both artistic and business points of view?

TT: Yes. And for the better. They will bring fidelity back to the music. In the cultural whirlwind of the Clinton scandal—with the moral unrest—I think that the women will bring a leveling to all the upheaval. Sort of put guidelines and make music one of the tools to maybe subdue some of this rage that has been, you know, stirred for the last twenty-five years since women have decided to become independent.

JS: Teri, let's change the subject to your activities in recent times. Have you been gigging regularly since your return to New York in 1982?

TT: There were some steadies, and then there were times when there was nothing. You know, I'd spend all summer on the Jersey shore. I was at Pier 52 for a year and a half.

JS: Have you had any long-standing musical associations during this period?

TT: I was with Grover Mitchell's Band[7] for five years: 1985 to 1990. We went to Paris; it was a wonderful two weeks. We did a lot of stuff domestically, like the Grand Ole Opry. But then, you know, I can't say that we had the steady gigs that would keep you alive. So there was Barry Harris. He had the Jazz Cultural Theatre, and I'd play there on occasion. I worked the Stanhope Hotel in '84 for a good six to eight months. Kinda closed down the room—I should've picked Mickey Mantle's. (*Laughs.*) I had the two offers at the same time, and I opted for the Stanhope. I've had to declare not bankruptcy, but Chapter 13 on a couple of occasions.

JS: Do you take non-music jobs to try and make ends meet?

TT: Not really. If I did a job it was always related to music. I had a lot of help, too. I had friends who'd say, "Look, I know you need this." Most of the stuff that I have had happen to me has come through friends. Never the big agent, or the big manager. I've got a song cookin' now called "Something Came from Out of the Blue and Pulled Me Out of the Red."

WE: Before we wrap up, let me ask you about family matters. You're a grandmother, I understand?

TT: Yes. My oldest grandchild is seventeen. And my oldest child is forty-three. I wasn't with the oldest kids that much. My mother helped me out in that area. But the baby son, who's twenty-seven now, I took him everyplace. I wanted to prove that I could take him, expose him to all this variety of life, and still have him come out with his head screwed on right. And he's fine. The other kids are fine, too.

WE: If you had the chance, would you live any part of your life differently?

TT: I probably would never have gotten married and would never had kids. Now that they're here, I wouldn't give them up for anything in the world.

JS: Regardless, you are finally independent.

TT: I'm on my own now, yes. It's better late than never, but I still have the energy. I knew in the beginning it was gonna be a long haul. I prepared for it and just tried to keep the craft honed and the body in good shape. And the mind fairly sane. I don't need to be that sane. (*Laughs.*)

JS: The best is yet to come.

TT: That's what I'm looking forward to. I feel that, and I'm going for it. Whole hog this time.

Epilogue: Recorded March 25, 2000

WE: Let's talk about some of the events in your life since our first interview. Did you first meet Suzi Reynolds, your current manager, in 1995?

TT: I met her ten years before that, but I can't say that I remember—I probably had a couple of glasses of wine. We were attending a benefit for Melba Liston,[8] and Suzi said that she walked up to me and introduced herself. She wanted to know if she could have my phone number, and did I give lessons?[9] I probably exchanged numbers with her and told her to call me sometime. That's where it was left for ten years, until she ran into me in 1995 in the Blue Note. I was doing a benefit sponsored by the Jazz Foundation of America. She walked up again and said, "I think I can help you." I said, "I have an agent." She said "That's fine. I just want to help you." And I said, "Well, then we'll talk." The first of the year, we did. We've kind of been there ever since, you know.

WE: Did she just take over management of your career, or did she also become a personal friend?

TT: She became a personal friend. Because neither one of us had a great deal going at the time. She had other clients and they were working, but it was one of those things where she wasn't gettin' rich by any means. I basically was out of work.

WE: Gigs had dried up?

TT: Maybe they hadn't, but I didn't know where they were. There were certain gigs around town; you'd go after them, and you'd wind up on a waiting list of some kind. But, you know, I was finally able to shake things loose. She took me to Arthur's. That was the beginning.

JS: How did you wind up back in a recording studio?

TT: There was a man from Switzerland that wanted to set up a branch office for his record company over here. Suzi brought him into Arthur's; he heard me and decided he wanted to record me.

JS: When was that recording session?

TT: The summer of 1997.

JS: That date resulted in *I'll Be Easy to Find*?

TT: Yes. That ultimately Verve bought. I was diagnosed with cancer in September of '97, so everything was put on hold after that.

WE: Did you suspect something was wrong before the diagnosis?

TT: I had symptoms. But we had looked and looked, and nobody could attribute them to anything serious. A doctor finally traced them where they lived.

WE: Did you quickly have to adopt a hospital mode of existence?

TT: Absolutely, and ever since. I came immediately to the doctors. They started aggressive treatment. I had thirty-eight radiations and two chemos right in the very beginning. The upshot is, after the surgery I knew I needed to do that contest.[10] I knew if I didn't do it, I would lose a great deal.

JS: Suzi entered your name into the Monk competition?

TT: She came to me and asked me first. I thought she was out of her mind, and I told her so. I said, "I don't think I'll have the strength to do it." Because I had the surgery June 3rd [1998] and this was, you know, the first or second week in July she's telling me this. She said, "Well, it's not gonna come off until September." And I said, "Well, I still don't think I'll have the strength, but at least it'll give me something to look forward to." And I knew there was an age limit[11] and figured there was no way that I was even eligible. When I found out they changed it, I said, "Why not?" (*Laughs.*)

JS: Obviously you felt stronger as the time approached.

TT: Strong enough. I wouldn't have done it if I hadn't really felt like I could do it. I mean, it wasn't "I'll do it if it kills me." It was really that I thought I could do it. I thought it would be a *marvelous* thing for Teri Thornton to win. It was a thing where winning can mean so much, whereas not even trying counts for nothing. So this is my middle name, "the cockeyed optimist." (*Laughs.*)

WE: How was the competition organized?

TT: There were three hundred in the beginning. It narrowed down to fifteen. I was part of that fifteen. Then it's live at the Blues Alley[12] for the semi-final. Out of the fifteen, they picked five, and then we came back to compete for the finals at the Baird Auditorium, part of the Smithsonian. That took about five days.

WE: After you finished your performance at the finals, how long did you have to wait to hear the results?

TT: Well, it was a good hour. I was standing there shaking. Billy Dee Williams was holding on to my elbow. I couldn't sweat. I had none. (*Laughs.*) I was tense. Oh boy, I was tense. We needed to win. Simple as that. We needed a door-opener.

JS: Did you know going in that Verve had an interest in you?

TT: I knew nothing about Verve at the time. In fact, Verve was there, and their statement to me was, you know, the same old thing: they were looking for young, fresh talent. Someone they can get a lot of years out of. They came to see Jane Monheit, who was the second-prize winner.

WE: After the competition, you had club dates in Boston and New York. Any other projects on the horizon?

TT: I was supposed to go out with an all-star band at the end of April or June. I canceled everything. They've got all this stuff that's wonderful lined up for me. These people hopefully will be there when I'm a lot stronger. I've got no voice now. I've got to put on some weight. I gain ten or fifteen pounds, then we'll start to talk. I weigh 98 pounds. When I checked into the facility, I weighed 168.

WE: How are you feeling?

TT: Well, I'm not dying, even though I might look like it. That's the funny thing about it. They're giving me shots to work up my appetite, and they're doing pretty good. I've got a refrigerator full of junk. (*Laughs.*) I just lost the hair in the last thirty days or so.

JS: What type of cancer were you diagnosed with?

TT: It was bladder cancer. They took out the bladder. They got rid of the cancer and the bladder all at once.

JS: Why are you still undergoing chemo treatment?

TT: Well, I had phlebitis in my right leg. Now it's normal. They're saying I probably really don't need another one, and then my voice will come back as soon as I regain weight. They're reversing all the stuff that has been wrong with me for the last forty-five years, *one by one*. They just took me off my heart medicine; I don't need it anymore.

WE: When we met you in 1995, you were desperate to rebuild your career. Do you feel now that a lot of those dreams have come true?

TT: Yes. I do. I also feel like all of this is to put me in a better position to enjoy and to perpetuate. Because a lot of this would have gone unnoticed, and I could have got caught out on the road with some really serious illnesses.

WE: So your hospitalization, as far as you're concerned, is . . .

TT: . . . a blessing in disguise.

WE: Do you have dreams that remain unfulfilled?

TT: Not really. I mean, my dreams are simple dreams. First of all, when I think of from whence I came, nobody ever knew that I would do any of this. I've crammed I don't know how many lifetimes into this one. I've got three great kids; I've got six great grandkids. I've had a career with some recognition. I've been able to maintain a private life without a whole lot of trouble. So many, many blessings.

WE: Do you want to perform again?

TT: Oh, absolutely. I love a good audience that you can turn on.

WE: You'd even get back on the road, maybe with that all-star band?

TT: Sure. I'm a road rat to the core. (*Laughs.*)

Devil May Care. Fantasy OJCCD-1017-2 (1961, reissued 1999).

Teri Thornton Sings Somewhere in the Night. Dauntless DM4306 (1963). (Unfortunately out of print, but this wonderful record is worth searching for in used vinyl bins.)

*Open Highway. Koch Jazz KOC-CD-8589 (1963, reissued 2001). (The original album is augmented by several singles that display Thornton venturing into country, bossa nova, and R&B.)

I'll Be Easy to Find. Verve 314 547 598-2 (1999).

Notes

1. Dauntless Records.

2. *Way Out,* Johnny Griffin Quartet, 1958; Riverside (Fantasy).

3. *Devil May Care,* 1961; Riverside Records.

4. In charge of Artist and Repertoire at Dauntless.

5. Recorded and released 1963; Columbia Records. Reissued in 2001, Sony Music Entertainment Inc., and Koch Jazz.

6. 1977–1979.

7. The Basie ghost band.

8. Jazz trombonist Melba Liston had suffered a paralyzing stroke.

9. At the time, Suzi Reynolds was a professional jazz singer who had recently moved to NYC.

10. The 1998 Thelonious Monk Institute of Jazz Vocal Competition, held in Washington, D.C.

11. Prior to the 1998 competition, the age limit was thirty.

12. A Washington, D.C., club.

Cassandra Wilson

Cassandra Wilson

Many critics cite Cassandra Wilson as the most important jazz vocalist to emerge in the 1990s. Wilson's output of thirteen albums as a leader and forty as a principal contributor feature her unorthodox vocal interpretations in addition to her talents as a songwriter. Because Wilson has her vocal finger in so many pies, she enjoys an audience diverse in age and race.

Cassandra Wilson was born in Jackson, Mississippi, on December 4, 1955, to a father who was a professional jazz musician and a schoolteacher mother who loved the Motown sound. Under their shepherding, she dutifully took piano lessons, but it was the guitar that finally earned her affection. Among Wilson's early musical influences were Betty Carter and Joni Mitchell. As a teenager, she combined playing lead roles in high school musicals with work in R&B and top-twenty cover bands.

Wilson graduated from Jackson State University with a degree in mass communications, and in 1981 she moved to New Orleans, where she took a staff job at a local television station. After hours, she immersed herself in the Crescent City music scene until 1982, when, encouraged by trumpeter Woody Shaw, she relocated to New York City.

In 1985, Wilson signed with JMT, a German label associated with the M-Base collective. After two eclectic collaborations with saxophonist Steve Coleman, she caught the attention of the critical press in 1988 with *Blue Skies*, a somewhat eccentric but memorable rendering of standards, with support that included drummer Terri Lyne Carrington.

In 1993, with her reputation in rapid ascent, she signed with Blue Note. The kaleidoscopic album that ensued, *Blue Light 'Til Dawn*,[1] created a stir as it defied categorization. It garnered rave reviews from critics while earning Wilson a following far beyond core jazz listeners. Her next recording, *New Moon Daughter*,[2] heightened her image as a synthesizer of musical genres, and won a Grammy in 1997. On this album,

Wilson's world music sensibility is showcased as she incorporates the Irish bozouki, accordion, and resophonic guitar[3] to accompany vocal makeovers of tunes long associated with country-western or rock and roll.

The long-shadowed low register that Wilson's singing voice mostly occupies is utterly distinctive and alternately comforting and chilling to witness. Her phrasing is languid, with a tendency toward bent vowels and elongated consonants that express a sultriness coaxed by rural blues. Her accompaniment is often unconventional and occasionally astringent; one of her strengths is the effortless way she insinuates her voice into the interplay among supporting instruments.

At the time of this interview, Wilson was touring as a featured vocalist in Wynton Marsalis's *Blood on the Fields.* More recently she has returned to her roots with the highly touted 2002 CD *Belly of the Sun,*[4] which was recorded in the Mississippi Delta with indigenous musicians. Cassandra Wilson's record of finishing at or near the top of the *Down Beat* Critics Polls since 1996 attests to her considerable skills as a musician, but perhaps the defining moment in the mainstream sanctioning of her career occurred in 2000, when *Time* magazine named her "America's Best Singer."

Recorded October 20, 1996

WE: Cassandra, let's start by comparing Anita O'Day's version of "Skylark,"[5] which I just played for you, with your recent recording[6] of the same tune. If I might venture a thought, O'Day's sounds very outgoing, public, if you will, while yours strikes me as more private, like a diary entry.

CW: I would guess that this is around the beginning of her career? Perhaps the '40s?

WE: The recording is from 1941.

CW: It has that kind of a "lightness of being" about it. It's kinda sweet and innocent. There's a certain naïveté in it, and I'm in my middle part. (*Laughter.*) I don't know if I want to say how old I am. But I'm probably older now than she was when she performed that. My version *is* a lot more intimate. The song is one of those songs for me. Whenever I sing it, I feel as if I'm tapping into something that's taken me a minute to get to. It's a kind of "jaded vulnerability." You know, those two words don't go together, but that's what I feel when I'm singing this song. It's like, okay, I've been through these love experiences, and yet I'm still hopeful and still thinking that possibly there *is* someone out there for me. I think that's maybe what you hear in my interpretation.

WE: So it could be like a diary entry.

CW: Oh, yeah. Definitely. Definitely.

WE: Do you take each one of the songs that you sing and personalize it to that extent?

CW: You have to internalize it, I think; you have to personalize it. If you don't do that, I don't think you're being true to the tradition of the music. I think you have to absorb it and then place yourself inside of the song. What does the song mean to you? In order to get across to people the emotion of the song, it's very important to identify with it.

WE: Let's talk about selection of material. Some vocalists are keenly aware of choosing songs that will advance their identity as a performer. Do you do this?

CW: Oh, I don't enter into a project thinking about choosing songs that are going to suit my personality. I think I'm just the opposite. It's hard to describe the process, but I look at songs as choosing me, instead of the other way around. It's not really an ego trip where "Oh, this song is going to sound great the way *I* sing it." I listen to the signs: if songs come back to me, if they keep popping up, if someone keeps mentioning a particular song, then I'll investigate that song. Or if it sticks in my memory. That's the way I choose a song. I think about the song itself and then play with structure—just have a good time with it. That's the first thing, to find the spaces in that particular song that excite me, and that's when the work begins.

WE: Is the way the words go together in a song important to you? Does a lyric have to be smart, witty, or have a turn of phrase that appeals to you for you to sing it?

CW: Yeah, sure. All of those things. But the most important thing about a lyric is its musicality. That's what makes lyrics lyrics, and prose and poetry prose and poetry. They're two different things. A lyric can be strong poetically yet not mesh with the music, not have a life of its own musically. I think that's just as important as the content. There has to be a musicality, a flow inside of the lyric.

WE: How do you approach writing your own lyrics?

CW: Most of the lyrics I write, I write for myself. Sometimes it's just working out some kind of problem that I have, or an idea that I have. This is how I feel about relationships, or death, or God. You know, universal themes.

WE: Do you think your writing has become more focused over the years?

CW: Yes, it has. I don't find myself as scattered. I think I have been a bit abstract in just pulling lyrics from out of the air and throwing them with some music and saying, "Oh, this sounds good; I'll do that." (*Laughs.*) I take more time with the lyrics that I write now. There's more craftsmanship involved in creating a lyric; I think there's more continuity in the lyric.

WE: Has the literary tradition of the South been an influence on your approach to a lyric?

CW: Perhaps unconsciously. I guess there's no conscious effort to make a connection between that tradition and what I'm doing, but perhaps it seeps in there anyway. My mother was a teacher for forty years, and she turned me on to Shakespeare when I was twelve. She was really big on reading, and I've been reading since I was a toddler. I'm sure that kind of sensibility about lyrics stems from that.

WE: With reference to the South, I have a question about the longstanding African-American tradition of "Gumbo Ya Ya." As I understand it, Gumbo Ya Ya is a conversational stew, a way of reaching wisdom that is collective, non-linear, and is, in its form, reminiscent of Dixieland. With such an emphasis on community, how do you think the concept of the soloist managed to emerge in jazz?

CW: I think it's just the natural evolution of the music. I think it's just two sides of the same coin. There's a collective effort in the music, and then there's the individual effort. Sometimes they come together, and sometimes they're weighed differently, you know, depending on the context. But there's a strong tradition of "collective individuality" (*chuckles*)— if that makes sense—inside of the music. Being able to improvise at the same time with other people is something that I think is very unique to jazz. And, of course, there's lots of earlier evidence of that. I don't know if it's as strong now as it was back at the inception of the music. But musicians still grapple with that—the collective sound—and how the individual expresses himself inside of that collective sound.

WE: So it's an issue that hasn't been resolved?

CW: Oh, no, it's always going to be an issue with musicians.

WE: In terms of a collective sound, talk about your experience working with AIR.[7]

CW: I don't remember (*laughs*) much of what I did. I have to go back and listen to it; a lot of it's difficult for me to listen to. I think I need probably some more years to go back to that and try to figure out exactly what happened. But being with Henry Threadgill in that context was a part of a period in my musical life when I was searching. I was always attracted to the avant-garde, and particularly Henry's brand of avant-garde—which, you know, has got all of the elements in it. It's got the blues; there's a strong blues foundation in it. It still is very enigmatic to me. I jumped inside of it and tried to imagine myself in it and dealt with it. I guess I will have to let other people judge what kind of work that was. But I'm very proud of it. We did one album, and that was *New Air; Air Show No. 1.*[8] I don't know if there's gonna be a "2" or a "3." (*Laughs.*) We did some touring in Italy and Germany. Then we recorded the album, and the pieces were extraordinary. Yeah, I really learned a lot from that time with him.

WE: Continuing on the theme of synthesizing the polarities of the individual and the collective, let's talk about your work with Steve Coleman. Were you deliberately attempting to mesh your voice with the M-Base[9] instrumentalists?

CW: M-Base was a great moment for me musically, because it was when I started to come into my own as far as chops go. Really being able to deal with the music the same way that the musicians were. Steve Coleman gave me a lot of confidence to do that. I spent a lot of time studying with him, and we used to get together with [trumpeter] Graham Haynes. They would do Gillespie and Parker stuff, or Miles and Parker stuff—you know, the solis. I would just listen; sometimes I'd imitate, and sometimes he'd try to get me to start to transcribe the solos. I never got into it to that extent, but that was the beginning of really absorbing that kind of improvisation. For a vocalist, that's a really tough thing to tackle, and that was the beginning of our relationship. I was introduced to the mixed-meter thing through him, and that was the beginning of really creating that whole other repertoire, that whole other approach to the music, turning it upside down. And it really was still an extension of the AACM[10] and the other group from out of St. Louis.

WE: BAG?

CW: Yeah, BAG.[11] It was an extension of that. I think what we were doing was incorporating more the music of our time into it, you know, James Brown, the Funkadelics, the Motown sound. All of that was being thrown into the bag, and it was *really* an exciting time musically. You know, all of the approaches that each *one* of us had—[pianist] Geri Allen and her own way of attacking it; [guitarist] Jean-Paul Bourelly, [bassist] Lonnie Plaxico was involved, Graham Haynes, as I said before. That's a long story. (*Laughs.*) That's a big block of time to think about.

But that was, I guess, the group of people that I bonded with, you know, most during my entire time in New York. And I felt very comfortable. It was a place for vocalists to be, and I couldn't really step inside of the Wynton Marsalis crowd because they weren't really into vocalists. They didn't really respect the vocal tradition. You know, I think they respected it, but it was like, ah, "little girl, nice, cute girl singer." Whereas Coleman and those guys were really about relearning what the voice does, and Steve would always question me about my approach to singing. I often wondered why is this guy who is this incredible musician *so* obsessed with my process, and I understood that he really respected that process. It was a very intuitive process when we first met, and more and more I gained knowledge of the language of the music and pretty soon we were able to communicate really well on theory, on structure, on how to create wild sorts of scenarios for songs.

WE: Do you see yourself currently as extending what you did with M-Base at that time?

CW: I think, yeah, I am extending what I did with M-Base. The place of the voice inside the music may be a *little* different now. I think it is more in the foreground, but there's still that sensibility of being a part of an ensemble. Not being a voice that's just sticking out completely separate from the textures, but inside of the textures.

WE: Would that be more difficult to do with a big band?

CW: No, I'd love to do a big band recording. *My* idea of a big band recording. (*Laughter.*) No, I'd like to play around with that idea. I think working with Wynton Marsalis on *Blood on the Fields* has really gotten me accustomed to that. It's just like this big block of sound that you're dealing with. I've never had to do that before, and being able to manipulate that kind of environment is something I would like to figure out.

WE: Preceding M-Base, the AACM was devoted to advancing what they called "Great Black Music." Do you relate more to the strict jazz tradition or to the more expansive, AACM-like approach?

CW: I think it's all the same thing. I think we just have different names for it, that's all. The music is really one big river, and we have tributaries of that river, but it all comes from the same source. I've always looked at music that way. I think the AACM just represents a specific time and a specific group of musicians, but the music that they have created and fostered over the years, it's all related, you know.

WE: So instead of being a modern jazz musician, in the mold of Gillespie and Parker, your eclecticism makes you postmodern, correct?

CW: (*Laughter.*) I don't know if I think that hard about what I do, to be honest with you. I don't even use those words, "modern" and "postmodern." I hear people use "postmodern," and I'm supposed to be somewhere up in that, but when they use it I have no idea what they're talking about. (*Laughs.*) I don't really think about it.

WE: And there is no reason why you should. However, part of postmodern theory has to do with the death of the author, including the notion of originality. And yet when you were working with Steve Coleman, he purportedly urged you to find your own voice, to innovate.[12] That's a very modern concept, the self-conscious process toward becoming your own person.

CW: There's a paradox in that. I think in becoming your own musical person, it's about surrendering. That's what I learned finally, that you can't push the process of becoming an individual. It has to be something that evolves, and the more self-conscious you are, the harder it is for the making of that voice to happen. I think that's something that I learned, especially with these last two projects. I had been trying so hard to create a sound with the tail end of the M-Base movement. You know, I was trying so hard to still fit inside of that context that I really was not able to find a context for myself until after that. I didn't see the forest for the trees, I guess—when I was inside of it. There was all this music that was being made, and there were times when I felt that I was lost inside of it. I could never *really* understand why I still felt that way, and I think it was because I wasn't learning the lesson that M-Base was initially teaching, which is that you can play with it all. There shouldn't be any dogma attached to it; there shouldn't be any correct way of doing it. But I stayed inside of that context because it was familiar, you know, lots of horns, the piano still there. You know, the very complex mixed-meter thing with maybe people being in two different meters inside of the same group. I was so involved in that that I couldn't really hear my voice after awhile. It was not until I peeled all those layers away in *Blue Light* [13] that I began to actually hear myself, and I also retained some of what I had learned from that experience in M-Base. I could now do it without the physical trappings being there. I could now abstract and play around with meter without it being so exact and so obvious and so apparent. I could do it inside of another context.

WE: Let me ask you about *Blue Skies*,[14] which was a set of standards. Was that an attempt to make you more accessible?

CW: It was probably a little bit of that. It's like come on, come back in, show us what you actually can do. What's the foundation? And I took the challenge. I also thought to myself that I really wanted to do standards. That I really wanted to do an album of standards with Mulgrew Miller and Terri Lyne Carrington and Lonnie Plaxico. I had them in mind from the very beginning; those were the people that I wanted to work with. It's fun when you get together with people like that.

WE: Do you feel that *Blue Light 'Til Dawn* and *New Moon Daughter* are more mature, and contain more of your identity than the JMT recordings?

CW: Well, I couldn't say that, because my identity was in the JMT recordings. It was just another time; it was my identity at that time. I feel more confident about what I'm doing now, and I feel more relaxed with myself, so much so that I am able to interact with an audience more. And I think that's really important for a singer. I think I felt distance from an audience because I was so busy trying to be obtuse for a long time (*laughter*), or trying to be really complicated or really smart, you know, with the music. I think that when I came to *Blue Light,* I let a lot of that go. I really, you know, just sat back and let it all happen. I think it was just a part of my maturation, learning how to perform for an audience. You know, for a jazz singer, it takes a long time. It's not something that you instantly have. It's a process. I feel that at this age I'm finally beginning to *really* connect with an audience, and it's much sweeter now for me. It was a lot more painful before, and I think a lot of times the music was set up so that I didn't have to give up so much. It was kind of protecting me from giving up so much, because it was *so* sophisticated and it was *so* complex that I really didn't have a chance to open up.

WE: So you were hiding in the music, to some extent?

CW: Yes. Hiding in the music.

WE: I've been very careful to use the term "vocalist" during this conversation, since it's my understanding that you are not happy when people refer to you as a "singer."[15]

CW: (*Laughter.*) That's been blown way out of proportion.

WE: That's what I wanted to know. I prefer not to be paranoid anymore, if you don't mind.

CW: No, not at all. (*Laughs.*) I use the word "singer" occasionally. I started that really to communicate to musicians. It was a word, a buzzword, that I wanted to use to let them know: "Okay, this is a musician who happens to sing." That's really where all of that started, so that when you walk in the door, they don't have this preconceived notion of what you're capable of.

WE: Referring again to Anita O'Day, she was an early feminist who refused to wear gowns and be dolled up. Instead, she wore a band uniform. That was because, I believe, she wanted to be thought of as a vocalist rather than as "the girl singer." Did you know about that?

CW: No, I didn't know about that. Yeah, I can definitely get with that. That makes perfect sense, because you can't enter into that world if you are all dolled up. It's really hard to enter into that world, and I always wanted so desperately to be inside of that world, not merely being an ornamentation, but to be inside in the trenches with the musicians dealing with the music.

WE: Let's talk a bit about your younger days. What kind of musical environment did your parents provide as you were growing up?

CW: Well, my first experience with music was through my father's collection of records. He was a big Miles Davis fan, and the first album I heard was *Sketches of Spain*.[16] I remember being fascinated by the album cover, and the music. I remember the album cover to this day, and its style.

WE: Was it the single figure of Miles, or the bands of ocher and red?

CW: Ocher—I love that word for yellow.

WE: You like ocher?

CW: Yeah. I paint a little bit. Well it was odd, that figure of the single musician with an instrument; there was always a lot of mystery surrounding the music. My father worked a lot then. He was a musician, and I was fascinated with his life and the way that he would dart in and out of the house. (*Laughs.*) The musicians would come over, and they'd be hanging out. There was like a private language that they had that was really fascinating to me. I was a little girl, so I couldn't enter into that world, but my father would give me sneak peeks at it from time to time. He'd take me to a gig occasionally. He would share with me his albums. He wouldn't so much talk about the music as just sit and listen to it. It was my mother's idea for me to start taking piano lessons, because I was so fascinated with music. I was, like, about six years old, and they got a piano for me and I started taking piano lessons. I think my mother wanted me to get some instruction and learn about classical music, European classical music. I took lessons for seven years. My father really never got involved in that; he just watched. He would come to the recitals, and he was really proud of me and everything.

I got tired of the music lessons after seven years; I got tired of the paper, really. My father had a lot of guitars around the house, so I picked up a guitar and I was playing around with it. He said, "Do you want to learn how to play the guitar?" I said, "Yeah, will you teach me?" He said "No." (*Laughs.*) He had these Mel Bay Method Books and he just said, "Here, teach yourself." And I think it was really interesting to me the way he did that. He realized that I had had enough of a certain way of learning music, and I think he wanted to rekindle that initial spark that I had. I think that's why he encouraged me to just pick up the guitar and play it. You know, get what you can from these books, but just play the guitar. Become intimate with the instrument without any formal instruction. So there was a balance for me. One side I had the formal instruction with piano, and then, on the other side, it was just like this very intuitive approach to the guitar that I still have. I have knowledge of the strings and what notes the strings are, and if we're in standard tuning I can tell you basically what the chords are. Once I get out, once I create a tuning, I have no idea where I am. It's all by the ear.

WE: With all that background in music, why did you choose mass communications as a college major?

CW: I think at that point I didn't want to have any more lessons. I think I didn't want to study music in school because I didn't want to lose the joy that I had for it. I'd seen a lot of students on campus who were involved in the music department, and they were all really very stuffy, and I just didn't feel the need to do that. I actually wanted to pursue another love of mine, which was filmmaking. But at that time, at Jackson State University, they had a concentration in radio and television, not so much in film. So I got into the television aspect of it.

WE: Nonetheless, did you maintain a sense that music eventually would play an important role in your life?

CW: I just knew music would always be there, because it had been my life. But at that time, my mother—of course, you know what mothers do; they say, "Listen, I don't think you're going to be able to make it out there as a musician or as a singer. You've got to have something to fall back on." That's the phrase, "fall back on." I took her advice; and I agreed with her. I couldn't really envision at that time becoming—I didn't want to pursue R&B, and jazz was kind of a—God, it's kind of an ethereal-type thing, you know. It's not something I felt you could make a living at. From my vantage being in Jackson, Mississippi, I didn't see it at that time. I didn't imagine it, so I studied mass communications with the idea that I would get involved in television, and that would be my bread and butter.

WE: Looking deeper into your roots, your grandmother was an important figure in your life. Do you have any special memories of her you care to relate?

CW: There's one that I always like to tell about my grandmother singing in church. I would stand beside her, and she couldn't carry a note in a bag. But she would sing as if her life depended on it. She had this incredible passion when she sang, and I would just—you know, I was a kid—and I would just sit back and look at her. I think I caught a lot of that. She didn't care whether she was singing in tune; she came from out of the tradition of the Holy Rollers and the Sanctified Church. They had more of an African-based religion, a brand of Christianity with the ring shouts—there's more dancing and there's music. They were, I think, perhaps closest to the old African religions. They probably retained more of those religions than anybody else. And still Christianity, but the deities didn't go anywhere, they were there still, just with different faces, different names. She came from that tradition. My parents started going to a Presbyterian church. So these are black folks when they're beginning to sing out of the hymnals and they're singing the usual, what is it the Presbyterian, the Methodist, those things they sing: (*sings*) "Praise God from whom all blessings flow," you know, that kind of thing. And so they're singing that, but she's singing the music still with the same kind of energy she would have been using in another context.

WE: She's singing in the Presbyterian church as if she were back with the Holy Rollers?

CW: (*Laughter.*) Yeah, yeah.

WE: She must have gotten stares.

CW: Oh, yeah, she did! Because she would sing so loud and so out of tune. It was the Holy Spirit, I believe it, it was the Holy Spirit. It would catch her.

WE: Has the passion of your grandmother been translated into a sacred underpinning for your own work?

CW: Oh yeah, definitely.

WE: How do you communicate this orientation to a listener?

CW: The release being surrendering, or being a vessel. I find that when I do sing in the studio there's a trance-type thing that I go into. I know it's a trance; it's hard to talk about it. You can't really describe it other than it's just being able to let go and allow the music to happen. What's the word I'm looking for, not being self-conscious?

WE: Kind of an alpha state?

CW: Yeah. An alpha state. You feel just as if you're there but you're not there.

WE: What happens when you're performing in front of an audience?

CW: Oh! It *really* happens then. It happens more.

WE: Why is that? Because of the energy from the audience?

CW: Yeah. Because then the audience is a part of the ritual. The more people you have that are connected to that, whether they know it or not, they're giving up energy to that moment. When you get people together inside of an auditorium, a closed space, where you have a control over the environment, the variables, then you are able to connect.

WE: Would it be accurate to say that when you perform, you want to create a sacred atmosphere?

CW: Yeah. I believe that music is the language of the spirit. I think it's the way that we can all communicate with one another, and we all communicate with that realm.

WE: Let's return to the subject of Miles Davis. [We listened to "Saeta," from *Sketches of Spain,* 1959–1960, Columbia.] Was Miles a major influence?

CW: Definitely. I think he's been the strongest influence in my musical life. It's funny; I didn't really realize it until a few years ago. That this is some of the first music that I heard as a child, and I didn't put it together. I didn't connect the dots until recently, that Miles has always been there and I've always been attracted to him and I've always just instantly connected with his approach to music. Not his personality (*laughs*), not his lifestyle, but the way that he spoke through his horn. I've always connected with it and loved it and cherished it.

WE: Did you know Miles?

CW: I didn't really meet Miles—I opened for him in Chicago at the Chicago Jazz Festival. That was the year he passed away. I remember standing in the corridor and looking at him in the distance. He had on his glasses, and I thought that he was looking at me, but I couldn't tell. He was leanin' up against the wall, and he had his horn in his hand. I thought maybe he gestured to me somehow, but I don't know if he did. I couldn't say that he did. And I was too intimidated to walk up to him and say, "Hi, how you doin'?" But I did have this real funny dream about him three or four years later. I dreamt that he and I were hanging out in Chicago. He had on this beautiful trench coat, and we were trying to get from some place in Chicago to another place. I said, "Miles, let's catch this taxi that's comin' up." He said (*imitating Miles's hoarse voice*), "No, I'm not going to get in that car." (*Laughter.*) He said something about teaching me, and, you know, that was the dream. But he said he wouldn't get in a car, and I took that as a sign not to get into certain cars. (*Laughter.*) You know, use my intuition more.

WE: If Miles was your primary musical influence, who comes in second?

CW: I couldn't go there.

WE: Then it just opens up?

CW: Yeah, it just opens up.

WE: Didn't you think you were Charlie Parker reborn when you were first starting out?[17]

CW: (*Laughter.*) I said that to Steve to go one up on him one day in conversation. He was teasing me about me not being able to sing "Donna Lee" correctly at a jam session, and I teased him back. I said, "Well, you say you're into Bird, but you're not bench-pressing changes the way that Bird would." And he said, "I've been studying Bird all my life. I know Bird, I know Bird." I said, "Well, I *am* Bird." (*Laughter*.)

I didn't really believe that, but I imagine that since Bird died in March of '55 and I was born in December of '55—oh, God! I just dated myself—that's like ten months of gestation. Time for a spirit to leave and then come back in. It was a joke, but there was a period when I was heavily into Bird. There's also a period when I was heavily into Betty Carter as a result of getting into Bird—or was it the other way around? I think at first it was Betty that I really got into, and then I decided to go further back and check out Bird. I mean, note for note, the shape of the solos. Yeah, there was a period of that, there was a period where I was into Ella Fitzgerald.

WE: So you were scatting more then?

CW: Yeah. You know, having that kind of articulation. I was really into it. There was a period for Sarah Vaughan; there was a period for Billie Holiday; there was a period for Nancy Wilson; there was a period for Joni Mitchell. Among instrumentalists, there was a period for Monk. I would just sit and listen to Monk all day. One of the first albums I heard was *Monk's Dream*.[18] I remember the cover for that one, too.

[At this point, we listened to "I Could Write a Book" by Betty Carter, from *The Audience with Betty Carter*, recorded 1979; Verve Records, John Hicks on piano.]

CW: Oh, this is one of my favorite albums. (*She sings along*.) I can sing this song exactly the way she does. I used to. It's way out of my range, though. John Hicks!

WE: You once commented in a *Down Beat* "blindfold test"[19] about the way Betty Carter "curves" her music.

CW: (*Laughs*.) See, that's me, talking in shapes again. I talk about music in shapes and colors.

WE: When you use the term "curves," are you referring to Carter's treatment of pitch?

CW: Yeah.

WE: In certain places it sounds like she is actually going flat.

CW: Yeah. She is.

WE: Purposefully?

CW: Yes.

WE: Is that part of a jazz vocal tradition, or is that totally Betty Carter?

CW: I think it's totally Betty. I think that's what Betty brought to the music. It's just this reckless abandon when it comes to pinpointing a note. A note for her is bigger than a little dot. It's like, there's this side of the note and then there's that side of the note. It's a thick thing. You know, it's not just a single dot that has to sit in the middle of some place in A 440.[20] I've heard many instrumentalists do the same thing. I think it's difficult to get with the human voice, though. I think it's harder for people to accept; it's harder for their ears to accept when you have a singer who bends like that and really stretches a note without comin' back. She'll stretch it and she won't come back. She'll make it flat and she won't rectify it. She just lets it stay there.

Some people would say she just has a problem with intonation. It never bothered me, and I'm pretty fierce about that. I can tell when things are out of tune and when it *annoys* me, you see. But Betty has a way of phrasing, and her approach to rhythm is really very innovative for a vocalist. She certainly impressed me with the way that she deals with phrasing and shaping; what she does, how she shapes it. It's not so much what you do, but it's where you place it inside of the bar. Over-the-bar phrasing she does a lot, and she does it really well. It's the way she paints. That's what she's doin' with that line, she's painting it. There's a little dip down there.

WE: You're describing an art form, it seems to me. I don't hear much pop music that possesses those creative qualities. Am I missing something?

CW: No, I don't think so at all. Most of it is mundane. Most of it is so watered down. It still comes from the same thing, though. I think the foundation of American popular music *is* blues and jazz. Everything else is a derivative after that uniquely American form. You know, just as Rodgers and Hammerstein wrote really kind of cute music for the musicals, John Coltrane walks up and takes one of those pieces and turns it into a masterpiece. So it comes from the same source, but there are people who deliver it on different levels, you know, and in different ways. There's the music for mass consumption, which is very light and very, well, when you talk about white artists, then they have to deliver it in a way that's comfortable for them and comfortable for their time. But they still can't do it without borrowing from the primary resource, which is jazz and blues.

WE: Let's talk about your career as a woman in this music. Have you met with obstacles due to your gender, and have they been compounded because you're African-American?

CW: I never thought about the obstacles, to be honest with you, because obstacles have always been like a challenge to me. So I don't internalize it; I don't really take the time to think about it. Comin' from the South, you know, being a black woman from the South, there are *at birth* obstacles, so you get into the habit of seeing them, and after a while it becomes "Oh, there's another obstacle. I think I'll just step by it." (*Chuckles.*) You know, talking about my grandmother and my mother, and the history of the women in our family, the impact that that has had on my life *is* clearly that there have always been obstacles. My mother often says that if my grandmother had been a man, she would have been lynched. Because she *was* always so very outspoken. *Not* ever intimidated by white people. Dealing with what she had to deal with, she was an incredible woman; and there *were* no obstacles. You look at the fact that my mother's grandmother was a slave, and my mother's a doctor of education now. Enjoying a rather quiet middle-class lifestyle. So, if you look at what has happened in that span of time, then what's an obstacle? That's what I would say: What *is* an obstacle? It's how you deal with it, how you manipulate it, and it *can* be worked with. I have run into sexism, racism, all kinds of isms, and it just doesn't really affect my life. I think it's a personal problem that people have, so I don't really let it enter.

WE: Is it safe to say that any young woman who wants to enter the jazz world, regardless of race, will likely face gender issues?

CW: Always. There are gender issues, period. In the music world, in the jazz world, maybe there's a disproportionate amount of gender issues to deal with because there are so many more men that control this business, who are involved in the music, than there are women. I mean disproportionate as compared to, you know, the population as a whole. Yeah, there are gonna be those issues to deal with. And I don't give any advice on that other than to meet it head-on and to come prepared for the fight. Make sure you have all of the weapons that you need. Make sure you have a *full* knowledge of the music. Make sure that you can communicate with musicians, and don't give them any excuse. Have your chops together. Don't allow your being a woman to interrupt your getting as much information as you can about what you do.

WE: Some of the women musicians I have spoken with expressed the view that a feminine aesthetic exists which doesn't have to be gender-specific. Do you share that view?

CW: That's a good question. I don't know, I'm thinking about that. I had a discussion with Wynton Marsalis about improvisation, and I found myself using words like "a feminine approach" to improvisation. And I had another conversation with a journalist about the same thing, and he said, "Well, why did you use that, why would you break it down to feminine and masculine?" I said, "I don't know why." But I think there is a feminine approach to things, and then there's a masculine approach to things, and we have to balance that. I think every human being has to balance that. I think that now what we have in jazz is too much of an emphasis on the masculine approach to music and not enough of an emphasis on a feminine approach. And I think because there's male and female, there are two distinct ways of approaching things, ways of knowing, ways of dealing with the music.

WE: Can you elaborate on the point that the masculine approach is dominant in jazz?

CW: I can give an example of what I *think* that means. I think of Miles as very feminine. I think that [music is] where he put his feminine energy, and it's clear because of the roundness of it, which we tend to identify with the feminine principle: circular motions, cycles, roundness instead of lines. Men are more linear. Nowadays you have musicians who are very strict about how they improvise, and it's really more for show of how they mastered the instrument than approaching the music intuitively or emotionally. I hate to associate that with the feminine approach, but I think that's what it is. There are men who, I like to use the term, "bench-press changes." It's a way of showing off their dexterity. "I can do this, I can do this." Well, you can do that, but what are you saying? What's the emotion that you're getting across? It's always this kind of spartan approach to music; it's more warlike than it is full and whole and warm and inviting.

WE: What's your opinion of women's jazz festivals?

CW: I have never played in a women's jazz festival. I have been a part of a women's jazz series that they have at the Schomburg.[21] That's the closest I've ever come to it. I have a prejudice, though, I'm afraid. Because there's a dearth of women musicians out there performing, I think that there's not as great a standard for the music, unfortunately. *Because* we're just now coming to the music, I think that there's overcompensation, and then there's undercompensation. I've never been to one of these festivals, but I've heard people talk about the festivals just for women. I'm not really into that. I like to see everybody together—the male and the female. I don't want to see an all-man's festival, although that's what it turns out to be invariably when you have a jazz festival. (*Laughs.*) Although people do make efforts to bring in women, to make sure there is a balance.

WE: A final question. We spoke of Betty Carter earlier, but in relation to your songwriting and the overall spiritual dimensions of your work, I can't help thinking that Abbey Lincoln may be important to you. Is she an inspiration?

CW: Yeah, definitely. Abbey's like a culture-bearer. I think hearing Abbey for the first time, I was able to make a connection. Because she's a singer that comes to mind first when we talk about the African retention and being able to carry that in the music. And it's very apparent; you don't have to really dig deep. It's right in front of your face. Abbey *is* the culture-bearer, and she tells the stories. She is the griot. She's not big on the vocal acrobatics, you know, but she represents, for me, the missing link in terms of the blues and jazz and the whole evolution of the music. When I listen to Abbey, it all makes sense to me. It all comes together more. I can hear the ancestors in the music. It's something about the quality of her voice, too, that's very deep and dark and plaintive. Nina Simone has a similar quality. Betty doesn't have that. Betty is a great vocalist, she has the chops, but she doesn't have that same quality that Abbey has. Abbey can just reach through a song and pull your heart out. Betty does that for me in another way—just the sheer beauty of the music. But Abbey, there's a story to what she does, and there's a history, and it's a very full history.

WE: Have you told her that?

CW: Noooo. She knows I love her. I'm always really shy when I'm around her. I hang on her every word, so I don't talk very much when I'm around her. I just like to listen. And learn.

Selected Discography

Blue Skies. JMT 834 419-2 (1988).
Blue Light 'Til Dawn. Blue Note CDP0777 8135722 (1993).
New Moon Daughter. Blue Note CDP 7243 8 32861 2 6 (1995).
*Traveling Miles. Blue Note 7243 8 54123 2 5 (1998).

Notes

1. 1993; Blue Note.
2. 1995; Blue Note.
3. A resophonic guitar has a metal plate in place of the sound hole making for a bright sound. This guitar is often referred to as a dobro guitar.
4. Blue Note.
5. Recorded 1941 with the Gene Krupa Band.
6. From *New Moon Daughter.*
7. Trio composed of Henry Threadgill, saxes and woodwinds; Fred Hopkins, bass; Steve McCall, drums. AIR, with this personnel, lasted from 1971 to 1982.
8. 1986; Black Saint.
9. A Brooklyn, New York–based collective, M-Base stands for "Macro-Basic Array of Structured Extemporization."
10. Association for the Advancement of Creative Musicians, a Chicago-based organization.
11. Black Artists Group.
12. Greg Tate, "Cassandra Wilson, Moon Daughter," *Essence,* July 1996, p. 120.
13. *Blue Light 'Til Dawn,* 1993; Blue Note Records.
14. 1988; JMT Records.
15. *Essence.*
16. 1959–1960; Columbia Records.
17. Charisse Jones, "Singing a Song of the South," *New York Times,* September 29, 1994.
18. 1962; Columbia Records.
19. *Down Beat,* December 1993, p. 60.
20. "A 440" means perfectly in tune.
21. Arts and Cultural Center in Harlem devoted to black culture.

Dahl, Linda. *In the Moment: Jazz in the 1980s.* New York and Oxford: Oxford University Press, 1986. (See "Leading Lady [Abbey Lincoln]" and "Woman's Work," devoted in part to Sheila Jordan.)

———. *Stormy Weather: The Music and Lives of a Century of Jazzwomen.* New York: Limelight Editions, 1989. (Coverage of Clora Bryant, Dottie Dodgion, Sheila Jordan.)

Davis, Francis. *Outcats: Jazz Composers, Instrumentalists, and Singers.* New York and Oxford: Oxford University Press, 1990. (See "Sunshine Too," about Sheila Jordan, and "Outchicks," devoted in part to Jane Ira Bloom.)

Driggs, Frank. *Women in Jazz: A Survey.* Stash Records Liner Notes, New York; 1977.

Feather, Leonard. *The Jazz Years: Earwitness to an Era.* New York: DaCapo Press, 1987. (Some coverage of Clora Bryant in a chapter entitled "Melba to Stacy.")

———. *The Passion for Jazz.* New York: Horizon Press, 1980. (See pp. 144–148 for information about JoAnne Brackeen.)

Gourse, Leslie. *Madam Jazz: Contemporary Women Instrumentalists.* New York and Oxford: Oxford University Press, 1995. (Coverage of Jane Ira Bloom, JoAnne Brackeen, Terri Lyne Carrington, Virginia Mayhew, Marion McPartland, and Maria Schneider.)

Handy, D. Antoinette. *Black Women in American Bands and Orchestras.* 2nd ed. Metuchen, N.J.: Scarecrow Press, 1998. (Coverage of Clora Bryant and Terri Lyne Carrington.)

———. *The International Sweethearts of Rhythm.* Metuchen, N.J.: Scarecrow Press, 1983.

Lock, Graham. *Forces in Motion: Anthony Braxton and the Meta-reality of Creative Music.* London: Quartet Books, 1988. (See pp. 179–188 for information about Marilyn Crispell.)

Placksin, Sally. *American Women in Jazz, 1900 to the Present: Their Words, Lives, and Music.* New York: Seaview Books, 1982. (Coverage of Jane Ira Bloom, JoAnne Brackeen, Clora Bryant, Dottie Dodgion, and Sheila Jordan.)

Stokes, W. Royal. *Living the Jazz Life: Conversations with Forty Musicians about Their Careers in Jazz.* New York: Oxford University Press, 2000. (Includes chapters on JoAnne Brackeen, Regina Carter, Shirley Horn, Ingrid Jensen, and Diana Krall.)

Tucker, Sherrie. *Swing Shift: "All-Girl" Bands of the 1940s.* Durham, N.C.: Duke University Press, 2000. (Coverage of Clora Bryant.)

Page numbers in italics refer to illustrations.

WAYNE ENSTICE is Professor and former Director at the School of Art, University of Cincinnati. His studio work has been exhibited nationally, and is included in public and private collections. He has co-authored a book on the art of drawing and contributed numerous articles of art criticism for book anthologies, journals, and catalogues. His previous book on jazz, *Jazz Spoken Here* (co-authored with Paul Rubin), was published by Louisiana State University Press (1992) and DaCapo Press in New York (1994). An excerpt from *Jazz Spoken Here* appeared in *Reading Jazz: A Gathering of Autobiography, Reportage, and Criticism from 1919 to Now*, edited by Robert Gottlieb, Pantheon Books, New York (1996).

JANIS STOCKHOUSE is a graduate of the Indiana University School of Music, and has been Director of Bands at Bloomington High School North in Bloomington, Indiana, since 1981. Under her tutelage, this school's jazz bands and combos have been honored at festivals throughout the Midwest as well as at the Lionel Hampton Jazz Festival in Moscow, Idaho. Over the past several years, many of her students have been winners in the annual *Down Beat* Student Awards competition. In 2002, Bloomington North's Big Band performed at the North Sea Jazz Festival in The Netherlands. Stockhouse is a member of the Young Talent Resource Team of the International Association for Jazz Education.